FINANCIAL TIM
MANAGEMEI..

Knowledge   Skills   Understanding

Financial Times Management is a new business created to deliver the knowledge, skills and understanding that will enable students, managers and organisations to achieve their ambitions, whatever their needs, wherever they are.

Financial Times Pitman Publishing, part of Financial Times Management, is the leading publisher of books for practitioners and students in business and finance, bringing cutting-edge thinking and best practice to a global market.

To find out more about Financial Times Management and Financial Times Pitman Publishing, visit our website at:

www.ftmanagement.com

Cases and Materials in Employment Law

SECOND EDITION

Gwyneth Pitt

Professor of Law and
Head of Department of Law
University of Huddersfield

FINANCIAL TIMES
PITMAN PUBLISHING

LONDON · HONG KONG · JOHANNESBURG
MELBOURNE · SINGAPORE · WASHINGTON DC

FINANCIAL TIMES MANAGEMENT
128 Long Acre, London WC2E 9AN
Tel: +44 (0)171 447 2000
Fax: +44 (0)171 240 5771
Website: www.ftmanagement.com

A Division of Financial Times Professional Limited

First published in Great Britain 1994
Second edition published 1998

© Financial Times Professional Limited 1998

The right of Gwyneth Pitt to be identified as Author
of this Work has been asserted by her in accordance
with the Copyright, Designs and Patents Act 1988.

ISBN 0 273 62702 3

British Library Cataloguing in Publication Data
A CIP catalogue record for this book can be obtained from the British Library.

10 9 8 7 6 5 4 3 2 1

Typeset by Land & Unwin (Data Sciences) Ltd
Printed and bound in Great Britain by Bell and Bain Ltd, Glasgow

The Publishers' policy is to use paper manufactured from sustainable forests.

Contents

Preface

There are two main reasons for producing a collection of cases and materials. One is to develop students' legal reasoning skills by getting them to sift out arguments and reasons from lengthy judgments. The other is to provide the reader with a portable library containing the most important primary materials. The latter remains the objective of this book. It contains extracts from over 200 British and EC cases together with British and European legislative provisions and excerpts from Reports, Command Papers and other sources. The aim has been to provide the reader with as complete a set of basic employment law materials as is possible within a book of this size.

There have been huge changes in the law since the last edition, in particular in discrimination law, transfers of undertakings and trade union law. Some are the result of legislation, such as the Disability Discrimination Act and the revised rules on consultation over transfers and redundancies. Others result from decisions of British courts and the European Court of Justice, involving important clarifications of unfair dismissal and redundancy as well as discrimination and equal pay. Over 30 new cases have been included in this edition to take account of these developments, and the indulgence of the publishers has meant that it has been possible on the whole to add new material without having to excise older cases which remain relevant and significant.

The consolidation of employment law in the Employment Rights Act 1996 and the Trade Union and Labour Relations (Consolidation) Act 1992 is convenient in many ways, but can be a source of confusion for students looking at case reports referring to earlier incarnations of statutory provisions. Another advantage of this collection is that it has been possible either to substitute the current references or at least to provide cross-references to present statutory provisions.

Linking commentary should permit the book to be used as a free-standing tool; however, it is apt for the use as the basis for a case method course supplemented with references to periodical and other literature. It has been designed to function also as a companion to my text, *Employment Law*, 3rd edition, published by Sweet & Maxwell in 1997.

The rate of change in employment law is unlikely to abate, given the massive increase in applications to tribunals, the changes promised by the new Labour Government and the continuing development of European Community law. British acceptance of the Social Charter is bound to give added impetus to legislative change. Nevertheless, in preparing this book I have been struck by how much can now be regarded as relatively settled, as shown by the fact that the majority of cases extracted here are at Court of Appeal level or higher. I hope that readers will find the book interesting and useful.

Gwyneth Pitt
March 1998

Acknowledgements

The publishers and the Author would like to express their thanks to the following copyright owners who kindly gave permission for the publishing of extracts:

ACAS
The Commissioner for the Rights of Trade Union Members
The Controller of Her Majesty's Stationery Office

Extracts from *The Law Reports, The Weekly Law Reports, The Appeal Cases* and the *Industrial Cases Reports* are reproduced with the permission of The Incorporated Council of Law Reporting for England and Wales.

Extracts from the *All England Reports* are reproduced with the permission of Butterworth Law Publishers Ltd.

The extract from the *Common Market Law Reports* is reproduced with the permission of Sweet & Maxwell.

Extracts from the *Industrial Law Reports* are reproduced with the permission of IRS/Eclipse Group Limited.

Extracts from the *EOC Code of Practice on Equal Pay* are reproduced with the permission of the Equal Opportunities Commission.

Extracts from the European Convention on Human Rights are reproduced with the permission of the Council of Europe.

The extract from *Prudential Assurance Co Ltd* v *Lorenz* is reproduced with the permission of Charles Knight Publishing.

Articles 2 and 20 of the Universal Declaration of Human Rights are reproduced with the permission of the UN Information Centre.

Table of cases

(Note: where a case is substantially extracted or discussed, the name is shown in heavy type. The page number is also in heavy type.)

Table of legislation

(Note: Materials reproduced are indicated in **bold**)

UK Statutory Instruments

International Treaties and European Community Legislation

Table of abbreviations

ACAS	Advisory, Conciliation and Arbitration Service	ITF	International Transport Workers' Federation
ASLEF	Associated Society of Locomotive Engineers and Firemen	NALGO	National Association of Local Government Officers
CAC	Central Arbitration Committee	NATSOPA	National Society of Operative Printers Graphical and Media Personnel
CBI	Confederation of British Industry	NUJ	National Union of Journalists
CCT	Compulsory Competitive Tendering	NUM	National Union of Mineworkers
CO	Certification Officer	NUPE	National Union of Public Employees
COHSE	Confederation of Health Service Employees	NUR	National Union of Railwaymen
CRE	Commission for Racial Equality	RMT	Rail Maritime and Transport Union
DDA	Disability Discrimination Act 1995	RPA	Redundancy Payments Act 1965
EA	Employment Act	RRA	Race Relations Act 1976
EAT	Employment Appeal Tribunal	SDA	Sex Discrimination Act 1975
EC	European Community	SOGAT	Society of Graphical and Allied Trades 1982
ECHR	European Convention on Human Rights	TGWU	Transport and General Workers' Union
ECJ	European Court of Justice	TSSA	Transport and Salaried Staffs Association
EOC	Equal Opportunities Commission	TUC	Trades Union Congress
EPA	Employment Protection Act 1975	TULRCA	Trade Union and Labour Relations (Consolidation) Act 1992
EPCA	Employment Protection (Consolidation) Act 1978	TULRA	Trade Union and Labour Relations Act 1974
EQPA	Equal Pay Act	TUPE	Transfer of Undertakings (Protection of Employment) Regulations 1981
ERA	Employment Rights Act 1996		
EU	European Union		
HSWA	Health and Safety at Work etc. Act	TURERA	Trade Union Reform and Employment Rights Act 1993
ILO	International Labour Organization		
ITA	Industrial Tribunals Act 1996	UDHR	Universal Declaration of Human Rights

1 Introduction

Every reader of this book will be or has been an employee or an employer at some point, so employment law is a subject to which we can relate our own experiences and perhaps find answers to troubling questions. Employment law is a subject which above others is at the interface of law and politics. It is pretty well impossible to study employment law without engaging at the same time with the politics and social context of industrial relations issues. Even if it were possible, it would be artificial and really rather sterile to attempt to do so. Resulting from this, employment law is a dynamic subject, constantly changing and forcing us to reassess our theories and understanding. Finally, it is an excellent example of the influence of European Community law within the national legal system and thus serves as a model for learning about the process of EC integration and as a concrete exemplar for the evaluation of this interplay.

In this chapter, salient features of the British industrial relations scene will be sketched as a foundation and the sources of employment law identified and introduced. This brief introduction is intended to provide an underpinning for the discussion of the law and would repay initial reading. The rest of the chapter gives an account of the main institutions of employment law: the organisations and officials who have responsibilities in defined areas. It may be convenient to defer reading about many of these until they come into focus through a substantive employment law issue.

CHARACTERISTICS OF THE BRITISH EMPLOYMENT SCENE

In 1996 the labour force in the UK, including those seeking work, stood at 28.8 million people. Of these, 2.3 million were unemployed. Unemployment running at a level of about 8–10 per cent has been a depressing characteristic of the British labour market in the 1980s and up to the present, compared with almost full employment in the 1950s and 1960s. Women now constitute over 43 per cent of the labour force and are likely to become a greater proportion, for two reasons. First, the main area of growth in employment has been in part-time work in the service sector – jobs which are more likely to be taken by women, and second, women are increasingly returning to work after the birth and early years of their children, and they are coming back earlier.

The number of self-employed workers has risen to 3.7 million, partly as a result of the Conservative Government's encouragement of small businesses, and partly because of the lack of vacancies in the employed labour market. As to the kinds of business in which people are employed, there has been a continuing decline in traditional manufacturing industry (now accounting for 18 per cent of employees) and a growth (although not at the same rate) in new technology industries and the service sector. About three-quarters of all employment is now in the service sector. The balance between private sector and public sector employment shifted terrifically in the 1980s because of the Conservative Government's commitment to privatisation. Thus by 1996 only about five and a half million, well under a quarter of the employed labour force, was employed in the public sector, 45 per cent of whom were employed in the National Health Service.

As the public sector has traditionally had high levels of trade union density, the drive towards privatisation has resulted in declining levels of membership, particularly where privatisation results in a move away from traditional patterns of national negotiation of terms and conditions to individual contracts. Derecognition of trade unions has taken place in the water industry, and in other former nationalised industries for supervisory categories of staff. Trade union membership has declined markedly from a high point of 13.3 million in 1979 to a little over 8 million in 1995. The decline of employment in traditional areas of high union density, such as the public sector and heavy manufacturing industry, is one reason. Other reasons are: general unemployment, since people out of work rarely maintain their union membership; the unwillingness of companies in new technology and new service industry, especially inward investors to the UK, to recognise and negotiate with trade unions, and the anti-union legislation of the 1980s which severely impeded their power to take action in furtherance of industrial disputes. Whether this decline is irreversible, or whether a more favourable environment for trade unions created by a combination of a new Labour Government and encouragement at European Community level will result in an increase in membership, remains to be seen.

SOURCES OF EMPLOYMENT LAW

The pivotal relationship of employment law, that of employer and worker, is a contract. Thus the law of contract, which is essentially common law (meaning case law rather than statute law), is central to the study of employment law. Since the early 1960s, the relationship has been transformed through numerous statutory reforms. However, most have been predicated on the existence of the contract of employment, and in situations where the interpretation of a statute is unclear or there appears to be a gap in the law, it is still to the law of contract that courts and tribunals look to supply the deficiency.

Thus the primary sources for the study of employment law are an amalgam of case law and statute law. Two major consolidations mean that today, the bulk of statutory provisions relevant to the individual employment relationship are to be found in the Employment Rights Act 1996 (ERA) and the bulk of statute law applicable to trade unions is found in the Trade Union and Labour Relations (Consolidation) Act 1992. Further reforms to individual and collective labour law have tended to work by amendment to these statutes, which is helpful only if you have an up-to-date version of them: such amended versions are found most conveniently in the statute books emanating from the major legal publishers and on the computer information retrieval system, LEXIS.

Employment law is an area of English law which has been substantially affected by Britain's membership of the European Community. Accession to the Treaty of Rome, the principal treaty constituting the EC, entails obligations to accept EC law and where necessary to change English law to be in accordance with it. English courts and tribunals have a duty to apply EC law, preferring it over English law in case of conflict and interpreting English law in accordance with EC law as far as possible. Thus EC directives and regulations and decisions of the European Court of Justice (ECJ), as well as the Treaty of Rome as amended, are also primary sources of employment law.

Other international treaties influence British law in a different way. The UK is a member of the International Labour Organization and has ratified many ILO Conventions. These are treaties which should then be brought into effect in British law. A failure to do so does not involve court proceedings in the way that a failure to implement EC law does, but creates at the very least a strong moral and diplomatic pressure to conform. The position is similar with relation to the European Convention on Human Rights (ECHR), although for this treaty there is a mechanism whereby an individual can sue the state for non-compliance. The new Labour Government produced its proposals to incorporate the ECHR into British law in autumn 1997.

Finally, non-statutory materials such as Codes of Practice issued by competent authorities must be considered. These do not create direct legal obligations, but must be taken into account where relevant in any legal proceedings. In so far as a failure to follow a code may help to establish liability, there is a strong if indirect pressure to comply.

INSTITUTIONS OF EMPLOYMENT LAW

Advisory, Conciliation and Arbitration Service (ACAS)

Trade Union and Labour Relations (Consolidation) Act 1992

247. (1) There shall continue to be a body called the Advisory, Conciliation and Arbitration Service (referred to in this Act as 'ACAS').

(2) ACAS is a body corporate of which the corporators are the members of its Council.

(3) Its functions, and those of its officers and servants, shall be performed on behalf of the Crown, but not so as to make it subject to directions of any kind from any Minister of the Crown as to the manner in which it is to exercise its functions under any enactment ...

COMMENT

(1) ACAS was established in 1974. It took over the conciliation, arbitration and advisory roles which had previously been carried out by the Department of Employment, and also the wider remit of examination and improvement of the institutions and procedures for the conduct of industrial relations which had belonged to the Commission on Industrial Relations. Both the CBI and TUC were agreed that there was a need for a conciliation and arbitration procedure that was independent of

government, so that it would not be affected by government incomes policies. Hence the importance of s 247(3).

(2) ACAS was put on a statutory footing by the Employment Protection Act 1975, although the provisions relating to it are now to be found in TULRCA. It has a chairperson (who may be part-time) and nine part-time members, three of whom are chosen after consultation with employers' representatives and three chosen after consultation with trade unions. It has five regional offices in England and offices in Wales and Scotland. Its original staff were transferees from the Department of Employment. It now has just under 600 staff, which is about the same as when it was first set up, although its work has increased substantially since then.

(3) Under TULRCA s 209, ACAS has a general duty to promote the improvement of industrial relations. However, its duty 'to encourage the extension of collective bargaining' was abolished by TURERA in 1993.

(4) Until 1993 ACAS made no charge for any of its services. However, a TURERA amendment introduced TULRCA s 251A allowing ACAS to make charges and giving the Secretary of State power to order it to do so in respect of specified functions. So far, apart from some publications, charges have been made only in respect of some conferences and workshops organised by ACAS: the 1996 Annual Report reveals that about two-thirds of these were chargeable in the previous year.

Advice
Trade Union and Labour Relations (Consolidation) Act 1992

213. (1) ACAS may, on request or otherwise, give employers, employers' associations, workers and trade unions such advice as it thinks appropriate on matters concerned with or affecting or likely to affect industrial relations.

COMMENT

(1) ACAS carries out its advisory functions in four main ways. First, it provides a telephone advisory service which anyone can use to raise general employment queries. In its 1996 Annual Report ACAS reported nearly half a million inquiries, which is double the level of the 1980s.

(2) Second, it publishes information leaflets, advisory handbooks and advisory leaflets. Its handbooks, *Employing People* (for small firms), *Discipline at Work* and *Employment Handbook*, have been widely used and influential. Most are available free from ACAS offices. These advisory and informational publications are to be distinguished from their Codes of Practice (which are dealt with below). The Codes of Practice have a recognised legal status which the other publications do not possess.

(3) Third, it gives advice on collective matters. The growth of mergers and acquisitions, privatisation of public sector industries and decentralisation of bargaining have all given rise to a need for new bargaining arrangements in circumstances where there is considerable potential for conflict. ACAS can frequently advise the parties before problems arise and encourage them to reach agreed solutions.

(4) Finally, ACAS runs an information service, organises conferences and seminars and provides speakers on aspects of its work.

Conciliation

Trade Union and Labour Relations (Consolidation) Act 1992

210. (1) Where a trade dispute exists or is apprehended ACAS may, at the request of one or more parties to the dispute or otherwise, offer the parties to the dispute its assistance with a view to bringing about a settlement.

(2) The assistance may be by way of conciliation or by other means, and may include the appointment of a person other than an officer or servant of ACAS to offer assistance to the parties to the dispute with a view to bringing about a settlement.

(3) In exercising its functions under this section ACAS shall have regard to the desirability of encouraging the parties to a dispute to use any appropriate agreed procedures for negotiation or the settlement of disputes.

COMMENT

(1) While ACAS does not have to wait to be asked to provide its conciliation services, the system is voluntary. Historically it derives from the Conciliation Act 1896, and the guiding principle is that the parties are encouraged to achieve a voluntary settlement first if possible.

(2) The collective conciliation service offered by ACAS seems to be well regarded: 1,306 requests for this were received in 1996, and ACAS reported that industrial action was avoided in 89 per cent of these cases.

(3) Additionally ACAS provides conciliation officers to act in individual employment disputes. Most statutory employment protection legislation stipulates that cases will be referred to ACAS before industrial tribunal proceedings. This area has grown dramatically in recent years, from 60,605 references in 1991 to 100,399 in 1996, of which 46 per cent concerned unfair dismissal.

Arbitration

Trade Union and Labour Relations (Consolidation) Act 1992

212. (1) Where a trade dispute exists or is apprehended ACAS may, at the request of one or more of the parties to the dispute and with the consent of all the parties to the dispute, refer all or any of the matters to which the dispute relates for settlement to the arbitration of—

(a) one or more persons appointed by ACAS for that purpose (not being officers or employees of ACAS), or

(b) the Central Arbitration Committee....

COMMENT

(1) ACAS engages in both arbitration and mediation. The difference is that in arbitration the parties commit themselves in advance to accepting the arbitrator's decision. In mediation, while again the issue is being referred to a third party for

decision (rather than the parties reaching their own decision with the assistance of a third party, which is conciliation), the parties are not bound to accept the mediator's recommendations, only to consider them. Mediation can also be successful in resolving disputes, sometimes through providing an acceptable solution on at least some issues, sometimes through clarifying matters and pointing a way forward.

(2)   Perhaps in line with the reduction in industrial action, requests for arbitration and mediation have dropped in recent years. In its 1996 Annual Report ACAS related that it received 117 requests, the majority from the private sector.

(3)   ACAS staff do not themselves act as arbitrators: they are drawn from a panel of independent arbitrators maintained by ACAS or arbitration is provided through the CAC.

Codes of Practice

Trade Union and Labour Relations (Consolidation) Act 1992

199.   (1)   ACAS may issue Codes of Practice containing such practical guidance as it thinks fit for the purpose of promoting the improvement of industrial relations.

(2)   In particular, ACAS shall in one or more Codes of Practice provide practical guidance on the following matters—
   (a)   the time off to be permitted by an employer to a trade union official in accordance with section 168 (time off for carrying out trade union duties);
   (b)   the time off to be permitted by an employer to a trade union member in accordance with section 170 (time off for trade union activities); and
   (c)   the information to be disclosed by employers to trade union representatives in accordance with sections 181 and 182 (disclosure of information for purposes of collective bargaining).

(3)   The guidance mentioned in subsection (2)(a) shall include guidance on the circumstances in which a trade union official is to be permitted to take time off under section 168 in respect of duties connected with industrial action; and the guidance mentioned in subsection (2)(b) shall include guidance on the question whether, and the circumstances in which, a trade union member is to be permitted to take time off under section 170 for trade union activities connected with industrial action.

(4)   ACAS may from time to time revise the whole or any part of a Code of Practice issued by it and issue that revised Code.

COMMENT

(1)   In pursuance of its powers under this section ACAS has issued three Codes of Practice: on Disciplinary Practice and Procedures in Employment (No 1, 1977); on Disclosure of Information to Trade Unions for Collective Bargaining Purposes (No 2, 1977), and on Time Off for Trade Union Duties and Activities (No 3, revised 1991).

(2)   Where ACAS wishes to issue a Code of Practice, it must first publish a draft for consultation and consider any representations made to it. It must then be submitted to the Secretary of State for approval; if it is not approved, it goes no further, but reasons must be given. If the Secretary of State gives approval, the Code is laid before Parliament. Unless Parliament passes a resolution to the contrary within 40 days, the

Code is brought into force by statutory instrument (TULRCA s 200). An attempted revision of the Disciplinary Code of Practice failed to get through this procedure, but was published instead as the Advisory Handbook *Discipline at Work*. However, it therefore has a different status from a Code.

Trade Union and Labour Relations (Consolidation) Act 1992

207.　(1)　A failure on the part of any person to observe any provision of a Code of Practice issued under this Chapter shall not of itself render him liable to any proceedings.

　　　(2)　In any proceedings before an industrial tribunal or the Central Arbitration Committee any Code of Practice issued under this Chapter by ACAS shall be admissible in evidence, and any provision of the Code which appears to the tribunal or Committee to be relevant to any question arising in the proceedings shall be taken into account in determining that question.

　　　(3)　In any proceedings before a court or industrial tribunal or the Central Arbitration Committee any Code of Practice issued under this Chapter by the Secretary of State shall be admissible in evidence, and any provision of the Code which appears to the court, tribunal or Committee to be relevant to any question arising in the proceedings shall be taken into account in determining that question.

COMMENT

(1)　ACAS is not the only body empowered to issue Codes of Practice. The Health and Safety Commission may issue Codes of Practice on health and safety issues, the Commission for Racial Equality (CRE) and the Equal Opportunities Commission (EOC) have authority to issue Codes in their fields also, and under TULRCA s 203 the Secretary of State has power to issue Codes for the purpose of promoting the improvement of industrial relations or to promote what are considered to be desirable practices in relation to the conduct of trade union ballots and elections. The Secretary of State has issued Codes of Practice on Picketing (revised 1991), the Closed Shop (1983), and Industrial Action Ballots and Notice to Employers (1995). These were seen as controversial issues where ACAS was unwilling to risk its reputation for impartiality by drawing up a Code which would certainly upset one side or the other.

Central Arbitration Committee (CAC)

Trade Union and Labour Relations (Consolidation) Act 1992

259.　(1)　There shall continue to be a body called the Central Arbitration Committee.

　　　(2)　The functions of the Committee shall be performed on behalf of the Crown, but not so as to make it subject to directions of any kind from any Minister of the Crown as to the manner in which it is to exercise its functions.

　　　(3)　ACAS shall provide for the Committee the requisite staff (from among the officers and servants of ACAS) and the requisite accommodation, equipment and other facilities.

COMMENT

(1)　The CAC was established by the Employment Protection Act 1975. Then, as now, it was constituted as a fairly small organisation within ACAS; however, it had the distinctive function of being a decision-making body. Under the Employment Protection Act 1975, it had some important issues to decide.

(2) (a) First, there was a procedure whereby a trade union could complain to the CAC if the employer refused to recognise it. The CAC had power to order recognition with the sanction of an order for improved terms and conditions for the workforce if the employer did not comply. The whole procedure was repealed by the Employment Act 1980 – one of the first acts of the incoming Conservative Government.

(b) Second, under Schedule 11 of the Employment Protection Act an application could be made to the CAC to order an employer to give terms and conditions to the workforce comparable to those pertaining generally in the trade or in the trade in that locality. This was an extension of the Fair Wages Resolution procedure: the Fair Wages Resolution of Parliament called for government contractors to pay fair wages, defined in a similar way.

This was widely used in the 1970s as a way of circumventing statutory incomes policies, and was anathema to a government committed to free market ideals. Schedule 11 was repealed in 1980 and the Fair Wages Resolution followed it into oblivion in 1982.

(3) That left two principal functions, which still exist. As seen already, disputes can be referred to the CAC for arbitration under TULRCA s 212. While this happens occasionally, it seems that most arbitration requests go to ACAS. Finally, the CAC retains jurisdiction over disclosure of information disputes. Trade unions which are recognised by employers for collective bargaining purposes have a right to certain kinds of information under TULRCA ss 181–185 (discussed in Chapter 5). Any dispute over such disclosure is referred to the CAC. Its Annual Report for 1995 showed that an average of 22 complaints per year have been handled since the jurisdiction was introduced in 1976. However, there were 30 new complaints in 1995.

Certification Officer

The original duties of the Certification Officer in relation to trade unions were inherited from the Registrar of Friendly Societies and the short-lived Registrar of Trade Unions. Ever since they were recognised as lawful bodies, trade unions have been subject to a voluntary registration system which originally was of importance merely in giving them certain tax advantages. The duty of checking that they were qualified for entry on the register and maintaining the register was placed first with the Registrar of Friendly Societies. When the Industrial Relations Act 1971 was in force, this duty was transferred to the Registrar of Trade Unions, an office created by that Act. The unpopularity of the Industrial Relations Act with trade unions was focused on a refusal to register under the Act; when it was repealed in 1974 it was felt necessary to create a new system and a new official – the Certification Officer.

The duty of the Certification Officer to maintain a list of trade unions is now in TULRCA s 2. A trade union may apply to the Certification Officer for a certificate that it is an independent trade union (a status whose significance is discussed in

Chapter 10) and the Certification Officer must adjudicate on the claim. In addition, he is responsible for seeing that unions submit annual returns, keep proper accounting records and have their accounts properly audited.

The other duties of the Certification Officer are: dealing with complaints by union members that accurate membership registers have not been kept, or that ballots to elect union officials have not been properly held; ensuring that statutory procedures on political funds and on merger ballots are observed (and dealing with any complaints of breach); and, finally, carrying out parallel functions in respect of employers' associations. Increasing statutory regulation of all these areas has meant that the workload of the Certification Officer has increased substantially in the last decade.

Commissioner for the Rights of Trade Union Members

The office of Commissioner for the Rights of Trade Union Members was created by the Employment Act 1988 (see now TULRCA ss 266–272).

Ninth Annual Report of the Commissioner for the Rights of Trade Union Members 1996–97

The Commissioner may provide assistance to any union members (and, in the case of elections, candidates) who are taking, or contemplating taking, proceedings against their union or an official or trustee of the union in a complaint that the union:

- has, without the support of a properly-conducted secret ballot, called for industrial action by the member and other members – or is likely to do so;
- has not observed statutory requirements in respect of elections to its principal executive committee, and those of President and General Secretary or equivalent positions or the requirements in respect of its membership register;
- has applied its funds for electoral or party political purposes without a properly constituted political fund;
- has failed to comply with the rules approved by the Certification Officer in any ballot, or proposed ballot, on a political resolution;
- has failed to bring or continue any proceedings to recover union property applied to pay or indemnify an individual for a penalty imposed for an offence or for contempt of court;
- has denied the members their statutory right of access to its accounting records;
- has failed to secure that certain offenders do not hold a position in the union to which section 45B of TULRCA applies; or
- the trustees have caused or permitted, or propose to cause or permit, an unlawful application of the union's funds or property or have complied with or are proposing to comply with an unlawful direction.

The Commissioner may also grant assistance when trade union members complain that their union has failed or is likely to fail to observe the requirements of its own rule book in relation to:

- appointment or election of a person to, or the removal of a person from, any office;
- disciplinary proceedings by the union (including expulsion);
- the authorising or endorsing of industrial action;
- the balloting of members;
- the application of the union's funds or property;

- the imposition, collection or distribution of any levy for the purposes of industrial action; or
- the constitution or proceedings of any committee, conference or other body.

(Assistance may only be granted where the Commissioner considers that the breach of rule about which the members are complaining is one which affects or may affect other members of the union or that similar breaches of the rules have been or may be committed in relation to other members of the union.)

Assistance provided by the Commissioner can help ensure that union members are able to protect their rights by an application to the High Court (or in Scotland the Court of Session). Where assistance is granted the member need not be placed at a disadvantage by a lack of ability to obtain legal advice or pay for the cost of legal action.

The assistance which the Commissioner can provide includes:

- paying for legal advice and representation:
- making arrangements for legal advice or representation; or
- a combination of both of the above.

Assistance is only available to individuals who are able to bring relevant proceedings to court in their own right. At the members' discretion, the words 'assisted by the Commissioner for the Rights of Trade Union Members' can be added after their names in the title of proceedings – although the Commissioner is never an actual party to those proceedings.

Once the Commissioner has agreed to pay for legal advice or representation in particular proceedings, the assisted person need incur no further significant costs in taking those proceedings, or in any steps preliminary to those proceedings.

Anyone granted assistance will be given a choice about the arrangements to be made. For example, assisted persons will be able to decide to use their own legal advisers/representatives and be reimbursed by the Commissioner, or to have the Commissioner arrange for legal advice to be provided on their behalf.

In granting assistance the Commissioner will always indicate the extent of that assistance – for example, up to what stage in any current or prospective court proceedings it will be available.

In general the Commissioner has a wide discretion to decide whether to grant assistance. However, the Commissioner is required to grant assistance for court proceedings in connection with a complaint about a membership register, or election or political funds ballots where a declaration of the Certification Officer has already been obtained and the Commissioner is satisfied that the proposed proceedings have a reasonable prospect of success ...

COMMENT

(1) The Commissioner's powers to assist trade union members were originally limited to the matters laid out in the first set of bullet points; they were extended to the matters in the second paragraph by the Employment Act 1990.

(2) In 1996–97 the number of enquiries to the Commissioner's Office rocketed from the previous annual level of 300–400 to 2,379. However, over 2,000 of these were general enquiries about the Commissioner's role or how to apply for advice, and followed a concerted publicity campaign; the underlying trend, therefore, remains the same. The grand total of 74 applications for assistance were received in that year, of which only seven were actually deemed worthy of assistance. This cost the taxpayer over £225,000. At a time when legal aid is not available to an employee who wants to challenge her dismissal in an industrial tribunal, it seems bizarre that public money

should be poured into claims against trade unions, particularly when all the evidence suggests that there is no real problem.

Commissioner for Protection Against Unlawful Industrial Action

Not deterred by the lack of take-up of the assistance of the Commissioner for the Rights of Trade Union Members, the Conservative Government introduced another new office in 1993. A TURERA amendment to TULRCA s 266 created the Commissioner for Protection Against Unlawful Industral Action, whose role is to provide assistance to third parties suing to prevent industrial action which is either unlawful or which does not have the support of a ballot (see Chapter 13, below).

Annual Report of the Commissioner for Protection Against Unlawful Industrial Action 1996–97

Applications and Enquiries

During the reporting year 384 people were in touch either with the Commissioner's office or with his staff on exhibition stands to obtain general information on the role of the Commissioner, to outline a possible grievance, or to obtain further information by way of the Commissioner's publicity material.

Two formal applications for assistance were received during the reporting year.

One application was granted assistance. This application concerned the threatened withdrawal of teaching to a secondary school pupil. The pupil had been excluded from school by both the head teacher and the school governors, but was returned to the school following his parents' successful application to the Local Education Authority's Appeals Committee. Strike action was threatened by members of a teaching union in protest at the pupil's re-admission. The case was continuing at 31 March 1997.

The second application was found to relate to matters outside the scope of the Commissioner's powers to consider, and the application was refused.

COMMENT

(1)   In addition to the above, the Commissioner's office issued 1,027 information sheets, 233 guides and 369 annual reports. It all cost the taxpayer £91,388.

Commission for Racial Equality (CRE) and Equal Opportunities Commission (EOC)

Sex Discrimination Act 1975

53.   (1)   There shall be a body of Commissioners named the Equal Opportunities Commission, consisting of at least eight but not more than fifteen individuals each appointed by the Secretary of State on a full-time or part-time basis, which shall have the following duties—

      (a)   to work towards the elimination of discrimination,

      (b)   to promote equality of opportunity between men and women generally, and

      (c)   to keep under review the working of this Act and the Equal Pay Act 1970

> and, when they are so required by the Secretary of State or otherwise think it necessary, draw up and submit to the Secretary of State proposals for amending them. ...

54. (1) The Commission may undertake or assist (financially or otherwise) the undertaking by other persons of any research, and any educational activities, which appear to the Commission necessary or expedient for the purposes of section 53(1).

   (2) The Commission may make charges for educational or other facilities or services made available by them.

(RRA ss 43 and 45 are in similar terms, *mutatis mutandis*.)

COMMENT

(1) In addition the Commissions have powers to issue Codes of Practice with the approval of the Secretary of State and each has issued one code: the CRE Code of Practice for the Elimination of Racial Discrimination and the Promotion of Equality of Opportunity in Employment came into force in 1984 and the EOC Code of Practice for the Elimination of Discrimination on the Grounds of Sex and Marriage and the Promotion of Equality of Opportunity in Employment came into force in 1985.

(2) The Commissions may also assist individuals in bringing claims under the legislation, and as much of the legislation is complex, this is an important power. Two other aspects of their duties warrant special mention.

Discriminatory advertisements

Sex Discrimination Act 1975

38. (1) It is unlawful to publish or cause to be published an advertisement which indicates, or might reasonably be understood as indicating, an intention by a person to do any act which is or might be unlawful by virtue of Part II or III.

   (2) Subsection (1) does not apply to an advertisement if the intended act would not in fact be unlawful.

   (3) For the purposes of subsection (1), use of a job description with a sexual connotation (such as 'waiter', 'salesgirl', 'postman' or 'stewardess') shall be taken to indicate an intention to discriminate, unless the advertisement contains an indication to the contrary.

   (4) The publisher of an advertisement made unlawful by subsection (1) shall not be subject to any liability under that subsection in respect of the publication of the advertisement if he proves—

      (a) that the advertisement was published in reliance on a statement made to him by the person who caused it to be published to the effect that, by reason of the operation of subsection (2), the publication would not be unlawful, and

      (b) that it was reasonable for him to rely on the statement.

   (5) A person who knowingly or recklessly makes a statement such as is referred to in subsection (4) which in a material respect is false or misleading commits an offence, and shall be liable on summary conviction to a fine not exceeding level 5 on the standard scale.

COMMENT

(1) RRA s 29 is in similar terms, except that instead of SDA s 38(3), RRA s 29(3) is concerned to prevent discriminatory advertisements for jobs abroad.

(2) Only the two Commissions have power to take action in respect of discriminatory advertisements.

Investigations

Under SDA ss 57–61 and RRA ss 48–52, the two Commissions have power to carry out investigations, either of their own motion, or at the instigation of the Secretary of State. Before doing so, they must draw up terms of reference and give appropriate notice. Investigations may be general or 'named-person' investigations; if the former, a general notice must be published; if the latter, the persons or organisations involved must be notified and given an opportunity to make representations about it.

Where an investigation is to be carried out, the Commissions have extensive powers to obtain information.

Industrial tribunals

Industrial Tribunals Act 1996

1. (1) The Secretary of State may by regulations make provision for the establishment of tribunals, to be known as industrial tribunals. ...

    (2) Industrial tribunals shall exercise the jurisdiction conferred on them by or by virtue of this Act or any other Act, whether passed before or after this Act.

COMMENT

(1) Industrial tribunals were set up with very limited jurisdiction in 1964. Today they have jurisdiction over almost all individual disputes based on statutory claims and hear thousands of cases every year. They are organised in 11 regions, with the Central Office of Industrial Tribunals being in Bury St Edmunds, and sit the year round. Under the Employment Rights (Dispute Resolution) Bill, which was before Parliament at the time of writing, industrial tribunals will be renamed 'employment tribunals'.

(2) Under the Industrial Tribunals Act 1996 s 3, the Secretary of State has power to extend industrial tribunal jurisdiction to actions for breach of contract. The Industrial Tribunals (Extension of Jurisdiction) Order 1994 provided that contract claims could be brought in industrial tribunals, provided that the claim arose on, or was outstanding, when the contract was terminated, was for no more than £25,000 in total, and was made within three months of termination. Certain breach of contract claims were excluded: terms concerned with provision of living accommodation; restraint of trade; intellectual property; or breach of confidence.

(3) Tribunals are principally governed by the Industrial Tribunals (Constitution and Rules of Procedure) Regulations 1993. The procedural requirements are laid down in Schedule 1 of those Regulations.

(4) The first stage of tribunal proceedings is for the applicant to submit her claim, usually on the standard form IT1. The claim is copied to the respondent, who must reply within 21 days and to ACAS, who will assign a conciliation officer to help the parties reach a settlement, if they want.

(5) Before a full hearing, the tribunal may order a pre-hearing review, either on the application of one of the parties, or of its own motion, if it considers that a particular contention is unlikely to succeed. It is hoped that cases with no prospect of success can be weeded out at this stage. If having considered the representations of the parties (but not any evidence), the tribunal thinks that a particular contention is unlikely to succeed it can order the relevant party to pay a deposit of up to £150 as a condition of continuing the case. The case will then be heard by a fresh tribunal; if the contention is proceeded with and lost, the deposit may be used towards any costs order against the relevant party.

(6) The Employment Rights (Dispute Resolution) Bill makes provision for ACAS to draw up a voluntary arbitration scheme as an alternative method of dealing with unfair dismissal disputes.

Industrial Tribunals (Constitution and Rules of Procedure) Regulations 1993

Schedule 1

9.   (1)   The tribunal shall, so far as it appears to it appropriate, seek to avoid formality in its proceedings and shall not be bound by any enactment or rule of law relating to the admissibility of evidence in proceedings before the courts of law. The tribunal shall make such enquiries of persons appearing before it and witnesses as it considers appropriate and shall otherwise conduct the hearing in such manner as it considers most appropriate for the clarification of the issues before it and generally to the just handling of the proceedings. ...

COMMENT

(1)   While tribunals have considerable discretion as to procedure and are less formal than ordinary courts, their proceedings do tend to follow normal court practice.

(2)   Thus the case is usually opened by the party with the burden of proof presenting her case and calling witnesses who may be cross-examined by the other side. After both sides have presented their evidence, they make closing statements and the tribunal retires to consider its decision.

Industrial Tribunals (Constitution and Rules of Procedure) Regulations 1993

Schedule 1

10.   (1)   Where a tribunal is composed of three members its decision may be taken by a majority; and if a tribunal is composed of two members only, the chairman shall have a second or casting vote.

       (2)   The decision of a tribunal, which may be given orally at the end of a hearing or reserved, shall be recorded in a document signed by the chairman.

(3)   The tribunal shall give reasons for its decision in a document signed by the chairman. That document shall contain a statement as to whether the reasons are given in summary or extended form and where the tribunal—
(a)   makes an award of compensation, or
(b)   comes to any other determination by virtue of which one party is required to pay a sum to another (excluding an award of costs or allowances),
the document shall also contain a statement of the amount of compensation awarded, or of the sum required to be paid, followed either by a table showing how the amount or sum has been calculated or by a description of the manner in which it has been calculated.

(4)   The reasons for the decision of the tribunal shall be given in summary form except where—
(a)   the proceedings involved the determination of an issue arising under or relating to the 1970 Act, the 1975 Act, the 1986 Act or the 1976 Act or the Disability Discrimination Act 1995;
(b)   a request that the reasons to be given in extended form is made orally at the hearing by a party;
(c)   such a request is made in writing by a party after the hearing either—
(i)   before any document recording the reasons in summary form is sent to the parties, or
(ii)   within 21 days of the date on which that document was sent to the parties; or
(d)   the tribunal considers that reasons given in summary form would not sufficiently explain the grounds for its decision;
and in those circumstances the reasons shall be given in extended form. ...

COMMENT

(1)   A tribunal is usually composed of three members: a solicitor or barrister of seven years' standing in the chair and two lay members drawn from either side of industry. It is possible, and not very uncommon, for the two lay members to outvote the lawyer.

(2)   The power to award costs is limited and rarely exercised; it is usually the applicant who is regarded as having persisted unnecessarily and acted frivolously, vexatiously or unreasonably, but it is recognised that there is often little point in awarding costs against someone of limited means. If the claim is an unfair dismissal or redundancy claim, the applicant is often still unemployed by the time of the hearing.

(3)   There is a power to request a review on grounds defined in para 11; additionally, either party has a right of appeal to the Employment Appeal Tribunal.

Employment Appeal Tribunal (EAT)

Industrial Tribunals Act 1996

20.   (1)   The Employment Appeal Tribunal ("The Appeal Tribunal") shall continue in existence.
(2)   The Appeal Tribunal shall have a central office in London but may sit at any time and in any place in Great Britain.
(3)   The Appeal Tribunal shall be a superior court of record and shall have an official

seal which shall be judicially noticed.

21. (1) An appeal lies to the Appeal Tribunal on any question of law arising from any decision of, or arising in any proceedings before, an industrial tribunal under or by virtue of—

(a) the Equal Pay Act 1970,

(b) the Sex Discrimination Act 1975,

(c) the Race Relations Act 1976,

(d) the Trade Union and Labour Relations (Consolidation) Act 1992,

(e) the Disability Discrimination Act 1995, or

(f) the Employment Rights Act 1996.

(2) No appeal shall lie except to the Appeal Tribunal from any decision of an industrial tribunal under or by virtue of the Acts listed in subsection (1).

(3) Subsection (1) does not affect any provision contained in, or made under, any Act which provides for an appeal to lie to the Appeal Tribunal (whether from an industrial tribunal, the Certification Officer or any other person or body) otherwise than on a question to which that subsection applies.

22. (1) The Appeal Tribunal shall consist of—

(a) such number of judges as may be nominated from time to time by the Lord Chancellor from the judges (other than the Lord Chancellor) of the High Court and the Court of Appeal,

(b) at least one judge of the Court of Session nominated from time to time by the Lord President of the Court of Session, and

(c) such number of other members as may be appointed from time to time by Her Majesty on the joint recommendation of the Lord Chancellor and the Secretary of State ("appointed members").

(2) The appointed members shall be persons who appear to the Lord Chancellor and the Secretary of State to have special knowledge or experience of industrial relations either—

(a) as representatives of employers, or

(b) as representatives of workers (within the meaning of the Trade Union and Labour Relations (Consolidation) Act 1992).

(3) The Lord Chancellor shall, after consultation with the Lord President of the Court of Session, appoint one of the judges nominated under subsection (1) to be the President of the Appeal Tribunal.

(4) No judge shall be nominated a member of the Appeal Tribunal except with his consent.

COMMENT

(1) It will be noted that appeals to the EAT lie only on a question of law. As a matter of policy, to reduce the number of appeals and keep down costs, the concept of a question of law is interpreted very restrictively.

(2) In its early years, the EAT saw itself as having an important role in fleshing out the rather bare provisions of the law on unfair dismissal to give guidance to employers and industrial tribunals as to what was required. That approach was frowned on by the Court of Appeal, which took many opportunities to warn against putting a gloss on the words of the statute.

(3)   Both these issues relate particularly to the law of unfair dismissal and are therefore discussed further in Chapter 8.

The European Community (EC) and European Union (EU)

Treaty of Rome (Treaty establishing the European Economic Community)

Article 100

The Council shall, acting unanimously on a proposal from the Commission, issue directives for the approximation of such provisions laid down by law, regulation or administrative action in Member States as directly affect the establishment or functioning of the common market.

   The European Parliament and the Economic and Social Committee shall be consulted in the case of directives whose implementation would, in one or more Member States, involve the amendment of legislation.

Article 100A

1.   By way of derogation from Article 100 and save where otherwise provided in this Treaty, the following provisions shall apply for the achievement of the objectives set out in Article 8A. The Council shall, acting by a qualified majority on a proposal from the Commission in co-operation with the European Parliament and after consulting the Economic and Social Committee, adopt the measures for the approximation of the provisions laid down by law, regulation or administrative action in Member States which have as their object the establishment and functioning of the internal market.

2.   Paragraph 1 shall not apply to fiscal provisions, to those relating to the free movement of persons nor to those relating to the rights and interests of employed persons.

3.   The Commission, in its proposals envisaged in paragraph 1 concerning health, safety, environmental protection and consumer protection, will take as a base a high level of protection.

4.   If, after the adoption of a harmonisation measure by the Council acting by a qualified majority, a Member State deems it necessary to apply national provisions on grounds of major needs referred to in Article 36, or relating to protection of the environment or the working environment, it shall notify the Commission of these provisions.

   The Commission shall confirm the provisions involved after having verified that they are not a means of arbitrary discrimination or a disguised restriction on trade between Member States.

   By way of derogation from the procedure laid down in Articles 169 and 170, the Commission or any Member State may bring the matter directly before the Court of Justice if it considers that another Member State is making improper use of the powers provided for in this Article.

5.   The harmonisation measures referred to above shall, in appropriate cases, include a safeguard clause authorising the Member States to take, for one or more of the non-economic reasons referred to in Article 36, provisional measures subject to a Community control procedure.

Article 117

Member States agree upon the need to promote improved working conditions and an improved standard of living for workers, so as to make possible their harmonisation while the improvement is being maintained.

They believe that such a development will ensue not only from the functioning of the common market, which will favour the harmonisation of social systems, but also from the procedures provided for in this Treaty and from the approximation of provisions laid down by law, regulation or administrative action.

Article 118

Without prejudice to the other provisions of this Treaty and in conformity with its general objectives, the Commission shall have the task of promoting close co-operation between Member States in the social field, particularly in matters relating to:
- employment;
- labour law and working conditions;
- basic and advanced vocational training;
- social security;
- prevention of occupational accidents and diseases;
- occupational hygiene;
- the right of association, and the collective bargaining between employers and workers.

To this end, the Commission shall act in close contact with Member States by making studies, delivering opinions and arranging consultations both on problems arising at national level and on those of concern to international organisations.

Before delivering the opinions provided for in this Article, the Commission shall consult the Economic and Social Committee.

Article 118A

1. Member States shall pay particular attention to encouraging improvements, especially in the working environment, as regards the health and safety of workers, and shall set as their objective the harmonisation of conditions in this area, while maintaining the improvements made.

2. In order to help achieve the objective laid down in the first paragraph, the Council, acting by a qualified majority on a proposal from the Commission, in co-operation with the European Parliament and after consulting the Economic and Social Committee, shall adopt, by means of directives, minimum requirements for gradual implementation, having regard to the conditions and technical rules obtaining in each of the Member States.

   Such directives shall avoid imposing administrative, financial and legal constraints in a way which would hold back the creation and development of small and medium-sized undertakings.

3. The provisions adopted pursuant to this Article shall not prevent any Member State from maintaining or introducing more stringent measures for the protection of working conditions compatible with this Treaty.

Article 118B

The Commission shall endeavour to develop the dialogue between management and labour at European level which could, if the two sides consider it desirable, lead to relations based on agreement.

Article 177

The Court of Justice shall have jurisdiction to give preliminary rulings concerning:
  (a) the interpretation of this Treaty;
  (b) the validity and interpretation of acts of the institutions of the Community;
  (c) the interpretation of the statutes of bodies established by an act of the Council,
where those statutes so provide.

   Where such a question is raised before any court or tribunal of a Member State, that court or tribunal may, if it considers that a decision on the question is necessary to enable it to give judgment, request the Court of Justice to give a ruling thereon.

   Where any such question is raised in a case pending before a court or tribunal of a Member State, against whose decisions there is no judicial remedy under national law, that court or tribunal shall bring the matter before the Court of Justice.

Article 189

In order to carry out their task the Council and the Commission shall, in accordance with the provisions of this Treaty, make regulations, issue directives, take decisions, make recommendations or deliver opinions.

   A regulation shall have general application. It shall be binding in its entirety and directly applicable in all Member States.

   A directive shall be binding, as to the result to be achieved, upon each Member State to which it is addressed, but shall leave to the national authorities the choice of form and methods.

   A decision shall be binding in its entirety upon those to whom it is addressed.

   Recommendations and opinions shall have no binding force.

COMMENT

(1) Britain joined the EC in 1972. In 1986 the Single European Act introduced Article 100A, which permits qualified majority voting in some circumstances, and Articles 118A and 118B.

(2) During the 1980s the other eleven members of the EC were keen to move further on harmonisation and improvement of working conditions, but this was constantly resisted by the British government. Thus in 1989, the Social Charter was agreed by eleven Member States without the UK, and the European Union Treaty (the Treaty of Maastricht), which was intended, among other things, to revise the social policy articles of the Treaty of Rome, could not do so because of British opposition. The result was that all 12 members agreed the Treaty of Maastricht, but the social policy provisions had to be put in a separate Social Policy Protocol (the Social Chapter) annexed to the main treaty, to which the UK was not a signatory.

(3) European Community law prevails over inconsistent British law, whether subsequent or prior to the EC rule (*Factortame* v *Secretary of State for Transport*).

English courts and tribunals have an obligation to apply EC law and to interpret English law in accordance with EC law as far as possible. In case of doubt, cases may be referred to the European Court of Justice (ECJ). The effects of this, and in particular, the results when a state does not implement EC directives, are illustrated in the discussion of sex discrimination law in Chapter 2.

The International Labour Organization (ILO)

(1)   The International Labour Organization (ILO) was established as an organ of the League of Nations in 1919 at the Treaty of Versailles. It is charged with the duty of promoting fair working conditions in all countries. With the demise of the League of Nations after the Second World War and its replacement by the United Nations, the ILO was reconstituted with a separate legal status, its constitution being based on the original treaty provisions.

(2)   The ILO works through international treaties: Conventions or Recommendations agreed by two-thirds of the representatives of member states at its conferences. It is up to the Conference to decide whether a particular proposal should take the form of a Convention or a Recommendation. In general, those matters which are fairly non-controversial go into Conventions, but more radical proposals are put in a Recommendation. It is thus common to find a Convention and a Recommendation on the same subject-matter emanating from the same conference.

(3)   Representatives of member states undertake to bring any Conventions or Recommendations to the attention of their government for consideration within a year of their being agreed. However, member states are not obliged to accept the requirements of these instruments unless they ratify them. On receiving a certain number of ratifications, the Convention or Recommendation comes into force and the member state is then under an obligation to ensure that municipal (state) law conforms to it.

(4)   In the case of non-ratification, there is nothing the ILO can do except to call for reports from time to time on the subject covered by the instrument. It is not necessarily under-developed countries which refuse to ratify: the USA has only ever ratified seven Conventions. If a state fails to comply with its obligations, the sanctions are essentially diplomatic: there is no court and there are no individual rights of redress. However, given that it agreed in the first place, on the whole it is to be expected that a state will comply.

(5)   If a state no longer wishes to be bound by a Convention which it has ratified, it must give notice of withdrawal. The process is called denunciation. The state may not act in a manner contrary to the Convention until the notice period has expired. The UK gave notice in the mid-1980s to denounce the Convention on protection of minimum terms and conditions so that it could pass the Wages Act restricting the powers and ambit of wages councils.

2 The law of discrimination

The right not to be discriminated against on grounds such as gender and race is usually justified on two grounds. First, that these are irrelevant to a person's ability; second, that it is unfair to treat someone less favourably on grounds of an unalterable characteristic. These justifications have implications beyond the labour market, and the right not to be discriminated against on irrelevant grounds has been recognised in all the major human rights treaties as a basic human right. More recently, the United Kingdom has followed the lead of other countries, especially the United States, by legislating against discrimination on grounds of disability (the Disability Discrimination Act 1995). As you will notice, this has not been universally recognised as a matter of human rights in the treaties. For disability discrimination, the second justification is stronger than the first, and this is reflected in the legislation.

Universal Declaration of Human Rights 1948

Article 2

Everyone is entitled to all the rights and freedoms set forth in this Declaration, without distinction of any kind, such as race, colour, sex, language, religion, political or other opinion, national or social origin, property, birth or other status.

COMMENT

(1) See also the International Covenant on Economic, Social and Cultural Rights 1966 (one of two treaties expanding the basic rights in the UDHR) and ILO Convention No 111 concerning Discrimination in Respect of Employment and Occupation 1958.

European Convention on Human Rights 1950

Article 14

The enjoyment of the rights and freedoms set forth in this Convention shall be secured without discrimination on any ground such as sex, race, colour, language, religion, political or other opinion, national or social origin, association with a national minority, property, birth or other status.

COMMENT

(1) The ECHR emanates from the Council of Europe, an association of European democracies which is quite separate from, and has a wider membership than, the EC. Proceedings for breach of the Convention can be taken via the European Commission on Human Rights to the European Court of Human Rights at Strasbourg. Member states have a choice as to whether to allow their nationals an individual right of redress under the Convention: the UK does permit this. The Labour Government has announced proposals to incorporate The European Convention on Human Rights into English law in autumn 1997.

(2) The most important treaty binding on the UK which has enforcement provisions is the Treaty of Rome which is the treaty establishing the European Economic Community. It contains a basic principle of equality for men and women (Article 119, extracted on p 210) which has since been expanded via the Equal Treatment Directive.

EC Council Directive No. 76/207 on the implementation of the principle of equal treatment for men and women as regards access to employment, vocational training and promotion, and working conditions (the Equal Treatment Directive) 1976

Article 1

1. The purpose of this Directive is to put into effect in the Member States the principle of equal treatment for men and women as regards access to employment, including promotion, and to vocational training and as regards working conditions and, on the conditions referred to in paragraph 2, social security. This principle is hereinafter referred to as 'the principle of equal treatment.'
2. With a view to ensuring the progressive implementation of the principle of equal treatment in matters of social security, the Council, acting on a proposal from the Commission, will adopt provisions defining its substance, its scope and the arrangements for its application.

Article 2

1. For the purposes of the following provisions, the principle of equal treatment shall mean that there shall be no discrimination whatsoever on grounds of sex either directly or indirectly by reference in particular to marital or family status.
2. This Directive shall be without prejudice to the right of Member States to exclude from its field of application those occupational activities and, where appropriate, the training leading thereto, for which, by reason of their nature or the context in which they are carried out, the sex of the worker constitutes a determining factor.
3. This Directive shall be without prejudice to provisions concerning the protection of women, particularly as regards pregnancy and maternity.
4. This Directive shall be without prejudice to measures to promote equal opportunity for men and women, in particular by removing existing inequalities which affect women's opportunities in the areas referred to in Article 1(1).

Article 3

1. Application of the principle of equal treatment means that there shall be no discrimination whatsoever on grounds of sex in the conditions, including selection criteria, for access to all jobs or posts, whatever the sector or branch of activity, and to all levels of the occupational hierarchy....

Article 5

1. Application of the principle of equal treatment with regard to working conditions, including the conditions governing dismissal, means that men and women shall be guaranteed the same conditions without discrimination on grounds of sex. ...

COMMENT

(1)   The enforcement of this Directive will be considered later in the chapter. Since much discrimination takes place at the point of entry to the labour market, it makes sense to look at the issue here, before going on to examine the relationship of employer and employee.

(2)   The Treaty of Amsterdam, agreed in 1997, amends The Treaty of Rome to insert a new Article 6A, giving power to the Council to act against discrimination on grounds of race or ethnic origin, religion, disability, age or sexual orientation. Any such action will require the unanimous agreement of member states, and the article will not have direct effect.

SEX AND RACE DISCRIMINATION

Discrimination on grounds of gender in the labour market was not really addressed until the Sex Discrimination Act 1975. The Sex Disqualification (Removal) Act of 1919 merely permitted women to enter certain professions (such as medicine and the law) from which they had effectively been barred before; it did not attempt to prevent discrimination against women. The first Race Relations Act in 1965 did not cover race discrimination at work; this was added only in 1968. The present law is to be found in the Race Relations Act 1976.

The Sex Discrimination Act (SDA) and Race Relations Act (RRA) were drafted according to the same model; it is therefore convenient to examine their provisions together.

The protected groups

Sex Discrimination Act 1975

2. (1)   Section 1, and the provisions of Parts II and III relating to sex discrimination against women, are to be read as applying equally to the treatment of men, and for that purpose shall have effect with such modifications as are requisite.

    (2)   In the application of subsection (1) no account shall be taken of special treatment afforded to women in connection with pregnancy or childbirth.

82. (1) In this Act, unless the context otherwise requires —
'employment' means employment under a contract of service or of apprenticeship or a contract personally to execute any work or labour ...

COMMENT

(1) Discrimination in employment against married people is also prohibited by the
SDA (s 3).

(2) Note that the Act adopts a symmetrical model of discrimination: discrimination
against men is just as unlawful as discrimination against women. This is in accordance
with European Community law.

Kalanke v Freie Hansestadt Bremen

[1995] IRLR 660 · European Court of Justice

The City of Bremen's Law on the Equal Treatment of Men and Women in the Public Service
provided that for any appointment, women having the same qualifications as men applying
for the same post were to be given priority in sectors where women were underrepresented.
'Underrepresented' was defined as meaning fewer than half of the staff in any particular
personnel group. On this basis, Mr Kalanke, holder of a diploma in horticulture and a
landscape gardener, was passed over in favour of Ms Glissmann, holder of a similar diploma,
despite, he alleged, his qualifications and experience being superior. The German court
asked whether the Bremen law contravened the Equal Treatment Directive.

Judgment of the Court: '... The national court asks, essentially, whether Article 2(1) and (4)
of the Directive precludes national rules such as those in the present case which, where
candidates of different sexes shortlisted for promotion are equally qualified, automatically
give priority to women in sectors where they are underrepresented, underrepresentation
being deemed to exist when women do not make up at least half of the staff in the individual
pay brackets in the relevant personnel group or in the function levels provided for in the
organisation chart.

In its order for reference, the national court points out that a quota system such as that
in issue may help to overcome in the future the disadvantages which women currently face
and which perpetuate past inequalities, inasmuch as it accustoms people to seeing women
also filling certain more senior posts. The traditional assignment of certain tasks to women
and the concentration of women at the lower end of the scale are contrary to the equal rights
criteria applicable today. In that connection, the national court cites figures illustrating the
low proportion of women in the higher career brackets among city employees in Bremen,
particularly if sectors such as education, where the presence of women in higher posts is
now established, are excluded.

The purpose of the Directive is, as stated in Article 1(1), to put into effect in the Member
States the principle of equal treatment for men and women as regards, inter alia, access to
employment, including promotion. Article 2(1) states that the principle of equal treatment
means that 'there shall be no discrimination whatsoever on grounds of sex either directly or
indirectly'.

A national rule that, where men and women who are candidates for the same promotion
are equally qualified, women are automatically to be given priority in sectors where they are
underrepresented, involves discrimination on grounds of sex.

It must, however, be considered whether such a national rule is permissible under Article
2(4), which provides that the Directive 'shall be without prejudice to measures to promote

equal opportunity for men and women, in particular by removing existing inequalities which affect women's opportunities'.

That provision is specifically and exclusively designed to allow measures which, although discriminatory in appearance, are in fact intended to eliminate or reduce actual instances of inequality which may exist in the reality of social life (see *Commission* v *France*).

It thus permits national measures relating to access to employment, including promotion, which give a specific advantage to women with a view to improving their ability to compete on the labour market and to pursue a career on an equal footing with men.

As the Council considered in the third recital in the preamble to Recommendation 84/635/EEC of 13 December 1984 on the promotion of positive action for women, 'existing legal provisions on equal treatment, which are designed to afford rights to individuals, are inadequate for the elimination of all existing inequalities unless parallel action is taken by governments, both sides of industry and other bodies concerned, to counteract the prejudicial effects on women in employment which arise from social attitudes, behaviour and structures.'

Nevertheless, as a derogation from an individual right laid down in the Directive, Article 2(4) must be interpreted strictly (see *Johnston* v *Chief Constable of the Royal Ulster Constabulary*).

National rules which guarantee women absolute and unconditional priority for appointment or promotion go beyond promoting equal opportunities and overstep the limits of the exception in Article 2(4) of the Directive.

Furthermore, in so far as it seeks to achieve equal representation of men and women in all grades and levels within a department, such a system substitutes for equality of opportunity as envisaged in Article 2(4) the result which is only to be arrived at by providing such equality of opportunity.

The answer to the national court's questions must therefore be that Article 2(1) and (4) of the Directive precludes national rules such as those in the present case which, where candidates of different sexes shortlisted for promotion are equally qualified, automatically give priority to women in sectors where they are underrepresented, underrepresentation being deemed to exist when women do not make up at least half of the staff in the individual pay brackets in the relevant personnel group or in the function levels provided for in the organisation chart. ...'

COMMENT

(1)   The ECJ subsequently backtracked from this position somewhat in *Marschall* v *Land Nordrein-Westfalen*.

(2)   In recent cases the ECJ has taken to describing the principle of non-discrimination on grounds of sex as a fundamental principle of Community law. This has led to some extension of the scope of protected groups, as the next case shows.

P v *S and Cornwall CC*

[1996] IRLR 347 European Court of Justice

The applicant was employed as a manager of an educational establishment operated by the Council and had been taken on as a male employee. She was dismissed when she indicated that she was to undergo a sex change operation. She claimed that this was a breach of the Equal Treatment Directive, but the United Kingdom argued that transsexuals were not within its scope.

Advocate-General's Opinion: '... While it is quite true that the Directive prohibits any discrimination whatsoever on grounds of sex, it is equally indisputable that the wording of the principle of equal treatment which it lays down refers to the traditional man/woman dichotomy.

In order to ascertain whether the Directive can, as the industrial tribunal suggests, be so interpreted as to cover discrimination against transsexuals too, it must, in any event, be determined in the first place whether the unfavourable treatment of transsexuals constitutes discrimination on grounds of sex. It will then be necessary to decide whether it is only discrimination between men and women which is covered by the expression 'discrimination on grounds of sex' or, more generally, all unfavourable treatment connected with sex.

I shall start by calling to mind the proposition, which has ever stronger support in medical and scientific circles, that it is necessary to go beyond the traditional classification and recognise that, in addition to the man/woman dichotomy, there is a range of characteristics, behaviour and roles shared by men and women, so that sex *itself* ought rather to be thought of as a continuum. From that point of view, it is clear that it would not be right to continue to treat as unlawful solely acts of discrimination on grounds of sex which are referrable to men and women in the traditional sense of those terms, while refusing to protect those who are also treated unfavourably precisely because of their sex and/or sexual identity.

The argument just put forward, attractive as it is, requires a redefinition of sex which merits deeper consideration in more appropriate circles; consequently, this is not the path that I propose that the Court should follow. I fully realise that from time immemorial a person's sex has merely been ascertained, without need of the law to define it. The law dislikes ambiguities, and it is certainly simpler to think in terms of Adam and Eve.

Having said that, I regard as obsolete the idea that the law should take intro consideration, and protect, a woman who has suffered discrimination in comparison with a man, or vice versa, but denies that protection to those who are also *discriminated against*, again by reason of sex, merely because they fall outside the traditional man/woman classification.

The objection is taken too much for granted, and has been raised on several occasions in these proceedings, that the factor of sex discrimination is missing, on the grounds that 'female transsexuals' are not treated differently from 'male transsexuals'. In short, both are treated unfavourably, hence there can be no discrimination at all. A survey of the relevant case law confirms that point of view, albeit with some exceptions.

I am not convinced by that view. It is quite true that even if P had been in the opposite situation, that is to say changing from female to male, it is possible that she would have been dismissed anyway. One fact, however, is not just possible, but certain: P would not have been dismissed if she had remained a man.

So how can it be claimed that discrimination on grounds of sex was not involved? How can it be denied that the cause of discrimination was precisely, and solely, sex? To my mind, where unfavourable treatment of a transsexual is related to (or rather is caused by) a change of sex, there is discrimination by reason of sex or on grounds of sex, if that is preferred.

On this subject I cannot do other than recall that the prohibition of discrimination on grounds of sex is an aspect of the principle of equality, a principle which requires no account to be taken of discriminatory factors, principally sex, race, language and religion. What matters is that, in like situations, individuals should be treated alike.

Consequently, the principle of equality prohibits unequal treatment of individuals based on certain distinguishing factors, and these specifically include sex. This means that importance may not and must not be given to sex as such, so as to influence in one way or another the treatment afforded, for example, to workers. That is the reasoning on which my Opinion in *Kalanke* is based, in which, as I recall, I declared myself opposed to employment and promotion quotas for women, because I believe that the principle of non-discrimination on grounds of sex permits only those exceptions which, because they aim at attaining *substantive* equality, are justified by the objective of ensuring acual equality between persons.

In the present case, what is required is at least a rigorous application of the principle of equality so that, therefore, any connotations relating to sex and/or sexual identity cannot be in any way relevant. Moreover, in trying to justify their relevance, it would be very hard to argue, and in any event it has not been claimed, that the abilities and role of the person in question were adversely affected by her change of sex.

I must add that, for the purposes of this case, sex is important as a convention, a social parameter. The discrimination of which women are frequently the victims is not of course due to their physical characteristics, but rather to their role, to the image which society has of women. Hence the rationale for less favourable treatment is the social role which women are supposed to play and certainly not their physical characteristics. In the same way it must be recognised that the unfavourable treatment suffered by transsexuals is most often linked to a negative image, a moral judgment which has nothing to do with their abilities in the sphere of employment.

Such a situation is still less acceptable when the social change and scientific advances made in this area in recent years are taken into consideration. Whilst it is true, as I have already said, that transsexuals are in fact not very significant in statistical terms, it is equally true that for that very reason it is vital that they should have at least a minimum of protection. On this view, to maintain that the unfavourable treatment suffered by P was not on grounds of sex because it was due to her change of sex or else because in such a case it is not possible to speak of discrimination between the two sexes would be a quibbling formalistic interpretation and a betrayal of the true essence of that fundamental and inalienable value which is equality. …'

Judgment of the Court: '… The United Kingdom and the Commission submit that to dismiss a person because he or she is a transsexual or because he or she has undergone a gender-reassignment operation does not constitute sex discrimination for the purposes of the Directive.

In support of that argument, the United Kingdom points out in particular that it appears from the order for reference that the employer would also have dismissed P if P had previously been a woman and had undergone an operation to become a man.

The European Court of Human Rights has held that 'the term "transsexual" is usually applied to those who, whilst belonging physically to one sex, feel convinced that they belong to the other; they often seek to achieve a more integrated, unambiguous identity by undergoing medical treatment and surgical operations to adapt their physical characteristics to their psychological nature. Transsexuals who save been operated upon thus form a fairly well-defined and identifiable group' (*Rees* v *United Kingdom*).

The principle of equal treatment 'for men and women' to which the Directive refers in its title, preamble and provisions means, as Articles 2(1) and 3(1) in particular indicate, that there should be 'no discrimination whatsoever on grounds of sex'.

Thus, the Directive is simply the expression, in the relevant field, of the principle of equality, which is one of the fundamental principles of Community law.

Moreover, as the Court has repeatedly held, the right not to be discriminated against on grounds of sex is one of the fundamental human rights whose observance the Court has a duty to ensure (see, to that effect, *Defrenne* v *Sabena (No 3)*, and joined cases *Razzouk and Beydoun* v *Commission*).

Accordingly, the scope of the Directive cannot be confined simply to discrimination based on the fact that a person is of one or other sex. In view of its purpose and the nature of the rights which it seeks to safeguard, the scope of the Directive is also such as to apply to discrimination arising, as in this case, from the gender reassignment of the person concerned.

Such discrimination is based, essentially if not exclusively, on the sex of the person concerned. Where a person is dismissed on the ground that he or she intends to undergo, or has undergone, gender reassignment, he or she is treated unfavourably by comparison with persons of the sex to which he or she was deemed to belong before undergoing gender reassignment.

To tolerate such discrimination would be tantamount, as regards such a person, to a failure to respect the dignity and freedom to which he or she is entitled, and which the Court has a duty to safeguard.

Dismissal of such a person must therefore be regarded as contrary to Article 5(1) of the Directive, unless the dismissal could be justified under Article 2(2). There is, however, no material before the Court to suggest that this was so here.

It follows from the foregoing that the reply to the questions referred by the industrial tribunal must be that, in view of the objective pursued by the Directive, Article 5(1) of the Directive precludes dismissal of a transsexual for a reason related to a gender reassignment. ...'

COMMENT

(1)   The claim here was based on the Equal Treatment Directive. This directive has vertical, not horizontal, direct effect, meaning that only workers employed by an 'emanation of the state' can sue their employer for its breach. However, the county council is clearly an emanation of the state of these purposes.

(2)   While the actual result in the case may be applauded, the reasoning is less than convincing. Both the Advocate-General and the ECJ talk about a fundamental principle of equality; however, only discrimination on grounds of sex is covered by Community law, and a fundamental principle of equality which did not cover race would seem to be rather impoverished.

(3)   Both Community law and British discrimination law have hitherto insisted on there being at least a hypothetical comparison with how someone of the opposite sex would have fared: do you consider that this point is adequately dealt with here?

(4)   The decision in this case has prompted two references to the ECJ on the question of whether discrimination on grounds of homosexuality is contrary to Community law. The Court of Appeal had earlier held it was not in *R* v *Secretary of State, ex p Smith*.

Race Relations Act 1976

1.   (1)   A person discriminates against another in any circumstances relevant for the purposes of any provision of this Act if—
      (a)   on racial grounds he treats that other less favourably than he treats or would treat other persons; or
      (b)   he applies to that other a requirement or condition which he applies or would apply equally to persons not of the same racial group as that other but—
          (i)   which is such that the proportion of persons of the same racial group as that other who can comply with it is considerably smaller than the

proportion of persons not of that racial group who can comply with it; and

    (ii) which he cannot show to be justifiable irrespective of the colour, race, nationality or ethnic or national origins of the person to whom it is applied; and

    (iii) which is to the detriment of that other because he cannot comply with it.

  (2) It is hereby declared that, for the purposes of this Act, segregating a person from other persons on racial grounds is treating him less favourably than they are treated.

3. (1) In this Act, unless the context otherwise requires—

'racial grounds' means any of the following grounds, namely colour, race, nationality or ethnic or national origins;

'racial group' means a group of persons defined by reference to colour, race, nationality or ethnic or national origins, and references to a person's racial group refer to any racial group into which he falls.

  (2) The fact that a racial group comprises two or more distinct racial groups does not prevent it from constituting a particular racial group for the purposes of this Act….

COMMENT

(1) The term 'employment' is defined in exactly the same way as in the SDA in RRA s 78(1).

(2) Most employment protection law is confined to employees, as will be seen in the next chapter. This legislation casts its net much wider.

Mandla v *Dowell Lee*

[1983] ICR 385 House of Lords

An orthodox Sikh boy, required by the rules of his religion to wear a turban, was refused admission to an independent school, on the grounds that wearing a turban would breach the school's rules on uniform. The main issue before the House of Lords was whether Sikhs qualified as a racial group within the meaning of the Act.

Lord Fraser: '… It is not suggested that Sikhs are a group defined by reference to colour, race, nationality or *national* origins. In none of these respects are they distinguishable from many other groups, especially those living, like most Sikhs, in the Punjab. The argument turns entirely upon whether they are a group defined by "*ethnic* origins". It is therefore necessary to ascertain the sense in which the word "ethnic" is used in the Act of 1976. We were referred to various dictionary definitions. The *Oxford English Dictionary* (1897 ed.) gives two meanings of "ethnic". The first is "Pertaining to nations not Christian or Jewish; gentile, heathen, pagan". That clearly cannot be its meaning in the Act of 1976, because it is inconceivable that Parliament would have legislated against racial discrimination intending that the protection should not apply either to Christians or (above all) to Jews. Neither party contended that that was the relevant meaning for the present purpose. The second meaning given in the *Oxford English Dictionary* (1897 ed.) was "Pertaining to race; peculiar to a race or nation; ethnological". A slightly shorter form of that meaning (omitting "peculiar to a race or nation") was given by the *Concise Oxford Dictionary* in 1934 and was expressly accepted by Lord Denning MR as the correct meaning for the present purpose. Oliver and Kerr LJJ also accepted that meaning as being substantially correct, and Oliver LJ said that the word "ethnic" in its popular meaning involved "essentially a racial concept – the concept of something with which the members of the group are born; some fixed or inherited characteristic". The respondent, who appeared on his own behalf, submitted that that was the relevant meaning of "ethnic" in the Act of 1976, and that it did not apply to Sikhs because they were essentially a religious group, and they shared their racial characteristics with other religious groups, including Hindus and Muslims, living in the Punjab. ...

For a group to constitute an ethnic group in the sense of the Act of 1976, it must, in my opinion, regard itself, and be regarded by others, as a distinct community by virtue of certain characteristics. Some of these characteristics are essential; others are not essential but one or more of them will commonly be found and will help to distinguish the group from the surrounding community. The conditions which appear to me to be essential are these: (1) a long shared history, of which the group is conscious as distinguishing it from other groups, and the memory of which it keeps alive; (2) a cultural tradition of its own, including family and social customs and manners, often but not necessarily associated with religious observance. In addition to those two essential characteristics the following characteristics are, in my opinion, relevant; (3) either a common geographical origin, or descent from a small number of common ancestors; (4) a common language, not necessarily peculiar to the group; (5) a common literature peculiar to the group; (6) a common religion different from that of neighbouring groups or from the general community surrounding it; (7) being a minority or being an oppressed or a dominant group within a larger community, for example a conquered people (say, the inhabitants of England shortly after the Norman conquest) and their conquerors might both be ethnic groups.

A group defined by reference to enough of these characteristics would be capable of including converts, for example, persons who marry into the group, and of excluding apostates. Provided a person who joins the group feels himself or herself to be a member of it, and is accepted by other members, then he is, for the purposes of the Act, a member. That appears to be consistent with the words at the end of section 3(1): "references to a person's racial group refer to any racial group into which he falls". In my opinion, it is possible for a person to fall into a particular racial group either by birth or by adherence, and it makes no difference, so far as the Act of 1976 is concerned, by which route he finds his way into the group.

My Lords, I have attempted so far to explain the reasons why, in my opinion, the word "ethnic" in the Act of 1976 should be construed relatively widely, in what was referred to by Mr Irvine as a broad, cultural/historic sense. The conclusion at which I have arrived by construction of the Act itself is greatly strengthened by consideration of the decision of the Court of Appeal in New Zealand (Richmond P, Woodhouse and Richardson JJ) in *King-Ansell* v *Police* ...

Richardson J said:

"The real test is whether the individuals or the group regard themselves and are regarded by others in the community as having a particular historical identity in terms of their colour or their racial, national or ethnic origins. That must be based on a belief shared by members of the group."

And the same learned judge said:

"a group is identifiable in terms of its ethnic origins if it is a segment of the population distinguished from others by a sufficient combination of shared customs, beliefs, traditions and characteristics derived from a common or presumed common past, even if not drawn from what in biological terms is a common racial stock. It is that combination which gives them an historically determined social identity in their own eyes and in the eyes of those outside the group. They have a distinct social identity based not simply on group cohesion and solidarity but also on their belief as to their historical antecedents."

My Lords, that last passage sums up in a way upon which I could not hope to improve the views which I have been endeavouring to express. It is important that courts in English-speaking countries should, if possible, construe the words which we are considering in the same way where they occur in the same context, and I am happy to say that I find no difficulty at all in agreeing with the construction favoured by the New Zealand Court of Appeal ...

The respondent admitted, rightly in my opinion, that, if the proper construction of the word "ethnic" in section 3 of the Act of 1976 is a wide one, on lines such as I have suggested, the Sikhs would qualify as a group defined by ethnic origins for the purposes of the Act. It is, therefore, unnecessary to consider in any detail the relevant characteristics of the Sikhs. They were originally a religious community founded about the end of the 15th century in the Punjab by Guru Nanak, who was born in 1469. But the community is no longer purely religious in character. Their present position is summarised sufficiently for present purposes in the opinion of the learned judge in the county court in the following passage:

"The evidence in my judgment shows that Sikhs are a distinctive and self-conscious community. They have a history going back to the 15th century. They have a written language which a small proportion of Sikhs can read but which can be read by a much higher proportion of Sikhs than of Hindus. They were at one time politically supreme in the Punjab."

The result is, in my opinion, that Sikhs are a group defined by a reference to ethnic origins for the purpose of the Act of 1976, although they are not biologically distinguishable from the other peoples living in the Punjab. That is true whether one is considering the position before the partition of 1947, when the Sikhs lived mainly in that part of the Punjab which is now Pakistan, or after 1947, since when most of them have moved into India ...'

COMMENT

(1) Both the SDA and RRA cover the provision of goods and services, including education, as well as employment. This decision constitutes an important clarification of the law. However, whether or not a group passes the test has been treated as a question of fact rather than of law, meaning that on the whole there can be no appeal from the decision of an industrial tribunal.

(2) With this qualification in mind, it may be noted that the following groups have been held to constitute ethnic groups within the meaning of the RRA: Jews (*Seide* v *Gillette Industries*); gypsies (*CRE* v *Dutton*), and the Welsh (*Gwynedd CC* v *Jones*); but not Rastafarians (*Dawkins* v *Department of the Environment*). There have been conflicting views as regards Muslims at tribunal level, but as yet no reported decision on appeal. (In *Walker* v *Hussain*, the EAT proceeded on the basis that Muslims did not consitute a racial group, but the point was not argued.)

Definition of discrimination

Three kinds of discrimination are identified in the legislation, which are universally known as 'direct discrimination', 'indirect discrimination' and 'discrimination by way of victimisation'.

Direct discrimination

Sex Discrimination Act 1975

1.   (1)   A person discriminates against a woman in any circumstances relevant for the purposes of any provision of this Act if—

   (a)   on the ground of her sex he treats her less favourably than he treats or would treat a man ...

COMMENT

(1)   Direct discrimination against married people (SDA s 3(1)(a)) and on racial grounds (RRA s 1(1)(a)) are similarly defined: see the extracts above. The slight difference in wording in RRA s 1(1)(a) ('on racial grounds' rather than 'on grounds of his race') gives a wider protection as shown by *Showboat* v *Owens*, where a white manager was held to have been treated less favourably on grounds of race when he was dismissed for refusing to obey an order to exclude young blacks from an amusement arcade.

(2)   The meaning of 'on the ground of her sex' has caused difficulty, now resolved by a bare 3–2 majority in the House of Lords in *James* v *Eastleigh BC*.

James v *Eastleigh BC*

[1990] ICR 554 House of Lords

Mr and Mrs James were both aged 61. Because she had reached state pension age while he had not, she received free admission to the municipal swimming pool, but he had to pay 75p to get in.

Lord Bridge: '... At first glance this may seem to be a very trivial matter. But the truth is to the contrary. It is an important test case brought with the backing of the Equal Opportunities Commission in performance of their statutory functions under the Act. The phrase "pensionable age" is a term of art derived from the definition in section 27(1) of the Social Security Act 1975 where it means: "(a) in the case of a man, the age of 65; and (b) in the case of a woman, the age of 60." In this sense it not only governs the age at which persons can first qualify for their state pensions, but is also used as the basis on which men and women qualify for a variety of concessions to the elderly such as free or reduced travel and free prescriptions under the National Health Service. The commission's purpose in this litigation is to establish the principle for which they contend that in any sphere of activity in which discrimination on the ground of sex is prohibited by the Sex Discrimination Act 1975 the practice of denying to men between the ages of 60 and 65 benefits which are offered to women between those ages is unlawful unless it is authorised by other express statutory provisions ...

   In the Court of Appeal the case took an entirely new turn and the court found in favour of the council on a ground first raised in argument by the court themselves. It had been common ground in the county court that the concession offered by the council to persons of pensionable age was discriminatory in favour of women and against men under section 1 of the Sex Discrimination Act 1975. But the Court of Appeal held that the council's less favourable treatment of a man than a woman was not "on the ground of his sex" and that there had accordingly been no direct discrimination contrary to section 1(1)(a)....

The Vice-Chancellor summarised Mr Lester's submissions for the plaintiff as follows,

"Mr Lester, for the plaintiff, forcefully submitted that there is direct discrimination in this case. He submitted that discrimination is 'on the ground of' sex within section 1(1)(a) if the sex of the plaintiff is a substantial cause of the less favourable treatment. In this context, he says, the correct question is 'what would the position have been but for the sex of the plaintiff?' If the position would be different if the plaintiff's sex were different, that is direct discrimination."

I hope I do justice to the judgment if I recite only what seem to me to be the two essential passages, rejecting these submissions as follows,

"In my judgment section 1(1)(a) is looking to the case where, subjectively, the defendant has treated the plaintiff less favourably because of his or her sex. What is relevant is the defendant's reason for doing an act, not the causative effect of the act done by the defendant.

There is a further objection to Mr Lester's construction of the section. If there is direct discrimination in every case where there is a substantial causative link between the defendant's treatment and the detriment suffered by the plaintiff as a result of his sex I can see no room for the operation of subsection (1)(b). In every case in which a sexually neutral condition in fact operates differentially and detrimentally to one sex as opposed to the other, the imposition of such condition would be a substantial cause of detriment to the plaintiff by reason of his or her sex, i.e. it would fall within Mr Lester's causation test and therefore constitute direct discrimination under subsection (1)(a). This plainly was not the intention of Parliament which was drawing a clear distinction between, on the one hand, those cases where the defendant expressly or covertly acts by reference to the sex of the plaintiff and, on the other, those cases where the defendant acted on grounds not expressly or covertly related to sex but his actions have caused a disparate impact as between the sexes."

The fallacy, with all respect, which underlies and vitiates this reasoning is a failure to recognise that the statutory pensionable age, being fixed at 60 for women and 65 for men, is itself a criterion which directly discriminates between men and women in that it treats women more favourably than men "on the ground of their sex". This was readily conceded' by Mr Beloff and is indeed self-evident. It follows inevitably that any other differential treatment of men and women which adopts the same criterion must equally involve discrimination "on the ground of sex". As Mr Beloff was again constrained to concede, the council would certainly have discriminated directly in favour of women and against men on the ground of their sex if they had *expressly* made their concession of free entry to the swimming pool available to women aged 60 and to men aged 65. He submits that the availability of the statutory concept of pensionable age in the Social Security Act 1975 to denote the criterion on which the concession is based and the fact that pensionable age, although now discriminatory, will not necessarily always remain so, enables the council to escape the charge of direct discrimination "on the ground of sex". But this simply will not do. The expression "pensionable age" is no more than a convenient shorthand expression which refers to the age of 60 in a woman and to the age of 65 in a man. In considering whether there has been discrimination against a man "on the ground of his sex" it cannot possibly make any difference whether the alleged discriminator uses the shorthand expression or spells out its full meaning.

The Court of Appeal's attempt to escape from these conclusions lies in construing the phrase "on the ground of her sex" in section 1(1)(a) as referring subjectively to the alleged discriminator's "reason" for doing the act complained of. As already noted, the judgment had earlier identified the council's reason as "to give benefits to those whose resources would be likely to have been reduced by retirement" and "to aid the needy, whether male or female". But to construe the phrase, "on the ground of her sex" as referring to the alleged discriminator's reason in this sense is directly contrary to a long line of authority confirmed by your Lordships' House in *Reg* v *Birmingham City Council, ex parte Equal Opportunities Commission*. In that case the council, as local education authority, was held to have discriminated against girls under section 1(1)(a). At the council's independent, single-sex grammar schools there were more places available for boys than girls. Consequently the council were obliged to set a higher pass mark for girls than boys in the grammar school entrance examination. In his speech, expressing the unanimous opinion of the House, Lord Goff of Chieveley said,

> "The first argument advanced by the council before your Lordship's House was that there had not been, in the present case, less favourable treatment of the girls on the grounds of sex. Here two points were taken. It was submitted ... (2) that, if that burden had been discharged, it still had to be shown that there was less favourable treatment on grounds of sex, and that involved establishing an intention or motive on the part of the council to discriminate against the girls. In my opinion, neither of these submissions is well-founded.... As to the second point, it is, in my opinion, contrary to the terms of the statute. There is discrimination under the statute if there is less favourable treatment on the ground of sex, in other words if the relevant girl or girls would have received the same treatment as the boys but for their sex. The intention or motive of the defendant to discriminate, though it may be relevant so far as remedies are concerned ... is not a necessary condition of liability; it is perfectly possible to envisage cases where the defendant had no such motive, and yet did in fact discriminate on the ground of sex ..."

Lord Goff's test, it will be observed, is not subjective, but objective. Adopting it here the question becomes: "Would the plaintiff, a man of 61, have received the same treatment as his wife but for his sex?" An affirmative answer is inescapable ...

The question of indirect discrimination under section 1(1)(b) arises only where the "requirement or condition" applied by the alleged discriminator to a person of one sex is applied by him equally to a person of the other sex. Pensionable age cannot be regarded as a requirement or condition which is applied equally to persons of either sex precisely because it is itself discriminatory between the sexes. Whether or not the proportion of men of pensionable age resorting to the council's swimming pool was smaller than the proportion of women of pensionable age was quite irrelevant. Women were being treated more favourably than men because they attained the age to qualify for free admission five years earlier than men ...'

(Lord Ackner and Lord Goff delivered concurring judgments; Lord Griffiths and Lord Lowry dissented.)

COMMENT

(1) Suppose that everything that was red was also round. Would the two qualities still be different? Would action taken on grounds of redness also be action taken on grounds of roundness? Is that the situation here?

(2)   Suppose that the gender-based criterion affects no members of one group but only some members of the other group. Is action on the basis of this criterion direct discrimination? What if a woman suffers discrimination on the grounds that she is pregnant?

This has given the courts great difficulty, especially because SDA s 5(3) provides:

'A comparison of the cases of persons of different sex or marital status under section 1(1) or 3(1) must be such that the relevant circumstances in the one case are the same, or not materially different, in the other.'

Webb v EMO Air Cargo (UK) Ltd

[1994] IRLR 482 European Court of Justice

Judgment of the Court: '1. By order of 26 November 1992, received at the court on 4 February 1993, the House of Lords referred to the court for a preliminary ruling under art 177 of the EEC Treaty a question on the interpretation of the [Equal Treatment Directive] on the implementation of the principle of equal treatment for men and women as regards access to employment, vocational training and promotion, and working conditions.

2. That question was raised in proceedings between Mrs Webb and EMO Air Cargo (UK) Ltd (hereinafter 'EMO').

3. It appears from the order for reference that in 1987 EMO employed 16 persons. In June one of the four employees working in the import operations department, Mrs Stewart, found that she was pregnant. EMO decided not to wait until her departure on maternity leave before engaging a replacement whom Mrs Stewart could train during the six months prior to her going on leave. Mrs Webb was recruited with a view, initially, to replacing Mrs Stewart following a probationary period. However, it was envisaged that Mrs Webb would continue to work for EMO following Mrs Stewart's return. The documents before the court show that Mrs Webb did not know she was pregnant when the employment contract was entered into.

4. Mrs Webb started work at EMO on 1 July 1987. Two weeks later, she thought that she might be pregnant. Her employer was informed of this indirectly. He then called her in to see him and informed her of his intention to dismiss her. Mrs Webb's pregnancy was confirmed a week later. On 30 July she received a letter dismissing her in the following terms: "You will recall that at your interview some four weeks ago you were told that the job for which you applied and were given had become available because of one of our employees becoming pregnant. Since you have only now told me that you are also pregnant I have no alternative other than to terminate your employment with our company."

5. Mrs Webb then brought proceedings before the industrial tribunal, pleading direct discrimination on grounds of sex and, in the alternative, indirect discrimination.
...

14. The House of Lords found that the special feature of this case lay in the fact that the pregnant woman who was dismissed had been recruited precisely in order to replace, at least initially, an employee who was herself due to take maternity leave. The national court is uncertain whether it was unlawful to dismiss Mrs Webb on the ground of her pregnancy, or whether greater weight should be attached to the reasons for which she was recruited.

15. Taking the view that it should construe the applicable domestic legislation so as to accord with the interpretation of Directive 76/207, as laid down by the court, the House of Lords stayed proceedings and submitted the following question for a preliminary ruling:

"Is it discrimination on grounds of sex contrary to Council Directive (EEC) 76/207 for an employer to dismiss a female employee ('the appellant') (a) whom he engaged for the specific purpose of replacing (after training) another female employee during the latter's forthcoming maternity leave, (b) when, very shortly after appointment, the employer discovers that the appellant herself will be absent on maternity leave during the maternity leave of the other employee, and the employer dismisses her because he needs the job holder to be at work during that period, (c) had the employer known of the pregnancy of the appellant at the date of appointment, she would not have been appointed, and (d) the employer would similarly have dismissed a male employee engaged for this purpose who required leave of absence at the relevant time for medical or other reasons?

16. As is apparent from the documents before the court, the question submitted for a preliminary ruling relates to a contract of employment concluded for an indefinite period.

17. According to art 1(1), the purpose of Directive 76/207 is to put into effect in the member states the principle of equal treatment for men and women as regards access to employment, including promotion, and vocational training and as regards working conditions.

18. Article 2(1) of directive 76/207 states that "the principle of equal treatment shall mean that there shall be no discrimination whatsoever on grounds of sex either directly or indirectly by reference in particular to marital or family status". Under art 5(1), "application of the principle of equal treatment with regard to working conditions, including the conditions governing dismissal, means that men and women shall be guaranteed the same conditions without discrimination on grounds of sex".

19. As the court ruled in *Handels-og Kontorfunktionærernes Forbund i Danmark* v *Dansk Arbejdsgiverforening* (the *Hertz* case) and confirmed in its judgment in *Habermann-Beltermann* v *Arbeiterwohlfahrt, Bezirksverband Ndb/Opf eV*, the dismissal of a female worker on account of pregnancy constitutes direct discrimination on grounds of sex.

20. Furthermore, by reserving to member states the right to retain or introduce provisions which are intended to protect women in connection with 'pregnancy and maternity', art 2(3) of Directive 76/207 recognises the legitimacy, in terms of the principle of equal treatment, first, of protecting a woman's biological condition during and after pregnancy and, second, of protecting the special relationship between a woman and her child over the period which follows pregnancy and childbirth (see the *Habermann-Beltermann* case and *Hofmann* v *Barmer Ersatzkasse*).

21. In view of the harmful effects which the risk of dismissal may have on the physical and mental state of women who are pregnant, have recently given birth or are breastfeeding, including the particularly serious risk that pregnant women may be prompted voluntarily to terminate their pregnancy, the Community legislature subsequently provided, pursuant to art 10 of Council Directive (EEC) 92/85 of 19 October 1992 on the introduction of measures to encourage improvements in the safety and health at work of pregnant workers and workers who have recently given birth or are breastfeeding, for special protection to be given to women by prohibiting dismissal during the period from the beginning of their pregnancy to the end of their maternity leave.

22. Furthermore, art 10 of Directive 92/85 provides that there is to be no exception to, or derogation from, the prohibition on the dismissal of pregnant women during that period, save in exceptional cases not connected with their condition.

23. The answer to the question submitted by the House of Lords, which concerns Directive 76/207, must take account of that general context.

24. First, in response to the House of Lords' inquiry, there can be no question of comparing the situation of a woman who finds herself incapable, by reason of pregnancy discovered very shortly after the conclusion of the employment contract, of performing the task for which she was recruited with that of a man similarly incapable for medical or other reasons.

25. As Mrs Webb rightly argues, pregnancy is not in any way comparable with a pathological condition, and even less so with unavailability for work on non-medical grounds, both of which are situations that may justify the dismissal of a woman without discriminating on grounds of sex. Moreover, in the *Hertz* case the court drew a clear distinction between pregnancy and illness, even where the illness is attributable to pregnancy but manifests itself after the maternity leave. As the court pointed out, there is no reason to distinguish such an illness from any other illness.

26. Furthermore, contrary to the submission of the United Kingdom, dismissal of a pregnant woman recruited for an indefinite period cannot be justified on grounds relating to her inability to fulfil a fundamental condition of her employment contract. The availability of an employee is necessarily, for the employer, a precondition for the proper performance of the employment contract. However, the protection afforded by Community law to a woman during pregnancy and after childbirth cannot be dependent on whether her presence at work during maternity is essential to the proper functioning of the undertaking in which she is employed. Any contrary interpretation would render ineffective the provisions of Directive 76/207.

27. In circumstances such as those of Mrs Webb, termination of a contract for an indefinite period on grounds of the woman's pregnancy cannot be justified by the fact that she is prevented, on a purely temporary basis, from performing the work for which she has been engaged (see the *Habermann-Beltermann* case and the Advocate General's opinion in this case).

28. The fact that the main proceedings concern a woman who was initially recruited to replace another employee during the latter's maternity leave but who was herself found to be pregnant shortly after her recruitment cannot affect the answer to be given to the national court.

29. Accordingly, the answer to the question submitted must be that art 2(1) read with art 5(1) of Directive 76/207 precludes dismissal of an employee who is recruited for an unlimited term with a view, initially, to replacing another employee during the latter's maternity leave and who cannot do so because, shortly after recruitment, she is herself found to be pregnant....'

Webb v *EMO Air Cargo (UK) Ltd (No. 2)*

[1995] IRLR 645 House of Lords

Lord Keith: '... The reasoning in my speech in the earlier proceedings was to the effect that the relevant circumstance which existed in the present case and which should be taken to be present in the case of the hypothetical man was unavailability for work at the time when the worker was particularly required, and that the reason for the unavailability was not a relevant circumstance. So it was not relevant that the reason for the woman's unavailability was pregnancy, a condition which could not be present in a man.

The ruling of the European Court proceeds on an interpretation of the broad principles dealt with in Articles 2(1) and 5(1) of the Directive 76/207/EEC. Sections 1(1)(a) and 5(3) of the Act of 1975 set out a more precise test of unlawful discrimination and the problem is how to fit the terms of that test into the ruling. It seems to me that the only way of doing so is to hold that, in a case where a woman is engaged for an indefinite period, the fact that the reason why she will be temporarily unavailable for work at a time when to her knowledge her services will be particularly required is pregnancy is a circumstance relevant to her case, being a circumstance which could not be present in the case of the hypothetical man. It does not necessarily follow that pregnancy would be a relevant circumstance in the situation where the woman is denied employment for a fixed period in the future during the whole of which her pregnancy would make her unavailable for work, nor in the situation where after engagement for such a period the discovery of her pregnancy leads to cancellation of the engagement.

My Lords, for these reasons I would allow the appeal and remit the case to the industrial tribunal to assess compensation....'

(Lord Griffiths, Browne-Wilkinson, Mustill and Slynn agreed with Lord Keith.)

COMMENT

(1)   Following this case, it is now clear that discrimination on grounds of pregnancy is sex discrimination, regardless of the comparison issue.

(2)   Lord Keith seemed to leave open the door for a different decision if a fixed-term contract was involved. However, the EAT declined to go through it in *Caruana* v *Manchester Airport*.

(3)   The 'sick man' comparison has not disappeared for all purposes, however. In *Hertz* v *Aldi Marked* the ECJ held that it was not unlawful sex discrimination to dismiss a woman for sickness absence resulting from pregnancy where a man would have been dismissed for a similar level of absence through illness (see also *Larsson* v *Føtex Supermarked*).

(4)   To some extent, this particular issue has been overtaken by the Pregnant Workers Directive (see below, Chapter 6). Dismissal on grounds of pregnancy is automatically unfair under ERA s 99. However, the sex discrimination claim remains important because (a) it applies to recruitment and problems arising during employment as well as to dismissal, and (b) there is no limit on compensation for dismissal claims.

Sexual and racial harassment

While the terms sexual harassment and racial harassment are not to be found in British legislation, and cannot be regarded as terms of art, it is clear that harassment can amount to less favourable treatment on grounds of sex or race and thus constitute direct discrimination.

Porcelli v Strathclyde Regional Council

[1986] ICR 564 Court of Session

Lord President (Lord Emslie): '... From the findings of the industrial tribunal it appears that in August 1980 there were three laboratory technicians on the staff at Bellahouston Academy, including the applicant. Her two colleagues were female. By December 1982 these two ladies had left the school and their places were taken by two men, Coles and Reid, who were of the same status as the applicant although they did not have as many years of experience. The industrial tribunal had no doubt that from the moment when they arrived in the school Coles and Reid pursued a policy of vindictive unpleasantness towards the applicant for the deliberate purpose of making her apply for a transfer to another school, and they went on to say that they had no doubt that they treated the applicant quite shamefully and that it must have been a singularly unpleasant and distressing period of time for her when she had to work alongside them ... it is found that Coles subjected her to treatment which can be described, in popular language, as "sexual harassment". The applicant's evidence about this treatment was accepted by the industrial tribunal who found that they could not, on any matter, place any reliance upon the evidence of Coles and Reid. Since it is agreed that the evidence given by the applicant was in accordance with the particulars averred in support of her application it will be convenient to quote them in full:

> "Shortly after the incident of my personal belongings being thrown out by Mr Coles and Mr Reid, Mr Coles began subjecting me to sexual harassment. During morning and afternoon teabreaks in the technicians' room I became aware of him deliberately staring at me and following me with his eyes when I moved about the room. He also began to make suggestive remarks. He would, for example, pick up a screw nail and ask me if I would like a screw. Another example was when he picked up a glass rod holder – which is shaped like a penis – and asked if I had any use for it. On several occasions he opened the Daily Record at page 3 and commented on my physical appearance in comparison with that of the nude female depicted in the newspaper. The atmosphere in the technicians' room became so unpleasant for me that I stopped using it during break times when Mr Coles and Mr Reid were there. After I had stopped using the technicians' room Mr Coles began to harass me in the preparation room. It was his practice to come behind me and take me unawares so that when I turned round he would brush against me. In addition to sexually harassing me Mr Coles began to behave in an intimidating way towards me. On several occasions he deliberately allowed swing doors to slam back in my face when I was carrying apparatus and could not protect myself...".

For the employers the submission was that in the proved circumstances of this case the industrial tribunal was clearly of opinion that the episodes of "sexual harassment" of the applicant by Coles were merely part of a single campaign against her founded upon dislike for her as a colleague. Such treatment of the applicant was not, accordingly, to be seen as having been meted out to her because she was a woman but because she was heartily disliked by Coles and Reid as a person and as a colleague. In any event, said counsel for the employers, the industrial tribunal correctly understood and applied section 1(1)(a) in that they went on to decide upon the evidence that Coles and Reid would have treated an equally disliked male colleague just as unfavourably as they had treated the applicant. In these circumstances the appeal tribunal was not entitled to interfere with their decision to dismiss the applicant's application because it cannot be seen to be flawed by an error of approach in law.

After some initial hesitation which I freely confess I have come to be of opinion that for the reasons advanced by the Dean of Faculty for the applicant the submissions for the employers fall to be rejected. Section 1(1) (a) is concerned with "treatment" and not with the motive or objective of the person responsible for it. Although in some cases it will be obvious that there is a sex related purpose in the mind of a person who indulges in unwanted and objectionable sexual overtures to a woman or exposes her to offensive sexual jokes or observations that is not this case. But it does not follow that because the campaign pursued against the applicant as a whole had no sex related motive or objective, the treatment of the applicant by Coles, which was of the nature of "sexual harassment" is not to be regarded as having been "on the ground of her sex" within the meaning of section 1(1)(a). In my opinion this particular part of the campaign was plainly adopted against the applicant because she was a woman. It was a particular kind of weapon, based upon the sex of the victim, which, as the industrial tribunal recognised would not have been used against an equally disliked man. Indeed, I do not understand from the reasons of the industrial tribunal that they were not entirely satisfied upon that matter, and they were in my opinion well entitled to be so satisfied upon a proper interpretation of section 1(1)(a). As I read their reasons the decision against the applicant, which they reached with evident regret, proceeded only upon their view that Coles and Reid would have treated an equally disliked male colleague just as unfavourably as they had treated the applicant. It is at this point, in my opinion, that their decision is vulnerable.

The industrial tribunal reached their decision by finding that Coles' and Reid's treatment of an equally disliked male colleague would have been just as unpleasant. Where they went wrong, however, was in failing to notice that a material part of the campaign against the applicant consisted of sexual harassment, a particularly degrading and unacceptable form of treatment which it must be taken to have been the intention of Parliament to restrain. From their reasons it is to be understood that they were satisfied that this form of treatment – sexual harassment in any form – would not have figured in a campaign by Coles and Reid directed against a man. In this situation the treatment of the applicant fell to be seen as very different in a material respect from that which would have been inflicted on a male colleague, regardless of equality of overall unpleasantness, and that being so it appears to me that upon a proper application of section 1(1)(a) the industrial tribunal ought to have asked themselves whether in that respect the applicant had been treated by Coles (on the ground of her sex) "less favourably" than he would have treated a man with whom her position fell to be compared. Had they asked themselves that question it is impossible to believe that they would not have answered it in the affirmative. In the result it has not been shown that the appeal tribunal were not entitled to substitute their own decision in the applicant's favour for that of the industrial tribunal and I am of opinion that the appeal by the employers should be refused.'

COMMENT

(1)   This was the first case on sexual harassment to be appealed. Lord Grieve and Lord Brand delivered concurring judgments.

(2)   In 1991 the EC Commission issued a Recommendation and a Code of Practice on the protection of dignity at work, containing useful guidance on the definition of sexual harassment.

Commission Recommendation on Protecting the Dignity of Women and Men at Work

91/131/EEC

Article 1

It is recommended that the Member State take action to promote awareness that conduct of a sexual nature, or other conduct based on sex affecting the dignity of women and men at work, including conduct of superiors and colleagues, is unacceptable if —

(a)   such conduct is unwanted, unreasonable and offensive to the recipient;

(b)   a person's rejection of or submission to such conduct on the part of employers or workers (including superiors or colleagues) is used explicitly or implicitly as a basis for a decision which affects that person's access to vocational training, access to employment, continued employment, promotion, salary or other employment decisions; and/or

(c)   such conduct creates an intimidating, hostile or humiliating work environment for the recipient;

and that such conduct may, in certain circumstances, be contrary to the principle of equal treatment within the meaning of Articles 3, 4 and 5 of Directive 76/207/EEC.

Article 2

It is recommended that Member States should take action, in the public sector, to implement the Commission's Code of Practice on the protection of the dignity of women and men at work, annexed hereto. The action of the Member States, in thus initiating and pursuing positive measures designed to create a climate at work in which women and men respect one another's human integrity, should serve as an example to the private sector.

Article 3

It is recommended that Member States encourage employers and employee representatives to develop measures to implement the Commission's Code of Practice on the protection of the dignity of women and men at work....

Commission Code of Practice on Protecting the Dignity of Women and Men at Work

2   Definition

Sexual harassment means 'unwanted conduct of a sexual nature, or other conduct based on sex affecting the dignity of women and men at work'. This can include unwelcome physical, verbal or non-verbal conduct.

Thus, a range of behaviour may be considered to constitute sexual harassment. It is unacceptable if such conduct is unwanted, unreasonable and offensive to the recipient; a person's rejection of or submission to such conduct on the part of employers or workers (including superiors or colleagues) is used explicitly or implicitly as a basis for a decision which affects that person's access to vocational training or to employment, continued employment, promotion, salary or any other employment decisions; and/or such conduct creates an intimidating, hostile or humiliating working environment for the recipient.

The essential characteristic of sexual harassment is that it is unwanted by the recipient, that it is for each individual to determine what behaviour is acceptable to them and what they regard as offensive. Sexual attention becomes sexual harassment if it is persisted in once it has been made clear that it is regarded by the recipient as offensive, although one incident of harassment may constitute sexual harassment if sufficiently serious. It is the unwanted nature of the conduct which distinguishes sexual harassment from friendly behaviour, which is welcome and mutual.

COMMENT

(1)   While Recommendations do not have binding effect on member states, they should be taken into account by national courts where Community law is relevant: *Grimaldi* v *Fonds des Maladies Professionelles*. This definition was referred to as a useful source by the EAT in *Wadman* v *Carpenter Farrer*.

De Souza v Automobile Association

[1986] ICR 514 Court of Appeal

The employee, who was of Asian origin, had either overheard herself being referred to as 'the wog' or had been told about it.

May LJ: '... In his submissions on behalf of the employee, Mr Sedley suggested that the real question for determination was whether an ethnic minority employee who is upset when she hears herself spoken of or referred to as "the wog" by a member of her employer's staff thereby suffers, or is capable of suffering, a "detriment" within the meaning of section 4(2)(c) of the Race Relations Act 1976. This issue was not separately presented to the industrial tribunal but it has now been properly identified both by the appeal tribunal and also by Oliver LJ, who gave leave to appeal. Mr Sedley was prepared to accept that the phrase "any other detriment" in section 4(2)(c) must be read in context and submitted that a detriment occurs to an employee within that paragraph of the subsection whenever a person is subjected to some disadvantage in the context of his or her employment. Where, as the industrial tribunal found in this case, the gratuitous insult showed that all was not well in the department at the time of the remark and that there was an element of racial prejudice there, what Mr Sedley described as a hostile working environment had been demonstrated, which was clearly a disadvantage in the context of the employee's employment. When the insult is based on race, it becomes a detriment by way of racial discrimination by virtue of section 1(1)(a) and thus the case is made out. If there were any doubt whether an insult could have been contemplated by Parliament as being within the concept of detriment, Mr Sedley submitted that this was resolved by the declaratory provision in section 57(4) that damages under the Act may include compensation for injury to feelings, whether or not they include compensation under any other head ...

We were referred to a number of authorities, amongst them *Ministry of Defence* v *Jeremiah.* That was a case under section 6(2)(b) of the Sex Discrimination Act 1975, which in so far as is presently material is in the same terms as section 4(2)(c) of the Race Relations Act 1976. A male employee complained that he was being discriminated against compared with female employees doing nominally the same job, in that he and his fellows were required to do a particularly dirty part of the job which their female colleagues were not. The question arose whether the men were being subjected "to any other detriment". Brandon LJ said: "I do not regard the expression 'subjecting ... to any other detriment' ... as meaning anything more than 'putting under a disadvantage.' " Brightman LJ in his turn said: "I think a detriment exists if a reasonable worker would or might take the view that the duty was in all the circumstances to his detriment."

In *Kirby* v *Manpower Services Commission*, a case before the Employment Appeal Tribunal under the Act of 1976, the "detriment" relied on was being moved by the manager of a Job Centre from the position of a first tier clerk interviewing applicants for jobs to that of filing clerk inside the office where the complainant had no contact with the public. The appeal tribunal held, following *Jeremiah's* case, that this would have been a sufficient detriment within the statute, but also held that the complainant had not been treated less favourably than anyone else, white or coloured, would have been treated in the same circumstances.

In *BL Cars Ltd* v *Brown* a black employee had been arrested and then granted bail. The employers feared that he would attempt to re-enter their plant, possibly using a false name. The chief security officer, therefore, issued instructions to those responsible at the gates of the plant, which included a thorough check on the identity of every black employee trying to enter the premises. Some 28 people complained that this instruction subjected them to a detriment which contravened the Act of 1976. Some of these were employed by BL Cars Ltd and some by contractors. The Commission for Racial Equality also issued a complaint that the instruction was unlawful. An industrial tribunal decided as a preliminary point that the mere issue of a written instruction could occasion detriment to individual employees. On appeal the appeal tribunal, again following *Jeremiah's* case, upheld the industrial tribunal's decision.

In each of these cases the detriment or disadvantage to the employee was in connection with what Mr Sedley described as his employment context. In the first, it was having to do dirty work: in the second, it was losing the more congenial work at the counter and having to work as a filing clerk in the rear office: in the third, it was being thoroughly checked when coming in to work, substantially more thoroughly than were white fellow employees. Apart from the actual decisions in these cases, I think that this necessarily follows upon a proper construction of section 4, and in particular section 4(2)(c) of the Act. Racially to insult a coloured employee is not enough by itself, even if that insult caused him or her distress; before the employee can be said to have been subjected to some "other detriment" the court or tribunal must find that by reason of the act or acts complained of a reasonable worker would or might take the view that he had thereby been disadvantaged in the circumstances in which he had thereafter to work.'

(Neill and Slade LJJ agreed.)

COMMENT

(1)   Should injury to feelings be considered as an adequate detriment to constitute discrimination?

(2)   What are the characteristics of the reasonable employee in this regard?

(3)   It will be clear from *Porcelli* that sexual harassment is by no means always a problem of management exploiting subordinate workers. How far is an employer liable for the acts of employees, customers and other third parties which may be unknown and which would be disapproved of if they were known?

Sex Discrimination Act 1975

41.   (1)   Anything done by a person in the course of his employment shall be treated for the purposes of this Act as done by his employer as well as by him, whether or not it was done with the employer's knowledge or approval....

      (3)   In proceedings brought under this Act against any person in respect of an act alleged to have been done by an employee of his it shall be a defence for that person to prove that he took such steps as were reasonably practicable to prevent the employee from doing that act, or from doing in the course of his employment acts of that description.

(RRA s 32 is in parallel terms.)

Jones v Tower Boot Co Ltd

[1997] IRLR 168   Court of Appeal

Waite LJ: '... In April 1992 a 16-year-old boy started work at the employers' shoe factory, as a last operative. He was of mixed ethnic parentage and was joining a workforce which had not previously employed anyone of ethnic minority origin. From this outset he was subjected by fellow-employees to harassment of the gravest kind. He was called by such racially offensive names as "chimp" amd "monkey". A notice had been stuck on his back reading "Chipmonks are go". Two employees whipped him on the legs with a piece of welt and threw metal bolts at his head. One of them burnt his arm with a hot screwdriver, and later the same two seized his arm again and tried to put it in a lasting machine, where the burn was caught and started to bleed again. Unable to endure this treatment, the boy left the job after four weeks. He made a complaint against the employers of racial discrimination, contending that his fellow employees had subjected him to a discriminatory detriment on racial grounds under s 4(2)(c) of the Race Relations Act 1976 ("racial harassment"), for which the employers were responsible by virtue of s 32(1) of the Act as representing acts done by the employees in the course of their employment. The employers sought to resist the claim on the ground that the relevant acts had been outside the scope of the employee's employment; or on the alternative ground that all reasonably practicable steps to avoid them for the purposes of s 32(3) ("the reasonable steps defence") had been taken.

On appeal to the Employment Appeal Tribunal the employers did not challenge the industrial tribunal's primary findings of fact as to the treatment given to the complainant or the finding that such treatment amounted to racial harassment. Nor was any challenge directed to the industrial tribunal's finding that the reasonable steps defence had not been made out. The sole ground of appeal was that the industrial tribunal had been wrong to regard the racial harassment as having been "done by a person in the course of his employment" for the purposes of s 32(1). The Employment Appeal Tribunal (Buckley J, Mrs Boyle and Mr Blyghton) were divided on that issue. The majority (the judicial chairman and Mrs Boyle) regarded this ground of appeal as being made out. They stated their reasons thus:

> "That phrase ['the course of employment'] has, and had at the time the draftsman penned s 32, a well-established meaning in law. We would have seen no reason not to adopt that meaning in the present context, in any event. Since it has been adopted by other decisions of this tribunal and by the Court of Appeal, see *Irving* v *The Post Office*, we shall certainly do so.
>
> We were referred to *Bracebridge Engineering* v *Darby* by Mr Whitmore on behalf of Mr Jones. That case conveniently cites *Aldred* v *Nacanco* in which the Court of Appeal quoted the well-known statement of principle set out in *Salmond on Torts* 18th edition at page 437 ... The nub of the test is whether the unauthorised wrongful act of the servant is so connected with that which he was employed to do as to be a mode of doing it. That has to be judged by reference to all the circumstances of the case. Applying that test to the facts of this case we cannot, by any stretch of the imagination, see how the acts complained of by Mr Jones, including deliberate branding with a hot screwdriver and whipping, could be described as an improper mode of performing authorised tasks. With respect, the industrial tribunal cannot have applied the law correctly and paragraph 9 of the reasons illustrates that. In answer to [counsel for the employers] Mr Buckhaven's submission that the acts were outside the scope of employment the tribunal held – 'if we accept the breadth of Mr Buckhaven's submission ... no act carried out by an employee can become the liability of the employer unless it was expressly authorised.' We presume the tribunal must have been referring to acts of the type in question, that is, acts such as assault not usually regarded as modes of carrying out employment tasks, otherwise the comment makes no sense. But to hold that an act is in the course of employment on this basis is to rewrite the accepted legal test. In any event, *Bracebridge* itself illustrates how such an act, in that case an indecent assault, could be in the course of employment. We are bound to say *Bracebridge* seems to stretch the test to its limit but the explanation for the decision clearly lies in the fact that the perpetrators were, at the time, involved in disciplinary supervision. That was not so in the present case and we conclude that Mr Jones's fellow-employees were not acting in the course of employment and their misdeeds cannot be laid at the door of [the employers] by reason of s 32(1)."

The minority view was summed up by Mr Blyghton in these words:

"One has to ask the question: 'Under what circumstances could a claim for racial discrimination succeed if it could be held that such actions do not occur in the course of employment?' The very strict common-law principles of vicarious liability were not intended to be rigidly applied in such cases; hence the code of practice."

In this appeal the complainant, with the backing of the Commission for Racial Equality, submits that Mr Blyghton was right and the majority was wrong. He does not base that claim (as he might have done) on the narrow objection that even if the majority was right in regarding the acts of physical assault as being outside the conventional tortious test for vicarious liability, they failed to consider whether the verbal abuse stood in a different category. He bases it (as in my opinion he is fully entitled to do) upon a challenge to the entire notion that the words "in the course of his employment" in s 32(1) are to be given a restricted meaning which would limit them to instances where the impugned conduct on the part of the employee would attract tortious liability to the employer under the common-law doctrine of vicarious liability.

The issue on this appeal

The effect of that challenge is to require an answer to this question. When an industrial tribunal is considering whether for the purposes of s 32(1) any conduct complained of does or does not amount to a "thing done by a person in the course of his employment", is the tribunal bound to answer that by reference to:

(a)   the words "course of employment" in the sense in which they are employed in everyday speech; or

(b)   the principles laid down by case law for the establishment of vicarious liability by an employer for the torts committed by an employee during the course of his employment?

That is an issue of widespread importance. The fact that the mechanism of the relevant sections of the Race Relations Act is matched exactly by corresponding provisions in the Sex Discrimination Act 1975 means that the issue needs to be resolved in relation to all acts of harassment on the grounds of race or sex which occur in an employment context.

The governing principles of statutory construction

Two principles are in my view involved. The first is that a statute is to be construed according to its legislative purpose, with due regard to the result which it is the stated or presumed intention of Parliament to achieve and the means provided for achieving it ("the purposive construction"); and the second is that words in a statute are to be given their normal meaning according to general use in the English language unless the context indicates that such words have to be given a special or technical meaning as a term of art ("the linguistic construction"). It will be convenient to deal with those separately.

The purposive construction

The legislation now represented by the Race and Sex Discrimination Act currently in force broke new ground in seeking to work upon the minds of men and women and thus affect their attitude to the social consequences of difference between the sexes or distinction of skin colour. Its general thrust was educative, persuasive, and (where necessary) coercive. The relief accorded to the victims (or potential victims) of discrimination went beyond the ordinary remedies of damages and an injunction – introducing, through declaratory powers in the court or tribunal and recommendatory powers in the relevant Commission, provisions with a proactive function, designed as much to eliminate the occasions for discrimination as to compensate its victims or punish its perpetrators. These were linked to a code of practice of which courts and tribunals were to take cognisance. Consistently with the broad front on which it operates, the legislation has traditionally been given a wide interpretation – see for example *Savjani* v *IRC* where Templeman LJ said of the Race Relations Act:

"…the Act was brought in to rememdy a very great evil. It is expressed in very wide terms, and I should be slow to find that the effect of something which is humiliatingly discriminatory in racial matters falls outside the ambit of the Act."

Since the getting and losing of work, and the daily funtioning of the workplace, are prime areas for potential discrimination on grounds of race or sex, it is not surprising that both Acts contain specific provisions to govern the field of employment. Those provisions are themselves wide-ranging – as is evidenced, for example, by the inclusion of contract workers without employee status within the scheme of the legislation. There is no indication in the Act that by dealing specifically with the employment field Parliament intended in any way to limit the general thrust of the legislation.

A purposive construction accordingly requires s 32 of the Race Relations Act (and the corresponding s 41 of the Sex Discrimination Act) to be given a broad interpretation. It would be inconsistent with that requirement to allow the notion of the "course of employment" to be construed in any sense more limited than the natural meaning of those everyday words would allow.

The linguistic construction

Mr Buckhaven's argument is attractively simple. Vicarious liability is a doctrine of tortious liability which has been applied by the common law to the employment context. Part Three of the Race Relations Act applies expressly to discrimination in the employment field. The two fields are the same. Words and phrases that have acquired a familiar and particular meaning through case law applied to employers' liability in the former context must therefore have been intended by Parliament to have the same meaning when applied to employers' liability in the latter context.

Mr Allen QC, while acknowledging that there is a broad conceptual similarity between the employers' responsibility that applies in both contexts, submits that substantial differences emerge when vicarious liability in tort is analysed and contrasted with the statutory scheme of which s 32 forms part. The employer's authority, for example, is a crucial element in vicarious liability in tort – as evidenced by the statement in *Salmond* (20th edition) in paragraph 21.5 that:

"A master is not responsible for a wrongful act done by his servant unless it is done in the course of his employment. It is deemed to be so done if it is either (1) a wrongful act authorised by the master, or (2) a wrongful and unauthorised way of doing some act authorised by the master."

That is to be contrasted with the position under s 32(1) of the Race Relations Act, where all actions by a person in the course of employment are attributed to the employer " whether or not … done with the employer's knowledge or approval". Mr Allen points to other distinctions, such as the greater range of remedies available under the statute (including damages for injury to feelings) than those available in tort against an employer at common law, and the total absence from the concept of vicarious liability in tort of any provision corresponding to the reasonable steps defence under s 32(3).

I am persuaded that Mr Allen's submission is to be preferred, and that there is here no sufficient similarity between the two contexts to justify, on a linguistic construction, the reading of the phrase "course of employment" as subject to the gloss imposed on it in the common law context of vicarious liability.

The position apart from authority

Both approaches to statutory construction therefore lead to the same interpretation. But even more compelling, in my view, is the anomaly which would result (as the minority member Mr Blyghton pointed out) from adopting any other interpretation. Mr Buckhaven accepts (indeed in his written argument he relies upon) the fact that an inevitable result of construing "course of employment" in the sense for which he contends will be that the more heinous the act of discrimination, the less likely it will be that the employer would be liable. That, he argues, is all to the good. Parliament must have intended the liability of employers to be kept within reasonable bounds.

I would reject that submission entirely. It cuts across the whole legislative scheme and underlying policy of s 32 (and its counterpart in sex discrimination), which is to deter racial and sexual harassment in the workplace through a widening of the net of responsibility beyond the guilty employees themselves, by making all employers additionally liable for such harassment, and then supplying them with the reasonable steps defence under s 32(3) which will exonerate the conscientious employer who has used his best endeavours to prevent such harassment, and will encourage all employers who have not yet undertaken such endeavours to take the steps necessary to make the same defence available in their own workplace. The recent decision of the Employment Appeal Tribunal in *Burton and Rhule v De Vere Hotels* provides a useful illustration of the matters to which employers need to be alert if they are to be able to take advantage of the reasonable steps defence in a harassment context.

The case law

Mr Buckhaven submits that the whole question is in any event concluded by authority at the level of this court which is binding on us. The case is *Irving* v *The Post Office*. That was a case in which a Post Office employee had neighbours who were black. He fell into dispute with them. While sorting mail at his place of work, he came across a letter addressed to them, and made use of that opportunity to write a racially offensive remark on the envelope before it was placed for delivery. The neighbours, having received the letter in the ordinary course of post, complained to the Post Office who conducted an investigation, identified the culprit and disciplined him. The neighbours brought a complaint of racial discrimination against the Post Office, which was heard in the county court by an Assistant Recorder sitting with two assessors. The complaint was dismissed, and the Court of Appeal (Fox LJ and Sheldon J) dismissed the neighbours' appeal from that decision.

No record of the arguments heard on that appeal has survived. It is undoubtedly the case, however, that both judgments proceeded on the basis that any issue as to the liability of the Post Office for the action of their employee depended upon establishing vicarious liability in the sense in which that concept is used in the law of tort. It is also the case, however, that in neither judgment is a single reference made to s 32 of the Race Relations Act. Indeed the Act itself is not mentioned at all in Sheldon J's judgment, and only in general terms by Fox LJ at the beginning and end of his judgment. There is a reference to s 32(1) at the head of the Law Report, but it is evident from glancing at other reports in the series that such references are introduced by the editors for the assistance of their readers and for indexing purposes, and form no part of any judicial statement.

The only realistic inference that can be drawn, in my judgment, is that the Court of Appeal in that case dealt with the issue on the basis of vicarious liability as applied in the law of tort because both counsel invited them to do so. The issue that is now before the court, therefore, never arose for consideration. *Irving* is accordingly not an authority for the purpose for which reliance is sought to be placed on it. It does not preclude us from holding that the majority of the Employment Appeal Tribunal was in error, and that there is no authority which requires the reference to "course of employment" in s 32(1) to be construed restrictively by reference to the case law governing an employer's vicarious liability in tort.

Conclusion

It would be particularly wrong to allow racial harassment on the scale that was suffered by the complainant in this case at the hands of his workmates – treatment that was wounding both emotionally and physically – to slip through the net of employer responsibility by applying to it a common-law principle evolved in another area of the law to deal with vicarious responsibility for wrongdoing of a wholly different kind. To do so would seriously undermine the statutory scheme of the Discrimination Acts and flout the purposes which they were passed to achieve.

The tribunals are free, and are indeed bound, to interpret the ordinary, and readily understandable, words "in the course of employment" in the sense in which every layman would understand them. This is not to say that when it comes to applying them to the infinite variety of circumstance which is liable to occur in particular instances – within or without the workplace, in or out of uniform, in or out of rest-breaks – all laymen would necessarily agree as to the result. That is what makes their application so well suited to decision by an industrial jury. The application of the phrase will be a question of fact for each industrial tribunal to resolve, in the light of the circumstances presented to it, with a mind unclouded by any parallels sought to be drawn from the law of vicarious liability in tort.

I, too, would allow the appeal and restore the order of the industrial tribunal.'

(McCowan LJ delivered a concurring judgment; Potter LJ agreed.)

Burton v *De Vere Hotels*

[1996] IRLR 596   Employment Appeal Tribunal

Bernard Manning has been invited to be guest speaker at a dinner for 400 men, held at the respondent's hotel. His speech, not surprisingly, contained a great deal of racially offensive matter and he noticed the two applicants, Afro-Caribbean waitresses, and made sexually and racially offensive comments about them. They sued their employer for racial harassment. Manning, of course, was not an employee of the hotel, nor in any contractual relationship with it: how could the hotel be responsible for this racial harassment?

Smith J: '… We do accept that, in practice, where an employer is shown to have actual knowledge that racial harassment of an employee is taking place, or deliberately or recklessly closes his eyes to the fact that it is taking place, if he does not act reasonably to prevent it, he will readily be found to have subjected his employee to the detriment of racial harassment.

However, we do not think that foresight and culpability are the means by which the employer's duty is to be defined. The duty is not to subject the employee to racial harassment. We think that the statutory test is best understood by consideration of the true meaning of the word "subjecting". We do not think "subjecting" is a word which connotes action or decision, as Mr Wilkie submitted. Rather we think it connotes "control". A person "subjects" another to something if he causes or allows that thing to happen in circumstances where he can control whether it happens or not. An employer subjects an employee to the detriment of racial harassment if he causes or permits the racial harassment to occur in circumstances in which he can control whether it happens or not.

We do not think it is necessary or appropriate that any particular degree of foresight on the part of the employer need be established. Indeed we think that it is undesirable that concepts of the law of negligence should be imported into the statutory torts of racial and sexual discrimination. However, we can see that on occasions what the employer knew or foresaw might be relevant to what control the employer could exercise. Lack of possible foresight and the unexpected nature of an event might be relevant to the question of whether the event was under the employer's control. But foresight of the events or the lack of it cannot be determinative of whether the events were under the employer's control. An employer might foresee that racial harassment is a real possibility and yet be able to do very little, if anything, to prevent it from happening or protect his employees from it. For example, the employer of a bus or train conductor may recognise that the employee will face a real risk of racial harassment at times. Yet the prevention of such an event will be largely beyond the control of the employer. All he will be able to do is to make his attitude to such behaviour known to the public and to offer his employees appropriate support if harassment occurs. On the other hand, if the harassment occurs even quite unexpectedly, but in circumstances over which the employer has control, a tribunal may well find that he has subjected his employee to it.

We think that the question of whether an employer has subjected his employee to racial harassment, where a third party is primarily responsible for the harassment, should be decided by the tribunal in its capacity as an industrial jury. The tribunal should ask themselves whether the event in question was something which was sufficiently under the control of the employer that he could, by the application of good employment practice, have prevented the harassment or reduced the extent of it. If such is their finding, then the employer has subjected the employee to the harassment.

We turn, as invited by the parties, to apply these principles to the tribunal's findings of fact in this case. Mr Pemberton told the tribunal that he would never allow young female staff to go into a function where he knew a performer might tell sexually explicit jokes. He was there clearly describing what he saw as good employment practice. The tribunal said that he ought to have warned his assistant managers to keep a look-out for Mr Manning and withdraw the young waitresses if things became unpleasant. He did not do so because he did not give the matter a thought. He should have done. Events within the banqueting hall were under the control of Mr Pemberton's assistants. If they had been properly instructed by him, these two young women would not have suffered any harassment. They might possibly have heard a few offensive words before they were withdrawn, but that would have been all.

We are unanimously of the view that on this occasion the employer "subjected" the appellants to the racial harassment which they received from Mr Manning and the guests.

For those reasons we allow this appeal and remit the case to the tribunal for the assessment of compensation.'

COMMENT

(1)   A high standard of vicarious liability is considered necessary since it would be too easy otherwise for employers to deny responsibility for discriminatory practices in the workplace. The Court of Appeal's rejection of the common law concept of vicarious liability in *Jones* v *Tower Boot* was clearly vitally important in maintaining this. Note also the extension of liability explicit in *Burton* v *De Vere Hotels*.

(2)   The best way that employers can protect themselves from complaints of discrimination is to have an effective equal opportunities policy, properly promulgated among the workforce – see *Balgobin* v *Tower Hamlets LBC*. So far as harassment is concerned, the EC Code of Practice contains practical advice and leaflets are available also from the EOC and CRE.

Indirect discrimination

Sex Discrimination Act 1975

1.   (1)   A person discriminates against a woman in any circumstances relevant for the purposes of any provision of this Act if —

  (b)   … he applies to her a requirement or condition which applies or would apply equally to a man but —

  (i)   which is such that the proportion of women who can comply with it is considerably smaller than the proportion of men who can comply with it, and

  (ii)   which he cannot show to be justifiable irrespective of the sex of the person to whom it is applied, and

  (iii)   which is to her detriment because she cannot comply with it.

COMMENT

(1)   Indirect discrimination against married people (SDA s 3) and on racial grounds (RRA s 1) are defined in parallel terms – see p 28.

(2)   This form of discrimination – called graphically but not entirely accurately 'adverse impact discrimination' – is based on the decision of the US Supreme Court in *Griggs* v *Duke Power Co*, which held that application tests which screened out many more blacks than whites and were not job-related were discriminatory.

Home Office v *Holmes*

[1984] ICR 678 Employment Appeal Tribunal

The applicant was employed as an executive officer in the civil service, one of 250 employed in the immigration and nationality department at Croydon. All were required to be full-time. Having experienced difficulty in working full-time after the birth of her first child, Holmes asked to go part-time when she returned after the birth of her second child. When her request was refused, she claimed under the SDA.

Waite J: '… The first question the industrial tribunal members asked themselves was this: did the requirement of full-time work in the employee's contract of employment amount to a requirement or condition? There was no dispute that if it did, it was one which applied or was applicable within her grade and her department equally to a man. The tribunal took the view, in answer to that question, that her obligation to work full-time was, indeed, a condition or requirement within the terms of section 1(1)(b) of the Act. They said it was an essential term of her engagement because unless she went on working full-time she would not be allowed to continue in her job.

The second question they asked themselves was whether this requirement or condition (i.e. the requirement of full-time work) was such that the proportion of women who could comply with it was considerably smaller than the proportion of men who could comply with it. They reached the answer to that one unhesitatingly. It was yes; and the reason was that despite the changes in the role of women in modern society, it is still a fact that the raising of children tends to place a greater burden upon them than it does upon men.

Next, they posed for themselves the question whether the Home Office had been able to show the requirement or condition to be justifiable irrespective of the sex of the person to whom it was applied. This question brought them into that area of detailed evidence which we have already mentioned. They very carefully considered departmental reports and other relevant data and statistics including the recommendations emanating from a joint review group established by the Civil Service National Whitley Council. They heard on this same issue, too, the oral evidence on the Home Office side of two senior representatives: and on the employee's side the evidence of her union representative and herself. Their finding was that, in all the circumstances, they had no hesitation in preferring the evidence on those issues put forward on behalf of the employee, and they therefore found that the Home Office had been unable to show the requirement or condition of full-time work to be a justifiable one.

Then the industrial tribunal turned to the last of the questions demanded of them by section 1 of the Act. They asked themselves whether the requirement or condition of full-time service was to her detriment because she could not comply with it. That was an issue on which very little evidence was required, and they expressed their finding briefly. They took the view that the requirement was to her detriment and that she could not comply with it, adding the comment that her parental responsibilities prevented her carrying out a normal full-time week's work, and that in trying to fulfil all of these at the same time she had had to suffer excessive demands on her time and energy ...

The scheme of the anti-discrimination legislation involves casting a wide net throwing upon employers the onus of justifying the relevant requirement or condition in particular instances. One must be careful, however, not to fall into the error of assuming that because the net is wide, the catch will necessarily be large. Mr Goldsmith eloquently invited us to envisage the shock to British industry and to our national and local government administration which, he submitted, would be bound to be suffered if, in addition to all their other problems, they now had to face a shoal of claims by women full-time workers alleging that it would be discriminatory to refuse them part-time status. In answer to that we emphasise, as did the industrial tribunal in the last sentence of their decision, that this one case of the employee and her particular difficulties within her particular grade in her particular department stands very much upon its own. It is easy to imagine other instances, not strikingly different from hers, where the result would not be the same. There will be cases where the requirement for full-time staff can be shown to be sufficiently flexible as arguably not to amount to a requirement or condition at all. There will be cases where a policy favouring full-time staff exclusively within a particular grade or department is found to be justified. There will be cases where no actual or no sufficient detriment can be proved by the employee. All such cases will turn upon their own particular facts. We only decide today that in this case the industrial tribunal were right, in our view, in saying that a case of unlawful discrimination had been made out.'

COMMENT

(1)   This case shows the importance of the claim for indirect discrimination and its potential for challenging working practices which have the effect of excluding women and minorities. As many commentators think that it is ingrained institutional practices which are more of a problem than deliberate discrimination, it is essential that apparently neutral requirements should be liable to scrutiny.

(2)   However, the decision is also a graphic illustration of the power of individual industrial tribunals, since decisions on whether the conditions in subsection (b) are met are treated as factual and therefore cannot be attacked unless the tribunal misdirects itself on the law or reaches a perverse conclusion. In *Clymo* v *Wandsworth LBC*, a different division of the EAT drew attention to the fact that *Home Office* v

Holmes was an unreserved decision, and expressed the view that:

'in many working structures, whether in industry or public bodies, local government or elsewhere, there will be a grade or position where the job or appointment by its very nature requires full-time attendance. At one end of the scale if a cleaner was required to work full-time it would clearly be a requirement or condition. Whereas in the case of a managing director it would be part of the nature of the appointment ...'

See also *Briggs* v *NE Education and Library Board.*

Perera v Civil Service Commission (No. 2)

[1983] ICR 428 Court of Appeal

The complainant was Sri Lankan by birth and had lived in the UK since 1973. In Sri Lanka he had gained a science degree and a baccalaureate in law; he had then qualified and practised as an advocate. In the UK he had also been called to the Bar and had a qualification from the Institute of Cost and Management Accountants. He was employed as an executive officer in the civil service but had failed in numerous attempts to move into the legal service, accountancy section or even to achieve promotion in his existing work. He brought proceedings alleging racial discrimination over his rejection for the post of legal assistant.

It was found that in making their selection, the interview board took into account four factors: experience in the UK; command of English; whether the candidate had, or had applied for, British nationality; and age. He claimed that use of these factors tended to screen out people from his racial group. The issue was whether he could establish that a 'requirement or condition' had been applied to him which had such a discriminatory effect.

Stephenson LJ: '... The matters which have to be established by an applicant who claims that he has been discriminated against indirectly are, first of all, that there has been a requirement or condition, as the complainant put it, a "must": something which has to be complied with. Here there was a requirement or condition for candidates for the post of legal assistant in the Civil Service: it was that the candidate should be either a qualified member of the English Bar or a qualified solicitor of the Supreme Court of this country – an admitted man or a barrister; and those conditions or requirements – those "musts" – were fulfilled by the complainant. But, as he admitted in his argument before the appeal tribunal and before this court, there is no other express requirement or condition, and he has to find a requirement or condition in the general combination of factors which he says the interview board took into account. He cannot formulate, as in my judgment he has to, what the particular requirement or condition is which he says has been applied to him and to his attempt to obtain a post of legal assistant. That is the hurdle which, as it seems to me, he is unable to get over. If he were able to prove a particular requirement or condition, he would then have to prove that it had been applied by the board ...

I do not find that the industrial tribunal singled out the four factors which are singled out by the appeal tribunal and on which the complainant so strongly relies. But in my opinion none of those factors could possibly be regarded as a requirement of a condition in the sense that the lack of it, whether of British nationality or even of the ability to communicate well in English, would be an absolute bar. The whole of the evidence indicates that a brilliant man whose personal qualities made him suitable as a legal assistant might well have been sent forward on a short list by the interview board in spite of being, perhaps, below standard on his knowledge of English and his ability to communicate in that language.

That is only an illustration, but once it appears clear from the evidence that the industrial tribunal were entitled to conclude that it was personal qualities for which the interviewing board were mainly looking, and it was personal qualities, as stated in the chairman's report and as was made clear by the markings of all the members of the board, which, in the opinion of the board, the complainant lacked, and that that was the reason for not sending him forward on the short list, the case of indirect discrimination which the complainant seeks to make, in my opinion, falls to the ground.

As I have said. I think the appeal tribunal correctly stated the law as to indirect discrimination. I agree with them that there was no application here of any requirement or condition, and no evidence of it. In my judgment the complainant has failed to prove what he has to prove in order to show a case of indirect discrimination.'

(Orr LJ delivered a concurring judgment and Sir George Baker agreed.)

COMMENT

(1)   This seems to drive a coach and horses through the protection provided in the legislation by permitting free rein to discriminatory preferences. It is surely not good enough to say that 'a brilliant man [sic] whose personal qualities made him suitable might well have been sent forward' despite a poor showing on one of the preferred factors. This may be true, but it is certainly discriminatory if brilliance is required of members of minority groups, but only ordinary ability of the majority. It states what is often the complaint (or sometimes the misguided boast) of women and minorities – that they have to be twice as good to be accepted.

The law should clearly be that any factor which figures in the employment decision should not be discriminatory. However, *Perera* has since been followed in *Meer* v *Tower Hamlets LBC*, with some regret being expressed, and is binding unless reviewed by the House of Lords.

(2)   It must be borne in mind that showing a requirement to be discriminatory is not the end of the story: the employer may be able to justify it; this is discussed below. What is claimed here is that any factor having a discriminatory effect should be put to the test of justification.

(3)   The next stage in proving a claim of indirect discrimination is to show that the requirement or condition is such that the proportion of women or married people or members of the racial group who can comply with it is 'considerably smaller' than the proportion of men, unmarried people or members of other racial groups. This involves identifying relevant groups for comparison and an analysis of statistics which may involve numeracy beyond that acquired by the average lawyer or tribunal member.

Price v *Civil Service Commission*

[1978] ICR 27 Employment Appeal Tribunal

Price applied for a job as executive officer in the civil service. The further particulars about the post stated that applicants should be aged between 17½ and 28. She was 35. She claimed that the age limit indirectly discriminated against women, who were frequently out of the labour market looking after young children between those ages.

Phillips J: 'The argument [in the industrial tribunal] went further, and was that since the number of women and the number of men in the population is not widely different it was impossible to say that the proportion of women who can comply with the age condition was considerably smaller than the proportion of men, because all men and all women had equal opportunity to comply with it. In paragraph 11 of the decision the industrial tribunal put it like this:

"We have unanimously decided that Mr Howard's submission on behalf of the [Civil Service Commission] must be upheld on both grounds. We are of the view that the only requirement or condition was that applicants should be between the specified age groups. Since the applicant conceded that the proportion of women within these groups was not considerably smaller than the proportion of men we are of the view that this concession is fatal to her case. In so far as the statistics are concerned, as Mr Howard submitted, no one can really say whether these women with children really wanted a job or chose to stay at home. If one takes the up-to-date statistics provided by the [Civil Service Commission] we find that indeed more women than men applied for ... executive officer posts than men. If they could apply for those posts then it follows that they could have applied for any other kind of job. It is also worthwhile recording that during 1976 53.7 per cent of women were accepted as against 46.3 per cent of men."

The appeal tribunal are not in agreement. Mr Alderton accepts this conclusion, and would dismiss the appeal. The majority take a different view, which is set out in the remainder of this judgment and which is theirs alone.

The industrial tribunal further decided that the statistics produced in evidence did not establish to their satisfaction why it was that fewer women applied for posts than men, and whether it was not that they chose not to do so, rather than that they were prevented from doing so. They were also impressed by the fact that during 1976, according to statistics produced of applications for executive officers, of those accepted 53.7 per cent were women as against 46.3 per cent who were men. We do not regard this last point as significant, since the complaint is not that over the whole range of appointment between 17½ and 28 years fewer women were successful than men, but that the age bar at 28 was more disadvantageous to women than to men ...

Knowledge and experience suggest that a considerable number of women between the mid-twenties and the mid-thirties are engaged in bearing children and in minding children, and that while many find it possible to take up employment many others, while desiring to do so, find it impossible, and that many of the latter as their children get older find that they can follow their wish and seek employment. This knowledge and experience is confirmed by some of the statistical evidence produced to the industrial tribunal (and by certain additional statistical evidence put in by consent of the parties on the hearing of the appeal). This demonstrates clearly that the economic activity of women with at least one Advanced Level falls off markedly about the age of 23, reaching a bottom at about the age of 33 when it climbs gradually to a plateau at about 45.

Basing ourselves on this and other evidence, we should have no hesitation in concluding that our own knowledge and experience is confirmed, and that it is safe to say that the condition is one which it is in practice harder for women to comply with than it is for men. We should be inclined to go further and say that there are undoubtedly women of whom it may be properly said in the terms of section 1(1)(b)(i) that they "cannot" comply with the condition, because they are women; that is to say because of their involvement with their children. But this is not enough to enable the applicant to satisfy the requirements of sub-paragraph (i). The difficulty we have is in saying whether the proportion of women who can comply with the condition is *considerably smaller* than the proportion of men who can comply with it. It follows from what we have said earlier that we do not agree with the approach of the industrial tribunal to this question, and it follows that there has never been a finding of fact based upon the evidence correctly approached and interpreted.

At one stage of the hearing we thought that it might be in order for us to make a finding ourselves on the basis of the evidence given to the industrial tribunal, together with that put in by consent on the hearing of the appeal. At the end of the day we have come to the conclusion that we ought not to do so. The difficulty is that most of the evidence is statistical, and is of a kind which needs to be analysed and interpreted, since it is designed for other purposes, and it is not entirely easy to draw relevant conclusions. We think it *does* confirm the likelihood that women are put into difficulties by the condition, and that there are women who would wish to apply to be an executive officer and could do so in, say, their thirties, but cannot do so in their late twenties. The difficulty is to quantify this in the terms of a "considerably smaller" result. We find that it would be unsafe for us to reach a conclusion without having had the benefit of hearing the statistician give evidence and be subjected to cross-examination upon the proper analysis and inferences to be drawn from the statistics.

Accordingly we propose to allow the appeal and to remit the case to be heard afresh, bearing in mind the terms of this judgment and such guidance as we have been able to give. It may perhaps be helpful to mention one other matter. The industrial tribunal, in paragraph 12 of their reasons, rightly point out that when considering section 1(1)(b)(i) and considering the proportion of women and the proportion of men, it may be proper to consider as the "pool" of women or men available for the purpose something less than total female and male population. We agree with that, though, as we have pointed out, the industrial tribunal themselves in the present case proceeded on the footing that it was appropriate to take into account the whole population, male and female respectively. We doubt whether that was the right approach, though we do not wish to lay down a proposition binding upon the industrial tribunal which will hear the remitted case. It seems to us, as at present advised, there would be a good deal in the present case for saying that the appropriate "pool" is that of qualified men and qualified women as the case may be.'

COMMENT

(1)   The case shows how easy it is to get dazzled by looking at the wrong statistics. If in this case the pool of actual applicants had been considered rather than the pool of *potential* (that is, qualified) applicants, the decision would have been different.

(2)   In this case, note that the EAT was considering the economic activity of people with one 'A' level. It is fortunate that the relevant statistics were available: applicants cannot rely on tribunals taking it as read that family responsibilities put barriers in the way of women's employment. Naturally, getting hold of the statistics and having expert analysis of them will add to the costs of presenting the case.

(3)   Problems in identifying the correct pool for comparison have led to some peculiar decisions, of which *Kidd* v *DRG Ltd* is probably the most notorious. Guidance has been given by the Court of Appeal.

Jones v University of Manchester

[1993] IRLR 218 Court of Appeal

Ralph Gibson LJ: '… Mr McMullen relied upon the decision of this Court in *Jones* v *Chief Adjudication Officer*. This decision was not available when this case was before the IT; and it was not cited in July 1990, if indeed it was available, before the EAT. That case was concerned with the provisions of the Social Security Act 1975, the Overlapping Benefit Regulations of 1979 and the EEC Social Security Directive 79/7. The question was whether the effect of the regulation involved discrimination on ground of sex either directly or indirectly. Lord Justice Mustill, with whose judgment Nourse LJ and Butler-Sloss LJ agreed, said:

> "What we must consider is whether, if one looks not at individuals but at the population of claimants as a whole, it can be seen that there is indirect discrimination. The parties agree ... that what was called the "demographic" argument represents one way in which indirect discrimination can be established. As I understand it, the process for establishing discrimination on this basis takes the following shape (... I will assume that the complaint stems from the failure of a woman to satisfy a relevant positive qualification for selection, and that only one such qualification is in issue):
>
> 1. Identify the criterion for selection. 2. Identify the relevant population, comprising all those who satisfy all the other criteria for selection. (I do not know to what extent this step in the process is articulated in the cases. To my mind it is vital to the intellectual soundness of the demographic argument.) 3. Divide the relevant population into groups representing those who satisfy the criterion and those who do not. 4. Predict statistically what proportion of each group should consist of women. 5. Ascertain what are the actual male/female balances in the two groups. 6. Compare the actual with the predicted balances. 7. If women are found to be under-represented in the first group and over-represented in the second, it is proved that the criterion is discriminatory."

Mr McMullen submitted that the process there described was required by the provisions of s 1(1)(b); that the IT had not followed it; and no sufficient material was before this Court to enable this Court to be sure that, if applied, the decision of the IT was clearly justified.

I respectfully agree with the explanation by Mustill LJ of the shape which the process for establishing indirect discrimination upon the demographic argument may properly take. It is clear from the judgment that that chain of reasoning was not in issue in that case and was agreed by the parties to be sound. The decision does not, in my judgment, compel this Court to hold that that chain of reasoning is the only process by which an IT may, without error, reach the conclusion that indirect discrimination has on the facts of a particular case been made out to their satisfaction, under s 1(1)(b) of the Act.

In *R* v *Sec of State for Education ex parte Schaffter* Schiemann J gave his view of the proper application of s 1(1) in more simple terms: he, in effect, omitted stages (iv) and (v) from the process described by Mustill LJ. Thus he said:

> "... The subsection would seem to indicate that what you should do is to establish: first, the proportion of all women who can comply with the requirement – I shall call this X%; secondly, the proportion of all men who can comply with the requirement – I shall call this Y%; thirdly, compare X and Y and determine whether one is considerably smaller than the other."

We have been told that s 1(1) has not before been considered by this Court with reference to the concept of the pool. The language of the section has been set out above. In order to compare the proportion of women who can comply with the requirement with the proportion of men who can comply with it, it is necessary to determine the relevant total. In my judgment, the relevant total is the number of men and women referred to in the subsection; ie those men and women to whom the person, ie the employer in this case, applies or would apply the requirement. In this case, that means all men and women graduates with the relevant experience. I do not accept that the relevant total is all men and women: the employer would have no occasion to apply the requirement to any men or women other than those who are able to comply with the requirements of the advertisement other than the requirement in question. That is in accordance with the view of Mustill LJ.

Further, I do not accept that the relevant total is merely of those men and women who can comply with the requirement. The section refers not to the number of men and the number of women who can comply with the requirement but to the proportion of men and of women. That shows, in my judgment, that those men and those women who can comply with the requirement are to be considered as a proportion of another number, and that that number must be the relevant total of men and women to whom the requirement is or would be applied…'.

COMMENT

(1)   If a requirement or condition has a discriminatory effect, the employer may still have a defence if it is justifiable.

Hampson v *Department of Education and Science*

[1989] ICR 179 Court of Appeal

The plaintiff, whose national origin was Hong Kong Chinese, had qualified as a teacher in Hong Kong. There she had taken a two-year initial teacher training course, had taught for eight years and then taken a further one-year course. Her application for qualified teacher status in the UK was rejected by the Secretary of State on the grounds that it was not sufficiently comparable to the three-year training course in Britain. She claimed that the insistence on a three-year training course indirectly discriminated against her. The EAT found that the requirement was discriminatory, but that it was justifiable. She appealed.

Balcombe LJ: '… In *Ojutiku* v *Manpower Services Commission* this court was concerned with the meaning of "justifiable" where it appears in section 1(1)(b)(ii) of the Act of 1976 and of course that decision is binding on us in so far as it decides that meaning: see *In re State of Norway's Application* (*No 2*). However, I regret that I do not find, in two of the judgments in *Ojutiku*, any clear decision as to that meaning. The first judgment was that of Eveleigh LJ. He dealt with the question in the following passage.

> "Mr Macdonald argued that in order to justify it, the employer, on whom admittedly lies the burden of proof, has to show that the requirement was necessary for the good of the employer's business. He referred the court to *Steel* v *Union of Post Office Workers* …
>
> I myself would not accept that it is essential, or at least that it is always essential, for the employer to prove that the requirement is necessary for the good of his business. It may well be that in a particular case that is the argument which is advanced by the employer; it does not follow that that is what the statute demands. I am very hesitant to suggest another expression for that which is used in the statute, for fear that it will be picked up and quoted in other cases and built upon thereafter, with the result that at the end of the day there is a danger of us all departing far from the meaning of the word in the statute. For myself, it would be enough simply to ask myself: is it justifiable? But if I have to give some explanation of my understanding of that word, I would turn to a dictionary definition which says 'to adduce adequate grounds for'; and it seems to me that if a person produces reasons for doing something, which would be acceptable to right-thinking people as sound and tolerable reasons for so doing, then he has justified his conduct."

Kerr LJ said,

"The complainants submitted that 'justifiable' in section 1(1)(b)(ii) means 'necessary as a matter of business' or 'something in the nature of a legitimate business necessity'; and in this connection they relied on an American judgment, *Rowe* v *General Motors Corporation*, a decision of the United States Court of Appeals, Fifth Circuit. They also relied on certain passages in the decision of the appeal tribunal in *Steel* v *Union of Post Office Workers*. So far as the American case is concerned, it should be borne in mind that the United States legislation appears to have no counterpart to the provision which is crucial in this case, section 1(1)(b)(ii); and it is also to be noted that in that case actual discrimination was established against the employers in question as the result of a prior practice of direct discrimination, which undoubtedly caused coloured employees to suffer by not having been able to get the same experience for the purposes of promotion as their white colleagues. For myself, I do not see how *Rowe* v *General Motors Corporation* could in any event be applied in the context of the English legislation unless the facts were similar, which they are not in this case. In *Steel* v *Union of Post Office Workers* the point under consideration involved the corresponding provisions in the same terms of the Sex Discrimination Act 1975. It seems to me that the appeal tribunal in that case put something of a gloss on the word 'justifiable' by suggesting that it was equivalent or close to having the same meaning as 'necessary'. But that gloss was rightly shaded, to put it no higher, by another decision of the appeal tribunal in *Singh* v *Rowntree MacKintosh Ltd*, in which the approach was in effect that 'justifiable' means 'reasonably necessary in all the circumstances'. In the same way as Eveleigh L J, I decline to put any gloss on the word 'justifiable', which is a perfectly easily understandable ordinary word, except that I would say that it clearly applies a lower standard than the word 'necessary'. This is also an ordinary word which is often used in legislation, but it has not been used in this case."

With all due respect to Eveleigh and Kerr L J J, I derive little help from these judgments. "Justifiable" and "justify" are words which connote a value judgment, as is evident from the dictionary definition cited by Eveleigh LJ – "to produce *adequate* grounds for", but neither Lord Justice indicates what test should be applied. Kerr LJ says it applies a lower standard than "necessary", but does not indicate how much lower. It was, however, accepted by Mr Carlisle, and rightly so, that whatever test is to be applied it is an objective one: it is not sufficient for the employer to establish that he considered his reasons adequate. However I do derive considerable assistance from the judgment of Stephenson LJ, who referred to:

"the comments, which I regard as sound, made by Lord McDonald, giving the judgment of the Employment Appeal Tribunal in Scotland in *Singh* v *Rowntree MacKintosh Ltd*, on the judgment of the appeal tribunal given by Phillips J in *Steel* v *Union of Post Office Workers*, to which Eveleigh and Kerr L J J have referred. What Phillips J there said is valuable as rejecting justification by convenience and requiring the party applying the discriminatory condition to prove it to be justifiable in all the circumstances on balancing its discriminatory effect against the discriminator's need for it. But that need is what is reasonably needed by the party who applied the condition; ..."

In my judgment "justifiable" requires an objective balance between the discriminatory effect of the condition and the reasonable needs of the party who applies the condition. This construction is supported by the recent decision of the House of Lords in *Rainey* v *Greater Glasgow Health Board*, a case under the Equal Pay Act 1970, and turning on the provisions of section 1(3) of that Act which at the material time was in the following terms:

"An equality clause shall not operate in relation to a variation between the woman's contract and the man's contract if the employer proves that the variation is genuinely due to a material difference (other than the difference of sex) between her case and his."

The House of Lords held, applying the decision of the European Court in *Bilka-Kaufhaus GmbH* v *Weber von Hartz*, that to justify a material difference under section 1(3) of the Equal Pay Act 1970, the employer had to show a real need on the part of the undertaking, objectively justified, although that need was not confined to economic grounds: it might, for instance, include administrative efficiency in a concern not engaged in commerce or business. Clearly it may, as in the present case, be possible to justify by reference to grounds other than economic or administrative efficiency. Lord Keith of Kinkel, who gave the leading speech, with which all the other Law Lords agreed, said, in reference to an argument based on section 1(1)(b)(ii) of the Sex Discrimination Act 1975, which is identical, mutatis mutandis, to section 1(1)(b)(ii) of the Act of 1976:

"This provision has the effect of prohibiting indirect discrimination between women and men. In my opinion it does not, for present purposes, add anything to section 1(3) of the Act of 1970, since, upon the view which I have taken as to the proper construction of the latter, a difference which demonstrated unjustified indirect discrimination would not discharge the onus placed on the employer. Further, there would not appear to be any material distinction in principle between the need to demonstrate objectively justified grounds of difference for purposes of section 1(3) and the need to justify a requirement or condition under section 1(1)(b)(ii) of the Act of 1975."

Mr Sedley constructed an elaborate argument designed to show that *Ojutiku* had been overruled by *Rainey*. This argument will be found set out in detail in the judgment of the appeal tribunal. However I do not find it necessary to consider this argument further here. For my part I can find no significant difference between the test adopted by Stephenson LJ in *Ojutiku* and that adopted by the House of Lords in *Rainey*. Since neither Eveleigh LJ nor Kerr LJ in *Ojutiku* indicated what they considered the test to be – although Kerr LJ said what it was not – I am content to adopt Stephenson LJ's test as I have expressed it above, which I consider to be consistent with *Rainey*. It is obviously desirable that the tests of justifiability applied in all these closely related fields should be consistent with each other ...'

(Nourse and Parker LJJ concurred. The Court of Appeal found against the plaintiff on another ground. She appealed successfully to the House of Lords, where the issue of justifiability was not discussed.)

COMMENT

(1)   This represents the most authoritative statement to date on the standard of justifiability. Do you think that the standard is clear?

(2)   The final requirement in an indirect discrimination claim is that the condition must be to the detriment of the complainant because she cannot comply with it. The meaning of 'can comply' was discussed in *Mandla* v *Dowell Lee*.

Mandla v Dowell Lee

[1983] ICR 385   House of Lords

(The facts of this case are given on p 29.)

Lord Fraser: '... *"Can comply"*

It is obvious that Sikhs, like anyone else, "can" refrain from wearing a turban, if "can" is construed literally. But if the board cultural/historic meaning of ethnic is the appropriate meaning of the word in the Act of 1976, then a literal reading of the word "can" would deprive Sikhs and members of other groups defined by reference to their ethnic origins of much of the protection which Parliament evidently intended the Act to afford to them. They "can" comply with almost any requirement or condition if they are willing to give up their distinctive customs and cultural rules. On the other hand, if ethnic means inherited or unalterable, as the Court of Appeal thought it did, then "can" ought logically to be read literally. The word "can" is used with many shades of meaning. In the context of section 1(1)(b)(i) of the Act of 1976 it must, in my opinion, have been intended by Parliament to be read not as meaning "can physically", so as to indicate a theoretical possibility, but as meaning "can in practice" or "can consistently with the customs and cultural conditions of the racial group". The latter meaning was attributed to the word by the Employment Appeal Tribunal in *Price* v *Civil Service Commission* on a construction of the parallel provision in the Sex Discrimination Act 1975. I agree with their construction of the word in that context. Accordingly I am of opinion that the "No turban" rule was not one with which the second appellant could, in the relevant sense, comply ...'

Discrimination by victimisation

Race Relations Act 1976

2.   (1)   A person ('the discriminator') discriminates against another person ('the person victimised') in any circumstances relevant for the purposes of any provision of this Act if he treats the person victimised less favourably than in those circumstances he treats or would treat other persons, and does so by reason that the person victimised has—

(a)   brought proceedings against the discriminator or any other person under this Act; or

(b)   given evidence or information in connection with proceedings brought by any person against the discriminator or any other person under this Act; or

(c)   otherwise done anything under or by reference to this Act in relation to the discriminator or any other person; or

(d)   alleged that the discriminator or any other person has committed an act which (whether or not the allegation so states) would amount to a contravention of this Act,

or by reason that the discriminator knows that the person victimised intends to do any of those things, or suspects that the person victimised has done, or intends to do, any of them.

(2)   Subsection (1) does not apply to treatment of a person by reason of any allegation made by him if the allegation was false and not made in good faith.

(SDA s 4 is in parallel terms.)

COMMENT

(1)   The need to protect complainants and witnesses from retaliation is obvious and should, it is submitted, be extended to all areas of employment protection legislation.

(2)   In *Aziz* v *Trinity Street Taxis* the Court of Appeal held that the applicant had not

been discriminated against contrary to s 2 when the *motive* of the discriminator was not based on race. This seems a suspect line of reasoning given the interpretation of direct discrimination in *James* v *Eastleigh BC*.

(3)   See also *Waters* v *Metropolitan Police Commissioner*, where the applicant, a police officer, was allegedly victimised for complaining of sexual harassment by another officer outside working hours. Because this was outwith his course of employment, so that the employer would not have been responsible for it, it was held that any victimisation of her for bringing the complaint was not covered by SDA s 4.

Exceptions

Genuine occupational qualifications

There are limited circumstances where being a woman or a member of a particular racial group can be regarded as a genuine job qualification.

Sex Discrimination Act 1975

7.   (1)   In relation to sex discrimination—

      (a)   section 6(2)(a) or (c) does not apply to any employment where being a man is a genuine occupational qualification for the job, and

      (b)   section 6(2)(a) does not apply to opportunities for promotion or transfer to, or training for, such employment.

    (2)   Being a man is a genuine occupational qualification for a job only where—

      (a)   the essential nature of the job calls for a man for reasons of physiology (excluding physical strength or stamina) or, in dramatic performances or other entertainment, for reasons of authenticity, so that the essential nature of the job would be materially different if carried out by a woman; or

      (b)   the job needs to be held by a man to preserve decency or privacy because—

        (i)   it is likely to involve physical contact with men in circumstances where they might reasonably object to its being carried out by a woman, or

        (ii)   the holder of the job is likely to do his work in circumstances where men might reasonably object to the presence of a woman because they are in a state of undress or are using sanitary facilities; or

      (ba)   the job is likely to involve the holder of the job doing his work, or living, in a private home and needs to be held by a man because objection might reasonably be taken to allowing to a woman—

        (i)   the degree of physical or social contact with a person living in the home, or

        (ii)   the knowledge of intimate details of such a person's life,

      which is likely, because of the nature or circumstances of the job or of the home, to be allowed to, or available to, the holder of the job; or

      (c)   the nature or location of the establishment makes it impracticable for the holder of the job to live elsewhere than in premises provided by the employer, and—

        (i)   the only such premises which are available for persons holding that kind of job are lived in, or normally lived in, by men and are not equipped with separate sleeping accommodation for women and sanitary facilities which could be used by women in privacy from men, and

(ii) it is not reasonable to expect the employer either to equip those premises with such accommodation and facilities or to provide other premises for women; or

(d) the nature of the establishment, or of the part of it within which the work is done, requires the job to be held by a man because—

(i) it is, or is part of, a hospital, prison or other establishment for persons requiring special care, supervision or attention, and

(ii) those persons are all men (disregarding any woman whose presence is exceptional), and

(iii) it is reasonable, having regard to the essential character of the establishment or that part, that the job should not be held by a woman; or

(e) the holder of the job provides individuals with personal services promoting their welfare or education, or similar personal services, and those services can most effectively be provided by a man, or

(g) the job needs to be held by a man because it is likely to involve the performance of duties outside the United Kingdom in a country whose laws or customs are such that the duties could not, or could not effectively, be performed by a woman, or

(h) the job is one of two to be held by a married couple....

Race Relations Act 1976

5. (1) In relation to racial discrimination—

(a) section 4(1)(a) or (c) does not apply to any employment where being of a particular racial group is a genuine occupational qualification for the job; and

(b) section 4(2)(b) does not apply to opportunities for promotion or transfer to, or training for, such employment.

(2) Being of a particular racial group is a genuine occupational qualification for a job only where—

(a) the job involves participation in a dramatic performance or other entertainment in a capacity for which a person of that racial group is required for reasons of authenticity; or

(b) the job involves participation as an artist's or photographic model in the production of a work of art, visual image or sequence of visual images for which a person of that racial group is required for reasons of authenticity; or

(c) the job involves working in a place where food or drink is (for payment or not) provided to and consumed by members of the public or a section of the public in a particular setting for which, in that job, a person of that racial group is required for reasons of authenticity; or

(d) the holder of the job provides persons of that racial group with personal services promoting their welfare, and those services can most effectively be provided by a person of that racial group....

COMMENT

(1)   The SDA used to contain a blanket exclusion for employment in a private household (such as still exists under RRA s 4(3)), and also exempted any employer with no more than five employees. In *Commission of the EC* v *UK*, these provisions were successfully challenged as being in breach of the Equal Treatment Directive. Thus in the Sex Discrimination Act 1986, the limitation for employers with no more than five employees was repealed and a narrower formulation given to the private household exemption (SDA s 7(2)(ba)). However, the fact that no change was made to the corresponding RRA provision starkly illustrates both a lack of commitment to genuine equal opportunity and the relative powerlessness of EC law in relation to race discrimination compared with sex discrimination.

(2)   In addition to these grounds, the SDA makes special provision for the police, prison officers and ministers of religion (ss 17–19) and the RRA contains an exception for seamen recruited abroad (s 9).

(3)   How far can it be a GOQ that the employing organisation wishes to boost its image among a particular section of the population – such as women or ethnic minorities – and therefore wants to recruit personnel from those groups to promote its credibility?

Lambeth LBC v *Commission for Racial Equality*

[1990] ICR 768 Court of Appeal

The council advertised the posts of group manager and assistant head of housing benefits in its housing department, stating that the posts were open only to Afro-Caribbean and Asian applicants. It argued that being of one of those racial groups was a genuine occupational qualification for the job under s 5(2)(d) because over half the council's tenants were of Afro-Caribbean or Asian origin and it had been decided that there was a need to make the housing benefits system more sensitive to the needs and experiences of black people.

Balcombe L J: '...I am wholly unpersuaded that one of the two main purposes of the Act is to promote positive action to benefit racial groups. The purpose of the Act, as stated in its long title, is "to make fresh provision with respect to discrimination on racial grounds and relations between people of different racial groups", and the substance of the operative Parts (I to IV) of the Act is to render acts of racial discrimination unlawful. It is true that sections 35, 37 and 38 do allow for limited acts of positive discrimination which would otherwise be unlawful, but that does not constrain us to give to section 5(2)(d) a meaning which its words do not naturally bear. If section 5(2)(d) had been intended to provide for positive action in the particular field to which it relates, one would have expected to find it grouped together with sections 35, 37 and 38, rather than as the last paragraph in a group relating to dramatic performances (e.g. the casting of "Othello") or restaurants (e.g. a Chinese take-away) where membership of a racial group is required for reasons of authenticity.

The only other reported decision in which section 5(2)(d) has been considered is *Tottenham Green Under Fives' Centre* v *Marshall*, another decision of the appeal tribunal. In giving the judgment of the tribunal in that case, Wood J said,

"The purpose of the Act of 1976 is to eliminate discrimination on racial grounds, and in construing section 5 it is important not to give too wide a construction, which would enable it to provide an excuse or cloak for undesirable discrimination: on the other hand where genuine attempts are being made to integrate ethnic groups into society, too narrow a construction might stifle such initiatives."

In their judgment in the present case the appeal tribunal cited that passage and said that they saw no reason to change their view of the purpose of the Act. I agree with this view. However, I should make it clear that by doing so I express no view of the case for or against positive action in favour of ethnic minorities in order to counter the effects of past discrimination; I confine my attention to the present meaning of the Act of 1976.

Finally, in this connection I would mention that, subject to the specified exceptions, any discriminatory advertisement is unlawful, even though the act of discrimination advertised might itself be lawful.

"Personal services promoting their welfare"

The services provided by the local authority's housing benefits department undoubtedly promote the welfare of the recipients of those benefits, but the rest of the phrase is qualified by the word "personal". "Personal" is defined by the *Oxford English Dictionary* as:

"Of, pertaining to, concerning or affecting the individual or self (as opposed, variously, to other persons, the general community, etc ....); individual; private; one's own."

The use of the word "personal" indicates that the identity of the giver and the recipient of the services is important. I agree with the appeal tribunal when they say that the Act appears to contemplate direct contact between the giver and the recipient – mainly face-to-face or where there could be susceptibility in personal, physical contact. Where language or a knowledge and understanding of cultural and religious background are of importance, then those services may be most effectively provided by a person of a particular racial group ...

However, I also agree with the appeal tribunal that the decision in any particular case whether the holder of a particular job provides persons of a particular group with personal services promoting their welfare is a question of mixed law and fact, and that unless the industrial tribunal have come to a decision which is wrong in law, neither the appeal tribunal nor this court can interfere. The industrial tribunal held that the holders of the jobs advertised, being managerial positions, did not provide personal services promoting the welfare of persons of a particular racial group. I can find no error of law in that decision. On this ground alone I would dismiss this appeal ...

For the reasons already given I would dismiss this appeal. I would add one final point which counsel for the commission conceded in the final paragraph of his skeleton argument. The recognition that the particular posts required knowledge of and sensitivity to the particular problems of an ethnic minority was a legitimate and laudable stance by the local authority. However, the method adopted to achieve the end was unlawful.'

(Mann LJ delivered a concurring judgment and Mustill LJ agreed.)

COMMENT

(1) The decision seems to indicate that on the whole the GOQ exceptions will be construed narrowly, although see also *Tottenham Green Under Fives' Centre* v *Marshall (No 2)*.

(2) Note that only the Commissions have power to take action in the case of discriminatory advertisements.

(3)   A limited amount of positive discrimination is permitted under RRA ss 37–38 and SDA ss 47–48. These sections allow for one sex or racial group to receive encouragement to apply or to be given training where in the previous 12 months no one, or relatively few, people from that group have been employed on the work in question.

Provision in relation to death or retirement

The SDA s 6(4) originally exempted all provision in relation to death or retirement from compliance with the Act. This was thought to be permissible under EC law and was justified on the ground that different pension ages and benefits for men and women had historically been permitted and that pension funds and other arrangements would be thoroughly upset if equality was required.

Some inroads were made on this through the ECJ's wide interpreting of the meaning of pay in Article 119 of the Treaty of Rome (see further Chapter 7 at p 253). However, one of the cases which blew the ship of tradition out of the water was *Marshall* v *Southampton and SW Hants Area Health Authority*.

Marshall v Southampton and SW Hants Area Health Authority

[1986] ICR 335 European Court of Justice

The applicant was employed as a senior dietician by the health authority. It was an implied term of her contract of employment that normal retiring age was the age at which state pensions became payable: namely, 60 for women and 65 for men. The applicant did not wish to retire at 60; she was allowed to stay on until she was 62, but then she was dismissed. She claimed that her dismissal was contrary to the Equal Treatment Directive 1976 (extracted on pp 22–3).

'... Decision
21.   By the first question the Court of Appeal seeks to ascertain whether or not article 5(1) of Council Directive 76/207/EC [the Equal Treatment Directive] must be interpreted as meaning that a general policy concerning dismissal, followed by a state authority, involving the dismissal of a woman solely because she has attained or passed the qualifying age for a state pension, which age is different under national legislation for men and for women, constitutes discrimination on grounds of sex, contrary to that directive ...

32.   The court observes in the first place that the question of interpretation which has been referred to it does not concern access to a statutory or occupational retirement scheme, that is to say the conditions for payment of an old age or retirement pension, but the fixing of an age limit with regard to the termination of employment pursuant to a general policy concerning dismissal. The question therefore relates to the conditions governing dismissal and falls to be considered under Council Directive 76/207/EC.

33.   Article 5(1) of Council Directive 76/207/EC provides that application of the principle of equal treatment with regard to working conditions, including the conditions governing dismissal, means that men and women are to be guaranteed the same conditions without discrimination on grounds of sex.

34.   In its judgment in *Burton* v *British Railways Board* the court has already stated that the term "dismissal" contained in that provision must be given a wide meaning. Consequently, an age limit for the compulsory dismissal of workers pursuant to an employer's

general policy concerning retirement falls within the term "dismissal" construed in that manner, even if the dismissal involves the grant of a retirement pension.

35. As the court emphasised in its judgment in the *Burton* case, article 7 of Council Directive 79/7/EC expressly provides that the directive does not prejudice the right of member states to exclude from its scope the determination of pensionable age for the purposes of granting old age and retirement pensions and the possible consequences thereof for other benefits falling within the statutory social security schemes. The court thus acknowledged that benefits tied to a national scheme which lays down a different minimum pensionable age for men and women may lie outside the ambit of the aforementioned obligation.

36. However, in view of the fundamental importance of the principle of equality of treatment, which the court has re-affirmed on numerous occasions, article 1(2) of Council Directive 76/207/EC, which excludes social security matters from the scope of that directive, must be interpreted strictly. Consequently, the exception to the prohibition of discrimination on grounds of sex provided for in article 7(1)(a) of Council Directive 79/7/EC applies only to the determination of pensionable age for the purposes of granting old age and retirement pensions and the possible consequences thereof for other benefits.

37. In that respect it must be emphasised that, whereas the exception contained in article 7 of Council Directive 79/7/EC concerns the consequences which pensionable age has for social security benefits, this case is concerned with dismissal within the meaning of article 5 of Council Directive 76/207/EC.

38. Consequently, the answer to the first question referred to the court by the Court of Appeal must be that article 5(1) of Council Directive 76/207/EC must be interpreted as meaning that a general policy concerning dismissal involving the dismissal of a woman solely because she has attained the qualifying age for a state pension, which age is different under national legislation for men and for women, constitutes discrimination on grounds of sex, contrary to that directive.'

COMMENT

(1) Because the Equal Treatment Directive was held to have 'vertical' but not 'horizontal' effect, for the reasons given in the decision, the result was a disparity of treatment between women employed in the public and private sectors. The Sex Discrimination Act 1986 had to be passed quickly in order to amend SDA s 6(4) and the corresponding provision in the Equal Pay Act 1970 (s 6) so that it became illegal to have differential retirement ages for women and men. This came into force on 7 November 1987.

(2) After *Marshall*, retirement ages had to be the same (although they could be lower than 65), but it remained lawful to have different pensionable ages and benefits. So far as occupational schemes are concerned, this discrimination was held to be unlawful in the other epoch-making case, *Barber* v *Guardian Royal Exchange*, p 255. For the time being, different pensionable ages under the state scheme remain lawful.

(3) For women forced to retire before men in the period between the *Marshall* decision and the coming into force of the Sex Discrimination Act 1986, it was most important to know whether or not their employer was an emanation or organ of the state or not. The issue could well be relevant in the future, wherever there are allegations that the state has not complied with an EC Directive which an individual seeks to enforce directly. The leading decision is *Foster* v *British Gas*.

Foster v *British Gas plc*

[1991] ICR 463 House of Lords

Lord Templeman: '... In the present case each of the appellants, all of whom are women, were employed by the British Gas Corporation ('the BGC') for whose liabilities the respondent British Gas plc is now responsible. The BGC had a policy that female employees shall retire at the age of 60 and male employees at the age of 65: the appellants were compulsorily retired when they respectively reached the age of 60 between 27 December 1985 and 22 July 1986. It is clear that this policy infringed the Equal Treatment Directive. In these proceedings the appellants claim compensation for unlawful discrimination.

This House referred the following question to the European Court of Justice for a preliminary ruling under Article 177 of the European Economic Community Treaty:

"Was the BGC (at the material time) a body of such a type that the appellants are entitled in English courts and Tribunals to rely directly upon [the Equal Treatment Directive]?"

The European Court of Justice gave its ruling on 12 July 1990 (Case C-188/89) and the relevant contents of that ruling are as follows:

"... the Court has held in a series of cases that unconditional and sufficiently precise provisions of a Directive could be relied on against organisations or bodies which were subject to the authority or control of the State or had special powers beyond those which result from the normal rules applicable to relations between individuals ...

20. It follows from the foregoing that a body, whatever its legal form, which has been made responsible, pursuant to a measure adopted by the State, for providing a public service under the control of the State and has for that purpose special powers beyond those which result from the normal rules applicable in relations between individuals is included in any event among the bodies against which the provisions of a Directive capable of having direct effect may be relied upon....

22. The answer to the question referred by the House of Lords must therefore be that Article 5(1) of Council Directive of 9 February 1976 may be relied upon in a claim for damages against a body, whatever its legal form, which has been made responsible, pursuant to a measure adopted by the State, for providing a public service under the control of the State and has for that purpose special powers beyond those which result from the normal rules applicable in relations between individuals."

Accordingly it falls to this House now to determine whether the BGC was a body which was made responsible pursuant to a measure adopted by the State, for providing a public service under the control of the State and had for that purpose special powers beyond those which result from the normal rules applicable in relations between individuals.

By the Gas Act 1972, replacing the Gas Act 1965 and since repealed by the Gas Act 1986 and orders made thereunder, the BGC was established as a body corporate. The Secretary of State was authorised to make regulations with regard to the appointment and tenure and vacation of office by members of the Corporation. Section 2 provided that:

"(1) It shall be the duty of the Corporation to develop and maintain an efficient, co-ordinated and economical system of gas supply for Great Britain, and to satisfy, so far as it is economical to do so, all reasonable demands for gas in Great Britain."

Thus the BGC was a body which was made responsible pursuant to a measure adopted by the State, for providing a public service.

By s 4 the BGC was directed to report to the Minister who was authorised to:

"... give to the Corporation such directions as he considers appropriate for securing that the management of the activities of the Corporation and their subsidiaries is organised in the most efficient manner; and it shall be the duty of the Corporation to give effect to any such directions."

By s 7 the Secretary of State was authorised to:

"... give to the Corporation directions of a general character as to the exercise and performance by the Corporation of their functions ... in relation to matters which appear to him to affect the national interest, and the Corporation shall give effect to any such directions."

By s 8 the Corporation was ordered to make an annual report to the Minister, if so directed by the Minister, in such form as might be specified in the direction on the exercise and performance by the Corporation of its functions during the year and on its policy and programmes. Under Part II of the Act of 1972 the Secretary of State was given general control over the finances of the Corporation and, in particular, was authorised to direct the Corporation to pay over to him so much of excess revenue of the Corporation as appeared to him surplus to the Corporation's requirements.

In my opinion by these provisions the BGC performed its public service of providing a gas supply under the control of the State. The Corporation was not independent; its members were appointed by the State; the Corporation was responsible to the Minister acting on behalf of the State, and the Corporation was subject to directions given by the Secretary of State.

By s 29 of the Act of 1972:

"... no person other than the Corporation shall ... supply gas to any premises except with the consent of the Corporation and in accordance with such conditions as may be attached to that consent."

This section conferred on the BGC "special powers beyond those which result from the normal rules applicable in relations between individuals".

Accordingly, the BGC was, in my opinion, a body which was made responsible pursuant to a measure adopted by the State, for providing a public service under the control of the State and had, for that purpose, special powers beyond those which resulted from the normal rules applicable in relations between individuals and therefore the BGC cannot take advantage of the failure of the State to comply with the Equal Treatment Directive....'

(Lord Ackner, Lord Jauncey and Lord Keith agreed with Lord Templeman.)

COMMENT

(1) It will be appreciated that one result of the widespread privatisation that took place in the 1980s is a reduction of possible government liability in these kinds of circumstances.

Problems of proof

King v *Great Britain-China Centre*

[1991] IRLR 513 Court of Appeal

The applicant was a Chinese woman who had been brought up in the UK. She applied for the post of deputy director of the Centre. Despite seeming to be very well-qualified for the post, she was not even short-listed for interview. The industrial tribunal found that she had received less favourable treatment than other candidates (she had not been called for interview) and there was a difference of race; as the employer had not satisfied them that the less favourable treatment was not on grounds of race, they considered that her claim for direct discrimination was made out.

The employer appealed successfully to the EAT on the grounds that the burden of proof remained throughout on the applicant, but that the tribunal had acted as if the employer had the burden of disproving discrimination. Ms King appealed to the Court of Appeal.

Neill LJ: '... In the course of the hearing the Court was referred to a number of authorities. It will be convenient to consider them in chronological order. I propose to start with *Khanna* v *Ministry of Defence*, where the applicant, who had been born in India, had made 22 unsuccessful applications for promotion. On the last occasion he brought proceedings alleging unlawful racial discrimination and relying on the fact that the person selected had less experience than he had. The judgment of the Employment Appeal Tribunal was delivered by Browne-Wilkinson J.... the President suggested that in future Industrial Tribunals might find it easier to forget about the rather nebulous concept of the "shift in the evidential burden". A little later he continued:

> "In this case the industrial tribunal would, we suspect, have found the case rather more straightforward if, looking at all the evidence as a whole, they had simply decided whether the complaint had been established. No useful purpose is served by stopping to reach a conclusion on half the evidence. The right course in this case was for the industrial tribunal to take into account the fact that direct evidence of discrimination is seldom going to be available and that, accordingly, in these cases the affirmative evidence of discrimination will normally consist of inferences to be drawn from the primary facts. If the primary facts indicate that there has been discrimination of some kind, the employer is called on to give an explanation and, failing clear and specific explanation being given by the employer to the satisfaction of the industrial tribunal, an inference of unlawful discrimination from the primary facts will mean the complaint succeeds ... Those propositions are, we think, most easily understood if concepts of shifting evidential burdens are avoided.
>
> So, in this case, the industrial tribunal has drawn the inference of possible discrimination from the fact that there was no obvious reason why the applicant should not have got the job ... To decide that there has been discrimination in the fact of sworn evidence that there was no such discrimination is unpalatable: equally, racial discrimination does undoubtedly exist, and it is highly improbable that a person who has discriminated is going to admit the fact, quite possibly even to himself. The judicial function, however unpalatable, is to resolve such conflicts by a decision if possible."

Later the same year in *Chattopadhyay* v *Headmaster of Holloway School* the Employment Appeal Tribunal considered the case of an Indian teacher who had applied unsuccessfully for the post of head of history at Holloway School. Browne-Wilkinson J referred to the rather special nature of proceedings involving allegations of discrimination contrary to the 1976 Act and continued:

> "As has been pointed out many times, a person complaining that he has been unlawfully discriminated against faces great difficulties. There is normally not available to him any evidence of overtly racial discriminatory words or actions used by the respondent. All that the applicant can do is to point to certain facts which, if unexplained, are consistent with his having been treated less favourably than others on racial grounds. In the majority of cases it is only the respondents and their witnesses who are able to say whether in fact

the allegedly discriminatory act was motivated by racial discrimination or by other, perfectly innocent, motivations. It is for this reason that the law has been established that if an applicant shows that he has been treated less favourably than others in circumstances which are consistent with that treatment being based on racial grounds, the industrial tribunal should draw an inference that such treatment was on racial grounds, unless the respondent can satisfy the Industrial Tribunal that there is an innocent explanation."

The decision in *Khanna* (supra) was commented upon in two later cases in the Court of Appeal. In *Morris* v *London Iron and Steel Co Ltd* May LJ said that he did not find the case of *Khanna* "an easy or satisfactory one" or "entirely satisfactory". He reiterated that the burden of proof lay on the complainant to make out a case of unlawful discrimination.

A year later in *North West Thames Regional Health Authority* v *Noone* May LJ repeated his comment that he did not find the decision in *Khanna* "altogether satisfactory". He then continued as follows:

"In these cases of alleged racial discrimination it is always for the complainant to make out his or her case. It is not often that there is direct evidence of racial discrimination, and these complaints more often than not have to be dealt with on the basis of what are the proper inferences to be drawn from the primary facts. For myself I would have thought that it was almost common sense that, if there is a finding of discrimination and of difference of race and then an inadequate or unsatisfactory explanation by the employer for the discrimination, usually the legitimate inference will be that the discrimination was on racial grounds."

This is an important passage and it is to be noted that it was set out in full in paragraph 8 of the industrial tribunal's reasons in the instant case. But it is also relevant to observe:

(a) that in *Noone* (supra) Balcombe LJ referred with apparent approval to the passages in the judgments of Browne-Wilkinson J in *Khanna* and *Chattopadhyay* which I have already set out; and

(b) that in *West Midlands Passenger Transport Executive* v *Singh* Balcombe LJ, delivering the judgment of the Court of Appeal in a case involving an application for discovery, cited the same passage in Browne-Wilkinson J's judgment in *Chattopadhyay* in support of the proposition that "cases based on racial, or sexual, discrimination have a number of special features."

In the course of the argument we were referred to other recent cases including *London Borough of Barking & Dagenham* v *Camara, Baker* v *Cornwall County Council* and the valuable judgment of Wood J in the Employment Appeal Tribunal in *British Gas plc* v *Sharma*. From these several authorities it is possible, I think, to extract the following principles and guidance:

(1) It is for the applicant who complains of racial discrimination to make out his or her case. Thus if the applicant does not prove the case on the balance of probabilities he or she will fail.

(2) It is important to bear in mind that it is unusual to find direct evidence of racial discrimination. Few employers will be prepared to admit such discrimination even to themselves. In some cases the discrimination will not be ill-intentioned but merely based on an assumption "he or she would not have fitted in".

(3) The outcome of the case will therefore usually depend on what inferences it is proper to draw from the primary facts found by the tribunal. These inferences can include, in appropriate cases, any inferences that it is just and equitable to draw in accordance with s 65(2)(b) of the 1976 Act from an evasive or equivocal reply to a questionnaire.

(4) Though there will be some cases where, for example, the non-selection of the applicant

for a post or for promotion is clearly not on racial grounds, a finding of discrimination and a finding of a difference in race will often point to the possibility of racial discrimination. In such circumstances the tribunal will look to the employer for an explanation. If no explanation is then put forward or if the tribunal considers the explanation to be inadequate or unsatisfactory it will be legitimate for the tribunal to infer that the discrimination was on racial grounds. This is not a matter of law but, as May LJ put it in *Noone*, "almost common sense".

(5) It is unnecessary and unhelpful to introduce the concept of a shifting evidential burden of proof. At the conclusion of all the evidence the tribunal should make findings as to the primary facts and draw such inferences as they consider proper from those facts. They should then reach a conclusion on the balance of probabilities, bearing in mind both the difficulties which face a person who complains of unlawful discrimination and the fact that it is for the complainant to prove his or her case.

I return to the facts of the present case. Miss King is an ethnic Chinese. So were four other of the 30 candidates. Eight candidates were called for interview. None of these eight candidates was an ethnic Chinese. The majority of the tribunal were satisfied that Miss King's paper qualifications fulfilled the requirements set out in the advertisement and in the job specification, and that she had been treated less favourably than the candidates called for interview, particularly candidates 5 and 7. The majority were also impressed by the fact that no ethnic Chinese had ever been employed by the centre.

In these circumstances the Tribunal were clearly entitled to look to the centre for an explanation of the fact that Miss King was not even called for an interview. The majority, however, found the explanation unsatisfactory and were also dissatisfied with the reply to the questionnaire. They therefore concluded that Miss King had made out her case.

It is not now said that the conclusion of the majority was perverse. But it is submitted that they misdirected themselves, the submission being based on the language used in the reasons and in particular in the underlined passages. I have considered this submission with great care and I have taken account of the fact that the submission was accepted by the President of the Employment Appeal Tribunal and by two very experienced lay members of that Tribunal. In the end I am quite satisfied that reading the relevant parts of the reasons as a whole the majority's decision was not flawed by an error of law. They clearly had in mind that it was for Miss King to make out her case: see the reference to *Noone* in paragraph 8 of the reasons. They were entitled to look to the centre for an explanation of the fact that Miss King was not selected for interview. They were not satisfied with the explanation and they were entitled to say so. It was therefore legitimate for them to draw an inference that the discrimination was on racial grounds. This process of reasoning did not involve a reversal of the burden of proof but merely a proper balancing of the factors which could be placed in the scales for and against a finding of unlawful discrimination.'

(Nourse LJ and Sir John Megaw agreed.)

COMMENT

(1) Because of the difficulties which tribunals have experienced in approaching these issues, both the CRE and EOC have argued that the burden of proof should be on the employer to disprove discrimination. While this would be contrary to the general principle that it is for he who alleges to make good his allegation, it is argued that it would be justified because the facts lie peculiarly within the employer's knowledge. However, there is considerable opposition to these proposals. In 1996 the

EC Commission presented a draft directive on the burden of proof, as it was introduced under the Social Chapter, which would provide for the burden to shift.

(2)   In his third principle, Neill LJ refers to the questionnaire. Under RRA s 65 and SDA s 74 the Secretary of State was given power to prescribe a questionnaire which an aggrieved party could send to an employer seeking further information about the reasons for its decisions or actions. Adverse inferences may be drawn from a failure to respond, or evasive or equivocal answers.

(3)   The questionnaire procedure is established by the Race Relations (Questions and Replies) Order 1977 and the Sex Discrimination (Questions and Replies) Order 1975; the form of the questionnaire is set out in the Schedules to the Orders.

Opinions differ as to the value of the questionnaire. In this case, evasive answers to the questionnaire clearly told against the employer.

(4)   One of the biggest difficulties facing a rejected candidate is finding out about the other candidates: only with this information is it possible to form a judgement as to whether you were unfairly passed over. However, much of this information is confidential. In *Science Research Council* v *Nassé* the House of Lords held that a claim of confidentiality should not necessarily defeat a claim for discovery. The test is whether or not the information is required to dispose fairly of the proceedings.

(5)   However, it should be noted further that discovery will not be ordered if it would be oppressive. In *West Midlands PTE* v *Singh* Balcombe LJ said:

> "Discovery may be oppressive in two respects. (1) It may require the provision of material not readily to hand which can only be made available with difficulty and at great expense ... (2) It is also possible that the effect of discovery may be to require the party ordered to make discovery to embark on a course which will add unreasonably to the length and cost of the hearing."

This was said in relation to the compilation of statistics, which is considered next.

CRE Code of Practice for the Elimination of Racial Discrimination and the Promotion of Equality of Opportunity in Employment

Monitoring equal opportunity

1.33.   It is recommended that employers should regularly monitor the effects of selection decisions and personnel practices and procedures in order to assess whether equal opportunity is being achieved.

1.34.   The information needed for effective monitoring may be obtained in a number of ways. It will best be provided by records showing the ethnic origins of existing employees and job applicants. It is recognised that the need for detailed information and the methods of collecting it will vary according to the circumstances of individual establishments. For example, in small firms or in firms in areas with little or no racial minority settlement it will often be adequate to assess the distribution of employees from personal knowledge and visual identification.

1.35.   It is open to employers to adopt the method of monitoring which is best suited to their needs and circumstances, but whichever method is adopted, they should be able to show that it is effective. In order to achieve the full commitment of all concerned the chosen method should be discussed and agreed, where appropriate, with trade union or employee representatives.

1.36. Employers should ensure that information on individuals' ethnic origins is collected for the purpose of monitoring equal opportunity alone and is protected from misuse.

1.37. The following is the comprehensive method recommended by the CRE.
Analyses should be carried out of:

    (a) the ethnic composition of the workforce of each plant, department, section, shift and job category, and changes in distribution over periods of time;

    (b) selection decisions for recruitment, promotion, transfer and training, according to the racial group of candidates, and reasons for these decisions.

1.38. Except in cases where there are large numbers of applicants and the burden on resources would be excessive, reasons for selection and rejection should be recorded at each stage of the selection process, e.g. initial shortlisting and final decisions. Simple categories of reasons for rejection should be adequate for the early sifting stages.

1.39. Selection criteria and personnel procedures should be reviewed to ensure that they do not include requirements or conditions which constitute or may lead to unlawful indirect discrimination.

1.40. This information should be carefully and regularly analysed and, in order to identify areas which may need particular attention, a number of key questions should be asked.

1.41. Is there evidence that individuals from any particular racial group:

    (a) do not apply for employment or promotion, or that fewer apply than might be expected?

    (b) are not recruited or promoted at all, or are appointed in a significantly lower proportion than their rate of application?

    (c) are under-represented in training or in jobs carrying higher pay, status or authority?

    (d) are concentrated in certain shifts, sections or departments?

1.42. If the answer to any of these questions is yes, the reasons for this should be investigated. If direct or indirect discrimination is found action must be taken to end it immediately. (ss 4, 28)

1.43. It is recommended that deliberate acts of unlawful discrimination by employees are treated as disciplinary offences.

COMMENT

(1) Collection of statistics and monitoring the results is recommended also by the EOC Code of Practice on the Elimination of Discrimination on the Grounds of Sex and Marriage and the Promotion of Equality of Opportunity in Employment 1985 paras 37–40.

(2) Failure to comply with the Codes is not of itself unlawful, but is to be taken into account in any proceedings under the legislation.

West Midlands Passenger Transport Executive v *Singh*

[1988] ICR 614 Court of Appeal

The applicant, a Sikh, had been employed as an inspector by the PTE since 1977. He applied for promotion to one of 13 senior inspector posts in 1985 but was rejected. He instituted proceedings for racial discrimination and sought discovery of statistics relating to the ethnic origins, qualifications and experience of all 55 applicants for the posts and the documentation (anonymised) on the short-listing decision process. The employers agreed to this, but resisted a further request for similar information relating to all posts in broadly comparable grades between 1983 (when an equal opportunities policy had been adopted) and the end of 1985 when he applied for promotion. The decision of the court was given by Balcombe LJ.

Balcombe LJ: '... The issue is whether evidence that a particular employer has or has not appointed any or many coloured applicants in the past is material to the question whether he has discriminated on racial grounds against a particular complainant; and whether discovery devoted to ascertaining the percentage of successful coloured applicants within successful white applicants should be ordered. Or as the Employment Appeal Tribunal put it in their judgment:

> "Assuming for the purpose of argument that no single coloured applicant who has applied over the last 18 months for a succession of these jobs has succeeded in obtaining them, is that fact in any way logically probative that in the present application made by the applicant there may be race discrimination? Put another way, is it open to an industrial tribunal to draw an inference from a long history of unsuccessful applications by coloured applicants that an employer has adopted a discriminatory policy and has exercised it in the particular case..."

Direct discrimination involves that an individual is not treated on his merits but receives unfavourable treatment because he is a member of a group. Statistical evidence may establish a discernible pattern in the treatment of a particular group: if that pattern demonstrates a regular failure of members of the group to obtain promotion to particular jobs and to under-representation in such jobs, it may give rise to an inference of discrimination against the group. That is the reason why the Race Relations Code of Practice which came into effect on 1 April 1984 ... recommends ethnic monitoring of the workforce and of applications for promotion and recruitment, a practice adopted by the employers in their own organisation. Statistics obtained through monitoring are not conclusive in themselves, but if they show racial or ethnic imbalance or disparities, then they may indicate areas of racial discrimination.

If a practice is being operated against a group then, in the absence of a satisfactory explanation in a particular case, it is reasonable to infer that the complainant, as a member of the group, has himself been treated less favourably on ground of race. Indeed, evidence of discriminatory treatment against the group in relation to promotion may be more persuasive of discrimination in the particular case than previous treatment of the applicant, which may be indicative of personal factors peculiar to the applicant and not necessarily racially motivated.

It has been a regular feature of cases conducted before industrial tribunals in race discrimination cases for employers to give evidence that persons holding responsible positions include both white and non-white as demonstrating that they have a policy of non-discrimination and as providing evidence from which an industrial tribunal could decide in a particular case that the particular applicant had not been discriminated against: – see the judgment of the Employment Appeal Tribunal.

The validity of this practice, and its probative effect, have been approved by this court in *Owen & Briggs* v *James*, approving a similar approach by the Employment Appeal Tribunal in that case ... If evidence of a non-discriminatory attitude on the part of an employer is accepted as having probative force, as being likely to have governed his behaviour in the particular case, then evidence of a discriminatory attitude on his part may also have probative effect.

The suitability of candidates can rarely be measured objectively: often subjective judgments will be made. If there is evidence of a high percentage rate of failure to achieve promotion at particular levels by members of a particular racial group, this may indicate that the real reason for refusal is a conscious or unconscious racial attitude which involves stereotyped assumptions about members of that group.

Mr. Beloff, for the employers, submitted that the statistical material ordered by the Employment Appeal Tribunal was not relevant, because it was not logically probative of the question in issue, namely, whether the employers discriminated against the applicant on racial grounds when they denied him promotion in December 1985. The fact that the statistical evidence might show that the employers had between October 1984 and December 1985 rejected all coloured applicants for the post of traffic supervisor would not of itself prove racial discrimination; in every case there may have been good, non-racial, reasons for the rejection of the particular applicant. And, even if there had been racial discrimination by the employers on other occasions, it would not of itself prove racial discrimination against the applicant on this particular occasion. As a matter of strict logic both these propositions are true. Nevertheless, the courts do not apply so stringent a test in deciding on the relevance of material to be used as evidence. "Relevant (i.e. logically probative or disprobative) evidence is evidence which makes the matter which requires proof more or less probable": see *Reg.* v *Kilbourne per* Lord Simon of Glaisdale cited with approval by Lord Hailsham of St. Marylebone in *Reg.* v *Boardman*; see also the dictum of Lord Wilberforce in *Reg.* v *Boardman*, "in judging whether one fact is probative of another, experience plays as large a place as logic".

A number of cases on "similar fact" evidence, in both the criminal and the civil field, were cited to us. We did not find these of assistance in answering the question with which we are faced. We are satisfied, for the reasons set out above, that the statistical material ordered is relevant to the issues in this case, in that (i) it may assist the applicant in establishing a positive case that treatment of coloured employees was on racial grounds, which was an effective cause for their, and his, failure to obtain promotion; (ii) it may assist the applicant to rebut the employers' contention that they operated in practice an equal opportunities policy which was applied in his case.'

COMMENT

(1)   In so far as it is inconsistent with this decision, *Jalota* v *Imperial Metals Industry (Kynoch) Ltd* was overruled.

Remedies

Sex Discrimination Act 1975

65.   (1)   Where an industrial tribunal finds that a complaint presented to it under section 63 is well-founded the tribunal shall make such of the following as it considers just and equitable—

   (a)   an order declaring the rights of the complainant and the respondent in relation to the act to which the complaint relates;

   (b)   an order requiring the respondent to pay to the complainant compensation of an amount corresponding to any damages he could have been ordered by a county court or by a sheriff court to pay to the complainant if the complaint had fallen to be dealt with under section 66;

(c)   a recommendation that the respondent take within a specified period action appearing to the tribunal to be practicable for the purpose of obviating or reducing the adverse effect on the complainant of any act of discrimination to which the complaint relates.

COMMENT

(1)   RRA s 56 is in parallel terms. At one time, compensation was limited to the maximum unfair dismissal award.

Compensation
Marshall v Southampton & South West Hants AHA (No 2)
[1993] IRLR 445 European Court of Justice

It will be recalled that Ms Marshall won her claim that discriminatory retirement ages breached the Equal Treatment Directive (above, p 65). In these proceedings, dealing with the amount of compensation, she challenged the statutory limit. The House of Lords referred the case to the ECJ.

Judgment of the Court: '… she appealed to the House of Lords, which decided to stay the proceedings and to submit to the Court of Justice the following questions for a preliminary ruling:

"1. Where the national legislation of a Member State provides for the payment of compensation as one remedy available by judicial process to a person who has been subjected to unlawful discrimination of a kind prohibited by Council Directive 76/207/EEC of 9 February 1976 ('the Directive'), is the Member State guilty of a failure to implement Article 6 of the Directive by reason of the imposition by the national legislation of an upper limit of £6,250 on the amount of compensation recoverable by such a person?
2.   Where the national legislation provides for the payment of compensation as aforesaid, is it essential to the due implementation of Article 6 of the Directive that the compensation to be awarded:
(a)   should not be less than the amount of the loss found to have been sustained by reason of the unlawful discrimination, and
(b)   should include an award of interest on the principal amount of the loss so found from the date of the unlawful discrimination to the date when the compensation is paid?
3.   If the national legislation of a Member State has failed to implement Article 6 of the Directive in any of the respects referred to in questions 1 and 2, is a person who has been subjected to unlawful discrimination as aforesaid entitled as against an authority which is an emanation of the Member State to rely on the provisions of Article 6 as overriding the limits imposed by the national legislation on the amount of compensation recoverable?"
…

The first and second questions
In its first question, the House of Lords seeks to establish whether it is contrary to Article 6 of the Directive for national provisions to lay down an upper limit on the amount of compensation recoverable by a victim of discrimination.

In its second question, the House of Lords asks whether Article 6 requires (a) that the compensation for the damage sustained as a result of the illegal discrimination should be full and (b) that it should include an award of interest on the principal amount from the date of the unlawful discrimination to the date when compensation is paid.

The Court's interpretation of Article 6 as set out above provides a direct reply to the first part of the second question relating to the level of compensation required by that provision.

It also follows from that interpretation that the fixing of an upper limit of the kind at issue in the main proceedings cannot, by definition, constitute proper implementation of Article 6 of the Directive, since it limits the amount of compensation a priori to a level which is not necessarily consistent with the requirement of ensuring real equality of opportunity through adequate reparation for the loss and damage sustained as a result of discriminatory dismissal.

With regard to the second part of the second question relating to the award of interest, suffice it to say that full compensation for the loss and damage sustained as a result of discriminatory dismissal cannot leave out of account factors, such as the effluxion of time, which may in fact reduce its value. The award of interest, in accordance with the applicable national rules, must therefore be regarded as an essential component of compensation for the purposes of restoring real equality of treatment.

Accordingly, the reply to be given to the first and second questions is that the interpretation of Article 6 of the Directive must be that reparation of the loss and damage sustained by a person injured as a result of discriminatory dismissal may not be limited to an upper limit fixed a priori or by excluding an award of interest to compensate for the loss sustained by the recipient of the compensation as a result of the effluxion of time until the capital sum awarded is actually paid.

The third question
In its third question, the House of Lords seeks to establish whether a person who has been injured as a result of discriminatory dismissal may rely, as against an authority of the State acting in its capacity as employer, on Article 6 of the Directive in order to contest the application of national rules which impose limits on the amount of compensation recoverable by way of reparation.

It follows from the considerations set out above as to the meaning and scope of Article 6 of the Directive, that that provision is an essential factor for attaining the fundamental objective of equal treatment for men and women, in particular as regards working conditions, including the conditions governing dismissal, referred to in Article 5(1) of the Directive, and that, where, in the event of discriminatory dismissal, financial compensation is the measure adopted in order to restore that equality, such compensation must be full and may not be limited a priori in terms of its amount.

Accordingly, the combined provisions of Article 6 and Article 5 of the Directive give rise, on the part of a person who has been injured as a result of discriminatory dismissal, to rights which that person must be able to rely upon before the national courts as against the State and authorities which are an emanation of the State.

COMMENT

(1) As a result of this decision the Sex Discrimination and Equal Pay (Remedies) Regulations 1993 were passed, lifting the limit on compensation and allowing the award of interest. Although it was not legally necessary to do the same for race discrimination, the position was equalised by the Race Relations (Remedies) Act 1994 and the Race Relations (Interest on Awards) Regulations 1994.

Recommendations

A recommendation can be made in addition to a declaration and an award of compensation. However, the tribunal's power to make recommendations has been interpreted fairly strictly.

North West Thames RHA v *Noone*

[1988] ICR 813 Court of Appeal

The complainant was a Sri Lankan doctor who had worked in England, specialising in pathology, for many years. She applied for a post as a consultant microbiologist with the health authority, but was not appointed. The industrial tribunal found that this was on grounds of race. As well as awarding compensation, the industrial tribunal wished to make a recommendation to the effect that the next time a vacancy for a consultant microbiologist occurred, it should not be advertised, so that Noone would in all likelihood be the only candidate.

Under the National Health Service (Appointment of Consultants) Regulations 1982, all consultancy posts had to be advertised, although the Secretary of State had power to dispense with this requirement.

May LJ: '... What is sought in this appeal in lieu of the recommendation made by the industrial tribunal in November 1985 is in effect a recommendation that the health authority should seek the Secretary of State's dispensation from the advertisement requirement when next a vacant consultant microbiologist post arises. In those circumstances, as Mrs Smith put it in the course of her argument before us today, that would mean that the complainant in whose favour we have found discrimination made out, should have an advantage in seeking appointment to the vacant post. Without the advertisement the field would be limited to her and, as was accepted in the course of the argument, to anybody else who, without an advertisement, heard of the vacancy and was minded to apply for it. But without the advertisement one can see that the field of those seeking the vacant post would be smaller than it might have been had the post been advertised. Of course that always proceeds on the premise, first, that the Secretary of State agreed to the request of the health authority to dispense with the advertising requirement under regulation 5(1) of the Regulations of 1982. If he does not, then nothing happens at all. The position is precisely the same as it would be without any recommendation.

In my judgment, however, the proposed recommendation for which the complainant seeks an order on this appeal is subject to one fundamental objection, in addition to a number of others into which I do not propose to go. The fundamental objection is this, that any such recommendation would set at nought the statutory procedure set out for the benefit of the National Health Service, the various professions concerned in that service, the public and others qualified for the vacant post, for making that particular consultant appointment, and on that ground alone, which is, as I think, fundamental, I for my part would dismiss this appeal in so far as I have indicated it relates to the third type of relief under section 56(1)(c) of the Race Relations Act 1976 ...'

(Balcombe and Stocker LJJ delivered concurring judgments.)

COMMENT

(1)   This does not amount to saying that a tribunal could never order that the next vacancy be offered to the applicant, because there were special rules applicable here.

However, in *British Gas* v *Sharma*, the EAT struck down such a recommendation saying that it would be positive discrimination and could amount to direct discrimination against other applicants. Leaving aside the fact that if the post was not advertised, there would probably be no other applicants, the argument is misconceived, for there is no general requirement that employers should advertise posts. Suppose I employ 20 workers in my factory; as a favour to a friend, I promise her that I will offer the next vacancy to her unemployed child. Would that be contrary to discrimination law?

The wording of the Acts does not seem to preclude a tribunal making a recommendation of this kind, which might seem to many to be the most appropriate kind of compensation for discrimination which has cost someone a post. It is unfortunate that the trend seems to be running against this.

(2) In *Irvine* v *Prestcold Ltd* a tribunal recommended that the applicant should be promoted to the next vacancy, or alternatively should be paid the difference in salary between the two posts until she was promoted to that or an equivalent post. This was overturned on appeal, both because the recommendation should be limited to a 'specified period' and because any compensation for pecuniary loss should be the subject of a compensation award, not a recommendation.

DISABILITY DISCRIMINATION

The Disability Discrimination Act 1995 came into force in December 1996, replacing the Disabled Persons (Employment) Act 1944 and attempting for the first time to provide comprehensive protection against discrimination for people with disabilities in fields such as education, transport, and the supply of goods and services, as well as employment. Although discrimination on grounds of disability has not been prohibited by the treaties on human rights, it was the denial of civil liberties inherent in the previous position which provided the mainspring for the movement which led to this Act, inspired by the movement in the United States which led to the influential Americans with Disabilities Act 1990. The DDA is amplified by two sets of regulations, a Code of Practice and Guidance on the Act. Both the Code and the Guidance are to be taken into account by courts and tribunals.

Scope of protection

The Act applies to people with disabilities.

Disability Discrimination Act 1995

1.   (1)   Subject to the provisions of Schedule 1, a person has a disability for the purposes of this Act if he has a physical or mental impairment which has a substantial and long-term adverse effect on his ability to carry out normal day-to-day activities.

       (2)   In this Act "disabled person" means a person who has a disability.

2.   (1)   The provisions of this Part and Parts II and III apply in relation to a person who has had a disability as they apply in relation to a person who has that disability.

       ...

Disability Discrimination (Meaning of Disability) Regulations 1996

3.   (1)   Subject to paragraph (2) below, addiction to alcohol, nicotine or any other substance is to be treated as not amounting to an impairment for the purposes of the Act.

       (2)   Paragraph (1) above does not apply to addiction which was originally the result of administration of medically prescribed drugs or other medical treatment.

4.   (1)   For the purposes of the Act the following conditions are to be treated as not amounting to impairments—

          (a)   a tendency to set fires,

          (b)   a tendency to steal,

          (c)   a tendency to physical or sexual abuse of other persons,

          (d)   exhibitionism, and

          (e)   voyeurism.

       (2)   Subject to paragraph (3) below for the purposes of the Act the condition known as seasonal allergic rhinitis shall be treated as not amounting to an impairment.

       (3)   Paragraph (2) above shall not prevent that condition from being taken into account for the purposes of the Act where it aggravates the effect of another condition.

5.   For the purposes of paragraph 3 of Schedule 1 to the Act a severe disfigurement is not to be treated as having a substantial adverse effect on the ability of the person concerned to carry out normal day-to-day activities if it consists of—

          (a)   a tattoo (which has not been removed), or

          (b)   a piercing of the body for decorative or other non-medical purposes, including any object attached through the piercing for such purposes.

COMMENT

(1)   According to the Guidance, 'substantial' means 'more than "minor" or "trivial"', and factors such as the time taken to do something, or the manner of doing it are among the things to be taken into account in deciding how substantial an effect is.

(2)   In the case of progressive illnessess (such as multiple sclerosis, muscular dystrophy or infection with HIV, all of which are specifically mentioned in the Act), the effects may not at first be substantial, or there may be periods of remission. People with such disabilities will nevertheless receive the protection of the Act as soon as the illness manifests itself in any adverse effect on their normal day-to-day activities (Sch 1, para 8).

(3)   'Long-term effect' is defined in Schedule 1 as capable of lasting for a year or more, or the rest of the applicant's life, although its severity may vary over time.

(4)   Normal day-to-day activities are exhaustively defined as involving mobility; manual dexterity; physical co-ordination; continence; ability to lift, carry or move everyday objects; speech, hearing and eyesight; memory or ability to learn, concentrate or understand; perception of the risk of personal danger (Sch 1, para 4).

(5)   Severe disfigurement is included as a disability (Sch 1, para 3), but note that self-inflicted disfigurements are not.

(6)   Employers with fewer than 20 employees are exempt from the provisions of the Act.

Meaning of discrimination

Two forms of unlawful discrimination are set out in the Act.

Disability Discrimination Act 1995

5.   (1)   For the purposes of this Part, an employer discriminates against a disabled person if—
     (a)   for a reason which relates to the disabled person's disability, he treats him less favourably than he treats or would treat others to whom that reason does not or would not apply; and
     (b)   he cannot show that the treatment in question is justified.
    (2)   For the purposes of this Part, an employer also discriminates against a disabled person if—
     (a)   he fails to comply with a section 6 duty imposed on him in relation to the disabled person; and
     (b)   he cannot show that his failure to comply with that duty is justified.
    (3)   Subject to subsection (5), for the purposes of subsection (1) treatment is justified if, but only if, the reason for it is both material to the circumstances of the particular case and substantial.
    (4)   For the purposes of subsection (2), failure to comply with a section 6 duty is justified if, only if, the reason for the failure is both material to the circumstances of the particular case and substantial. ...

6.   (1)   Where—
     (a)   any arrangements made by or on behalf of an employer, or
     (b)   any physical feature of premises occupied by the employer,
     place the disabled person concerned at a substantial disadvantage in comparison with persons who are not disabled, it is the duty of the employer to take such steps as it is reasonable, in all the circumstances of the case, for him to have to take in order to prevent the arrangements or feature having that effect.
     ...

Code of Practice: Disability Discrimination 1996

What adjustments might an employer have to make?

4.20   **The Act gives** a number of examples of 'steps' which employers may have to take, if it is reasonable for them to have to do so in all the circumstances of the case **(s 6(3))**. Steps other than those listed here, or a combination of steps, will sometimes have to be taken. The steps in the Act are—

*   *making adjustments to premises*

    An employer might have to make structural or other physical changes such as: widening a doorway, providing a ramp or moving furniture for a wheelchair user; relocating light switches, door handles or shelves for someone who has difficulty in reaching; providing appropriate contrast in decor to help the safe mobility of a visually impaired person.

*   *allocating some of the disabled person's duties to another person*

Minor or subsidiary duties might be reallocated to another employee if the disabled person has difficulty in doing them because of the disability. For example, if a job occasionally involves going onto the open roof of a building an employer might have to transfer this work away from an employee whose disability involves severe vertigo.

- *transferring the person to fill an existing vacancy*

  If an employee becomes disabled, or has a disability which worsens so she cannot work in the same place or under the same arrangements and there is no reasonable adjustment which would enable the employee to continue doing the current job, then she might have to be considered for any suitable alternative posts which are available. (Such a case might also involve reasonable retraining.)

- *altering the person's working hours*

  This could include allowing the disabled person to work flexible hours to enable additional breaks to overcome fatigue arising from the disability, or changing the disabled person's hours to fit with the availability of a carer.

- *assigning the person to a different place of work*

  This could mean transferring a wheelchair user's work station from an inaccessible third floor office to an accessible one on the ground floor. It could mean moving the person to other premises of the same employer if the first building is inaccessible.

- *allowing the person to be absent during working hours for rehabilitation, assessment or treatment*

  For example, if a person were to become disabled, the employer might have to allow the person more time off during work, than would be allowed to non-disabled employees, to receive physiotherapy or psychoanalysis or undertake employment rehabilitation. A similar adjustment might be appropriate if a disability worsens or if a disabled person needs occasional treatment anyway.

- *giving the person, or arranging for him to be given, training*

  This could be training in the use of particular pieces of equipment unique to the disabled person, or training appropriate for all employees but which needs altering for the disabled person because of the disability. For example, all employees might need to be trained in the use of a particular machine but an employer might have to provide slightly different or longer training for an employee with restricted hand or arm movements, or training in additional software for a visually impaired person so that he can use a computer with speech output.

- *acquiring or modifying equipment*

  An employer might have to provide special equipment (such as an adapted keyboard for a visually impaired person or someone with arthritis), or an adapted telephone for someone with a hearing impairment or modified equipment (such as longer handles on a machine). There is no requirement to provide or modify equipment for personal purposes unconnected with work, such as providing a wheelchair if a person needs one in any event but does not have one: the disadvantage in such a case does not flow from the employer's arrangements or premises.

- *modifying instructions or reference manuals*

  The way instruction is normally given to employees might need to be revised when telling a disabled person how to do a task. The format of instructions or manuals may need to be modified (eg produced in braille or on audio tape) and instructions for people with learning disabilities may need to be conveyed orally with individual demonstration.

- *modifying procedures for testing or assessment*

  This could involve ensuring that particular tests do not adversely affect people with particular types of disability. For example, a person with restricted manual dexterity might be disadvantaged by a written test, so an employer might have to give that person an oral test.

- *providing a reader or interpreter*

  This could involve a colleague reading mail to a person with a visual impairment at particular times during the working day or, in appropriate circumstances, the hiring of a reader or sign language interpreter.

- *providing supervision*

  This could involve the provision of a support worker, or help from a colleague, in appropriate circumstances, for someone whose disability leads to uncertainty or lack of confidence.

COMMENT

(1)   One of the major concerns for employers about the Act is what it may cost them to make adjustments. This is also dealt with in the Code.

Code of Practice: Disability Discrimination 1996

When is it 'reasonable' for an employer to have to make an adjustment?
4.21   Effective and practicable adjustments for disabled people often involve little or no cost or disruption and are therefore very likely to be reasonable for an employer to have to make. *The Act lists* a number of factors which may, in particular, have a bearing on whether it will be reasonable for the employer to have to make a particular adjustment (**s 6(4)**). These factors make a useful checklist, particularly when considering more substantial adjustments. The effectiveness and practicability of a particular adjustment might be considered first. If it is practicable and effective, the financial aspects might be looked at as a whole—cost of the adjustment and resources available to fund it. Other factors might also have a bearing. The factors in the Act are listed below.

- *The effectiveness of the step in preventing the disadvantage*
4.22   It is unlikely to be reasonable for an employer to have to make an adjustment involving little benefit to the disabled employee.

  A disabled person is significantly less productive than his colleagues and so is paid less. A particular adjustment would improve his output and thus his pay. It is more likely to be reasonable for the employer to have to make that adjustment if it would significantly improve his pay, than if the adjustment would make only a relatively small improvement.

- *The practicability of the step*

4.23   It is more likely to be reasonable for an employer to have to take a step which is easy to take than one which is difficult.

> It might be impracticable for an employer who needs to appoint an employee urgently to have to wait for an adjustment to be made to an entrance. How long it might be reasonable for the employer to have to wait would depend on the circumstances. However, it might be possible to make a temporary adjustment in the meantime, such as using another, less convenient entrance.

- *The financial and other costs of the adjustment and the extent of any disruption caused*

4.24   If an adjustment costs little or nothing and is not disruptive, it would be reasonable unless some other factor (such as practicability or effectiveness) made it unreasonable. The costs to be taken into account include staff and other resource costs. The significance of the cost of a step may depend in part on what the employer might otherwise spend in the circumstances.

> It would be reasonable for an employer to have to spend at least as much on an adjustment to enable the retention of a disabled person—including any retraining—as might be spent on recruiting and training a replacement.

4.25   The significance of the cost of a step may also depend in part on the value of the employee's experience and expertise to the employer.

> Examples of the factors that might be considered as relating to the value of an employee would include—
>
> - the amount of resources (such as training) invested in the individual by the employer;
> - the employee's length of service;
> - the employee's level of skill and knowledge;
> - the employee's quality of relationships with clients;
> - the level of the employee's pay.

4.26   It is more likely to be reasonable for an employer to have to make an adjustment with significant costs for an employee who is likely to be in the job for some time than for a temporary employee.

4.27   An employer is more likely to have to make an adjustment which might cause only minor inconvenience to other employees or the employer than one which might unavoidably prevent other employees from doing their job, or cause other significant disruption.

- *The extent of the employer's financial or other resources*

4.28   It is more likely to be reasonable for an employer with substantial financial resources to have to make an adjustment with a significant cost, than for an employer with fewer resources. The resources in practice available to the employer as a whole should be taken into account as well as other calls on those resources. The reasonableness of an adjustment will depend, however, not only on the resources in practice available for the adjustment but also on all other relevant factors (such as effectiveness and practicability).

4.29   Where the resources of the employer are spread across more than one 'business unit' or 'profit centre' the calls on them should also be taken into account in assessing reasonableness.

A large retailer probably could not show that the limited resources for which an individual shop manager is responsible meant that it was not reasonable for the retailer to have to make an adjustment at that shop. Such an employer may, however, have a number—perhaps a large number— of other disabled employees in other shops. The employer's expenditure on other adjustments, or his potential expenditure on similar adjustments for other existing disabled employees, might then be taken into account in assessing the reasonableness of having to make a new adjustment for the disabled employee in question.

4.30   It is more likely to be reasonable for an employer with a substantial number of staff to have to make certain adjustments, than for a smaller employer.

It would generally be reasonable for an employer with many staff to have to make significant efforts to reallocate duties, identify a suitable alternative post or provide supervision from existing staff. It could also be reasonable for a small company covered by the Act to have to make any of these adjustments but not if it involved disproportionate effort.

* *The availability to the employer of financial or other assistance to help make an adjustment*

4.31   The availability of outside help may well be a relevant factor.

An employer, in recruiting a disabled person, finds that the only feasible adjustment is too costly for him alone. However, if assistance is available eg from a Government programme or voluntary body, it may well be reasonable for him to have to make the adjustment after all.

A disabled person is not required to contribute to the cost of a reasonable adjustment. However, if a disabled person has a particular piece of special or adapted equipment which he is prepared to use for work, this might make it reasonable for the employer to have to take some other step (as well as allowing use of the equipment).

An employer requires his employees to use company cars for all business travel. One employee's disability means she would have to use an adapted car or an alternative form of transport. If she has an adapted car of her own which she is willing to use on business, it might well be reasonable for the employer to have to allow this and pay her an allowance to cover the cost of doing so, even if it would not have been reasonable for him to have to provide an adapted company car, or to pay an allowance to cover alternative travel arrangements in the absence of an adapted car.

Other factors
4.32   Although the Act does not mention any further factors, others might be relevant depending on the circumstances. For example—

* *effect on other employees*

Employees' adverse reaction to an adjustment being made for the disabled employee which involves something they too would like (such as a special working arrangement) is unlikely to be significant.

- *adjustments made for other disabled employees*

  An employer may choose to give a particular disabled employee, or group of disabled employees, an adjustment which goes beyong the duty—that is, which is more than it is reasonable for him to have to do. This would not mean he necessarily had to provide a similar adjustment for other employees with a similar disability.

- *the extent to which the disabled person is willing to cooperate*

  An employee with a mobility impairment works in a team located on an upper floor, to which there is no access by lift. Getting there is very tiring for the employee, and the employer could easily make a more accessible location available for him (though the whole team could not be relocated). If that was the only adjustment which it would be reasonable for the employer to have to make but the employee refused to work there then the employer would not have to make any adjustment at all.

Justification

The standard of justification is set out in DDA s 5 (above) and amplified with numerous examples in the Code of Practice. The Disability Discrimination (Employment) Regulations 1996 specifically provide that paying a disabled worker less as a result of a generally applicable performance-related pay system will be justified.

Discrimination in pension schemes both in eligibility conditions and amount of benefits is to be regarded as justified if the reason for it is that the cost of providing the benefit is projected to be 'substantially greater' than it would be for a comparable person without the disability (reg 4). Nonetheless, under reg 5 the disabled worker can still be required to make the same contributions as other workers even if not eligible for the same benefits.

Enforcement and remedies

Enforcement is through individual application to industrial tribunals within three months of the alleged act of discrimination, as with the SDA and RRA. However, unlike the EOC and CRE, the National Disability Council has no enforcement powers.

As with the other anti-discrimination statutes, declaration, recommendation and compensation (unlimited) are the available remedies.

3 Defining the contract of employment

In Chapter 2 we saw that the law against discrimination in employment protects anyone who has or seeks a contract personally to execute any work or labour. Contracts for personal labour must now be subdivided to distinguish between workers providing personal service under a *contract of employment* (called employees) and workers personally providing work on a *self-employed* basis (independent contractors). It is possible that there may be a final category of workers providing personal service who are neither employees nor self-employed.

Why must these distinctions be made? There are five main reasons. First, certain terms are implied by law into all contracts of employment; second, employment protection rights (such as the right to claim unfair dismissal) are available only to employees; third, liability for tax and National Insurance contributions is different for employees and the self-employed; fourth (and relatedly), only employees are entitled to many social security benefits, and finally, the employer's duty of care to, and responsibility for the acts of, employees is much greater than the corresponding duty to and responsibility for independent contractors.

EMPLOYEES AND INDEPENDENT CONTRACTORS
Who is an employee?

Employment Rights Act 1996

230.   (1) In this Act 'employee' means an individual who has entered into or works under (or, where the employment has ceased, worked under) a contract of employment.
(2) In this Act 'contract of employment' means a contract of service or apprenticeship, whether express or implied, and (if it is express) whether it is oral or in writing.

COMMENT

(1)   These definitions are not very helpful, as they give no indication of how a contract of service is to be identified. The answer must be found at common law, and various factors may be identified from the extracts below.

(2)   Note that for statutory purposes a contract of apprenticeship is to be treated as a contract of employment. This means, for example, that an apprentice who is not kept on at the end of the training period has the right to claim redundancy or unfair dismissal (though see *North East Coast Shiprepairers Ltd* v *Secretary of State*).

In the extracts which follow, note the factors regarded as relevant to whether or not the contract is a contract of employment as opposed to a contract for services.

Yewens v Noakes

(1880) 6 QBD 530 Court of Appeal

Bramwell LJ: 'A servant is a person subject to the command of his master as to the manner in which he shall do his work.'

Walker v Crystal Palace Football Club

[1910] 1 KB 87 Court of Appeal

Cozens-Hardy MR: 'The question in this appeal is whether the particular respondent here, who has been a party to a written form of agreement, is a workman entitled to compensation under the Workmen's Compensation Act. The man in question is a professional football player. The present appellants are the Crystal Palace Football and Athletic Club Ltd. Amongst their objects as provided by the memorandum of association in this: "To promote the game of football and to establish games and to maintain a team of football players either professional or amateur or partly of the one and partly of the other."...

Now, that being the relation between the parties, the agreement is in these terms: "The club hereby agrees to engage the said G Walker from 1 May 1908 until 30 April 1909 for the purpose of playing football with the Crystal Palace Football Club Limited provided always and it is hereby agreed and declared that the said G Walker shall not....;" and then there is a limitation that the man shall not be a publican or reside in a public-house or take part in professional running or any other sport without the consent in writing of the club. First of all the club agrees to engage the man. Then what does the man do? "The said G Walker hereby agrees to serve the club for the purpose and period aforesaid and not to engage himself to play football for any other person or club during the said period", and at the expiration of that period the club is to have the first offer to re-engage his services. Then in consideration of such service the club agrees to pay the man so much per week, and the man agrees that he will during the period aforesaid "play in all matches when required by the club and will keep himself temperate, sober, and in good playing form and attend regularly to training and observe the training and general instructions of the club and do all that may by the club be deemed necessary to fit himself as an efficient football player and will in all respects conform to the rules and laws of the Football Association". Then there is a proviso that if the man refuses or neglects "to play in club matches when required as aforesaid or if he shall refuse or neglect to obey the training and general instructions of the club he shall pay to the club a sum not exceeding five pounds as liquidated damages".

Before going further it is right to say that the regulations or instructions there referred to are also in print, and it is quite clear, without going through those regulations in detail, that the man agrees to devote his whole time, to attend regularly on certain days and hours, not merely for the purpose of playing, but for the purpose of training, and there are a number of detailed regulations which the man is bound to observe and comply with ...

It has been argued before us very forcibly by Mr Russell that there is a certain difference between an ordinary workman and a man who contracts to exhibit and employ his skill where the employer would have no right to dictate to him in the exercise of that skill; e.g. the club in this case would have no right to dictate to him how he should play football. I am unable to follow that. He is bound according to the express terms of his contract to obey all general directions of the club, and I think in any particular game in which he was engaged he would also be bound to obey the particular instructions of the captain or whoever it might be who was the delegate of the authority of the club for the purpose of giving those instructions. In my judgment it cannot be that a man is taken out of the operation of the Act simply because in doing a particular kind of work which he is employed to do, and in doing which he obeys general instructions, he also exercises his own judgment uncontrolled by anybody. I think this appeal must be dismissed.'

Farwell LJ: 'I agree.

The appellants ... say there is no contract of service with an employer because the football player is at liberty to exercise his own initiative in playing the game. That appears to me to be no answer. There are many employments in which the workman exercises initiative, but he may or may not be bound to obey the directions of his employer when given to him. If he has no duty to obey them, it may very well be that there is no service, but here not only is the agreement by the player that he will serve, but he also agrees to obey the training and general instructions of the club. I cannot doubt that he is bound to obey any directions which the captain, as the delegate of the club, may give him during the course of the game – that is to say, any direction that is within the terms of his employment as a football player.'

Stevenson Jordan & Harrison v *MacDonald & Evans*

[1952] 1 TLR 101 Court of Appeal

Denning LJ: 'I fully agree with all that my Lord has said on all the issues in this case. It raises the troublesome question: What is the distinction between a contract of service and a contract for services? The test usually applied is whether the employer has the right to control the manner of doing the work. Thus in *Collins* v *Herts CC*, Hilbery J said:

> "The distinction between a contract for services and a contract of service can be summarised in this way: In the one case the master can order or require what is to be done, while in the other cases, he can not only require what is to be done but how it shall be done."

But in *Cassidy* v *Ministry of Health*, Somervell LJ pointed out that that test is not universally correct. There are many contracts of service where the master cannot control the manner in which the work is to be done, as in the case of the captain of a ship. Somervell LJ went on to say that "One perhaps cannot get much beyond this 'Was the contract a contract of service within the meaning which an ordinary person would give under the words?' ." I respectfully agree. As my Lord has said, it is almost impossible to give a precise definition of the distinction. It is often quite easy to recognise a contract of service when you see it, but very difficult to say wherein the difference lies. A ship's master, a chauffeur and a reporter on the staff of a newspaper are all employed under a contract of service; but a ship's pilot, a taxi-man and a newspaper contributor are employed under a contract for services. One feature which seems to me to run through the instances is that, under a contract of service, a man is employed as part of the business and his work is done as an integral part of the business: whereas under a contract for services his work, although done for the business, is not integrated into it but is only accessory to it.'

COMMENT

(1)   The 'integration' or 'organisation' test propounded by Lord Denning in *Stevenson Jordan & Harrison* v *MacDonald & Evans* was intended to overcome the deficiencies of the 'control' test. However, today it may frequently be misleading, if not useless. It has become increasingly common for businesses to contract out parts of their operation, rather than having the function performed by employees. One of the reasons for this is that it saves them the overheads and potential liabilities associated with having employees. The function is still as necessary or integral as ever it was. An example might be a road haulage company subcontracting the maintenance and repair of its vehicles rather than having its own garage and mechanics. Clearly the maintenance of the lorries would continue to be integral to the road haulage business, but the workers carrying it out would not be employees.

Market Investigations v *Minister of Social Security*

[1969] 2 QB 173 Queen's Bench Division

The company was involved in market research. In addition to its permanent staff, it employed interviewers to carry out over 8,000 interviews a year, who worked as and when called upon. The issue was whether these interviewers were employees of the company, in which case the company was liable to pay National Insurance contributions on their behalf; the position of one interviewer was used as a test case, and it was held that they were employees.

Cooke J: '...I think it is fair to say that there was at one time a school of thought according to which the extent and degree of the control which B was entitled to exercise over A in the performance of the work would be a decisive factor. However, it has for long been apparent that an analysis of the extent and degree of such control is not in itself decisive. Thus in *Collins* v *Hertfordshire County Council*, it had been suggested that the distinguishing feature of a contract of service is that the master cannot only order or require what is to be done but also how it shall be done. The inadequacy of this test was pointed out by Somervell LJ in *Cassidy* v *Ministry of Health*, where he referred to the case of a certified master of a ship. The master may be employed by the owners under what is clearly a contract of service, and yet the owners have no power to tell him how to navigate his ship. As Lord Parker CJ pointed out in *Morren* v *Swinton and Pendlebury Borough Council*, when one is dealing with a professional man, or a man of some particular skill and experience, there can be no question of an employer telling him how to do work; therefore the absence of control and direction in that sense can be of little, if any, use as a test....

In *United States of America* v *Silk*, the question was whether certain men were "employees" within the meaning of that word in the Social Security Act, 1935. The judges of the Supreme Court decided that the test to be applied was not "power of control, whether exercised or not, over the manner of performing service to the undertaking", but whether the men were employees "as a matter of economic reality".

The observations of Lord Wright, of Denning LJ and of the judges of the Supreme Court suggest that the fundamental test to be applied is this: "Is the person who has engaged himself to perform these services performing them as a person in business on his own account?" If the answer to that question is "Yes", then the contract is a contract for services. If the answer is "No", then the contract is a contract of service. No exhaustive list has been compiled and perhaps no exhaustive list can be compiled of the considerations which are relevant in determining that question, nor can strict rules be laid down as to the relative weight which the various considerations should carry in particular cases. The most that can be said is that control will no doubt always have to be considered, although it can no longer be regarded as the sole determining factor; and that factors which may be of importance are such matters as whether the man performing the services provides his own equipment, whether he hires his own helpers, what degree of financial risk he takes, what degree of responsibility for investment and management he has, and whether and how far he has an opportunity of profiting from sound management in the performance of his task.

The application of the general test may be easier in a case where the person who engages himself to perform the services does so in the course of an already established business of his own; but this factor is not decisive, and a person who engages himself to perform services for another may well be an independent contractor even though he has not entered into the contract in the course of an existing business carried on by him.'

Ferguson v *John Dawson & Partners (Contractors) Ltd*

[1976] 1 WLR 1213 Court of Appeal

Megaw LJ: 'On April 19, 1972, the plaintiff, Mr Michael Joseph Ferguson, fell some 15 feet from a flat roof on which he was working. He suffered serious injuries. He claimed damages for breach of statutory duty from the defendants, John Dawson & Partners (Contractors) Ltd.

The action was heard by Boreham J at Leeds. On July 28, 1975, the judge gave judgment for the plaintiff for £30,387.88, including interest. The defendants appeal on issues as to liability. There is no appeal as to the amount of damages ...

I turn to the other issue. Was the plaintiff employed by the defendants? For the plaintiff it is submitted that he was employed by the defendants under a contract of service. For the defendants it is contended that the contract was a contract for services, and that therefore the defendants were not under a statutory duty to him to provide a guard for the working place. For if it were a contract for services the plaintiff would not have been "employed" by the defendants, and in the circumstances of this accident regulation 3 (1)(a) would not have brought regulation 28(1) into effect so as to impose on the defendants a duty towards the plaintiff. Regulation 28(1) is brought into operation only in relation to " ... the falling or slipping of persons, ... " (which this accident was) so far as the requirements of that regulation " ... affect ... any workman employed by him, ..." – "him", here, being the defendants. Regulation 3(1)(b) has a wider scope as regards the persons who are under the duty, but it is confined to "the falling of materials and articles".

It is conceded by the defendants that, if the plaintiff was employed under a contract of service, they were, subject only to the issue as to "appreciable time", under a duty to the plaintiff; they failed to carry out that duty, and that failure was the cause of the accident. But, say the defendants, the plaintiff was employed under a contract for services: he was "self-employed": he owed a statutory duty to himself to take the statutory precautions: *Smith* v *George Wimpey & Co Ltd*. It was for him, under the regulations, not for the defendants, to ensure that the guard-rail was erected. The defendants were under no such duty.

What is the basis for that contention? The judge accepted the evidence given by Mr Murray, the defendants' site agent, as to the circumstances in which the plaintiff came to work for the defendants in January 1972, some three months before the accident happened. The evidence was simply this: the plaintiff came with four other Irishmen, already working for the defendants, and asked, or perhaps one of his friends asked, if he could "come along". Mr Murray's evidence is: "I said he could start on Monday and that was it. But I did inform him there were no cards, we were purely working as a lump labour force." ...

Mr Murray accepted that he was responsible for "hiring and firing". In other words, as between the defendants and the workmen, including the plaintiff, he could dismiss them. There would be no question of his being able to determine a contract between the defendants and a subcontractor. He could move men from site to site, if he was so minded, and in support of the existence of that contractual right on behalf of the defendants he gave instances of having done so. If tools were required for the work, it was for the defendants to provide them. Again, as confirmation of that contractual obligation Mr Murray gave evidence of instances where the plaintiff had required tools for the work which he had been required to do, and the defendants had provided them. It was for Mr Murray to tell the workmen, including the plaintiff, what particular work they were to do: "I tell him what to take and what to do." The centurion in St Matthew's Gospel says to the man under him: " 'Do this,' and he doeth it." The man under him is a servant, not an independent contractor. All these things are in relation to the contractual relationships existing. "I tell him what to do", and he does it on Mr Murray's instructions because, when legal analysis has to be applied, it is a term of the contract that the plaintiff shall carry out the defendants' instructions what to do when they tell him to do it. The men, including the plaintiff, were employed on an hourly basis. The money paid to them would be correctly described as "a wage".

In my judgment, on the tests laid down in the authorities, all of this indicates beyond doubt that the reality of the relationship was of employer and employee – a contract of service. I do not propose to lengthen this judgment by examining afresh the criteria, so fully discussed in so many cases. The judge, as I have already said, based himself on the judgment of MacKenna J in *Ready Mixed Concrete (South East) Ltd* v *Minister of Pensions and National Insurance.* Another judgment which I have found very helpful is that of Cooke J in *Market Investigations Ltd* v *Minister of Social Security.*

My own view would have been that a declaration by the parties, even if it were incorporated in the contract, that the workman was to be, or was to be deemed to be, self-employed, an independent contractor, ought to be wholly disregarded – not merely treated as not being conclusive – if the remainder of the contractual terms, governing the realities of the relationship, showed the relationship of employer and employee. The Roman soldier would not have been a self-employed labour only subcontractor because of any verbal exchange between him and the centurion when he enlisted. I find difficulty in accepting that the parties, by a mere expression of intention as to what the legal relationship should be, can in any way influence the conclusion of law as to what the relationship is. I think that it would be contrary to the public interest if that were so, for it would mean that the parties, by their own whim, by the use of a verbal formula, unrelated to the reality of the relationship, could influence the decision on whom the responsibility for the safety of workmen, as imposed by statutory regulations, should rest.'

(Browne LJ agreed that F was an employee. Lawton LJ dissented.)

Massey v *Crown Life Insurance Co*

[1978] ICR 590   Court of Appeal

Lord Denning MR: ' … What was the position of Mr Massey?

He was the manager of the Ilford branch of the insurance company. For a couple of years, from 1971 to 1973, the company treated him as though he were a servant. They gave him a memorandum under [ERA s 1]. They paid him wages; and, before paying him, they deducted the tax, national insurance and graduated pension contributions from the amount they paid him. Further, they had a pension scheme of their own and he had to make contributions towards his pension. Being regarded as a servant, he was taxed for his income tax payments under Schedule E.

But in 1973 Mr Massey went to his accountant who advised him to change his relationship with the company. The accountant said: "I think you would be much better off if you so arranged your affairs so as to be self-employed instead of being a servant. Then you will come under Schedule D instead of Schedule E." That is what was proposed. The company would pay him the full amount each week: they would not deduct tax or national insurance contributions or anything like that. It would be for him to account for tax to the Inland Revenue under Schedule D.

He went to the company and told them: "I have been advised by my accountants to change over to Schedule D. Will you agree?" They said: "Oh, yes; we are agreeable." So it was put through. It was done in this way. Instead of being called "Mr John L Massey", he was called "John L Massey & Associates". It was really just the same man under another name. He registered that new name with the Register of Business Names. With that new name he entered into a new agreement with the company. So far as his duties were concerned, the new agreement was in almost identical terms as the previous one. As a result of that new agreement, Mr Massey said he was no longer a servant, he was an independent contractor and, therefore, liable to be taxed under Schedule D. The position was placed before the Inland Revenue, and the Inland Revenue seem to have thought it was all right …

In November 1975 Mr Massey was dismissed. Thereafter he said: "I want to claim for unfair dismissal." A claim for unfair dismissal was quite admissible if he was employed by the company under a contract of service, but not if he was employed under a contract for services. So here he was claiming as a servant whereas, for the last two years, he had been paid on the basis that he was an independent contractor.

The law, as I see it, is this: if the true relationship of the parties is that of master and servant under a contract of service, the parties cannot alter the truth of that relationship by putting a different label upon it. If they should put a different label upon it and use it as a dishonest device to deceive the revenue, I should have thought it was illegal and could not be enforced by either party and they could not get any advantage out of it – at any rate not in any case where they had to rely upon it as the basis of a claim: see *Alexander* v *Rayson*. An arrangement between two parties to put forward a dishonest description of their relationship so as to deceive the revenue would clearly be illegal and unenforceable.

On the other hand, if the parties' relationship is ambiguous and is capable of being one or the other, then the parties can remove that ambiguity, by the very agreement itself which they make with one another.

…I would only say a word about the recent case of *Ferguson* v *John Dawson & Partners (Contractors) Ltd*. That case turned on its facts. Boreham J held that the real relationship of the parties was that of master and servant and that they had put the wrong label on it by regarding him as working on "the lump". The majority of this court accepted that view. But Lawton LJ thought that the partners had deliberately put the right label on their relationship. The man was on "the lump". He had had all the benefits of it by avoiding tax. It was contrary to public policy that, when he had an accident, he could throw over that relationship and claim that he was only a servant.

In most of these cases, I expect that it will be found that the parties do deliberately agree for the man to be "self-employed" or "on the lump". It is done especially so as to obtain the tax benefits. When such an agreement is made, it affords strong evidence that that is the real relationship. If it is so found, the man must accept it. He cannot afterwards assert that he was only a servant.

In the present case there is a perfectly genuine agreement entered into at the instance of Mr. Massey on the footing that he is self-employed. He gets the benefit of it by avoiding tax deductions and getting his pension contributions returned. I do not see that he can come along afterwards and say it is something else in order to claim that he has been unfairly dismissed. Having made his bed as being self-employed, he must lie on it. He is not under a contract of service.

I agree entirely with the industrial tribunal and with the Employment Appeal Tribunal that he does not qualify to claim for unfair dismissal in this case, and I would dismiss the appeal.'

Lane v Shire Roofing Co Ltd

[1995] IRLR 493 Court of Appeal

The plaintiff suffered serious head injuries when he fell off his ladder while tiling the roof of a porch at a domestic house. Had scaffolding been provided, he would have had a safer position from which to work. He alleged negligence on the part of the company for failing to provide him with scaffolding to do the job.

Henry LJ: '... The next question is whether the respondents owed to the plaintiff the common law or statutory duty of an employer to his employees, or whether the appellant when doing that job was acting as an independent contractor. When it comes to the question of safety at work, there is a real public interest in recognising the employer/employee relationship when it exists, because of the responsibilities that the common law and statutes such as the Employers' Liability (Compulsory Insurance) Act 1969 places on the employer.

The judge was to find that the appellant was not an employee, but was an independent contractor. In that event the appellant would have been responsible for his own safety; the respondent would have owed him no duty of care, and would have had no responsibility (statutory or at common law) for the safety of the work done by the appellant. That was the context in which the question was asked.

We were taken through the standard authorities on this matter: *Readymix Concrete (South East) Ltd* v *Minister of Pensions and National Insurance*; *Market Investigations Ltd* v *Minister of Social Security*; and *Ferguson* v *Dawson & Partners (Contractors) Ltd*, to name the principal ones. Two general remarks should be made. The overall employment background is very different today (and was, though less so, in 1986) than it had been at the time when those cases were decided. First, for a variety of reasons there are more self-employed and fewer in employment. There is a greater flexibility in employment with more temporary and shared employment. Second, there are perceived advantages for both workman and employer in the relationship between them being that of independent contractor. From the workman's point of view, being self-employed brings him into a more benevolent and less prompt taxation regime. From the employer's point of view, the protection of employees' rights contained in the employment protection legislation of the 1970s brought certain perceived disincentives to the employer to take on full-time long-term employees. So even in 1986 there were reasons on both sides to avoid the employee label. But, as I have already said, there were, and are, good policy reasons in the safety at work field to ensure that the law properly categorises between employees and independent contractors.

That line of authority shows that there are many factors to be taken into account in answering this question, and, with different priority being given to those factors in different cases, all depends on the facts of each individual case. Certain principles relevant to this case, however, emerge.

First, the element of control will be important: who lays down what is to be done, the way in which it is to be done, the means by which it is to be done, and the time when it is done? Who provides (ie hires and fires) the team by which it is done, and who provides the material, plant and machinery and tools used?

But it is recognised that the control test may not be decisive – for instance, in the case of skilled employees, with discretion to decide how their work should be done. In such cases the question is broadened to whose business was it? Was the workman carrying on his own business, or was he carrying on that of his employers? The American Supreme Court, in *United States of America* v *Silk* asks the question whether the men were employees 'as a matter of economic reality'. The answer to this question may cover much of the same ground as the control test (such as whether he provides his own equipment and hires his own helpers) but may involve looking to see where the financial risk lies, and whether and how far he has an opportunity of profiting from sound management in the performance of his task (see *Market Investigations* v *Minister of Social Security*, supra).

And these questions must be asked in the context of who is responsible for the overall safety of the men doing the work in question. Mr Whittaker, of the respondents, was cross-examined on these lines and he agreed that he was so responsible. Such an answer is not decisive (though it may be indicative) because ultimately the question is one of law, and he could be wrong as to where the legal responsibility lies (see *Ferguson* v *Dawson*, supra).

The facts that the judge had to consider were as follows. The appellant was a builder/roofer/carpenter who had since 1982 traded as a one-man firm, P J Building. He had obtained self-employed fiscal status, with a right to the 714 tax exemption certificates issued by the Inland Revenue. As a one-man firm he solicited work through advertisements, and when engaged by clients would of course be responsible for estimating, buying in materials, and matters of that kind. But that work had dried up. His public liability insurance had lapsed. At the time he answered the repondents' advertisement he was usually working for others.

The respondent company (which was the corporate manifestation of its proprietor, Mr Whittaker) was a newly established roofing contractor. It was in its early days of trading, and Mr Whittaker did not wish to take on too many long-term employees – he considered it prudent and advantageous to hire for individual jobs. In September of 1986 he obtained a large roofing sub-contract in Marlow. He advertised for men to work that contract. The appellant answered that advertisement, and was employed by him at the daily rate of £45. He started work on that job at some time in September. It seems, though the evidence is not entirely clear on this, that that job was nearly over when, at the respondents' request, he left that job to do the Sonning Common porch re-roofing job. As he had been promised no work from the respondents after the Marlow job, it is right to consider the question whether he was an employee in the context of the Sonning Common job.

The building contract in relation to that job had been entered into by the respondents, through Mr Whittaker, and the householders, Mr and Mrs Bird, for an agreed price of £389 (plus VAT). (As will be seen, the economic realities of that price were that if, to do it safely, scaffolding had to be hired and erected, the job would be loss-making to the respondents.) Mr Whittaker then visited the site with the appellant, agreed to pay him an all-in fee of £200 for the job, and discussed (as we shall see) with him what was necessary in the way of plant (using that phrase to embrace ladders, scaffolds and trestles) to do the job. And Mr Whittaker accepted in cross-examination that it was his responsibility to supply aids such as scaffolds and trestles. Had two men been employed on that job, Mr Whittaker would have provided the other. The appellant brought to that job all his personal roofing and carpentry tools (including a slate cutter) but of course he provided no materials or plant. He brought his own ladder.

The judge's reasons for finding that the appellant was an independent contractor, not an employee, were these:

"The defendant company (which was really Mr Whittaker's company) had only been in operation for six months and it would obviously be of advantage to him to be able to enter into contracts with other people for specific works without having a continuous payroll for those parts. I consider it important that the plaintiff himself had his own genuine roofing business, so that he was a roofing specialist, and he had the benefit of 714 certificates so that he could pay his own tax and was paid gross. He continued with that system while he was working on contracts for the defendant company. I note that the plaintiff was obviously capable of working without supervision and that Mr Whittaker relied upon him to do so, although it seems that Mr Whittaker was subsequently rather disappointed with the quality of the plaintiff's work and subsequently thought that the plaintiff had more experience with clay tiles than the artificial slates which he was using on the final contract. There was no guarantee given by Mr Whittaker of continuing work for the defendant, no provision for notice or dismissal and, as pointed out by Mr Matthews, that would have been unnecessary if this was genuine sub-contracting work, because each job had to be taken on its own and there was no guarantee that the plaintiff would be employed thereafter, though both the plaintiff and Mr Whittaker were obviously anticipating that further jobs would arise which Mr Whittaker could give to the plaintiff. In all the circumstances, therefore, I find that the plaintiff was an independent contractor throughout the time that he was working for the defendant company and in particular, of course, on the contract in question at the Birds's."

Each of those four reasons given by the judge would apply equally to the work being done under a short-term single job contract of employment. All of them concentrate on what Mr Whittaker wanted, and not on whose business it was. Mr Matthews, for the respondents, rightly distinguishes between a *Ferguson* v *Dawson* situation, where an employer engages men on "the lump" to do labouring work (where the men are clearly employees, whatever their tax status may be), and when a specialist sub-contractor is employed to perform some part of a general building contract. That team or individual clearly will be an independent contractor. He submits that the appellant in this case falls somewhere in between. With that I would agree, but would put this case substantially nearer "the lump" than the specialist sub-contractor. Though the degree of control that Mr Whittaker would use would depend on the need he felt to supervise and direct the appellant (who was just someone answering the advertisement) the question "Whose business was it?" in relation to the Sonning Common job could only in my judgment be answered by saying that it was the respondents' business and not the appellant's. In my judgment, therefore, they owed the duties of employers to the appellant. Consequently, for my part I would find that the first ground of appeal against the judge's judgment succeeds. ...'

(Auld and Nourse LJJ agreed.)

COMMENT

(1)   *Lane* v *Shire Roofing* seems to mark a decisive shift in the approach to this issue. What reasons are put forward for suggesting that the question of whether Lane was an employee or not should be more closely scrutinised in this situation than in others? Are either or both of these reasons convincing, in your opinion? (See the note by McKendrick in (1996) 25 ILJ 136.)

(2)   The test as stated by Cooke J in *Market Investigations* v *Minister of Social Security* – is the person in question a person in business on his own account? – has been cited with approval on numerous subsequent occasions, one of the most important recent examples being the Privy Council's judgment in *Lee* v *Chung* (below, p 100). It could be criticised as circular, merely restating the question in a different

form. However, it is submitted that the test is useful in that it focuses on the entrepreneurial aspect that one would expect to find in an independent contractor. This has been rather overlooked in some cases, especially those involving casual workers (see, for example, *O'Kelly* v *Trusthouse Forte*, below).

(3)   Quite a long list of factors relevant to the nature of the contract can be drawn up. Is it possible to say that any of them are absolutely essential? The requirement for personal service probably is necessary, but it is submitted that no other factor is capable of being decisive one way or the other. There is a view that mutuality of obligation is also essential: this is examined in the extracts which follow.

Casual Workers

Fluctuating demand may lead an employer to rely heavily on workers who are not permanently employed. Seasonal work, such as fruit-picking, is an obvious example, but demand varies considerably in the hotel and catering industry, photograph developing and other service areas. Many homeworkers also fall into this category of regular, but not permanent, workers. Are they employees? The problem is that while they expect to be given work and the employer expects to have work for them, there is no legal obligation on the employer to offer nor on them to accept.

O'Kelly v *Trusthouse Forte*

[1984] QB 90 Court of Appeal

The banqueting division of the company employed only 34 permanent staff at Grosvenor House in London, relying on staffing functions with casual staff who were drafted in for each occasion. Some of these were more casual than others: the applicants in the case, who were claiming unfair dismissal, were on a list of about 100 'regular casuals' who were given preference when work was available. In addition there was another list of about 200–300 casual staff who were used less frequently. The applicants claimed that they had been dismissed for trade union activities: this is an exceptional situation where unfair dismissal may be claimed without the necessity for two years' continuous employment. The issue in the case was therefore whether the 'regular casuals' were employees. The factors taken into account by the industrial tribunal were quoted in the judgment of Ackner LJ.

Ackner LJ: 'In making their assessment, the industrial tribunal took into account the following factors which they considered consistent with a contract of employment:

   (a) The applicants provided their services in return for remuneration for work actually performed. They did not invest their own capital or stand to gain or lose from the commercial success of the functions organised by the banqueting department. (b) They performed their work under the direction and control of [the company]. (c) When the casual workers attended at functions they were part of [the company's] organisation and for the purpose of ensuring the smooth running of the business they were represented in the staff consultation process. (d) When working they were carrying on the business of [the company]. (e) Clothing and equipment were provided by [the company]. (f) The applicants were paid weekly in arrear and were paid under deduction of income tax and social security contributions. (g) Their work was organised on the basis of a weekly rota and they required permission to take time off from rostered duties. (h) There was a disciplinary and grievance procedure. (i) There was holiday pay or an incentive bonus calculated by reference to past service.

The following additional factors in the relationship the industrial tribunal considered were *not inconsistent* with the contract of employment:

(j) The applicants were paid for work actually performed and did not receive a regular wage or retainer. The method of calculating entitlement to remuneration is not an essential aspect of the employment relationship. (k) Casual workers were not remunerated on the same basis as permanent employees and did not receive sick pay and were not included in [the company's] staff pension scheme and did not receive the fringe benefits accorded to established employees. There is, however, no objection to employers adopting different terms and conditions of employment for different categories of employee (e.g. different terms for manual and managerial staff). (l) There were no regular or assured working hours. It is not a requirement of employment that there should be "normal working hours": see [ERA ss 88–89]. (m) Casual workers were not provided with written particulars of employment. If it is established that casual workers are employees there is a statutory obligation to furnish written particulars.

The following factors were considered by the industrial tribunal to be *inconsistent* with a contract of employment:

(n) The engagement was terminable without notice on either side. (o) The applicants had the right to decide whether or not to accept work, although whether or not it would be in their interest to exercise the right to refuse work is another matter. (p) [The company] had no obligation to provide any work. (q) During the subsistence of the relationship it was the parties' view that casual workers were independent contractors engaged under successive contracts for services. (r) It is the recognised custom and practice of the industry that casual workers are engaged under a contract for services.'

Sir John Donaldson MR: ' ... In the instant appeal the industrial tribunal directed itself to:

"consider all aspects of the relationship, no single factor being in itself decisive and each of which may vary in weight and direction, and having given such balance to the factors as seems appropriate, to determine whether the person was carrying on business on his own account."

This is wholly correct as a matter of law and it is not for this court or for the appeal tribunal to re-weigh the facts.

The industrial tribunal then concluded that there was no contract of employment extending over a series of engagements. This conclusion was based upon an evaluation of the large number of factors set out in their reasons, but it is clear that the majority attached great importance to the fact that, as they saw it, there was no mutuality of obligation and that in the industry casual workers were not regarded as working under any overall contract of employment.

The appeal tribunal refused to interfere with this conclusion and in my judgment they were right to do so. So far as mutuality is concerned, the "arrangement", to use a neutral term, could have been that the company promised to offer work to the regular casuals and, in exchange, the regular casuals undertook to accept and perform such work as was offered. This would have constituted a contract. But what happened in fact could equally well be attributed to market forces. Which represented the true view could only be determined by the tribunal which heard the witnesses and evaluated the facts. Again, although how the industry and its casual workers regarded their status is not directly material, any generally accepted view would be part of the contractual matrix and so indirectly material, although in no way decisive. This again was a matter for the industrial tribunal.

Although I, like the appeal tribunal, am content to accept the industrial tribunal's conclusion that there was no overall or umbrella contract, I think that there is a shorter answer. It is that giving the applicants' evidence its fullest possible weight, all that could emerge was an umbrella or master contract *for*, not *of*, employment. It would be a contract to offer and accept individual contracts of employment and, as such, outside the scope of the unfair dismissal provisions.

This leaves the question of whether the applicants entered into individual contracts of employment on each occasion when they worked for the company and it is here that the appeal tribunal and the industrial tribunal parted company. The appeal tribunal dealt with this aspect of the matter by saying:

> "For whatever reason, the industrial tribunal have not dealt with the point, nor have they weighed the factors bearing on the question: 'was each contract for services?' in the same careful way in which they weighed those factors when looking at the nature of an overall contract of employment. In our judgment, the mere assertion by the industrial tribunal that it was a succession of contracts for services entered into by independent contractors cannot stand as good in law in the absence of any reason for that conclusion. We must therefore consider the point and reach our own decision on it."

This, in my judgment, does less than justice to the decision of the industrial tribunal. It had weighed the relevant factors governing the relationship between the parties with great care in the course of determining whether any umbrella contract was one of employment or for the provision of services. It had rejected the umbrella contract on the grounds that there was no contract at all, but it had also concluded:

> "the applicants were in business on their own account as independent contractors supplying services and are not qualified for interim relief because they were not employees who worked under a contract of employment."

This, unless erroneous in law, was wholly sufficient reason for holding that the individual contracts, which clearly existed, were contracts for the provision of services.

(Ackner and Fox LJJ delivered concurring judgments.)

COMMENT

(1)   In a case like this, it seems that there are at least three possibilities:

   (a)   that there is no contract to offer work (or to accept), but that there is a contract when the worker is actually at work, and it is a contract of employment;
   (b)   as in (a), but the daily contract is not a contract of employment;
   (c)   that the work takes place within the overall framework of a contract, and this global contract is a contract of employment.

Possibility (c) was held to be the best fit for the facts in *Airfix Footwear Ltd* v *Cope*. It may have started out as a situation like (a), but had gone on so long that the overall arrangement could be said to have hardened the parties' expectations into binding legal obligations. In *O'Kelly* the industrial tribunal, laying emphasis on mutuality of obligation, held that the casuals were not employees. The EAT agreed with them that there was no overall or global contract, but held that on the occasions when they were actually at work, the contracts were contracts of employment: that is, that the situation was as in possibility (a) above. The Court of Appeal restored the decision of the industrial tribunal.

(2)   There are two strands in the Court of Appeal's decision: first, they seem to agree with the conclusions that the industrial tribunal reached on the facts; but even more importantly they considered that the EAT had no jurisdiction to overturn the industrial tribunal's decision because it was a decision on a question of fact not a question of law. The classification of this issue as a question of fact has not escaped criticism, principally on the grounds that it means different industrial tribunals could reach different conclusions on very similar facts but that there could be no appeal from their decisions (compare *Nethermere (St Neots) Ltd* v *Gardiner* with *O'Kelly*, for example). This kind of inconsistency is undesirable (see further Pitt, *Law, Fact and Casual Workers* 101 LQR 217 (1985)).

(3)   It is clear that where a contract is in writing, its nature and construction is a question of law, not of fact (*Davies* v *Presbyterian Church of Wales*). This makes the position even more inconsistent. However, when the issue came before the Privy Council, they upheld the approach of the Court of Appeal.

Lee v Chung

[1990] ICR 409 Privy Council

A stonemason was injured while working on a construction site for the employers. The employers argued that he was a casual worker, not an employee and that therefore they were not liable to him. While the employer provided him with tools and told him where to work, thereafter he was left to get on with the job without supervision. He was usually paid according to the amount of work done, but was expected to be on site during normal working hours when they had work for him. He was free to work for other employers and did so, but he always gave priority to this employer.

At the original hearing the trial judge held that Lee was an independent contractor (on which point Hong Kong law and English law are identical). The Privy Council had to decide whether it had any jurisdiction to alter that decision.

Lord Griffiths: ' ... Upon these findings of fact their Lordships would have had no hesitation, if sitting as a court of first instance, in concluding that the applicant was working for the first respondent as an employee and not as an independent contractor. All the tests, or perhaps it is better to call them indicia, mentioned by Cooke J in *Market Investigations Ltd* v *Minister of Social Security*, point towards the status of an employee rather than an independent contractor. The applicant did not provide his own equipment, the equipment was provided by his employer. He did not hire his own helpers: this emerged with clarity in his evidence when he explained that he gave priority to the first respondent's work and if asked by the first respondent to do an urgent job he would tell those he was working for that they would have to employ someone else: if he was an independent contractor in business on his own account, one would expect that he would attempt to keep both contracts by hiring others to fulfil the contract he had to leave. He had no responsibility for investment in, or management of, the work on the construction site, he simply turned up for work and chipped off concrete to the required depth upon the beams indicated to him on a plan by the first respondent. There is no suggestion in the evidence that he priced the job which is normally a feature of the business approach of a subcontractor; he was paid either a piece-work rate or a daily rate according to the nature of the work he was doing. It is true that he was not supervised in his work, but this is not surprising, he was a skilled man and he had been told the beams upon which he was to work and the depth to which they were to be cut and his work was measured to see that he achieved that result. There was no question of his being called upon to exercise any skill or judgment as to which beams required chipping or as to the depths that they were to be cut. He was simply told what to do and left to get on with it as, for example, would a skilled turner on a lathe who was required to cut a piece of metal to certain dimensions.

Taking all the foregoing considerations into account the picture emerges of a skilled artisan earning his living by working for more than one employer as an employee and not as a small businessman venturing into business on his own account as an independent contractor with all its attendant risks ...

Whether or not a person is employed under a contract of service is often said in the authorities to be a mixed question of fact and law. Exceptionally, if the relationship is dependent solely upon the true construction of a written document it is regarded as a question of law: see *Davies* v *Presbyterian Church of Wales*. But where, as in the present case, the relationship has to be determined by an investigation and evaluation of the factual circumstances in which the work is performed, it must now be taken to be firmly established that the question of whether or not the work was performed in the capacity of an employee or as an independent contractor is to be regarded by an appellate court as a question of fact to be determined by the trial court. At first sight it seems rather strange that this should be so, for whether or not a certain set of facts should be classified under one legal head rather than another would appear to be a question of law. However, no doubt because of the difficulty of devising a conclusive test to resolve the question and the threat of the appellate courts being crushed by the weight of appeals if the many borderline cases were considered to be questions of law, it was held in a series of decisions in the Court of Appeal and in the House of Lords under the English Workmen's Compensation Acts 1906 and 1925 that a finding by a county court judge that a workman was, or was not, employed under a contract of service was a question of fact with which an appellate court could only interfere if there was no evidence to support his finding ...

Their Lordships conclude that reliance upon these two dicta culled from cases of a wholly dissimilar character, may have misled the courts below in their assessment of the facts of this case and amount in the circumstances to an error of law justifying setting aside what are to be regarded as concurrent findings of fact.

Their Lordships are further of the opinion that the facts of the present case point so clearly to the existence of a contract of service that the finding that the applicant was working as an independent contractor was, to quote the words of Viscount Simonds in *Edwards* v *Bairstow*, "a view of the facts which could not reasonably be entertained" and is to be regarded as an error of law.'

COMMENT

(1) Note the approval of Cooke's test in *Market Investigations* v *Minister of Social Security* in this case.

(2) While confirming that the nature of the contract is to be treated as a question of fact unless the contract is in writing, it is notable that in this case the Privy Council *did* overturn the original decision. Does this indicate a slight loosening of the standards for review?

(3) In this case there was no issue over continuity of employment because an employer has a duty to take reasonable care for an employee's safety from day one. Thus the question of mutual obligation was largely disregarded, even though Lee was a casual worker. Where continuity is required, casual workers may sometimes be assisted by ERA s 86(4), which provides that where a worker has been employed for three months or more on fixed-term contracts of one month or less (which would include daily contracts), the contract is to be treated as an indefinite contract: see *Brown* v *Chief Adjudication Officer*.

(4) How far the EAT can interfere with the decision of an industrial tribunal is a big issue in unfair dismissal cases also, and is addressed again in Chapter 8.

CONTINUITY OF EMPLOYMENT

In the last section we saw the difficulties for casual workers in establishing that they are employed under a contract of employment. Even if they can establish that they are employees, they may still fail if they are held to be working under a series of separate contracts such that they cannot show the requisite period of continuous employment. Two years of continuous employment is required for the principal statutory rights such as unfair dismissal, redundancy and maternity rights.

Establishing sufficient continuity used to involve two things: first, that the employee worked for sufficient hours per week for the week to count towards the overall period, and second, that enough weeks were strung together without a disqualifying break. The hours requirement meant that part-time workers were frequently excluded and it was attacked by the EOC on grounds of sex discrimination. It was common ground that the great majority of part-time workers were women, so that the provisions resulted in indirect discrimination against women.

R v *Secretary of State for Employment, ex parte EOC*

[1995] 1 AC 1   House of Lords

Lord Keith: '... The original reason for the threshold provisions of the [ERA] appears to have been the view that part-time workers were less committed than full-time workers to the undertaking which employed them. In his letter of 23 April 1990 the Secretary of State stated that their purpose was to ensure that a fair balance was struck between the interest of employers and employees. These grounds are not now founded on as objective justification for the thresholds. It is now claimed that the thresholds have the effect that more part-time employment is available than would be the case if employers were liable for redundancy pay and compensation for unfair dismissal to employees who worked for less than eight hours a week or between eight and 16 hours a week for under five years. It is contended that if employers were under that liability they would be inclined to employ less part-time workers and more full-time workers, to the disadvantage of the former.

The bringing about of an increase in the availability of part-time work is properly to be regarded as a beneficial social policy aim and it cannot be said that it is not a necessary aim. The question is whether the threshold provisions of the [ERA] have been shown, by reference to objective factors, to be suitable and requisite for achieving that aim. As regards suitability for achieving the aim in question, it is to be noted that the purpose of the thresholds is said to be to reduce the costs to employers of employing part-time workers. The same result, however, would follow from a situation where the basic rate of pay for part-time workers was less than the basic rate for full-time workers. No distinction in principle can properly be made between direct and indirect labour costs. While in certain circumstances an employer might be justified in paying full-time workers a higher rate than part-time workers in order to secure the more efficient use of his machinery (see *Jenkins* v *Kingsgate (Clothing Productions) Ltd (No. 2)*) that would be a special and limited state of affairs. Legislation which permitted a differential of that kind nationwide would present a very different aspect and considering that the great majority of part-time workers are women would surely constitute a gross breach of the principle of equal pay and could not possibly be regarded as a suitable means of achieving an increase in part-time employment. Similar considerations apply to legislation which reduces the indirect cost of employing part-time labour. Then as to the threshold provisions being requisite to achieve the stated aim, the question is whether on the evidence before the Divisional Court they have been proved actually to result in greater availability of part-time work than would be the case without them. In my opinion that question must be answered in the negative. The evidence for the Secretary of State consisted principally of an affidavit by an official in the Department of Employment which set out the views of the Department but did not contain anything capable of being regarded as factual evidence demonstrating the correctness of these views. One of the exhibits to the affidavit was a report with draft Directives prepared by the Social Affairs Commissioner of the European Commission in 1990. This covered a wide range of employment benefits and advantages, including redundancy pay and compensation for unfair dismissal, but proposed a qualifying threshold for those benefits of eight hours of work per week. The basis for that was stated to be the elimination of disproportionate administrative costs and regard to employers' economic needs. These are not the grounds of justification relied on by the Secretary of State. The evidence put in by the EOC consisted in large measure in a Report of the House of Commons Employment Committee in 1990 and a Report of the House of Lords Select Committee on the European Communities on Part-Time and Temporary Employment in 1990. These revealed a diversity of views upon the effect of the threshold provisions on part-time work, employers' organisations being of the opinion that their removal would reduce the amount available with trade union representatives and some employers and academics in the industrial relations field taking the opposite view. It also appeared that no other Member State of the European Community, apart from the Republic of Ireland, had legislation providing for similar thresholds. The Republic of Ireland, where statute at one time provided for an 18-hour per week threshold, had recently introduced legislation reducing this to eight hours. In the Netherlands the proportion of the workforce in part-time employment was, in 1988, 29.8% and in Denmark 25.5%, neither country having any thresholds similar to those in the [ERA]. In France, legislation was introduced in 1982 providing for part-time workers to have the same rights as full-time workers, yet between 1983 and 1988 part-time work in that country increased by 36.6%, compared with an increase of 26.1% over the same period in the United Kingdom. While various explanations were suggested on behalf of the Secretary of State for these statistics, there is no means of ascertaining whether these explanations have any validity. The fact is, however, that the proportion of part-time employees in the national workforce is much less than the proportion of full-time employees, their weekly remuneration is necessarily much lower, and the number of them made redundant or unfairly dismissed in any year is not likely to be unduly large. The conclusion must be that no objective justification for the thresholds in the [ERA] has been established.

...

In the light of the foregoing I am of the opinion that the appeal by the EOC should be allowed and that declarations should be made in the following terms:

1. That the provisions of the Employment Protection (Consolidation) Act 1978 whereby employees who work for fewer than 16 hours per week are subject to different conditions in respect to qualification for redundancy pay from those which apply to employees who work for 16 hours per week or more are incompatible with Article 119 of the Treaty of Rome and the Council Directive 75/117/EEC of 10 February 1975 [the Equal Pay Directive].

2. That the provisions of the Employment Protection (Consolidation) Act 1978 whereby employees who work for fewer than 16 hours per week are subject to different conditions in respect of the right to compensation for unfair dismissal from those which apply to employees who work for 16 hours per week or more are incompatible with the Council Directive 76/207/EEC of 9 February 1976 [the Equal Treatment Directive].'

(Lord Browne-Wilkinson delivered a concurring speech; Lord Lowry and Lord Slynn agreed with Lord Keith; Lord Jauncey dissented.)

COMMENT

(1)   Note the robust approach of the House of Lords here to the 'evidence' put forward to justify the exclusion of part-timers.

(2)   As a result of this decision, the Employment Protection (Part-Time Employees) Regulations 1995 were made, abolishing threshold hours requirements for all statutory claims. The ERA s 212(1) now provides that:

'Any week during the whole or part of which an employee's relations with his employer are governed by a contract of employment counts in computing the employee's period of employment.'

(3)   In *Biggs* v *Somerset CC* the Court of Appeal held that part-timers could not bring redundancy or unfair dismissal claims in respect of pre-1994 dismissals because their claims would be out of time. To the argument that at the time of their dismissals such part-time applicants could not claim because the legislation excluded them, the Court responded that the decision in *R* v *Secretary of State, ex p EOC* showed that the legislation had always been unlawful, so they could have challenged it then. This is the effect of the declaratory theory of law which pertains in the United Kingdom.

(4)   Following this case, a more radical attack was launched, arguing that the requirement of two years' continuous employment for unfair dismissal was itself discriminatory.

R v Secretary of State, ex parte Seymour-Smith and Perez

[1997] IRLR 315 House of Lords

The two applicants were dismissed in 1991, when they had between one and two years' continuous employment. The qualifying period for claiming unfair dismissal was raised from one year to two in 1985 by the Unfair Dismissal (Variation of Qualifying Period) Order 1985. The Court of Appeal granted them a declaration that the order raising the limit was incompatible with the Equal Treatment Directive; however, it considered that it could not find it to be incompatible with Article 119 without referring to the ECJ the question of whether unfair dismissal compensation could be regarded as 'pay' within the meaning of the Article.

Lord Hoffman: '... 1. *The Equal Treatment Directive*
Mr Allen QC, who appeared for the employees, submitted that the declaration of incompatibility with the Equal Treatment Directive made by the Court of Appeal would affect the legal rights of his clients. They would be able to go back to the industrial tribunal and argue that the Order, being incompatible with Community law, should not be given effect. This would leave them in possession of their rights under the original legislation by which they qualified after one year of employment. He said that even if your Lordships were not fully persuaded that a directive could have this effect, the contrary was not *acte clair* and the question should be referred to the Court of Justice.

For the purposes of the preliminary point, it must be assumed that the Order brought English law into conflict with the terms of the Directive. But, by virtue of a consistent jurisprudence expressed in a series of decisions of the Court of Justice, it is in my view *acte clair* that a directive, as such, has no effect upon the private rights of parties such as the employees in this case and their employers. The position is otherwise when the question concerns the rights and duties of the citizen as against the State or one of its emanations ...

... The effect of the decisions in *Marshall* and *Faccini Dori* is that, except in proceedings which bring into question the legal relations between the individual and the State or its emanations, directives do not give rise to rights or restrictions which without further enactment are required to be given legal effect. Accordingly, section 2(4) does not enable them to affect the validity or construction of domestic legislation such as the Order. Mr Allen's distinction between using a directive as a source of rights and as a means of disapplying a restriction on rights which would otherwise be available in domestic law is in my view quite unworkable. It would produce arbitrary results according to whether domestic legislation was framed by reference to positive conditions or as a general rule subject to exceptions, even though the substantive effective was precisely the same.

I therefore think that it is *acte clair* that a declaration such as was made by the Court of Appeal would not enable the employees to pursue their proceedings in the industrial court. Would it serve any other purpose? ...

The difficulty is that the declaration made by the Court of Appeal was not that United Kingdom Legislation was incompatible with Community law. It was that such incompatibility existed in May of 1991. This was founded upon evidence that the two-year qualifying period had a considerably greater adverse impact upon women than upon men during the years 1985–1991. Non constat that it was having such a discriminatory effect at the time of the judgment in the summer of 1995. On the contrary, the evidence showed that by 1993 the gap between the ratios of men and women who qualified had narrowed.

Thus the declaration made by the Court of Appeal neither enabled the employees to sue for unfair dismissal nor told the Government (or any other interested party) that United Kingdom legislation needed to be changed because it was incompatible with Community law ...

... The second contention is that the Court of Appeal declaration can found a *Francovich* claim against the State. In the *Equal Opportunities Commission* case, this House refused to make a declaration on similar grounds. Lord Keith of Kinkel said,

> "In my opinion it would be quite inappropriate to make any such declaration. If there is any individual who believes that he or she has a good claim to compensation under the *Francovich* principle, it is the Attorney-General who would be defendant in any proceedings directed to enforcing it, and the issues raised would not necessarily be identical with any of those which arise in the present appeal."

For my part, I can see no grounds upon which this reasoning does not apply to the present case.

2 Article 119 of the Treaty

Mr Elias [counsel for the Secretary of State] accepted that if the Order was contrary to the terms of article 119, the employees have directly enforceable rights which they are entitled to assert in the industrial tribunal. For that very reason, he says that the House should not entertain the question in proceedings for judicial review. The industrial tribunal is the more appropriate forum. He relied upon the *Equal Opportunities Commission* case, in which the House refused to entertain an application for judicial review by a second applicant, a Mrs Day, who was employed by the Hertfordshire County Council. Since the Council counted as an emanation of the State for the purposes of the *Marshall* principle, Mrs Day was entitled to rely upon the Directive in proceedings against her employer in an industrial tribunal. Lord Keith of Kinkel said,

> "Mrs Day's claim against her employers is a private law claim, and indeed she has already started proceedings to enforce it in the appropriate industrial tribunal, these having been adjourned to await the outcome of the present case."

I interpolate that the employees in this case are in the same position. ...

... I agree, for the reasons so cogently stated by Lord Keith of Kinkel, that a person claiming to be entitled as a matter of private law to compensation for unfair dismissal should ordinarily bring her proceedings in the industrial tribunal, even if they will raise an issue of incompatibility between domestic and Community law. But this is an exceptional case. The question of compatibility with article 119 was raised for the first time in the Court of Appeal. I need not discuss the reasons why it was raised so late: the Court of Appeal was satisfied that it was right to give leave to amend. Subject to the question of the meaning of "pay", it raised the same issues as the question of incompatibility with the Directive and could be resolved on the evidence which had been put before the Divisional Court. The position is the same before this House and the parties have come prepared to deal with it. I therefore think it would be wrong for the House to tell the employees at this stage that they must start again before the Industrial Tribunal. The House should in my view entertain the appeal. But the parties are agreed that it is necessary to enable the House to give judgment that the European Court of Justice should be requested to give preliminary rulings on certain questions on the construction of article 119. Your Lordships have received the submissions of the parties on the drafting of those questions and, having considered those submissions, I would propose that the following questions be referred:

1. Does an award of compensation for breach of the right not to be unfairly dismissed under national legislation such as the [ERA] constitute "pay", within the meaning of article 119 of the EC Treaty?
2. If the answer to question 1 is "yes", do the conditions determining whether a worker has the right not to be unfairly dismissed fall within the scope of article 119 or that of Directive 76/207?
3. What is the legal test for establishing whether a measure adopted by a Member State has such a degree of disparate effect as between men and women as to amount to indirect discrimination for the purposes of article 119 of the EC Treaty unless shown to be based upon objectively justified factors other than sex?
4. When must this legal test be applied to a measure adopted by a Member State? In particular at which of the following points in time, or at what other point in time, must it be applied to the measure:
    (a) When the measure is adopted.
    (b) When the measure is brought into force.
    (c) When the employee is dismissed.

5. What are the legal conditions for establishing the objective justification, for the purposes of indirect discrimination under article 119, of a measure adopted by a Member State in pursuance of its social policy? In particular, what material need the Member State adduce in support of its grounds for justification?

I would therefore discharge the declaration made by the Court of Appeal and adjourn further consideration of the appeal until after the judgment of the Court of Justice. For the convenience of your Lordships and the parties I would suggest that further argument should not necessarily be before the same Appellate Committee.'

(Lords Mustill, Jauncey, Slynn and Nicholls agreed with Lord Hoffmann.)

COMMENT

(1)   This opinion was given in March 1997. It usually takes at least a year for the ECJ to reach a decision in a case referred to it. Until that decision is made, employees dismissed with less than two years' service have to claim within the statutory limitation periods in order to preserve their rights. Such claims are normally adjourned pending the ECJ's decision, but if dismissed for want of jurisdiction, it is important for applicants to appeal, again observing the statutory time limits.

(2)   In the meantime, the existing qualification periods apply to all claims for statutory employment protection rights. It is unlikely that all continuity requirements will be lifted, so the concept of continuous employment remains important.

Employment Rights Act 1996

210. ...

(4)   Subject to sections 215 to 217, a week which does not count in computing the length of a period of continuous employment breaks continuity of employment.

(5)   A person's employment during any period shall, unless the contrary is shown, be presumed to have been continuous.

COMMENT

(1)   Generally by changing jobs you will lose the continuity built up with your previous employer. However, if a business is sold as a going concern to a new owner who keeps on the existing workforce, continuity will be preserved. This is dealt with in detail in Chapter 9.

(2)   If you change jobs but remain with the same employer (if you are promoted, for example) your continuity is not affected by the change.

(3)   The ERA s 216 makes special provision for strikes and other industrial action:

(1)   A week does not count under s 212 if during the week, or any part of the week, the employee takes part in a strike.

(2)   The continuity of an employee's period of employment is not broken by a week which does not count under this Chapter ... if during the week, or any part of the week, the employee takes part in a strike. ...

(3) The continuity of the employee's period of employment is not broken by a week if during the week, or any part of the week, the employee is absent from work because of a lock-out by the employer. ...

Even where there is no contract of employment in existence, continuity can still be preserved in certain circumstances laid down in ERA s 212(3):

...

212 (3) ... any week ... during the whole or part of which an employee is—
    (a) incapable of work in consequence of sickness or injury,
    (b) absent from work on account of a temporary cessation of work,
    (c) absent from work in circumstances such that, by arrangement or custom, he is regarded as continuing in the employment of his employer for any purpose, or
    (d) absent from work wholly or partly because of pregnancy or childbirth, counts in computing the employee's period of employment.
  (4) Not more than twenty-six weeks count under subs (3)(a) or (subject to subs (2)) subs (3)(d) between any periods falling under subs (1).

COMMENT

(1) Usually when people are absent through sickness the contract will continue. Section 212(3)(a) is only necessary to preserve continuity where the contract has actually been terminated but the employee returns to the same employer within twenty-six weeks.

(2) Casual workers often seek to rely on 'temporary cessation of work' to preserve their continuity between contracts. Clearly there is a lot of room for disagreement over how temporary a break is. Guidance was given by the House of Lords in *Ford* v *Warwickshire CC*.

Lord Diplock: ' ... My Lords, since [ERA s 212(3)] only applies to an interval of time between the coming to an end of one contract of employment and the beginning of a fresh contract of employment, the expression "absent from work", where it appears in [s 212(3)](b), (c) and (d), must mean not only that the employee is not doing any actual work for his employer but that there is no contract of employment subsisting between him and his employer that would entitle the latter to require him to do any work. So in this context the phrase "the employee is ... absent from work on account of a temporary cessation of work" as descriptive of a period of time, as it would seem to me, must refer to the interval between (1) the date on which the employee who would otherwise be continuing to work under an existing contract of employment is dismissed because for the time being his employer has no work for him to do, and (2) the date on which work for him to do having become again available, he is re-engaged under a fresh contract of employment to do it; and the words "on account of a temporary cessation of work" refer to the reason why the employer dismissed the employee, and make it necessary to inquire what the reason for the dismissal was. The fact that the unavailability of work had been foreseen by the employer sufficiently far in advance to enable him to anticipate it by giving to the employee a notice to terminate his contract of employment that is of sufficient length to satisfy the requirements of [ERA s 86] (which may be as long as 12 weeks), cannot alter the reason for the dismissal or prevent the absence from work following upon the expiry of the notice from being "on account of a temporary cessation of work" …

From the fact that there is no work available for the employee to do for the employer during the whole of the interval between the end of one fixed term contract of employment and the beginning of the next, and that this was the reason for his non-employment during that interval, it does not necessarily follow that the interval constitutes a *"temporary cessation of work"*. In harmony with what this House held in *Fitzgerald* v *Hall, Russell & Co Ltd*, [s 212(3)(b)], in cases of employment under a succession of fixed term contracts of employment with intervals in between, requires one to look back from the date of the expiry of the fixed term contract in respect of the non-renewal of which the employee's claim is made over the whole period during which the employee has been intermittently employed by the same employer, in order to see whether the interval between one fixed term contract and the fixed term contract that next preceded it was short in duration relative to the combined duration of those two fixed term contracts during which work had continued; for the whole scheme of the Act appears to me to show that it is in the sense of "transient", i.e. lasting only for a relatively short time, that the word "temporary" is used in [s 212(3)(b)]. So, the continuity of employment for the purposes of the Act in relation to unfair dismissal and redundancy payments is not broken unless and until, looking backwards from the date of the expiry of the fixed term contract on which the employee's claim is based, there is to be found between one fixed term contract and its immediate predecessor an interval that cannot be characterised as short relatively to the combined duration of the two fixed term contracts. Whether it can be so characterised is a question of fact and degree and so is for decision by an industrial tribunal rather than by the Employment Appeal Tribunal or an appellate court of law …

My Lords, as I indicated at the outset, the length of successive fixed term contracts on which part-time lecturers are employed and the intervals between them vary considerably with the particular course that the part-time lecturer is engaged to teach; so it by no means follows that a similar concession would be made or would be appropriate in each of their cases. It also follows from what I have said that successive periods of seasonal employment of other kinds under fixed term contracts, such as employment in agriculture during harvest-time or in hotel work during the summer season will only qualify as continuous employment if the length of the period between two successive seasonal contracts is so short in comparison with the length of the season during which the employee is employed as properly to be regarded by the industrial tribunal as no more than a *temporary* cessation of work in the sense that I have indicated.'

(3) Note from this that not only must the absence be temporary, judged with hindsight according to the duration of the whole relationship, but the reason for the absence must be a temporary cessation of work. If there was work available, then even if the absence was temporary, continuity is not preserved under [s 212(3)(b)] (*Byrne* v *Birmingham City DC*).

(4)   It has been argued that the trend towards the greater use of atypical workers has the effect of shifting the risks associated with market-driven business from the employer to the worker, in that the employer does not guarantee the atypical worker regular employment and protected pay levels (see Collins, 'Independent Contractors and the Challenge of Vertical Disintegration to Employment Protection Laws' (1990) 10 OJLS 353). If so, is this a fair allocation of risk?

4 Contract of employment – formation and content

FORMATION

No particular formalities are required for making a contract of employment; it is usual, however, for the process of offer and acceptance to follow some sort of selection procedure, which will often involve advertisement, written application and interview. Job applicants are generally asked for the names of someone who may be approached to give a reference, and the present or former employer is the most obvious person.

This can create something of a problem for an employee, especially if there are reasons for suspecting that the former employer may not be wholly favourable. First, employers have no general obligation to give references about employees at all. Second, the applicant has no right to see the reference (unless it is kept in a computerised form, when there is a right of access under the Data Protection Act 1984). Third, even if the reference contains defamatory matter which is untrue, the employer will be protected from liability provided that the reference was published only to the person with an interest in seeing it (the new employer) and the statements in it were not made maliciously: the employer providing the reference has qualified privilege. Can the employee sue for negligence if the reference is inaccurate?

Spring v *Guardian Assurance plc*

[1994] IRLR 460 House of Lords

Until his dismissal in July 1989, Spring had been employed as sales director and office manager by Corinium, the third defendants in the case. Corinium were authorised agents for the sale of Guardian Assurance insurance policies, and Spring was authorised as a representative for their sale in accordance with the rules of the then statutory regulatory body, LAUTRO.

After his dismissal, Spring tried to set up his own business selling Scottish Amicable policies. LAUTRO rules required insurance companies to take up references on potential representatives, and also instructed insurance companies giving references to other companies to make full and frank disclosure of relevant matters.

Scottish Amicable therefore approached Guardian Assurance for a reference. It was drawn up by a Guardian Assurance compliance officer who had no personal knowledge of Spring. She relied on information given to her by his former boss, who disliked him and had in fact dismissed him, and two other company officials. The reference, which impugned Spring's honesty and stated that he had been involved in serious mis-selling, was aptly described by the trial judge as 'the kiss of death' to his career in insurance.

It was found that the reference was inaccurate and that those giving the information on which it was based had acted negligently, albeit not maliciously. Spring sued Guardian Assurance. Did they owe him a duty of care?

Lord Woolf: '... I am able, from the outset, to focus on the important issues of principle to which this appeal gives rise. They are:

1. Whether a person who suffers loss as a result of being the subject of an inaccurate reference is ever able to recover damages for that loss in an action for negligence, or whether he is confined to seeking damages for defamation or injurious falsehood. (The difference in practice between an action for negligence and an action for defamation or injurious falsehood is that in an action based on defamation or injurious falsehood it will be necessary to establish that the person responsible for giving the reference was motivated by malice, while in the case of an action based on negligence it will be sufficient to establish that it was due to a lack of care in ascertaining the facts on which the reference is based on the part of the person giving the reference or those for whom he is responsible.)

2. Whether, in the appropriate circumstances, in a contract for service or services a term can be implied requiring an employer to exercise due care in the preparation of a reference relating to a person who is, or has been, in his service.

I do not consider it is of any significance whether Mr Spring was employed by, or acting under a contract for services with, Corinium. Certain of the documents suggest he was self-employed and the judge held he was acting under a contract for services. However, this is wholly inconsistent with the nature of his role with the company, which was that of a sales director (designate) and office manager. However, whether he was a servant or self-employed, his activities in selling insurance policies would be as a company representative, subject to the LAUTRO Rules; and the person who was responsible for compiling the reference, Mrs Debra Lee-Moore, had delegated to others the task of collecting the information on which the reference was based. As a matter of convenience, I will treat him as an employee, but it should be appreciated that my views would be the same if he was acting under a contract for services. ...

The claim based on negligence

The claim here is in respect of economic loss. Before there can be a duty owed in respect of economic loss, it is now clearly established that it is important to be able to show foreseeability of that loss, coupled with the necessary degree of proximity between the parties. It is also necessary to establish that in all the circumstances it is fair, just and reasonable for a duty to be imposed in respect of the economic loss. Deferring for the moment consideration of the consequences of there being possible alternative causes of action of defamation and injurious falsehood and the related public policy considerations, there can really be no dispute that Mr Spring can establish the necessary foreseeability and proximity.

It is clearly foreseeable that if you respond to a request for a reference by giving a reference which is inaccurate, the subject of the reference may be caused financial loss. Where the reference is required by a prospective employer, the loss will frequently result from a failure to obtain that employment. The prospect of such loss is considerably increased if the reference relates to an applicant, like Mr Spring, for a position as a company representative in an industry which is subject to a rule which is in equivalent terms to rule 3.5 of the LAUTRO Rules. That rule provides:

"(1) A person shall not be appointed as a company representative of a member unless the member has first taken reasonable steps to satisfy itself that he is of good character and of the requisite aptitude and competence, and those steps shall … include … taking up of references relating to character and experience.

(2) A member which receives an inquiry for a reference in respect of a person whom another member or appointed representative is proposing to appoint shall make full and frank disclosure of all relevant matters which are believed to be true to the other member or the representative."

His Honour Judge Lever, at first instance, accepted Mr Spring's counsel's description of the reference as being "the kiss of death" to Mr Spring's career in insurance. This was the inevitable consequence of the reference. The reference related to a time and was based upon events which occurred while Mr Spring was working for Corinium and was engaged in selling policies issued by Guardian. The relationship between Mr Spring and the respondents could hardly be closer. Subject to what I have to say hereafter, it also appears to be uncontroversial that if an employer, or former employer, by his failure to make proper inquiries, causes loss to an employee, it is fair, just and reasonable that he should be under an obligation to compensate that employee for the consequences. This is the position if an employer injures his employee physically by failing to exercise reasonable care for his safety and I find it impossible to justify taking a different view where an employer, by giving an inaccurate reference about his employee, deprives an employee, possibly for a considerable period, of the means of earning his livelihood. The consequences of the employer's carelessness can be as great in the long term as causing the employee a serious injury.

…

In *Hedley Byrne* v *Heller,* their Lordships extended the circumstances giving rise to a duty of care so as to protect the recipient from an inaccurate reference in those situations where the relationship between the person giving and receiving the reference is " 'equivalent to contract', that is, where there is an assumption of responsibility in circumstances in which, but for the absence of consideration, there would be a contract." In such a situation it is necessary to distinguish "between social and professional relationships and between those which are of a contractual character and those which are not." It may also "be material to consider whether the adviser is acting purely out of good nature or whether he is getting his reward in some indirect form" (per Lord Devlin). Applying that guidance to the different situation of the relationship between the person giving and the person who is the subject of the reference, it is immediately clear that a distinction can be drawn between cases where the subject of the reference is an employee (I use that term hereafter to include a person engaged on a contract for services as well as a contract of service) or an ex-employee, and where the relationship is social and has never been contractual. In the latter situation all that the person who is the subject of the reference may be able to rely on is the fact that the referee gave the reference. That, I can well understand, may not be considered sufficient to create the required degree of proximity. The proximity would be closer to that in *Hedley Byrne*, if the reference had been given by a purely social acquaintance at the *request* of the subject of the reference. While the request may or may not be sufficient to create the required proximity, it can still be distinguished from the present class of case. Here the relationship is of a different order because there is or has been a contract of employment or services. Of course the period which elapses between the end of the engagement and the giving of the reference is capable of reducing the degree of proximity.

In addition, the relationship is one where the employer should, as I have already indicated, appreciate that the terms of any reference which he gives could materially affect the ability of the subject of the reference to find alternative employment. Furthermore, in a contemporary employment context it is appropriate to regard the employer as obtaining an indirect benefit from giving a reference. Employers in industry, commerce and the professions are all dependent on the reciprocity which exists among employers as to the giving of references on prospective recruits. Without that reciprocity recruitment of staff would be more difficult. It would also directly affect an employer's ability to recruit staff if it became known that he was not prepared to assist those he has previously engaged by giving them references. Employees are unlikely to regard as attractive employment at the end of which they would find themselves without a reference.

The duty imposed by the LAUTRO Rules is not for the protection of employees. It is for the protection of the public. An employee cannot therefore rely on the rules directly. However, they nonetheless demonstrate the importance now attached in the insurance industry to references being given and obtained. To be of value they need to be full, frank and, by implication, accurate references.

Finally, no difficulty is created by the fact that before the reference was given the employment had come to an end. Mr Spring was dismissed on 26 July 1989 and the reference which has resulted in these proceedings was the consequence of his seeking an appointment as a representative almost immediately thereafter on 2 August 1989. The reference was sent on 21 November 1989 and, as Judge Lever said, "the inevitable happened". Mr Spring was rejected first by Scottish Amicable and then by two other insurance companies. This all occurred within a reasonable time of the employment ending.

I therefore now turn to examine the two factors which make the issues in this case difficult to resolve. The first of those factors is the existence of the alternative causes of action in defamation and injurious falsehood which are available to a person in Mr Spring's position who believes he has been caused damage by an inaccurate reference. (I will treat both these alternative causes of action under the heading of defamation, since it is their common characteristic that to succeed a plaintiff must prove malice which creates the difficulty.) The second factor is closely related to the first. It is the public policy consequences which would follow from there being a remedy in negligence.

The defamation issue

There would be no purpose in extending the tort of negligence to protect the subject of an inaccurate reference if he was already adequately protected by the law of defamation. However, because of the defence of qualified privilege, before an action for defamation can succeed (or, for that matter, an action for injurious falsehood) it is necessary to establish malice. In my judgment, the result of this requirement is that an action for defamation provides a wholly inadequate remedy for an employee who is caused damage by a reference which, due to negligence, is inaccurate. This is because it places a wholly disproportionate burden on the employee. Malice is extremely difficult to establish. This is demonstrated by the facts of this case. Mr Spring was able to establish that one of his colleagues, who played a part in compiling the information on which the reference was based, had lied about interviewing him, but this was still insufficient to prove malice. Without an action for negligence the employee may, therefore, be left with no practical prospect of redress, even though the reference may have permanently prevented him from obtaining employment in his chosen vocation.

If that the law provided a remedy for references which are inaccurate due to carelessness this would be beneficial. It would encourage the adoption of appropriate standards when preparing references. This would be an important advantage, as frequently an employee will be ignorant that it is because of the terms of an inaccurate reference, of the contents of which he is unaware, that he is not offered fresh employment.

The availability of a remedy without having to prove malice will not open the floodgates. In cases where the employee discovers the existence of the inaccurate reference, he will have a remedy if, but only if, he can establish, instead of malice, that the reason for the inaccuracy is the default of the employer, in the sense that he has been careless. To make an employer liable for an inaccurate reference, but only if he is careless, is, I would suggest, wholly fair. It would balance the respective interests of the employer and employee. It would amount to a development of the law of negligence which accords with the principles which should control its development. It would, in addition, avoid a rather unattractive situation continuing of a recipient of a reference, but not the subject of a reference, being able to bring an action for negligence. It would also recognise that while both in negligence and defamation it is the untrue statement which causes the damage, there is a fundamental difference between the torts. An action for defamation is founded upon the inaccurate terms of the reference itself. An action for negligence is based on the lack of care of the author of the reference. ...

[Public policy]

It is obviously in accord with public policy that references should be full and frank. It is also in accord with public policy that they should not be based upon careless investigations. In the case of references for positions of responsibility this is particularly important. That is confirmed by the LAUTRO Rules. It has also to be accepted that some referees may be more timid in giving full and frank references if they feel there is a risk of their being found liable for negligence. However, there is already such a possible liability in respect of a negligently favourable reference, so all that needs to be considered is the possible adverse consequences of a negligently unfavourable reference. For reasons to which I have already referred, I consider there is little practical likelihood of no reference at all being given nowadays. Certainly this could not happen in the case of appointments to which the LAUTRO Rules apply.

However, the real issue is not whether there would be any adverse effect on the giving of references. Rather the issue is whether the adverse effects, when balanced against the benefits which would flow from giving the subject a right of action, sufficiently outweigh the benefits to justify depriving the subject of a remedy unless he can establish malice. In considering this issue it is necessary to take into account contemporary practices in the field of employment; the fact that nowadays most employment is conditional upon a reference being provided. There are also the restrictions on unfair dismissal which mean that an employee is ordinarily not capable of being dismissed except after being told of what is alleged against him and after he has been given an opportunity of giving an explanation. There is also the widespread practice, especially in the Civil Service, of having annual reports which the subject is entitled to see – which practice, apparently even in an ongoing employment situation, is not defeated by any lack of candour. There is now an openness in employment relationships which did not exist even a few years ago.

There is also the advantage, already referred to, of it being appreciated that you cannot give a reference which could cause immense harm to its subject without exercising reasonable care.

A further consideration mentioned by the President is the undesirability of infringing freedom of speech. This is a consideration at least as important to the common law as it is under the international conventions by which it is also protected. Here it is necessary to bear in mind that, as is the case with all fundamental freedoms, the protection is qualified and not absolute. Freedom of speech does not necessarily entitle the speaker to make a statement without exercising reasonable care. Freedom of speech has to be balanced against the equally well-recognised freedom both at common law and under the conventions that an individual should not be deprived of the opportunity of earning his livelihood in his chosen occupation. A development of the law which does no more than protect an employee from being deprived of employment as a result of a negligent reference would fully justify any limited intrusion on freedom of speech.

When I weigh these considerations I find that public policy comes down firmly in favour of not depriving an employee of a remedy to recover the damages to which he would otherwise be entitled as a result of being a victim of a negligent reference.

Under this head there remains to be considered whether it is preferable for the law in this area to be developed by Parliament or by the courts. It is an area of law where previous decisions of the courts have already clearly identified the tests which should be applied in deciding whether the law should be developed. It is also an area where a case-by-case approach is particularly appropriate and so, as happened in *Hedley Byrne*, it appears to me desirable for the courts to provide the remedy which I believe is clearly required.

The claim based on the breach of contract

As I indicated earlier, it is possible to approach this appeal as being primarily one involving a contractual issue. This was the preferred approach of Lord Bridge of Harwich in *Scally* v *Southern Health and Social Services Board*, in a speech, with which other members of the House agreed, from which I obtained singular assistance. In that case, Lord Bridge stated the obverse of the proposition that I have previously advanced when he said "if a duty of the kind in question was not inherent in the contractual relationship, I do not see how it could possibly be derived from the tort of negligence". In *Scally* it was decided that where a contract of employment negotiated between employers and a representative body contained a particular term conferring on an employee a valuable contingent right to a pension, of the benefit of which he could not be expected to be aware unless the term was brought to his attention, there was an implied obligation on the employer to take reasonable steps to publicise that term. Accordingly, when the employer failed to notify the employee of his pension rights, which were therefore lost, he was entitled to recover damages for breach of contract in respect of that loss.

In the course of his speech, Lord Bridge drew a distinction "between the search for an implied term necessary to give business efficacy to a particular contract and the search, based on wider considerations, for a term which the law will imply as a necessary incident of a definable category of contractual relationship". He also referred to the difficulty which would arise if the implied term "must necessarily be too wide in its ambit to be acceptable as of general application". He indicated that he believed that "this difficulty is surmounted if the category of contractual relationship in which the implication will arise is defined with sufficient precision".

Lord Bridge then proceeded to define the situation on the basis of the relationship of employer and employee where the circumstances he specified existed. As I understand the *Scally* case, it recognises that, just as in the earlier authorities the courts were prepared to imply by necessary implication a term imposing a duty on an employer to exercise due care for the physical well-being of his employees, so in the appropriate circumstances would the court imply a like duty as to his economic well-being, the duty as to his economic well-being giving rise to an action for damages if it is breached.

Here, it is also possible to specify circumstances which would enable a term to be implied. The circumstances are:

(i)   The existence of the contract of employment or services.

(ii)   The fact that the contract relates to an engagement of a class where it is the normal practice to require a reference from a previous employer before employment is offered.

(iii)   The fact that the employee cannot be expected to enter into that class of employment except on the basis that his employer will, on the request of another prospective employer made not later than a reasonable time after the termination of a former employment, provide a full and frank reference as to the employee.

This being the nature of the engagement, it is necessary to imply a term into the contract that the employer would, during the continuance of the engagement or within a reasonable time thereafter, provide a reference at the request of a prospective employer which was based on facts revealed after making those reasonably careful enquiries which, in the circumstances, a reasonable employer would make.

In this case Mr Spring's employers were in breach of that implied term. Although the person actually writing the reference was not negligent, she delegated the task of ascertaining the facts to others, and as is the case with the employer's duty to exercise reasonable care for the safety of his employee, the employer cannot escape liability by so delegating his responsibility.

It only remains for me to underline what I anticipate is already clear, that is, that the views which I have expressed are confined to the class of case with which I am now dealing. Some of the statements I have made I appreciate could be applied to analogous situations. However, I do not intend to express any view either way as to what will be the position in those analogous situations. I believe that they are better decided when, and if, a particular case comes before the court. This approach can lead to uncertainty, which is undesirable. However, that undesirable consequence is in my view preferable to trying to anticipate the position in relation to other situations which are not the subject matter of this appeal.

I would allow this appeal and remit the case to the Court of Appeal so that that Court can deal with the question of causation.'

(Lord Slynn and Lowry delivered concurring speeches; Lord Goff concurred, but based his decision only on the *Hedley Byrne* duty rather than the wider duty of care. Lord Keith dissented.)

COMMENT

(1)   Note the suggestion that the duty of care in this situation would be the same for an employee and an independent contractor.

(2)   Do employers have an obligation to give references, according to Lord Woolf? Are there any situations where the provider of a reference would not owe a duty of care to the subject of the reference?

(3)   What policy reasons are identified as relevant to the decision? Do you agree with the judge's assessment of them?

(4)   Under the Rehabilitation of Offenders Act 1974 s 4(2) a referee has a duty not to mention any spent conviction or ancillary circumstances; the referee will be protected from any legal liability in such a case. However, by regulations there are a number of exceptions to this basic position.

WRITTEN PARTICULARS OF TERMS

Employment Rights Act 1996

1.   (1)   Where an employee begins employment with an employer, the employer shall

give to the employee a written statement of particulars of employment.

(2) The statement may (subject to s 2(4)) be given in instalments and (whether or not given in instalments) shall be given not later than two months after the beginning of the employment.

(3) The statement shall contain particulars of—
   (a) the names of the employer and employee,
   (b) the date when the employment began, and
   (c) the date on which the employee's period of continuous employment began (taking into account any employment with a previous employer which counts towards that period).

(4) The statement shall also contain particulars, as at a specified date not more than seven days before the statement (or the instalment containing them) is given, of—
   (a) the scale or rate of remuneration or the method of calculating remuneration,
   (b) the intervals at which remuneration is paid (that is, weekly, monthly or other specified intervals),
   (c) any terms and conditions relating to hours of work (including any terms and conditions relating to normal working hours),
   (d) any terms and conditions relating to any of the following—
      (i) entitlement to holidays, including public holidays, and holiday pay (the particulars given being sufficient to enable the employee's entitlement, including any entitlement to accrued holiday pay on the termination of employment, to be precisely calculated),
      (ii) incapacity for work due to sickness or injury, including any provision for sick pay, and
      (iii) pensions and pension schemes,
   (e) the length of notice which the employee is obliged to give and entitled to receive to determine his contract of employment,
   (f) the title of the job which the employee is employed to do or a brief description of the work for which he is employed,
   (g) where the employment is not intended to be permanent, the period for which it is expected to continue or, if it is for a fixed term, the date when it is to end,
   (h) either the place of work or, where the employee is required or permitted to work at various places, an indication of that and of the address of the employer,
   (j) any collective agreements which directly affect the terms and conditions of the employment including, where the employer is not a party, the persons by whom they were made....

COMMENT

(1) The requirement to give employees a written statement of their principal terms and conditions has existed in some form since 1963. It has been extended over the years, and was most recently amended in 1993 by TURERA in order to give effect to the EC Directive on the Proof of the Employment Relationship (91/533/EEC), adopted in 1991.

(2) Although the employer has two months in which to provide the statement, the

employee actually becomes entitled to it after one month of employment: ERA s 198.

(3)   Apart from information on notice periods, sick pay, pensions and collective agreements, for which the employee may be referred to another document, the information must now be provided in a separate document for each individual employee. This is in line with the former Conservative Government's thinking revealed in the White Paper, *People, Jobs and Opportunities* (Cm 1810, 1992), that employers should be encouraged towards individual rather than collective bargaining.

(4)   In case of dispute between the parties, what is the status of the written statement?

Status of the written statement

System Floors v Daniel

[1981] IRLR 475 Employment Appeal Tribunal

The employer disputed the starting date in the employee's written statement.

Browne-Wilkinson P: '...The first issue is whether the Industrial Tribunal was right in holding that the statement was a contract and fell within the decision of the Court of Appeal in *Gascol Conversions Ltd* v *Mercer*. The statement was served under the statutory provisions now included in ss 1 to 4 of the [Employment Rights Act 1996]. Under [s 1(3)], an employer is required, in a statement which must be served under that section, to specify the date when the employment began.

There is some authority as to the effect of the statutory particulars of the terms of employment. In *Turriff Construction Ltd* v *Bryant* the Divisional Court had to consider for the purposes of redundancy payment what effect was to be given to the number of hours worked specified in a statutory statement. Speaking of the statutory predecessor of [ERA s 1], Lord Parker, giving the decision of the Court, said this:

> "It is of course quite clear that the statement made pursuant to s 4 of the Act of 1963 is not a contract. It is not even conclusive evidence of the terms of a contract."

Again, the Divisional Court in *Parkes Classic Confectionery Ltd* v *Ashcroft* overruled the decision of an Industrial Tribunal which had held that where the terms of the contract of employment had been varied, but the employer had failed to serve particulars of the changes in the terms in accordance with what is now s 4 of the [1996 Act], the employer was not entitled to rely on the varied contract. The Divisional Court held that notwithstanding the failure to serve the necessary statutory statement and notwithstanding that that might be a criminal offence, there was nothing in the Act to provide that a change of contractual terms should be ineffectual between the parties merely because the employer had failed to give written notice of the change.

It seems to us, therefore, that in general the status of the statutory statement is this. It provides very strong *prima facie* evidence of what were the terms of the contract between the parties, but does not constitute a written contract between the parties. Nor are the statements of the terms finally conclusive: at most, they place a heavy burden on the employer to show that the actual terms of contract are different from those which he has set out in the statutory statement.

Against that background we turn to consider the decision of the Court of Appeal in *Gascol Conversions Ltd* v *Mercer* which was the basis of the Industrial Tribunal's decision in this case. In that case there was an agreed variation in the terms on which the employees were engaged. When the Industrial Relations Act 1971 came into operation the employer became bound to give a written statement of particulars, and in pursuance of that obligation the employer sent a new contract of employment to each of their men. Each man was given a copy to keep, and he was required to sign a document in these terms: "I confirm receipt of a new contract of employment dated 25.2.72, which sets out as required under the Industrial Relations Act 1971 the terms and conditions of my employment." Mr Mercer signed such a document. The Court of Appeal held that in those circumstances the document constituted a binding written contract and that accordingly no evidence was admissible to show that the terms of the contract were otherwise. In our view that case does not cover the present case. In that case Mr Mercer had signed a document which he confirmed was a new contract of employment and that it set out the terms and conditions of his employment. The Court of Appeal treated that as being a contract in writing, as indeed it was, having been signed by both parties. But in the case of an ordinary statutory statement served pursuant to the statutory obligation, the document is a unilateral one merely stating the employer's view of what those terms are. In the absence of an acknowledgement by the parties that the statement is itself a contract and that the terms are correct (such as that contained in the *Mercer* case), the statutory statement does not itself constitute a contract in writing.

In the present case, all that Mr Daniel did was to sign an acknowledgement that he had received the statement. In no sense did he sign it as a contract or acknowledge the accuracy of the terms in it. We therefore think that the Industrial Tribunal erred in law in treating the date of commencement mentioned in the statement as decisive because it was a contractual term. In our view the statement is no more than persuasive, though not conclusive, evidence of the date of commencement.'

COMMENT

(1)   The difference between *System Floors* v *Daniel* and *Gascol Conversions Ltd* v *Mercer* lies in the nature of the document signed. Do you think that the relevance of the form is likely to be appreciated by employers and employees?

(2)   What if no written statement is given, or the employee disputes its accuracy? Under ERA s 11 the employee may apply to an industrial tribunal, which has power to determine the particulars which ought to have been included, or to amend inaccurate particulars.

In *Mears* v *Safecar Security* the Court of Appeal suggested that if no particulars had been included on a specific issue, and if there was no evidence of what the parties had agreed on it, then the industrial tribunal should 'invent' the relevant particulars, 'by deciding which term fits in best with all the circumstances of the case, which may be getting near to deciding what is a reasonable term, or a term which, to quote the industrial tribunal's decision, "would be sensible if the parties had in fact agreed it" ' (*per* Stephenson LJ at p 653). This surprising encouragement to judicial creativity has since been disapproved by another Court of Appeal in *Eagland* v *British Telecommunications plc*. Pointing out that Stephenson LJ's remarks were strictly *obiter*, Parker LJ said:

'There is in *Mears*'s case clearly an indication, albeit obiter, by Lord Justice Stephenson, with whom Lord Justice O'Connor and Sir Stanley Rees agreed, that the Tribunal is under a statutory duty to invent terms if there are no materials upon which they can say a term could be found to be agreed expressly or by implication or by the general conduct of the parties. It is to be noted that in that passage Lord Justice Stephenson does not distinguish between mandatory terms and non-mandatory terms. The terms with which we are concerned in this case are all non-mandatory terms. With respect to the Lord Justice, I have no hesitation in saying that, so far as non-mandatory terms are concerned, the Tribunal have no power to include any such terms. What they would have power to do – but it is a wholly different matter – is to say that, because the contract turned out to be a contract of employment, it was a necessary legal incident of that contract that the ordinary requirements of such a relationship be included. But the requirements of such a relationship do not include disciplinary rules, pension, sick pay or holiday pay and in my judgment they have no power to impose upon an employer any such terms if it be the fact, as it undoubtedly was, that either it had been agreed that there should be no pension, sick pay, holiday pay, or disciplinary rules, or the matter had not been agreed at all. The wording of the section makes it perfectly plain, as indeed must be the case at common law, that there may be no such terms and there is nothing in any section of the Act which empowers or requires the Tribunal to impose upon the parties terms which had not been agreed when the statute recognises that it may be the case that no such terms have been agreed.

So far as mandatory terms are concerned, it may be difficult to see how the matter can ever arise, subject only to this. There may be a case where there is, for example, provision as to the length of notice. In such a case the Tribunal would in my view have power to conclude that there must be reasonable notice. It may also have power to decide, as would a court of law, the length of such notice, which would be a question of fact. But I do not consider that even in mandatory cases the Tribunal have power to impose on parties terms which have not been agreed.

This may be piling obiter upon obiter, since my conclusion is that, quite apart from the guidance, the appeal must fail on the facts, the Tribunal having concluded the matter in a manner which in my judgment cannot be faulted. But it is undesirable that there should remain in the authorities guidance which appears to me to have been arrived at without paying any attention to the distinction between mandatory and non-mandatory terms and when the guidance was given without argument on the point. We have in this Court heard argument on the point and it is therefore desirable that we should correct the matter in so far as it is possible.'

(3)   Another possible course of action for a dissatisfied employee is shown in the next case.

W A Goold (Pearmak) Ltd v McConnell

[1995] IRLR 516 Employment Appeal Tribunal

The company had a wholesale jewellery business and employed the two applicants as salesmen on a salary and commission basis. Following financial difficulties a new managing director was taken on to reorganise and improve the business. Changes introduced to the payment system resulted in a substantial drop in the applicants' take-home pay and they sought to discuss this with management.

Their own manager did nothing about it, and approaches to the new managing director got a negative response. Finally, they attempted to get an interview with the company chairman, but were told that any appointment had to be made through the managing director. The employees resigned and claimed unfair dismissal. The claim depended on their being able to show that the company had committed a fundamental breach of contract.

Morison J: '... The industrial tribunal asked itself the right question, namely, and I quote:

"Whether the [employers] were in such serious breach of their obligations under the contracts of employment as to entitle the [employees] to leave as they did."

They noted that neither man was provided with a written statement of the terms and conditions of his employment, which would have specified the method of pursuing a grievance. In his written statement, which was admitted in evidence, the employers' chairman said he was well-known to see any employee who has a grievance or other problem. As the tribunal noted, the employees tried to speak to the chairman, but were rebuffed. The tribunal was of the view that any grievance procedure should have incorporated within it some kind of time limit, so as to ensure that grievances were nipped in the bud. In the absence of any grievance procedure in the contract of employment, the employees' grievances, instead of being considered and dealt with promptly, were allowed to fester in an atmosphere of prevarication and indecision. The industrial tribunal concluded, and I quote:

"We think that this failure by the [employers] amounted to a breach of contract."

It seems to us quite clear that the breach of contract identified by the industrial tribunal related to the way the employees' grievances were dealt with. Their process of reasoning was that Parliament requires employers to provide their employees with written particulars of their employment in compliance with the statutory requirements. Section 3(1) of the [Employment Rights Act 1996] provides that the written statement required under s 1 of the Act shall include a note specifying, by description or otherwise, to whom and in what manner the employee may apply if he is either dissatisfied with any disciplinary decision or has any other grievance, and an explanation of any further steps in the grievance procedure. It is clear therefore, that Parliament considered that good industrial relations requires employers to provide their employees with a method of dealing with grievances in a proper and timeous fashion. This is also consistent, of course, with the codes of practice. That being so, the industrial tribunal was entitled, in our judgment, to conclude that there was an implied term in the contract of employment that the employers would reasonably and promptly afford a reasonable opportunity to their employees to obtain redress of any grievance they may have. It was in our judgment rightly conceded at the industrial tribunal that such could be a breach of contract.

Further, it seems to us that the right to obtain redress against a grievance is fundamental for very obvious reasons. The working environment may well lead to employees experiencing difficulties, whether because of the physical conditions under which they are required to work, or because of a breakdown in human relationships, which can readily occur when people of different backgrounds and sensitivities are required to work together, often under pressure.

There may well be difficulties arising out of the way that authority and control is exercised – sometimes by people who themselves have insufficient experience and training to exercise such power wisely. ...'

(The EAT upheld the tribunal's finding that they had been unfairly dismissed.)

Variation of the contract

Employment Rights Act 1996

4.   (1)   If after the material date, there is a change in any of the matters particulars of which are required by sections 1 to 3 to be included or referred to in a statement under section 1, the employer shall give to the employee a written statement containing particulars of the change. ...

  (3)   A statement under subsection (1) shall be given at the earliest opportunity and, in any event, not later than—

   (a)   one month after the change in question ...

COMMENT

While s 4 requires notification of changes, it does not give the employer the authority unilaterally to make changes in the contract.

Burdett-Coutts v *Hertfordshire County Council*

[1984] IRLR 91   Queen's Bench Division

Kenneth Jones J: 'In about 1982 the defendants, the Hertfordshire County Council, were minded to reduce the incomes of certain of their employees who have been referred to as "the dinner ladies". Six of those dinner ladies now appear as plaintiffs in this action. Let me say immediately that I am not concerned to inquire in any way into the reasonableness or unreasonableness of either the defendants or of the plaintiffs, or of the representatives of the union who were seeking to safeguard the plaintiffs' interests; I am concerned solely with the contractual relationship between the plaintiffs and the defendants.

What the plaintiffs say very shortly is that the defendants have broken the contracts of employment which they have entered into with the plaintiffs and, by reason of that breach, the plaintiffs are entitled to damages taking the form of arrears of wages and a declaration that the defendants were not entitled lawfully to act as they have done in this case ...

What ... happened was that the defendants wrote to each of these ladies a letter ... This letter is central to the whole of this case and I propose to read much of it. It is dated 5.1.83. The significance of that date is that it was at least 12 weeks before 31.3.83. The letter continues:

"Dear Madam,
   Amendment of contract of service – general kitchen assistant.
   I refer to my letters of 8 and 19.10.82 concerning the proposals made by the Education Committee for changes in the working arrangements of school meal staff and mid-day supervisory assistants. In adopting these proposals the Committee were concerned to seek to maintain the school meals service and to avoid the redundancies which other courses of action would have involved. Consultation with the appropriate unions have not resulted in any changes in the proposals and it is now necessary for me to give you detailed notice of the variations in your contract of service. As you know, your appointment as a general kitchen assistant is subject to such terms and conditions determined by the National Joint Council, and Essex and Hertfordshire Provincial Local Authority Services as are adopted by the County Council from time to time, together with such other terms as the County Council may from time to time lay down. I am now writing to inform you that these terms and conditions of service will be amended by the County Council from 31.3.83 as follows."

There are then set out details of the amendments which relate to (a) rates of pay and meals entitlement, (b) the working week year, (c) payment of wages. I can summarise all those detailed amendments by saying that they each involve, and were designed to involve, a reduction in the pay of the employees. The letter continues:

"This letter is the formal notice of these changes in your contract of service which take effect on 31.3.83. I do hope you will understand why the County Council have to change your conditions of service as set out above, as a means of preserving both the school meals service and employment. I hope you will continue in the school meals service."

That letter was signed by the County Education Officer.

Mr Pardoe does not suggest that the County Council was in any way entitled to make these amendments to the contract of service within the terms of the document containing the terms and conditions of employment. He submits, with great clarity, that this letter properly construed is a letter giving notice to the addressee of the termination of her employment on 31.3.83 and offering to re-employ her with effect from that date on the new terms set out in that letter.

There can, of course, be no doubt whatsoever that what was in the mind of the County Education Officer was that all his dinner ladies should continue with their jobs and should accept a reduction in their wages. It may be that he was not concerned primarily with the precise method as to which that was to be carried out. Put another way, this was a letter written not by a lawyer but by a layman.

Mr Higgs, on behalf of the plaintiffs, says that that is not the correct interpretation to be put upon this letter and this letter, although in practical terms is offering the employee the choice of accepting a reduction in pay or leaving, looked at properly it is an attempt by the defendant unilaterally to vary the terms of the contracts of employment. As such it amounted to a fundamental breach of that contract which had the effect of repudiating the contract and putting the employee in the position where she could either refuse to accept that repudiation, or she could have accepted it and left.

I am bound to say that, in reading this letter, I can see nowhere within it any words which can be construed as giving notice to the employee to terminate her employment. The words of the letter are clear beyond a peradventure. It is giving "detailed notice of the variations in your contract of service". It is informing the addressee that these terms and conditions will be amended by the County Council. The letter is expressed to be "formal notice of these changes in your contract of service". Those words are apt, and apt only, to describe an attempt by the employer to vary unilaterally the terms of the contract of employment. Of course it was present in the author's mind that the addressee may fall into line and be content to carry on at a reduced wage, or that they may prefer to leave, so he understandably ended his letter by saying, "I hope you will continue in the school meals service"; but it is stretching words beyond meanings they are capable of bearing to say that the letter having given notice of termination of employment that was an offer of re-employment. I have therefore come to the conclusion that the defendants sought to repudiate the contracts of employment.

What happened afterwards was that these ladies allowed 31 March to pass and stayed at their posts, taking the lower sums which were paid to them. Mr Pardoe relies upon that activity by the employees as being an acceptance of the new contract of employment which he says was offered in the letter … Since I have held that there was no such offer in the letter, … then there is no occasion for me to consider whether the conduct of these ladies constituted an acceptance of such an offer. But the argument could have been put in a slightly different way and have the same effect in the end; that these ladies, by implication, have waived their right to treat the contract as having been brought to an end and have, as I say, by implication after that entered into some fresh contract. I cannot accept that that is a true construction to put on their activities because it has been made abundantly clear to the defendants from a date prior to 31.3.83 that they were not in any way prepared to accept the new terms, or amendments, which had been put forward by the defendants ...

What is the position? In my judgment the defendants have sought unilaterally to impose amendments to the contracts of employment here. By so doing they are in breach of those contracts and have repudiated them. The plaintiff, faced with the choice which every innocent party to a contract has, has not accepted that repudiation but is standing on the original contract and saying, as she is entitled to say, 'I can now recover the total wages which should have been paid to me under the original contract' ...

Accordingly, I give judgment in this case for the arrears of wages and return of excess monies ... I also find that the plaintiffs, each of them, are entitled ... to a declaration that the defendants sought ... to vary unilaterally the terms of the plaintiffs' contract of employment, and that they were not entitled in law so to do.'

COMMENT

(1)   The case illustrates the point that variation of a contract requires the agreement of both parties. However, what if the construction argued for by the Council had been accepted by the court? Would the dismissals have been fair? There is no clear answer. In May 1991 Rolls Royce announced that it would dismiss its 34,000 strong workforce and offer them new contracts, essentially because the company wanted to institute a pay freeze, which would have been a breach of contract. The outcry was such that the company backed down and the legality of its action was never tested. But some commentators thought that the workers would have had a good claim for redundancy and/or unfair dismissal (see, for example, John McGlyne, 'A technical hitch' (1991) 141 NLJ 705).

(2)   In this case it was also plain that the employees had not acquiesced in the new situation and so could not be taken to have accepted the variation impliedly. But what if the employee makes no protest when the employer purports to vary the contract unilaterally?

Jones v Associated Tunnelling Co Ltd

[1981] IRLR 477 Employment Appeal Tribunal

J started working for the company in 1964. From 1969 he was employed at the Hem Heath Colliery, about 12 miles from his home. When work at that colliery ceased in 1980 his employers sought to move him to another colliery which was a similar distance from his home. J claimed that they had no right to move him and that he was redundant. The employers relied on an express mobility clause that had been notified to him in updated versions of his written statement of terms and conditions of employment in 1973 and 1976. J had never objected that these were inaccurate and the employers claimed that he had therefore acquiesced in the variation.

Browne-Wilkinson P: ' ... We therefore reach the conclusion that we are entitled to hold, and do hold, that the right term to imply into Mr Jones's contract from the outset was that he could be required to work at any place within reasonable daily commuting distance from his home ...

It is therefore not necessary for us to reach any concluded view as to whether the Industrial

Tribunal was right in holding that, even if under the original contract Mr Jones's place of work could not be changed, by continuing to work without objection Mr Jones must be taken to have assented to a variation in his terms of employment including the introduction of the mobility clause. However, since the case may go further and the Court of Appeal may take a different view on the implied term, we must state our reservations about the Industrial Tribunal's view on such variations. The statutory "statement of terms and conditions of employment" is not itself a contract but merely contains the employer's statement of what has previously been agreed. As such, the first of such statements to be issued is often compelling evidence of what terms have in fact been agreed. But where there are two or more statements which are not in identical terms, the later statement can only be evidence of an agreed variation of the original terms. Such variation may be either express or implied. If, as in the present case, there is no evidence of any oral discussion varying the original terms, the fact that a statement of terms and conditions containing different terms has been issued cannot be compelling evidence of an express oral variation. The most that can be said is that by continuing to work without objection after receiving such further statement, the employee may have impliedly agreed to the variation recorded in the second statement or is estopped from denying it.

In our view, to imply an agreement to vary or to raise an estoppel against the employee on the grounds that he has not objected to a false record by the employers of the terms actually agreed is a course which should be adopted with great caution. If the variation relates to a matter which has immediate practical application (e.g. the rate of pay) and the employee continues to work without objection after effect has been given to the variation (e.g. his pay packet has been reduced) then obviously he may well be taken to have impliedly agreed. But where, as in the present case, the variation has no immediate practical effect the position is not the same. It is the view of both members of this Tribunal with experience in industrial relations (with which the Chairman, without such experience, agrees) that it is asking too much of the ordinary employee to require him either to object to an erroneous statement of his terms of employment having no immediate practical impact on him or be taken to have assented to the variation. So to hold would involve an unrealistic view of the inclination and ability of the ordinary employee to read and fully understand such statements.

Even if he does read the statement and can understand it, it would be unrealistic of the law to require him to risk a confrontation with his employer on a matter which has no immediate practical impact on the employee. For those reasons, as at present advised, we would not be inclined to imply any assent to a variation from mere failure by the employee to object to the unilateral alteration by the employer of the terms of employment contained in a statutory statement.'

COMMENT

(1)   This reasoning has frequently been applied since: see, for example, *Aparau* v *Iceland Frozen Foods*. However, note the qualification in *Crédit Suisse Asset Management* v *Armstrong* in relation to employees 'of experience and sophistication'.

CUSTOM AND PRACTICE AS A SOURCE OF CONTRACT TERMS

Sagar v *Ridehalgh*

[1931] 1 Ch 310 Court of Appeal

The plaintiff was employed by the defendant company as a weaver. He sued when one shilling was deducted from his wages for bad work. The employers claimed that they were entitled to deduct for bad work either because this was the longstanding practice in their mill, or because it was customary in the Lancashire cotton weaving trade.

Lawrence LJ: ' … The employers based their contention on two alternative grounds: either that the established practice of making reasonable deductions for bad work in the defendants' mill was incorporated into the plaintiff's contract of service by reason of his having agreed to be employed upon the same terms as the other weavers in that mill, or else that the general usage of making reasonable deductions for bad work prevailing in the cotton weaving trade of Lancashire was so well known and understood that every weaver engaging in that trade must be taken to have entered upon his employment on the footing of that usage.

As regards the first of these grounds, it is clearly established by the evidence of Mr George Ridehalgh that the practice of making reasonable deductions for bad work has continuously prevailed at the defendants' mill for upwards of thirty years, and that during the whole of that time all weavers employed by the defendants have been treated alike in that respect. The practice was therefore firmly established at the defendants' mill when the plaintiff entered upon his employment there. Further, I think that it is clear that the plaintiff accepted employment in the defendants' mill on the same terms as the other weavers employed at that mill … Although I entirely agree with the learned judge in finding it difficult to believe that the plaintiff did not know of the existence of the practice at the mill, I think that it is immaterial whether he knew of it or not, as I am satisfied that he accepted his employment on the same terms as to deductions for bad work as the other weavers at the mill.

In the result, I have come to the conclusion that the practice of making reasonable deductions for bad work prevailing at the defendants' mill was incorporated in the plaintiff's contract of service.

Further, I am of opinion that the second ground is also established by the evidence – namely, that the practice in the defendants' mill is in accordance with the general usage of making reasonable deductions for bad work prevailing in the weaving trade of Lancashire, which usage, in the absence of any stipulation to the contrary, would be incorporated into every contract of service as a weaver in a Lancashire cotton mill without special mention. This usage seems to me to receive recognition in the Joint Rules for the Settlement of Trade Disputes appended to the Uniform List of Prices (to which Rules both the plaintiff and the defendants were subject: see p 3 of the plaintiff's particulars delivered on May 8, 1929) inasmuch as r. 4 expressly provides that in the case of an underpayment by the employer of the Uniform List of Prices where the employer either admits the underpayment or refuses to consent to an inspection of the work, the workman is to be at liberty to take whatever action he thinks fit without the necessity of bringing the matter before either the Local or Central Employers Committee …

Farwell J [the judge at first instance] has held that the usage is not a good usage, because it is neither universal nor reasonable nor certain, and accordingly does not comply with the tests laid down in *Devonald* v *Rosser & Sons*. If I am right in thinking that the plaintiff's contract of service incorporated the established practice at the defendants' mill, the question whether the general usage in the trade is good or bad does not arise, but as I may be wrong on this point, and as the question has been fully argued and dealt with by the learned judge in his judgment, I think it right that I should shortly express my views upon it. In the first place, it is to be noticed that in *Hart* v *Riversdale Mill Co* the justices found that "deductions for bad work are, and have been for many years, the usage and custom in the cotton weaving trade of Lancashire, and have always been, and are, an incident of a weaver's contract of service, and have always been, and are, taken into account in calculating the correct wages". The Court of Appeal decided that this usage was not illegal under the Truck Acts and gave effect to it. This decision is binding both on Courts of first instance and on this Court, and in my opinion covers the present case....

In the next place, I am of opinion that the usage is not, as held by the learned judge, unreasonable. The deductions are not arbitrary deductions at the will and pleasure of the employers; they are limited to cases where there has been bad work, and they are limited to an amount which does not exceed the actual or estimated damage or loss occasioned to the employer by the act or omission of the workman. The workman is free to prove that his work was good and that no deduction ought to be made, or to prove that any particular deduction exceeds the amount of the actual or estimated damage or loss to the employer ... The ground upon which the learned judge held that the usage was bad for uncertainty is because the amount of the deductions for bad work is left to the discretion of the employers, and because the maximum amount of such deductions is the actual loss occasioned to the employers, which could not in most cases be ascertained until after the payment of the wages. In the first place, I think it is clear that the maximum amount of the deduction is not only the actual but also the estimated loss occasioned to the employer, and that the workman is free to dispute the accuracy of such actual or estimated loss. In the next place, a trade usage allowing an employer to make deductions for bad work at his discretion not exceeding a certain defined limit does not, in my opinion, render the usage uncertain. It would be altogether unreasonable if the usage were to make certain definite deductions in every case. There are degrees of negligence, and it is reasonable that employers should not exact the full amount of the loss occasioned to them in every case. From a business point of view there is no uncertainty about such a usage. A Lancashire weaver knows, and has for very many years past known, precisely what his position was as regards deductions for bad work on accepting employment in a Lancashire mill. There would be no uncertainty in his mind on this point as to the effect of his engagement.'

COMMENT

(1) Note the three criteria used by the court for deciding whether or not a customary term should be recognised.

(2) A customary practice must start somewhere, either with the employer or the employees. If it is the employer, note the qualification suggested by the EAT in *Duke* v *Reliance Systems*:

'A policy adopted by management unilaterally cannot become a term of the employees' contracts on the grounds that it is an established custom and practice unless it is at least shown that the policy has been drawn to the attention of the employees or has been followed without exception for a substantial period.'

(3) Today the requirement to provide employees with a written statement of their

main terms and conditions means that it must be fairly unlikely that a customary term will be invoked. In the next case, employees who tried to rely on a customary term in fact had a different axe to grind.

Cresswell v *Board of Inland Revenue*

[1984] 2 All ER 713 Chancery Division

The Board of Inland Revenue wanted to computerise all its PAYE operations. The plaintiff employees and their union feared that the new technology would lead to job losses. Having failed to get assurances from the Board that there would be no compulsory redundancies as a result of the computerisation, they refused to co-operate with it, claiming *inter alia* that it was a term of the contract that they could not be required to carry out tasks except in the manner that they had habitually been carried out by custom and practice.

Walton J: ' ... I now turn straight away to a consideration of the main point on which counsel for the plaintiffs relied. He put his case in this way, that although it is undoubtedly correct that an employer may, within limits, change the manner in which his employees perform the work which they are employed to do, there may be such a change in the method of performing the task which the employee was recruited to perform proposed by the employer as to amount to a change in the nature of the job. This would mean that the employee was being asked to perform work under a wholly different contract and this cannot be done without his consent ...

It is a very fine line from counsel's submissions to the submission that employees have a vested right to preserve their working obligations completely unchanged as from the moment when they first begin work. This cannot surely, by any stretch of the imagination, be correct. That it is not so is very clearly shown by *O'Neill* v *Merseyside Plumbing Co Ltd*. In that case the employee had entered the services of his employers in 1947 and remained (apart from absence for national service) in their employment until 1972. Throughout all that time he worked as a gas fitter, i.e. for something approaching a quarter of a century. Then his employers directed him to work at a hospital site as a general plumber and he refused on the ground that he was incompetent to perform the plumbing work required. He submitted that the purported transfer to work of a different kind from that to which he was accustomed made him redundant. He claimed redundancy and the hearing in the National Industrial Relations Court was on an appeal by him from an industrial tribunal. The court held that the crucial question to be asked was whether he was employed as a plumber or as a specialist gas fitter; in other words, what were his terms of employment? What was it that he was employed to do? For if he was employed as a general plumber then, although he had always previously worked as a gas fitter, "the employers were plainly entitled to require him to do other forms of plumbing work, and the cause of his dismissal was quite simply that he refused to do that which he was required to do under his contract of employment"...

Granted that down to the present the work of each of these three grades has been done manually, with pen, paper and pocket calculator, if the employer changes this so as largely to remove the necessity to use pen and paper but requires the person concerned to use a computer instead or, in some cases, in addition, is the nature of the job thereby fundamentally changed? I do not think that the drawing of parallels with other situations really assists because, at the end of the day, it is the precise impact which is made by the computerisation programme on the day-to-day work of these three grades which is in question. However there is, I think, one important point. When dealing with other examples counsel for the plaintiffs made the point that the requirements of the employer might be such that the employee was genuinely unable to comply therewith. He instanced, for example, a typist engaged on audio typing who might be unable, with the best will in the world, to readapt to a word processor. What then?

That kind of case can be left to be dealt with when it arises, although *O'Neill's* case would certainly not suggest that if the employee had been originally engaged as a typist simpliciter there would really be much doubt about the matter.

But there can really be no doubt as to the fact that an employee is expected to adapt himself to new methods and techniques introduced in the course of his employment (cf *North Riding Garages Ltd* v *Butterwick*). Of course, in a proper case the employer must provide any necessary training or retraining. I think the probable answer to counsel's point is simply that it will, in all cases, be a question of pure fact whether the retraining involved the acquisition of such esoteric skills that it would not be reasonable to expect the employee to acquire them. In an age when the computer has forced its way into the schoolroom and where electronic games are played by schoolchildren in their own homes as a matter of everyday occurrence, it can hardly be considered that to ask an employee to acquire basic skills as to retrieving information from a computer or feeding such information into a computer is something in the slightest esoteric or, even nowadays, unusual.

In any event in the present case one remarkable feature, comparable to that of the dog which did not bark in the night, is that from first to last in all the voluminous evidence put in by the plaintiffs, there is no suggestion whatsoever that the plaintiffs themselves, or anybody else in any similar category in all the 14 districts covered by the present scheme, found any real difficulty in accepting the necessary instruction in the use of COP I and putting it into practice as they had been doing for some little time at the end of last year.

Whatever the change in working methods may be, it is one which, of course with proper instruction (which I think the employer must be under a duty to provide and which has, of course, been provided in the present case), the three grades concerned have, one and all, taken in their stride.'

COMMENT

(1)   Usually changes in working methods will be introduced by agreement with the workforce, their agreement being secured by offering some consideration for it, like higher wages. This case arose through a failure to agree in the collective bargaining process.

(2)   How extensive should the duty of adaptability be? Should it make a difference if the employee *cannot* adapt rather than *will not* adapt? See Napier, 'Computerisation and Employment Rights'(1992) 21 ILJ 1 for a discussion of some of these issues.

TERMS IMPLIED AT COMMON LAW

The common law, meaning the law created by judges, is an important source of employment obligations. Courts have decided that certain kinds of terms are to be regarded as part of every contract of employment as a necessary incident of the relationship of employer and employee. Implied terms can be overridden by express agreement to the contrary, but these terms frequently apply where there is no express agreement between the parties. They are traditionally expressed in terms of duties of employer and employee.

The advantage of common law terms is their flexibility: judges can adapt the law to take account of changing circumstances. The disadvantage, however, is that the law may be uncertain as a result. Employees may further feel that judges are more likely to exercise their creativity in favour of employers rather than workers – a point worth bearing in mind in considering the extracts which follow. The traditional tests for implying terms is whether it is necessary in order to give business efficacy to the contract (*The Moorcock*) or that it is so obvious that it goes without saying (*Southern Foundries* v *Shirlaw*): do the implied terms discussed below all pass that test?

Duty to provide work?

Probably the most fundamental duty of the employer is the duty to pay wages. The aspect of that duty considered here is whether it is enough if the employer pays wages or must she also provide work for the employee to perform?

Turner v *Sawdon*

[1901] 2 KB 653 Court of Appeal

The plaintiff was taken on as a sales representative by the defendants for a period of four years on a fixed annual salary. After two years the defendants withdrew his authority to act, although they were willing to continue paying his salary. He sued for breach of contract.

A L Smith MR: ' ... The action is by a man who was in the employment of the defendants, and it was not brought for wages, because it is clear that the defendants were always ready and willing to pay all that was due under the contract. The real question which the plaintiff thought to raise, and which was raised, was whether beyond the question of remuneration there was a further obligation on the masters that, during the period over which the contract was to extend, they should find continuous, or at least some, employment for the plaintiff. In my opinion such an action is unique – that is an action in which it is shewn that the master is willing to pay the wages of his servant, but is sued for damages because the servant is not given employment. In *Turner* v *Goldsmith* the wages were to be paid in the form of commission, and that impliedly created a contract to find employment for the servant. This contract is different, being to employ for wages which are to be paid at a certain rate per year. I do not think this can be read otherwise than as a contract by the master to retain the servant, and during the time covered by the retainer to pay him wages under such a contract. It is within the province of the master to say that he will go on paying the wages, but that he is under no obligation to provide work. The obligation suggested is said to arise out of the undertaking to engage and employ the plaintiff as their representative salesman. It is said that if the salesman is not given employment which allows him to go on the market his hand is not kept in practice, and he will not be so efficient a salesman at the end of the term. To read in an obligation of that sort would be to convert the retainer at fixed wages into a contract to keep the servant in the service of his employer in such a manner as to enable the former to become *au fait* at his work. In my opinion, no such obligation arose under this contract, and it is a mistake to stretch the words of the contract so as to include in what is a mere retainer an obligation to employ the plaintiff continuously for the term of his service.'

Devonald v *Rosser*

[1906] 2 KB 728 Court of Appeal

The plaintiff worked as a rollerman in the defendants' tinplate works. He was paid by piece work: that is, he had no fixed salary but was paid according to the amount of work he produced. His contract stipulated that either party had to give a month's notice to terminate.

Because of a downturn in trade, the defendants closed the works and then gave him a month's notice. He claimed damages for breach of an implied agreement to give him work to do during this six-week period. The defendants claimed that as he was a piece worker, if he did no work he was not entitled to any pay; they denied the existence of the implied agreement.

Lord Alverstone CJ: 'In this case I am of opinion that Jelf J came to a perfectly right conclusion, but I wish to add a few observations of my own in confirmation of his view. I entirely agree with Mr Bailhache that the implication which is to be drawn from this contract is one which, to use the language of Bowen LJ in *The Moorcock*, is raised "from the presumed intention of the parties with the object of giving to the transaction such efficacy as both parties must have intended that at all events it should have", that "what the law desires to effect by the implication is to give such business efficacy to the transaction as must have been intended at all events by both parties who are business men". I am content to accept that test in deciding whether or not this contract involves the implication which is necessary to enable the plaintiff to recover. Now, in order to determine that question, the only facts that are material to be considered are that the plaintiff was in the defendants' regular employment, that he was paid by piece work, and that he was employed upon the terms of a rule which provides that "No person regularly employed shall quit or be discharged from these works without giving or receiving twenty-eight days' notice in writing, such notice to be given on the first Monday of any calendar month." I put out of consideration rule 11, as to the workmen being employed on other than their own special work in case of emergency, as it is not necessary to rely upon it, but in my opinion there is nothing in it which contradicts the implication which, to my mind, is involved in the language of the former rule. No distinction in principle can be drawn between wages by time and wages by piece. Piece work is only a method of ascertaining the amount of the wages which is to be paid to the workman. What, then, is the obligation of the employers under such a contract as the present? On the one hand we must consider the matter from the point of view of the employers who I agree will under ordinary circumstances desire to carry on their works at a profit, though not necessarily at a profit in every week, for it is matter of common knowledge that masters have frequently to run their mills for weeks and months together at a loss in order to keep their business together and in hopes of better times. On the other hand, we have to consider the position of the workman. The workman has to live; and the effect of the defendants' contention is that if the master at any time found that his works were being carried on at a loss, he might at once close down his works and cease to employ his men, who, even if they gave notice to quit the employment, would be bound to the master for a period of at least twenty-eight days during which time they would be unable to earn any wages at all. I agree with Jelf J that that is an unreasonable contention from the workman's point of view. In my opinion the necessary implication to be drawn from this contract is at least that the master will find a reasonable amount of work up to the expiration of a notice given in accordance with the contract. I am not prepared to say that that obligation is an absolute one to find work at all events, for the evidence shewed that it was subject to certain contingencies, such as breakdown of machinery and want of water and materials. But I am clearly of opinion that it would be no excuse to the master, for non-performance of his implied obligation to provide the workman with work, that he could no longer make his plates at a profit either for orders or for stock. It is to be observed that the question how the works are to be carried on, whether they are going to work short or full time, or whether for stock or current orders, is a matter which rests entirely in the hands of the master. The men have absolutely nothing to say to it.'

Collier v *Sunday Referee Publishing Co*

[1940] 2 KB 647 King's Bench Division

The plaintiff was engaged for two years as chief sub-editor of the *Sunday Referee*. When his contract still had more than a year to run the publication was sold to new owners, who ceased to publish it. They continued to pay him, as long as he came to the office at certain times, in case they wanted him to do anything. He stopped doing this, they stopped paying and he sued for breach of contract.

Asquith J: 'The plaintiff argues that by ceasing to publish the *Sunday Referee* the defendants disabled themselves from performing further their contractual obligation, which was to employ him as chief sub-editor of that newspaper. The defendants contend that they were not bound to provide the plaintiff with work, but merely to continue to pay his salary, retaining the right to call on him to do work for them; that they did continue to pay his salary until November, 1939, but that at that time the plaintiff finally repudiated his alleged obligation to work for them when required so to do; and that the contract of service, alive until then, was terminated by such repudiation, and with it went any obligation on their part to pay further salary.

It is true that a contract of employment does not necessarily, or perhaps normally, oblige the master to provide the servant with work. Provided I pay my cook her wages regularly she cannot complain if I choose to take any or all of my meals out. In some exceptional cases there is an obligation to provide work. For instance, where the servant is remunerated by commission, or where (as in the case of an actor or singer) the servant bargains, among other things, for publicity, and the master, by withholding work, also withholds the stipulated publicity: see, for instance, *Marbe* v *George Edwardes (Daly's Theatre) Ltd*; but such cases are anomalous, and the normal rule is illustrated by authorities such as *Lagerwall* v *Wilkinson, Henderson & Clarke Ltd*, and *Turner* v *Sawdon & Co*, where the plaintiffs (a commercial traveller and a salesman respectively, retained for a fixed period and remunerated by salary) were held to have no legal complaint so long as the salary continued to be paid, notwithstanding that owing to their employers' action they were left with nothing to do. The employers were not bound to supply work to enable the employee, as the phrase goes, to "keep his hand in", or to avoid the reproach of idleness, or even to make a profit out of a travelling allowance. In such a case there is no breach of contract, but the result is much the same as if there had been, because in either event the plaintiff is entitled to a sum or sums which are measured *prima facie* by the amount of salary in respect of the unexpired period of service.

I do not hold that in the present case there was in the contract of employment an implied stipulation for publicity and an obligation to provide work for the purpose of providing publicity.'

(The plaintiff's claim was ultimately upheld on the different ground that he was an office-holder, and by destroying the office the defendants were in breach of contract.)

COMMENT

(1) The extracts above explain the traditional view on whether there is a duty to provide work. However, the story would not be complete without reference to the one-judge campaign of Lord Denning to create a general right to work – usually in order to supply what in his eyes was some deficiency in existing rules. The apotheosis of this approach is his judgment in *Langston* v *AUEW*.

Langston v *AUEW*

[1974] ICR 180 Court of Appeal

The plaintiff, who was employed by Chrysler UK, refused to belong to the defendant trade union, as was his right under the legislation at that time. Rather than risk a confrontation with the union if they let him work or attract heavy penalties if they dismissed him, Chrysler UK paid him his wages, but instructed him to stay away from the workplace. He sued the union for inducing a breach of his contract of employment. The case came to the Court of Appeal on the preliminary point of whether the employers were in fact in breach of contract by paying his wages but not allowing him to work.

Lord Denning MR: '... In the second place, Mr Harvey suggested that there was no evidence of breach of contract. This was based on the fact that Chryslers had not dismissed Mr Langston. They had only suspended him from work. And they had paid him full wages. So it was said there was no breach of contract. In this regard we were referred to *Collier* v *Sunday Referee Publishing Co Ltd*, where Asquith J said:

> "It is true that a contract of employment does not necessarily, or perhaps normally, oblige the master to provide the servant with work. Provided I pay my cook her wages regularly, she cannot complain if I choose to take any or all of my meals out."

Asquith J went on to refer to two cases where a commercial traveller and a salesman:

> "were held to have no legal complaint so long as the salary continued to be paid, notwithstanding that owing to their employer's action they were left with nothing to do. The employers were not bound to supply work to enable their employee, as the phrase goes, to 'keep his hand in', or to avoid the reproach of idleness, or even to make a profit out of a travelling allowance."

That was said 33 years ago. Things have altered much since then. We have repeatedly said in this court that a man has a right to work, which the courts will protect: see *Nagle* v *Feilden* and *Hill* v *CA Parsons & Co Ltd*. I would not wish to express any decided view, but simply state the argument which could be put forward for Mr Langston. In these days an employer, when employing a skilled man, is bound to provide him with work. By which I mean that the man should be given the opportunity of doing his work when it is available and he is ready and willing to do it. A skilled man takes a pride in his work. He does not do it merely to earn money. He does it so as to make his contribution to the well-being of all. He does it so as to keep himself busy, and not idle. To use his skill, and to improve it. To have the satisfaction which comes of a task well done. Such as Longfellow attributed to *The Village Blacksmith*:

> "Something attempted, something done,
> Has earned a night's repose."

The *Code of Practice* [1972, repealed 1991] contains the same thought. It says, at paragraph 9:

> "... management should recognise the employee's need to achieve a sense of satisfaction in his job and should provide for it so far as practicable."

A parallel can be drawn in regard to women's work. Many a married woman seeks work. She does so when the children grow up and leave the home. She does it, not solely to earn money, helpful as it is: but to fill her time with useful occupation, rather than sit idly at home waiting for her husband to return. The devil tempts those who have nothing to do.

To my mind, therefore, it is arguable that in these days a man has, by reason of an implication in the contract, a right to work. That is, he has a right to have the opportunity of doing his work when it is there to be done. If this be correct, then if any person knowingly induces the employer to turn the man away – and thus deprive him of the opportunity of doing his work – then that person induces the employer to break his contract. It is none the less a breach, even though the employer pays the man his full wages. So also when fellow workers threaten to walk out unless a man is turned off the job, they threaten to induce a breach of contract. At any rate, the man who is suspended has a case for saying that they have induced or threatened to induce the employer to break the contract of employment.'

COMMENT

(1)   This is not a masterpiece of legal reasoning. Lord Denning omits to indicate that he gave the principal judgment in the two cases cited, so to use them as authority is rather to pull himself up by his bootstraps. In any case, there is no reference to a right to work in *Hill* v *Parsons*, where Lord Denning, discussing the situation of an employee whose contract was kept alive during a notice period, actually said, 'If the company did not want him to come to work, the court would not order the company to give him work.'

(2)   Following the Court of Appeal's decision on the preliminary point, the case returned to the National Industrial Relations Court for a decision on the substance. The NIRC decided that Langston was really a piece worker and therefore entitled to be given work within the principle of *Devonald* v *Rosser*.

(3)   Thus in general, it would seem that there is no right to work, except in the two exceptional cases mentioned by Asquith J in *Collier* v *Sunday Referee*. However, although in that case Asquith J denied any duty to provide work in order that the employee should be able 'to keep his hand in', it may be that a third exception along these lines is being recognised.

Provident Financial Group plc v Hayward

[1989] ICR 160 Court of Appeal

The defendant was employed as financial director of the plaintiff company under a contract which required him to give six months' notice to terminate. He gave notice which was due to expire in December. However, having stopped working for the company in September, he proposed to start work for another employer as financial controller before the notice period expired. The plaintiff company, which was continuing to pay his salary during the notice period, sought an injunction to prevent him going to the new employer.

Dillon LJ: ' ... the case has a wider importance because these clauses are imposed on many senior executives and it may be that such executives are hardly in a position to negotiate over the terms of their contracts of service. We have heard full argument on both sides about the validity of the clause and the considerations that the court ought to have in mind when enforcement of the clause is in question. The practice of long periods of "garden leave" is obviously capable of abuse. It is a weapon in the hands of the employers to ensure that an ambitious and able executive will not give notice if he is going to be unable to work at all for anyone for a long period of notice. Any executive who gives notice and leaves his employment is very likely to take fresh employment with someone in the same line of business not through any desire to act unfairly or to cheat the former employer but to get the best advantage of his own personal expertise ...

The wide clause prohibiting working for anyone else would, as it seems to me, not be enforced by the courts even though the employee was offered full pay if it appeared that the other business for which the employee wished to work before the expiration of his notice had nothing whatever to do with the business of the employers. Extreme examples are easy to think of. In an extreme case it would be most unlikely that the employer would go to the court seeking to enforce the covenant. The employer would be happy to save the expense of paying the employee if the employee was going off to other employment which even the employer recognised could not conceivably affect the employer. But it is very common for employers to have somewhat exaggerated views of what will or may affect their businesses and, if the employer were to come to the court seeking to enforce the covenant, the court would be fully entitled in my view to say, if it took that view of the facts, that the proposed other employment is in truth objectively considered and despite the fears of the employer, nothing whatever to do with the employer and, therefore, it is not appropriate as a matter of discretion to grant an injunction. It is not enough just that the employee has contracted in certain terms and will not starve if the terms are enforced against him while the employer continues to pay him in full. The employee has a concern to work and a concern to exercise his skills. That has been recognised in some circumstances concerned with artists and singers who depend on publicity, but it applies equally, I apprehend, to skilled workmen and even to chartered accountants.'

Duty to maintain mutual trust and confidence

Recognition of such a duty has occurred comparatively recently. The extracts which follow chart its development.

Robinson v Crompton Parkinson

[1978] ICR 401 Employment Appeal Tribunal

The employee, an electrician of many years' standing, was 'wrongly, unfairly and improperly' accused of theft from his employer. After he was acquitted in a criminal trial he sought an apology from his employer. When it was not forthcoming he left and claimed unfair dismissal.

Kilner Brown J: ' ... It seems to us, although there is no direct authority to which we have been referred, that the law is perfectly plain and needs to be re-stated so that there shall be no opportunity for confusion in the future. In a contract of employment, and in conditions of employment, there has to be mutual trust and confidence between master and servant. Although most of the reported cases deal with the master seeking remedy against a servant or former servant for acting in breach of confidence or in breach of trust, that action can only be upon the basis that trust and confidence is mutual. Consequently where a man says of his employer, "I claim that you have broken your contract because you have clearly shown you have no confidence in me, and you have behaved in a way which is contrary to that mutual trust which ought to exist between master and servant", he is entitled in those circumstances, it seems to us, to say that there is conduct which amounts to a repudiation of the contract....'

(The case was remitted to the industrial tribunal for a rehearing.)

Post Office v *Roberts*

[1980] IRLR 347 Employment Appeal Tribunal

A senior official wrote a bad report on the employee, judging her to be unfit for promotion. This was written without proper consideration of the employee's record. It led to her being refused a transfer to another branch, although the true reason for this refusal was not made known to her until some time later. She left and an industrial tribunal found that she had been unfairly dismissed.

Talbot J: ' ... The final point of complaint made by Mr Carr is that the Industrial Tribunal's finding of a breach of the obligation of mutual trust and confidence is erroneous, in that the conduct relied upon was incapable in law of amounting to a repudiation. In this respect the main burden of his submission was that, for the obligation of mutual trust and confidence to be destroyed, there must be deliberate conduct or bad faith in the appraisal reports. Though there was a finding that Mr O'Keefe had failed to discharge his responsibilities it was not deliberate and it was not in bad faith. To support this submission Mr Carr cited a number of authorities: the first was *Isle of Wight Tourist Board* v *Coombes*. In that case the respondent had been a personal secretary to the appellant's director and in the course of an argument that director had spoken to another employee about her, saying that she was an "intolerable bitch on a Monday morning". The Employment Appeal Tribunal held that the relationship between the director and his personal secretary must be one of complete confidence and they must trust and respect each other, that in calling his secretary a "bitch" the employer's director had shattered that relationship. Thus, they confirmed the Industrial Tribunal's decision that there had been a constructive dismissal.

We do not find in that decision any hint of the need for the conduct to be deliberate and intentional or prompted by bad faith.

The next case was *Courtaulds Northern Textiles Ltd* v *Andrew*. Again this was a case where words had been spoken in an argument. The words spoken by the assistant manager of the respondent were "You can't do the bloody job anyway". Again the Employment Appeal Tribunal, in this case Arnold J presiding, referred to the implied term of the contract of employment that "the employers will not without proper reason and cause conduct themselves in a manner calculated or likely to destroy or seriously damage the relationship of confidence and trust between the parties". That part of the headnote is borne out in the judgment which appears at paragraph 10. We will read the latter part of that dictum, where Arnold J said:

"We think that, thus phrased, the implied term (as regards 'calculated') extends only to an obligation not to conduct themselves in such a manner as is intended, although not intended by itself, to destroy or seriously damage the relationship in question ..."

The next authority was *F C Gardner Ltd* v *Beresford*. In substance, the complaint in that appeal was that there had been no increase in pay for two years. Phillips J, giving the judgment of the Employment Appeal Tribunal, referred to the obligation on an employer not to behave arbitrarily, capriciously, or inequitably in matters of remuneration. Certainly, we can see no complaint about that; that is absolutely right. But that is not this case. In the headnote (and this is borne out by the judgment) it is stated:

"On the other hand, if there was evidence to support a finding that the employers were deliberately singling the respondent out for special treatment inferior to that given to everybody else and that they were doing it arbitrarily, capriciously and inequitably, that might well lead the Industrial Tribunal to say that she had a good claim even under the new test for constructive dismissal."

Again we fail to see why that plain and sensible dictum applied to the question of remuneration states a general principle that applies to cases of the kind with which we are dealing.

Then there was the authority of *Robinson* v *Crompton Parkinson Ltd.* In that appeal Kilner Brown J referred to this obligation of mutual trust and confidence. He said, in his judgment:

> "It seems to us, although there is no direct authority to which we have been referred, that the law is perfectly plain and needs to be re-stated so that there shall be no opportunity for confusion in the future. In a contract of employment, and in conditions of employment, there has to be mutual trust and confidence between master and servant. Although most of the reported cases deal with the master seeking remedy against a servant or former servant for acting in breach of confidence or in breach of trust, that action can only be upon the basis that trust and confidence is mutual. Consequently where a man says of his employer, 'I claim that you have broken your contract because you have clearly shown you have no confidence in me, and you have behaved in a way which is contrary to that mutual trust which ought to exist between master and servant', he is entitled in those circumstances, it seems to us, to say that there is conduct which amounts to a repudiation of the contract."

In stating that principle, in our view Kilner Brown J does not set out any requirement that there should be deliberation, or intent, or bad faith.

Finally, there are very important words in a part of the judgment in *Palmanor Ltd* v *Cedron*, the words appearing in the judgment of Slynn J. It is a short quotation and reads as follows:

> "It seems to us that in a case of this kind the Tribunal is required to ask itself the question whether the conduct was so unreasonable that it really went beyond the limits of the contract. We observed that in the course of the argument on behalf of the employee, it was submitted that the treatment that he was accorded was a repudiation of the contract ..."

(The employer's appeal was dismissed.)

Woods v WM Car Services

[1981] ICR 666 Employment Appeal Tribunal

The applicant was employed as chief secretary and accounts clerk. Following a take-over of the business, the new employers first put pressure on her to take a drop in salary, then to work longer hours, both of which she refused. Then they dropped the word 'chief' from her title and gave her additional duties. She left and claimed unfair dismissal.

Browne-Wilkinson J: '...In our view it is clearly established that there is implied in a contract of employment a term that the employers will not, without reasonable and proper cause, conduct themselves in a manner calculated or likely to destroy or seriously damage the relationship of confidence and trust between employer and employee: *Courtaulds Northern Textiles Ltd* v *Andrew*. To constitute a breach of this implied term it is not necessary to show that the employer intended any repudiation of the contract: the tribunal's function is to look at the employer's conduct as a whole and determine whether it is such that its effect, judged reasonably and sensibly, is such that the employee cannot be expected to put up with it: see *British Aircraft Corporation Ltd* v *Austin* and *Post Office* v *Roberts* ...

The conduct of the parties has to be looked at as a whole and its cumulative impact assessed: *Post Office* v *Roberts*.

We regard this implied term as one of great importance in good industrial relations ... '

(The EAT upheld the decision of the industrial tribunal that on the facts there was no fundamental breach of contract in this case. The Court of Appeal dismissed the employee's appeal.)

Lewis v Motorworld Garages Ltd

[1986] ICR 157 Court of Appeal

In November 1981 the employee was demoted without warning, lost his office and had his pay structure altered detrimentally. This was a fundamental breach of contract by the employer, but the employee elected to affirm the contract by continuing to work. Over the next months the employee was persistently and unfairly criticised and threatened with dismissal. The employer purported to give him a final warning in August 1982; this was the last straw and the employee left and claimed unfair dismissal.

Glidewell LJ: 'The principles to be found in the relevant authorities can, I believe, be summarised as follows.

(1)   In order to prove that he has suffered constructive dismissal, an employee who leaves his employment must prove that he did so as the result of a breach of contract by his employer, which shows that the employer no longer intends to be bound by an essential term of the contract: see *Western Excavating (ECC) Ltd* v *Sharp*.

(2)   However, there are normally implied in a contract of employment mutual rights and obligations of trust and confidence. A breach of this implied term may justify the employee in leaving and claiming he has been constructively dismissed: see *Post Office* v *Roberts* and *Woods* v *WM Car Services (Peterborough) Ltd per* Browne-Wilkinson J.

(3)   The breach of this implied obligation of trust and confidence may consist of a series of actions on the part of the employer which cumulatively amount to a breach of the term, though each individual incident may not do so. In particular in such a case the last action of the employer which leads to the employee leaving need not itself be a breach of contract; the question is, does the cumulative series of acts taken together amount to a breach of the implied term? (See *Woods* v *WM Car Services (Peterborough) Ltd*.) This is the "last straw" situation.

(4)   The decision whether there has been a breach of contract by the employer so as to constitute constructive dismissal of the employee is one of mixed law and fact for the industrial tribunal. An appellate court, whether the Employment Appeal Tribunal or the Court of Appeal, may only overrule that decision if the industrial tribunal have misdirected themselves as to the relevant law or have made a finding of fact for which there is no supporting evidence or which no reasonable tribunal could make: see *Pedersen* v *Camden London Borough Council (Note)* and *Woods* v *WM Car Services (Peterborough) Ltd* both in the Court of Appeal, applying the test laid down in *Edwards* v *Bairstow*.

This case raises another issue of principle which, so far as I can ascertain, has not yet been considered by this court. If the employer is in breach of an express term of a contract of employment, of such seriousness that the employee would be justified in leaving and claiming constructive dismissal, but the employee does not leave and accepts the altered terms of employment: and if subsequently a series of actions by the employer might constitute together a breach of the implied obligation of trust and confidence: is the employee then entitled to treat the original action by the employer which was a breach of the express terms of the contract as a part – the start – of the series of actions which, taken together with the employer's other actions, might cumulatively amount to a breach of the implied terms? In my judgment the answer to this question is clearly "yes".'

(The case was remitted to a different industrial tribunal for a rehearing.)

COMMENT

(1)   It is now well established that there is an implied term applying to both parties that they should not do anything which would be destructive of the mutual trust and confidence which is necessary for the continuance of the contract. There is no end to the possible actions which could be attacked on this ground, as the variety of the situations in the extracts indicates.

(2)   It is noticeable that all these cases arose because the employees left and claimed that they had been unfairly dismissed. Until recently, this was true of almost all the cases where this implied term had been invoked. However, in a landmark decision, the House of Lords held that its breach could alternatively give rise to a remedy in damages.

Malik v Bank of Credit and Commerce International

[1997] IRLR 462 House of Lords

Lord Nicholls: 'My Lords,
   This is another case arising from the disastrous collapse of Bank of Credit and Commerce International SA in the summer of 1991. Thousands of people around the world suffered loss. Depositors lost their money, employees lost their jobs. Two employees who lost their jobs were Mr Raihan Nasir Mahmud and Mr Qaiser Mansoor Malik. They were employed by BCCI in London. They claim they lost more than their jobs. They claim that their association with BCCI placed them at a serious disadvantage in finding new jobs. So in March 1992 they sought to prove for damages in the winding up of BCCI. The liquidators rejected this 'stigma' head of loss in their proofs. Liability for notice money and statutory redundancy pay was not in dispute.
   Mr Mahmud had worked for the bank for 16 years. At the time of his dismissal he was manager of the bank's Brompton Road branch. Mr Malik was employed by the bank for 12 years. His last post was as the head of deposit accounts and customer services at BCCI's Leadenhall branch. On 3 October 1991 they were both dismissed by the provisional liquidators, on the ground of redundancy.
   Mr Mahmud and Mr Malik appealed to the court against the liquidators' decision on their proofs. The registrar directed the trial of a preliminary issue: whether the applicants' evidence disclosed a reasonable cause of action or sustainable claim for damages. The Judge, Evans-Lombe J, gave a negative answer to this question. So did the Court of Appeal, comprising Glidewell, Morritt and Aldous LJJ.
   Before this House, as in the courts below, the issue is being decided on the basis of an agreed set of facts. The liquidators do not admit the accuracy of these facts, but for the purpose of this preliminary issue it is being assumed that the bank operated in a corrupt and dishonest manner, that Mr Mahmud and Mr Malik were innocent of any involvement, that following the collapse of BCCI its corruption and dishonesty became widely known, that in

consequence Mr Mahmud and Mr Malik were at a handicap on the labour market because they were stigmatised by reason of their previous employment by BCCI, and that they suffered loss in consequence.

In the Court of Appeal and in your Lordships' House the parties were agreed that the contracts of employment of these two former employees each contained an implied term to the effect that the bank would not, without reasonable and proper cause, conduct itself in a manner likely to destroy or seriously damage the relationship of confidence and trust between employer and employee. Argument proceeded on this footing, and ranged round the type of conduct and other circumstances which could or could not constitute a breach of this implied term. The submissions embraced questions such as the following: whether the trust-destroying conduct must be directed at the employee, either individually or as part of a group; whether an employee must know of the employer's trust-destroying conduct while still employed; and whether the employee's trust must actually be undermined. Furthermore, and at the heart of this case, the submissions raised an important question on the damages recoverable for breach of the implied term, with particular reference to the decisions in *Addis* v *Gramophone Co Ltd* and *Withers* v *General Theatre Corporation Ltd.*

A dishonest and corrupt business
These questions are best approached by focusing first on the particular conduct of which complaint is made. The bank operated its business dishonestly and corruptly. On the assumed facts, this was not a case where one or two individuals, however senior, were behaving dishonestly. Matters had gone beyond this. They had reached the point where the bank itself could properly be identified with the dishonesty. This was a dishonest business, a corrupt business.

It is against that background that the position of an innocent employee has to be considered. In my view, when an innocent employee of the bank learned the true nature of the bank's business, from whatever source, he was entitled to say: "I wish to have nothing more to do with this organisation. I am not prepared to help this business, by working for it. I am leaving at once." This is my intuitive response in the case of all innocent employees of the business, from the most senior to the most junior, from the most long serving to the most recently joined. No one could be expected to have to continue to work with and for such a company against his wish.

This intuitive response is no more than a reflection of what goes without saying in any ordinary contract of employment, namely, that in agreeing to work for an employer the employee, whatever his status, cannot be taken to have agreed to work in furtherance of a dishonest business. This is as much true of a doorkeeper or cleaner as a senior executive or branch manager.

An implied obligation
Two points can be noted here. First, as a matter of legal analysis, the innocent employee's entitlement to leave at once must derive from the bank being in breach of a term of the contract of employment which the employee is entitled to treat as a repudiation by the bank of its contractual obligations. That is the source of his right to step away from the contract forthwith.

In other words, and this is the necessary corollary of the employee's right to leave at once, the bank was under an implied obligation to its employees not to conduct a dishonest or corrupt business. This implied obligation is no more than one particular aspect of the portmanteau, general obligation not to engage in conduct likely to undermine the trust and confidence required if the employment relationship is to continue in the manner the employment contract implicitly envisages.

Second, I do not accept the liquidators' submission that the conduct of which complaint is made must be targeted in some way at the employee or a group of employees. No doubt that will often be the position, perhaps usually so. But there is no reason in principle why this must always be so. The trust and confidence required in the employment relationship can be undermined by an employer, or indeed an employee, in many different ways. I can see no justification for the law giving the employee a remedy if the unjustified trust-destroying conduct occurs in some ways but refusing a remedy if it occurs in others. The conduct must, of course, impinge on the relationship in the sense that, looked at objectively, it is likely to destroy or seriously damage the degree of trust and confidence the employee is reasonably entitled to have in his employer. That requires one to look at all the circumstances.

Breach
The objective standard just mentioned provides the answer to the liquidators' submission that unless the employee's confidence is actually undermined there is no breach. A breach occurs when the proscribed conduct takes place: here, operating a dishonest and corrupt business. Proof of a subjective loss of confidence in the employer is not an essential element of the breach, although the time when the employee learns of the misconduct and his response to it may affect his remedy. ...

Continuing financial losses
Exceptionally, however, the losses suffered by an employee as a result of a breach of the trust and confidence term may not consist of, or be confined to, loss of pay and other premature termination losses. Leaving aside injured feelings and anxiety, which are not the basis of the claim in the present case, an employee may find himself worse off financially than when he entered into the contract. The most obvious example is conduct, in breach of the trust and confidence term, which prejudicially affects an employee's future employment prospects. The conduct may diminish the employee's attractiveness to future employers.

The loss in the present case is of this character. BCCI promised, in an implied term, not to conduct a dishonest or corrupt business. The promised benefit was employment by an honest employer. This benefit did not materialise. Proof that Mr Mahmud and Mr Malik were handicapped in the labour market in consequence of BCCI's corruption may not be easy, but that is an assumed fact for the purpose of this preliminary issue.

There is here an important point of principle. Are financial losses of this character, which I shall call 'continuing financial losses', recoverable for breach of the trust and confidence term? This is the crucial point in the present appeals. In my view, if it was reasonably foreseeable that a particular type of loss of this character was a serious possibility, and loss of this type is sustained in consequence of a breach, then in principle damages in respect of the loss should be recoverable.

In the present case the agreed facts make no assumption, either way, about whether the appellants' handicap in the labour market was reasonably foreseeable by the bank. On this there must be scope for argument. I would not regard the absence of this necessary ingredient from the assumed facts as a sufficient reason for refusing to permit the former employees' claims to proceed further.

The contrary argument of principle is that since the purpose of the trust and confidence term is to preserve the employment relationship and to enable that relationship to prosper and continue, the losses recoverable for breach should be confined to those flowing from the premature termination of the relationship. Thus, a breach of the term should not be regarded as giving rise to recoverable losses beyond those I have described as premature termination losses. In this way, the measure of damages would be commensurate with, and not go beyond, the scope of the protection the trust and confidence term is intended to provide for the employee.

This is an unacceptably narrow evaluation of the trust and confidence term. Employers may be under no common law obligation, through the medium of an implied contractual term of general application, to take steps to improve their employees' future job prospects. But failure to improve is one thing, positively to damage is another. Employment, and job prospects, are matters of vital concern to most people. Jobs of all descriptions are less secure than formerly, people change jobs more frequently, and the job market is not always buoyant. Everyone knows this. An employment contract creates a close personal relationship, where there is often a disparity of power between the parties. Frequently the employee is vulnerable. Although the underlying purpose of the trust and confidence term is to protect the employment relationship, there can be nothing fairly onerous or unreasonable in requiring an employer who breaches the trust and confidence term to be liable if he thereby causes continuing financial loss of a nature that was reasonably foreseeable. Employers must take care not to damage their employees' future employment prospects, by harsh and oppressive behaviour or by any other form of conduct which is unacceptable today as falling below the standards set by the implied trust and confidence term. ...'

(Lord Steyn delivered a concurring opinion. Lord Goff, Mackay and Mustill agreed with both opinions.)

COMMENT

(1)   The most dramatic feature of the decision in this case is that it indicates a way of getting round the limitation on damages for wrongful dismissal set out by the House of Lords in *Addis* v *Gramophone Co*. This aspect of the case is considered below (p 268).

(2)   Lord Steyn noted that this was the first time that the implied duty to maintain mutual trust and confidence had been considered by the House of Lords. He commented:

'The evolution of the implied term of trust and confidence is a fact. It has not yet been endorsed by your Lordships' House. It has proved a workable principle in practice. It has not been the subject of adverse criticism in any decided cases and it has been welcomed in academic writings. I regard the emergence of the implied obligation of mutual trust and confidence as a sound development.'

(3)   Note in particular the discussion of the parameters of the implied term in Lord Nicholls's opinion, and the decisions reached.

Duty to obey lawful and reasonable orders

Laws v *London Chronicle*

[1959] 1 WLR 698 Court of Appeal

The plaintiff was employed on the advertising staff of the company. She attended a meeting where there was an argument between D, the advertising manager, and B, chairman and managing director of the company. D left the room, telling her to go with him. B told her to stay. She went, and was dismissed without notice as a result. Dismissal without notice is justifiable if the employee has committed a fundamental breach of contract.

Lord Evershed MR: 'It is the corner-stone of Mr Stable's case that there was in truth nothing that a self-respecting employer could do but to dismiss summarily: for here was an order given – "Stay where you are" – and disobeyed. Mr Stable has cited authority – of antiquity, but none the less of respectability – to show that disobedience (as he contends) of any order that is lawful entitles the employer to dismiss the servant summarily. In *Turner* v *Mason* a domestic servant – quite deliberately, because she had made a request which was rejected – absented herself during a certain night when she should have been on duty; and her plea of justification was that her mother was desperately ill – though it is not clear that she so informed her employer. She was dismissed; and the court of Queen's Bench affirmed the view that the dismissal was justified. I will not read the judgments of Parke CB and Barons Alderson and Rolfe: but it would in my judgment be going too far to say that any of those judges laid it down as a proposition of law that every act of disobedience of a lawful order must entitle the employer to dismiss. I think that cannot be extracted from the judgments; and I am satisfied that it is too narrow a proposition as one of law.

The law to be applied is stated (for example) in the paragraphs of Halsbury's Laws of England, 3rd ed., Vol. 25, at pp. 485 and 486, to which Mr Stable referred us in reply; and I will cite a sentence or two as a foundation to what follows. "Wilful disobedience to the lawful and reasonable order of the master justifies summary dismissal." Then, a little later, "Misconduct, inconsistent with the due and faithful discharge by the servant of the duties for which he was engaged, is good cause for his dismissal, but there is no fixed rule of law defining the degree of misconduct which will justify dismissal." Later, again, "There is good ground for the dismissal of a servant if he is habitually neglectful in respect of the duties for which he was engaged." And in one of the footnotes on that page there is a further statement, in reference to *Edwards* v *Levy*, observing that in that case "it was pointed out that a single instance of insolence in the case of a servant in such a position as that of a newspaper critic would hardly justify dismissal".

To my mind, the proper conclusion to be drawn from the passages I have cited and the cases to which we have been referred is that, since a contract of service is but an example of contracts in general, so that the general law of contract will be applicable, it follows that the question must be – if summary dismissal is claimed to be justifiable – whether the conduct complained of is such as to show the servant to have disregarded the essential conditions of the contract of service. It is, no doubt, therefore, generally true that wilful disobedience of an order will justify summary dismissal, since wilful disobedience of a lawful and reasonable order shows a disregard – a complete disregard – of a condition essential to the contract of service, namely, the condition that the servant must obey the proper orders of the master, and that unless he does so the relationship is, so to speak, struck at fundamentally....

On the facts, the court held that the special circumstances surrounding her single act of disobedience indicated that she had not shown an intention not to comply with the contract and had therefore not committed a fundamental breach of contract.

COMMENT

(1)   An order is not lawful and reasonable if it requires the employee to do something outside the terms of his contract. Many employment disputes arise because it is not clear whether compliance with an order from management is within the employee's contract or not, as the next case shows.

O'Brien v Associated Fire Alarms Ltd

[1968] 1 WLR 1916 Court of Appeal

This was a claim for redundancy payments: the redundancy aspects of the case are dealt with on p 336.

Salmon LJ: 'These three men all lived close to Liverpool, and they had each been employed for many years by the respondents. During the whole time they were so employed, they had worked in and around Liverpool. Each night they went home after the day's work was done. The time came when the work in and around Liverpool tended to diminish, but there was work that required to be done in Barrow. The men were ordered to go and do this work in Barrow. They refused. As a result of their conduct in refusing to go to Barrow, the employers dismissed them.

Now clearly if under the contract of employment the employers were entitled to order them to go to Barrow and they refused to go there, the employers would be entitled to dismiss them ...

The Industrial Tribunal, in the course of its very careful decision, came to the conclusion that it was an implied term of the contract of employment that these men could be ordered to work in any part of the area controlled from the respondents' Liverpool office. That area ran from Whitehaven in the north down to mid-Wales in the south. It was a very large area, and Barrow was undoubtedly within it. Barrow was about 150 miles from Liverpool and the jobs which the appellants were ordered to do there would have entailed their being away from home for about 13 weeks.

Whether a term should be implied into a contract is a question of law. Whether the implication should be made in law no doubt depends upon the facts. In my view there were no facts proved in evidence from which it was permissible for the tribunal to draw the inference in law that it was a term of the men's employment that they could be asked to work anywhere within what I have referred to as the area controlled from the respondents' Liverpool office ...

I would have thought that as the material circumstances in which these contracts of employment were entered into are shrouded in mystery, it is permissible, if one is seeking to reconstruct the contract, to look at what happened while the men were being employed. The fact is that never during all the years in which they worked for the respondents were they ever asked to work anywhere except in the conurbation of Liverpool or those parts of Cheshire which they could reach from their homes so that they returned to their homes every night. This, of course, would be by no means conclusive about the terms of their employment if there were any evidence the other way, but it is all there is as to where they could be required to work. This indicates (and there is nothing to the contrary) that what they were doing during the year of their employment was all that they could be required to do in accordance with the terms of their employment. There is no evidence that the terms of their employment gave their employers the power to order them to do anything else ... '

COMMENT

(1)   It makes sense for employers to include requirements of flexibility and mobility expressly in the contract if required, and to provide the information, in permanent form, to the employees as now required in ERA s 1. This should head off disputes.

Morrish v *Henly's Ltd*

[1973] ICR 482 National Industrial Relations Court

Sir Hugh Griffiths: ' … For nearly four years the employee had been employed as a stores driver, and he drove one vehicle all the time. It was his duty to draw diesel oil for the vehicle as and when it was required. On the morning of August 2 he drew five gallons of diesel oil from one of his employers' forecourt pumps and recorded that upon a document called a monthly fuel invoice. He entered on that document the date, the number of the vehicle, the amount and grade of fuel, and he signed it. Next day he drew another five gallons but when he went to record it on the invoice he discovered that the figure of five gallons he had entered on the previous day had been altered to seven. He changed it back to five. Later that day he found that the entry had again been altered to seven, and again he changed it to five. Still later he saw that a further entry had been made which showed that on August 2 two gallons of diesel had been drawn by the vehicle he was driving on that day, and that entry was signed by the manager, Mr Wilkes. The employee had by that time learned that the manager had made the previous alterations to his figure of five, and so, after crossing out the number of his vehicle against the entry of two gallons, he went to see the manager. A heated interview ensued. The manager explained that there was no suggestion that the employee had in fact drawn seven gallons and not five gallons, but that there was a deficiency of two gallons in the forecourt pumps and the alteration was merely to cover that deficiency and the forecourt staff. The employee was not willing to have an entry recorded which showed that two gallons of diesel had been put into the vehicle which he was driving, when that was not in fact the case, even if it was against the signature of the manager. The manager told him that, as he would not accept his instructions to leave the record showing two gallons attributed to that vehicle, he had no alternative but to give him notice; and that he did. On those facts the tribunal held that the employee had been unfairly dismissed.

The employers contended that, as there was evidence before the tribunal that it was a common practice to alter the records in that way to cover deficiencies, it was unreasonable of the employee to object, and he should have accepted the manager's instructions. Accordingly, his refusal to do so was an unreasonable refusal to obey an order, which justified dismissal.

We cannot accept this submission. It involves the proposition that it is an implied term of an employee's contract of service that he should accept an order to connive at the falsification of one of his employers' records. The proposition only has to be stated to be seen to be untenable. In our view, the employee was fully entitled to refuse to be in any way party to a falsification of that record and the tribunal were manifestly right in holding that he had been unfairly dismissed … '

Duty of fidelity

In common with other agents, employees owe fidelity to their employers: this means that they must at all times show good faith in their dealings with the employer and on the employer's behalf. Specific aspects of the duty of fidelity warrant separate consideration.

Secret profits
Boston Deep Sea Fishing v *Ansell*

(1888) 39 ChD 339 Court of Appeal

The defendant was managing director of the plaintiff company until his dismissal for failing to have the fishing smacks properly repaired and for overcharging for repairs. At the trial it was found that these allegations were unsubstantiated; however, by that time the company had discovered that some months previously the defendant had received a commission from a shipbuilder on a contract he had arranged on behalf of the plaintiff company for the construction of new boats.

Bowen LJ: ' … In the present instance we have first of all to consider what was done by the managing director, and, in the next place, if we find that the managing director has taken and received a commission behind the back of his company and without the knowledge of his company, and kept it, we have to pronounce our opinion upon the question of whether or not in law that is an ample reason for his dismissal.

Now, with regard to the facts relating to Earle's Shipbuilding Company, they stand beyond all dispute. The managing director has received a profit, and he has received a profit which was unknown to his own employers. How does that bear upon the condition which is implied in every contract of service or agency such as his – the condition that he will faithfully and truly discharge his duty towards his employer, and that if he does not so discharge it, the employer is to be at liberty to elect whether he will determine the service, or in spite of the fault continue the erring servant in his employ?

… there can be no question that an agent employed by a principal or master to do business with another, who, unknown to that principal or master, takes from that other person a profit arising out of the business which he is employed to transact, is doing a wrongful act inconsistent with his duty towards his master, and the continuance of confidence between them. He does the wrongful act whether such profit be given to him in return for services which he actually performs for the third party, or whether it be given to him for his supposed influence, or whether it be given to him on any other ground at all; if it is a profit which arises out of the transaction, it belongs to his master, and the agent or servant has no right to take it, or keep it, or bargain for it, or to receive it without bargain, unless his master knows it. It is said if the transaction be one of very old date, that in some way deprives the master of his right to treat it as a breach of faith. As the Lord Justice has pointed out, the age of the fraud may be a reason in the master's mind for not acting on his rights; but it is impossible to say that because a fraud has been concealed for six years, therefore the master has not a right when he discovers it to act upon his discovery, and to put an end to the relation of employer and employed with which such fraud was inconsistent. I, therefore, find it impossible to adopt Mr Justice Kekewich's view, or to come to any other conclusion except that the managing director having been guilty of a fraud on his employers was rightly dismissed by them, and dismissed by them rightly even though they did not discover the fraud until after they had actually pronounced the sentence of dismissal.'

COMMENT

(1)   While this case involved the managing director of a company – the most senior employee – it is clear that the duty is not confined to directors but applies to every employee.

(2)   In this case the reason relied on at first by the company for dismissing him was

inadequate but they were allowed to rely instead on a reason discovered *after* he had been dismissed. The importance of this point will be seen later in the discussion of dismissal law (see Chapter 8).

Disclosure of misconduct
Bell v *Lever Bros*

[1932] AC 161 House of Lords

B and S were appointed chairman and vice-chairman respectively of Niger Company, a company almost wholly owned by Lever Bros, for a fixed term of five years. At a point when their contracts still had two years to run, Lever Bros arranged to sell the company; they therefore entered compensation agreements with B and S, who were paid £50,000 for the loss of their contracts. It later transpired that B and S had been using their position and inside knowledge to deal in the company's goods on their own account, making a profit of £1,360. 'No defence can be offered for this piece of misconduct', said Lord Atkin. 'The appellants were acting in a business in which their employers were concerned; their interests and their employers' conflicted; they were taking a secret advantage out of their employment, and committing a grave breach of duty both to Levers and to the Niger Company. The jury have found that had the facts been discovered during the service, Levers could and would have dismissed them, and no objection can be taken to this finding.'

However, the facts were not discovered at the time, only afterwards. Lever Bros claimed back the compensation and an amount equivalent to the secret profits that they had made. There was no argument but that this latter sum should be disgorged. The issue was whether the compensation should be returned. At this time, juries commonly sat in civil cases and made findings of fact. The jury here found as a fact that at the time that they negotiated their 'golden parachutes' with Lever Bros, the two employees did not have in mind their earlier misconduct and that therefore they were not guilty of fraudulent misrepresentation.

There are complex questions of contract law in the case which, happily, we can ignore. The issue for us is whether the compensation agreement could be set aside on the ground that the employees were in breach of duty in failing to disclose their misconduct. By a 3–2 majority, the House of Lords held that they were not.

Lord Atkin: ' ... It now becomes necessary to deal with the second point of the plaintiffs – namely, that the contract of March 19, 1929 could be avoided by them in consequence of the non-disclosure by Bell of his misconduct as to the cocoa dealings. Fraudulent conceal-ment has been negatived by the jury; this claim is based upon the contention that Bell owed a duty to Levers to disclose his misconduct, and that in default of disclosure the contract was voidable. Ordinarily the failure to disclose a material fact which might influence the mind of a prudent contractor does not give the right to avoid the contract. The principle of *caveat emptor* applies outside contracts of sale. There are certain contracts expressed by the law to be contracts of the utmost good faith, where material facts must be disclosed; if not, the contract is voidable. Apart from special fiduciary relationships, contracts for partnership and contracts of insurance are the leading instances. In such cases the duty does not arise out of contract; the duty of a person proposing an insurance arises before a contract is made, so of an intending partner. Unless this contract can be brought within this limited category of contracts *uberrimae fidei* it appears to me that this ground of defence must fail. I see nothing to differentiate this agreement from the ordinary contract of service; and I am aware of no authority which places contracts of service within the limited category I have mentioned. It seems to me clear that master and man negotiating for an agreement of service are as unfettered as in any other negotiation. Nor can I find anything in the relation of master and servant, when established, that places agreements between them within the protected category. It is said that there is a contractual duty of the servant to disclose his past faults. I agree that the duty in the servant to protect his master's property may involve the duty to report a fellow servant whom he knows to be wrongfully dealing with that property. The servant owes a duty not to steal, but having stolen, is there superadded a duty to confess that he has stolen? I am satisfied that to imply such a duty would be a departure from the well established usage of mankind and would be to create obligations entirely outside the normal contemplation of the parties concerned. If a man agrees to raise his butler's wages, must the butler disclose that two years ago he received a secret commission from the wine merchant; and if the master discovers it, can he, without dismissal or after the servant has left, avoid the agreement for the increase in salary and recover back the extra wages paid? If he gives his cook a month's wages in lieu of notice can he, on discovering that the cook has been pilfering the tea and sugar, claim the return of the month's wages? I think not. He takes the risk; if he wishes to protect himself he can question his servant, and will then be protected by the truth or otherwise of the answers.'

Sybron Corp v Rochem Ltd

[1983] ICR 801 Court of Appeal

Roques was employed as manager of the European zone of Sybron, an American chemicals company. He was party to a conspiracy in which he and other senior employees of Sybron secretly set up competing companies (including Rochem Ltd) to which they diverted contracts and opportunities which should have gone to Sybron. Roques's fraud was not discovered until after he had been permitted to take early retirement with pension and insurance benefits which Sybron now sought to recover. It was argued for Roques that, following *Bell* v *Lever Bros*, he was under no duty to disclose his misconduct. After quoting a passage from Lord Atkin's judgment in that case reproduced above, Stephenson LJ continued as follows.

Stephenson LJ: ' ... So there again, what that judge is saying about the duty to report a fellow servant is linked to the question of a duty to report his own wrongdoing, but it is I think significant that Lord Atkin is agreeing that the duty of a servant to protect his master's property "may involve the duty to report a fellow servant whom he knows to be wrongfully dealing with that property", although Lord Atkin was of the firm view that the servant had no such duty to report his own wrongful conduct. It is, as I have already indicated, puzzling that it never seems to have occurred to counsel or to any of the many judges who dealt with *Bell* v *Lever Bros Ltd*, that they might have to consider the duty of Bell to report Snelling's misconduct, or Snelling's duty to report Bell's.

But the question was not there considered, let alone decided, and there is the direct authority of a decision of this court, in a case in which *Bell* v *Lever Bros Ltd* was considered, that there is in certain circumstances a duty to report the misconduct of fellow servants. That case is *Swain* v *West (Butchers) Ltd*. There the plaintiff was employed for a term of five years as a general manager of the defendant company. His contract of service provided, *inter alia*, that he would do all in his power to promote, extend and develop the interests of the company. The managing director gave the plaintiff certain unlawful orders, which orders the plaintiff carried out. The matter came to the notice of the chairman of the board of directors who, in an interview with the plaintiff, told the plaintiff that if he gave conclusive proof of the managing director's dishonesty he would not be dismissed. The plaintiff duly supplied the information required and was then dismissed, the defendants alleging fraud and dishonesty. The plaintiff did not deny the allegations, but he brought an action for breach of contract and wrongful dismissal on the grounds that under the terms of a verbal agreement between the plaintiff and the chairman it was not open to the defendants to rely upon information given by the plaintiff relating to his own fraud and dishonesty. It was held that it was the plaintiff's duty, as part of his contract of service, to report to the board of directors any acts which were not in the interests of the company; that there was therefore no consideration for the alleged verbal agreement and the defendant company was not prevented from relying upon the information received from the plaintiff ...

It follows from that decision, which is consistent with *Bell* v *Lever Bros Ltd* and is binding upon us, that there is no general duty to report a fellow-servant's misconduct or breach of contract; whether there is such a duty depends on the contract and on the terms of employment of the particular servant. He may be so placed in the hierarchy as to have a duty to report either the misconduct of his superior, as in *Swain* v *West (Butchers) Ltd*, or the misconduct of his inferiors, as in this case. Mr Munby will not have it that Mr Roques's "No. 2" was subordinate to Mr Roques, or that the other managers involved in the conspiracy were his subordinates or inferiors; but on this point I agree with Walton J [the judge at first instance] and I refer, again without apology and with approval, to the way in which he put the matter in his judgment below:

"I do not think that there is any general duty resting upon an employee to inform his master of the breaches of duty of other employees; the law would do industrial relations generally no great service if it held that such a duty did in fact exist in all cases. The duty must, in my view, depend upon all the circumstances of the case, and the relationship of the parties to their employer and *inter se*. I think it would be very difficult to have submitted, with any hope of success, that Messrs Bell and Snelling, having been appointed to rescue the affairs of their employers' African subsidiary in effect jointly, ought to have denounced each other."

That is a reference to the finding that Messrs Bell and Snelling were, according to the report of the case in the House of Lords, in joint management and therefore one was not subordinate to the other. Walton J goes on:

"However, where there is an hierarchical system, particularly where the person in the hierarchy whose conduct is called into question is a person near the top who is responsible to his employers for the whole of the operation of a complete sector of the employers' business – here the European zone – then in my view entirely different considerations apply. That the principle of disclosure extends at least as far as I think it extends (and perhaps further, but that is of no consequence for present purposes) has been decided once and for all, so far as this court is concerned, by *Swain* v *West (Butchers) Ltd*, a decision of the Court of Appeal. *Bell* v *Lever Bros Ltd* was very much in the forefront of everybody's mind in that case, but none of the Lords Justices thought it had any bearing on the case before them."

After reading, pretty well in full, the judgment of Greene LJ, from which I have read extracts, Walton J went on:

"This judgment has, if I may respectfully say so, the great merit of common sense. A person in a managerial position cannot possibly stand by and allow fellow servants to pilfer the company's assets and do nothing about it, which is really what Mr Munby's submissions would come to when applied to the present type of case. Certainly at all events where the misconduct is serious and the servant is not discharged immediately it must be quite obvious that, as part of his duties generally, the senior employee is under a duty to report what has happened as soon as he finds out, and further to indicate which steps (if any) he has taken to prevent a repetition thereof.

Of course, this all depends upon the duties of the relevant employee under his contract of service. In the present case there was a well-recognised reporting procedure, where-under the zone controller, Mr Roques, was expected to make reports as to the state of matters in his zone every month. It may possibly be argued that in such a case the duty to report was not an immediate duty but one to be fulfilled at the next reporting date; so be it, because even if this is correct no such report was ever made by Mr Roques to his superiors.

I therefore reach the not very surprising conclusion that Mr Roques was under a duty to report all he knew about the misdeeds of his subordinate employees, commencing with those of Mr Bove, as soon as he found out about them, and that he did not do so, deliberately and fraudulently, because he was one of the conspirators himself. The duty which lay upon him was, I repeat, not a duty to report his own misdeeds – this may well be regarded as negatived by *Bell* v *Lever Bros Ltd* – but to report those of his fellow conspirators."

Sorry as I am for Mrs Roques, I am happy to find that the law is not so outrageous as to enable Mr Roques to keep the £13,000. What Mr Roques did disentitled him, and I am afraid his wife, from keeping the money, and the plaintiffs are entitled to the declaration and orders for which they have asked, against these two defendants.'

COMMENT

(1)   While there is no general implied duty to disclose one's own misconduct, it has been suggested that since *Bell* v *Lever Bros* developments in the law of directors' duties mean that directors, or at least managing directors, should be regarded as having such a duty. This was doubted *obiter* by Goff L J in *Horcal* v *Gatland* (Court of Appeal).

(2)   Would the duty to disclose other employees' misconduct apply to the supervisor of a workshop aware of falsification of time sheets by her subordinates? Would it apply to a personnel manager aware that the sales manager (of equal status) was cheating on expenses? Should it?

(3)   The strong culture against telling tales seems to be behind Walton J's remark that a general duty to inform 'would do industrial relations generally no great service'. Is there anything that an employer not happy with this situation can do?

(4)   Does it make sense to have a duty in certain circumstances to disclose someone else's misconduct but not your own?

(5)   There is a good discussion of some of these issues in Freedland, 'High Trust, Pensions and the Contract of Employment' (1984) 13 ILJ 25.

Competition

When your working day is finished, you are free to do whatever you want, and what you do is none of your employer's business. True or false?

Hivac v *Park Royal Scientific Instruments*

[1946] Ch 169 Court of Appeal

The plaintiff company had a virtual monopoly in the manufacture of midget valves. Discovering that some of their employees were doing similar work for a competitor, the defendant company, in their spare time, the plaintiffs sought an injunction to stop the defendants employing these workers.

Lord Greene MR: '… It has been said on many occasions that an employee owes a duty of fidelity to his employer. As a general proposition that is indisputable. The practical difficulty in any given case is to find exactly how far that rather vague duty of fidelity extends. Prima facie it seems to me on considering the authorities and the arguments that it must be a question on the facts of each particular case. I can very well understand that the obligation of fidelity, which is an implied term of the contract, may extend very much further in the case of one class of employee than it does in others. For instance, when you are dealing, as we are dealing here, with mere manual workers whose job is to work five and a half days for their employer at a specific type of work and stop their work when the hour strikes, the obligation of fidelity may be one the operation of which will have a comparatively limited scope. The law would, I think, be jealous of attempting to impose on a manual worker restrictions, the real effect of which would be to prevent him utilising his spare time. He is paid for five and a half days in the week. The rest of the week is his own, and to impose upon a man, in relation to the rest of the week, some kind of obligation which really would unreasonably tie his hands and prevent him adding to his weekly money during that time would, I think, be very undesirable. On the other hand, if one has employees of a different character, one may very well find that the obligation is of a different nature. A manual worker might say: "You pay me for five and a half days work. I do five and a half days work for you. What greater obligation have I taken upon myself? If you want in some way to limit my activities during the other day and a half of the week, you must pay me for it." In many cases that may be a very good answer. In other cases it may not be a good answer because the very nature of the work may be such as to make it quite clear that the duties of the employee to his employer cannot properly be performed if in his spare time the employee engages in certain classes of activity….

It appears to me the question we have to consider resolves itself into these elements. First of all, what was done here was done in the spare time of the employees. That leads to this: we have to consider what implication, if any, needs to be read into the contract of service with regard to the employee's use of his spare time. Does that implication in any way restrict him, or, rather (which is the practical question here) did that implication make it a breach of duty on his part to do what he did, with the consequential result that the defendants, in persuading the employees to do what they did, procured a breach of contract? I think the judgment of Maugham LJ in *Wessex Dairies Ltd* v *Smith*, which is quite deliberately placed by him on a broad ground, does lead to this. Although the case before him was concerned with an employee who had done certain things in his employer's time, I cannot find that in his reasoning that was regarded as an essential part of the offence. I cannot read the judgment as meaning that if the roundsman had on a Saturday afternoon, when his work was over, gone round to all these customers and canvassed them, he would have been doing something he was entitled to do. It would be a curious result if, quite apart from making use of the list of customers or his special knowledge or anything of that kind, he could set himself during his spare time deliberately to injure the goodwill of his master's business by trying to get his customers to leave him. Then again the question here is not a question of getting the customers to leave the business but a question of building up a rival in business to the prejudice of the goodwill of the employer's business.

I am not ashamed to confess that in the course of the argument my mind has fluctuated considerably on this question. As I see it, the court stands in a sense between Scylla and Charybdis, because it would be most unfortunate if anything we said, or any other court said, should place an undue restriction on the right of the workman, particularly a manual workman, to make use of his leisure for his profit. On the other hand, it would be deplorable if it were laid down that a workman could, consistently with his duty to his employer, knowingly, deliberately and secretly set himself to do in his spare time something which would inflict great harm on his employer's business. I have endeavoured to raise the questions in the way that they appeal to me and, on the best consideration I can give to the matter, I think that the plaintiffs are prima facie right in this case ... '

COMMENT

(1)   This defines the scope of the employee's *implied* duty while still employed. It is open to the employer to prevent employees working in competition by use of an appropriate express term. However, restraining ex-employees is more difficult, as any term may be struck down as being in unlawful restraint of trade. This topic is outside the scope of this book: see Pitt (1997), *Employment Law*, 3rd edn, p 103.

(2)   An intention to leave and set up in competition is not in itself a breach of the duty of fidelity: *Laughton* v *Bapp Industrial Supplies*. Contrast *Lancashire Fires* v *S A Lyons*.

(3)   One of the issues in this case was the possible leakage of confidential information to the competitor. The duty not to disclose confidential information is another aspect of the duty of fidelity.

Confidential information

An employee has an implied duty not to disclose confidential information. This can apply to ex-employees as well. The greatest difficulty is establishing what is confidential information.

Faccenda Chicken v Fowler

[1986] ICR 297 Court of Appeal

Fowler had been employed as sales manager by the plaintiff company, and had established a system whereby sales staff delivered fresh chickens to customers from refrigerated vans. He left and set up in competition, employing a number of other sales staff who were also former employees of the plaintiffs. They all knew the names and addresses of the plaintiff's customers, the routes taken by the vans and when they called, the customers' regular requirements and the prices charged. The plaintiffs argued that this package of sales information was confidential information and that Fowler and the other former employees should be restrained from using it. Neill LJ delivered the judgment of the court. Look for the definition of three kinds of information, the factors which suggest that the information is confidential and the difference between the duty of an employee and an ex-employee.

Neill LJ: 'In these two appeals it will be necessary to consider the interaction of three separate legal concepts. (1) The duty of an employee during the period of his employment to act with good faith towards his employer: this duty is sometimes called the duty of fidelity. (2) The duty of an employee not to use or disclose after his employment has ceased any confidential information which he has obtained during his employment about his employer's affairs. (3) The prima facie right of any person to use and to exploit for the purpose of earning his living all the skill, experience and knowledge which he has at his disposal, including skill, experience and knowledge which he has acquired in the course of previous periods of employment …

In the course of his submissions in support of the appeal Mr Dehn took us on an instructive and valuable tour of many of the cases dealing with the law of confidence in the context of the relationship between employer and employee and also referred us to some of the cases on restrictive covenants.

It is not necessary, however, for us for the purpose of this judgment to travel this ground again. It is sufficient to set out what we understand to be the relevant principles of law. Having considered the cases to which we were referred, we would venture to state these principles:

(1)   Where the parties are, or have been, linked by a contract of employment, the obligations of the employee are to be determined by the contract between him and his employer: cf. *Vokes Ltd* v *Heather*.

(2)   In the absence of any express term, the obligations of the employee in respect of the use and disclosure of information are the subject of implied terms.

(3)   While the employee remains in the employment of the employer the obligations are included in the implied term which imposes a duty of good faith or fidelity on the employee. For the purposes of the present appeal it is not necessary to consider the precise limits of this implied term, but it may be noted: (a) that the extent of the duty of good faith will vary according to the nature of the contract: see *Vokes Ltd* v *Heather*, (b) that the duty of good faith will be broken if an employee makes or copies a list of the customers of the employer for use after his employment ends or deliberately memorises such a list, even though, except in special circumstances, there is no general restriction on an ex-employee canvassing or doing business with customers of his former employer: see *Robb* v *Green* and *Wessex Dairies Ltd* v *Smith*.

(4)   The implied term which imposes an obligation on the employee as to his conduct after the determination of the employment is more restricted in its scope than that which imposes a general duty of good faith. It is clear that the obligation not to use or disclose information may cover secret processes of manufacture such as chemical formulae (*Amber Size & Chemical Co Ltd* v *Menzel*), or designs or special methods of construction (*Reid & Sigrist Ltd* v *Moss and Mechanism Ltd*), and other information which is of a sufficiently high degree of confidentiality as to amount to a trade secret.

The obligation does not extend, however, to cover all information which is given to or acquired by the employee while in his employment, and in particular may not cover information which is only "confidential" in the sense that an unauthorised disclosure of such information to a third party while the employment subsisted would be a clear breach of the duty of good faith.

This distinction is clearly set out in the judgment of Cross J in *Printers & Finishers Ltd* v *Holloway* where he had to consider whether an ex-employee should be restrained by injunction from making use of his recollection of the contents of certain written printing instructions which had been made available to him when he was working in his former employers' flock printing factory. In his judgment he said:

"In this connection one must bear in mind that not all information which is given to a servant in confidence and which it would be a breach of his duty for him to disclose to another person during his employment is a trade secret which he can be prevented from using for his own advantage after the employment is over, even though he has entered into no express covenant with regard to the matter in hand. For example, the printing instructions were handed to Holloway to be used by him during his employment exclusively for the plaintiffs' benefit. It would have been a breach of duty on his part to divulge any of the contents to a stranger while he was employed, but many of these instructions are not really 'trade secrets' at all. Holloway was not, indeed, entitled to take a copy of the instructions away with him; but in so far as the instructions cannot be called 'trade secrets' and he carried them in his head, he is entitled to use them for his own benefit or the benefit of any future employer."

The same distinction is to be found in *E Worsley & Co Ltd* v *Cooper* where it was held that the defendant was entitled, after he had ceased to be employed, to make use of his knowledge of the source of the paper supplied to his previous employer. In our view it is quite plain that this knowledge was nevertheless "confidential" in the sense that it would have been a breach of the duty of good faith for the employee, while the employment subsisted, to have used it for his own purposes or to have disclosed it to a competitor of his employer.

(5) In order to determine whether any particular item of information falls within the implied term so as to prevent its use or disclosure by an employee after his employment has ceased, it is necessary to consider all the circumstances of the case. We are satisfied that the following matters are among those to which attention must be paid:

(a) The nature of the employment. Thus employment in a capacity where 'confidential' material is habitually handled may impose a high obligation of confidentiality because the employee can be expected to realise its sensitive nature to a greater extent than if he were employed in a capacity where such material reaches him only occasionally or incidentally.

(b) The nature of the information itself. In our judgment the information will only be protected if it can properly be classed as a trade secret or as material which, while not properly to be described as a trade secret, is in all the circumstances of such a highly confidential nature as to require the same protection as a trade secret eo nomine. The restrictive covenant cases demonstrate that a covenant will not be upheld on the basis of the status of the information which might be disclosed by the former employee if he is not restrained, unless it can be regarded as a trade secret or the equivalent of a trade secret: see, for example, *Herbert Morris Ltd* v *Saxelby per* Lord Parker of Waddington and *Littlewoods Organisation Ltd* v *Harris per* Megaw LJ.

We must therefore express our respectful disagreement with the passage in Goulding J's judgment where he suggested that an employer can protect the use of information in his second category, even though it does not include either a trade secret or its equivalent, by means of a restrictive covenant. As Lord Parker of Waddington made clear in *Herbert Morris Ltd* v *Saxelby* in a passage to which Mr Dehn drew our attention, a restrictive covenant will not be enforced unless the protection sought is reasonably necessary to protect a trade secret or to prevent some personal influence over customers being abused in order to entice them away …

It is clearly impossible to provide a list of matters which will qualify as trade secrets or their equivalent. Secret processes of manufacture provide obvious examples, but innumerable other pieces of information are *capable* of being trade secrets, though the secrecy of some information may be only short-lived. In addition, the fact that the circulation of certain information is restricted to a limited number of individuals may throw light on the status of the information and its degree of confidentiality.

(c)   Whether the employer impressed on the employee the confidentiality of the information. Thus, though an employer cannot prevent the use or disclosure *merely* by telling the employee that certain information is confidential, the attitude of the employer towards the information provides evidence which may assist in determining whether or not the information can properly be regarded as a trade secret. It is to be observed that in *E Worsley & Co Ltd* v *Cooper* Morton J attached significance to the fact that no warning had been given to the defendant that 'the source from which the paper came was to be treated as confidential'.

(d)   Whether the relevant information can be easily isolated from other information which the employee is free to use or disclose. In *Printers & Finishers Ltd* v *Holloway* Cross J considered the protection which might be afforded to information which had been memorised by an ex-employee. He put on one side the memorising of a formula or a list of customers or what had been said (obviously in confidence) at a particular meeting, and continued:

"The employee might well not realise that the feature or expedient in question was in fact peculiar to his late employer's process and factory; but even if he did, such knowledge is not readily separable from his general knowledge of the flock printing process and his acquired skill in manipulating a flock printing plant, and I do not think that any man of average intelligence and honesty would think that there was anything improper in his putting his memory of particular features of his late employer's plant at the disposal of his new employer."

For our part we would not regard the separability of the information in question as being conclusive, but the fact that the alleged 'confidential' information is part of a package and that the remainder of the package is not confidential is likely to throw light on whether the information in question is really a trade secret.

These then are the principles of law which we consider to be applicable to a case such as the present one. We would wish to leave open, however, for further examination on some other occasion the question of whether additional protection should be afforded to an employer where the former employee is not seeking to earn his living by making use of the body of skill, knowledge and experience which he has acquired in the course of his career, but is merely selling to a third party information which he acquired in confidence in the course of his former employment ...

We find ourselves unable to accept Mr Dehn's submissions either as to the information about prices or as to the sales information as a whole. We can well appreciate that in certain circumstances information about prices can be invested with a sufficient degree of confidentiality to render that information a trade secret or its equivalent. The price put forward in a tender document is an obvious example. But there may be many other cases where the circumstances show that a price or prices are matters of great importance and highly confidential.

Information about the price to be charged for a new model of a car or some other product or about the prices negotiated, for example, for various grades of oil in a highly competitive market in which it is known that prices are to be kept secret from competitors occur to us as providing possible further instances of information which is entitled to protection as having the requisite degree of confidentiality.

But in the present case the following factors appear to us to lead to the clear conclusion that neither the information about prices nor the sales information as a whole had the degree of confidentiality necessary to support the plaintiffs' case. We would list these factors as follows. (1) The sales information contained some material which the plaintiffs conceded was not confidential if looked at in isolation. (2) The information about the prices was not clearly severable from the rest of the sales information. (3) Neither the sales information in general, nor the information about the prices in particular, though of some value to a competitor, could reasonably be regarded as plainly secret or sensitive. (4) The sales information, including the information about prices, was necessarily acquired by the defendants in order that they could do their work. Moreover, as the judge observed in the course of his judgment, each salesman could quickly commit the whole of the sales information relating to his own area to memory. (5) The sales information was generally known among the van drivers who were employees, as were the secretaries, at quite a junior level. This was not a case where the relevant information was restricted to senior management or to confidential staff. (6) There was no evidence that the plaintiffs had ever given any express instructions that the sales information or the information about prices was to be treated as confidential. We are satisfied that, in the light of all the matters set out by the judge in his judgment, neither the sales information as a whole nor the information about prices looked at by itself fell within the class of confidential information which an employee is bound by an implied term of his contract of employment or otherwise not to use or disclose after his employment has come to an end.

Accordingly these appeals must be dismissed.'

COMMENT

(1)   While the duty not to disclose confidential information is usually seen as a duty of employees, it is worth noting that in an appropriate case it may apply to the employer. In *Dalgleish* v *Lothian and Borders Police Board* the Court of Session Outer House thought it probable that the Police Board would be in breach of such a duty if it disclosed the names and addresses of its employees to the Lothian Regional Council, thus enabling the Council to identify public employees who had failed to pay the community charge (poll tax).

(2)   Most cases about the abuse of confidential information come up in this context, where the employee has set up in competition or has gone to work for a competitor. However, there is another situation where employees may be tempted to disclose confidential information: where they want to go public on wrongdoing by their employer.

Whistle-blowing

In the United States the term 'whistle-blower' has become common for employees who reveal damaging information about their employers. Is it a breach of the duty of fidelity?

Initial Services Ltd v Putterill

[1968] 1 QB 396 Court of Appeal

The former sales manager of the company passed documents to the *Daily Mail* alleging that the company had entered price-fixing agreements with other companies, contrary to the Restrictive Trade Practices Act 1956. The company sued for damages and an injunction to prevent further disclosure on the grounds that the defendant was in breach of his duty of confidence. His defence was that the disclosure was in the public interest.

Lord Denning MR: ' ... The plaintiffs sought to strike out several of the paragraphs in Mr Putterill's defence. The master and the judge refused to strike them out. The plaintiffs appeal to this court.

In support of the appeal, Mr Michael Kerr said that in the employment of every servant there is implied an obligation that he will not, before or after his service, disclose information or documents which he has received in confidence. Now I quite agree that there is such an obligation. It is imposed by law. But it is subject to exceptions. Take a simple instance. Suppose a master tells his servant: "I am going to falsify these sale notes and deceive the customers. You are not to say anything about it to anyone." If the master thereafter falsifies the sale notes, the servant is entitled to say: "I am not going to stay any longer in the service of a man who does such a thing. I will leave him and report it to the customers." It was so held in *Gartside* v *Outram*.

Mr Michael Kerr suggested that this exception was confined to cases where the master has been "guilty of a crime or fraud". But I do not think that it is so limited. It extends to any misconduct of such a nature that it ought in the public interest to be disclosed to others. Wood VC put it in a vivid phrase: "There is no confidence as to the disclosure of iniquity."

In *Weld-Blundell* v *Stephens*, Bankes LJ rather suggested that the exception is limited to the proposed or contemplated commission of a crime or a civil wrong. But I should have thought that was too limited. The exception should extend to crimes, frauds and misdeeds, both those actually committed as well as those in contemplation, provided always – and this is essential – that the disclosure is justified in the public interest. The reason is because "no private obligations can dispense with that universal one which lies on every member of the society to discover every design which may be formed, contrary to the laws of the society, to destroy the public welfare": see *Annesley* v *Anglesea (Earl)*.

The disclosure must, I should think, be to one who has a proper interest to receive the information. Thus it would be proper to disclose a crime to the police; or a breach of the Restrictive Trade Practices Act to the registrar. There may be cases where the misdeed is of such a character that the public interest may demand, or at least excuse, publication on a broader field, even to the press ... '

Salmon LJ: ' ... [The plaintiffs] elected not to sue for defamation; and of course they were under no obligation to choose any particular form of action once they resorted to the courts. What they said was that the information and the documents which had been passed on by Mr Putterill to the *Daily Mail* had been passed on by him to the newspaper in breach of confidence, that the newspaper knew that what they were given by Mr Putterill was in breach of his duty of confidence to his employers, and the plaintiffs asked for damages against both Mr Putterill and the newspaper on that basis alone and for an injunction and delivery up of any confidential material that had been handed over.

It is to be observed that whether or not the information was true is of no consequence in that action. The plaintiffs, if they are entitled to succeed on this form of action, are, as they put it, just as much entitled to succeed whether the information that was given by Mr Putterill to the newspaper was true or false. So presumably there will be no issue, if and when this action comes to trial, as to whether in fact the plaintiffs had entered into agreements to which the Restrictive Trade Practices Act 1956, applied, as to whether or not they were in breach of their statutory obligations in failing to reveal such agreements to the registrar or as to whether or not they falsely put out a circular saying their increase in prices was in the main to cover the burden cast upon them by the selective employment tax … '

COMMENT

(1)   On a motion for striking out, such as this was, the court will find against the plaintiff if the defendant's argument has any chance at all of success. Thus the Court of Appeal did not have to reach a final view on this case, it had only to be satisfied that the defence was arguable, which it clearly was.

(2)   While it is clear that there is a defence of disclosure in the public interest, it is still not entirely clear how far it goes. Must the whistle-blower be acting in good faith? Must the disclosure be to the proper authorities, as Lord Denning seems to suggest? Does it make a difference if the whistle-blower is being paid, for example by a newspaper? Does the information which is disclosed have to be true? The best way of dealing with the problem is probably to require the employee or former employee to go to the proper authorities, as in the next case.

Re a Company's Application

[1989] ICR 449 Chancery Division

The defendant had been employed as compliance officer by the plaintiff, a financial services company, and among his duties he had to ensure that the company complied with regulations laid down by FIMBRA (the Financial Investment Managers and Brokers' Regulatory Authority). Having ceased to be an employee of the company, he told them that he was planning to go to FIMBRA over alleged breaches of their regulations and to the Inland Revenue with information about tax fiddles. The company alleged that he was trying to blackmail them into paying him £10,000 to remain silent and sought an injunction to prevent all disclosure.

Scott J: ' … The case has been based by Mr Shipley on the duty of confidentiality that undoubtedly was owed by the defendant to the plaintiff in the course of and arising out of his employment. It is easy to agree that details about the plaintiff's clients' personal affairs should be regarded as confidential information and should be so treated by all the plaintiff's employees.

If this were a case in which there were any question or threat of general disclosure by the defendant of confidential information concerning the way in which the plaintiff carries on its business or concerning any details of the affairs of any of its clients, there could be no answer to the claim for an injunction; but it is not general disclosure that the defendant has in mind. He has in mind only disclosure to FIMBRA, the regulatory authority, and, in relation to a particular case that he has identified in his affidavit, the Inland Revenue. I ask myself whether an employee of a company carrying on the business of giving financial advice and of financial management to members of the public under the regulatory umbrella provided by FIMBRA owes a duty of confidentiality that extends to barring disclosure of information to FIMBRA.

It is part of the plaintiff's case, although not essential to its confidential information cause of action, that the defendant in communicating with FIMBRA will be motivated by malice. The defendant's professed intention is, in the plaintiff's view, associated with the blackmail attempt made by the defendant. At the present stage, and until cross~examination, I must accept that that may be true. It is not necessarily true. The defendant's explanation may be a genuine one. But the plaintiff's case may be true. It may be the case that the information proposed to be given, the allegations proposed to be made by the defendant to FIMBRA, and for that matter by the defendant to the Inland Revenue, are allegations made out of malice and based upon fiction or invention.

But if that is so, then I ask myself what harm will be done. FIMBRA may decide that the allegations are not worth investigating. In that case, no harm will have been done. Or FIMBRA may decide that an investigation is necessary. In that case, if the allegations turn out to be baseless, nothing will follow the investigation. And if harm is caused by the investigation itself, it is harm which is implicit in the regulatory role of FIMBRA. It may be that what is put before FIMBRA includes some confidential information. But that information would, as it seems to me, be information which FIMBRA could at any time obtain by the spot checks that it is entitled to carry out. I doubt whether an employee of a financial services company such as the plaintiff owes a duty of confidence which extends to an obligation not to disclose information to the regulatory authority FIMBRA.

So far as the Inland Revenue is concerned, the point is a narrower one. The Inland Revenue is not concerned in any general way with the business of a financial services company. It is concerned with tax. It is concerned with assets, with capital and income. If confidential details which did not relate to fiscal matters were disclosed to the Inland Revenue, that would, in my opinion, be as much a breach of the duty of confidentiality as the disclosure of that information to any other third party. But if what is disclosed to the Inland Revenue relates to fiscal matters that are the concern of the Inland Revenue, I find it difficult to accept that the disclosure would be in breach of a duty of confidentiality ...

I think it would be contrary to the public interest for employees of financial services companies who thought that they ought to place before FIMBRA information of possible breaches of the regulatory system, or information about possible fiscal irregularities before the Inland Revenue, to be inhibited from so doing by the consequence that they might become involved in legal proceedings in which the court would conduct an investigation with them as defendants into the substance of the information they were minded to communicate.

If it turns out that the defendant's allegations are groundless and that he is motivated by malice then, as it seems to me, he will be at serious risk of being found liable in damages for defamation or malicious falsehood. But that is for the future. The plaintiff's application before me for an injunction is based on the proposition that the disclosure by the defendant of the information will be in breach of his duty of confidence. In my judgment, however, the defendant's undoubted duty of confidence does not extend so as to bar the disclosures to FIMBRA and the Inland Revenue of matters that it is the province of those authorities to investigate ... '

An injunction was granted preventing disclosure to anyone except FIMBRA and the Inland Revenue.

Duty to co-operate?

We have seen that an employee has a duty to obey lawful and reasonable orders (*Laws v London Chronicle*, p 143), that to some extent they must be prepared to adapt (*Cresswell v Board of Inland Revenue*, p 129) and that they have a duty to maintain mutual trust and confidence (*Robinson v Crompton Parkinson*, p 136). It is perhaps not surprising, therefore, that it is now argued that employees have a positive duty to co-operate with their employer. This has potentially wide implications.

Ticehurst v *British Telecommunications plc*

[1992] IRLR 219 Court of Appeal

In the course of a pay dispute, the Society of Telecom Executives (STE) instructed its members to withdraw goodwill, essentially meaning that they should do nothing outside their existing contracts. After some months, BT announced that it would no longer accept non-co-operation and that any employee not prepared to sign an undertaking to work normally would be sent home and not paid. The plaintiff, who had been sent home without pay, claimed her lost wages. It was conceded that, apart from refusing to give the required undertaking, no action or omission on her part amounting to a breach of her contract could be established.

The judgment of the court was given by Ralph Gibson LJ.

Ralph Gibson LJ: ' ... The analysis which I respectfully find most apt to define the relevant duties of Mrs Ticehurst under her contract of employment as a manager employed by BT, is that stated by Buckley LJ [in *Secretary of State* v *ASLEF (No 2)*], namely "an implied term to serve the employer faithfully within the requirements of the contract". It is, I think, consistent with the judgments of Lord Denning and Roskill LJ. It was not suggested that there is any express term in the contract of employment of Mrs Ticehurst, or anything else in the general circumstances of this case, which would make it wrong to imply such a term into her contract. It is, in my judgment, necessary to imply such a term in the case of a manager who is given charge of the work of other employees and who therefore must necessarily be trusted to exercise her judgment and discretion in giving instructions to others and in supervising their work. Such a discretion, if the contract is to work properly, must be exercised faithfully in the interests of the employers.

Next, it seems to me clear that participation by Mrs Ticehurst in the concerted action of withdrawal of goodwill, as it was devised and carried out by STE and the members, would constitute a breach of that term if Mrs Ticehurst was intending to continue to participate in it. For example, a manager who intends, when opportunity offers, to consider how much choice she has in performing any task within those listed by STE and then to choose that which would cause the most inconvenience to her employers, is intending, in my judgment, to break her obligation to serve her employers faithfully. Similarly, the doing of the other acts listed in paragraphs 8, 10 and 11 of the statement of the facts above, not from a genuine intention or interest but so as to cause disruption, would be a breach of that obligation. In addition to those acts by Mrs Ticehurst herself, she was intending after 12 April (if she was intending to continue in the action of the withdrawal of goodwill) to continue, as a committee member of the Stone branch of STE, to advise and encourage other members of STE at Stone to carry on that action by herself distributing STE documents and by being available to answer questions of members by telephone. Her name and telephone number were included in documents distributed by the Stone branch committee for that purpose.

I do not accept the submission of Mr Elias that there can be no breach of the implied term for faithful service unless the intended disruption of BT's undertaking was achieved by the action taken, whether to the extent of rendering the business unmanageable or to some other level of disruption. The term is breached, in my judgment, when the employee does an act, or omits to do an act, which it would be within her contract and the discretion allowed to her not to do, or to do, as the case may be, and the employee so acts or omits to do the act, not in honest exercise of choice or discretion for the faithful performance of her work but in order to disrupt the employer's business or to cause the most inconvenience that can be caused. We need not consider the position which would arise if the ill-intentioned course of conduct is shown to have had no significant consequences adverse to the employer and to be incapable of causing any such adverse consequences in future. This action by way of withdrawal of goodwill did have adverse consequences (see paragraph 28 of the facts above) and the fact that STE was asserting that the effect of the action was greater than that in fact achieved does not cause the conduct not to have been a breach of contract ... '

(Because she was in breach of contract, her claim for lost wages was unsuccessful.)

COMMENT

(1)   The 'other acts listed in the statement of the facts' in addition to the withdrawal of goodwill were to apply for any job vacancies within British Telecom for which the employee might possibly be qualified, to apply for any likely-looking training course, to ask for a written statement of pension entitlement, to ask for written details of bonus schemes and similar activities which were designed to swamp the administration. None on its own would be a breach of contract.

(2)   On this analysis, the duty to co-operate is another facet of the duty of fidelity. The Court of Appeal's decision here is in one sense wider than in *Secretary of State v ASLEF (No. 2)*, in that it holds conduct to be a breach even where there is no allegation that any specific duty of the employee has been performed wrongly or has been neglected. However, it may also be construed more narrowly, in that the Court places emphasis on her managerial role, and the discretion that it entails.

(3)   Would it be right to draw a distinction between employees with a high degree of discretion in how they carry out their work (who generally have correspondingly higher salaries) and employees with virtually no discretion, holding that the former, but not the latter, have an implied duty to co-operate with their employer?

5 Collective bargaining

INTRODUCTION

First of all, let us look at a definition of collective bargaining, taken from the Donovan Commission Report in 1968. A Royal Commission chaired by Lord Donovan was set up in 1965 to review the law relating to industrial relations. It carried out a comprehensive programme of research, so that its report constitutes an authoritative survey of law and industrial relations in the UK at that time. In the following extract, note the different levels of bargaining, the overlap between them and the distinction between substantive and procedural collective agreements.

Report of the Royal Commission on Trade Unions and Employers' Associations 1965–1968 (the Donovan Commission) Cmnd 3623

31. The relationship between trade unions and employers' associations arises principally in the process of negotiating and applying collective agreements, and the rules established by these agreements form a considerable part of the framework within which managers and workers deal with each other. 'Collective bargain' is a term coined by Beatrice Webb to describe an agreement concerning pay and conditions of work settled between trade unions on the one hand and an employer or association of employers on the other. Thus it covers any negotiations in which employees do not negotiate individually, and on their own behalf, but do so collectively through representatives.

32. The best-known type of collective agreement in this country is the industry-wide agreement (a more precise term than 'national agreement'). This is an agreement between an employers' association (or in some instances two or more associations) and a trade union (or, more commonly, two or more unions or a federation of unions) which is intended to operate throughout an industry. Where industry-wide bargaining is practised the resulting agreements can be classified into substantive agreements, which deal with matters such as rates of pay, hours of work, overtime rates and holiday arrangements, and procedural agreements dealing with the procedures for reaching substantive agreements and for dealing with disputes which may arise in the establishments within the industry. Substantive agreements and disputes procedures are almost invariably written down and often printed in a handbook of agreements for the industry. Some industries have agreed formal constitutions for joint bodies at industry level which meet regularly to deal with such matters as negotiating or amending substantive agreements. Where they exist, these constitutions are generally included in the handbooks.

Other industries prefer to rely on arranging *ad hoc* meetings for negotiating and revising substantive agreements.

33. Some large corporations which do not belong to employers' associations negotiate their own substantive and procedural agreements with the unions. A few of these agreements, like that of the Ford Motor Company, operate throughout the undertaking and cover more workers than many industry-wide agreements. Some of the major oil companies, on the other hand, negotiate separate agreements for each of their refineries. In a few instances, including the National Coal Board, an agreement with a single corporation is also an industry-wide agreement.

34. Companies in membership of employers' associations (usually called 'federated' companies) may negotiate agreements with unions representing their employees to supplement industry-wide agreements, either substantive or procedural, but such agreements are relatively rare. More commonly bargaining to supplement industry-wide agreements takes place between managers and representatives of particular groups of workers. In a company possessing two or more factories it is normal for managers in each factory to deal separately with representatives of groups of their own workers. This type of bargaining we refer to as 'workplace bargaining'. In some instances workers are represented by full-time trade union district officials in workplace bargaining. More commonly, however, their spokesmen are representatives chosen from among themselves, usually called 'shop stewards', and full-time officials are called in only where managers and shop stewards cannot reach agreement. Many of these agreements affect only one group of workers in a single shop, and may be settled between a shop steward and a foreman or departmental manager. This is 'workshop' or 'shop floor' bargaining. Most industry-wide disputes procedures give some guidance on the conduct of workplace bargaining, although often in practice this guidance is not strictly observed.

35. Workplace agreements may be written down, but are rarely collected together into a single coherent document. Many of them, especially shop floor agreements, are oral. These oral agreements are difficult to distinguish from 'custom and practice'. This is the body of customary forms of behaviour among groups of workers which managers have permitted to grow up and are therefore assumed to accept. Examples of matters widely covered by custom and practice are 'tea-breaks' and tasks reserved for members of a given craft. These customs play an important part in shop floor industrial relations, and some have their origin in oral agreements.

36. The pay and conditions of an individual employee may therefore be the result of collective bargains struck at one or more (even, conceivably, all) of the foregoing levels.

COMMENT

(1)   For employees, the advantage of collective bargaining is that the combined power of many employees can even up the otherwise unequal bargaining position between employer and worker. What is in it for the employer?

Kahn-Freund's Labour and the Law 3rd ed 1983, edited P Davies and M Freedland, p 69

... it is not difficult to summarise the purposes of collective bargaining: by bargaining collectively with organised labour, management seeks to give effect to its legitimate expectation that the planning of production, distribution, etc., should not be frustrated through interruptions of work. By bargaining collectively with management, organised labour seeks to give effect to its legitimate expectations that wages and other conditions of work should be such as to guarantee a stable and adequate form of existence and as to be compatible with the physical integrity and moral dignity of the individual, and also that jobs should be reasonably secure. This definition is not intended to be exhaustive. It is intended to indicate (and this is important for the law) that the principal interest of management in collective bargaining has always been the maintenance of industrial peace over a given area and period, and that the principal interest of labour has always been the creation and the maintenance of certain standards over a given area and period, standards of distribution of work, of rewards, and of stability of employment.

COMMENT

(1) Traditionally, therefore, the trade-off has been that the employer can expect that no industrial action will take place without procedures laid down in collective agreements being carried out first. The agreement is seen as an industrial peace treaty.

(2) Because of the contribution of collective bargaining to orderly industrial relations, the policy of successive governments and therefore of the law was that the process should be encouraged. However, the policing of collective agreements was not seen as the law's business.

Report of the Royal Commission on Trade Unions and Employers' Associations 1965–1968 (the Donovan Commission) Cmnd 3623

39. Until recent times it was a distinctive feature of our system of industrial relations that the State remained aloof from the process of collective bargaining in private industry. It left the parties free to come to their own agreement. It imposed some, but few, restrictions on the right of employees to strike or of employers to resort to a lock-out. The parties to the collective agreement themselves rarely intend that their bargain shall be a legally enforceable contract, but rather that it shall be binding in honour only. The law goes out of its way to provide that such bargains between employers' associations and trade unions shall not be directly enforceable.

40. This abstentionist attitude has reflected a belief that it is better in the long run for the law to interfere as little as possible in the settlement of questions arising between employers and workmen over pay and conditions of work. Parliament has long been committed to the view that the best means of settling such questions is voluntary collective bargaining and has equipped Governments in various ways to support, assist and promote collective bargaining.

41. One example of support for collective agreements is the Fair Wages Resolution of the House of Commons. The first was passed in 1891, and the Resolution at present in force was adopted in 1946. Its basic purpose is to ensure that employers engaged on Government contracts do not give their employees terms and conditions inferior to those established generally. Other examples are the Terms and Conditions of Employment Act 1959, under which an employer may be required under certain

conditions to observe terms and conditions not less favourable than those established for his trade or industry by collective bargaining; and the statutory obligation placed on the boards of nationalised industries to seek agreement with trade unions over the establishment of negotiating machinery for settling terms and conditions of work for their employees.

COMMENT

(1)   The Donovan Commission considered that collective bargaining needed reform because the overlap between national agreements and local arrangements led to considerable confusion. However, overall they remained convinced that voluntary collective bargaining was the best policy for orderly industrial relations.

(2)   As well as the two measures of state support mentioned in the extract, collective bargaining was also encouraged by the wages council system (designed, among other things, to foster collective bargaining in industries with low levels of unionisation) and through government-provided conciliation and arbitration systems. In 1975 the Labour Government extended this support further, in particular by providing a legal mechanism for trade unions to demand recognition from an unwilling employer.

However, under the Conservative Government of the 1980s the position shifted considerably. The Fair Wages Resolution, the provisions requiring observance of established terms and conditions and the legal recognition procedure were all repealed. Wages councils were abolished by TURERA 1993 and the duty of ACAS to promote collective bargaining was repealed at the same time. The attitude of the Conservative Government towards collective bargaining was made clear in Green and White Papers.

People Jobs and Opportunity Cm 1810 (1992) (White Paper)

4.3   In the 1960s and 1970s, the way in which pay was determined for the great majority of employees ran counter to the objectives of rewarding individual effort and performance, and increasing job opportunities and choice through the operation of a more efficient labour market. The combination of centralised, industry-wide collective bargaining and Government policies to limit the growth of earnings by imposing uniform 'pay limits' resulted in a strong trend towards identical pay increases, regardless of individual employees' contributions to the organisations for which they worked.

4.4   Since 1979 the Government has taken a series of steps to reverse this damaging trend. In the first place, pay determination has been freed from Government interference through the discredited mechanism of past 'incomes policies'. Secondly … the Government, through its employment legislation, has provided effective protection for employers and employees alike against the abuses of trade union power which created such an imbalance of bargaining power in the 1970s: employers are now free to decide for themselves whether or not to recognise and negotiate with trade unions, just as employees are now free to decide for themselves whether or not to join a trade union. Thirdly, the Government has taken specific steps to encourage the spread of profit-related pay. Finally it has set an example, as an employer, in taking initiatives to move pay determination away from centralised collective bargaining and make it more responsive to local needs.

4.5   As a result, the 1980s have seen a number of important developments:
- there has been a marked decline in the number of people whose pay is determined by national collective agreements. Data from the New Earnings Survey shows that the coverage of major national collective agreements dropped substantially – from 47 per cent in 1983 to 34 per cent in 1991. Moreover, those covered by such agreements did relatively worse than those who were not. In 1983 those covered earned £3 a week more than those who were not covered. By 1991 the picture was reversed, with those covered earning £7.50 a week less than those who were not;
- there is an increasing trend to move away from collective bargaining altogether: external research suggests that by 1990 some 42 per cent of the workforce was not covered, either directly or indirectly, by collective bargaining; more and more companies are negotiating pay on an individual basis with each of their employees on the basis of relevant skills and performance;
- even where collective bargaining persists, pay determination has become increasingly decentralised to local level; there are now much greater regional variations in pay within organisations where previously employees were paid at the same rate regardless of differences in labour market conditions;
- new forms of performance pay, merit pay and other incentives such as employee share ownership and profit-sharing are becoming more widespread at all levels. A recent study found that 47 per cent of companies surveyed used performance related pay for all their white collar workers and 30 per cent had an element of merit pay for manual workers;
- there has been a widening in skill differentials after reaching a low-point in the mid 1970s. For instance, the average pay of foremen and technicians has risen from around 30 per cent above the unskilled rate in 1976 to about 50 per cent above in 1990.

4.6   These are all valuable and healthy developments. They mean that pay determination is increasingly responsive to individual effort. Furthermore, they are making an important contribution to improving the effective operation of the labour market on which the expansion of job opportunities and choice crucially depends. It is, therefore, essential that these developments should be built upon in the 1990s.

The way forward for the 1990s
4.7   The Government will be ready to take further action, as necessary, to remove any obstacles to these developments and to stimulate progress in such areas as profit-related pay. It will continue to encourage employers to move away from traditional, centralised collective bargaining towards methods of pay determination which reward individual skills and performance; respond to the wish of individual employees to negotiate their own terms and conditions of employment; and take full account of business circumstances.

COMMENT

(1)   As this demonstrates, the policy of the Conservative Government was to discourage collective bargaining in favour of individualised contracts and greater variations in pay and conditions. It had some success in this policy, although it remains

true that collective agreements are the most important source of contract terms for a majority of workers. In law, this raises the question of how terms in an agreement between a trade union and an employer can affect a third party, namely the employee, who may not even be a member of the union. As between the employer and the trade union, the issue is whether either side can enforce the agreement if the other side wants to renege. These questions will be considered next.

COLLECTIVE AGREEMENTS AND THE INDIVIDUAL EMPLOYEE

It is a basic principle of the law of contract that agreements are binding only on the parties to the agreement – this is the doctrine of privity of contract. Even if a contract is made for the benefit of a third party, the third party cannot enforce it. So if a trade union and an employer were to agree that the employees' pay should be increased by five per cent, the employees could not sue to enforce that agreement. In fact, as we will see, collective agreements between trade unions and employers are hardly ever legally binding contracts in the first place, which provides another reason why an employee could not enforce the agreement. Yet everyone knows that the agreement is intended to have an effect: how can this be translated into law?

Union as agent

Can it be argued that the union negotiates the collective agreement as agent for its members? If so, that could bring them into contractual relations with the employer. Since we think of the union as acting on behalf of the workers, this initially seems an attractive proposition. It faces two main difficulties, however. First, by no stretch of the imagination could the union be regarded as acting on behalf of workers who were not members of the union – yet collective agreements typically apply to all the workers in a bargaining unit, whether they are members or not. Second, it is unrealistic to suppose that in joining a trade union, members intend to give it virtually unlimited authority to enter agreements on their behalf.

Burton Group v *Smith*

[1977] IRLR 351 Employment Appeal Tribunal

It was argued that notice to a trade union had been received by the union as agent for its member.

Arnold J: ' … There is no reason at all why, in a particular case, union representatives should not be the agents of an employee to make a contract, or to receive a notice, or otherwise effect a binding transaction on his behalf. But that agency so to do does not stem from the mere fact that they are union representatives and that he is a member of the union; it must be supported in the particular case by the creation of some specific agency, and that can arise only if the evidence supports the conclusion that there was such an agency. It is sufficient to say that in this case there was no evidence before the Tribunal of the existence of such an agency … '

COMMENT

(1)   This correctly represents the law on this matter. For an example where the agency of the union was accepted, see *Edwards* v *Skyways*.

Incorporation into individual contracts

Since the agency argument will operate only in very limited circumstances, the usual question is whether or not the collective agreement has become incorporated into the individual's own contract of employment. If so, then the term can be enforced by and against the individual like any other contract term. The simplest case is where the incorporation of the collective agreement is expressly agreed between the parties.

Marley v *Forward Trust*

[1986] ICR 891 Court of Appeal

The company decided to close the Bristol office where the applicant was employed and to redeploy him to London. Under a collective agreement between the employers and the trade union ASTMS, employees redeployed in a redundancy situation were allowed six months in which to assess the suitability of the new job, and could opt instead for redundancy terms if they were unhappy. Having tried the new job for two months, the applicant decided to take redundancy instead. The company argued that the terms of the collective agreement were not binding.

Dillon LJ: ' … When the employee's contract of employment was taken over by the respondent employers, Forward Trust Group Ltd in December 1981, possibly as a result of a group reconstruction or a takeover of the previous employer, the employee was given a letter which made it plain that the terms and conditions of his employment were being published in a new personnel manual. When, in June 1983, he was promoted to field supervisor operating from the south west regional head office of the employers, the particulars of his terms of employment [were] set out again and again those details were contained in various sections of the personnel manual. One of those sections was section A10, and section A10 provides categorically that redundancies will be handled in accordance with the procedure outlined in section A25 of the personnel manual. Section A25 sets out the terms of the collective agreement between the employers and the trade union ASTMS to which Lawton LJ has referred. It sets it out verbatim and that includes clause 11: "This agreement is binding in honour only and it is not intended to give rise to any legal obligation." That may, no doubt, have been so as between the employers and the union, but the terms of the agreement are incorporated into the personnel manual in section A25 and they must have legal effect thereby as terms of the contract between the employee and the employers.

I, therefore, am unable to accept the conclusion of the industrial tribunal and of the Employment Appeal Tribunal that clause 11 prevented the employee enforcing those terms. If there was a redundancy situation he was entitled to the benefit of the terms set out in section A25 in relation to a redundancy situation … '

(Lawton LJ delivered a concurring judgment; Woolf LJ agreed.)

COMMENT

(1)   Here there was a double incorporation. Marley's contract incorporated the personnel manual and the personnel manual incorporated the collective agreement.

(2)   The collective agreement contained a term (clause 11) to the effect that it was not intended to be a legally binding agreement as between the union and the employer. While not strictly necessary (see below), this kind of provision is not uncommon. The collective agreement had been reproduced verbatim in the personnel manual, hence the argument that the term saying that it was not binding was also incorporated. That argument, which would involve a paradox of the Cretan liar variety, was sensibly rejected by the Court.

(3)   It is a consequence of the non-binding nature of collective agreements that either the union or the employer can terminate them at any time. What effect does this have on individual employees?

Robertson v British Gas

[1983] ICR 351 Court of Appeal

British Gas appealed against a decision that they were liable to pay arrears of pay to the employee under an incentive bonus scheme. The incentive bonus scheme had been contained in a collective agreement and had undergone some variation over the years. British Gas had terminated the collective agreement containing the latest version at the end of 1981.

The employee relied on his letter of appointment which stated 'Incentive bonus scheme conditions will apply … ' as incorporating entitlement into his contract of employment. His written statement of terms and conditions said, 'Any payment which may, from time to time, become due in respect … of incentive bonuses … will be calculated in accordance with the rules of the scheme in force at the time.' The letter of appointment and the written statement are the two sets of contractual documents referred to by the judge.

Kerr LJ: ' … Turning to the two sets of contractual documents in this case, and without distinguishing between them, it seems to me to be clear that both of them were designed to operate in the context of some agreed collective scheme concerning bonus payments, with conditions (in the case of the first document) and rules in force (in the case of the second document), whose terms are to be treated as incorporated into the individual contracts evidenced by these documents. Both of them proceed on the basis that there will be an incentive bonus and that its amount and the terms governing it are to be found in an agreed collective scheme in force from time to time. Such an agreement was in force at the time when both these documents came into existence, and from time to time the terms of the scheme were thereafter varied by some further collective agreement between the trade union side and the employer's side. I agree with Mr Sedley's submission that, when the terms of the collective agreements were varied by consent between the two sides, then the new terms clearly became incorporated into the individual contracts of employment. But what does not follow, in my view, is that the contracts of the individual workmen can be varied by some unilateral variation or abrogation or withdrawal from the collective agreement by either side.

It is true that collective agreements such as those in the present case create no legally enforceable obligation between the trade union and the employers. Either side can withdraw.

But their terms are in this case incorporated into the individual contracts of employment, and it is only if and when those terms are varied collectively by agreement that the individual contracts of employment will also be varied. If the collective scheme is not varied by agreement, but by some unilateral abrogation or withdrawal or variation to which the other side does not agree, then it seems to me that the individual contracts of employment remain unaffected. This is another way of saying that the terms of the individual contracts are in part to be found in the agreed collective agreements as they exist from time to time, and, if these cease to exist as collective agreements, then the terms, unless expressly varied between the individual and the employer, will remain as they were by reference to the last agreed collective agreement incorporated into the individual contracts.

In the present case this construction is reinforced by the fact that, although it looks from the documents as though the incentive bonus scheme is merely one small part of the total terms of the individual contracts of employment, it provides in fact an integrated and general framework for a very large number of the mutual rights and obligations of the parties. Indeed, it becomes virtually impossible to determine what the full terms of these individual contracts of employment are if you once take away the agreed collective scheme for an incentive bonus as an integral part of these contracts.

For all these reasons I have no doubt that the judge came to the right conclusion, and I would equally dismiss this appeal.'

COMMENT

(1) Presumably if the contractual documents had said something like, 'any incentive bonus payments will be subject to the collective agreement in force for the time being', the employer would have been excused liability after terminating the agreement. Support for this view may be gleaned from the decision of the Court of Session in *Cadoux* v *Central Regional Council*. See also *Airlie* v *City of Edinburgh DC*.

(2) The case illustrates the major problem likely to arise in the context of express incorporation: what precisely has been incorporated? For another example, see *Gascol Conversions* v *Mercer*, where the issue was whether a local agreement which had in fact been acted on took precedence over a national collective agreement.

(3) Where there is no express incorporation of the terms of a collective agreement, it may be possible to rely instead on implied incorporation. That is, the circumstances may indicate that the collective agreement should be treated as incorporated into the contract of employment. This is essentially a question of fact.

Alexander v Standard Telephones & Cables Ltd (No 2)

[1991] IRLR 286 Queen's Bench Division

Faced with the need to make 112 redundancies, the company, after consultation with the relevant unions, selected on the basis of several criteria: length of service, skill, aptitude, performance, attendance record and approach to work. Two groups of employees selected challenged the lawfulness of their dismissals. These were cable operators, of whom Mr Alexander was representative (the *Alexander* action), and maintenance workers, of whom Mr Wall was representative (the *Wall* action).

Hobhouse J: '... The various plaintiffs dispute that they were lawfully dismissed. They make no complaint about the conduct of the consultation procedures that were gone through prior to their dismissal, nor do they complain about their selection for dismissal if the criteria adopted by the company were the proper criteria. Nor do they say in these actions that they were unfairly dismissed. What the plaintiffs say is that the company was only entitled to select employees for compulsory redundancy on the basis of seniority, or as it is commonly known, "last in first out". If that criterion had been applied they would not have been selected for dismissal; they were among the more senior employees. They say that it was a requirement of the collective agreements between the company and the relevant union or unions covering the maintenance workers and the cable operators that selection for redundancy should be on the basis of seniority alone and they further say that provision of each collective agreement was incorporated into their individual contracts of employment. Accordingly each plaintiff says that his dismissal was wrongful and in breach of contract from the defendant company.

...

The so-called "normative effect" by which it can be inferred that provisions of collective agreements have become part of individual contracts of employment is now well recognised in employment law (see, for example, *Harvey on Industrial Relations and Employment Law*). However, serious difficulties still arise because the principle still has to be one of incorporation into the individual contracts of employment and the extraction of a recognisable contractual intent as between the individual employee and his employer. The mere existence of collective agreements which are relevant to the employee and his employment does not include a contractual intent (see for example per Ackner LJ, *Robertson* v *British Gas*). The contractual intent has to be found in the individual contract of employment and very often the evidence will not be sufficient to establish such an intent in a manner which satisfies accepted contractual criteria and satisfies ordinary criteria of certainty. Where the relevant subject-matter is one of present day-to-day relevance to the employer and employee, as for example wage rates and hours of work, the continuing relationship between employer and employee, the former paying wages and providing work, the latter working and accepting wages, provides a basis for inferring such a contractual intent. Where, as in the case of redundancy, the situation is one which does not have daily implications but only arises occasionally the inference will be more difficult to sustain. Here, there had not previously been any question of compulsory redundancies. There was no previously tested position by which a local custom could be demonstrated, nor was there any previous situation involving any of the relevant individuals, or for that matter any other employees of the defendants from which it could be inferred as a matter of individual contractual intent, that individual contracts of employment were to include as a matter of contractual right and obligation selection for redundancy on the seniority principle. It must be borne in mind that although the present plaintiffs would be the beneficiaries of the application of such a principle, by a parity of reasoning there would be other employees who would be disadvantaged. Similarly, there is no necessity to infer an intention to incorporate since collective agreements have a function and value of their own which exists wholly independently of any individual contract of employment (see, for example, the reasoning of the Judicial Committee in *Young* v *Canadian Northern Railway*).

...

The principles to be applied can therefore be summarised. The relevant contract is that between the individual employee and his employer; it is the contractual intention of those two parties which must be ascertained. In so far as that intention is to be found in a written document, that document must be construed on ordinary contractual principles. In so far as there is no such document or that document is not complete or conclusive, their contractual intention has to be ascertained by inference from the other available material including collective agreements. The fact that another document is not itself contractual does not prevent it from being incorporated into the contract if that intention is shown as between the employer and the individual employee. Where a document is expressly incorporated by general words it is still necessary to consider, in conjunction with the words of incorporation, whether any particular part of that document is apt to be a term of the contract; if it is inapt, the correct construction of the contract may be that it is not a term of the contract. Where it is not a case of express incorporation, but a matter of inferring the contractual intent, the character of the document and the relevant part of it and whether it is apt to form part of the individual contract is central to the decision whether or not the inference should be drawn.

In the present cases I have concluded that the wording of the only document directly applicable to the individual plaintiffs, the statutory statements, is not sufficient to effect an express incorporation of the provisions relating to redundancy in the collective agreements: accordingly it is a matter of considering whether or not to *infer* that the selection procedures and the principle of seniority have been incorporated into the individual contracts of employment and this has to be decided having regard to the evidence given and an evaluation of the character of the relevant provisions in the collective agreements. …'

COMMENT

(1)   On the evidence, the judge considered that this inference could not be established because the collective agreement was not appropriate for incorporation. This brings us to the remaining issue: can the whole of a collective agreement be regarded as incorporated, and so enforceable by an individual employee?

What terms are incorporated?

Young v *Canadian Northern Railway*

[1931] AC 83 Privy Council

Y was made redundant in contravention of a collective agreement ('Wage Agreement No. 4') which provided that selection for redundancy should be on the basis of 'last in, first out' – that is, that those employees with longest service should be retained. The opinion of the Privy Council was given by Lord Russell.

Lord Russell: ' … There can be no doubt upon the evidence that in fact, the provisions of Wage Agreement No. 4 were applied by the railway company to all its employees in its locomotive and car department. One extract from the evidence of the general manager (Mr Tisdale) makes this clear: "(A.) I understand your question to be this: Is the agreement that was negotiated between the railway companies and Division 4 applicable to all the men in the shop? (Q.) Yes? (A.) The answer is Yes."

Their Lordships, however, are unable to treat these matters as establishing contractual liability by the railway company to the appellant. The fact that the railway company applied the agreement to the appellant is equally consistent with the view that it did so, not because it was bound contractually to apply it to him, but because as a matter of policy it deemed it expedient to apply it to all.

If the conduct of the railway company in applying the provisions of the agreement to the appellant could be explained only by the existence of a contractual obligation to the appellant so to do, it would be not only permissible, but necessary to hold that the existence of the contractual obligation had been established. In the circumstances, however, of the present case, their Lordships find themselves unable so to decide.

But the matter does not quite rest there. When Wage Agreement No. 4 is examined, it does not appear to their Lordships to be a document adapted for conversion into or incorporation with a service agreement, so as to entitle master and servant to enforce *inter se* the terms thereof. It consists of some 188 "rules", which the railway companies contract with Division No. 4 to observe. It appears to their Lordships to be intended merely to operate as an agreement between a body of employers and a labour organisation by which the employers undertake that as regards their workmen, certain rules beneficial to the workmen shall be observed. By itself it constitutes no contract between any individual employee and the company which employs him. If an employer refused to observe the rules, the effective sequel would be, not an action by any employee, not even an action by Division No. 4 against the employer for specific performance or damages, but the calling of a strike until the grievance was remedied.'

Alexander v *Standard Telephones & Cables Ltd (No 2)*

[1991] IRLR 286 Queen's Bench Division

The facts are given above (p 171).

Hobhouse J: '... In the case *National Coal Board* v *National Union of Mineworkers*, to which some individual employees were also parties, Mr Justice Scott reviewed the authorities on incorporation at pp 453 and following. In that case there was an express provision in the individual contracts of employment that the employees' "wages and conditions of service shall be regulated by and subject to such national, district and pit agreements as are for the time being in force". The question was the application of that clear contractual intent; the question in the action therefore was: what was the extent of he resultant incorporation? He drew a distinction which was derived from the argument of Mr Dehn before him.

"He seeks, however, to draw a distinction between the terms of a collective agreement which are of their nature apt to become enforceable terms of an individual's contract of employment and terms which are of their nature inapt to become enforecable by individuals. Terms of collective agreements fixing rates of pay, or hours of work, would obviously fall into the first category. Terms ... dismissing an employee also would fall into the first category. But conciliation agreements setting up machinery designed to resolve by discussions between employers' representatives and union representatives, or by arbitral proceedings, questions arising within the industry, fall, submitted Mr Dehn, firmly in the second category. The terms of conciliation schemes are not intended to become contractually enforceable by individual workers whether or not referred into the individual contracts of employment.

...

A collective agreement between an employer and a union providing machinery for collective bargaining and for resolving industrial disputes may be of very great importance to each and every worker in the industry. But it is not likely to be an agreement intended to be legally enforceable as between employer and union, and it is almost inconceivable to my mind that it could have been intended to become legally enforceable at the suit of an individual worker. In the procedures laid down by the 1946 Scheme, for instance, no part is played by an individual mineworker. The machinery is designed to be invoked and operated either by the NCB or by the NUM with the co-operation of the other. It simply does not lend itself at all to enforceability at the suit of an individual mineworker."

Therefore, even in a case which involved wide express words of incorporation the court considered it necessary to look at the content and character of the relevant parts of the collective agreement in order to decide whether or not they were incorporated into the individual contracts of employment.

...

Turning to the collective agreements themselves it is convenient to take the *Wall* agreement first. It expressly states that it is a"procedure" agreement. Thus, on a simplistic application of the language of Mr Justice Scott, one would conclude that it was not apt to be incorporated. However, it is of course necessary to examine the character of the agreement and its relevant parts more closely before reaching a conclusion. It is undoubtedly primarily a policy document applicable to the relationship between the unions and the company. It also is specifically concerned with procedure. Thus the third clause under the heading "Joint consultation" lays down a procedure and it is within that scheme that individuals are to be selected for compulsory redundancy. Indeed, all the first five clauses of the agreement are clearly inappropriate for application to or incorporation in individual contracts of employment.

Clauses 7 to 10 are also inapt for such incorporation. The reference to temporary workers is merely to exclude them from the scope of the agreement. The re-employment clause merely says that the company will give consideration to re-employment, at a later date, of employees made compulsorily redundant; this is neither expressed as a contractual obligation nor could it form part of a present contract of employment. As regards transfer allowances the clause contemplates that the company may make offers of employment in another division of the company to some individuals as an alternative to redundancy and states that if such an offer should be made it will include assistance in making the transfer. This again is not apt to be a term of an existing contract of employment as it involves the choice of the company to make an offer and it is only from the making of that offer and its acceptance that any individual right can subsequently arise. As regards the provision relating to employees who leave early, it merely provides that employees will normally be required to observe their contractual obligations under their contracts of employment; therefore again it is not apt for incorporation.

In this context, where none of the other clauses of the collective agreement are apt to be incorporated into the individual contract of employment, it would require some cogent indication in clause 6 [dealing with selection for redundancy] that it was to have a different character and to be incorporated into the individual contracts of employment. The plaintiff's submissions gain nothing from the context within which clause 6 is to be found; indeed the context strongly detracts from their case. The first part of clause 6 is a statement of policy – looking for volunteers, giving priority to employees taking early retirement or affected by ill-health. Likewise paragraph 6.2 is again expressed in policy terms having regard to inter-union relationships and to the requirements of the company's on-going business; it is stated to be "the mutual objective". Whilst this again is not inconsistent with giving paragraph 6.1 contractual effect, it does detract from that implication. Paragraph 6.1, the critical paragraph, is expressed in terms which are capable of giving rise to individual rights. It says that selection for compulsory redundancy "will be made on the basis of service" within the relevant group. Therefore the plaintiffs can reasonably argue that as individuals they are entitled, on account of their seniority, not to be selected. However, I consider that the wording of paragraph 6.1 is too weak, when considered in the context in which it occurs in clause 6 itself and within the context and consultation scheme of the procedure agreement as a whole, to support the inference of incorporation. Clear and specific express words of incorporation contained in a primary contractual document could displace this conclusion, but on any view the wording of the statutory statements in the present case do not suffice.

It follows that the *Wall* plaintiffs' case of breach of contract must fail. They cannot establish the contractual right under their individual contracts of employment which they need in order to succeed in their action for damages for breach of contract against the defendants. ...'

COMMENT

(1)   The judge dismissed the *Alexander* action for similar reasons.

(2)   In *Marley* v *Forward Trust* the court proceeded on the basis that the redundancy agreement applied without discussing the point. However, that was not a selection agreement. In *Lee* v *GEC Plessey* a provision for payment of enhanced severance pay in a collective agreement was held to be apt for incorporation, and in *Airlie* v *City of Edinburgh DC*, where the employees' written statements expressly incorporated the collective agreement, the Scottish EAT rejected the argument that this did not incorporate all parts of it, even though some clauses were clearly inapt. Two points may be made: first, it is submitted that the criteria for redundancy selection so closely affect individuals that such a provision ought always to be regarded as appropriate for incorporation; second, that there is an unfortunate lack of certainty as to the principles for the incorporation of collective agreements.

(3)   All aspects of handling a redundancy situation, especially the method of selection, are obviously important to individuals. In view of the state of the authorities, it seems that trade unions would be well advised to have some formulation of key terms in a redundancy agreement drawn up in a manner which is suitable for incorporation in individual contracts, and to ensure that express incorporation takes place.

No-strike clauses

At the beginning of this chapter we noted that the advantage for employers in collective bargaining is promotion of industrial peace. Today employers, especially foreign companies, want collective agreements which do not merely require procedures to be followed before industrial action is instituted, but which prohibit industrial action altogether. As this is a significant inroad on employees' freedom of action, it is subject to statutory safeguard.

Trade Union and Labour Relations (Consolidation) Act 1992

180.   (1)   Any terms of a collective agreement which prohibit or restrict the right of workers to engage in a strike or other industrial action, or have the effect of prohibiting or restricting that right, shall not form part of any contract between a worker and the person for whom he works unless the following conditions are met.

(2)   The conditions are that the collective agreement—
   (a)   is in writing,
   (b)   contains a provision expressly stating that those terms shall or may be incorporated in such a contract,
   (c)   is reasonably accessible at his place of work to the worker to whom it applies and is available for him to consult during working hours, and
   (d)   is one where each trade union which is a party to the agreement is an independent trade union;
   and that the contract with the worker expressly or impliedly incorporates those terms in the contract.

(3)   The above provisions have effect notwithstanding anything in section 179 and notwithstanding any provision to the contrary in any agreement (including a collective agreement or a contract with any worker).

COMMENT

(1)   If workers take part in a strike or industrial action despite a no-strike clause incorporated in their contracts of employment, they will actually be no worse off than they would be anyway. As we will see (Chapter 12), almost all industrial action is a breach of contract for which employees can be lawfully dismissed and for which they may be liable for damages. The damages would not be increased because of the existence of such a term, and courts will not order workers to return to work.

(2)   Suppose a collective agreement required that the employer should receive a period of notice before any industrial action. Would this be a term suitable for incorporation into individual contracts?

ENFORCEABILITY BETWEEN UNION AND EMPLOYER

As indicated in the extract from the Donovan Commission Report (p 163), collective agreements have traditionally been regarded as unenforceable in law. This view is now enshrined in TULRCA s 179.

Trade Union and Labour Relations (Consolidation) Act 1992

179.   (1)   A collective agreement shall be conclusively presumed not to have been intended by the parties to be a legally enforceable contract unless the agreement—

(a)   is in writing, and

(b)   contains a provision which (however expressed) states that the parties intend that the agreement shall be a legally enforceable contract.

(2)   A collective agreement which does satisfy those conditions shall be conclusively presumed to have been intended by the parties to be a legally enforceable contract....

COMMENT

(1)   In a seminal judgment in *Ford* v *AUEFW*, Geoffrey Lane J held that collective agreements were not legally binding because the parties did not intend to create legally binding relations, referring specifically to the views of Kahn-Freund and the Donovan Commission.

(2)   The advantage seen by some in making collective agreements legally enforceable is that strikes on matters covered by the agreement would be unlawful so long as the agreement remained in force. This is certainly how it works in some countries, such as the United States; however, note that it is not an essential term to include in a legally enforceable collective agreement and it is possible to have a no-strike clause without having a legally enforceable collective agreement (cf TULRCA s 180, above). Furthermore, even if a 'peace obligation' is included, it will probably

not prevent strikes about matters outside the agreement. On this, see Roy Lewis, 'Strike-free Deals and Pendulum Arbitration' (1990) 28 BJIR 32.

(3)   As the reason for non-enforceability is the intention of the parties, it becomes rather difficult to see how legislation can change the position. A statute cannot force parties to enter contracts if they do not want to. The Industrial Relations Act 1971 attempted to do so: the result was a rash of disclaimers in agreements, usually known by their acronym, TINA LEA (This Is Not A Legally Enforceable Agreement). This was repealed by TULRA 1974, being replaced by the forerunner of TULRCA s 179 above. The Conservative Government considered more than once whether the law should be changed to 'encourage' employers and unions to enter legally enforceable agreements (see the Green Paper *Industrial Relations in the 1990s* Cm 1602 (1991) Ch 8). The advantages claimed were not only the 'peace obligation' but also that it would bring the UK into line with most of the rest of Europe and North America, and would be easier for foreign companies investing in the UK to understand.

(4)   It is, of course, possible for foreign investors to insist on legally binding collective agreements, and some have made this a condition of recognising trade unions at new plants. Peace obligations are often, but not always, included. Another feature of this development is an insistence on 'single union deals'. To avoid the confusion and delay inherent in having to negotiate with many trade unions (in *Ford v AUEFW*, the company recognised 19 unions), companies are beginning to offer recognition only to one union, which will represent all grades of workers.

(5)   Collective bargaining can only take place in a situation where both parties are prepared to negotiate. This means that the employer must be prepared to recognise the union. It is to this that we now turn.

RECOGNITION OF TRADE UNIONS

Recognition of trade unions means recognition by an employer for the purposes of collective bargaining. If the employer refuses to recognise the union, there is little that it can do and little advantage for employees in belonging to it. Hence the importance for a trade union in being recognised.

Trade Union and Labour Relations (Consolidation) Act 1992

178.   (1)   In this Act 'collective agreement' means any agreement or arrangement made by or on behalf of one or more trade unions and one or more employers or employers' associations and relating to one or more of the matters specified below; and 'collective bargaining' means negotiations relating to or connected with one or more of those matters.

  (2)   The matters referred to above are—

  (a)   terms and conditions of employment, or the physical conditions in which any workers are required to work;

  (b)   engagement or non-engagement, or termination or suspension of employment or the duties of employment, of one or more workers;

  (c)   allocation of work or the duties of employment between workers or groups of workers;

(d) matters of discipline;

(e) a worker's membership or non-membership of a trade union;

(f) facilities for officials of trade unions; and

(g) machinery for negotiation or consultation, and other procedures, relating to any of the above matters, including the recognition by employers or employers' associations of the right of a trade union to represent workers in such negotiation or consultation or in the carrying out of such procedures.

(3) In this Act 'recognition', in relation to a trade union, means the recognition of the union by an employer, or two or more associated employers, to any extent, for the purpose of collective bargaining; and 'recognised' and other related expressions shall be construed accordingly.

COMMENT

(1) Where a trade union is recognised within the meaning of s 178 it qualifies for certain useful rights: the right to disclosure of information for collective bargaining (TULRCA s 181 (see below)); the right to appoint a safety representative (Health and Safety at Work Act 1974 s 2(4)); and the right to time off for their officials and members (TULRCA ss 168, 170). Recognised unions are also entitled to be consulted over health and safety issues (HSWA s 2(6),(7)) and used to have exclusive rights to consultation over redundancies and transfers of undertakings (TULRCA s 188 and TUPE reg 10). However, in these latter situations an employer may now bypass the union and instead consult other employee representatives (see below, Chapter 9).

(2) Apart from a brief period between 1975 and 1980, there has been no legal mechanism for a trade union to insist upon recognition by the employer, unlike many other countries, such as the United States. An employer who is not attracted by the inherent virtues of the trade union may be persuaded by industrial action to recognise, but that is fast becoming an unrealistic option. Small wonder that some trade unions have sought to argue that recognition has taken place without the employer even being aware of it.

National Union of Gold, Silver and Allied Trades v Albury Bros Ltd

[1979] ICR 84 Court of Appeal

The company, a jewellers' firm, made three employees redundant. The union claimed that it should have been consulted, but the company argued that it did not recognise the union. The facts relied on by the union as showing recognition were (1) that the company belonged to an employers' association which negotiated national terms and conditions with the union; (2) that the managing director of the company had exchanged letters and had a few meetings with the union's district secretary about the wages of a particular trainee.

Lord Denning MR: 'On the history, the question arose whether on that discussion and on those few talks and letters the employers had recognised the union for the purpose of collective bargaining. That is the one point in this case. If they had recognised them, they ought to have gone through all the statutory procedure for handling redundancies. If they had not recognised them, then they were under no such obligation.

This is a new point under a new Act. Both the industrial tribunal and the Employment

Appeal Tribunal have held that there was no recognition. Only three cases have come before the appeal tribunal on it. The first one was at the end of 1976 before the Scottish tribunal – *Transport and General Workers' Union* v *Dyer*. The next one was *Joshua Wilson & Bros Ltd* v *Union of Shop, Distributive and Allied Workers*. Finally *National Union of Tailors and Garment Workers* v *Charles Ingram & Co Ltd*. Reading through those cases, there is general agreement and consensus of opinion in these respects: a recognition issue is a most important matter for industry; and therefore an employer is not to be held to have recognised a trade union unless the evidence is clear. Sometimes there is an actual agreement of recognition. Sometimes there is an implied agreement of recognition. But at all events there must be something sufficiently clear and distinct by conduct or otherwise so that one can say, "They have mutually recognised one another, the trade union and the employers, for the purposes of collective bargaining."

Then one comes to this particular case. Were those few letters and the one meeting recognition of the trade union? It is agreed by Mr Sedley that if the employers had simply banged the door and told the union representative to go off, that would not be recognition. Is it recognition when Mr Albury goes along with the letter in his hand and is ready to discuss the wages? It seems to me that that is not sufficient. Nor is it sufficient if he starts discussing the wages of one particular man, Stephen Rickard. There must be something a great deal more than that.

As I said at the beginning, an act of recognition is such an important matter involving such serious consequences on both sides, both for the employers and the union, that it should not be held to be established unless the evidence is clear upon it, either by agreement or actual conduct clearly showing recognition. The conduct in this case does not come clearly up to that. I would therefore dismiss the appeal.

I should mention that Mr Sedley did suggest that owing to some of the regulations of the federation there might be an agency and that the employers' association was the agent of Albury Brothers Ltd to recognise the union. That was not pressed before us; I must say that there is nothing in it. This association was in no way the agent of the employers. The fact that there was an agreement between the employers' association and the union certainly does not impose recognition on the members of it. I think the appeal should be dismissed.'

(Eveleigh LJ and Sir David Cairns delivered concurring judgements.)

COMMENT

(1)   It seems clear that recognition will not be found to have occurred unless the employer has definitely agreed to it. As noted already, the trend is in the other direction. In recent years a number of employers (especially newly privatised industries that were previously nationalised) have derecognised trade unions.

(2)   It seems likely that the new Labour Government will legislate for some sort of union right to recognition, but it is not clear what form it will take. (See Hall, 'Beyond recognition? Employee representation and EU Law' (1996) 25 ILJ 15.)

Disclosure of information to trade unions

In order to bargain effectively, trade unions need information about the business of the employer. One of the measures of statutory support for collective bargaining which has survived is the requirement that an employer should disclose certain kinds of information to any trade union which is recognised for collective bargaining. This is not much of an inroad on the privacy of employers, for an employer who does not wish to disclose information can avoid doing so by refusing to recognise the union.

Trade Union and Labour Relations (Consolidation) Act 1992

181....

(2) The information to be disclosed is all information relating to the employer's undertaking which is in his possession, or that of an associated employer, and is information—

(a) without which the trade union representatives would be to a material extent impeded in carrying on collective bargaining with him, and

(b) which it would be in accordance with good industrial relations practice that he should disclose to them for the purposes of collective bargaining. ...

182. (1) An employer is not required by section 181 to disclose information—

(a) the disclosure of which would be against the interests of national security, or

(b) which he could not disclose without contravening a prohibition imposed by or under an enactment, or

(c) which has been communicated to him in confidence, or which he has otherwise obtained in consequence of the confidence reposed in him by another person, or

(d) which relates specifically to an individual (unless that individual has consented to its being disclosed), or

(e) the disclosure of which would cause substantial injury to his undertaking for reasons other than its effect on collective bargaining, or

(f) obtained by him for the purpose of bringing, prosecuting or defending any legal proceedings.

ACAS Code of Practice 2

Disclosure of information to trade unions for collective bargaining purposes (1977)

11. Collective bargaining within an undertaking can range from negotiations on specific matters arising daily at the work place affecting particular sections of the workforce, to extensive periodic negotiations on terms and conditions of employment affecting the whole workforce in multiplant companies. The relevant information and the depth, detail and form in which it could be presented to negotiators will vary accordingly. Consequently, it is not possible to compile a list of items that should be disclosed in all circumstances. Some examples of information relating to the undertaking which could be relevant in certain collective bargaining situations are given below:

(i) *Pay and benefits*: principles and structure of payment systems; job evaluation systems and grading criteria; earnings and hours analysed according to work-group, grade, plant, sex, out-workers and homeworkers, department or division, giving, where appropriate, distributions and make-up of pay showing any additions to basic rate of salary; total pay bill; details of fringe benefits and non-wage labour costs.

(ii) *Conditions of service*: policies on recruitment, redeployment, redundancy, training, equal opportunity, and promotion; appraisal systems; health, welfare and safety matters.

(iii) *Manpower*: numbers employed analysed according to grade, department, location, age and sex; labour turnover; absenteeism; overtime and short-time; manning standards; planned changes in work methods, materials, equipment or organisation; available manpower plans; investment plans.

 (iv) *Performance*: productivity and efficiency data; savings from increased productivity and output; return on capital invested; sales and state of order book.

 (v) *Financial*: cost structures; gross and net profits; sources of earnings; assets; liabilities; allocation of profits; details of government financial assistance; transfer prices; loans to parent or subsidiary companies and interest charged.

12. These examples are not intended to represent a check list of information that should be provided for all negotiations. Nor are they meant to be an exhaustive list of types of information as other items may be relevant in particular negotiations.

Restrictions on the duty to disclose

13. Trade unions and employers should be aware of the restrictions on the general duty to disclose information for collective bargaining.

14. Some examples of information which if disclosed in particular circumstances might cause substantial injury are: cost information on individual products; detailed analysis of proposed investment, marketing or pricing policies; and price quotas or the make-up of tender prices. Information which has to be made available publicly, for example under the Companies Acts, would not fall into this category.

15. Substantial injury may occur if, for example, certain customers would be lost to competitors, or suppliers would refuse to supply necessary materials, or the ability to raise funds to finance the company would be seriously impaired as a result of disclosing certain information. The burden of establishing a claim that disclosure of certain information would cause substantial injury lies with the employer.

COMMENT

(1) If a trade union considers that an employer is in breach of the duty to disclose information, it may make a complaint to the Central Arbitration Committee. The CAC may refer the matter to ACAS for conciliation or may proceed to hear and determine the complaint (as it will also do if conciliation fails). Where the CAC upholds the complaint, it will specify the information which should have been disclosed and a timetable for its disclosure (TULRCA s 183).

(2) If the employer still refuses to disclose the information, the union must complain again to the CAC and may also bid for certain improvements to be included in the employees' terms and conditions of employment. If the CAC finds the further complaint well founded, it makes a declaration to that effect and may also award the improvements asked for (TULRCA ss 184–5). In effect, the employer is treated as having impeded the collective bargaining process and the sanction is not to force disclosure, but to give the workforce the kinds of improvements to their working conditions which could perhaps have been expected to result from proper collective bargaining.

(3) The ACAS Code does not of itself impose any legal obligations to disclose information, nor does failure to observe the Code render anyone liable; however, the Code must be taken into account in any proceedings before the CAC.

(4) The CAC's Annual Report for 1995 showed that it had received 30 new

complaints from trade unions over employers' failure to disclose information in the previous year. Compared with an average of 22 references per year since the disclosure of information provisions were introduced in 1976, this indicates that the jurisdiction continues to be important. The CAC noted that the market-testing of public services and performance-related pay were fertile sources of complaints.

(5)   Shareholders in companies get regular information, including financial information, about the company via its annual report. Employees have no right to similar information, although more enlightened employers today produce a version of the annual report for the employees. It is government policy to encourage this, at least indirectly, by requiring companies with more than 250 employees to report annually on what steps have been taken to inform and involve employees in the company's affairs (Companies Act 1985, Sch 7, para 11).

COLLECTIVE BARGAINING AND EUROPE

In contrast to the policy of the Conservative Government throughout the 1980s and early 1990s, it is European Union policy to encourage what is called 'the social dialogue' between both sides of industry, and even to use such agreements as a source of legal regulation, as the following extracts indicate.

Treaty of Rome Article 118B

The Commission shall endeavour to develop the dialogue between management and labour at European level which could, if the two sides consider it desirable, lead to relations based on agreement.

Treaty of European Union

Protocol on Social Policy

Article 2

1 With a view to achieving the objectives of Article 1, the Community shall support and complement the activities of the Member States in the following fields:

- improvement in particular of the working environment to protect workers' health and safety;
- working conditions;
- the information and consultation of workers;
- equality between men and women with regard to labour market opportunities and treatment at work;
- the integration of persons excluded from the labour market, without the prejudice of Article 127 of the Treaty establishing the European Community (hereinafter referred to as "the Treaty").

2 To this end, the Council may adopt, by means of directives, minimum requirements for gradual implementation, having regard to the conditions and technical rules obtaining in each of the Member States. Such directives shall avoid imposing administrative, financial and legal constraints in a way which would hold back the creation and development of small and medium-sized undertakings.

The Council shall act in accordance with the procedure referred to in Article 189c of the Treaty after consulting the Economic and Social Committee.

3 However, the Council shall act unanimously on a proposal from the Commission, after consulting the European Parliament and the Economic and Social Committee, in the following areas:

- social security and social protection of workers;
- protection of workers where their employment contract is terminated;
- representation and collective defence of the interests of workers and employers, including co-determination, subject to paragraph 6;
- conditions of employment for third-country nationals legally residing in Community territory;
- financial contributions for promotion of employment and job-creation, without prejudice to the provisions relating to the Social Fund.

4 A Member State may entrust management and labour, at their joint request, with the implementation of directives adopted pursuant to paragraphs 2 and 3.

In this case, it shall ensure that, no later than the date on which a directive must be transposed in accordance with Article 189, management and labour have introduced the necessary measures by agreement, the Member State concerned being required to take any necessary measure enabling it at any time to be in a position to guarantee the results imposed by that directive.

5 The provisions adopted pursuant to this Article shall not prevent any Member State from maintaining or introducing more stringent protective measures compatible with the Treaty.

6 The provisions of this Article shall not apply to pay, the right of association, the right to strike or the right to impose lock-outs.

COMMENT

(1) Article 118B was added to the Treaty of Rome by the Single European Act in 1986.

(2) The Protocol to the Treaty of European Union (also known as the Maastricht Treaty) was added in order to give effect to the Community Charter on the Fundamental Social Rights of Workers agreed in 1989 by all member states except for the United Kingdom. The United Kingdom refused to agree to the incorporation of measures to implement the Charter in the Treaty of European Union, so they had to appear in a Protocol which does not bind the United Kingdom. The Protocol allows the other member states to go ahead with legislation on the matters indicated in Article 2 without reference to the United Kingdom. Any resulting instruments will bind the other member states only. The 1994 Works Council Directive (94/95EC) was the first directive to be so agreed.

(3) The Labour Government has indicated its willingness in principle to sign up to the Protocol. In any case, the experience of the Works Councils Directive indicates the potential for such legislation to affect British employers and workers, because of the international dimension of many businesses.

6 Statutory employment protection rights

While collective bargaining has been seen for most of this century as the prime method for equalising the bargaining position between employers and workers, it is recognised that on its own it may not be enough. There are always industries where the workforce is transient or fragmented and where effective unionisation is difficult.

In the 1960s employees were given certain basic protections by statute: the right to a written statement of their main terms and conditions of employment, the right to compensation if dismissed for redundancy. In 1971 the Industrial Relations Act introduced the important right to claim for unfair dismissal. However, the mid-1970s saw a move to a different style of legislation which impinged to a much greater extent on the ongoing day-to-day relationship of employer and employee. The Sex Discrimination Act 1975 and the Race Relations Act 1976 can be seen as examples of this, but in this chapter we will concentrate on the range of statutory employment protection rights introduced by the Employment Protection Act 1975.

Part of the impetus for these rights came from the informal 'Social Contract' between the Labour Government of the day and the TUC. The idea was that unions should show restraint in their pay demands in return for receiving a legislative guarantee of certain positive rights. The principal individual rights introduced by the Employment Protection Act related to maternity, guarantees for certain kinds of lay-off and time off for a range of duties and activities. They are now to be found in the Employment Rights Act 1996.

MATERNITY RIGHTS

There are four rights relating to maternity: a right not to be dismissed on grounds of pregnancy; a right to time off for ante-natal care; a right to maternity pay, and a right to maternity leave. As yet they are not matched by rights for fathers.

No dismissal on grounds of pregnancy

Since 1975 there has been some provision intended to inhibit dismissal on grounds of pregnancy by rendering such dismissals automatically unfair. However, substantial amendments were made to existing provisions by TURERA in response to the Pregnant Workers Directive (92/85/EC), adopted in October 1992. This directive was the tenth to be adopted on the authority of the Health and Safety Framework Directive (89/391/EC). Because it was a health and safety measure it could be adopted by qualified majority voting instead of needing unanimity (as is required for directives on most employment matters). Italy and the UK abstained on the vote for this directive.

Employment Rights Act 1996

99.   (1)   An employee who is dismissed shall be regarded for the purposes of this Part as unfairly dismissed if —

   (a)   the reason (or, if more than one, the principal reason) for the dismissal is that she is pregnant or any other reason connected with her pregnancy,

   (b)   her maternity leave period is ended by the dismissal and the reason (or, if more than one, the principal reason) for the dismissal is that she has given birth to a child or any other reason connected with her having given birth to a child,

   (c)   her contract of employment is terminated after the end of her maternity leave period and the reason (or, if more than one, the principal reason) for the dismissal is that she took, or availed herself of the benefits of, maternity leave,

   (d)   the reason (or, if more than one, the principal reason) for the dismissal is a relevant requirement, or a relevant recommendation, as defined by section 66(2), or

   (e)   her maternity leave period is ended by the dismissal, the reason (or, if more than one, the principal reason) for the dismissal is that she is redundant and section 77 has not been complied with.

   (2)   For the purposes of subsection (1)(c) –

   (a)   a woman takes maternity leave if she is absent from work during her maternity leave period, and

   (b)   a woman avails herself of the benefits of maternity leave if, during her maternity leave period, she avails herself of the benefit of any of the terms and conditions of her employment preserved by section 71 during that period.

   (3)   An employee who is dismissed shall also be regarded for the purposes of this Part as unfairly dismissed if —

   (a)   before the end of her maternity leave period she gave to her employer a certificate from a registered medical practitioner stating that by reason of disease or bodily or mental disablement she would be incapable of work after the end of that period,

   (b)   her contract of employment was terminated within the period of four weeks beginning immediately after the end of her maternity leave period in circumstances in which she continued to be incapable of work and the certificate remained current, and

   (c)   the reason (or, if more than one, the principal reason) for the dismissal is that she has given birth to a child or any other reason connected with her having given birth to a child.

   (4)   Where —

   (a)   an employee has the right conferred by section 79,

   (b)   it is not practicable by reason of redundancy for the employer to permit

her to return in accordance with that right, and
(c) no offer is made of such alternative employment as is referred to in section
81,
the dismissal of the employee which is treated as taking place by virtue of
section 96 is to be regarded for the purposes of this Part as unfair.

COMMENT

(1)   There is now no qualifying period of service for this: the previous formulation
had been interpreted as subject to the condition of two years' continuous service. This
means that women dismissed for pregnancy after a short period of service will no
longer need to try to bring their cases under the Sex Discrimination Act. However, a
woman who is not *recruited* on grounds of pregnancy would still only be able to claim
under the Sex Discrimination Act; furthermore, compensation under that Act is
unlimited.

(2)   The previous law permitted the employer to dismiss for pregnancy if the woman
became incapable of performing her job properly. This exception is now abolished:
in such circumstances the woman will be entitled instead to immediate maternity leave
(see below).

Time off for ante-natal care

Employment Rights Act 1996

55.   (1)   An employee who –
(a)   is pregnant, and
(b)   has, on the advice of a registered medical practitioner, registered midwife
or registered health visitor, made an appointment to attend at any place
for the purpose of receiving ante-natal care,
is entitled to be permitted by her employer to take time off during the employee's
working hours in order to enable her to keep the appointment.
(2)   An employee is not entitled to take time off under this section to keep an
appointment unless, if her employer requests her to do so, she produces for
his inspection –
(a)   a certificate from a registered medical practitioner, registered midwife or
registered health visitor stating that the employee is pregnant, and
(b)   an appointment card or some other document showing that the appointment has been made ...

56.   (1)   An employee who is permitted to take time off under section 55 is entitled to
be paid remuneration by her employer for the period of absence at the
appropriate hourly rate ...

COMMENT

(1)   This right, for which there is no qualifying period of employment, was introduced in 1980 as a response to figures showing the UK to have one of the worst records

for perinatal deaths in the developed world. A study carried out by the Policy Studies Institute in 1989 showed that 84 per cent of the pregnant women surveyed who were working full time had made use of this right (S McRae, *Maternity Rights in Britain*, PSI 1991).

(2) Where the employer unreasonably refuses to grant paid time off under this section, the woman may apply to an industrial tribunal for a declaration and an award of compensation equal to the remuneration she would have had for the time off to which she was entitled (ERA s 57).

(3) Attendance at ante-natal classes is generally thought to be covered by s 55 – but only for women. Today, prospective fathers are also encouraged to attend at least some classes, but they are not entitled to time off to do so.

Statutory maternity pay

To understand what follows, it helps to know that until 1987, there were two different sources of maternity pay: women who had been employed for two years got six weeks' pay from their employers at a rate of 90 per cent of their usual pay; women who had fulfilled certain contribution requirements got a lower maternity allowance from the state. Women in the first category also qualified in the second, although the reverse was not always true.

Rather than have two organisations – the employer and the state – doing much the same thing and frequently duplicating each other's work, the Government decided to shift the whole administrative burden to the employer, as it already had done with sick pay. The system is broadly the same as it was; the lower of the two rates corresponds to the old maternity allowance and is equivalent to the statutory sick pay rate.

As a result of the Pregnant Workers Directive 1992, the right to maternity pay and maternity leave was extended to all women workers. The justification for this as a health and safety measure is found in the preamble to the directive.

EC Council Directive 92/85 on the introduction of measures to encourage improvements in the safety and health at work of pregnant workers and workers who have recently given birth or are breastfeeding (the Pregnant Workers Directive 1992)

...Whereas the vulnerability of pregnant workers, workers who have recently given birth or who are breastfeeding makes it necessary for them to be granted the right to maternity leave of at least 14 continuous weeks, allocated before and/or after confinement, and renders necessary the compulsory nature of maternity leave of at least two weeks, allocated before and/or after confinement;

Whereas the risk of dismissal for reasons associated with their condition may have harmful effects on the physical and mental state of pregnant workers, workers who have recently given birth or who are breastfeeding; whereas provision should be made for such dismissal to be prohibited;

Whereas measures for the organisation of work concerning the protection of the health of pregnant workers, workers who have recently given birth or workers who are breastfeeding would serve no purpose unless accompanied by the maintenance of rights linked to the employment contract, including maintenance of payment and/or entitlement to an adequate allowance;

Whereas, moreover, provision concerning maternity leave would also serve no purpose unless accompanied by the maintenance of rights linked to the employment contract and or entitlement to an adequate allowance; ...

COMMENT

(1)   As a result of this directive the relevant legislation in the United Kingdom (the Social Security Contributions and Benefits Act 1992, the Statutory Maternity Pay (General) Regulations 1986 and the Social Security (Maternity Allowance) Regulations 1987) have been amended so that every woman who has worked and made National Insurance contributions in at least 26 out of the 66 weeks before the expected week of childbirth will receive either statutory maternity pay (SMP) or the higher rate of maternity allowance. Unemployed or self-employed women may qualify for the lower rate of maternity allowance.

(2)   Note that the right to SMP is entirely independent of the right to maternity leave and is payable whether or not the woman intends to return to work. However, many employers have provision for some sort of contractual maternity pay in addition to SMP. Typically, it tops up SMP so that the woman receives her usual salary for a stipulated period, and is usually conditional on the woman returning to work afterwards. It seems to be a successful ploy: the PSI study found that three quarters of women receiving contractual maternity pay returned to work against an overall figure of 44 per cent (McCrae *op. cit.* above).

(3)   SMP is payable to women who have completed 26 weeks of continuous employment before the expected week of confinement, provided that their average earnings reach the threshold for paying National Insurance contributions (£62 in 1997). It is an entitlement to six weeks at 90 per cent of normal pay followed by 12 weeks at a rate equivalent to statutory sick pay (SSP) (£55.70 in 1997).

(4)   Women who have made National Insurance contributions in any 26 weeks of the 66 preceding the expected week of confinement are entitled to higher rate maternity allowance, which is the same as SSP (£55.70 in 1997).

(5)   This linkage between sick pay and maternity pay is authorised by the Pregnant Workers Directive (Article 11(3)), although the preamble pays lip service to the idea that pregnancy is not an illness ('. . . a technical point of reference with a view to fixing the minimum level of protection . . . should in no circumstances be interpreted as suggesting an analogy between pregnancy and illness'.) In the next case, it was argued that women on maternity leave should be entitled to full pay.

Gillespie v *Northern Health and Social Services Board*

[1996] IRLR 214 European Court of Justice

The plaintiffs took maternity leave in 1988, before the Pregnant Workers Directive had been adopted. A pay rise was awarded during the period in which they were receiving maternity pay, but their maternity pay was not increased accordingly. The Northern Ireland Court of

Appeal decided that it was necessary to refer a wider question to the European Court: whether women should be paid full pay during maternity leave.

Judgment of the Court: '. . . The Court of Appeal considered that settlement of the dispute before it required an interpretation of Article 119 of the Treaty, as well as of Directives 75/117 and 76/207 [The Equal Pay/Equal Treatment Directives]. It accordingly stayed proceedings and referred the following questions to the Court for a preliminary ruling:

1. Do the following provisions, or any of them, namely, (i) Article 119 of the Treaty of Rome, (ii) the Equal Pay Directive, or (iii) the Equal Treatment Directive ('the relevant provisions'), require that, while a woman is absent from work on the maternity leave provided for by the relevant national legislation or by her contract of service, she be paid the full pay to which she would have been entitled if at the time she had been working normally for her employer?

2. If the answer to question 1 is 'no', do the relevant provisions require that while a woman is on such leave the amount of her pay be determined by reference to certain particular criteria?

3. If the answer to question 2 is 'yes', what are those criteria?

4. If the answer to each of questions 1 and 2 is 'no', is it the position that none of the relevant provisions has any application or effect as respects the amount of pay to which a woman on such leave is entitled?

By those four questions, which should be considered together, the national court seeks in essence to ascertain whether it follows from the principle of equal pay, laid down in Article 119 of the Treaty and set out in detail in [the Equal Pay] Directive, or from the principle that pregnant women have a lawful right to protection, contained in [the Equal Treatment] Directive, that women on maternity leave must continue to receive full pay and, where appropriate, must receive a pay rise awarded before or during maternity leave. If there is no such requirement, the national court asks whether Community law none the less lays down specific criteria – and, if so, what criteria – for determining the amount of benefit to be paid to those women during maternity leave.

Article 119 of the Treaty and [the Equal Pay] Directive
According to Article 1 of [the Equal Pay] Directive, the principle that men and women should receive equal pay for equal work, as laid down in Article 119 of the Treaty and set out in detail in the Directive, is designed to eliminate, for the same work or for work to which equal value is attributed, all discrimination on grounds of sex with regard to all aspects and conditions of remuneration.

The definition in the second paragraph of Article 119 provides that the concept of pay used in the abovementioned provisions includes all consideration which workers receive directly or indirectly from their employers in respect of their employment. The legal nature of such consideration is not important for the purposes of the application of Article 119 provided that it is granted in respect of employment (see *Garland* v *British Rail Engineering Ltd*).

Consideration classified as pay includes, inter alia, consideration paid by the employer by virtue of legislative provisions and under a contract of employment whose purpose is to ensure that workers receive income even where, in certain cases specified by the legislature, they are not performing any work provided for in their contracts of employment (see *Arbeitwohlfahrt der Stadt Berlin eV* v *Bötel*, also *Kowalska v Freie und Hansestadt Hamburg*, and *Barber* v *Guardian Royal Exchange Assurance Group Ltd*.

It follows that since the benefit paid by an employer under legislation or collective agreements to a woman on maternity leave is based on the employment relationship, it constitutes pay within the meaning of Article 119 of the Treaty and [the Equal Pay] Directive.

Article 119 of the Treaty and Article 1 of [the Equal Pay] Directive therefore preclude regulations which permit men and women to be paid at different rates for the same work or for work of equal value.

It is well-settled that discrimination involves the application of different rules to comparable situations or the application of the same rule to different situations (see, in particular, *Finanzamt Köln-Alstadt* v *Schumacker.*

The present case is concerned with women taking maternity leave provided for by national legislation. They are in a special position which requires them to be afforded special protection, but which is not comparable either with that of a man or with that of a woman actually at work.

As to whether Community law requires women on maternity leave to continue to receive full pay or lays down specific criteria determining the amount of benefit payable during maternity leave, Council Directive 92/85/EEC of 19 October 1992 on the introduction of measures to encourage improvements in the safety and health at work of pregnant workers and workers who have recently given birth or are breastfeeding provides for various measures to protect inter alia the safety and health of female workers, especially before and after giving birth. Those measures include, as regards rights connected with contracts of employment, a continuous period of maternity leave of at least 14 weeks, including compulsory maternity leave of at least two weeks, and maintenance of a payment to, and/or entitlement to an adequate allowance for, female workers covered by the Directive.

However, that Directive does not apply ratione temporis to the facts of the present case. It was therefore for the national legislature to set the amount of the benefit to be paid during maternity leave, having regard to the duration of such leave and the existence of any other social advantages.

That being so, it follows that at the material time neither Article 119 of the EEC Treaty nor Article 1 of [the Equal Pay] Directive required that women should continue to receive full pay during maternity leave. Nor did those provisions lay down any specific criteria for determining the amount of benefit to be paid to them during that period. The amount payable could not, however, be so low as to undermine the purpose of maternity leave, namely the protection of women before and after giving birth. In order to assess the adequacy of the amount payable from that point of view, the national court must take account not only of the length of maternity leave but also of the other forms of social protection afforded by national law in the case of justified absence from work. There is nothing, however, to suggest that in the main proceedings the amount of the benefit granted was such as to undermine the objective of protecting maternity leave.

As to the question whether a woman on maternity leave should receive a pay rise awarded before or during that period, the answer must be 'yes'.

The benefit paid during maternity leave is equivalent to a weekly payment calculated on the basis of the average pay received by the worker at the time when she was actually working and which was paid to her week by week, just like any other worker. The principle of non-discrimination therefore requires that a woman who is still linked to her employer by a contract of employment or by an employment relationship during maternity leave must, like any other worker, benefit from any pay rise, even if backdated, which is awarded between the beginning of the period covered by reference pay and the end of maternity leave. To deny such an increase to a woman on maternity leave would discriminate against her purely in her capacity as a worker since, had she not been pregnant, she would have received the pay rise.

[The Equal Treatment] Directive

The national court also asks whether [the Equal Treatment] Directive applies to the facts of the case.

In that regard, it should be borne in mind that the benefit paid during maternity leave constitutes pay and therefore falls within the scope of Article 119 of the Treaty and [the Equal Pay] Directive. It cannot therefore be covered by [the Equal Treatment] Directive as well. That Directive, as is clear from its second recital in the preamble, does not apply to pay within the meaning of the abovementioned provisions.

In the light of the foregoing considerations, the answer to the four questions referred by the Court of Appeal in Northern Ireland must be that the principle of equal pay laid down in Article 119 of the Treaty and set out in detail in [the Equal Pay] Directive neither requires that women should continue to receive full pay during maternity leave, nor lays down specific criteria for determining the amount of benefit payable to them during that period, provided that the amount is not set so low as to jeopardise the purpose of maternity leave. However, to the extent that it is calculated on the basis of pay received by a woman the commencement of maternity leave, the amount of benefit must include pay rises awarded between the beginning of the period covered by reference pay and the end of maternity leave, as from the date on which they take effect. . . .

COMMENT

(1)   *Gillespie* thus establishes that women on maternity leave do not have a right to full pay, although if their pay is calculated by reference to full pay, they should get the benefit of any pay rise. When the case came back to the Northern Ireland Court of Appeal (*Gillespie* v *Northern Health and Social Services Board (No. 2)*) it was held that maternity pay set at the same level as statutory sickness benefit could not be said to be 'so low as to undermine the purpose of maternity leave'.

(2)   In another case heard at the same time, *Todd* v *Eastern Health and Social Services Board*, the Northern Ireland Court of Appeal held that the plaintiff had no grounds for complaint where her maternity pay was less than contractual sick pay.

Maternity leave

A right to maternity leave has existed since 1975, for employees who have had two years' service, in the shape of a right to return to their former job after a maximum of 40 weeks. Under the Pregnant Workers Directive, however, all workers are entitled to maternity leave, regardless of length of service. Thus TURERA substantially altered the previous provisions. Now, under ERA s 71, every female employee is entitled to 14 weeks' maternity leave, during which time her contract remains in force, with the exception of provisions as to remuneration. The detailed rules are in ERA ss 71–78. The former right to a longer period of maternity leave, for women who have completed two years' continuous employment by the eleventh week before the expected week of childbirth, is continued and governed by ERA ss 79–85. It is distinguished from the right introduced because of the Directive by being referred to in the Act as 'a right to return to work' rather than as maternity leave. One disappointment with the Directive is that it leaves it open to national legislation to set conditions for the exercise of the right to leave. British legislation requires up to four different notices to be given to the employer in connection with maternity leave, which must be in writing if the employer so stipulates, and with forfeiture being the penalty for non-compliance. This can have extremely harsh results as the next case shows.

Lavery v *Plessey Communications*

[1982] IRLR 180 Employment Appeal Tribunal

Ms Lavery began maternity leave on 11 February 1980. Her baby was due on 2 April, and so her employer anticipated that the final date by which she could return to work in exercise of statutory right was 27 October. In fact the baby was 18 days late, so she had until 8 November to exercise her statutory right to return. However, she did not realise this, and her employer did not know that the baby had been born later than 2 April.

At that time, to be entitled to return, a woman had to give seven days' notice of her intention to do so. The notice period has since been extended to 21 days (ERA s 82(1)).

Browne-Wilkinson J: '. . . In order to exercise her statutory right to return to work, Ms Lavery was required to give at least seven days' notice of the day on which she intended to return to work, being a day not more than 29 weeks after the date of actual confinement. On 22.10.80 Ms Lavery rang up her employers and told them that she was returning to work on 27 October, ie, she only gave five days' notice of her return. The employers, not being aware of the actual date of confinement, thought that the period of 29 weeks during which Ms Lavery was entitled to return expired on 27 October. They therefore took the view that, not having been given the required seven days' notice of return before 27 October, they were not obliged to offer any job to Ms Lavery, ie she had lost her statutory right. They told her on 22.10.80 that there was "no job for her". Ms Lavery did not understand her statutory rights: if she had done so, she could still have given the requisite seven days' notice to return before the 29 weeks period from the date of actual birth expired on 8 November. But she never gave any such notice.

Ms Lavery, having been refused her job back, applied to the Industrial Tribunal claiming, in effect, to enforce her statutory right to return to work. The Industrial Tribunal by a majority dismissed her claim. She appeals against that decision.

. . .

Before the Industrial Tribunal, the case for Ms Lavery was that, as she had given notice of her return more than seven days before the expiry of 29 weeks from the week of actual confinement, she had effectively exercised her statutory right to return even though she had only given five days' notice of the day on which she proposed to return. The Industrial Tribunal did not have the benefit of the very full argument that we have had. We do not really understand the basis on which they decided the case. All the members of the Industrial Tribunal appear to have taken the view that the outcome depended on whether (as the majority thought) Ms Lavery was to be held to blame for not informing the employers of the actual date of confinement or whether (as the minority member thought) the employers were to blame for not discovering the actual date of confinement before refusing to allow Ms Lavery to return. In our view those considerations are irrelevant to the decision of this case.

S 47 [cf now ERA s 82(1)] requires the employee to give seven days' notice of her proposal to return on a particular day – "the notified day of return". The notified day of return cannot be a date falling after the 29 weeks have expired, but it can be any day before. An employee is not bound to wait for the full 29 weeks to expire. She can return on any day she chooses, but she must first give the employer seven days' notice of her intention so to do. Her obligation is to notify the date on which she proposes to return, not the date on which her right expires. Plainly the purpose of such notice is to enable the employer to make arrangements to fit the employee (who may have been away for a very considerable period) back into his work force. The seven days' notice is notice by the employee of the exercise of her option to return and is plainly mandatory.

The remaining provisions of the Act dealing with "the right to return" are all geared to the "notified day of return". The remedy of an employee for the refusal of an employer to give effect to the statutory right to return to work is to complain of unfair dismissal under [ERA s 95. S 95] confers this right only on an employee who has "exercised her right to return in accordance with s 47" [cf s 82]. Under [ERA s 96] she is treated as having been employed until the notified day of return, as having been continuously employed down to that day and as having been dismissed as from that day. Therefore, if there is no notified day of return, there is no way in which the machinery of [s 96] can be made to operate. Moreover, where a case falls within [s 96] the statutory definitions of "dismissal" in [s 95] do not apply and references to the notified day of return are substituted for "the effective date of termination" and "the date of termination of employment": [ERA s 97(6)].

It is therefore clear that the giving of the seven days' notice under s 47(1) is of critical importance, since all the employees' other rights flow from it. Unless the requisite notice is given under s 47, there are no remedies available to her. No notice complying with s 47(1) has been given by Ms Lavery. It is in our view irrelevant that she could have given such notice within the 29 weeks period. Although we sympathise with Ms Lavery, there is no escaping the fact that she has not given the statutory notice upon which her statutory right to return to work depends.

...

These statutory provisions are of inordinate complexity exceeding the worst excesses of a taxing statute; we find that especially regrettable bearing in mind that they are regulating the everyday rights of ordinary employers and employees. We feel no confidence that, even with the assistance of detailed arguments from skilled advocates, we have now correctly understood them: it is difficult to see how an ordinary employer or employee is expected to do so. . . .'

COMMENT

(1)   The exasperated criticism expressed by Browne-Wilkinson J at the end of his judgment was endorsed by the Court of Appeal, which subsequently upheld the EAT's decision. The notice rules have since become, if anything, more complex than they were before because of the necessity to incorporate the newer universal right to 14 weeks' maternity leave.

(2)   The woman's right to return to her former job was watered down in 1980 because it was feared that it was too onerous for employers to hold jobs open. Employers were given a defence where it was not reasonably practicable to give her back her old job, provided that she was offered a suitable alternative. An employer with five or fewer employees did not even have to offer an alternative. This greatly reduced the value of the right to return to work. However, the new right to 14 weeks' maternity leave cannot be overridden in this way.

(3)   It is worth noting that a PSI survey in 1979 found that the rules then existing did not cause problems to the majority of employers: fewer than one in fifteen reported

any difficulty (W W Daniel, *Maternity Rights: the experience of employers*, PSI 1981). Since then, although the number of women returning to work after a period of maternity leave has risen considerably, the number of employers finding that it caused difficulties fell (McCrae, *op. cit.* above).

(4) If a woman gives notice of an intention to return after maternity leave and then does not do so, the employer has no redress for whatever inconvenience is caused. Many employers therefore give more generous maternity pay arrangements to women who express an intention of returning to work, as this has the effect of ensuring that the intention is turned into reality.

(5) Most other EU countries have had provisions for paternity leave and more extended family leave for some time. Proposals for a directive were consistently blocked by the United Kingdom in the 1980s. However, under the Protocol on Social Policy annexed to the Treaty of European Union, the procedure whereby a directive can be proposed by the social partners was invoked on this topic and resulted in a draft directive which was accepted by the Council in 1996. While this does not bind the United Kingdom at the moment, the present Government has indicated its willingness to sign up to the Social Chapter. It is thus likely that it will become binding in this country before too long.

GUARANTEE PAYMENTS AND SUSPENSION ON MEDICAL GROUNDS

Employment Rights Act 1996

28. **Right to guarantee payment**
(1) Where throughout a day during any part of which an employee would normally be required to work in accordance with his contract of employment the employee is not provided with work by his employer by reason of—
  (a) a diminution in the requirements of the employer's business for work of the kind which the employee is employed to do, or
  (b) any other occurrence affecting the normal working of the employer's business in relation to work of the kind which the employee is employed to do,
the employee is entitled to be paid by his employer an amount in respect of that day.
(2) In this Act a payment to which an employee is entitled under subsection(1) is referred to as a guarantee payment. ...

COMMENT

(1) The purpose of this provision is to give some kind of wage to employees laid off work through no fault of their own. It does not give employers a right to lay off workers: they may only do this if they have a contractual right to do so. Otherwise it would be a fundamental breach of contract by the employer (see p 266).

Even if the contract does permit the employer to lay off workers temporarily, to prevent excessive use of this power the ERA provides that the employee can leave and claim a redundancy payment under certain conditions (see p 357).

(2)   The right to claim a guarantee payment is not particularly generous. It is limited to a maximum of five days in any three-month period, and is subject to an upper limit which in September 1997 was only £14.50 gross per day (ERA s 31). Employers who have their own arrangements for lay-off payments can opt out of the statutory scheme as long as their schemes are at least as good, and quite a number of employers have done so.

(3)   The interplay between this and entitlement to jobseeker's allowance is also worth noting. Jobseeker's allowance (which is paid at a similar level to the maximum guarantee payment) is payable after three days of unemployment. Thus the overall effect is broadly to shift the burden of paying to the employer instead of the state for the first five days. The only real benefit to the employee is that she gets paid for the first three days that she is out of work. But if the lay-off persists beyond five days, she will have to wait three more days before becoming entitled to unemployment benefit, so this advantage may be marginal.

(4)   If the employer fails to make a guarantee payment, the employee can complain to an industrial tribunal (ERA s 34).

(5)   Under ERA s 64, an employee has a right to up to 26 weeks' pay where an employer has to shut down the business temporarily to meet health or safety requirements. In the absence of any contractual right to suspend without pay in these circumstances the employee would remain entitled to pay at the usual rate. However, if the employer does have the power to suspend without pay, these provisions provide some measure of income protection to the employees.

(6)   At present, the regulations specified in s 64(3) are:
   Control of Lead at Work Regulations 1980
   Ionising Radiation Regulations 1985
   Control of Substances Hazardous to Health Regulations 1988.

(7)   As with guarantee payments, the remedy for the employee is an application within three months to an industrial tribunal, which can order payment (ERA s 70).

TIME-OFF RIGHTS

A range of rights to time off work for particular reasons were introduced by the Employment Protection Act 1975. The one right introduced since then, the right to time off for ante-natal care, has been discussed already under maternity rights. The right to time off to look for work in a redundancy situation is discussed with the other redundancy provisions (p 358). This section covers the right to time off for trade union duties and activities, for safety representatives and for public duties.

Time off for trade union duties and activities

Paid time off

Trade Union and Labour Relations (Consolidation) Act 1992

168. (1) An employer shall permit an employee of his who is an official of an independent trade union recognised by the employer to take time off during his working hours for the purpose of carrying out any duties of his, as such an official, concerned with—

      (a) negotiations with the employer related to or connected with matters falling within section 178(2) (collective bargaining) in relation to which the trade union is recognised by the employer, or

      (b) the performance on behalf of employees of the employer of functions related to or connected with matters falling within that provision which the employer has agreed may be so performed by the trade union.

  (2) He shall also permit such an employee to take time off during his working hours for the purpose of undergoing training in aspects of industrial relations—

      (a) relevant to the carrying out of such duties as are mentioned in subsection (1), and

      (b) approved by the Trades Union Congress or by the independent trade union of which he is an official.

  (3) The amount of time off which an employee is to be permitted to take under this section and the purposes for which, the occasions on which and any conditions subject to which time off may be so taken are those that are reasonable in all the circumstances having regard to any relevant provisions of a Code of Practice issued by ACAS.

  (4) An employee may present a complaint to an industrial tribunal that his employer has failed to permit him to take time off as required by this section.

169. (1) An employer who permits an employee to take time off under section 168 shall pay him for the time taken off pursuant to the permission ...

COMMENT

(1) There is no qualifying period of service for this right. However, it is subject to the most important limitation that it applies only where the employer recognises the trade union, and recognition is voluntary not compulsory (see p 179).

(2) The right is limited first in that it must be connected with matters falling under TULRCA s 178(2). The ACAS Code of Practice No 3 (revised 1991) gives examples as follows:

para 12

      (a) terms and conditions of employment, or the physical conditions in which workers are required to work. Examples could include:

- pay
- hours of work
- holidays and holiday pay
- sick pay arrangements
- pensions
- vocational training

- equal opportunities
- notice periods
- the working environment
- utilisation of machinery and other equipment;

(b) engagement or non-engagement, or termination or suspension of employment or the duties of employment, of one or more workers. Examples could include:
- recruitment and selection policies
- human resource planning
- redundancy and dismissal arrangements;

(c) allocation of work or the duties of employment as between workers or groups of workers. Examples could include:
- job grading
- job evaluation
- job descriptions
- flexible working practices;

(d) matters of discipline. Examples could include:
- disciplinary procedures
- arrangements for representing trade union members at internal interviews
- arrangements for appearing on behalf of trade union members, or as witnesses, before agreed outside appeal bodies or industrial tribunals;

(e) trade union membership or non-membership. Examples could include:
- representational arrangements
- any union involvement in the induction of new workers;

(f) facilities for officials of trade unions. Examples could include any agreed arrangements for the provision of:
- accommodation
- equipment
- names of new workers to the union;

(g) machinery for negotiation or consultation and other procedures. Examples could include arrangements for:
- collective bargaining
- grievance procedures
- joint consultation
- communicating with members
- communicating with other union officials also concerned with collective bargaining with the employer.

(3) Second, since the Employment Act 1989, the right has also been restricted in that it must relate to matters for which the employer actually recognises the union for collective bargaining. This may be a narrower range of issues than those set out in TULRCA s 178(2) and ACAS Code No 3 para 12.

(4) Third, the time off must either be concerned with negotiations with the employer or the performance of other accepted functions on behalf of employees. Clearly this is wider than the actual negotiations themselves: the ACAS Code para 13 says:

13. The duties of an official of a recognised trade union must be connected with or related to negotiations or the performance of functions both in time and subject matter. Reasonable time off may be sought, for example to:
*   prepare for negotiations
*   inform members of progress
*   explain outcomes to members
*   prepare for meetings with the employer about matters for which the trade union has only representational rights.

See *British Bakeries* v *Adlington* and *London Ambulance Service* v *Charlton*: whether any such action is so concerned is a question of fact.

(5) Where paid time off for duties is unreasonably refused, the remedy is to apply to the industrial tribunal within three months of the refusal. In situations where the employee has been refused the time off altogether, the tribunal awards whatever it considers to be just and equitable 'having regard to the employer's default in failing to permit time off to be taken by the employee and to any loss sustained by the employee which is attributable to the matters complained of' (TULRCA s 172(2)). Where the employee has had the time off, but the employer refuses to pay, the tribunal awards lost wages. One problem which arises increasingly is whether the employer is liable to pay wages where the employee is carrying out trade union duties, but not in her normal working hours.

Kuratorium für Dialyse v Lewark

[1996] IRLR 637 European Court of Justice

The employee worked four days a week for the employer. When elected to the staff council, she went on a one-week training course, with her employer's consent. However, the employer only paid her for her usual four days, although the course lasted for five.

The employee argued that this was a breach of Article 119 of the Treaty of Rome and the Equal Pay Directive, on the grounds that the employer was thus treating part-time employees less favourably than full-timers (who would get full pay for time spent on the course), and that this amounted to sex discrimination because the vast majority of part-timers are women.

Judgment of the Court: 'It must be observed first of all that legal concepts and definitions established or laid down by national law cannot affect the interpretation or binding force of Community law, or, consequently, the scope of the principle of equal pay for men and women laid down in Article 119 of the Treaty and in the Directive and developed by the Court's case law (see the judgments in [*Arbeiterwohlfahrt der Stadt Berlin* v] *Bötel*, and in *Hoekstra* v *Bedrijfsvereniging Detailhandel*).

Secondly, as the Court has consistently held, the concept of pay within the meaning of Article 119 of the Treaty comprises any consideration, whether in cash or in kind, whether immediate or future, provided that the worker receives it, albeit indirectly, in respect of his employment from his employer, and irrespective of whether the worker receives it under a contract of employment, by virtue of legislative provisions or on a voluntary basis (see the judgments in *Bötel*, and in *Barber* v *Guardian Royal Exchange Assurance Group*).

As the Court held in *Bötel*, paragraph 14, although compensation such as that at issue in the main proceedings does not derive as such from the contract of employment, it is nevertheless paid by the employer by virtue of legislative provisions and under a contract of employment. Staff council members must necessarily be employees of the undertaking, to be able to serve on that undertaking's staff council.

It follows that compensation received for losses of earnings due to attendance at training courses imparting the information necessary for performing staff council functions must be regarded as pay within the meaning of Article 119, since it constitutes a benefit paid indirectly by the employer by reason of the existence of an employment relationship.

The German Government also considers, as does the referring court, that the legislation in question does not cause any difference in treatment between staff council members working part time and those working full time, since they all have the same protection against losses of earnings incurred through attending training courses.

The Court held in joined cases, [*Stadt Lengerich*] v *Helmig and others*, that there is unequal treatment whenever the overall pay of full-time employees is higher than that of part-time employees for the same number of hours worked on the basis of an employment relationship.

In the present case, it is indisputable that where training courses necessary for performing staff council functions are organised during the full-time working hours in force in the undertaking but outside the individual working hours of part-time workers serving on those councils, the overall pay received by the latter is, for the same number of hours worked, lower than that received by the full-time workers serving on the same staff councils.

Nor can it be objected that the time spent by staff council members on such training courses is not a direct consequence of the existence of a contract of employment, since it is sufficient for that time to be spent by reason of the existence of an employment relationship, which is indeed the case, as was found in paragraphs 22 and 23 in connection with the concept of pay.

Since a difference in treatment has been found to exist, it follows from settled case law that, if it were the case that a much lower proportion of women than men work full time, the exclusion of part-time workers from certain benefits would be contrary to Article 119 of the Treaty where, taking into account the difficulties encountered by women workers in working full time, that measure could not be explained by factors excluding any discrimination on grounds of sex (judgments in *Jenkins* v *Kingsgate (Clothing Productions) Ltd* and in *Bilka-Kaufhaus GmbH* v *Weber von Hartz*).

According to the order for reference, the official employment and social statistics show that at the end of June 1991 93.4% of all part-time workers were women and 6.6% were men. The Landesarbeitsgericht considered that in view of that very great difference between the numbers of men and women working part time, it was to be supposed that the proportion of men and women working part time among staff council members was at least similar.

As those figures have not been disputed, it must be considered that the application of legislative provisions such as those at issue in the main proceedings in principle causes indirect discrimination against women workers, contrary to Article 119 of the Treaty and to the Directive.

It would be otherwise only if the difference of treatment found to exist was justified by objective factors unrelated to any discrimination based on sex. On this point, the Court held in *Bötel*, cited above, that it remained open to the Member State to prove that the legislation was justified by such factors.

However, although in preliminary-ruling proceedings it is for the national court to establish whether such objective factors exist in the particular case before it, the Court of Justice, which has to provide the national court with helpful answers, may provide guidance based on the documents before the national court and on the written and oral observations which have been submitted to it, in order to enable the national court to give judgment (see the judgment in *Secretary of State for Social Security* v *Thomas and others*.

The German Government considers that, assuming that there is a proven difference of treatment, it is justified by the principle that staff council members are not paid, which is intended to ensure their independence. The unpaid and honorary nature of staff council functions and the principle that they must not confer any benefit or entail any disadvantage have the purpose of ensuring staff council members' independence from both internal and external pressures.

It is also apparent from the order for reference in the present case that the Bundesarbeitsgericht considers that the German legislature's wish to place the independence of staff councils above financial inducements for performing staff council functions, as expressed in the provisions at issue, is an aim of social policy.

Such a social policy aim appears in itself to be unrelated to any discrimination on grounds of sex. It cannot be disputed that the work of staff councils does indeed play a part in German social policy, in that the councils have the task of promoting harmonious labour relations within undertakings and in their interest. The concern to ensure the independence of the members of those councils thus likewise reflects a legitimate aim of social policy.

If a Member State is able to show that the measures chosen reflect a legitimate aim of its social policy, are appropriate to achieve that aim and are necessary in order to do so, the mere fact that the legislative provision affects far more women workers than men cannot be regarded as a breach of Article 119 (see the judgments in *De Weerd and others* and in *Megner and Scheffel*.

However, it should be noted that, as the Court held in *Bötel*, legislation such as that at issue is likely to deter workers in the part-time category, in which the proportion of women is undeniably preponderant, from performing staff council functions or from acquiring the knowledge necessary for performing them, thus making it more difficult for that category of worker to be represented by qualified staff council members.

In the light of all those considerations and taking into account the possibility of achieving the social policy aim in question by other means, the difference in treatment could be justified from the point of view of Article 119 of the Treaty and of the Directive only if it appeared to be suitable and necessary for achieving that aim. It is for the national court to ascertain whether that is so in the present case.

Consequently, where the category of part-time workers includes a much higher number of women than men, the prohibition of indirect discrimination in the matter of pay, as set out in Article 119 and in the Directive, precludes national legislation which, not being suitable and necessary for achieving a legitimate social policy aim, has the effect of limiting to their individual working hours the compensation which staff council members employed on a part-time basis are to receive from their employer for attending training courses which impart the knowledge necessary for serving on staff councils and are held during the full-time working hours applicable in the undertaking but which exceed their individual part-time working hours, when staff council members employed on a full-time basis receive compensation for attendance at the same courses on the basis of their full-time working hours.

COMMENT

(1) The ECJ's decision that this payment came within Article 119 must cast doubt on the EAT's decision in *Manor Bakeries* v *Nazir* that payment to union officials while attending a union conference was not within the equal pay principle.

(2) In addition to part-timers, this problem arises with shift workers, whose union duties may well be performed outside their normal working hours. See *Hairsine* v *Hull CC* and *Ryford* v *Drinkwater*.

(3)   It is possible for the tribunal to find that the union official was not entitled to pay for the time off but *was* entitled to unpaid time off, because it was for trade union activities. We consider this right next.

Unpaid time off
Trade Union and Labour Relations (Consolidation) Act 1992

170. (1)   An employer shall permit an employee of his who is a member of an independent trade union recognised by the employer in respect of that description of employee to take time off during his working hours for the purpose of taking part in—
  (a)   any activities of the union, and
  (b)   any activities in relation to which the employee is acting as a representative of the union.
  (2)   The right conferred by subsection (1) does not extend to activities which themselves consist of industrial action, whether or not in contemplation or furtherance of a trade dispute.
  (3)   The amount of time off which an employee is to be permitted to take under this section and the purposes for which, the occasions on which and any conditions subject to which time off may be so taken are those that are reasonable in all the circumstances having regard to any relevant provisions of a Code of Practice issued by ACAS.
  (4)   An employee may present a complaint to an industrial tribunal that his employer has failed to permit him to take time off as required by this section.

COMMENT

(1)   This right for trade union members is again limited to situations where the employer has chosen to recognise the trade union. Examples of the kind of activities covered are given in the ACAS Code:

  21.   The activities of a trade union member can be, for example:
  • attending workplace meetings to discuss and vote on the outcome of negotiations with the employer
  • meeting full-time officials to discuss issues relevant to the workplace
  • voting in properly conducted ballots on industrial action
  • voting in union elections.
  22.   Where the member is acting as a representative of a recognised union activities can be, for example, taking part in:
  • branch, area or regional meetings of the union where the business of the union is under discussion
  • meetings of official policy-making bodies such as the executive committee or annual conference
  • meetings with full-time officials to discuss issues relevant to the workplace.

(2)   Although the right is to unpaid time off only, the ACAS Code para 24 states, 'Nevertheless employers may want to consider payment in certain circumstances, for example to ensure that workplace meetings are fully representative.'

(3)   It is not surprising to find that taking part in industrial action is not something for which the employer must allow time off. However, it is not always easy to distinguish between what is a union activity and what is industrial action. This problem has received most attention where an employer has dismissed a union member for what the member claims is a protected union activity (see p 394). Note the ACAS Code para 39:

> 39.   Employers and unions have a responsibility to use agreed procedures to settle problems and avoid industrial action. Time off may therefore be permitted for this purpose particularly where there is a dispute. **There is no right to time off for trade union activities which themselves consist of industrial action**. However, where an official is not taking part in industrial action but represents members involved, normal arrangements for time off with pay for the official should apply.

(4)   Another problem is to define the line between trade union activity and political protest. Similar debates are encountered in deciding whether industrial action has occurred in the context of a trade dispute or a political dispute. The following decision is not wholly satisfactory, as the applicant refused to give evidence himself or to call any witnesses.

Luce v *Bexley LBC*

[1990] ICR 591 Employment Appeal Tribunal

When the bill which eventually became the Education Reform Act 1988 was going through Parliament, the Bexley division of the National Union of Teachers sought permission for six teachers to have a day's paid leave to attend a lobby of Parliament. The council refused and the applicant, one of the teachers involved, claimed that this was a contravention of s 168. The industrial tribunal held that the Parliamentary lobby was not a union activity within the meaning of the section.

Wood J: '...In the present case however, the tribunal decided against the applicant on the first issue and went no further. What then can we indicate which may be helpful to tribunals in approaching the phrase "any activities of an appropriate trade union of which the employee is a member"? First, and most importantly, we are satisfied that the issue is ultimately one of degree and therefore one of fact. This must be left to the good sense and experience of the industrial tribunal which is entitled to look at all the circumstances. Second, although we do not consider that the phrase should be understood too restrictively, we are satisfied that it cannot have been the intention of Parliament to have included any activity of whatever nature. The whole context of the phrase is within the ambit of the employment relationship between that employee and that employer and that trade union. Quite apart from the overall considerations which we have expressed above this seems to be emphasised by the provisions of [s 173(1)]. The time off is during the employee's normal working hours for which he would be contractually bound. Thus it seems to us that in a broad sense the activity should be one which is in some way linked to that employment relationship, i.e., between that employer, that employee and that trade union.

The ACAS Code of Practice 3, Time Off for Trade Union Duties and Activities (1977), offers some support to this approach at the start of paragraph 8. This section of the code is entitled "General consideration for time off arrangement" and the first sentence of that paragraph reads:

> The general purpose of the statutory provisions on time off for trade union duties and activities is to aid and improve the conduct of industrial relations.

We are satisfied that the decision of the schools subcommittee was far too sweeping without further consideration of the details of each case and is not justified. Lobbying is the presentation of arguments intended to persuade a Member of Parliament to vote in a particular way on a particular issue. It is to be contrasted with an approach which is in essence based upon mere protest.

The reasoning of the industrial tribunal can be found in the following passages of their decision:

> "18. ... sections 27 and 28 [now TULRCA ss 168–170] confer rights to time off for limited purposes only and we regard it as inconceivable that it was intended that the rights to time off given to ordinary trade union members should be entirely unlimited in purpose and should extend to, for example, activities with purely political or ideological ends. In relation to such activities, section 28(3), which requires consideration to be given to the purpose of the time off, would, in our view, put the employer in a particularly invidious position.
>
> 20. In our view, the terms 'trade union activity' and 'trade union activities' are to be construed as they are commonly understood when used to describe the purpose of time off, that is, as encompassing activities usually associated with trade unions and peculiarly within their province. Paragraph (a) of subsection (2) applies to such activities when they are carried out or organised by a trade union itself. But, in addition, a trade union member may seek time off for 'trade union activities' even though his or her trade union does no more than send representatives to a particular body, for example, if the employee is the union's representative on the committee of an industrial training board. Although the trade union activity in such a case is not that of the union itself, it is nevertheless caught by paragraph (b) of subsection (2).
>
> 21. We take the view that, so construed, the term 'trade union activities' covers a very broad range of activity and that there is much force in Mr Davies' submission that the examples of trade union activity given in paragraphs 21 and 22 of the Code of Practice are too narrow. We do not exclude the possibility that some activities directed at Parliament may fall within the scope of section 28. For example, a trade union may have developed in the ordinary course of its work for its members specialised technical knowledge relevant to a measure before Parliament concerned with health and safety at work. We consider that representations to Parliament arising out of the union's expertise concerning such a measure might well fall within the scope of section 28. In our view, however, time off to attend a lobby of Parliament intended to convey only political or ideological objections to proposed legislation cannot be regarded as time off for the purpose of taking part in 'trade union activity' as that term is commonly understood, even if the legislation is of vital concern to the members of the union concerned."

The industrial tribunal were constrained to make their findings of the nature and purpose of the proposed activity upon the very limited evidence proffered by the applicant and did so in the terms to which we have referred. Despite the able arguments of Mr Clayton we are not satisfied that the tribunal erred in law in their approach to the problems before them, and their conclusions were fully justified upon the evidence before them.'

COMMENT

(1) While the action failed in this case, it seems that some lobbying can count as a trade union activity.

(2) The 'general purpose of the statutory provisions' as stated in the 1977 version of the ACAS Code and mentioned in the judgment are put differently in paragraph 4 of the 1991 revised version:

> The general purpose of the statutory provisions and this Code of Practice is to aid and improve the effectiveness of relationships between employers and trade unions. Employers and unions have a joint responsibility to ensure that agreed arrangements seek to specify how reasonable time off for trade union duties and activities and for training can work to their mutual advantage.

(3) General considerations on time off for union duties and activities are found in Sections 4 and 5 of the Code of Practice.

Time off for safety representatives

Under the authority of the Health and Safety at Work, etc., Act 1974 s 2(4), the Safety Representatives and Safety Committees Regulations 1977 were made.

Safety Representatives and Safety Committees Regulations 1977

3.   Appointment of safety representatives
(1)   For the purposes of section 2(4) of the 1974 Act, a recognised trade union may appoint safety representatives from amongst the employees in all cases where one or more employees are employed by an employer by whom it is recognised.
(2)   Where the employer has been notified in writing by or on behalf of a trade union of the names of the persons appointed as safety representatives under this Regulation and the group or groups of employees they represent, each such safety representative shall have the functions set out in Regulation 4 below.
(3)   A person shall cease to be a safety representative for the purposes of these Regulations when—
    (a)   the trade union which appointed him notifies the employer in writing that his appointment has been terminated; or
    (b)   he ceases to be employed at the workplace but if he was appointed to represent employees at more than one workplace he shall not cease by virtue of this sub-paragraph to be a safety representative so long as he continues to be employed at any one of them; or
    (c)   he resigns.
(4)   A person appointed under paragraph (1) above as a safety representative shall so far as is reasonably practicable either have been employed by his employer throughout the preceding two years or have at least two years experience in similar employment.

4.   Functions of safety representatives
(1)   In addition to his function under section 2(4) of the 1974 Act to represent the employees in consultations with the employer under section 2(6) of the 1974 Act

(which requires every employer to consult safety representatives with a view to the making and maintenance of arrangements which will enable him and his employees to co-operate effectively in promoting and developing measures to ensure the health and safety at work of the employees and in checking the effectiveness of such measures), each safety representative shall have the following functions:—

(a)   to investigate potential hazards and dangerous occurrences at the workplace (whether or not they are drawn to his attention by the employees he represents) and to examine the causes of accidents at the workplace;

(b)   to investigate complaints by any employee he represents relating to that employee's health, safety or welfare at work;

(c)   to make representations to the employer on matters arising out of sub-paragraphs (a) and (b) above;

(d)   to make representations to the employer on general matters affecting the health, safety or welfare at work of the employees at the workplace;

(e)   to carry out inspections in accordance with Regulations 5, 6 and 7 below;

(f)   to represent the employees he was appointed to represent in consultations at the workplace with inspectors of the Health and Safety Executive and of any other enforcing authority;

(g)   to receive information from inspectors in accordance with section 28(8) of the 1974 Act; and

(h)   to attend meetings of safety committees where he attends in his capacity as a safety representative in connection with any of the above functions;

but, without prejudice to sections 7 and 8 of the 1974 Act, no function given to a safety representative by this paragraph shall be construed as imposing any duty on him.

(2)   An employer shall permit a safety representative to take such time off with pay during the employee's working hours as shall be necessary for the purposes of—

(a)   performing his functions under section 2(4) of the 1974 Act and paragraph (1)(a) to (h) above;

(b)   undergoing such training in aspects of those functions as may be reasonable in all the circumstances having regard to any relevant provisions of a code of practice relating to time off for training approved for the time being by the Health and Safety Commission under section 16 of the 1974 Act.

In this paragraph 'with pay' means with pay in accordance with the Schedule to these Regulations.

COMMENT

(1)   In 1994 the ECJ decided that consultation over redundancies and transfers was inadequate where representation was only possible through recognised trade unions (*EC Commission* v *UK*, discussed below, p 383). It therefore became clear that statutory provisions for employee safety representatives which applied only where there was a recognised union were also inadequate and that change was necessary.

(2)   However, in line with the former Conservative Government's policy of 'no gold-plating' when forced to introduce Community directives, it was decided not to take the straightforward course of extending the 1977 Regulations but instead to introduce new regulations which constituted a minimum compliance with the Framework Health and Safety Directive (89/391/EEC). Under the Health and Safety

(Consultation with Employees) Regulations 1996, workplaces without a recognised trade union have a right to elect safety representatives, but their role is more limited than that of union-appointed safety representatives.

(3)   In accordance with the Directive, protection from dismissal or discrimination on grounds of the exercise of their functions was also introduced for both kinds of safety representatives (see ERA, ss 44 and 100). See also the recommendation of the Cullen inquiry after the explosion of the *Piper Alpha* oil platform with great loss of life. It was alleged that workers who complained about safety standards were liable to lose their jobs or be otherwise victimised. The protection applies also to employer-designated safety representatives, or any employee who acts in good faith where either there is no safety representative or it is not practicable to contact the proper person.

(4)   The right to time off for union-appointed safety representatives is explained further by the Health and Safety Commission Codes of Practice *Safety Representatives and Safety Committees* (1978) and *Time Off for the Training of Safety Representatives* (1978).

Time off for public duties

Employment Rights Act 1996

50.   (1)   An employer shall permit an employee of his who is a justice of the peace to take time off during the employee's working hours for the purpose of performing any of the duties of his office.

(2)   An employer shall permit an employee of his who is a member of –
   (a)   a local authority,
   (b)   a statutory tribunal,
   (c)   a police authority,
   (ca)   the Service Authority for the National Criminal Intelligence Service or the Service Authority for the National Crime Squad,
   (d)   a board of prison visitors or a prison visiting committee,
   (e)   a relevant health body,
   (f)   a relevant education body, or
   (g)   the Environment Agency or the Scottish Environment Protection Agency,
   to take time off during the employee's working hours for the purposes specified in subsection (3).

(3)   The purposes referred to in subsection (2) are –
   (a)   attendance at a meeting of the body or any of its committees or sub-committees, and
   (b)   the doing of any other thing approved by the body, or anything of a class so approved, for the purpose of the discharge of the functions of the body or of any of its committees or sub-committees.

(4)   The amount of time off which an employee is to be permitted to take under this section, and the occasions on which and any conditions subject to which time off may be so taken, are those that are reasonable in all the circumstances having regard, in particular, to –
   (a)   how much time off is required for the performance of the duties of the office or as a member of the body in question, and how much time off is required

for the performance of the particular duty,
(b) how much time off the employee has already been permitted under this section or sections 168 and 170 of the Trade Union and Labour Relations (Consolidation) Act 1992 (time off for trade union duties and activities), and
(c) the circumstances of the employer's business and the effect of the employee's absence on the running of that business. . . .

COMMENT

(1)   The remedy is for the employee to complain to an industrial tribunal. One of the purposes of this provision was to try to bring about a wider representation of the community on public bodies. There is no Code of Practice on this, and an attempt by an industrial tribunal to supply the deficiency came to grief in the following case.

Corner v *Buckinghamshire CC*

[1978] ICR 836 Employment Appeal Tribunal

The employee, a teacher, was permitted 15 days a year to carry out his duties as a magistrate. He wanted more time, and brought an action claiming that he had not been permitted reasonable time off. The industrial tribunal, balancing the needs of the employer against the needs of the employee, considered that a reasonable compromise would be to give the employee 19 days' leave, but stipulating that all leave beyond the first ten days should be unpaid. Both sides appealed.

Slynn J: '...The employee's submission is that the industrial tribunal did not have the jurisdiction or the power to impose that condition as a part of their award. On behalf of the employers it is said that the sole power of an industrial tribunal ... is to make a declaration that a complaint that an employer has failed to permit an employee to take time off is well-founded, and in a suitable case to make an award of compensation, but that it is not open to the tribunal to go beyond that. In that case, apparently it is agreed by both parties, that there really was no discussion or issue about the number of days which might be taken unpaid. The employers said, quite simply, "15 and no more." The employee said, "I need more." Accordingly, it was open to the tribunal to say that there had been a refusal on the part of the employers to grant the employee time to carry out his duties as a justice of the peace. The question really is whether the industrial tribunal can go beyond that. It may be that in a suitable case, as is here accepted on behalf of the employers, in considering whether there has been a refusal to grant time, the industrial tribunal can look at the conditions subject to which an employer is prepared to grant time off (including conditions relating to pay) and could say that the conditions imposed by an employer were such that they really amounted to a refusal to allow time off to be taken. But this was not a matter which arose before this tribunal, and we all accept the submission of the employers and the employee, that it is not within the power of the industrial tribunal to do more than to make the declaration whether or not there has been a failure to permit the employee to take time off. The tribunal, as we understand it, does not have power to impose conditions upon the parties as to the way in which the time off shall be granted. It is not for the tribunal to re-write the terms of service between the employer and the employee. They may be able to consider whether the conditions are reasonable in deciding whether there has been a refusal but, in our judgment, beyond that they are not empowered to go.

We, accordingly, uphold the submission made here both by the employee and by the employers that the tribunal did not have jurisdiction to impose the condition in paragraph 21 of their decision, and that condition is deleted from their decision.'

COMMENT

(1)   It is perhaps unfortunate that a tribunal cannot arbitrate on what is reasonable if the parties disagree; however, there has been little litigation on this section, so presumably there are few problems in practice.

(2)   It is not specified in ERA s 50 that the leave must be paid. Interestingly, Slynn J here suggests *obiter* that a failure to pay wages could conceivably be regarded as amounting to a refusal of time off.

7 Equal pay

The Equal Pay Act 1970 was passed to address part of the problem of discrimination against women at work. It was at one time regarded as quite acceptable to pay a woman less than a man for exactly the same work and employers openly had a man's rate and a woman's rate for the job. Although the TUC supported the principle of equal pay as long ago as 1888, this did not translate into practical action. When the Equal Pay Act was passed, the average wage of full-time female workers was less than two-thirds that of full-time male workers.

Support for the basic principle of equality can be found in numerous international treaties and in ILO Convention No 100. However, the most important treaty obligation in practice has been that found in the Treaty of Rome.

Treaty establishing the European Economic Community (Treaty of Rome) 1957

Article 119

Each Member State shall during the first stage ensure and subsequently maintain the application of the principle that men and women should receive equal pay for equal work.

For the purpose of this Article, 'pay' means the ordinary basic or minimum wage or salary and any other consideration, whether in cash or in kind, which the worker receives, directly or indirectly, in respect of his employment from his employer.

Equal pay without discrimination based on sex means:

(a) that pay for the same work at piece rates shall be calculated on the basis of the same unit of measurement;

(b) that pay for work at time rates shall be the same for the same job.

COMMENT

(1) Article 119 is of crucial importance, because following British accession to the European Community, the Treaty of Rome became binding on the UK. This means it is the government's responsibility to ensure that British law is in accordance with EC law.

(2) The Equal Pay Act 1970 was the British attempt to enshrine the principle of equal pay for men and women in UK law. It was not brought into force until the end of 1975, when the Sex Discrimination Act 1975 also came into force. The five-year gap was to allow employers time to remove discrimination in their pay scales in a fairly gradual manner which it was hoped would not be too disruptive.

(3)   In *Defrenne* v *SABENA (No 2)* the ECJ held that Article 119 had direct effect in member states. This means that an individual has the right to ask an English court or tribunal to apply it in appropriate cases, even if there is no national legislation appearing to give it effect – or even if the national legislation appears to be inconsistent with it.

(4)   Article 119 has been amplified by two later Directives of the EC, the Equal Pay Directive 1975 and the Equal Treatment Directive 1976.

EC Council Directive No 75/117 on the approximation of the laws of the Member States relating to the application of the principle of equal pay for men and women (the Equal Pay Directive) 1975

Article 1

The principle of equal pay for men and women outlined in Article 119 of the Treaty, hereinafter called 'principle of equal pay', means, for the same work or for work to which equal value is attributed, the elimination of all discrimination on grounds of sex with regard to all aspects and conditions of remuneration.

In particular, where a job classification system is used for determining pay, it must be based on the same criteria for both men and women and so drawn up as to exclude any discrimination on grounds of sex.

Article 2

Member States shall introduce into their national legal systems such measures as are necessary to enable all employees who consider themselves wronged by failure to apply the principle of equal pay to pursue their claims by judicial process after possible recourse to other competent authorities.

Article 3

Member States shall abolish all discrimination between men and women arising from laws, regulations or administrative provisions which is contrary to the principle of equal pay.

Article 4

Member States shall take the necessary measures to ensure that provisions appearing in collective agreements, wage scales, wage agreements or individual contracts of employment which are contrary to the principle of equal pay shall be, or may be declared, null and void or may be amended.

Article 5

Member States shall take the necessary measures to protect employees against dismissal by the employer as a reaction to a complaint within the undertaking or to any legal proceedings aimed at enforcing compliance with the principle of equal pay.

Article 6

Member States shall, in accordance with their national circumstances and legal systems, take the measures necessary to ensure that the principle of equal pay is applied. They shall see that effective means are available to take care that this principle is observed.

Article 7

Member States shall take care that the provisions adopted pursuant to this Directive, together with the relevant provisions already in force, are brought to the attention of employees by all appropriate means, for example at their place of employment.

Article 8

1. Member States shall put into force the laws, regulations and administrative provisions necessary in order to comply with this Directive within one year of its notification and shall immediately inform the Commission thereof.
2. Member States shall communicate to the Commission the texts of the laws, regulations and administrative provisions which they adopt in the field covered by this Directive ...

COMMENT

(1)   In *Worringham* v *Lloyds Bank* and *Jenkins* v *Kingsgate* the ECJ stated that Article 1 of the Equal Pay Directive merely explains and does not extend Article 119. Thus an applicant may be able to bring a claim under Article 119 (which clearly has direct effect) and then rely on the Directive for further amplification if necessary.

(2)   The Equal Treatment Directive is extracted on p 22 As noted there, it has been held to have only 'vertical', not 'horizontal' direct effect – meaning that it can be relied on against the government or an 'emanation of the state', but not against anyone else.

(3)   Our consideration of the British legislation on equal pay must therefore include reference to EC law, both as an aid to interpretation and as a standard against which British law must be tested.

SCOPE OF THE EQUAL PAY ACT 1970

While the Equal Pay Act was passed because of discrimination against women, it applies to both men and women. It operates by deeming an 'equality clause' to be included in the contract, providing that terms in the woman's contract which are less favourable than those in the comparator man's contract (or which do not appear at all in the woman's contract) are to be equalised (EqPA s 1(1), (2)). There are three situations in which an equality clause may be relied upon; each will be considered in turn.

Like work

The first situation where equal pay can be claimed is—

Equal Pay Act 1970

1. ...   (2)   ...

        (a)   where the woman is employed on like work with a man in the same employment— ...

        (4)   A woman is to be regarded as employed on like work with men if, but only if

her work and theirs is of the same or a broadly similar nature, and the differences (if any) between the things she does and the things they do are not of practical importance in relation to terms and conditions of employment; and accordingly in comparing her work with theirs regard shall be had to the frequency or otherwise with which any such differences occur in practice as well as to the nature and extent of the differences.

Capper Pass Ltd v Lawton

[1977] ICR 83 Employment Appeal Tribunal

Phillips J: '... The employee worked as a cook in the kitchen from which the directors of the employers, and their guests, were served. She sought equality of treatment with Mr Smith and Mr Brattan, who were employed as assistant chefs in the kitchen serving the canteen at the employers' factory. She was the only cook in her kitchen. She had to provide lunch for between 10 and 20 persons per day, and the kitchen was of an appropriate semi-domestic sort. Mr Smith and Mr Brattan worked as assistant chefs under a head chef and between them provided 350 meals a day in six sittings: two for breakfast, two for lunch, and two for tea. The kitchen in which they worked was on an appropriate non-domestic scale. The facts upon which the complaint had to be decided were not in dispute, and, as the industrial tribunal said, it was a question of how to interpret them.

It is not necessary for the purposes of this judgment to set out the whole of the facts and circumstances. During the course of the argument Mr Bradley, for the employers, sum-marised the main differences between the work done by the employee and that done by Mr Smith and Mr Brattan under five heads, as follows: (i) the employee was the directors' cook, cooking on a domestic scale. The others were cooks in an industrial canteen. (ii) She worked a 40-hour week. The others worked a 45½-hour week, and one Saturday in three. (iii) She did not have to prepare food in advance on a large scale. They did. (iv) She only cooked lunch; they cooked breakfast, lunch and tea in two sittings; and (v) she was not answerable to a head chef, and to that extent might be admitted to have greater authority. She was answerable to the catering manager; they were answerable to the head chef. As against this, when the catering manager was on holiday the head chef deputised for him, so that one of the assistant chefs had to take over the head chef's functions, and similarly, when the head chef was on holiday, one of them had to take his place ...

The vital provision in determining whether a woman is employed on like work with a man is to be found in section 1(4), and we think that it may be helpful to say something about the proper approach to that provision.

It is obviously difficult, in an Act intended to prevent discrimination between men and women in terms and conditions of employment, to define the test which is to be applied in determining whether discrimination exists. It is easy to talk in general terms but very hard to lay down a clear test which can be applied satisfactorily in practice. One can see that it would be possible to prescribe tests of varying degrees of severity. The least favourable from a woman's point of view would be to require equality of treatment when men and women are doing the *same work*. More favourable would be to require equality where the work done by the man and woman, although different, was of *equal value*. The Act has chosen a middle course. Equality of treatment is required where the woman is employed on "like work" with the man. And "like work" is work which is of the *same* nature as, or of a broadly *similar* nature to, the man's work.

In cases of dispute this test, imposed by section 1(4), requires the industrial tribunal to make a comparison between the work done by the woman and the work done by the man. It is clear from the terms of the subsection that the work need not be of the *same* nature in order to be like work. It is enough if it is of a similar nature. Indeed, it need only be broadly similar. In such cases where the work is of a broadly similar nature (and not of the *same* nature) there will necessarily be differences between the work done by the woman and the work done by the man. It seems clear to us that the definition requires the industrial tribunal to bring to the solution of the question, whether work is of a broadly similar nature, a broad judgment. Because, in such cases, there will be such differences of one sort or another it would be possible in almost every case, by too pedantic an approach, to say that the work was not of a like nature despite the similarity of what was done and the similar kinds of skill and knowledge required to do it. That would be wrong. The intention, we think, is clearly that the industrial tribunal should not be required to undertake too minute an examination, or be constrained to find that work is not like work merely because of insubstantial differences.

It seems to us that in most cases the inquiry will fall into two stages *First*, is the work of the same, or, if not, "of a broadly similar" nature? This question can be answered by a general consideration of the type of work involved, and of the skill and knowledge required to do it. It seems to us to be implicit in the words of subsection (4) that it can be answered without a minute examination of the detail of the differences between the work done by the man and the work done by the woman. But, *secondly*, if on such an examination the answer is that the work is of a broadly similar nature, it is then necessary to go on to consider the detail and to inquire whether the differences between the work being compared are of "practical importance in relation to terms and conditions of employment". In answering that question the industrial tribunal will be guided by the concluding words of the subsection. But again, it seems to us, trivial differences, or differences not likely in the real world to be reflected in the terms and conditions of employment, ought to be disregarded. In other words, once it is determined that work is of a broadly similar nature it should be regarded as being like work unless the differences are plainly of a kind which the industrial tribunal in its experience would expect to find reflected in the terms and conditions of employment. This last point requires to be emphasised. There seems to be a tendency, apparent in some of the decisions of industrial tribunals cited to us, and in some of the arguments upon the hearing of this appeal, to weigh up the differences by reference to such questions as whether one type of work or another is or is not suitable for women, or is the kind of work which women can do, or whether the differences are important, and so on. These are not the tests prescribed by the Act. The only differences which will prevent work which is of a broadly similar nature from being "like work" are differences which in practice will be reflected in the terms and conditions of employment … '

COMMENT

(1)   Applying this to the facts, the EAT held that the tribunal had been correct in holding that Ms Lawton was entitled to equal pay. Note that this meant that she should get the same hourly rate, not the same overall pay.

(2)   This was the first case to reach the EAT on the meaning of like work. Its liberal approach to the interpretation of that phrase has subsequently been endorsed by the Court of Appeal.

Dugdale v *Kraft Foods Ltd*

[1977] ICR 48 Employment Appeal Tribunal

Four women employed as quality control inspectors claimed parity with the six male quality control inspectors who worked with them, but who received a higher basic wage. The women worked morning and afternoon shifts. The men also worked night shifts and on Sunday mornings. The night shifts were compulsory, once every three weeks, but they received a shift allowance of more than 25 per cent of the basic wage for this. The Sunday morning shift was optional, but all the men chose to work it. At this time, women were prevented by statute from working at night unless the employer got a specific exemption to allow it.

The industrial tribunal held that the work of the men and women was similar, but that working at night constituted a difference which meant that they were not employed on like work.

Phillips J: '... To summarise: it seems to us on the admitted facts to be clear that the appellants' work (or certainly Mrs Dugdale's) and that of the male quality control inspectors was of the same or a broadly similar nature, and that the question, then, was whether the differences between the things which the appellants did and the things which they did were of practical importance in relation to terms and conditions of employment. This involves a consideration of two separate matters: (1) the fact that the male quality control inspectors unlike the appellants worked at night and on Sunday morning, and (2) the nature of the work which they did on those occasions. It is not clear to us that the industrial tribunal in reaching its decision distinguished between these two matters.

It appears to us to be necessary to decide, as a matter of the construction of section 1(4), whether the first of these matters, i.e. the fact of doing work at a different time, falls within the words "the things she does and the things they do". To simplify the question by an example: take a factory in which a simple repetitive process of assembly takes place, employing men and women engaged upon identical work. Suppose that the men did, but the women did not, work at night and on a Sunday morning doing the same work. Undoubtedly, the women's work and the men's work would be of the same or a broadly similar nature. Prima facie, therefore, they would be employed on "like work". Does the fact that the men work at night and on Sunday morning, and the women do not, constitute a difference between the things which the women do and the things which the men do? It may be that either view is possible. A man, if asked what he does, might reply, "I assemble radio components," or he might reply, "I assemble radio components on the night shift." We have come to the conclusion that, in the context of the Equal Pay Act 1970 (as amended), the mere time at which the work is performed should be disregarded when considering the differences between the things which the woman does and the things which the man does Were it not so, the Act could never apply in cases where it must obviously have been intended to apply, where the men doing the same work are engaged on a night shift ...

It does not seem to us that this interpretation of section 1(4) would lead to any unfairness; rather the reverse. Where the work done is the same, and the only difference is the time at which it is done, the men will be compensated for the extra burden of working at night or on Sundays by the shift payment or premium. There seems to be no reason why the women should not have equality of treatment in respect of the basic wage, or in respect of the day shift payment, if any. In a case in which the men are not paid a shift payment or premium for night working or Sunday working, but are paid at an enhanced basic wage to reflect their readiness to work at nights or on Sundays, there seems to us to be no reason why, in giving effect to the equality clause in accordance with section 1(2)(a)(i), the terms in the women's contracts as to remuneration should not be so modified as to take account of the fact that the men do, and they do not, work at nights or on Sunday ... '

COMMENT

(1) The case was remitted to the industrial tribunal because it had not given sufficient consideration to whether the work done by the men on the night shift and Sunday mornings was different from the work done on the ordinary day shifts. For a case where the added responsibility which came from working a permanent night shift without a supervisor being available *was* held to be a difference of practical importance, see *Thomas* v *NCB*.

(2) What is to stop an employer getting round the *Dugdale* decision by paying a massive premium for night shifts worked by men? Then it is up to the woman to produce evidence to show that the premium is excessive. In *NCB* v *Sherwin* the EAT noted that 'the percentage taken to represent the differential properly attributable to night work is often of the order of 20 per cent', and also said:

> the disadvantage of working at night or at other inconvenient times, can be compensated by an additional night shift premium, or other appropriate arrangement; but there is no reason why the person, usually the man, should receive by way of remuneration a sum which is greater than necessary to recognise the fact that he works at night, or at other inconvenient times; and if he does there is no reason why the woman should not be remunerated to the extent of the excess.

(3) Most restrictions on women's working hours, including night work, were removed by the Sex Discrimination Act 1986.

Shields v E Coomes (Holdings) Ltd

[1978] ICR 1159 Court of Appeal

Lord Denning MR: 'E Coomes (Holdings) Ltd are bookmakers, alias turf accountants. They have 90 betting shops, 60 of them in South-East London, and the remaining 30 in South Coast towns, such as Ramsgate, where they have five. In 81 of the shops they have two counterhands, who are both women. But in nine of the shops one of the counterhands is a man, and the other is a woman. The reason why they have a man in those nine is because they are situated in areas where the company anticipate there may be trouble from customers and others: and a man is needed to cope with it, if it arises. One of these nine shops is in Sussex Street, Pimlico. The industrial tribunal describes it:

> "The company has a policy of employing some male counterhands at each of those nine shops, not only as a possible deterrent to attack or forcible entry or other trouble but also to ensure that, if trouble arises then physical help shall be available on the spot to repel it until such time as the police are given an opportunity of arriving ..."

The tribunal describes how the company took over this shop in 1973. The company were told that trouble had been experienced there before they took over, but they had not themselves had any trouble in their three years of ownership. The company said that this period of calm has been ensured by employing suitable male personnel, particularly on the counter where he was readily visible. The man was especially important when the shop was opened in the mornings as a cover or precaution against illegal entry when the opening of the shop made it most vulnerable to attack. The man was needed, too, from time to time, when cash had to be transported to and from their shop and other shops or head office.

Those findings make it clear that, at those nine shops in troublesome areas, the man fills a protective role. He does the same work at the counter as the woman counterhand. He takes the bets and receives and pays out the money. But, in his protective role, he works longer hours. He has to be at the shop when it is opened and most vulnerable, whereas the woman comes half-an-hour later. He is required to work a basic week of 37½ hours a week as compared with a woman counterhand who does 32½ hours.

Now here is the point: at 81 shops in trouble-free areas, the counterhands are all women and receive 92p per hour. But at the nine shops in troublesome areas the man counterhand is paid £1.06 per hour, and the woman 92p per hour ...

In this case the woman and the man were employed on work of a broadly similar nature. They were both counterhands. There were several differences between the things she did and the things which he did; for instance, he started at opening time and worked longer hours: but this did not, by itself, warrant a difference in the "rate for the job". He carried cash from shop to shop or to head office. But this difference was, by itself, "not of practical importance". The one difference of any significance between them was that the man filled a protective role. He was a watchdog ready to bark and scare off intruders. This difference, when taken with the others, amounted to differences which the majority of the industrial tribunal found were "real and existing and of practical importance". Accepting this finding, I do not think these differences could or did affect the "rate for the job". Both the woman and the man worked alongside one another hour after hour doing precisely the same work. She should, therefore, receive the same hourly rate as he. It is rather like the difference between a barman and a barmaid. They do the same work as one another in serving drinks. Each has his or her own way of dealing with awkward customers. Each is subject to the same risk of abuse or unpleasantness. But, whichever way each adopts in dealing with awkward customers, the job of each, as a job, is of equivalent rating. Each should, therefore, receive the same "rate for the job". It comes within section 1(4) as "like work".

It would be otherwise if the difference was based on any special personal qualification that he had, as, for instance, if he was a fierce and formidable figure, trained to tackle intruders. Then there might be a variation such as to warrant a "wage differential" under section 1(3). But no such special personal qualification is suggested. The only difference between the two jobs is on the ground of sex. He may have been a small nervous man, who could not say "boo to a goose". She may have been as fierce and formidable as a battle-axe. Such differences, whatever they were, did not have any relation to the terms and conditions of employment. They did not affect the "rate for the job".

I confess, however, that I have felt great difficulty in overcoming the finding of the industrial tribunal that the differences, especially the protective role of the man, were "real and existing and of practical importance". I thought for some time that this protective role should be rewarded by some additional bonus or premium. But my difficulties on this score have been resolved by giving supremacy to Community law. Under that law it is imperative that "pay for work at time rates shall be the same for the same job ... " (article 119); and that all discrimination on the grounds of sex shall be eliminated with regard to all aspects and conditions of remuneration: see Council Directive 75/117/EEC, article 1. The differences found by the majority of the industrial tribunal are all based on sex. They are because he is a man. He only gets the higher hourly rate because he is a man. In order to eliminate all discrimination, there should be an equality clause written into the woman's contract.

I would, therefore, dismiss the appeal.

Bridge LJ: 'The matter falls for decision, as already stated, under section 1 of the Equal Pay Act 1970. In comparing the applicant's position with that of her fellow counterhand, Mr Rolls, three possible questions fell to be answered, as they would in any case where a woman claims an equality clause by virtue of employment on like work with a man under section

1(2)(a). First, was their work of the same or a broadly similar nature? Second, if so, were any differences between the things she did and the things he did (regard being had to the frequency, nature and extent of such differences) of practical importance in relation to terms and conditions of employment? These first two questions arise under section 1(4), which defines like work. The legal burden of proving that she is employed on like work with a man rests on the woman claimant. But if the first question is answered in her favour, an evidential burden of showing differences of practical importance rests upon the employers. The third question under section 1(3) arises only if the woman has established that she is employed on like work with a man. Can the employer then prove that any variation between the woman's contract and the man's is genuinely due to a material difference (other than the difference of sex) between her case and his? If so, her claim to an equality clause is defeated.'

(Bridge LJ and Orr LJ concurred in holding that the applicant was entitled to equal pay.)

COMMENT

(1)   The three stage approach to like work cases set out by Bridge LJ is a helpful method of dealing with these cases. The third stage, the genuine material factor defence, is considered below.

(2)   On situations where it is alleged that the men have additional responsibilities see also *Electrolux Ltd* v *Hutchinson*.

Eaton Ltd v Nuttall

[1977] ICR 272 Employment Appeal Tribunal

The applicant was employed as one of six production schedulers, who were responsible for ordering materials to ensure that the manufacturing process proceeded smoothly. She earned £45.38 per week and claimed equal pay with a male production scheduler who earned £51.88 per week.

Phillips J: '... We turn now to the case as it proceeded before the industrial tribunal and to the point put forward in the notice of appeal. This matter is dealt with in paragraph 7 of the industrial tribunal's reasons. It is there stated:

"So far as [the applicant] is concerned it is suggested by the [employers] that the work she does involves a different and less degree of responsibility from that involved in the work done by the male production schedulers. The test by which this suggested difference in degree of responsibility is established is by gravity of consequence in the event of an error and we unanimously reject that as being the proper test for responsibility. The proper test is whether or not the same function is done with the same degree of competence; if it is, then the responsibility is the same."

Mr Turner suggested that in this passage the industrial tribunal were not rejecting responsibility as being always irrelevant but holding that in the circumstances of this case it was of no importance. We do not read the decision in this way, and it seems clear to us that the industrial tribunal were saying that it is always irrelevant to see whether the acts done by the woman and the man, albeit the same, may have very different consequences if badly done. The contention in the present case was that, whereas the applicant looked after 2,400 items up to the value of £2.50, Mr Biddle looked after 1,200 items of a value from £5 to £1,000, so that an error by him was likely to have far more serious consequences.

In our judgment the industrial tribunal came to a wrong conclusion on this point. Several decisions of the appeal tribunal have said that in applying section 1(4) of the Act the most important point to consider is what the woman does and what the man does, but we do not think that it is right to disregard the circumstances in which they do it, any more than it would be right to do so when applying section 1(5); and the circumstances in which a job is carried out would commonly be taken into account in an evaluation study. Thus in *Waddington* v *Leicester Council for Voluntary Service* when considering section 1(4), we said that it was wrong to ignore the responsibility for supervision taken by the woman and not by the man albeit that in the circumstances of that case it was difficult to pin-point particular acts done in performance of the duty to supervise. In earlier cases we have tried to discourage industrial tribunals from applying section 1(4) too narrowly, and this we strongly endorse; and we should expect them to act in that way when considering such matters as responsibility. Nonetheless this is a job aspect highly regarded by all groups of employers and employees alike, and we would think it not only unacceptable, but also wrong, to ignore it as a factor properly to be taken into account. The sort of situation where we think that the existence of a factor such as responsibility, in the case of one only of two persons whose work is being compared, might truly be decisive is where it can be seen to put one into a different grade from the other. For example, suppose two book-keepers working side by side doing, so far as actions were concerned, almost identical work, where on an examination of the importance of the work done it could be seen that one was a senior book-keeper and another a junior book-keeper. Such distinctions between two employees are often easy to spot in practice but difficult to distinguish only in the terms of what each of them does. That is the sort of case where we think that the existence of the factor of responsibility might be crucial. Accordingly we come to the conclusion that the industrial tribunal misdirected themselves on this point.'

(The case was remitted to a different industrial tribunal for rehearing.)

Work rated as equivalent under a job evaluation scheme

The second situation where a woman can claim equal pay is—

Equal Pay Act 1970

1. ...   (2) ...
        (b)   where the woman is employed on work rated as equivalent with that of a man in the same employment – ...
     (5)   A woman is to be regarded as employed on work rated as equivalent with that of any men if, but only if, her job and their job have been given an equal value, in terms of the demand made on a worker under various headings (for instance effort, skill, decision), on a study undertaken with a view to evaluating in those terms the jobs to be done by all or any of the employees in an undertaking or group of undertakings, or would have been given an equal value but for the evaluation being made on a system setting different values for men and women on the same demand under any heading.

COMMENT

(1)   Job evaluation studies permit the comparison of jobs involving entirely different duties. Given the *de facto* segregation in many parts of the labour market between

'women's jobs' and 'men's jobs', which means that in many cases there are no men with whom a woman could compare under a like work claim, job evaluation is an extremely important tool in achieving equal pay for women.

(2)   There is no single accepted method of carrying out job evaluation studies, nor a foolproof one. The main methods are discussed in the ACAS Guide No 1 on Job Evaluation, and are conveniently summarised in an Appendix to *Eaton Ltd* v *Nuttall*:

Eaton Ltd v Nuttall

[1977] ICR 272 Employment Appeal Tribunal

Phillips J:
'APPENDIX
As not all concerned are familiar with job evaluation, we set out below a note on the principal methods (*see*: ACAS Guide No. 1).

Job ranking. This is commonly thought to be the simplest method. Each job is considered as a whole and is then given a ranking in relation to all other jobs. A ranking table is then drawn up and the ranked jobs grouped into grades. Pay levels can then be fixed for each grade.

Paired comparisons. This is also a simple method. Each job is compared as a whole with each other job in turn and points (0, 1 or 2) awarded according to whether its overall importance is judged to be less than, equal to or more than the other. Points awarded for each job are then totalled and a ranking order produced.

Job classification. This is similar to ranking except that it starts from the opposite end; the grading structure is established first and individual jobs fitted into it. A broad description of each grade is drawn up and individual jobs considered typical of each grade are selected as "benchmarks". The other jobs are then compared with these benchmarks and the general description and placed in their appropriate grade.

Points assessment. This is the most common system in use. It is an analytical method, which, instead of comparing whole jobs, breaks down each job into a number of factors – for example, skills, responsibility, physical and mental requirements and working conditions. Each of these factors may be analysed further. Points are awarded for each factor according to a predetermined scale and the total points decide a job's place in the ranking order. Usually, the factors are weighted so that, for example, more or less weight may be given to hard physical conditions or to a high degree of skill.

Factor comparison. This is also an analytical method, employing the same principles as points assessment but using only a limited number of factors, such as skill, responsibility and working conditions A number of "key" jobs are selected because their wage rates are generally agreed to be "fair". The proportion of the total wage attributable to each factor is then decided and a scale produced showing the rate for each factor of each key job. The other jobs are then compared with this scale, factor by factor, so that a rate is finally obtained for each factor of each job. The total pay for each job is reached by adding together the rates for its individual factors.'

Bromley v H & J Quick Ltd

[1988] ICR 623 Court of Appeal

The employers carried out a job evaluation study, essentially by using a system of paired comparisons. The women applicants claimed that their work was of equal value to that of male comparators who had been ranked higher.

Dillon LJ: '... It is clear from the decision of the European Court in *Rummler* v *Dato-Druck GmbH* that the consideration of any job, and of the qualities required to perform that job, under a job evaluation study must be objective. See especially paragraphs 13 and 14, where it is said:

"13. It follows that the principle of equal pay requires essentially that the nature of the work to be carried out be considered objectively. Consequently, the same work or work to which equal value is attributed must be remunerated in the same manner whether it is carried out by a man or by a woman. Where a job classification system is used in determining remuneration, that system must be based on criteria which do not differ according to whether the work is carried out by a man or by a woman and must not be organised, as a whole, in such a manner that it has the practical effect of discriminating generally against workers of one sex.

14. Consequently, criteria corresponding to the duties performed meet the require-ments of article 1 of the Directive where those duties by their nature require particular physical effort or are physically heavy. In differentiating rates of pay, it is consistent with the principle of non-discrimination to use a criterion based on the objectively measurable expenditure of effort necessary in carrying out the work or the degree to which, reviewed objectively, the work is physically heavy."

The approach of English law to the construction of section 1(5) appears to be in line with the European law approach: see *Eaton Ltd* v *Nuttall* where Phillips J said:

"It seems to us that subsection (5) can only apply to what may be called a valid evaluation study. By that, we mean a study satisfying the test of being thorough in analysis and capable of impartial application ... One which does not satisfy that test, and requires the management to make a subjective judgment concerning the nature of the work before the employee can be fitted into the appropriate place in the appropriate salary grade, would seem to us not to be a valid study for the purpose of subsection (5)."

The same judge made observations to the same effect in *England* v *Bromley London Borough Council*. One has to be a little careful, however, in considering what is meant by "objective" since, so far as the evidence in the present case goes, there are no universally accepted external criteria available for measuring how much of a factor or quality is involved in a particular job or for measuring what relative weights ought to be attached to different factors or qualities involved, to differing extents, in various jobs. Every attempt at job evaluation will, as the expert witnesses seem to have agreed, inevitably at some stages involve value judgments, which are inherently to some extent subjective or "felt-fair"....

What section 1(5) does require is, however, a study undertaken with a view to evaluating jobs in terms of the demand made on a worker under various headings, for instance effort, skill and decision. To apply that to section 2A(2)(a) it is necessary, in my judgment, that both the work of the woman who has made application to the industrial tribunal and the work of the man who is her chosen comparator should have been valued in such terms of demand made on the worker under various headings. Mr Lester submitted that the method used on undertaking a study within section 1(5) must necessarily be analytical, a word he used in the sense of describing the process of dividing a physical or abstract whole into its constituent parts to determine their relationship or value. Sir Ralph Kilner Brown criticised the use of the word analytical as a gloss on the section. In my judgment, the word is not a gloss, but indicates conveniently the general nature of what is required by the section, viz. that the jobs of each worker covered by the study must have been valued in terms of the demand made on the worker under various headings.

(The Court of Appeal held unanimously that the job evaluation study in this case was invalid.)

COMMENT

(1)   In this case, the employer was trying to use the fact that the women's jobs had been rated lower than the men's as a defence to an equal value claim brought by the women workers. The equal value claim is discussed in the next section.

(2)   While it is not necessary to involve trade unions or other worker representatives, nor to provide a right of appeal against grading, it obviously makes sense in industrial relations terms, and usually would help to indicate the validity of the study.

(3)   In order for the employee to be able to rely on the job evaluation study, it must be shown that the study is complete, in the sense of having been agreed by the parties. In *O'Brien* v *Sim-Chem Ltd*, the study had been agreed, and rated the women's jobs in the same grade as the men's, but had not been implemented because of government pay policy; it was held that they could claim. However, in *Arnold* v *Beecham Group*, the study had been carried out but was not acceptable to the employer, the trade union and the majority of the workers covered by it. It could not be relied on.

(4)   Note the emphasis in the judgment on avoiding discriminatory weighting being given to criteria which tend to favour one sex (e.g. a requirement of strength tends to favour male workers, a requirement of manual dexterity tends to favour female workers). In *Rummler* v *Dato-Druck GmbH* the ECJ was faced with the difficult question whether, in assessing the effort associated with a job, it was appropriate to class it as 'heavy' if it would be for the average woman, even if not for the average man. The danger of using one sex as a benchmark and thus arriving at discriminatory slant is clear. The answer given by the ECJ, quoted in the judgment of Dillon LJ, was expanded as follows:

Rummler v Dato-Druck GmbH

[1987] ICR 774 European Court of Justice

'*Question 2 and 3*
18. It appears from the wording of those questions and from the grounds of the order for reference that the national court wishes in substance to know whether, in the event that the criteria of muscle demand or muscular effort and of the heaviness of the work are compatible with Council Directive (75/117/EEC), the fact that in determining to what extent work requires an effort or is demanding or heavy regard is had to the degree to which the work requires an effort or is demanding or heavy for women workers satisfies the requirements of the directive.
19. The defendant argues that regard must be had only to the objective nature of the work to be carried out and the objectively measurable demands it makes.
20. The United Kingdom adds that to use an absolute level of muscular effort or an absolute degree of heaviness of the work, which in fact amounts to using male points of reference, can constitute no more than indirect discrimination, which is not prohibited by article 119 of the EEC Treaty in so far as it is based on objectively justifiable grounds. Such grounds exist where an employer must, in order to attract workers to and retain them in a specific job, set the rate of pay for that job in accordance with the particular effort required by it.
21. The Commission considers that in this regard the directive contains no general legal

principle, so that national courts are not precluded from basing themselves mainly or exclusively on female values if the principle of non-discrimination so requires in order to avoid discrimination against women.

22. The answer to questions 2 and 3, seen in those terms, follows from what has already been said in answer to question 1, this is to say that nothing in the directive prevents the use in determining wage rates of a criterion based on the degree of muscular effort objectively required by a specific job or the objective degree of heaviness of the job.

23. The directive lays down the principle of equal pay for equal work. It follows that the work actually carried out must be remunerated in accordance with its nature. Any criterion based on values appropriate only to workers of one sex carries with it a risk of discrimination and may jeopardise the main objective of the directive, equal treatment for the same work. That is true even of a criterion based on values corresponding to the average performance of workers of the sex considered to have less natural ability for the purposes of that criterion, for the result would be another form of pay discrimination: work objectively requiring greater strength would be paid at the same rate as work requiring less strength.

24. The failure to take into consideration values corresponding to the average performance of female workers in establishing a progressive pay scale based on the degree of muscle demand and muscular effort may indeed have the effect of placing women workers, who cannot take jobs which are beyond their physical strength, at a disadvantage. That difference in treatment may, however, be objectively justified by the nature of the job when such a difference is necessary in order to ensure a level of pay appropriate to the effort required by the work and thus corresponds to a real need on the part of the undertaking: see *Bilka-Kaufhaus GmbH* v *Weber von Hartz*. As has already been stated, however, a job classification system must, in so far as the nature of the tasks in question permits, include other criteria which serve to ensure that the system as a whole is not discriminatory.

25. The answer to the second and third questions must therefore be that it follows from Council Directive (75/117/EEC) that (a) the criteria governing pay-rate classification must ensure that work which is objectively the same attracts the same rate of pay whether it is performed by a man or a woman; (b) the use of values reflecting the average performance of workers of one sex as a basis for determining the extent to which work makes demands or requires effort or whether it is heavy constitutes a form of discrimination on grounds of sex, contrary to the directive; (c) in order for a job classification system not to be discriminatory as a whole, it must, in so far as the nature of the tasks carried out in the undertaking permits, take into account criteria for which workers of each sex may show particular aptitude.'

COMMENT

(1) Does this answer the question posed? If so, is it a satisfactory answer?

Work of equal value

A claim based on a job evaluation scheme is subject to the serious drawback that there must have been a job evaluation study, but there is no mechanism compelling employers to carry one out. It is hardly surprising, therefore, that statistics on equal pay claims between 1976 and 1983 reveal that over 90 per cent were brought under the like work provisions, and also that the number of claims dropped substantially from 1,742 in 1976 to a mere 35 in 1983. It did not take long for most anomalies arising where men and women did similar work to be ironed out, and it was not possible for more fundamental problems to be addressed because of the limitation on claims for work rated as equivalent.

In 1982 the EC Commission successfully sued the United Kingdom on the ground that UK legislation on equal pay contravened Article 119 and the Equal Pay Directive 1975 (*EC Commission* v *UK*. As a result, the Equal Pay (Amendment) Regulations 1983 were passed, amending the Equal Pay Act to introduce a third situation where equal pay could be claimed:

Equal Pay Act 1970

1. ... (2) ...
    (c)   where a woman is employed on work which, not being work in relation to which paragraph (a) or (b) above applies, is, in terms of the demands made on her (for instance under such headings as effort, skill and decision), of equal value to that of a man in the same employment ...

COMMENT

(1)   Note that an equal value claim is expressed to be applicable only where one of the other two claims cannot be brought. This seemed to open up a considerable hole in the scheme until it was plugged by the House of Lords.

Pickstone v *Freemans plc*

[1988] ICR 697 House of Lords

Lord Keith: '... In the present case the respondent, Mrs Pickstone, who is employed by the appellant employers as a "warehouse operative", claims that her work as such is of equal value with that of a man, Mr Phillips, who is employed in the same establishment as a "checker warehouse operative", and who is paid £4.22 per week more than she is paid. However, it happens to be the fact that one man is employed in the establishment as a warehouse operative doing the same work as Mrs Pickstone. The employers maintain that the existence of this fact precludes Mrs Pickstone from claiming equal pay with Mr Phillips under section 1(2)(c) of the Act of 1970, as amended, notwithstanding that she may be performing work of equal value with his and notwithstanding that the difference in pay may be the result of discrimination on grounds of sex.

This argument is based on the words in paragraph (c) "not being work in relation to which paragraph (a) or (b) above applies". The employers say that the work on which Mrs Pickstone is employed is work to which paragraph (a) applies because it is like work with a man in the same employment, namely the one male warehouse operative. So Mrs Pickstone's work does not qualify under paragraph (c).

The question is whether the exclusionary words in paragraph (c) are intended to have effect whenever the employers are able to point to some man who is employed by them on like work with the woman claimant within the meaning of paragraph (a) or work rated as equivalent with hers within the meaning of paragraph (b), or whether they are intended to have effect only where the particular man with whom she seeks comparison is employed on such work. In my opinion the latter is the correct answer. The opposite result would leave a large gap in the equal work provision, enabling an employer to evade it by employing one token man on the same work as a group of potential women claimants who were deliberately paid less than a group of men employed on work of equal value with that of the women. This would mean that the United Kingdom had failed yet again fully to implement its obligations under article 119 of the Treaty and the Equal Pay Directive, and had not given full effect to the decision of the European Court in *Commission of the European Communities* v *United Kingdom of Great Britain and Northern Ireland.*

It is plain that Parliament cannot possibly have intended such a failure. The draft Regulations of 1983 were presented to Parliament as giving full effect to the decision in question. The draft Regulations were not subject to the Parliamentary process of consideration and amendment in Committee, as a Bill would have been. In these circumstances and in the context of section 2 of the European Communities Act 1972 I consider it to be entirely legitimate for the purpose of ascertaining the intention of Parliament to take into account the terms in which the draft was presented by the responsible Minister and which formed the basis of its acceptance. The terms in which it was presented to the House of Commons are set out in the speech of my noble and learned friend Lord Templeman. Much the same was said before the House of Lords. There was no suggestion that the exclusionary words in paragraph (c) were intended to apply in any other situation than where the man selected by a woman complainant for comparison was one in relation to whose work paragraph (a) or paragraph (b) applied. It may be that, in order to confine the words in question to that situation, some necessary implication falls to be made into their literal meaning. The precise terms of that implication do not seem to me to matter. It is sufficient to say that the words must be construed purposively in order to give effect to the manifest broad intention of the maker of the Regulations and of Parliament. I would therefore reject the employers' argument.

In the circumstances it is unnecessary to consider the ground upon which the Court of Appeal found in favour of the respondents, namely that article 119 was directly enforceable in such a way as to enable their claim to be supported irrespective of the true construction of the Regulations of 1983.

My Lords, for these reasons and those given by my noble and learned friends Lord Templeman and Lord Oliver of Aylmerton, I would dismiss the appeal.'

Lord Templeman: 'My Lords, the appellants, Freemans Plc ("the employers"), conduct a mail order business. The respondents are five women who work for the employers as "warehouse operatives"; their basic weekly wage is £77.66. Mr Phillips is a man who works for the employers as a "checker warehouse operative"; his basic weekly wage is £81.88. The respondents assert that the work carried out by the respondents is equal in value to the work of Mr Phillips in terms of the demands, effort, skill and decision-making involved. The respondents say that the difference of £4.22 between the respondents' pay and the pay of Mr Phillips is due to the difference of sex; the respondents are paid less because they are women. The respondents complained to an industrial tribunal that they were the victims of sex discrimination, contrary to the provisions of the Equal Pay Act 1970 and contrary to Community law. When the complaints of the respondents came before the tribunal, investigation might have shown that there was no discrimination, that the work of Mr Phillips was of greater value than the work of the respondents or that for some other reason the difference between the pay of Mr Phillips and the pay of the respondents was not due to the difference of sex. By agreement between the parties however, the industrial tribunal was asked to decide a preliminary point of law which is the subject of this appeal on assumed facts. The assumptions are that the respondents are factually correct in their complaint; that the work of the respondents is equal in value to the work of Mr Phillips; that the respondents are paid £4.22 less on the grounds of difference of sex and for no other reason; that, in short, the respondents are the victims of discrimination. It is unlawful under British law and under Community law for an employer to discriminate against a woman by paying her less than a man if the work of the woman is the same as or is equal in value to the work of the man. Nevertheless, the employers contend that under British law and under Community law, the respondents have no right to or, alternatively, no remedy for the discrimination which on the assumed facts is practised by the employer against the respondents and in favour of Mr Phillips. The employers' argument is based on the fact that it so happens that one of the employers' warehouse operatives is a man, doing the same work as the respondents. According to the employers this fact makes all the difference. The respondents are entitled to complain if they are discriminated against by reason of the fact that they are not paid the same as the man who does the same work. Therefore, it is argued, the respondents are not entitled to complain if they are discriminated against by reason of the fact that they are not paid the same as Mr Phillips who does work of equal value. The employers admit that if there were 15 warehouse operators and all the warehouse operators were women, paid £77.66, for work equal in value to the work of 10 checker warehouse operatives, all men, paid £81.88 and the difference was due to difference in sex, the respondents would be entitled to an increase in pay of £4.22. But the employers claim that if there were 14 women warehouse operatives, one male warehouse operative, and 10 checker warehouse operatives the respondents would be obliged to rest content with £77.66 and would have no remedy for the admitted discrimination based on difference in sex. The industrial tribunal and the Employment Appeal Tribunal accepted the argument of the employers. The Court of Appeal (Purchas and Nicholls LJJ and Sir Roualeyn Cumming-Bruce) decided that under Community law the respondents had an enforceable right on the assumed facts to equal pay with Mr Phillips for work of equal value. The employers appeal to this House …

The draft of the Regulations of 1983 was not subject to any process of amendment by Parliament. In these circumstances the explanations of the Government and the criticisms voiced by Members of Parliament in the debates which led to approval of the draft Regulations provide some indications of the intentions of Parliament. The debate on the draft Regulations in the House of Commons which led to their approval by Resolution was initiated by the Under Secretary of State for Employment who, in the reports of the House of Commons for 20 July 1983 said, *Hansard*, at column 479 et seq.:

"The Equal Pay Act allows a woman to claim equal pay with a man … if she is doing the same or broadly similar work, or if her job and his have been rated equal through job evaluation in effort, skill and decision. However, if a woman is doing different work from a comparable man, or if the jobs are not covered by a job evaluation study, the woman has at present no right to make a claim for equal pay. This is the gap, identified by the European Court, which we are closing …"

In the course of his speech at column 485, the Minister outlined the procedure which will apply if a claim is made under paragraph (c) in the following words:

"Under the amending Regulations which are the subject of this debate, an employee will be able to bring a claim for equal pay with an employee of the opposite sex working in the same employment on the ground that the work is of equal value. When this happens, conciliation will first be attempted, as in all equal pay claims. If conciliation is unsuccessful, the industrial tribunal will take the following steps. First, it will check that the work is not in fact so similar that the case can be heard under the current Act. Secondly, it will consider whether the jobs have already been covered by a job evaluation scheme and judged not to be of equal value. If this is the case, the claim may proceed, only if the original job evaluation scheme is shown to have been sexually discriminatory. Having decided that the case should proceed, the tribunal will first invite the parties to see if they can settle the claim voluntarily. If not, the tribunal will consider whether to commission an independent expert to report on the value of the jobs. It will not commission an expert's report if it feels that it is unreasonable to determine the question of value – for example, if the two jobs are quite obviously of unequal value. Nor ... will it commission an expert's report if the employer shows at this stage that inequality in pay is due to material factors other than sex discrimination..." .

Thus it is clear that the construction which I have placed upon the Regulations corresponds to the intentions of the Government in introducing the Regulations. In the course of the debate in the House of Commons, and in the corresponding debate in the House of Lords, no one suggested that a claim for equal pay for equal work might be defeated under the Regulations by an employer who proved that a man who was not the subject of the complaint was employed on the same or on similar work with the complainant. The Minister took the view, and Parliament accepted the view, that paragraph (c) will only apply if paragraphs (a) and (b) are first held by the tribunal not to apply in respect of the work of the woman and the work of the man with whom she seeks parity of pay. This is also the only view consistent with Community law.

In *von Colson and Kamann* v *Land Nordrhein-Westfalen* the European Court of Justice advised that in dealing with national legislation designed to give effect to a Directive:

"3 ... It is for the national court to interpret and apply the legislation adopted for the implementation of the Directive in conformity with the requirements of Community law, in so far as it is given discretion to do so under national law."

In *Duke* v *Reliance Systems Ltd* this House declined to distort the construction of an Act of Parliament which was not drafted to give effect to a Directive and which was not capable of complying with the Directive as subsequently construed by the European Court of Justice. In the present case I can see no difficulty in construing the Regulations of 1983 in a way which gives effect to the declared intention of the Government of the United Kingdom responsible for drafting the Regulations and is consistent with the objects of the EEC Treaty, the provisions of the Equal Pay Directive and the rulings of the European Court of Justice. I would dismiss the appeal.'

COMMENT

(1)   This is an important decision on substantive equal pay law, establishing as it does that a woman may choose another man with whom to compare for equal value notwithstanding that there is a man who does the same work as her. However, it is almost more interesting for the approach of the House of Lords to the interpretation of English and European law.

(2)   First, note the reference in the speeches to Hansard as an aid to construction. Traditionally Parliamentary materials were considered out of bounds to judges interpreting legislation (cf their Lordships' criticisms of Lord Denning for referring to Parliamentary debates in *Hadmor Productions Ltd* v *Hamilton*). This was taken further in *Pepper* v *Hart*, with the House of Lords granting a general dispensation to refer to Parliamentary proceedings as an aid to the construction of legislation.

(3)   Second, the willingness of the House to construe national legislation to be in accord with European Community law is worth noting. Lord Oliver said that his initial inclination had been to refer the case to the ECJ because the Court of Appeal's interpretation of the statute appeared to be correct: Lord Jauncey similarly; both were persuaded by the other speeches to go along with the views of Lords Keith and Templeman. (Lord Brandon also concurred, although apparently without having to wrestle with his conscience to the same extent.)

(4)   These and other issues are well discussed in Hepple and Byre, 'EEC labour law in the United Kingdom' (1989) 18 ILJ 129.

(5)   A woman will be precluded from claiming that her work is of equal value with a man's if a valid job evaluation study has been carried out which applies to them both and ranks their jobs unequally. It has been held that where the employer only institutes the job evaluation study after the woman has submitted her equal value claim, it is still capable of stopping the equal value claim in its tracks (*Dibro Ltd* v *Hore*).

Procedure for bringing an equal value claim

The procedure is complex, and best understood if broken down into a number of stages:

Stage 1

As with most other industrial tribunal proceedings, the originating application is sent to ACAS, who may try to help the parties reach a conciliated settlement of the issue.

Stage 2

Assuming that there is no settlement at stage 1:

Equal Pay Act 1970

2A.   (1)   Where on a complaint or reference made to an industrial tribunal under section 2 above, a dispute arises as to whether any work is of equal value as mentioned in section 1(2)(c) above the tribunal may either –

(a)   proceed to determine that question; or
(b)   unless it is satisfied that there are no reasonable grounds for determining that the work is of equal value as so mentioned, require a member of the panel of independent experts to prepare a report with respect to that question;

and, if it requires the preparation of a report under paragraph (b) of this subsection, it shall not determine that question unless it has received the report.

COMMENT

(1)   Until amendment in 1996, tribunals did not have the option of considering the case on its merits without commissioning an independent expert's report (unless the case was considered to have no reasonable prospect of success and was dismissed for that reason). The tribunal may not decide to go ahead without an expert's report

without listening to representations from the parties on the matter (Industrial Tribunals (Constitution etc) Regulations 1993 Sch 2 para 8A(3)).

Industrial Tribunals (Constitution and Rules of Procedure) Regulations 1993

Schedule 2

9. ...

(2E) A tribunal may, on the application of a party, if in the circumstances of the case, having regard to the considerations expressed in paragraph (1), it considers that it is appropriate so to proceed, hear evidence upon and permit the parties to address it upon the issue contained in subsection (3) of section 1 of the Equal Pay Act (defence of genuine material factor) before determining whether to require an expert to prepare a report under rule 8A. ...

COMMENT

(1) Another 1996 amendment removed the employer's opportunity to play the 'genuine material factor' card twice. The employer now has a choice of arguing it at the outset and hoping to get the claim dismissed without further delay (and expense), or waiting until the work has actually been adjudged to be of equal value before arguing a genuine material difference between the woman and the man. The former could prove a high risk strategy: *Enderby* v *Frenchay HA* went all the way to the ECJ on whether the employer could rely on a genuine material factor defence. The employer might have been better advised to argue instead that the jobs were not of equal value.

(2) The EAT confirmed that if the genuine material factor defence is made out, the claim should be dismissed without proceeding to an independent expert's report in *Reed Packaging* v *Boozer.*

Stage 3

Unless it has decided to determine the question without a report, the tribunal must require an independent expert from the panel assembled by ACAS to investigate and make a report.

Industrial Tribunals (Constitution and Rules of Procedure) Regulations 1993

Schedule 2

8A. ...

(4) Any requirement to prepare a report shall be made in writing and shall set out –
(a) the name and address of each of the parties;
(b) the address of the establishment at which the applicant is (or, as the case may be was) employed;
(c) the question;
(d) the identity of the person with reference to whose work the question arises;
(e) the date by which the expert is required to send his report to the tribunal; and

(f) the length of the intervals, during the currency of the requirement to prepare the report, before the expiration of which the expert must send progress reports pursuant to paragraph (8).

The Secretary shall send a copy of the requirement to each of the parties together with a notice informing them that a party who unreasonably delays the preparation of the expert's report may have an award of costs made against him, which may include an award in respect of the expert's fees, or have his originating application or notice of appearance struck out.

COMMENT

(1) The original version of this procedure required the expert to report within six weeks – a requirement honoured in the breach rather than the observance. It frequently took 18 months to get from commissioning the report to the reconvened hearing. This new procedure attempts to give the tribunal a more proactive role in ensuring that the progress of the expert's report is monitored. It is further hoped that the threat of penalties will discourage parties from delaying the process.

Stage 4

When the expert's report is ready, the tribunal reconvenes the hearing. It may accept the expert's report, or reject it if
(a) the expert has not complied with the correct procedures;
(b) the conclusion is perverse on the evidence;
(c) the report is unsatisfactory for some other material reason (para 13).

The expert can be called to be cross-examined on her report, and the parties have the right to appoint an expert of their own, who may also give evidence (para 9(2A), (2B)). This has become common practice, although it should be noted that the partisan experts cannot require co-operation from the other side as the tribunal-appointed expert can (*Lloyds Bank* v *Fox*).

If the tribunal rejects the report, it must commission another. It cannot decide without an expert's report. However, accepting the expert's report does not imply necessary acceptance of any conclusions in it, although usually they will be accepted (*Tennants Textile Colours* v *Todd*).

Choice of comparator

The applicant must claim equality with someone of the opposite sex who is 'in the same employment' as her. This is defined as follows:

Equal Pay Act 1970

1. ... (6) Subject to the following subsections, for the purposes of this section—
   (a) 'employed' means employed under a contract of service or of apprentice-ship or a contract personally to execute any work or labour, and related expressions shall be construed accordingly;

   ...

(c)   two employers are to be treated as associated if one is a company of which
the other (directly or indirectly) has control or if both are companies of
which a third person (directly or indirectly) has control,

and men shall be treated as in the same employment with a woman if they are
men employed by her employer or any associated employer at the same
establishment or at establishments in Great Britain which include that one and
at which common terms and conditions of employment are observed either
generally or for employees of the relevant classes.

Leverton v Clwyd CC

[1989] ICR 33 House of Lords

The applicant was employed by the council as a nursery nurse working 32½ hours a week
and having all school holidays (some 70 days a year) off. After obtaining discovery of the
contracts of 200 other council staff, she chose 11 male comparators, all of whom worked at
different establishments from her and who had significantly higher annual salaries. They
worked a 37-hour week and had about 30 days' holiday a year. All council employees were
employed on terms and conditions of employment derived from a national collective
agreement known as 'the purple book'.

Lord Bridge: '... On the question of whether the appellant was in the same employment as
the comparators working at different establishments, the view which prevailed with the
majority of the industrial tribunal, the Employment Appeal Tribunal and the majority of the
Court of Appeal was that the comparison called for by s 1(6) was between the terms and
conditions of employment of the appellant on the one hand and of the comparators on the
other and that it was only if this comparison showed their terms and conditions of employment to be "broadly similar" that the test applied by the phrase "common terms and conditions
of employment" in s 1(6) was satisfied. The majority of the industrial tribunal, affirmed by
the Employment Appeal Tribunal and the majority of the Court of Appeal, held that the
difference in this case in working hours and holidays was a radical difference in the "core
terms" of the respective contracts of employment which prevented the comparison from
satisfying the statutory test. The contrary view embraced by the dissenting members of the
industrial tribunal and by May LJ in the Court of Appeal was that the comparison called for
was much broader, viz a comparison between the terms and conditions of employment
observed at two or more establishments, embracing both the establishment at which the
woman is employed and the establishment at which the men are employed, and applicable
either generally, i.e. to all the employees at the relevant establishments, or to a particular
class or classes of employees to which both the woman and the men belong. Basing himself
implicitly on this view, the dissenting member of the industrial tribunal expressed his
conclusion in the matter tersely. Having referred to the purple book, he said:

> "... 3   Within that agreement there are nine sections and numerous clauses. They do
> not apply, with few exceptions, to any particular grade. It is clearly a general agreement
> and not specific to any particular group or class of employee. 4   It is, in my opinion,
> beyond doubt that the [appellant] and the comparators are employed on common terms
> and conditions, i.e. the APT & C Agreement, and clearly it is within the provisions of section
> 1(6) ..."

My Lords, this is an important difference in principle which depends on the true construction of s 1(6). I have no hesitation in preferring the minority to the majority view expressed
in the courts below. It seems to me, first, that the language of the subsection is clear and

unambiguous. It poses the question whether the terms and conditions of employment "observed" at two or more establishments (at which the relevant woman and the relevant men are employed) are "common", being terms and conditions of employment observed "either generally or for employees of the relevant classes". The concept of common terms and conditions of employment observed generally at different establishments necessarily contemplates terms and conditions applicable to a wide range of employees whose individual terms will vary greatly inter se. On the construction of the subsection adopted by the majority below the phrase "observed either generally or for employees of the relevant classes" is given no content. Terms and conditions of employment governed by the same collective agreement seem to me to represent the paradigm, though not necessarily the only example, of the common terms and conditions of employment contemplated by the subsection.

But if, contrary to my view, there is any such ambiguity in the language of s 1(6) as to permit the question whether a woman and men employed by the same employer in different establishments are in the same employment to depend on a direct comparison establishing a "broad similarity" between the woman's terms and conditions of employment and those of her claimed comparators, I should reject a construction of the subsection in this sense on the ground that it frustrates rather than serves the manifest purpose of the legislation. That purpose is to enable a woman to eliminate discriminatory differences between the terms of her contract and those of any male fellow employee doing like work, work rated as equivalent or work of equal value, whether he works in the same establishment as her or in another establishment where terms and conditions of employment common to both establishments are observed. With all respect to the majority view which prevailed below, it cannot, in my opinion, possibly have been the intention of Parliament to require a woman claiming equality with a man in another establishment to prove an undefined substratum of similarity between the particular terms of her contract and his as the basis of her entitlement to eliminate any discriminatory differences between those terms.

On the construction of s 1(6) which I would adopt there is a sensible and rational explanation for the limitation of equality claims as between men and women employed at different establishments to establishments at which common terms and conditions of employment are observed. There may be perfectly good geographical or historical reasons why a single employer should operate essentially different employment regimes at different establishments. In such cases the limitation imposed by s 1(6) will operate to defeat claims under s 1(6) as between men and women at the different establishments. I take two examples by way of illustration. A single employer has two establishments, one in London and one in Newcastle. The rates of pay earned by persons of both sexes for the same work are substantially higher in London than in Newcastle. Looking at either the London establishment or the Newcastle establishment in isolation there is no sex discrimination. If the women in Newcastle could invoke s 1 of the 1970 Act to achieve equality with the men in London this would eliminate differential in earnings which is due not to sex but to geography. Section 1(6) prevents them from doing so. An employer operates factory A where he has a long-standing collective agreement with the ABC union. The same employer takes over a company operating factory X and becomes an "associated employer" of the persons working there. The previous owner of factory X had a long-standing collective agreement with XYZ union which the new employer continues to operate. The two collective agreements have produced quite different structures governing pay and other terms and conditions of employment at the two factories. Here again s 1(6) will operate to prevent women in factory A claiming equality with men in factory X and vice versa. These examples are not, of course, intended to be exhaustive. So long as industrial tribunals direct themselves correctly in law to make the appropriate broad comparison, it will always be a question of fact for them, in any particular case, to decide whether, as between two different establishments, "common terms and conditions of employment are observed either generally or for employees of the relevant classes". Here the majority of the industrial tribunal misdirected themselves in law and their conclusion on this point cannot be supported ...

I cannot leave this case without adding a word about the procedure involved in equal value claims under s 1(2)(c) of the 1970 Act. If such a claim is referred to an expert under s 2A, the expert's job evaluation and the subsequent procedural steps which follow the presentation of his report under the special rules of procedure governing equal value claims in Sch 2 to the Industrial Tribunals ([Constitutional and] Rules of Procedure) Regulations [1993], will involve a lengthy, elaborate and, I apprehend, expensive process. The larger the number of comparators whose jobs have to be evaluated, the more elaborate and expensive the process is likely to be. Here, as already mentioned, the appellant spread her net very widely by claiming equality with 11 comparators. But, by the time the case reached the House, your Lordships were told that, if her appeal succeeded, she would only seek a reference to an expert in relation to four of the original comparators. This only goes to show what a lot of time and money would have been wasted if the matter had proceeded on a reference to an expert with respect to all the 11 comparators. I do not in any way criticise the industrial tribunal in this case for deciding under s 2A(1)(a) that they could not be satisfied that there were no reasonable grounds for determining her work to be of equal value with any one of the comparators. But I think that industrial tribunals should, so far as possible, be alert to prevent abuse of the equal value claims procedure by applicants who cast their net over too wide a spread of comparators. To take an extreme case, an applicant who claimed equality with A who earns £X and also with B who earns £2X could hardly complain if an industrial tribunal concluded that her claim of equality with A itself demonstrated that there were no reasonable grounds for her claim of equality with B. That said, however, it is right to point out that an employer's most effective safeguard against oppressive equal value claims is to initiate his own comprehensive job evaluation study under s 1(5), which, if properly carried out, will afford him complete protection.'

(Lord Templeman delivered a concurring speech. Lords Griffiths, Ackner and Goff agreed with Lord Bridge.)

COMMENT

(1) Although winning on the common terms and conditions point, the applicant ultimately failed because the employer made out the genuine material factor defence – see below.

(2) Note the warning given by Lord Bridge at the end of his judgment about the risks of choosing many comparators.

(3) The liberal interpretation given by the House of Lords here to the meaning of "common terms and conditions" is surely correct. However, the drift away from national or company-wide collective bargaining to plant bargaining or individual negotiation, noted in Chapter 5, carried the risk that it would be more difficult for workers to establish commonality across establishments. This was addressed by the House of Lords in the next case.

British Coal Corporation v Smith

[1996] IRLR 404 House of Lords

1,286 women employed as canteen workers and cleaners at 47 different establishments claimed equal pay with 150 male surface mineworkers and clerical staff at 14 different establishments. British Coal argued that common terms and conditions did not apply across the establishments because, while national bargaining was used to settle most terms, some things, such as entitlement to concessionary coal and incentive bonuses, were left to local bargaining. Thus surface mineworkers and clerical workers at different establishments did not have exactly the same terms and conditions.

Lord Slynn: '... The real question, however, is what is meant by "common terms of conditions of employment" ' and between whom do such terms and conditions have to be common?

It is plain and it is agreed between the parties that the woman does not have to show that she shares common terms and conditions with her comparator, either in the sense that all the terms are the same, since necessarily his terms must be different in some respect if she is to show a breach of the equality clause, or in regard to terms other than that said to constitute the discrimination.

It is accepted by the corporation that for the purposes of this appeal as between the different establishments common terms and conditions do in any event apply to the two classes of applicants, canteen workers and cleaners. What therefore has to be shown is that the male comparators at other establishments and at her establishment share common terms and conditions. If there are no such men at the applicant's place of work then it has to be shown that like terms and conditions would apply if men were employed there in the particular jobs concerned.

The corporation contends that the applicants can only succeed if they can show that common terms and conditions were observed at the two establishments for the relevant classes in the sense that they apply "across the board"; in other words the terms and conditions of the comparators (eg surface mineworkers) are "common in substantially all respects" for such workers at her pit and at the places of employment of the comparators. This in effect means that all the terms and conditions must be common, ie the same, subject only to de minimis differences.

The applicants reject this and contend that it is sufficient if there is a broad similarity of terms rather than that they are strictly coterminous.

Your Lordships have been referred to a number of dictionary definitions of "common", but I do not think that they help. The real question is what the legislation was seeking to achieve. Was it seeking to exclude a woman's claim unless, subject to de minimis exceptions, there was complete identity of terms and conditions for the comparator at his establishment and those which applied or would apply to a similar male worker at her establishment? Or was the legislation seeking to establish that the terms and conditions of the relevant class were sufficiently similar for a fair comparison to be made, subject always to the employer's right to establish a "material difference" defence under s 1(3) of the Act?

If it was the former then the woman would fail at the first hurdle if there was any difference (other than a de minimis one) between the terms and conditions of the men at the various establishments, since she could not then show that the men were in the same employment as she was. The issue as to whether the differences were material so as to justify different treatment would then never arise.

I do not consider that this can have been intended. The purpose of requiring common terms and conditions was to avoid it being said simply: "a gardener does work of equal value to mine and my comparator at another establishment is a gardener." It was necessary for the applicant to go further and to show that gardeners at other establishments and at her establishment were or would be employed on broadly similar terms. It was necessary but it was also sufficient.

...

If, as I consider, the terms and conditions do not have to be identical, but on a broad basis to be substantially comparable, then it seems to me that the industrial tribunal did not err in law in the way it directed itself and there was clearly material on which it could base its finding that the applicants and their comparators were in the same employment. On this issue accordingly in my view the applicants' cross-appeal succeeds. ...'

(Lords Keith, Browne-Wilkinson, Steyn and Hoffmann agreed with Lord Slynn.)

Macarthys Ltd v Smith

[1980] ICR 672 European Court of Justice

S was taken on as stockroom manager by the company at a salary of £50 per week. She discovered that her male predecessor in the post, who had left some four months earlier, had been paid £60 per week. There was no one else in a similar post with whom she could compare, so she claimed equal pay with her predecessor. The Court of Appeal took the view that the wording of the Equal Pay Act meant that the woman and her male comparator had to be employed at the same time. They referred the case to the European Court of Justice for answers to the following questions. First, whether the principle of equal pay was confined to situations where the man and woman were contemporaneously employed? Second, if it was not, did the woman have to identify an actual male to compare with, or could she seek comparison with how a (hypothetical) man would have been treated?

'DECISION

The interpretation of article 119 of the EEC Treaty

9. According to the first paragraph of article 119 the member states are obliged to ensure and maintain "the application of the principle that men and women should receive equal pay for equal work".

10. As the court indicated in *Defrenne v Sabena*, that provision applies directly, and without the need for more detailed implementing measures on the part of the Community or the member states, to all forms of direct and overt discrimination which may be identified solely with the aid of the criteria of equal work and equal pay referred to by the article in question. Among the forms of discrimination which may be thus judicially identified, the court mentioned in particular cases where men and women receive unequal pay for equal work carried out in the same establishment or service.

11. In such a situation the decisive test lies in establishing whether there is a difference in treatment between a man and a woman performing "equal work" within the meaning of article 119. The scope of that concept, which is entirely qualitative in character in that it is exclusively concerned with the nature of the services in question, may not be restricted by the introduction of a requirement of contemporaneity.

12. It must be acknowledged, however, that, as the Employment Appeal Tribunal properly recognised, it cannot be ruled out that a difference in pay between two workers occupying the same post but at different periods in time may be explained by the operation of factors which are unconnected with any discrimination on grounds of sex. That is a question of fact which it is for the court or tribunal to decide.

13. Thus the answer to the first question should be that the principle that men and women should receive equal pay for equal work, enshrined in article 119 of the EEC Treaty, is not confined to situations in which men and women are contemporaneously doing equal work for the same employer.

14. The second question put by the Court of Appeal and expressed in terms of alternatives concerns the framework within which the existence of possible discrimination in pay may be established. This question is intended to enable the court to rule upon a submission made by the employee and developed by her before the European Court of Justice to the effect that a woman may claim not only the salary received by a man who previously did the same work for her employer but also, more generally, the salary to which she would be entitled were she a man, even in the absence of any man who was concurrently performing, or had previously performed, similar work. The employee defined this term of comparison by reference to the concept of what she described as "a hypothetical male worker".

15. It is clear that the latter proposition, which is the subject of question 2(a), is to be classed as indirect and disguised discrimination, the identification of which, as the court explained in *Defrenne* v *Sabena*, implies comparative studies of entire branches of industry and therefore requires, as a prerequisite, the elaboration by the Community and national legislative bodies of criteria of assessment. From that it follows that, in cases of actual discrimination falling within the scope of the direct application of article 119, comparisons are confined to parallels which may be drawn on the basis of concrete appraisals of the work actually performed by employees of different sex within the same establishment or service.

16. The answer to the second question should therefore be that the principle of equal pay enshrined in article 119 applies to the case where it is established that, having regard to the nature of her services, a woman has received less pay than a man who was employed prior to the woman's period of employment and who did equal work for the employer.

17. From the foregoing it appears that the dispute brought before the national court may be decided within the framework of an interpretation of article 119 of the Treaty alone. In those circumstances it is unnecessary to answer the questions submitted in so far as they relate to the effect and to the interpretation of EEC Council Directive (75/117/EEC).'

COMMENT

(1)   The Equal Pay Act has not been amended in the light of this decision: what is necessary is for tribunals and courts now to interpret it so as not to include the requirement of contemporaneity. In suitable cases, it might be possible for a woman to compare herself with a successor receiving higher pay (see *Diocese of Hallam* v *Connaughton*).

(2)   Although the Court here suggests that a claim can be brought only on the basis of 'concrete appraisals of the work actually performed by employees of different sex', it is submitted that the jurisprudence of the Court has now moved on to the extent that comparison with a hypothetical male would be possible. It would be a question of how convincing (or concrete) was the evidence that a man would have been paid more.

(3)   A major problem for a woman in identifying suitable comparators is that she has no statutory right to gain information about the terms and conditions of her male colleagues. It is true that once she has mounted a claim she will be entitled to discovery of documents; but it is axiomatic that discovery will not be allowed for a 'fishing expedition' and so she will have to have adduced enough to make out a decent claim first. Her trade union may be able to be of assistance, but note the limitations on disclosure of information discussed above (p 182).

THE 'GENUINE MATERIAL FACTOR' DEFENCE

Equal Pay Act 1970

1. ...   (3)   An equality clause shall not operate in relation to a variation between the woman's contract and the man's contract if the employer proves that the variation is genuinely due to a material factor which is not the difference of sex and that factor—

   (a)   in the case of an equality clause falling within subsection (2)(a) or (b) above, must be a material difference between the woman's case and the man's; and

   (b)   in the case of an equality clause falling within subsection (2)(c) above, may be such a material difference.

COMMENT

(1)   This most important defence explains why it is that not everyone doing the same job gets the same pay. Most workers expect that factors such as seniority, merit or qualifications will also be taken into account and present management orthodoxy with its emphasis on performance-related pay would be impossible if workers had to be paid the same for the same job.

(2)   The onus is clearly on the employer to prove that the genuine material factor accounts for the variation in terms. While it is frequently said that this defence takes account of the 'personal equation', an examination of some of the things which are now well-recognised as capable of constituting a genuine material factor will indicate that the defence is wider than this.

(3)   In considering the validity of a defence under s 1(3), regard must be had to the statement of the ECJ in *Bilka-Kaufhaus GmbH* v *Weber von Hartz* that:

'... It is for the national court, which has sole jurisdiction to make findings of fact, to determine whether and to what extent the grounds put forward by an employer to explain the adoption of a pay practice which applies independently of a worker's sex but in fact affects more women than men may be regarded as objectively justified economic grounds.'

The implication is that a factor which is a genuine material factor must yet be justified on objective grounds if it has an indirectly discriminatory effect.

Market forces

Rainey v Greater Glasgow Health Board

[1987] ICR 129 House of Lords

In 1980 it was decided to establish a prosthetic fitting service within the National Health Service in Scotland. Some prosthetists were recruited from the National Health Service and were paid according to appropriate NHS scales; however, because it was not possible to recruit enough from this source, 20 prosthetists (all men) were recruited directly from the private sector.

In order to make the job attractive to them, these direct recruits were allowed to keep their former terms and conditions of employment and existing negotiating procedure. This meant that in 1980 the applicant, a female prosthetist subject to NHS scales, earned £4,773 p.a., whereas a man recruited from the private sector earned £6,680. There were no plans to phase out this differential, and by the time her equal pay claim was heard by an industrial tribunal in 1983, their salaries were £7,295 and £10,085 respectively. It was accepted that they were employed on like work.

Lord Keith: '... The main question at issue in the appeal is whether those circumstances are capable in law of constituting, within the meaning of section 1(3) of the Act of 1970, "a material difference (other than the difference of sex) between her case and his".

Counsel for the appellant argued that nothing can constitute such a difference which is not related to the personal circumstances of the two employees, such as their respective skills, experience or training. Reliance was placed upon the decision of the Court of Appeal in *Clay Cross (Quarry Services) Ltd* v *Fletcher*. In that case a woman sales clerk was employed at a lower wage than a male sales clerk who had been engaged at a later date. The employers relied, as being the material difference between her case and his, on the circumstance that the male clerk had been the only suitable applicant for the post and that he had refused to accept it unless he was paid the same wage as he had received in his previous job. The Employment Appeal Tribunal had accepted this as discharging the onus on the employers under section 1(3) of the Act of 1970, but their decision was reversed by the Court of Appeal. Lord Denning MR said,

"The issue depends on whether there is a material difference (other than sex) between her case and his. Take heed to the words 'between her case and his'. They show that the tribunal is to have regard to *her* and to *him* – to the personal equation of the woman as compared to that of the man – irrespective of any extrinsic forces which led to the variation in pay. As I said in *Shields* v *E Coomes (Holdings) Ltd*, section 1(3) applies when 'the personal equation of the man is such that he deserves to be paid at a higher rate than the woman'. Thus the personal equation of the man may warrant a wage differential if he has much longer length of service, or has superior skill or qualifications; or gives bigger output or productivity; or has been placed, owing to downgrading, in a protected pay category, vividly described as 'red-circled'; or to other circumstances personal to him in doing his job. But the tribunal is not to have regard to any extrinsic forces which have led to the man being paid more. An employer cannot avoid his obligations under the Act by saying: 'I paid him more because he asked for more', or 'I paid her less because she was willing to come for less.' If any such excuse were permitted, the Act would be a dead letter.

Those are the very reasons why there was unequal pay before the statute. They are the very circumstances in which the statute was intended to operate. Nor can the employer avoid his obligations by giving the reasons why he submitted to the extrinsic forces. As for instance by saying: 'He asked for that sum because it was what he was getting in his previous job', or, 'He was the only applicant for the job, so I had no option.' In such cases the employer may beat his breast, and say: 'I did not pay him more because he was a man. I paid it because he was the only suitable person who applied for the job. Man or woman made no difference to me.' Those are reasons personal to the employer. If any such reasons were permitted as an excuse, the door would be wide open. Every employer who wished to avoid the statute would walk straight through it."

Lawton LJ said,

"What does section 1(3) in its context in both the Equal Pay Act 1970 and the Sex Discrimination Act 1975 mean? The context is important. The overall object of both Acts is to ensure that women are treated no less favourably than men. If a woman is treated less favourably than a man there is a presumption of discrimination which can only be rebutted in the sphere of employment if the employer brings himself within section 1(3). He cannot do so merely by proving that he did not intend to discriminate. There are more ways of discriminating against women than by deliberately setting out to do so: see section 1(1)(b) of the Sex Discrimination Act 1975. If lack of intention had provided a lawful excuse for variation, section 1(3) would surely have been worded differently. The variation must have been genuinely due to (that is, caused by) a material difference (that is, one which was relevant and real) between – and now come the important words – her case and his. What is her case? And what is his? In my judgment, her case embraces what appertains to her *in* her job, such as the qualifications she brought to it, the length of time she has been in it, the skill she has acquired, the responsibilities she has undertaken and where and under what conditions she has to do it. It is on this kind of basis that her case is to be compared with that of the man's. What does not appertain to her job or to his are the circumstances in which they came to be employed. These are collateral to the jobs as such."

In my opinion these statements are unduly restrictive of the proper interpretation of section 1(3). The difference must be "material", which I would construe as meaning "significant and relevant", and it must be between "her case and his". Consideration of a person's case must necessarily involve consideration of all the circumstances of that case. These may well go beyond what is not very happily described as "the personal equation", i.e. the personal qualities by way of skill, experience or training which the individual brings to the job. Some circumstances may on examination prove to be not significant or not relevant, but others may do so, though not relating to the personal qualities of the employee. In particular, where there is no question of intentional sex discrimination whether direct or indirect (and there is none here) a difference which is connected with economic factors affecting the efficient carrying on of the employer's business or other activity may well be relevant … '

[The judge then discussed the decisions of the ECJ in *Jenkins* v *Kingsgate (Clothing Productions) Ltd* and *Bilka-Kaufhaus* v *Weber von Hartz*. Referring to the latter, he continued:]

'… It therefore appears that the European Court has resolved the doubts expressed by Browne-Wilkinson J in *Jenkins* v *Kingsgate (Clothing Productions) Ltd* and established that the true meaning and effect of article 119 in this particular context is the same as that there attributed to section 1(3) of the Act of 1970 by the Employment Appeal Tribunal. Although the European Court at one point refers to "economic" grounds objectively justified, whereas Browne-Wilkinson J speaks of "economic or other reasons", I consider that read as a whole the ruling of the European Court would not exclude objectively justified grounds which are other than economic, such as administrative efficiency in a concern not engaged in commerce or business.

The decision of the European Court on article 119 must be accepted as authoritative and the judgment of the Employment Appeal Tribunal on section 1(3) of the Act of 1970, which in my opinion is correct, is in harmony with it. There is now no reason to construe section 1(3) as conferring greater rights on a worker in this context than does article 119 of the Treaty. It follows that a relevant difference for purposes of section 1(3) may relate to circumstances other than the personal qualifications or merits of the male and female workers who are the subject of comparison.'

COMMENT

(1)   *Rainey* should be read in the light of a later EAT decision, *Benveniste* v *University of Southampton*, where it was held that once the financial exigency, which had been a genuine material factor justifying lower pay for a woman at the time of her appointment, had eased, she was entitled to equal pay.

(2)   Many commentators have criticised this decision on the grounds that to allow a defence of market forces will result in the perpetuation of unequal pay for women. The argument is that market forces will generally tend to put women in the lower pay groups for any job, because they are valued less, and that work done predominantly by women is consistently undervalued in comparison to work undertaken predomi- nantly by men. This issue was considered by the ECJ in *Enderby* v *Frenchay Health Authority*.

Enderby v Frenchay Health Authority

[1994] ICR 112 European Court of Justice

Judgment of the Court:
'1. By order of 30 October 1991, received by the Court of Justice on 17 April 1992, the Court of Appeal of England and Wales, pursuant to article 177 of the EEC Treaty, referred for a preliminary ruling questions concerning the interpretation of article 119 of the Treaty, enshrining the principle of equal pay for men and women.

2. Those questions were referred in the context of proceedings brought by the applicant, Dr. Pamela Enderby, against the Frenchay Health Authority and the Secretary of State for Health concerning the difference in pay between two jobs within the National Health Service.

3. The applicant, who is employed as a speech therapist by the health authority, considers that she is a victim of sex discrimination due to the fact that at her level of seniority within the National Health Service, namely, chief 3, members of her profession, which is over- whelmingly a female profession, are appreciably less well paid than members of comparable professions in which, at an equivalent professional level, there are more men than women. In 1986, she brought proceedings against her employer before an industrial tribunal, claiming that her annual pay was only £10,106 while that of a principal clinical psychologist and of a grade 3 principal pharmacist, jobs which were of equal value to hers, was £12,527 and £14,106 respectively.

4. The applicant's claim was dismissed by the industrial tribunal and then, on appeal, by

the appeal tribunal. The industrial tribunal considered that the differences in pay were the result of structures specific to each profession, and in particular the separate collective bargaining arrangements, which were not discriminatory. The appeal tribunal also considered that the differences were not attributable to discrimination. It held further that it had been established that the state of the employment market played some part in the difference in pay between speech therapists and pharmacists and that that was enough to justify the whole of the difference between those two professions.

5. On appeal, the Court of Appeal, considering that the outcome of the proceedings depended on the interpretation of article 119 of the Treaty, decided to refer questions to the Court of Justice for a preliminary ruling. In the statement of facts in its order, the Court of Appeal defined the job of principal speech therapist as "job A" and that of principal pharmacist as "job B," and assumed for the purpose of the present proceedings that those two different jobs were of equal value. It then asked the following questions:

"(1) Does the principle of equal pay enshrined in article 119 of the EEC. Treaty require the employer to justify objectively the difference in pay between job A and job B?

"(2) If the answer to question (1) is in the affirmative, can the employer rely as sufficient justification for the difference in pay upon the fact that the pay of jobs A and B respectively have been determined by different collective bargaining processes which (considered separately) do not discriminate on grounds of sex and do not operate so as to disadvantage women because of their sex?

"(3) If the employer is able to establish that at times there are serious shortages of suitable candidates for job B and that he pays the higher remuneration to holders of job B so as to attract them to job B but it can also be established that only part of the difference in pay between job B and job A is due to the need to attract suitable candidates to job B, (a) is the whole of the difference of pay objectively justified, or (b) is that part but only that part of the difference which is due to the need to attract suitable candidates to job B objectively justified, or (c) must the employer equalise the pay of jobs A and B on the ground that he has failed to show that the whole of the difference is objectively justified?"

...

The third question

24. In its third question, the Court of Appeal wishes to know to what extent—wholly, in part or not at all—the fact that part of the difference in pay is attributable to a shortage of candidates for one job and to the need to attract them by higher salaries can objectively justify that pay differential.

25. The court has consistently held that it is for the national court, which has sole jurisdiction to make findings of fact, to determine whether and to what extent the grounds put forward by an employer to explain the adoption of a pay practice which applies independently of a worker's sex but in fact affects more women than men may be regarded as objectively justified economic grounds: *Bilka-Kaufhaus GmbH* v *Weber von Hartz* and *Nimz* v *Freie und Hansestadt Hamburg.* Those grounds may include, if they can be attributed to the needs and objectives of the undertaking, different criteria such as the worker's flexibility or adaptability to hours and places of work, his training or his length of service: see *Handels-og Kontorfunktionærernes Forbund i Danmark* v *Dansk Arbejdsgiverforening* [the *Danfoss* case].

26. The state of the employment market, which may lead an employer to increase the pay of a particular job in order to attract candidates, may constitute an objectively justified economic ground within the meaning of the case law cited above. How it is to be applied in

the circumstances of each case depends on the facts and so falls within the jurisdiction of the national court.

27. If, as the question referred seems to suggest, the national court has been able to determine precisely what proportion of the increase in pay is attributable to market forces, it must necessarily accept that the pay differential is objectively justified to the extent of that proportion. When national authorities have to apply Community law, they must apply the principle of proportionality

28. If that is not the case, it is for the national court to assess whether the role of market forces in determining the rate of pay was sufficiently significant to provide objective justification for part or all of the difference.

29. The answer to the third question, therefore, is that it is for the national court to determine, if necessary by applying the principle of proportionality, whether and to what extent the shortage of candidates for a job and the need to attract them by higher pay constitutes an objectively justified economic ground for the difference in pay between the jobs in question. ...'

Grading structures and collective bargaining

An employer's grading structure could be the outcome of a job evaluation study – in which case we have seen that a woman would have no claim unless she argued that the study itself was discriminatory. Alternatively, it may be the product of collective bargaining, where the employer recognises a trade union, or it may be unilaterally imposed.

In the first case to reach the Court of Appeal on section 1 of the Equal Pay Act, it was held that provided the grading scheme was genuinely operated, it could constitute a genuine material difference justifying unequal pay (*National Vulcan Engineering Insurance Group Ltd* v *Wade*). This principle was later extended to situations where the reason for the difference was the fact that the man and the woman were subject to different grading schemes, or separate collective bargaining structures (see *Rainey*, above, and *Reed Packaging* v *Boozer*). As usual, however, this must be considered in the context of European Community law.

Handels-og Kontorfunktionaererernes Forbund i Danmark v Dansk Arbejdsgiverforening (acting for Danfoss) ('the Danfoss case')

[1991] ICR 74   European Court of Justice

Employees of Danfoss were paid individual supplements to their basic wages according to a collective agreement. The first set of supplements were on the basis of the worker's skill, independence, responsibility and quality of work. The second set of supplements were on the basis of training and length of service.

A study of 157 workers over a period of four years revealed that on average men earned 6.85 per cent more than women. The scheme was challenged as being in breach of Article 119 and the Equal Pay Directive.

'DECISION

10.   It is apparent from the documents before the court that the issue between the parties to the main proceedings has its origin in the fact that the system of individual supplements applied to basic pay is implemented in such a way that a woman is unable

to identify the reasons for a difference between her pay and that of a man doing the same work. Employees do not know what criteria in the matter of supplements are applied to them and how they are applied. They know only the amount of their supplemented pay without being able to determine the effect of the individual criteria. Those who are in a particular wage group are thus unable to compare the various components of their pay with those of the pay of their colleagues who are in the same wage group.

11. In those circumstances the questions put by the national court must be understood as asking whether the Equal Pay Directive must be interpreted as meaning that where an undertaking applies a system of pay which is totally lacking in transparency, it is for the employer to prove that his practice in the matter of wages is not discriminatory, if a female worker establishes, in a relation to a relatively large number of employees, that the average pay for women is less than that for men.

12. In that respect it must first be borne in mind that in *Commission v France* the court condemned a system of recruitment, characterised by a lack of transparency, as being contrary to the principle of equal access to employment on the ground that the lack of transparency prevented any form of supervision by the national courts.

13. It should next be pointed out that in a situation where a system of individual pay supplements which is completely lacking in transparency is at issue, female employees can establish differences only so far as average pay is concerned. They would be deprived of any effective means of enforcing the principle of equal pay before the national courts if the effect of adducing such evidence was not to impose upon the employer the burden of proving that his practice in the matter of wages is not in fact discriminatory.

14. Finally, it should be noted that under article 6 of the Equal Pay Directive member states must, in accordance with their national circumstances and legal systems, take the measures necessary to ensure that the principle of equal pay is applied and that effective means are available to ensure that it is observed. The concern for effectiveness which thus underlies the Directive means that it must be interpreted as implying adjustments to national rules on the burden of proof in special cases where such adjustments are necessary for the effective implementation of the principle of equality.

15. To show that his practice in the matter of wages does not systematically work to the disadvantage of female employees the employer will have to indicate how he has applied the criteria concerning supplements and will thus be forced to make his system of pay transparent.'

...

...The court in reply to the questions submitted to it by the industrial arbitration board by order of 12 October 1987, hereby rules:

Council Directive (75/117/EEC) on the approximation of the laws of the member states relating to the application of the principle of equal pay for men and women must be interpreted as meaning:

1. Where an undertaking applies a system of pay which is totally lacking in transparency, it is for the employer to prove that his practice in the matter of wages is not discriminatory, if a female worker establishes, in relation to a relatively large number of employees, that the average pay for women is less than that for men.

2. Where it appears that the application of criteria for additional payments such as mobility, training or the length of service of the employee systematically works to the disadvantage of female employees, the employer may justify recourse to the criterion of mobility if it is understood as referring to adaptability to variable hours and varying places of work, by showing that such adaptability is of importance for the performance of the specific tasks which are entrusted to the employee, but not if that criterion is understood as covering the quality of the work done by the employee; the employer may justify recourse to the criterion of training by showing that such training is of importance for the performance of the specific tasks which are entrusted to the employee; the employer does not have to provide special justification for recourse to the criterion of length of service.

Enderby v Frenchay Health Authority

[1994] ICR 112 European Court of Justice

(The facts are given above, p 240. The second question referred to the Court deals with the issue of collective bargaining.)

Judgment of the Court: '... *The second question*
20. In its second question, the Court of Appeal wishes to know whether the employer can rely as sufficient justification for the difference in pay upon the fact that the rates of pay of the jobs in question were decided by collective bargaining processes which, although carried out by the same parties, are distinct and which, considered separately, have no discriminatory effect.

21. As is clear from article 4 of Council Directive (75/117/EEC) of 10 February 1975 on the approximation of the laws of the member states relating to the application of the principle of equal pay for men and women, collective agreements, like laws, regulations or administrative provisions, must observe the principle enshrined in article 119 of the Treaty.

22. The fact that the rates of pay at issue are decided by collective bargaining processes conducted separately for each of the two professional groups concerned, without any discriminatory effect within each group, does not preclude a finding of prima facie discrimination where the results of those processes show that two groups with the same employer and the same trade union are treated differently. If the employer could rely on the absence of discrimination within each of the collective bargaining processes taken separately as sufficient justification for the difference in pay, he could, as the German Government pointed out, easily circumvent the principle of equal pay by using separate bargaining processes.

23. Accordingly, the answer to the second question is that the fact that the respective rates of pay of two jobs of equal value, one carried out almost exclusively by women and the other predominantly by men, were arrived at by collective bargaining processes which, although carried out by the same parties, are distinct, and, taken separately, have in themselves no discriminatory effect, is not sufficient objective justificiation for the difference in pay between those two jobs. ...'

British Coal Corporation v Smith

[1996] IRLR 404 House of Lords

The facts are given above, p 234. Having decided that the canteen staff and cleaners could compare themselves with the surface mineworkers, the next question was the genuine material factor defence.

Lord Slynn: '... On the appeal the corporation challenges the Court of Appeal's finding that the corporation had failed to establish that the variation in terms between surface mineworkers and canteen workers and cleaners, originating in separate bargaining structures, was on 1 January 1986 genuinely due to a material difference other than sex.

In the absence of a misdirection in law, it seems to me that this question essentially is one of fact for the industrial tribunal. The industrial tribunal rightly directed itself that the simple existence of separate pay structures was not in itself a defence. It was necessary to see "not just how the difference arises but also why it arose and, if necessary, why it persists" (paragraph 25(ii)). Thus, they said, they must decide whether the justification for admitted differences in benefits received by the applicants and their comparators satisfied objective criteria and was not one which occurred because of a difference of sex between applicant and comparator.

The industrial tribunal set out in detail the pay structures which had evolved since 1947. For the reasons which they gave they were satisfied that there was "no sexually discriminatory reason for the [different] treatment of the canteen workers in 1976–77 or in the earlier period". They found at paragraph 29(A)(i)(f):

"The mineworkers' structure has received periodic review. In particular there seemed to us to have been remarkably little consistency (as evidenced by the letter of 25 July 1980, to which we refer in paragraph 5(iv) above) in the acceptance of workers as surface mineworkers – even if they had hitherto been on Wages Council or other terms – with the result that some jobs, generally performed by men (eg gardener, general labourer) were or became surface mineworker grades (even if not performed at a pithead), while others, generally performed by women (eg canteen worker) or by men (clerical workers), even though performed at a pithead, were not so accepted. It is that inconsistency which no doubt has created ill-feeling and bitterness."

Having recited the evidence of a witness that it was known that in the 1980s a major rundown in the coal industry would take place which justified putting mineworkers in a special category, they said at paragraph 29(A)(ii)(b):

"We have since seen that decline occur; but it had not been completed to anything like the present degree at the times relevant for our consideration. Thus the justification pleaded by the respondent (and attested to by a witness who was in an important post at the relevant time) will inevitably be historical and we must prevent ourselves from assessing that justification with the benefit of hindsight."

They concluded:

"(c) It must be said that that justification may well hold good for underground mineworkers, we can see the reason for classing them differently in the economic conditions prevailing at the relevant times, together with the pressures which the respondent undoubtedly felt in dealing with a strong union. We accept that that justification is as good in later time (ie at all times relevant for our consideration) as it originally had been. We were not satisfied however that it remained an equally good justification for paying surface mineworkers, some of whom did jobs (eg gardener, cleaner) which were on a superficial comparison certainly no more arduous, strenuous or difficult than the jobs of the applicants in this class. We heard that men classed and paid as surface mineworkers had been absorbed into that category virtually at random, not predominantly because of previous underground service, but because the jobs existed; we heard of no woman being so absorbed even though she may have worked at a pithead while men absorbed into the surface mineworker category might well have worked away from the pithead.

(d) The justification for the different treatment of surface mineworkers and canteen workers was said by the respondent to be the desire to treat ancillary workers differently without regard for sex; that justification does not find favour with us at this stage of the proceedings. It seems to us as likely that the difference was due to an ingrained approach, based upon sex, which meant that women, whatever they did, would not be classed or categorised as surface mineworkers. It may well be that that approach has been condoned – even encouraged – by the NUM in the past, but it does not now prevent these applicants from making appropriate complaint under the equal value legislation.

(e) In the context specified, we are therefore bound to say that the respondent has failed to put before us clear objectives for treating surface mineworkers separately from canteen workers; Miss Wharf has set out cogent evidence for the treatment of underground mineworkers, but that evidence does not meet the complaints before us. We have recognised and reminded ourselves that it is not for us to make moral judgment upon the respondent's actions or, as Mr Goldsmith put it, to make judgments of fairness on pay structures or to restructure the respondent's business in accordance with our own views. We do understand that it is our function to ask whether the respondent has put before us aims which genuinely caused the differences in pay between these two categories of workers, whether he has described appropriate actions to achieve those aims and whether they were necessary to achieve those aims. Even having accepted Miss Wharf's evidence, we find that the respondent has failed to prove that the differences in pay arose because of 'reasonable necessity, objectively justified', as Lord Bridge of Harwich put it in *Leverton*'s case. As a result of that conclusion we find that the respondent has failed to prove a genuine material factor defence to claims by canteen workers for equal pay with surface mineworkers; their claims must therefore go forward to an independent expert for assessment."

The industrial members of the industrial tribunal added in addition to these reasons that they considered the corporation's failure to address the position of women canteen workers in comparison with surface mineworkers since 1976–77 as additional evidence for an inference of discrimination against the former category of workers. They thought that the failure to recognise women as performing work similar to that of some surface mineworkers was because of their sex.

The corporation says it was anxious to "ring-fence" those who should be considered as mineworkers and to separate them from other workers. They wanted to include ex-underground workers, and those who might be required to do their job underground from time to time such as carpenters and electricians. Canteen workers were wholly outside the ring-fence as were all ancillary workers, and that exclusion had nothing to do with the fact that they were women.

The corporation can point to the finding of the industrial tribunal as to the position between 1947 and 1986, but at the end of the day, and not just on the basis of the letter of 25 July 1980 from a corporation official which the tribunal referred to, but on the basis of the evidence of a witness, they concluded that as of 1 January 1986 the distinction had not been shown to be based on a material difference other than sex. So far as canteen workers and surface mineworkers are concerned, it seems to me that there was clearly evidence on which they could base their decision and there was no misdirection in law. It was perfectly open to them to conclude that the pay structure differentiation, because of the way in which the category of surface mineworkers had changed, was not shown in 1986 to have been due to a factor other than sex. They (both the whole tribunal and for a different reason the industrial members) were also entitled to accept, as clearly they did, that the differentiation was based on sex. Accordingly, in my view, the Court of Appeal reached the correct conclusion on this issue.

Although the corporation reaches the contrary result, it accepts that the issues in relation to the comparison between the cleaners and the surface mineworkers are substantially the same as those in the canteen worker/surface mineworker comparison. I agree that the issues are the same and that the cleaners, like the canteen workers, should succeed as to the issue under s 1(6) and 1(3) of the Act.'

(Lords Keith, Browne-Wilkinson, Steyn and Hoffman agreed with Lord Slynn.)

Performance-related pay

Employers may pay workers wholly or partly by results: commission on sales, payment by the piece and payments dependent on reaching specific targets are all forms of this. Would such a system constitute a genuine material factor justifying unequal pay for men and women?

Specialarbejderforbundet i Danmark v *Dansk Industri (acting for Royal Copenhagen)* ('the *Royal Copenhagen* case')

[1995] IRLR 648 European Court of Justice

Judgment of the Court: '... Royal Copenhagen is a ceramics producer employing some 1,150 workers, 40% men and 60% women, in the manufacture of such products. Its employees may be divided into three groups: turners, who use a variety of techniques to mould the porcelain clay mass; painters, who decorate the products; and unskilled workers, who are engaged in operating the kilns, sorting and polishing, transport within the factory and so forth.

The turners' group consists of some 200 persons and the painters' group 453 persons. Those groups may in turn be divided into a number of subgroups, such as, within the first group, automatic-machine operators, who man machines which automatically mould ceramic products; and, within the second, blue-pattern painters, who decorate the products by brush, and ornamental-plate painters, who spray-paint ornamental plates which already have a pattern and then remove the paint from certain parts of the pattern with a sponge.

All these employees are covered by the same collective agreement, under which they are in principle paid on a piecework basis; that is to say, the level of their pay is wholly or partially dependent on their output. They may however opt to be paid a fixed hourly rate which is the same for all the groups. In practice, approximately 70% of the turners and 70% of the painters are paid by the piece: their pay consists of a fixed element, paid as a basic hourly wage, and a variable element, paid by reference to the number of items produced.

The group of automatic-machine operators paid by the piece comprises 26 persons, all men, and accounts for approximately 18% of all turners paid by the piece. The group of blue-pattern painters paid by the piece comprises 156 persons, 155 women and one man, and accounts for approximately 49% of the group of painters paid by the piece. The group of ornamental-plate decorators paid by the piece comprises 51 persons, all women, and accounts for approximately 16% of the group of painters paid by the piece.

In April 1990, the average hourly pay of the automatic-machine operators paid by the piece was DKR 103.93, including a fixed element of DKR 71.69, with the highest earner receiving DKR 118 per hour and the lowest earner DKR 86 per hour. During the same period, the average hourly pay of the blue-pattern painters paid by the piece was DKR 91, including a fixed element of DKR 57, with the highest earner receiving DKR 125 per hour and the lowest DKR 72 per hour; and the average hourly pay of the ornamental-plate decorators paid by the piece was DKR 116.20, including a fixed element of DKR 35.85, with the highest earner receiving DKR 159 per hour and the lowest DKR 86 per hour.

The Specialarbejderforbundet considered that Royal Copenhagen was infringing the requirement of equal pay because the average hourly piecework pay of the group of blue-pattern painters, all but one of whom were women, was less than that of the group of automatic-machine operators, all of whom were men. It brought proceedings before the Faglige Voldgiftsret of Copenhagen, seeking an order that Royal Copenhagen acknowledge that the blue-pattern painters perform work of equal value to that of the automatic-machine operators and bring the average hourly piecework pay of the former up to the level of that of the latter.

...

The first question
The national court's first question asks whether Article 119 of the Treaty and the Directive apply to piecework pay schemes in which pay depends entirely or in large measure on the individual output of each worker.

Article 119, by stating expressly in subparagraph (a) of its third paragraph that equal pay without discrimination based on sex means that pay for the same work at piece rates is to be calculated on the basis of the same unit of measurement, itself provides that the principle of equal pay applies to piecework pay schemes.

Moreover the Court has already held that Article 119 prohibits any discrimination with regard to pay as between men and women, whatever the system which gives rise to such inequality (*Barber* v *Guardian Royal Exchange Assurance Group*).

That conclusion is borne out by the first paragraph of Article 1 of the Directive, which provides that the principle of equal pay for men and women means the elimination of all discrimination on grounds of sex "with regard to all aspects and conditions of remuneration".

The reply to the first question should accordingly be that Article 119 of the Treaty and the Directive apply to piecework pay schemes in which pay depends entirely or in large measure on the individual output of each worker. ...

It follows from paragraph 12 of this judgment that in a piecework pay scheme the principle of equal pay requires that the pay of two groups of workers, one consisting predominantly of men and the other predominantly of women, is to be calculated on the basis of the same unit of measurement.

Where the unit of measurement is the same for two groups of workers carrying out the same work or is objectively capable of ensuring that the total individual pay of workers in the two groups is the same for work which, although different, is considered to be of equal value, the principle of equal pay does not prohibit workers belonging to one or the other group from receiving different total pay if that is due to their different individual output.

It follows that in a piecework pay scheme the mere finding that there is a difference in the average pay of two groups of workers, calculated on the basis of the total individual pay of all the workers belonging to one or the other group, does not suffice to establish that there is discrimination with regard to pay.

It is for the national court, which alone is competent to assess the facts, to decide whether the unit of measurement applicable to the work carried out by the two groups of workers is the same or, if the two groups carry out work which is different but considered to be of equal value, whether the unit of measurement is objectively capable of ensuring that their total pay is the same. It is also for that court to ascertain whether a pay differential relied on by a worker belonging to a group consisting predominantly of women as evidence of sex discrimination against that worker compared with a worker belonging to a group consisting predominantly of men is due to a difference between the units of measurement applicable to the two groups or to a difference in individual output.

The Court has, however, held (*Enderby* v *Frenchay Health Authority*) that the burden of proof, which is normally on the worker bringing legal proceedings against his employer with a view to removing the discrimination of which he believes himself to be the victim, may be shifted when that is necessary to avoid depriving workers who appear to be the victims of discrimination of any effective means of enforcing the principle of equal pay. Thus in particular where an undertaking applies a system of pay which is wholly lacking in transparency, it is for the employer to prove that his practice in the matter of wages is not discriminatory if a female worker establishes, in relation to a relatively large number of employees, that the average pay for women is less than that for men (*Handels-og Kontorfunktionaererernes Forbund i Danmark* v *Dansk Arbejdsgiverforening* ("*Danfoss*"). Similarly, where significant statistics disclose an appreciable difference in pay between two jobs of equal value, one of which is carried out almost exclusively by women and the other predominantly by men, so that there is a prima facie case of sex discrimination, Article 119 of the Treaty requires the employer to show that that difference is based on objectively justified factors unrelated to any discrimination on grounds of sex (*Enderby*, cited above).

Admittedly, in a piecework pay scheme such a prima facie case of discrimination does not arise solely because significant statistics disclose appreciable differences between the average pay of two groups of workers, since those differences may be due to differences in individual output of the workers constituting the two groups.

If, however, in a system such as that in the main proceedings where the individual pay taken into account in calculating the average pay of the two groups of workers consists of a variable element depending on each worker's output and a fixed element differing according to the group of workers concerned (fourth question, paragraph (e)), it is not possible to identify the factors which determined the rates or units of measurement used to calculate the variable element in the pay (fourth question, paragraph (g)), the objective of not depriving workers of any effective means of enforcing the principle of equal pay may require the employer to bear the burden of proving that the differences found are not due to sex discrimination.

It is for the national court to ascertain whether, in the light in particular of those factors and the extent of the differences between the average pay of the two groups of workers, the conditions for so shifting the burden of proof are satisfied in the main proceedings. If so, it will be open to the employer for example to demonstrate that the pay differentials are due to differences in the choice by the workers concerned of their rate of work (fourth question, paragraph (c)) and to rely on major differences between total individual pay within each of those groups (fourth question paragraph (d)).

The reply to the second question in conjunction with paragraphs (c), (d), (e) and (g) of the fourth question should accordingly be that the principle of equal pay set out in Article 119 of the Treaty and Article 1 of the Directive means that the mere finding that in a piecework pay scheme the average pay of a group of workers consisting predominantly of women carrying out one type of work is appreciably lower than the average pay of a group of workers consisting predominantly of men carrying out another type of work to which equal value is attributed does not suffice to establish that there is discrimination with regard to pay. However, where in a piecework pay scheme in which individual pay consists of a variable element depending on each worker's output and a fixed element differing according to the group of workers concerned it is not possible to identify the factors which determined the rates or units of measurement used to calculate the variable element in the pay, the employer may have to bear the burden of proving that the differences found are not due to sex discrimination.

COMMENT

(1) The general message is that payment systems which result in women overall receiving less than men overall are suspect and will require the employer to produce objective justification for any differences. However, note that this is dependent on their jobs being adjudged to be of equal value in the first place.

Red-circling

A job evaluation study or any other review of grading systems may result in some jobs being graded as lower than they were before. In these circumstances, the employees are usually left on their existing wage (higher than others in the same grade) and the differential is gradually phased out over a period of time. The existing employees are placed in a protected category, or 'red-circled'. Another common situation of red-circling is where an employee who has become unable to do his (usually his) existing job is given lower grade work, but at the former wage (e.g. *Methven* v *Cow Industrial Polymers*).

It has long been accepted that this amounts to a genuine material difference, as long as the reason for the red-circling is not itself discriminatory.

Snoxell v *Vauxhall Motors Ltd*

[1977] ICR 700 Employment Appeal Tribunal

Until 1971 the company operated separate grades for men and women even for the same jobs. In 1971 they introduced an amended structure which was open to men and women. It was agreed that one of the male grades in the past had been given too high a status and so it was assimilated to a lower grade, but those in it were red-circled. Two women claimed equal pay arguing that the reason they were not in the red circle was because as women, before 1971 they could not join that grade.

Phillips J: '... Mr Lester submitted that section 1(3) is not a general escape clause designed to enable employers to phase in equal pay gradually; that was provided for in the Equal Pay Act 1970 itself which did not come into operation until December 29, 1975, five years after it was enacted. Nor, he submitted, could reliance be placed on section 1(3) where the facts said to constitute the difference other than sex could be shown to have their origin in sex discrimination. Thus in the present case, although the immediate cause of the discrimination lay in the fact that the male inspectors were red circled whereas Miss Snoxell and Mrs Davies were not, and although they were red circled in order to preserve their status for reasons unconnected with sex, it was necessary to look to see why Miss Snoxell and Mrs Davies were not also within the red circle. The answer was that, because they were women, they were not able to enter grade X2, and so did not qualify. Thus at the root of the difference relied upon lay sex discrimination, and it would be contrary to the purpose and intent of the Equal Pay Act 1970 to allow such an answer to the claim.

Mr Grabiner submitted that the reason for the red circling of the male inspectors had nothing to do with sex discrimination, but was intended merely to preserve their status, and that it was not brought into existence to discriminate against women. If there had been no circle, he submitted, all the men and the women would have been paid the same. The difference for the purpose of section 1(3) was the formation of the red circle. The substantive cause of the discrimination, he submitted, was the formation of the red circle, and it was the effective cause. Thus there was no discrimination, and a good answer to the claim was available to Vauxhall Motors Ltd under section 1(3).

Putting these arguments side by side it can be seen that the solution depends upon whether, in analysing the history of the difference in treatment of Miss Snoxell and Mrs Davies on the one hand and the red circle male inspectors on the other, one stops at the moment of the formation of the circle or looks further back to see why Miss Snoxell and Mrs Davies were not within it. The arguments presented to us have, not surprisingly, considered questions of causation, and it has been said that the inability of Miss Snoxell and Mrs Davies to join the red circle was, or was not, the effective cause of the current variation in the terms of their contracts of employment. It seems to us that this earlier discrimination can be said to be an effective cause of the current variation.

(It was held that the women were entitled to equal pay.)

Part-time working

Bilka-Kaufhaus GmbH v *Weber von Hartz*

[1987] ICR 110 European Court of Justice

'DECISION

The first question

24. In the first of its questions the national court asks whether a staff policy pursued by a department store company excluding part-time employees from an occupational pension scheme constitutes discrimination contrary to article 119 where that exclusion affects a far greater number of women than men.

25. In order to reply to that question reference must be made to the judgment of 31 March 1981 in *Jenkins* v *Kingsgate (Clothing Productions) Ltd.*

26. In that judgment the court considered the question whether the payment of a lower hourly rate for part-time work than for full-time work was compatible with article 119.

27. Such a practice is comparable to that at issue before the national court in this case: Bilka does not pay different hourly rates to part-time and full-time workers, but it grants only full-time workers an occupational pension. Since, as was stated above, such a pension falls within the concept of pay for the purposes of the second paragraph of article 119 it follows that, hour for hour, the total remuneration paid by Bilka to full-time workers is higher than that paid to part-time workers.

28. The conclusion reached by the court in its judgment of 31 March 1981 is therefore equally valid in the context of this case.

29. If, therefore, it should be found that a much lower proportion of women than of men work full-time, the exclusion of part-time workers from the occupational pensions scheme would be contrary to article 119 of the Treaty where, taking into account the difficulties encountered by women workers in working full-time, that measure could not be explained by factors which exclude any discrimination on grounds of sex.

30. However, if the undertaking is able to show that its pay practice may be explained by objectively justified factors unrelated to any discrimination on grounds of sex there is no breach of article 119.

31. The answer to the first question referred by the national court must therefore be that article 119 of the EEC Treaty is infringed by a department store company which

excludes part-time employees from its occupational pension scheme, where that exclusion affects a far greater number of women than men, unless the undertaking shows that the exclusion is based on objectively justified factors unrelated to any discrimination on grounds of sex.

Question 2 (a)

32. In its second question the national court seeks in essence to know whether the reasons put forward by Bilka to explain its pay policy may be regarded as "objectively justified economic grounds", as referred to in the judgment of 31 March 1981, where the interests of undertakings in the department store sector do not require such a policy.

33. In its observations Bilka argues that the exclusion of part-time workers from the occupational pension scheme is intended solely to discourage part-time work, since in general part-time workers refuse to work in the late afternoon and on Saturdays. In order to ensure the presence of an adequate workforce during those periods it was therefore necessary to make full-time work more attractive than part-time work, by making the occupational pension scheme open only to full-time workers. Bilka concludes that on the basis of the judgment of 31 March 1981 it cannot be accused of having infringed article 119.

34. In reply to the reasons put forward to justify the exclusion of part-time workers Mrs Weber von Hartz points out that Bilka is in no way obliged to employ part-time workers and that if it decides to do so it may not subsequently restrict the pension rights of such workers, which are already reduced by reason of the fact that they work fewer hours.

35. According to the Commission, in order to establish that there has been no breach of article 119 it is not sufficient to show that in adopting a pay practice which in fact discriminates against women workers the employer sought to achieve objectives other than discrimination against women. The Commission considers that in order to justify such a pay practice from the point of view of article 119 the employer must, as the court held in its judgment of 31 March 1981, put forward objective economic grounds relating to the management of the undertaking. It is also necessary to ascertain whether the pay practice in question is necessary and in proportion to the objectives pursued by the employer.

36. It is for the national court, which has sole jurisdiction to make findings of fact, to determine whether and to what extent the grounds put forward by an employer to explain the adoption of a pay practice which applies independently of a worker's sex but in fact affects more women than men may be regarded as objectively justified economic grounds. If the national court finds that the measures chosen by Bilka correspond to a real need on the part of the undertaking, are appropriate with a view to achieving the objectives pursued and are necessary to that end, the fact that the measures affect a far greater number of women than men is not sufficient to show that they constitute an infringement of article 119.

37. The answer to question 2(a) must therefore be that under article 119 a department store company may justify the adoption of a pay policy excluding part-time workers, irrespective of their sex, from its occupational pension scheme on the ground that it seeks to employ as few part-time workers as possible, where it is found that the means chosen for achieving that objective correspond to a real need on the part of the undertaking, are appropriate with a view to achieving the objective in question and are necessary to that end ...'

COMMENT

(1) In *Jenkins* v *Kingsgate*, evidence was given that about 90 per cent of all part-time workers are women. Therefore terms which are disadvantageous to part-time workers will indirectly discriminate against women. According to the ECJ this does not prevent it being a genuine material difference subject to the need for objective justitution.

(2) Under the Equal Pay Act as worded, it seemed that the concept of indirect discrimination did not apply. Thus if terms and conditions were not different for men and women, but had a disparate effect on women, it looked as if there was no complaint. As a result of the ECJ decision in *Jenkins* v *Kingsgate* and followed here, the Act must be read to include the concept of indirect discrimination.

(3) In *Kowalska* v *Freie und Hansestadt Hamburg* the ECJ held that exclusion of part-timers from the employer's redundancy payments scheme was indirect discrimination contrary to Article 119 and the Equal Pay Directive. It was held that the women should receive *pro rata* payments according to the number of hours worked. Similarly, in *Rinner-Kühn* v *FWW Spezial-Gebäudereinigung GmbH* the ECJ held that German legislation excluding part-time workers from the right to receive sick pay from their employers required objective justification. Largely on the strength of these decisions the EOC challenged the exclusion of workers working less than 16 hours per week (or 8 hours with five years' service) from the right to claim redundancy payments or unfair dismissal, and the method of calculating redundancy payments: see *R* v *Secretary of State for Employment, ex p EOC* above, p 102.

WHAT IS EQUALISED?

Hayward v *Cammell Laird Shipbuilders (No 2)*

[1988] ICR 464 House of Lords

Julie Hayward, employed as a cook by Cammell Laird, brought the first equal value claim in the country when in 1984 she claimed that her work was of equal value with male painters, thermal insulation engineers and joiners employed by the company. An industrial tribunal held that her work was of equal value and that the employer could not rely on there being a genuine material difference between the two cases because they had made it clear that they were not relying on that defence and could not change their minds.

There was a further hearing as to the form of relief that she should receive. The employers here sought to argue that what should be compared was the overall job packages of the employees. While her basic pay was lower, she had better terms in relation to sickness, holidays, paid meal breaks and benefits in kind. Taken overall, the employers argued that although her basic pay was £25 per week less than theirs, she was actually £11 per week better off!

Lord Mackay: '... I deal first with the issue between the parties arising on the United Kingdom legislation to which I have referred. The issue is whether in terms of the Equal Pay Act 1970, as amended, the woman who can point to a term of her contract which is less favourable than a term of a similar kind in the man's contract is entitled to have that term made not less favourable irrespective of whether she is as favourably treated as the man when the whole of her contract and the whole of his contract are considered, as the appellant submits, or whether, although she shows that a particular term of her contract is less favourable to her than a term of a similar kind in the man's contract, her claim can nevertheless be defeated if it is shown that the terms of her contract considered as a whole are not less favourable to her than the terms of the man's contract considered as a whole, as the respondents submit.

No authority dealing with this question was referred to in the argument before your Lordships. There is no definition of the word "term" in the legislation. In that situation I am of opinion that the natural meaning of the word "term" in this context is a distinct provision or part of the contract which has sufficient content to make it possible to compare it from the point of view of the benefits it confers with similar provision or part in another contract. For example, Miss Hayward was employed on her accepting terms set out in a letter to her from the respondents which includes the following:

"We can offer you a position on our staff as a cook at a salary of £5,165 per annum. The base rate on which overtime is based is £4,741 ..."

There is a provision in the letter setting out the normal hours of work, providing that the overtime payment shall be plain time rate plus a third (two-thirds on Saturday and Sunday).

The corresponding provision with regard to basic pay in the men's contracts is less specific and refers to a national agreement from which the rate of wages to be paid weekly in arrears is to be determined. Overtime payments are to be determined also in accordance with the national agreement.

It appears to me that it would be natural to compare the appellant's basic salary as set out in her contract with the basic salary determined under the men's contracts. I think it would be natural to treat the provision relating to basic pay as a term in each of the contracts.

However, one has to take account of the hours to be worked in order to earn this money and I think this consideration points to the importance of the provision in question being one which is capable of being compared from the point of view of the benefit it confers with a corresponding provision in another contract to see whether or not it is more beneficial than that provision. Accordingly, I am of opinion that the natural application of the word "term" to this contract is that it applies for example, to the basic pay, and that the appropriate comparison is with the hourly rate of basic pay ... '

Lord Goff: '... Now I fully appreciate that this construction of section 1(2) will always lead, where the section is held to apply, to enhancement of the relevant term in the woman's contract. Likewise, it will in the converse case lead to enhancement of the relevant term in the man's contract. This appears to me to be the effect of the philosophy underlying the subsection. I also appreciate that this may, in some cases, lead to what has been called mutual enhancement or leap-frogging, as terms of the woman's contract and the man's contract are both, so to speak, upgraded to bring them into line with each other. It is this effect which was found to be so offensive by both the Employment Appeal Tribunal and the Court of Appeal. They viewed with dismay the possibility of equality being achieved only by mutual enhancement, and not by an overall consideration of the respective contractual terms of both the man and the woman, at least in relation to a particular subject matter such as overall remuneration, considering that mutual enhancement transcended the underlying philosophy of the Equal Pay Act 1970 and that it could have a profoundly inflationary effect.

To these fears there are, I consider, two different answers on two different levels. The first answer is that given by Mr Lester, for the appellant, which is that the employer must, where he can, have recourse to section 1(3). I for my part, see great force in this argument ...

This brings me to my second answer, which is that, if the construction of section 1(2) which I prefer does not accord with the true intention of Parliament, then the appropriate course for Parliament is to amend the legislation to bring it into line with its true intention. In the meanwhile, however, the decision of your Lordships' House may have the salutary effect of drawing to the attention of employers and trade unions the absolute need for ensuring that the pay structures for various groups of employees do not contain any element of sex discrimination direct or indirect, because otherwise section 1(3) will not be available to mitigate the effects which section 1(2), in its present form, is capable of producing on its own.

For these reasons, I would allow the appeal.'

(Lords Bridge, Brandon and Griffiths agreed with Lords Mackay and Goff. The case was remitted to the industrial tribunal for determination accordingly.)

COMMENT

(1)   It is no longer open to Parliament to adopt the second solution to the problem of leap-frogging, for the approach requiring the equalisation of each different element in the remuneration package was explicitly endorsed by the ECJ in *Barber* v *Guardian Royal Exchange*.

Barber v *Guardian Royal Exchange*

[1990] ICR 616 European Court of Justice

Barber was made compulsorily redundant in 1980 aged 52. Under the company's severance terms, men aged 55 and women aged 50 got an immediate pension on redundancy, plus a small lump sum. Men aged under 55 and women aged under 50 had to wait until normal pension age for their pensions, but got a higher lump sum. Overall, the first option was more beneficial. If Barber had been a woman, he would have had an immediate pension, hence his claim, which was referred to the ECJ.

'DECISION

10. In its first question the Court of Appeal seeks to ascertain, in substance, whether the benefits paid by an employer to a worker in connection with the latter's compulsory redundancy fall within the scope of article 119 of the Treaty and the Equal Pay Directive or within the scope of the Equal Treatment Directive.

11. The court has consistently held (see, in particular, *Jenkins* v *Kingsgate (Clothing Productions) Ltd* that the first of those two Directives, which is designed principally to facilitate the application of the principle of equal pay outlined in article 119 of the Treaty, in no way alters the content or scope of that principle as defined in the latter provision. It is therefore appropriate to consider, in the first place, whether article 119 applies in circumstances such as those of this case.

12. As the court has held, the concept of pay, within the meaning of the second paragraph of article 119, comprises any other consideration, whether in cash or in kind, whether immediate or future, provided that the worker receives it, albeit indirectly, in respect of his employment from his employer: see, in particular, *Garland* v *British Rail Engineering Ltd.* Accordingly, the fact that certain benefits are paid after the termination of the employment relationship does not prevent them from being in the nature of pay, within the meaning of article 119 of the Treaty.

13. As regards, in particular, the compensation granted to a worker in connection with his redundancy, it must be stated that such compensation constitutes a form of pay to which the worker is entitled in respect of his employment, which is paid to him upon termination of the employment relationship, which makes it possible to facilitate his adjustment to the new circumstances resulting from the loss of his employment and which provides him with a source of income during the period in which he is seeking new employment.

14. It follows that compensation granted to a worker in connection with his redundancy falls in principle within the concept of pay for the purposes of article 119 of the Treaty.

15. At the hearing, the United Kingdom argued that the statutory redundancy payment fell outside the scope of article 119 of the Treaty because it constituted a social security benefit and not a form of pay.

16. In that regard it must be pointed out that a redundancy payment made by the employer, such as that which is at issue, cannot cease to constitute a form of pay on the sole ground that, rather than deriving from the contract of employment, it is a statutory or ex gratia payment.

17. In the case of statutory redundancy payments it must be borne in mind that, as the court held in *Defrenne* v *Sabena*, article 119 of the Treaty also applies to discrimination arising directly from legislative provisions. This means that benefits provided for by law may come within the concept of pay for the purposes of that provision.

18. Although it is true that many advantages granted by an employer also reflect considerations of social policy, the fact that a benefit is in the nature of pay cannot be called in question where the worker is entitled to receive the benefit in question from his employer by reason of the existence of the employment relationship.

19. In the case of ex gratia payments by the employer, it is clear from the *Garland* case that article 119 also applies to advantages which an employer grants to workers although he is not required to do so by contract.

20. Accordingly, without there being any need to discuss whether or not the Directive on Equal Treatment is applicable, the answer to the first question must be that the benefits paid by an employer to a worker in connection with the latter's compulsory redundancy fall within the scope of the second paragraph of article 119, whether they are paid under a contract of employment, by virtue of legislative provisions or on a voluntary basis.

The second question

21. In view of the answer given to the first question, the second question must be understood as seeking in substance to ascertain whether a retirement pension paid under a contracted-out private occupational scheme falls within the scope of article 119 of the Treaty, in particular where that pension is awarded in connection with compulsory redundancy.

22. It must be pointed out in that regard that, in *Defrenne* v *Belgian State* the court stated that consideration in the nature of social security benefits is not in principle alien to the concept of pay. However, the court pointed out that this concept, as defined in article 119, cannot encompass social security schemes or benefits, in particular retirement pensions, directly governed by legislation without any element of agreement within the undertaking or the occupational branch concerned, which are compulsorily applicable to general categories of workers.

23. The court noted that those schemes afford the workers the benefit of a statutory scheme, to the financing of which workers, employers and possibly the public authorities contribute in a measure determined less by the employment relationship than by considerations of social policy.

24. In order to answer the second question, therefore, it is necessary to ascertain whether those considerations also apply to contracted-out private occupational schemes such as that referred to in this case.

25. In that regard it must be pointed out first of all that the schemes in question are the result either of an agreement between workers and employers or of a unilateral decision taken by the employer. They are wholly financed by the employer or by both the employer and the workers without any contribution being made by the public authorities in any circumstances. Accordingly, such schemes form part of the consideration offered to workers by the employer.

26. Secondly, such schemes are not compulsorily applicable to general categories of workers. On the contrary, they apply only to workers employed by certain undertakings, with the result that affiliation to those schemes derives of necessity from the employment relationship with a given employer. Furthermore, even if the schemes in question are established in conformity with national legislation and consequently satisfy the conditions laid down by it for recognition as contracted-out schemes, they are governed by their own rules.

27. Thirdly, it must be pointed out that, even if the contributions paid to those schemes and the benefits which they provide are in part a substitute for those of the general statutory scheme, that fact cannot preclude the application of article 119. It is apparent from the documents before the court that occupational schemes such as that referred to in this case may grant to their members benefits greater than those which would be paid by the statutory scheme, with the result that their economic function is similar to that of the supplementary schemes which exist in certain member states, where affiliation and contribution to the statutory scheme is compulsory and no derogation is allowed. In its judgment in *Bilka-Kaufhaus GmbH* v *Weber von Hartz* the court held that the benefits awarded under a supplementary pension scheme fell within the concept of pay, within the meaning of article 119.

28. It must therefore be concluded that, unlike the benefits awarded by national statutory social security schemes, a pension paid under a contracted-out scheme constitutes consideration paid by the employer to the worker in respect of his employment and consequently falls within the scope of article 119 of the Treaty.

29. That interpretation of article 119 is not affected by the fact that the private occupational scheme in question has been set up in the form of a trust and is administered by trustees who are technically independent of the employer, since article 119 also applies to consideration received indirectly from the employer.

30. The answer to the second question submitted by the Court of Appeal must therefore be that a pension paid under a contracted-out private occupational scheme falls within the scope of article 119 of the Treaty.

The third and fifth questions

31. In these questions the Court of Appeal seeks in substance to ascertain, in the first place, whether it is contrary to article 119 of the Treaty for a man made compulsorily redundant to be entitled only to a deferred pension payable at the normal pensionable age when

a woman in the same position receives an immediate retirement pension as a result of the application of an age condition that varies according to sex in the same way as is provided for by the national statutory pension scheme. Secondly, the Court of Appeal wishes to ascertain, in substance, whether equal pay must be ensured at the level of each element of renumeration or only on the basis of a comprehensive assessment of the consideration paid to workers.

32.   In the case of the first of those two questions thus formulated, it is sufficient to point out that article 119 prohibits any discrimination with regard to pay as between men and women, whatever the system which gives rise to such inequality. Accordingly, it is contrary to article 119 to impose an age condition which differs according to sex in respect of pensions paid under a contracted-out scheme, even if the difference between the pensionable age for men and that for women is based on the one provided for by the national statutory scheme.

33.   As regards the second of those questions, it is appropriate to refer to the judgments in *Commission* v *France* and in *Handels-og Kontorfunktionaererernes Forbund i Danmark* v *Dansk Arbejdsgiverforening* in which the court emphasised the fundamental importance of transparency and, in particular, of the possibility of a review by the national courts, in order to prevent and, if necessary, eliminate any discrimination based on sex.

34.   With regard to the means of verifying compliance with the principle of equal pay, it must be stated that if the national courts were under an obligation to make an assessment and a comparison of all the various types of consideration granted, according to the circumstances, to men and women, judicial review would be difficult and the effectiveness of article 119 would be diminished as a result. It follows that genuine transparency, permitting an effective review, is assured only if the principle of equal pay applies to each of the elements of remuneration granted to men or women.

35.   The answer to the third and fifth questions submitted by the Court of Appeal must therefore be that it is contrary to article 119 of the Treaty for a man made compulsorily redundant to be entitled to claim only a deferred pension payable at the national pensionable age when a woman in the same position is entitled to an immediate retirement pension as a result of the application of an age condition that varies according to sex in the same way as is provided for by the national statutory pension scheme. The application of the principle of equal pay must be ensured in respect of each element of remuneration and not only on the basis of a comprehensive assessment of the consideration paid to workers ...'

COMMENT

(1)   Of a number of ECJ decisions giving a wide meaning to the term 'pay', this case was a landmark. At a stroke it rendered redundant most of the Occupational Social Security Directive (86/378/EC) which was designed to equalise the terms of employers' pension schemes, by holding that these benefits were 'pay' and therefore required equalisation under Article 119.

(2)   Immediately following the *Barber* decision it was unclear if, and how far, the decision had retrospective effect. The pensions industry was not slow to warn of catastrophe should a wide interpretation be adopted. In *Ten Oever* the ECJ held that

equal pension benefits were payable only in respect of periods of employment after 17 May 1990 (the date of the *Barber* judgment). This was the most restrictive possible interpretation of *Barber*, but accorded with the agreement reached by EU member states and recorded in the second Protocol to the Treaty of Maastricht. *Ten Oever* also made clear that benefits for the widows and widowers of pensioners were also within the principle of equality.

(3) In *Smith* v *Advel* and *Van den Akker* v *Stichting Shell* the ECJ further held that retirement ages could be equalised upwards without infringing Article 119. However, both men and women had to be given the benefit of the most generous terms in any transitional period.

(4) It was already clear from *Bilka-Kaufhaus* v *Weber von Hartz* that Article 119 covered access to pension schemes, so that the exclusion of part-time workers would be unlawful indirect sex discrimination unless the employer could produce objective justification for the inequality. In *Vroege* v *NCIV Institut voor Volkshuisvesting* and *Fisscher* v *Voorhuis Hengelo* the ECJ held that the access rights of part-timers could be backdated to 1976 (when Article 119 was first held to be directly effective) and that there was no 'minimum hours' requirement for these rights.

(5) These cases led to a flood of claims by part-timers in the United Kingdom. However, in *Preston* v *Wolverhampton Healthcare Trust* the Court of Appeal delivered two crushing blows to part-timers. First, it held that the normal six-month limitation period applied to these actions, thus excluding most claimants who had already left their employment. Second, it held that the usual two-year limit on backdated claims (EqPA s 2(5)) also applied, thus substantially limiting the value of such claims. On appeal, the House of Lords referred these issues to the ECJ.

(6) Not all issues relating to the meaning of 'pay' within Article 119 have been settled. Important questions remain to be answered, especially in relation to pensions. However, if the law is still opaque in some respects, it should at least be clear that the influence of European Community law is crucially important in this rapidly evolving area.

EQUAL PAY CODE OF PRACTICE

Having been given power to do so by TURERA, the EOC issued a Code of Practice on Equal Pay in 1996, which came into force on 26 March 1997. Its central recommendations are that employers should undertake a review of payment systems for possible sex bias and that they should adopt an Equal Pay Policy.

An eight-stage process is recommended for the review of payment systems:

1   Analyse the existing system to get a breakdown of all employees by sex, job title, grade, whether full- or part-time, basic pay and all other elements of remuneration.
2   Examine each element of the pay system against the above data.
3   Identify any elements in the pay system which the review indicates may be the source of discrimination.

4   Change any rules or practices (including collective agreements) which are thus identified as likely to give rise to discrimination. Consultation with employees and their representatives over this is recommended. Any other problems identified in Stages 1 to 3 should also be addressed.

5   Analyse the likely effects of any proposed changes to the pay system before implementation to identify and rectify any discrimination which could be caused.

6   Give equal pay to current employees.

7   Set up a regular monitoring system to allow checks of pay practices.

8   Draw up and publish an equal pay policy. Provide information so that employees are aware of how every element in their pay is calculated (transparency principle).

The Code gives an example of an equal pay policy.

Code of Practice on Equal Pay

Equal Opportunities Commission 1997

Annex A: Suggested equal pay policy

Equal Pay Statement

This organisation supports the principle of equal opportunities in employment and believes as part of that principle that male and female staff should receive equal pay for the same or broadly similar work, for work rated as equivalent and for work of equal value.

We understand that a right to equal pay between men and women free of sex bias is a fundamental principle of European Community law and is conferred by United Kingdom legislation.

We believe it is in our company's interest and good business practice that pay is awarded fairly and equitably.

We recognise that in order to achieve equal pay for employees doing equal work we should operate a pay system which is transparent, based on objective criteria and free from sex bias.

Action to implement policy

In order to put our commitment to equal pay into practice we will:

* examine our existing and future pay practices for all our employees including those in non-standard employment and those who are absent on pregnancy and maternity leave.
* carry out regular monitoring of the impact of our practices.
* inform employees of how these practices work and how their own pay is arrived at.
* provide training and guidance for managers and supervisory staff involved in decisions about pay and benefits.
* discuss and agree the equal pay policy with employees, trade unions or staff representatives where appropriate.

We intend through the above action to avoid unfair discrimination, to reward fairly the skills, experience and potential of all staff and thereby to increase efficiency, productivity and competitiveness and enhance the organisation's reputation and image.

8   Dismissal

Termination of a contract of employment may be a breach of contract by either party. Like any other claim for a breach of contract, the aggrieved party may sue the other in the High Court or county court; additionally, since 1994 many such claims can be taken to industrial tribunals. It is fairly rare for an employer to sue an employee who leaves, although there have been more cases in recent years. Usually pursuing the employee will be perceived as more trouble than it is worth, and the employer will instead direct effort at finding a replacement. The employee is more likely to sue for termination in breach of contract: in the industrial context, this is called an action for wrongful dismissal, and it will be considered first in this chapter.

Since 1965 employees have received some negative protection from the disaster of dismissal through statutory measures. They are described as 'negative protection' because they do not on the whole actually prevent dismissal; instead they stipulate that in certain circumstances the employee should receive a remedy, usually compensation. The first statutory measure was the Redundancy Payments Act 1965; claims for redundancy payments are considered in Chapter 9. The second, and more important, was the action for unfair dismissal, introduced by the Industrial Relations Act 1971. This will be considered secondly in this chapter. Finally, recent developments showing a revival of interest in common law claims will be examined.

WRONGFUL DISMISSAL

An employee can only claim for wrongful dismissal if the employer's termination of the contract was in breach. There is no breach of contract if *either* the employer gave adequate notice to terminate *or* if the employer terminated in face of a fundamental breach of contract by the employee.

Notice

Employment Rights Act 1996

86.   (1)   The notice required to be given by an employer to terminate the contract of employment of a person who has been continuously employed for one month or more—

      (a)   is not less than one week's notice if his period of continuous employment is less than two years,

      (b)   is not less than one week's notice for each year of continuous employment if his period of continuous employment is two years or more but less than twelve years; and

      (c)   is not less than twelve weeks' notice if his period of continuous employment is twelve years or more.

(2)   The notice required to be given by an employee who has been continuously employed for one month or more to terminate his contract of employment is not less than one week. ...

COMMENT

(1)   These are minimum periods of notice: if the contract stipulates a longer period, either party can sue if it is not given. Information about notice to be given on either side is one of the matters which must be included in the written statement given to the employee (ERA s 1(4)(e), p 118).

(2)   Giving pay in lieu of notice is regarded as being as good as giving notice; if it is accepted that the employee has no right to work then her only entitlement is to be paid. Hence pay for the notice period is as good as having notice. Compare *Devonald* v *Rosser*, above, p 131.

(3)   The requirement at common law is that both parties should give reasonable notice to terminate the contract. In *Hill* v *C A Parsons Ltd* the Court of Appeal held that reasonable notice for a chartered engineer with 35 years' service was six months: however, this was a rather unusual case. The court was anxious to keep his contract in existence until the Industrial Relations Act 1971 came into force so that Hill, who had been dismissed for refusing to join a trade union, would be able to claim unfair dismissal and the union's insistence on a closed shop arrangement would have become unlawful. Thus the decision has rarely been relied on since; however, it is also important for the revival of common law actions discussed later in this chapter (p 325) because it treats the employer's notice as invalid in some circumstances.

Justified summary dismissal

Dismissal without notice or with inadequate notice is called summary dismissal. If it is not justified by an adequate reason, it will constitute wrongful dismissal.

    Disobedience to a lawful and reasonable order is a prime example of conduct justifying summary dismissal: see the extract from *Laws* v *London Chronicle* and associated discussion, p 143. This is why taking industrial action is almost always a fundamental breach of contract and would therefore justify dismissal at common law. What else justifies summary dismissal?

Sinclair v *Neighbour*

[1967] 2 QB 279 Court of Appeal

The plaintiff had been employed for about a month as manager of one of the defendant's betting shops. He borrowed £15 from the till – putting in an IOU – to place a bet at a different betting shop. The following day (the bet having been successful) he returned the money to the till. When the defendant heard about the incident, he summarily dismissed the plaintiff.

Sellers LJ: ' … This case turns on the attitude which the employer could properly take to that conduct. It seems that the manager not infrequently used to telephone to the employer. He said he did it too often and so he did not think he would do it again over this matter. He took the money without asking. He thought that if he had asked, the employer might have lent him the money for some purposes, but that if he had told the employer that it was for betting the employer would not have agreed. He would not have permitted it. In my view, whether such taking of the money would have resulted in a conviction for larceny or for dishonest misappropriation of the money does not arise. On these facts a jury might have taken the view that they would not convict. But whether it is to be described as dishonest misconduct or not, I do not think matters. Views might differ. It was sufficient for the employer if he could, in all the circumstances, regard what the manager did as being something which was seriously inconsistent – incompatible – with his duty as the manager in the business in which he was engaged.

To take money out of the till in such circumstances is on the face of it incompatible and inconsistent with his duty. Some people might well say that to take money out of the till, when the manager knew that if he had asked if he could do it for the purpose which he might have had to disclose it would have been refused, is dishonest conduct. The question for this court to decide is whether, in the circumstances of this case, it was conduct in its nature, as it has been described, quite irrespective of any point of pleading, which justified the employer instantly dismissing the manager.

I think that it was. Counsel referred to some of the cases. I do not think that I need refer to them further. The whole question is whether that conduct was of such a type that it was inconsistent, in a grave way – incompatible – with the employment in which he had been engaged as a manager.

There was an aggravating feature, I think, in that there were in the office two others, including one boy who was only some 18 or 19 years of age who had said something about borrowing money out of the till and it was said that it had been done before. On a new manager coming in, I should have thought that the one thing that was incumbent upon him was to keep the till inviolate. The practice of taking money out of the till in that way, as all who have had experience in criminal courts know, can lead to endless trouble.

On the short facts of this case, and applying the law as I understand it, since we have been asked to do so, I would not hesitate to say that the dismissal was justified.'

Sachs LJ: '…It is well-established law that a servant can be instantly dismissed when his conduct is such that it not only amounts to a wrongful act inconsistent with his duty towards his master but is also inconsistent with the continuance of confidence between them. That was said by Bowen LJ in his classic judgment in *Boston Deep Sea Fishing and Ice Co* v *Ansell.*

Here we have a case where the manager of a betting shop, responsible for the conduct of the shop and of the other employees there, quite deliberately takes out of the till money for his own personal purposes, in circumstances which he knew quite well his employer, if asked, would not permit.

To state those facts quite simply seems to me enough to make plain that here indeed there was beyond a peradventure misconduct of a type which justified instant dismissal; and I agree with the judge's view where he uses the adjectives "utterly reprehensible" and "improper" in regard to that conduct … '

(Davies LJ delivered a concurring judgment.)

Wilson v Racher

[1974] ICR 428 Court of Appeal

The plaintiff was employed as head gardener by the defendant. On a Sunday afternoon, the defendant called over the plaintiff and wrongly and aggressively accused him of various derelictions of duty. An argument developed, and the plaintiff was provoked into swearing obscenely at his employer, who responded by summarily dismissing him.

Edmund Davies LJ: ' ... *Pepper* v *Webb*, a case which Mr Connell seemed to regard as affording some measure of support for his argument, appears to me, on the other hand, to do nothing of the kind. In that case also the plaintiff was a gardener, but there was a history of complaints of insolence and inefficiency from time to time. The culminating incident was when the employer asked the plaintiff what arrangements he had made in relation to a greenhouse in his absence during the weekend. The plaintiff said: "I couldn't care less about your bloody greenhouse or your sodding garden", and walked away. Harman LJ there said,

> "Now what will justify an instant dismissal? – something done by the employee which impliedly or expressly is a repudiation of the fundamental terms of the contract; and in my judgment if ever there was such a repudiation this is it. What is the gardener to do? He is to look after the garden and he is to look after the greenhouse. If he does not care a hoot about either then he is repudiating his contract. That is what it seems to me the plaintiff did, and I do not see, having done that, that he can complain if he is summarily dismissed. It is said on his behalf that one act of temper, one insolent outburst, does not merit so condign a punishment. But this, according to the defendant, his employer, and I think rightly on the evidence, was the last straw. He had been acting in a very unsatisfactory way ever since April."

And this was an incident which had occurred in June. That the court were there having regard not simply to the last incident of June 10, in isolation, but to the whole history, appears also from the other judgments, Russell LJ, for example saying,

> "I entirely agree that, against the background of what the plaintiff's counsel must admit the deputy county court judge found or assumed to be quite a number of disobediences and a certain amount of insolence, it must be taken as conduct repudiatory of the contract justifying summary dismissal."

The present case, too, has to be looked at against the whole background. On the judge's findings, here was a competent, diligent and efficient gardener who, apart from one complaint of leaving a ladder against a yew tree, had done nothing which could be regarded as blameworthy by any reasonable employer. Here, too, was an employer who was resolved to get rid of him; an employer who would use every barrel in the gun that he could find, or thought available; and an employer who was provocative from the outset and dealt with the plaintiff in an unseemly manner. The plaintiff lost his temper. He used obscene and deplorable language. He was therefore deserving of the severest reproof. But this was a solitary occasion. Unlike *Pepper* v *Webb*, there was no background either of inefficiency or of insolence. The plaintiff tried to avert the situation by walking away, but he was summoned back and the defendant continued his gadfly activity of goading him into intemperate language. Such are the findings of the county court judge.

In those circumstances, would it be just to say that the plaintiff's use of this extremely bad language on a solitary occasion made impossible the continuance of the master and servant relationship, and showed that the plaintiff was indeed resolved to follow a line of conduct which made the continuation of that relationship impossible? The judge thought the answer to that question was clear, and I cannot say that he was manifestly wrong. On the contrary, it seems to me that the parties could have made up their differences. The plaintiff apologised to Mrs Racher. There are no grounds for thinking that if the defendant had given him a warning that such language would not be tolerated, and further, if he had manifested recognition that he himself had acted provocatively, the damage done might well have been repaired and some degree of harmony restored. Perhaps there was such instinctive antipathy between the two men that the defendant would, nevertheless, have been glad to get rid of the plaintiff when October 23, 1972, arrived.

In my judgment, in the light of the findings of fact the judge arrived at a just decision. That is not to say that language such as that employed by the plaintiff is to be tolerated. On the contrary, it requires very special circumstances to entitle a servant who expresses his feelings in such a grossly improper way to succeed in an action for wrongful dismissal. But there were special circumstances here, and they were of the defendant's own creation. The plaintiff, probably lacking the educational advantages of the defendant, and finding himself in a frustrating situation despite his efforts to escape from it, fell into the error of explosively using this language. To say that he ought to be kicked out because on this solitary occasion he fell into such grave error would, in my judgment, be wrong. I am not persuaded that the judge was in error in holding that … it was wrongful dismissal, and that the plaintiff was entitled to the damages awarded. I would therefore be for dismissing the appeal.'

(Cairns and James LJJ concurred.)

ACAS Code of Practice No 1

Disciplinary Practice and Procedures in Employment (1977)

8.   Employees should be made aware of the likely consequences of breaking rules and in particular they should be given a clear indication of the type of conduct which may warrant summary dismissal.

ACAS Advisory Handbook

Discipline at Work (1987)

6.   *Deciding and implementing disciplinary action*
     … Employers should give all employees a clear indication of the type of misconduct which, in the light of the requirements of the employer's business, will warrant dismissal without the normal period of notice or pay in lieu of notice. So far as possible the types of offence which fall into this category (gross misconduct) should be clearly specified in the rules.
     A dismissal for gross misconduct should only take place after the normal investigation to establish all the facts. The employee should be told of the complaint and be given an opportunity to state his or her case and be represented.
     Gross misconduct is generally seen as misconduct serious enough to destroy the employment contract between the employer and the employee and make any further working relationship and trust impossible. It is normally restricted to very serious offences – for example, physical violence, theft or fraud – but may be determined by the nature of the business or other circumstances.

COMMENT

(1)   Gross misconduct is an evolving concept: in *Denco Ltd* v *Joinson* the EAT

suggested that unauthorised access to the employer's computer system was probably to be regarded as the kind of offence that any employee should know will be regarded as gross misconduct; however, they also suggested that employers should make their rules clear and post copies near all terminals.

(2) In considering what offences justify summary dismissal, it is worth referring back to the discussion of the implied duties of the employee under the contract in Chapter 4. In general, breach of the implied duties will be regarded as a fundamental breach of contract justifying immediate dismissal. In fact, many of the decisions establishing implied terms under the contract arose as claims for wrongful dismissal.

(3) In particular, note that in *Boston Deep Sea Fishing* v *Ansell* (p 147) conduct only discovered *after* the dismissal was held to justify the termination. This should be contrasted with the position for unfair dismissal (cf *Devis* v *Atkins* (p 303).

(4) Note that the ACAS Advisory Handbook, *Discipline at Work*, has no legal status. The guidance it gives on handling cases of gross misconduct is relevant to whether the dismissal would be unfair rather than to wrongful dismissal.

(5) An employer who is entitled to dismiss an employee for breach of contract may not substitute the lesser penalty of suspension without pay unless the right to suspend is incorporated into the employee's contract of employment (expressly or impliedly) (*Hanley* v *Pease*). See also the ACAS Code of Practice No 1 on Disciplinary Practice and Procedures in Employment para 12(c) (p 300).

(6) Suspension on full pay is not usually a breach of contract (see the discussion of the right to work (p 131)), and is often used to give time for investigation of very serious offences.

(7) Even where suspension is permitted by the contract, the employee may be able to claim a redundancy payment if it has continued for a lengthy period (see p 357).

Damages for wrongful dismissal

Addis v *Gramophone Co Ltd*

[1909] AC 488 House of Lords

The plaintiff was manager of the defendant's business in Calcutta, paid by a mixture of salary and commission and dismissable on six months' notice. The defendant gave him notice, but then prevented him from working out his notice period and earning any commission during that period. A jury awarded him £600 for wrongful dismissal and £340 for loss of commission.

Lord Loreburn LC: '... As to the damages of £600 for wrongful dismissal a variety of controversies arose. Did what happened entitle the plaintiff to treat the breach of contract as a wrongful dismissal? If yes, then did he elect to treat the contract of service as still continuing? Was it open to the defendants to raise the point having regard to the pleadings and the amendments to the pleadings, and the way the case was conducted at the trial, and the contents of the notice of appeal to the Court of Appeal? A subsidiary dispute was raised as to the way in which the case had been in fact conducted at the trial, as to which eminent counsel did not agree. A further controversy ensued, whether the £600 was intended to include salary for the six months, or merely damages because of the abrupt and oppressive way in which the plaintiff's services were discontinued, and the loss he sustained from the discredit thus thrown upon him. And, finally, a question of law was argued, whether or not such damages could be recovered in law.

My Lords, it is difficult to imagine a better illustration of the way in which litigation between exasperated litigants can breed barren controversies and increase costs in a matter of itself simple enough.

To my mind it signifies nothing in the present case whether the claim is to be treated as for wrongful dismissal or not. In any case there was a breach of contract in not allowing the plaintiff to discharge his duties as manager, and the damages are exactly the same in either view. They are, in my opinion, the salary to which the plaintiff was entitled for the six months between October, 1905, and April, 1906, together with the commission which the jury think he would have earned had he been allowed to manage the business himself. I cannot agree that the manner of dismissal affects these damages. Such considerations have never been allowed to influence damages in this kind of case. An expression of Lord Coleridge CJ has been quoted as authority to the contrary.(1) I doubt if the learned Lord Chief Justice so intended it. If he did I cannot agree with him.

If there be a dismissal without notice the employer must pay an indemnity; but that indemnity cannot include compensation either for the injured feelings of the servant, or for the loss he may sustain from the fact that his having been dismissed of itself makes it more difficult for him to obtain fresh employment. The cases relating to a refusal by a banker to honour cheques when he has funds in hand have, in my opinion, no bearing. That class of case has always been regarded as exceptional. And the rule as to damages in wrongful dismissal, or in breach of contract to allow a man to continue in a stipulated service, has always been, I believe, what I have stated. It is too inveterate to be now altered, even if it were desirable to alter it.

Accordingly I think that so much of the verdict of £600 as relates to that head of damages cannot be allowed to stand. As there is an additional dispute how much of it does relate to that head of damages, the best course will be to disallow the £600 altogether, and to state in the order that plaintiff is entitled to be credited, in the account which is to be taken, with salary from October, 1905, to April, 1906 ...'

(1)   The plaintiff by reason of his being dismissed during his apprenticeship with a slur on his character naturally would experience a greater difficulty in getting employment elsewhere: 25 QBD at p 108.

(Lords James, Atkinson, Gorell and Shaw agreed; Lord Collins dissented.)

COMMENT

(1)   This important decision stated the basic rule that compensation for wrongful dismissal is limited to monies which the employee would have been entitled to during the notice period, and nothing more. The justification for this is that since the employer could at any time terminate the contract lawfully by giving notice or pay in lieu of notice, this is all that the employee has lost through being wrongfully dismissed.

(2)   Thus where an employee with a five-year contract was dismissed after only two years, it was held that he could not claim the amount by which his salary would have been increased had he stayed, because he had no contractual entitlement to an increase. Nor could he claim an amount representing discretionary bonuses, precisely because they were discretionary (*Lavarack* v *Woods of Colchester Ltd*).

(3) However, a significant qualification to this position is contained in the House of Lords' decision in *Malik* v *BCCI* to the effect that damages may be payable for breach of the implied term of mutual trust and confidence.

Malik v *Bank of Credit and Commerce International*

[1997] IRLR 462 House of Lords

The employees, who were made redundant after the bank collapsed, claimed that their association with BCCI placed them at a serious disadvantage in finding new employment. The House of Lords held that by carrying on a dishonest and corrupt business an employer would be in breach of the implied term not to act in such a way as to damage or destroy the relationship of confidence and trust between employer and employee. This aspect of the case is considered above, p 140. Having found such a breach, what were the remedies?

Lord Nicholls: '...
Remedies: (1) acceptance of breach as repudiation
The next step is to consider the consequences which flow from the bank being in breach of its obligation to its innocent employees by operating a corrupt banking business. The first remedy of an employee has already been noted. The employee may treat the bank's conduct as a repudiatory breach, entitling him to leave. He is not compelled to leave. He may choose to stay. The extent to which staying would be more than an election to remain, and would be a waiver of the breach for all purposes, depends on the circumstances.

I need say no more about waiver in the present case. The assumed facts do not state whether the appellants first learned of the corrupt nature of BCCI after their dismissal on 3 October 1991, or whether they acquired this knowledge earlier, in the interval of three months between the appointment of the provisional liquidators on 5 July 1991 and 3 October 1991. If anything should turn on this, the matter can be investigated further in due course.

In the nature of things, the remedy of treating the conduct as a repudiatory breach, entitling the employee to leave, can only avail an employee who learns of the facts while still employed. If he does not discover the facts while his employment is still continuing, perforce this remedy is not open to him. But this does not mean he has no remedy. In the ordinary course breach of a contractual term entitles the innocent party to damages.

Remedies: (2) damages
Can an employee recover damges for breach of the trust and confidence term when he first learns of the breach after he has left the employment? The answer to this question is inextricably bound up with the further question of what damages are recoverable for a breach of this term. In turn, the answer to this further question is inextricably linked with one aspect of the decision in *Addis* v *Gramophone Co Ltd.* ...

Addis v *Gramophone Co*
Against this background I turn to the much discussed case of *Addis* v *Gramophone Co Ltd.* Mr Addis, it will be recalled, was wrongfully and contumeliously dismissed from his post as the defendant's manager in Calcutta. At trial he was awarded damages exceeding the amount of his salary for the period of notice to which he was entitled. The case is generally regarded as having decided, echoing the words of Lord Loreburn LC, that an employee cannot recover damages for the manner in which the wrongful dismissal took place, for injured feelings or for any loss he may sustain from the fact that his having been dismissed of itself makes it more difficult for him to obtain fresh employment. In particular, *Addis* is generally understood to have decided that any loss suffered by the adverse impact on the

employee's chances of obtaining alternative employment is to be excluded from an assessment of damages for wrongful dismissal: see, for instance, *O'Laoire* v *Jackel International Ltd (No 2)*, following earlier authorities; in Canada, the decision of the Supreme Court in *Vorvis* v *Insurance Corporation of British Columbia*; and, in New Zealand, *Vivian* v *Coca-Cola Export Corporation*; *Whelan* v *Waitaki Meats Ltd*, where Gallen J disagreed with the decision in *Addis*, and *Brandt* v *Nixdorf Computer Ltd*.

For present purposes I am not concerned with the exclusion of damages for injured feelings. The present case is concerned only with financial loss. The report of the facts in *Addis* is sketchy. Whether Mr Addis sought to prove that the manner of his dismissal caused him financial loss over and above his premature termination losses is not clear beyond a peradventure. If he did, it is surprising that their Lordships did not address this important feature more specifically. Instead there are references to injured feelings, the fact of dismissal of itself, aggravated damages, exemplary damages amounting to damages for defamation, damages being compensatory and not punitive, and the irrelevance of motive. The dissenting speech of Lord Collins was based on competence to award exemplary or vindictive damages.

However, Lord Loreburn's observations were framed in quite general terms, and he expressly disagreed with the suggestion of Lord Coleridge CJ in *Maw* v *Jones*, to the effect that an assessment of damages might take into account the greater difficulty which an apprentice dismissed with a slur on his character might have in obtaining other employment. Similarly general observations were made by Lord James of Hereford, Lord Atkinson, Lord Gorell and Lord Shaw of Dunfermline.

In my view these observations cannot be read as precluding the recovery of damages where the manner of dismissal involved a breach of the trust and confidence term and this caused financial loss. *Addis* v *Gramophone Co Ltd* was decided in the days before this implied term was adumbrated. Now that this term exists and is normally implied in every contract of employment, damages for its breach should be assessed in accordance with ordinary contractual principles. This is as much true if the breach occurs before or in connection with dismissal as at any other time.

This approach would accord, in its result, with the approach adopted by courts and tribunals in unfair dismissal cases when exercising the statutory jurisdiction, currently limited to a maximum of £11,300, to award an amount of compensation which the court or tribunal considers "just and reasonable" in all the circumstances. Writing on a clean slate, the courts have interpreted this as enabling awards to include compensation in respect of the manner and circumstances of dismissal if these would give rise to a risk of financial loss by, for instance, making the employee less acceptable to potential employers: see sections 123 and 124 of the Employment Rights Act 1996 and *Norton Tool Co Ltd* v *Tewson*.

I do not believe this approach gives rise to artificiality. On the contrary, the trust and confidence term is a useful tool, well established now in employment law. At common law damages are awarded to compensate for *wrongful* dismissal. Thus, loss which an employee would have suffered even if the dismissal had been after due notice is irrecoverable, because such loss does not derive from the wrongful element in the dismissal. Further, it is difficult to see how the mere fact of wrongful dismissal, rather than dismissal after due notice, could of itself handicap an employee in the labour market. All this is in line with *Addis*. But the manner and circumstances of the dismissal, as measured by the standards of conduct now identified in the implied trust and confidence term, may give rise to such a handicap. The law would be blemished if this were not recognised today. There now exists the separate cause of action whose absence Lord Shaw of Dunfermline noted with "a certain regret": see *Addis* v *Gramophone Co Ltd*. The trust and confidence term has removed the cause for his regret. ...

Conclusion

For these reasons I would allow these appeals. The agreed set of assumed facts discloses a good cause of action. Unlike the courts below, this House is not bound by the observations in *Addis* v *Gramophone Co Ltd* regarding irrecoverability of loss flowing from the manner of dismissal, or by the decision in *Withers* v *General Theatre Corporation Ltd*.

I add some cautionary footnotes, having in mind the assumed facts in the present case. First, when considering these appeals I have been particularly conscious of the potential difficulties which claims of this sort may present for liquidators. I am conscious that the outcome of the present appeals may be seen by some as opening the door to speculative claims, to the detriment of admitted creditors. Claims of handicap in the labour market, and the other ingredients of the cause of action now under consideration, may give rise to lengthy and costly investigations and, ultimately, litigation. If the claims eventually fail, liquidators may well be unable to recover their costs from the former employees. The expense of liquidations, and the time they often take, are matters already giving rise to concern. I am aware of the dangers here, but it could not be right to allow "floodgates" arguments of this nature to stand in the way of claims which, as a matter of ordinary legal principle, are well founded. After all, if the former employee's claim is well founded in fact as well as in law, he himself is a creditor and ought to be admitted as such.

Secondly, one of the assumed facts in the present case is that the employer was conducting a dishonest and corrupt business. I would like to think this will rarely happen in practice. Thirdly, there are many circumstances in which an employee's reputation may suffer from his having been associated with an unsuccessful business, or an unsuccessful department within a business. In the ordinary way this will not found a claim of the nature made in the present case, even if the business or department was run with gross incompetence. A key feature in the present case is the assumed fact that the business was dishonest or corrupt.

Finally, although the implied term that the business will not be conducted dishonestly is a term which avails all employees, proof of consequential handicap in the labour market may well be much more difficult for some classes of employees than others. An employer seeking to employ a messenger, for instance, might be wholly unconcerned by an applicant's former employment in a dishonest business, whereas he might take a different view if he were seeking a senior executive.

COMMENT

(1) As the case went to the House of Lords on an agreed set of hypothetical facts, the result meant only that the employees could go ahead with their claim. Whether they were successful would depend on whether they could prove the relevant facts.

(2) Lord Nicholls's speech is an interesting example of the techniques of legal reasoning used by a court which does not wish to follow an earlier decision. First, it is suggested that the earlier court did not really have this particular point in mind. Second, he points out that circumstances have changed: the implied term did not exist at the time of *Addis*. Third, it is morally right to take this position. Fourth, there is a fleeting and indirect reference to the Practice Statement. Finally, he implies that the decision will barely have any effect beyond the facts of this specific case. As to that, we shall see!

UNFAIR DISMISSAL

Royal Commission on Trade Unions and Employers' Associations 1965–1968 (the Donovan Commission) Cmnd 3623

521.   In the eye of the law employer and employee are free and equal parties to the contract of employment. Hence, either employer or employee has the right to bring the contract to an end in accordance with its terms. Thus, an employer is legally entitled to dismiss an employee whenever he wishes and for whatever reason, provided only that he gives due notice. At common law he does not even have to reveal his reason, much less to justify it.

522.   An employee has protection at common law against 'wrongful' dismissal, but this protection is strictly limited; it means that if an employee is dismissed without due notice he can claim the payment of wages he would have earned for the period of notice. From this payment will be deducted any amount which he earned (or through his fault failed to earn) during the period of notice. Beyond this, the employee has no legal claim at common law, whatever hardship he suffers as a result of his dismissal. Even if the way in which he is dismissed constitutes an imputation on his honesty and his ability to get another job is correspondingly reduced he cannot – except through an action for defamation – obtain any redress (see the decision of the House of Lords in *Addis* v *Gramophone Co*)....

524.   In practice of course many employees enjoy much greater security against dismissal than is implied in the law. Many employers dislike having to dismiss employees and do so only with reluctance when they feel that there is no alternative. Some employers have introduced formal procedures designed to ensure that employees are not dismissed without an opportunity to get their case reconsidered at a higher level, and in many well-organised industries trade unions can take up a dismissal which they think unjust through an agreed disputes procedure. Sometimes additional factors may have some influence, such as an acute shortage of labour or the possibility that action which seemed arbitrary would provoke a strike.

525.   There is nevertheless a very general feeling, shared by employers as well as trade unions, that the present situation is unsatisfactory, and it was reflected in the submissions of many who gave evidence to us. In 1964 the Government announced that they accepted Recommendation No 119 on Termination of Employment adopted by the International Labour Organization in 1963 and would discuss the provision of procedures to give effective safeguards against arbitrary dismissal with representatives of employers and trade unions. The Minister of Labour's National Joint Advisory Council subsequently set up a committee to examine dismissals and dismissal procedures. The committee's report was published in 1967, and the committee drew particular attention to a number of points about procedures in Great Britain as compared with the position in some other countries (see paragraph 121 of *Dismissal Procedures* published by HMSO 1967). They pointed out that in law employees are in general protected only against dismissal without due notice, there being no legal protection against being dismissed unfairly or without good reason. Provision by employers of a formal procedure for the handling of dismissals is not very common and is usually found only in large concerns, and this is particularly serious because the great majority of grievances about dismissals are bound to be matters dealt with within the individual concern. Disputes procedures laid down by industry-wide agreement have limitations; for example the delays in their operation may mean that a dismissed worker often takes another job and the case lapses without his grievance having been properly thrashed out. In less highly organised

sectors of employment there may be no disputes procedure and an employee may have no effective redress against dismissal. Finally, with rare exceptions employees have no right of appeal to an independent person or body.

526.   We share in full the belief that the present situation is unsatisfactory. In practice there is usually no comparison between the consequences for an employer if an employee terminates the contract of employment and those which will ensue for an employee if he is dismissed. In reality people build much of their lives around their jobs. Their incomes and prospects for the future are inevitably founded in the expectation that their jobs will continue. For workers in many situations dismissal is a disaster. For some workers it may make inevitable the breaking up of a community and the uprooting of homes and families. Others, and particularly older workers, may be faced with the greatest difficulty in getting work at all. The statutory provision for redundancy goes some way to recognise what is really at stake for an employee when his job is involved, but it is no less at stake if he is being dismissed for alleged incompetence or for misconduct than if he is being dismissed for redundancy. To this it is no answer that good employers will dismiss employees only if they have no alternative. Not all employers are good employers. Even if the employer's intentions are good, is it certain that his subordinates' intentions are always also good? And even when all concerned in management act in good faith, are they always necessarily right? Should their view of the case automatically prevail over the employee's?

527.   The passage we refer to above in the report of the committee on dismissals draws attention to the unsatisfactory situation in less highly organised sectors of employment. Elsewhere in this report we recommend measures to promote the growth of collective bargaining machinery on sound lines and in particular that any stipulation in a contract of employment that an employee should not belong to a trade union should by law be made void and of no effect. Clearly however the protection given by this enactment will be far from complete so long as it is open to an employer to dismiss an employee because he exercises his right to join a trade union or because, having joined, he takes a part in legitimate trade union activities. It is just where organisation is weak that the danger that this could happen is greatest.

528.   From the point of view of industrial peace, it is plain also that the present situation leaves much to be desired. In the period 1964–1966 some 276 unofficial strikes took place each year on average as a result of disputes about whether individuals should or should not be employed, suspended or dismissed. The committee on dismissals analysed stoppages – whether official or unofficial – arising out of dismissals *other than redundancies* over this period and found that there were on average 203 a year. It can be argued that the right to secure a speedy and impartial decision on the justification for a dismissal might have averted many of these stoppages, though some cases would no doubt still have occurred where workers were taking spontaneous action to try to prevent a dismissal being given effect.

529.   For all these reasons we believe it urgently necessary for workers to be given better protection against unfair dismissal.

COMMENT

(1)   The Donovan Commission's proposals led to the enactment of a right to claim unfair dismissal in the Industrial Relations Act 1971. The broad outlines of the law have been unchanged since: the present provisions are to be found in the Employment Rights Act 1996 Part X.

(2)   Not every worker has the right to claim unfair dismissal, and in case of doubt, the burden of proof is on the worker to establish that she is entitled to claim. Major exclusions are as follows:

- (a)   The applicant must be an employee (ERA s 94: see Chapter 3);
- (b)   The applicant must have been employed for two years (ERA s 108(1));
- (c)   The applicant must not be over normal retiring age: that is, the age at which employees in her position normally retire, or, if there is no normal retiring age, 65 (ERA s 109(1): see *Waite* v *GCHQ* on the meaning of 'normal retiring age').

(3)   In addition, certain categories of worker are excluded from the right to claim; the police; those who ordinarily work outside Great Britain; share fishermen; those excluded by national security considerations as certified by the Secretary of State; and anyone covered by a contracted-out dismissals procedure agreed between employers and independent trade unions (such contracting-out is permitted only if the scheme is at least as advantageous as the statutory scheme). Members of the armed forces may now claim unfair dismissal, except under s 100 (health and safety grounds) (ERA s 192).

(4)   Finally, if there is any dispute on the matter, it is for the employee to prove that she was dismissed.

The meaning of dismissal

Under ERA s 95, three kinds of termination will count as a dismissal which may therefore be the subject of a claim for unfair dismissal. Each will be examined in turn.

Termination with or without notice
Employment Rights Act 1996

95.   (1)   … an employee is dismissed by his employer if …

- (a)   the contract under which he is employed is terminated by the employer (whether with or without notice), or …

COMMENT

(1)   The fact that it is largely irrelevant for the purposes of an unfair dismissal claim whether or not notice to terminate was given marks a major distinction from the common law action for wrongful dismissal.

(2)   Difficulties in relation to dismissal under this head are only likely to arise if non-technical and perhaps equivocal language is used which the parties understand differently.

Tanner v *Kean*

[1978] IRLR 110 Employment Appeal Tribunal

The employee had been instructed not to use the company van outside working hours and had been lent £275 by the employer to buy a car. On discovering that the employee was still using the van for his part-time job at a country club, the employer lost his temper, swore at the employee and said, 'That's it, you're finished with me.' When the employee claimed for unfair dismissal, the employer denied that he had been dismissed.

Phillips J: ' ... In the present case the words are those set out in paragraph 1 of the Reasons: "What's my fucking van doing outside; you're a tight bastard. I've just lent you £275 to buy a car and you are too tight to put juice in it. That's it; you're finished with me." Part of the circumstances were that that was said in a country club to which Mr Tanner had taken the firm's van, and where he acted as a part-time doorman and had met Mr Kean, his employer. It seems to us – and although they do not say so, no doubt it seemed to the tribunal – that those words, in all the circumstances of the case, were not as a matter of law in one category or the other; in other words, whether what was said constituted a dismissal depended on all the circumstances of the case. In our judgment the test which has to be applied in cases of this kind is along these lines. Were the words spoken those of dismissal, that is to say, were they intended to bring the contract of employment to an end? What was the employer's intention? In answering that a relevant, and perhaps the most important, question is how would a reasonable employee, in all circumstances, have understood what the employer intended by what he said and did? Then in most of these cases, and in this case, it becomes relevant to look at the later events following the utterance of the words and preceding the actual departure of the employee. Some care, it seems to us, is necessary in regard to later events, and it might be put, we think, like this: that later events, unless relied on as themselves constituting a dismissal, are only relevant to the extent that they throw light on the employer's intention; that is to say, we would stress, his intention at the time of the alleged dismissal. A word of caution is necessary because in considering later events it is necessary to remember that a dismissal or resignation, once it has taken effect, cannot be unilaterally withdrawn. Accordingly, as it seems to us, later events need to be scrutinised with some care in order to see whether they are genuinely explanatory of the acts alleged to constitute dismissal, or whether they reflect a change of mind. If they are in the former category they may be valuable as showing what was really intended ... '

(The EAT held that the tribunal had not misdirected itself in holding on the facts that there had been no dismissal.)

COMMENT

(1)   It is worth noting that if an employer swears at an employee, it could be grounds for the employee to leave and claim constructive dismissal (see below).

(2)   Similar considerations are relevant where an employee has apparently resigned in anger (see below).

Expiry of a fixed term contract
Employment Rights Act 1996

95.   (1)   ... an employee is dismissed by his employer if
         ...
      (b)   he is employed under a contract for a fixed term and that term expires without being renewed under the same contract, or ...

197.   (1)   Part X does not apply to dismissal from employment under a contract for a fixed term of one year or more if —

(a) the dismissal consists only of the expiry of that term without its being renewed, and

(b) before the term so expires the employee has agreed in writing to exclude any claim in respect of rights under that Part in relation to the contract.

COMMENT

(1)   Expiry of a fixed-term contract is included in the definition of dismissal because otherwise there would be a major loophole in unfair dismissal protection. It would be possible for an employer to put staff on relatively short fixed-term contracts and then make entirely arbitrary decisions about whether or not to re-engage them, and the employee who was not kept on would have no redress, because technically there would have been no termination by the employer.

(2)   Non-renewal does not mean that the dismissal is unfair: only that there has been a dismissal, so that the employee has the possibility of claiming for unfair dismissal (assuming that she is otherwise qualified to claim). Its fairness or otherwise will depend on the reasons for non-renewal.

(3)   To protect employers from the cost and trouble of defending unmeritorious claims where the fixed term meets a genuine short-term need, ERA s 197 permits contracting-out of the right to claim for certain fixed-term contracts. Unfortunately there seems to be no way of ensuring that an employer only requires an employee to waive her rights where the fixed term need is genuine. It is therefore possible for employers to make at least a proportion of their staff fixed-term employees with no unfair dismissal or redundancy rights, who can therefore be let go at the end of their contracts with no repercussions. This means in effect that there can be two classes of employee, only one of which enjoys proper statutory protection rights.

(4)   Two problems have arisen in interpreting s 95(1)(b): first, how fixed does a term have to be for the contract to be regarded as a fixed-term contract? Second, can it still be a fixed-term contract even where it is also terminable by notice?

Wiltshire CC v NATFHE and Guy

[1980] ICR 455 Court of Appeal

Guy was employed for ten years as a part-time, hourly-paid teacher at a college of further education run by the council. Her appointment started in September each year and continued until the end of the courses she was teaching – usually in June. The council did not renew her contract for the 1976–77 session and she claimed that she had been unfairly dismissed. The employers argued that there was no dismissal, as this was not a fixed-term contract within the meaning of the legislation and in consequence, it simply terminated through performance without any action on their part. An industrial tribunal held that she had been employed on a fixed-term contract.

Lord Denning MR: ' … The county council thought that this finding was of general importance in the teaching profession. To clear it up they appealed to the appeal tribunal. Phillips J presided. They affirmed the decision of the industrial tribunal. But they put the case not only on the construction of this particular contract: but also on a much more general question.

Phillips J said that a contract of employment which came to an end on the happening of an uncertain future event would be a contract for a "fixed term." For example, he said (ibid), a contract of employment:

"for the duration of the present government, or during the life of the present Sovereign, or for some other period capable of being determined by reference to prescribed tests"

would be a contract for a fixed term.

That would be a very important extension of the words "fixed term". It was disapproved in the recent case of *Ryan* v *Shipboard Maintenance Ltd*. Kilner Brown J ventured to query the proposition of Phillips J. He declined to follow it. In that case a man was employed as a repairer on a ship, either in port or on the high seas. The job started and finished with the repairing of a ship, after which he received unemployment pay. The question was whether that was a contract for a fixed term or not. The appeal tribunal held it was not. Kilner Brown J said,

"... we take the view that it is stretching the meaning of the words beyond the intention of Parliament to say that it covers an event which can be identified in character but cannot be identified with a precise date in the future."

It does seem desirable for us to try and clear up the position. [ERA s 95(1)(b)] says that an employee shall be treated as dismissed "where under that contract he is employed for a fixed term, that term expires without being renewed under the same contract ... " [The present wording is slightly different: see above.] If you turn back to the Contracts of Employment Act 1972, section 4(4), the legislature clearly thought that, in order to be a "fixed term", there had to be a date stated at the beginning when the contract will expire. Section 4(4) says: "If the contract is for a fixed term, the statement given under subsection (1) of this section shall state the date when the contract expires."

This is in accord with what we said in *Dixon* v *British Broadcasting Corporation*. I said,

"... a 'fixed term' is sufficiently satisfied if the contract is for a specific stated period, even though it is determinable by notice within that period."

That is borne out by consideration of other clauses of the Schedule to the Act of 1974. I would also mention an interesting paragraph in the report of Lord Donovan's *Royal Commission on Trade Unions and Employers' Associations* 1965–1968. Paragraph 558 says:

"Most employees have contracts of employment for an indefinite period. However the need for protection against unfair deprivation of employment may also arise when the contract of employment has been entered into for a fixed period or for a particular purpose and its renewal is refused by the employer."

Although the Royal Commission recommended "a particular purpose" the legislature did not accept that recommendation. It limited the protection to contracts for a "fixed period". It did not extend the protection to a contract "for a particular purpose".

If I may seek to draw the matter together, it seems to me that if there is a contract by which a man is to do a particular task or to carry out a particular purpose, then when that task or purpose comes to an end the contract is discharged by performance. Instances may be taken of a seaman who is employed for the duration of a voyage – and it is completely uncertain how long the voyage will last. His engagement comes to an end on its completion. Also of a man who is engaged to cut down trees, and, when all the trees have been cut down, his contract is discharged by performance. In neither of those instances is there a contract for a fixed term. It is a contract which is discharged by performance. There is no "dismissal". A contract for a particular purpose, which is fulfilled, is discharged by performance and does not amount to a dismissal.

Phillips J mentioned contracts which are terminable on a completely uncertain event such as the duration of the government or the life of the sovereign, or something like that. It seems to me that such a contract is not employment for a fixed term at all. It does not come within the provision. It is not the subject of "dismissal" unless it is terminated by the employer under sub-paragraph (a) or the employee under sub-paragraph (c) of [s 95(1)].

So we come back to the facts of this particular case. Looking at it, it seems to me that this contract is capable of one or other of two alternative interpretations. On the one hand, it can be said that this is a contract for a fixed term, namely, for the session 1976–77, starting from the beginning of the autumn term and ending on the last day of the summer term: and during that session Mrs Guy is to teach such courses in such circumstances as may be required of her and be paid for such time as she has taught during that stated period. On that interpretation of the contract, it seems to me that it is a contract for a "fixed term". Even though her work may end early in June because there is no more work for her to do, nevertheless it is still a contract for a fixed term. That is one alternative interpretation.

On the other hand, it can be said that it is not for a fixed term at all. It is a contract whereby she is to do specific work – teaching the students on these courses. She is to do it during the academic session, but nevertheless the contract is only for those particular purposes. When those come to an end, then it is not a contract for a fixed term, but a contract which is discharged by performance.

On which side is the court to come down on those alternative solutions? The industrial tribunal and the Employment Appeal Tribunal thought that this was a contract for a "fixed term" from the beginning of the autumn term to the last day of the summer term. During that time she had to do such work as she was required to do. That seems to me to be an intelligible and sensible view. This court should not interfere with their decision. I would therefore dismiss the appeal.'

(Ackner and Lawton LJJ agreed.)

COMMENT

(1)   Note the reference to *Dixon* v *BBC*, where the Court of Appeal held that provision for termination by notice did not prevent a contract being classified as fixed-term.

Constructive dismissal

Employment Rights Act 1996

95.   (1)   ... an employee is dismissed by his employer if ...
      (c)   the employee terminates the contract under which he is employed (with or without notice) in circumstances in which he is entitled to terminate it without notice by reason of the employer's conduct.

Western Excavating Ltd v *Sharp*

[1978] QB 761 Court of Appeal

Lord Denning MR: 'Mr Sharp was only employed by the China-Clay Co for 20 months. He left of his own accord. Yet he has been awarded £658 as compensation for unfair dismissal. There seems something wrong about that award. What is it?

To fill in the details, the employee started work with the company on July 9, 1974. One of the terms was that, if he worked extra time, he could have time off in lieu. One day in February 1976 he wanted to play a card game for a team. He asked the foreman for three hours off. The foreman said that he could not have it that afternoon as there was a lot of work to be done. But the employee took it off and played his game of cards. Next morning – Friday, February 27, 1976 – the foreman dismissed him, giving him two weeks' notice for failing to carry out a reasonable order. The employee appealed to a panel set up by the company under its disciplinary procedure. On March 5, 1976, the panel allowed his appeal, saying:

"Having considered all the evidence presented to us, we are of the unanimous decision that the dismissal be withdrawn, as there was room for confusion the way the situation was left, but having regard to the seriousness of what has happened, we substitute the dismissal with five working days' suspension without pay."

Thus, the employee lost five days' pay. He does not dispute the justice of the panel's decision. But it left him in financial difficulties. He was living with a woman who was, in modern terminology, his "common law wife" and their two children. His take-home pay was £42.40 a week. He had no savings, but he had holiday pay accrued to him of £117.17 net.

As a result of the five days' loss of pay, the employee had no money to pay his household expenses. He went to the social security and was given £6.45. But that was not enough to carry on. So he went to his employers. He asked for an advance on his accrued holiday pay. He was told, quite correctly, that it was against company policy to pay holiday pay unless the holiday was itself actually taken. The employee then asked for a loan. He said he wanted £40. The welfare officer told him that the company could not make him a loan to that extent. The welfare officer suggested that he should see him again to discuss the details. That did not satisfy the employee. He said: "If the company cannot help me, I must sort it out myself. I shall have to obtain my holiday pay." That is just what he did. He went to see the workshop manager, and said: "I don't want to leave, but circumstances force me to do so. I am leaving and want my holiday pay now." So on March 11, 1976, the employee picked up his holiday pay of £117.17, and left. He went straight off to the industrial tribunal and made a complaint of unfair dismissal ...

[ERA s 95(1)(c)] has given rise to a vast body of case law as to what comes within it. It is spoken of as "constructive dismissal." It has given rise to a problem upon which there has been a diversity of views among chairmen of industrial tribunals and among the judges of the Employment Appeal Tribunal. On July 28, 1977, the Employment Appeal Tribunal attempted to settle these differences in *Wetherall (Bond St, W1) Ltd* v *Lynn* but they were unsettled again by the discovery of some obiter dicta in the Court of Appeal in *Turner* v *London Transport Executive*. This led the Employment Appeal Tribunal on October 4, 1977, to think that they ought to follow those obiter dicta and to give guidance accordingly. It is to be found in *Scott* v *Aveling Barford Ltd*. But this guidance was expressed to be given as an interim measure pending an authoritative statement of the law by the Court of Appeal or the Court of Session.

It is with diffidence that we approach the task. The rival tests are as follows.

The contract test
On the one hand, it is said that the words of [ERA s 95(1)(c)] express a legal concept which is already well settled in the books on contract under the rubric "discharge by breach". If the employer is guilty of conduct which is a significant breach going to the root of the contract of employment, or which shows that the employer no longer intends to be bound by one or more of the essential terms of the contract, then the employee is entitled to treat himself as discharged from any further performance. If he does so, then he terminates the contract by reason of the employer's conduct. He is constructively dismissed. The employee is entitled

in those circumstances to leave at the instant without giving any notice at all or, alternatively, he may give notice and say he is leaving at the end of the notice. But the conduct must in either case be sufficiently serious to entitle him to leave at once. Moreover, he must make up his mind soon after the conduct of which he complains: for, if he continues for any length of time without leaving, he will lose his right to treat himself as discharged. He will be regarded as having elected to affirm the contract.

The unreasonableness test

On the other hand, it is said that the words of [ERA s 95(1)(c)] do not express any settled legal concept. They introduce a new concept into contracts of employment. It is that the employer must act reasonably in his treatment of his employees. If he conducts himself or his affairs so unreasonably that the employee cannot fairly be expected to put up with it any longer, the employee is justified in leaving. He can go, with or without giving notice, and claim compensation for unfair dismissal.

It would seem that this new concept of "unreasonable conduct" is very similar to the concept of "unfairness" as described in TULRA 1974 Sched 1 para 6(8) [see now ERA s 98(4)] which says:

> "... the determination of the question whether the dismissal was fair or unfair, having regard to the reason shown by the employer, shall depend on whether the employer can satisfy the tribunal that in the circumstances (having regard to equity and the substantial merits of the case) he acted reasonably in treating it as a sufficient reason for dismissing the employee."

Those who adopt the unreasonableness test for dismissal say quite frankly that it is the same as the "unreasonableness" test for fairness. That was the view taken by Megaw LJ in *Turner's* case.

He said:

> "So far as (c) is concerned, in my judgment, the wording of this subparagraph is not a wording which involves, or implies, the same concept as the common law concept of fundamental breach of a contract resulting in its unilateral repudiation and acceptance of that unilateral repudiation by the innocent party. The employer's 'conduct' here is employer's conduct to be adjudged by the industrial tribunal by the criteria which they regard as right and fair in respect of a case in which the issue is whether or not there has been 'unfair' dismissal."

Previous cases

The only previous case in the Court of Appeal on the words is *Marriott* v *Oxford and District Co-operative Society Ltd (No 2)*. It was under the Redundancy Payments Act 1965. Section 3(1)(c) did not apply because it only applied where the employee terminated his contract *without* notice, whereas Marriott had terminated it *with* notice. So the court put it on section 3(1)(a). But since the amendment to the wording of paragraph (c), it would have been more properly brought under paragraph (c). It was not really an (a) case: but we had to stretch it a bit. It was not the employer who terminated the employment. It was the employee: and he was entitled to do so by reason of the employer's conduct.

All the other cases are in the Employment Appeal Tribunal. We have studied them all, but I hope I will be excused from going through them.

The result

In my opinion, the contract test is the right test. My reasons are as follows. (i) The statute itself draws a distinction between "dismissal" in [ERA s 95(1)(c)] and "unfairness" in [s 98(4)].

If Parliament intended that same test to apply, it would have said so. (ii) "Dismissal" in [s 95(1)(c)] goes back to "dismissal" in the Redundancy Payments Act 1965. Its interpretation should not be influenced by [s 98(4)] which was introduced first in 1971 in the Industrial Relations Act 1971. (iii) [Section 95(1)(c)] uses words which have a legal connotation, especially the words "entitled" and "without notice". If a non-legal connotation were intended, it would have added "justified in leaving at once" or some such non-legal phrase. (iv) [Section 95(1)(a) and (c)] deal with different situations. [Section 95(1)(a)] deals with cases where the employer himself terminates the contract by dismissing the man with or without notice. That is, when the employer says to the man: "You must go." [Section 95(1)(c)] deals with the cases where the employee himself terminates the contract by saying: "I can't stand it any longer. I want my cards." (v) The new test of "unreasonable conduct" of the employer is too indefinite by far. It has led to acute difference of opinion between the members of tribunals. Often there are majority opinions. It has led to findings of "constructive dismissal" on the most whimsical grounds. The Employment Appeal Tribunal tells us so. It is better to have the contract test of the common law. It is more certain: as it can well be understood by intelligent laymen under the direction of a legal chairman. (vi) I would adopt the reasoning of the considered judgment of the Employment Appeal Tribunal in *Wetherall (Bond St, W1) Ltd* v *Lynn*:

> "Parliament might well have said, in relation to whether the employer's conduct had been reasonable having regard to equity and the substantial merits of the case, but it neither laid down that special statutory criterion or any other. So, in our judgment, the answer can only be, entitled according to law, and it is to the law of contract that you have to look."

(vii)   The test of unreasonableness gives no effect to the words "without notice". They impose a legal test which no test of "unreasonableness" can do.

Conclusion
The present case is a good illustration of a "whimsical decision". Applying the test of "unreasonable conduct", the industrial tribunal decided by a majority of two to one in favour of the employee. All three members of the Employment Appeal Tribunal would have decided in favour of the employers, but felt that it was a matter of fact on which they could not reverse the industrial tribunal. So counting heads, it was four to two in favour of the employers, but yet the case was decided against them – because of the test of "unreasonable conduct".

If the contract test had been applied, the result would have been plain. There was no dismissal, constructive or otherwise, by the employers. The employers were not in breach at all. Nor had they repudiated the contract at all. The employee left of his own accord without anything wrong done by the employers. His claim should have been rejected. The decision against the employers was most unjust to them. I would allow the appeal, accordingly.'

(Lawton and Eveleigh LJJ agreed.)

COMMENT

(1)   Lord Denning's argument is compelling as a matter of statutory interpretation; however, many commentators would prefer a reasonableness test (was the employee justified in leaving?) rather than a contractual test (is the employer in fundamental breach of contract?) in this context (e.g. Hepple 'Restructuring Employment Rights' (1986) 15 ILJ 69, 79–83; Collins *Justice in Dismissal* (1992) 44–45).

(2)   At the same time, there is a strong view that reasonableness has come in through

the back door, by the development of an implied duty to maintain mutual trust and confidence. The evolution of this implied term was outlined in Chapter 4 (pp 136–43), where the point was made that almost all the cases dealing with it were cases where employees were claiming that they had been constructively dismissed. The argument goes that if the employer has behaved unreasonably (although it is not possible to point to a specific breach of contract), she may be found to have acted in such a way as to undermine mutual trust and confidence – and that will be a fundamental breach of contract.

(3)   A resignation which is not a response to a fundamental breach of contract by the employer will not constitute dismissal, nor will other modes of termination of the contract of employment, which will now be examined.

Resignation and termination by mutual agreement
Sheffield v Oxford Controls

[1979] ICR 396 Employment Appeal Tribunal

Sheffield was employed as director of the company, in which he also held shares; the majority of shares were held by his co-director and the co-director's wife. Sheffield's wife, who also worked for the company, had a dispute with the wife of Sheffield's co-director and was threatened with dismissal as a result. In an acrimonious discussion, Sheffield threatened to resign if his wife was dismissed. He was asked how much he wanted to go, and eventually £10,000 was agreed upon; it seems that it was also made clear that if he did not resign he would be dismissed. Sheffield agreed to go in return for the payment, but later brought an action for unfair dismissal claiming that he had been forced to resign.

Arnold J: ' … The principle of law has been stated in a number of cases. So far as we know we have been referred to all of them. They start with *East Sussex County Council* v *Walker* in the National Industrial Relations Court. That was a case about a school cook. What had happened there was that the cook was invited to resign; that it was indicated to her that her contract was to be terminated and that such determination should be brought about by her own letter of resignation; and that she wrote a letter of resignation. Those are the only relevant facts. Giving the judgment of the court, Brightman J said:

"In our judgment, if an employee is told that she is no longer required in her employment and is expressly invited to resign, a court of law is entitled to come to the conclusion that, as a matter of common sense, the employee was dismissed within the meaning of what was then section 3 of the Redundancy Payments Act 1965."

That being a case in fact about a redundancy payment, since the reason why the cook was invited to resign was that she had become redundant. Then the judge went on:

"Suppose that the employer says to the employee, 'Your job is finished; I will give you the opportunity to resign. If you don't you'll be sacked.' How, we would ask, is it possible to reach a conclusion other than that the employment is being terminated by the employer even though the employee takes the first and more respectable alternative of signing a letter of resignation rather than being the recipient of a letter of dismissal? We feel that in such circumstances there really can be no other conclusion than that the employer terminated the contract …"

So, we find that there was the sort of threat which is referred to in the decided cases; and the question is, what is the legal consequence of that finding?

The industrial tribunal concludes, in the course of their reasons, that as a result of what they describe as the shameful treatment meted out to the employee and Mrs Sheffield by the Raisons, the employee was, at the stage at which he initialled the heads of agreement, prepared to bow out of the industry in which they were all engaged "and the heads of agreement represent the terms upon which he was prepared to agree to terminate his employment with the company". The industrial tribunal support that by the observation:

> "Mrs Sheffield was not prepared to resign as she had been asked to do until he [Mr Sheffield] had agreed terms satisfactory to himself but directly he had, and had initialled the heads of agreement, she signed her resignation letter."

It is plain, we think, that there must exist a principle, exemplified by the four cases to which we have referred, that where an employee resigns and that resignation is determined upon by him because he prefers to resign rather than to be dismissed (the alternative having been expressed to him by the employer in the terms of the threat that if he does not resign he will be dismissed), the mechanics of the resignation do not cause that to be other than a dismissal. The cases do not in terms go further than that. We find the principle to be one of causation. In cases such as that which we have just hypothesised, and those reported, the causation is the threat. It is the existence of the threat which causes the employee to be willing to sign, and to sign, a resignation letter or to be willing to give, and to give, the oral resignation. But where that willingness is brought about by other considerations and the actual causation of the resignation is no longer the threat which has been made but is the state of mind of the resigning employee, that he is willing and content to resign on the terms which he has negotiated and which are satisfactory to him, then we think there is no room for the principle to be derived from the decided cases. In such a case he resigns because he is willing to resign as the result of being offered terms which are to him satisfactory terms on which to resign. He is no longer impelled or compelled by the threat of dismissal to resign, but a new matter has come into the history, namely, that he has been brought into a condition of mind in which the threat is no longer the operative factor of his decision; it has been replaced by the emergence of terms which are satisfactory. Therefore, we think that the finding that the employee had agreed to terms upon which he was prepared to agree to terminate his employment with the employers – terms which were satisfactory to him – means that there is no room for the principle and that it is impossible to upset the conclusion of the tribunal that he was not dismissed.'

COMMENT

(1)   Whether or not the employee left because of the threat or because of an inducement will be finely balanced at times, and will usually be treated as a question of fact for the industrial tribunal.

(2)   The position with termination 'by mutual agreement' is much the same. The question will be whether the agreement was genuine – and this will depend on whether the employee simply agreed in order to avoid being dismissed, or whether she received an inducement which caused her agreement.

(3)   As we will see, the definition of dismissal for the purpose of redundancy claims is the same as for unfair dismissal. In the case of voluntary redundancies, it was held in the unusual circumstances of *Birch* v *University of Liverpool* that the termination was by mutual agreement (the employees had received a very good severance package

which was stated to include any redundancy entitlement). However, usually this situation will count as dismissal, even if there are enhanced severance payments: the employee is to be taken as having volunteered to be dismissed, not to have resigned.

(4)   As with dismissal by an employer, if the employee speaks ambiguous words of resignation, or says in anger that she is leaving, the issue is what was really intended by the words, and whether a reasonable employer would have understood them in this sense (e.g. *Sovereign House Security* v *Savage*).

(5)   Also by analogy with the concept of dismissal, it has been argued that tribunals should recognise a concept of 'constructive resignation', which should not count as dismissal.

London Transport Executive v *Clarke*

[1981] ICR 355 Court of Appeal

Templeman LJ: 'The first question raised by this appeal is whether a contract of employment was terminated by the respondent employee, Mr Clarke, or by the appellant employers, London Transport Executive. If the contract was terminated by the employee within the meaning of [section 95 of the Employment Rights Act 1996] then he is not entitled to claim compensation for unfair dismissal. If the contract was terminated by the employers, then compensation is payable unless the employers have proved that the employee was fairly dismissed.

The employee absented himself from work for seven weeks without leave and it is agreed that by his conduct he repudiated his contract of employment. After he had been absent for four weeks, the employers took him off their books of employees and wrote to him to say so. The question is whether the contract of employment was terminated by the employee's conduct or by the employers' acceptance of his conduct as a repudiation of the contract.

The general rule is that a repudiated contract is not terminated unless and until the repudiation is accepted by the innocent party: see *Boston Deep Sea Fishing and Ice Co* v *Ansell*.

That case itself illustrates that contracts of employment cannot provide a general exemption to that rule because it would be manifestly unjust to allow a wrongdoer to determine a contract by repudiatory breach if the innocent party wished to affirm the contract for good reason. Thus in *Thomas Marshall (Exports) Ltd* v *Guinle*, which contains a full discussion of principles and of the conflicting authorities, a contract of employment was repudiated by the employee. The court could not enforce specific performance of the contract for personal services, but Sir Robert Megarry VC enforced against the wrongdoing employee at the behest of the innocent employer who had not accepted the repudiation a confidentiality and non-competition obligation which was only effective during the continuance of the contract. Repudiation cannot determine a contract of service or any other contract while there exists a reason and an opportunity for the innocent party to affirm the contract.

Mr Scrivener, who appeared for the employers, argued that a contract of employment was an exception to the general rule that a repudiated contract is only determined by the acceptance and not by the repudiation. If there was no exception at common law, there is at any rate, he argued, an exception for the purposes of the Act of 1978 so that a worker can determine a contract of employment by repudiating that contract. It is plain from the Act that an employer can determine a contract by the employer's breaches of contract, which give good reason for the worker to leave the employment, whether the worker gives notice or not; the conduct of the employer produces constructive dismissal which by [ERA s 95(1)(c)] constitutes a termination of the contract of employment by the employer. Similarly, says Mr Scrivener, although the Act does not expressly so provide, a worker who walks out or commits some similar breach of contract which is so fundamental that it amounts to a repudiation of the contract on his part is guilty of self-dismissal and in these circumstances it is the worker who terminates the contract and not the employer who can only stand helplessly by.

I can see no reason why a contract of employment or services should be determined by repudiation and not by the acceptance of repudiation. The argument has little practical importance at common law. The only difference which would exist at common law between self-dismissal and accepted repudiation is that self-dismissal would determine the contract when the worker walked out or otherwise committed a repudiatory breach of the contract whereas accepted repudiation determines the contract when the employer expressly or impliedly gives notice to the worker that the employer accepts the repudiation and does not wish to affirm the contract. But, in practice, at common law self-dismissal and acceptance of repudiation in contracts of service are usually simultaneous both being implied rather than express where affirmation of the contract would be meaningless; in any event, they involve similar consequences in almost all cases. A difficulty, however, arises under the [ERA] if Mr Scrivener's argument of a special category of determination of a contract by self-dismissal is correct. When a worker commits a breach of contract, neither he nor the employer nor in the final analysis the industrial tribunal may be entirely clear whether the breach is repudiatory or not. Whatever the nature of the breach, the worker may seek expressly or impliedly to persuade the employer to affirm the contract and to allow the worker to continue in or resume his employment. If the employer does not allow the worker to continue or resume his employment, then if Mr Scrivener is right an industrial tribunal must first decide whether the worker's breach of contract is repudiatory or not. If the breach of contract is so fundamental as to be repudiatory of the contract, then the tribunal must decide whether the repudiatory act is of a special kind which amounts to self-dismissal. If these matters are decided in favour of the employer, then the tribunal is not authorised to consider whether in the circumstances the refusal of the employer to affirm the contract and to allow the worker to continue or resume employment is fair or unfair unless, despite the finding of self-dismissal, the worker is able to establish conduct on the part of the employer which converts self-dismissal into constructive dismissal. If the tribunal decide that the breach of contract by the worker was not repudiatory or if the tribunal decide that the repudiatory breach was not of the special kind which amounts to self- dismissal, then they must conclude that the contract was terminated by the employer and they must then consider whether the employer satisfies the onus of proving that the termination of the contract which amounts to dismissal was in fact fair dismissal.

These complications arise, and only arise, if there is grafted on to the old common law rule that a repudiated contract is only terminated by acceptance, an exception in the case of contracts of employment. In my view any such exception is contrary to principle, unsupported by authority binding on this court and undesirable in practice. If a worker walks out of his job and does not thereafter claim to be entitled to resume work, then he repudiates his contract and the employer accepts that repudiation by taking no action to affirm the contract. No question of unfair dismissal can arise unless the worker claims that he was constructively dismissed. If a worker walks out of his job or commits any other breach of contract, repudiatory or otherwise, but at any time claims that he is entitled to resume or to continue his work, then his contract of employment is only determined if the employer expressly or impliedly asserts and accepts repudiation on the part of the worker. Acceptance can take the form of formal writing or can take the form of refusing to allow the worker to resume or continue his work. Where the contract of employment is determined by the employer purporting to accept repudiation on the part of the worker, the tribunal must decide whether the worker has been unfairly dismissed.

In my judgment, the acceptance by an employer of repudiation by a worker who wishes to continue his employment notwithstanding his repudiatory conduct constitutes the determination of the contract of employment by the employer; the employer relying on the repudiatory conduct of the worker must satisfy the tribunal in the words of [ERA s 98(4)] that in the circumstances, having regard to equity and the substantial merits of the case, the employer acted reasonably in treating the repudiatory conduct as sufficient reason for accepting repudiation and thus determining the contract.

In the present case the employee absented himself for seven weeks for what he no doubt considered was a good reason. The employers considered that the employee absented himself for a bad reason. After one month had elapsed the employers decided not to allow the employee to resume his work if and when he reported back and they wrote to the employee informing him of their decision. The employers thereby determined the employee's contract of employment and the question for the tribunal was whether he had been unfairly dismissed ...'

(Dunn LJ agreed; Lord Denning MR dissented.)

COMMENT

(1)   This decision is so clearly right, it is surprising to find that there were conflicting EAT decisions before it settled the matter. One of the major features of unfair dismissal law is that a dismissal may be unfair even though the employer would be justified in dismissing at common law, and vice versa. Had the concept of constructive resignation or self-dismissal been accepted, then the opportunity for tribunals to review the fairness of numbers of dismissals on grounds of misconduct would have been in doubt, for the employer would have argued that the misconduct was a fundamental breach and thus a self-dismissal.

(2)   A related problem arose in relation to contractual provisions which purported to end the contract of employment automatically on the happening of a certain event. This is common in certain kinds of ongoing contract – hire purchase agreements, for example, regularly provide that the contract will terminate automatically if the debtor goes bankrupt. Could it be used in relation to contracts of employment? In *Igbo* v *Johnson, Matthey Chemicals Ltd* the employee had asked for leave on top of her holiday entitlement in order to visit her family in Nigeria. The employers agreed, provided that she signed a letter stipulating that if she failed to return on the stated date, her contract of employment would terminate automatically. Requiring such agreements was common practice among employers to ensure that employees did not overstay their leave. The Court of Appeal held that the agreement contravened what is now ERA s 230, which provides:

'(1)   Any provision in an agreement (whether a contract of employment or not) is void in so far as it purports—

(a)   to exclude or limit the operation of any provision of this Act, or

(b)   to preclude a person from bringing any proceedings under this Act before an industrial tribunal.'

(3)   There are other situations which would either end the contract automatically or by frustration at common law for which special provision is made under the legislation.

First, where a company is dissolved or an employer who is an individual dies: here, for the purposes of redundancy law the employee will be treated as having been dismissed and may be entitled to a redundancy payment (ERA s 136(5); see Chapter 9).

Second, where a partnership is dissolved either through the death or retirement of a partner, the contract would once again be terminated at common law. However, under ERA s 139(4) the employee will be deemed to have been dismissed for redundancy unless taken on by the successors to the original partnership.

Frustration

The final situation to be considered where the contract of employment may be terminated without counting as a dismissal for the purposes of unfair dismissal is frustration. This is the common law doctrine applicable to all kinds of contracts which provides that if the contract becomes impossible to perform without the fault of either party, then both parties are discharged from further obligations under the contract.

Poussard v Spiers and Pond

(1876) 1 QBD 410 Queen's Bench Division

Madame Poussard was engaged to sing the principal female part in an opera at the Criterion Theatre. She was taken ill during the rehearsal period and was therefore unable to attend the final rehearsals or to perform on the opening night. The producers arranged for a substitute to cover the part on the basis that if the substitute were called on to perform on the opening night, she would then be given the engagement for the rest of the scheduled performances.

Mme Poussard had recovered sufficiently to perform by the fifth performance, but by that time the substitute had been given all the performances. Her husband and agent therefore brought this action alleging that the producers were in breach of contract.

The judgment of the court (Blackburn, Quain and Field JJ) was delivered by Blackburn J.

Blackburn J: ' ... We think that, from the nature of the engagement to take a leading, and, indeed, the principal female part (for the prima donna sang her part in male costume as the Prince de Conti) in a new opera which (as appears from the terms of the engagement) it was known might run for a longer or shorter time, and so be a profitable or losing concern to the defendants, we can, without the aid of the jury, see that it must have been of great importance to the defendants that the piece should start well, and consequently that the failure of the plaintiff's wife to be able to perform on the opening and early performances was a very serious detriment to them.

This inability having been occasioned by sickness was not any breach of contract by the plaintiff, and no action can lie against him for the failure thus occasioned. But the damage to the defendants and the consequent failure of consideration is just as great as if it had been occasioned by the plaintiff's fault, instead of by his wife's misfortune ...

Now, in the present case, we must consider what were the courses open to the defendants under the circumstances. They might, it was said on the argument before us (though not on the trial), have postponed the bringing out of the piece till the recovery of Madame Poussard, and if her illness had been a temporary hoarseness incapacitating her from singing on the Saturday, but sure to be removed by the Monday, that might have been a proper course to pursue. But the illness here was a serious one, of uncertain duration, and if the plaintiff had at the trial suggested that this was the proper course, it would, no doubt, have been shewn that it would have been a ruinous course; and that it would have been much better to have abandoned the piece altogether than to have postponed it from day to day for an uncertain time, during which the theatre would have been a heavy loss.

The remaining alternatives were to employ a temporary substitute until such time as the plaintiff's wife should recover; and if a temporary substitute capable of performing the part adequately could have been obtained upon such a precarious engagement on any reasonable terms, that would have been a right course to pursue; but if no substitute capable of performing the part adequately could be obtained, except on the terms that she should be permanently engaged at higher pay than the plaintiff's wife, in our opinion it follows, as a matter of law, that the failure on the plaintiff's part went to the root of the matter and discharged the defendants.

We think, therefore, that the fifth question put to the jury, and answered by them in favour of the defendants, does find all the facts necessary to enable us to decide as a matter of law that the defendants are discharged ... '

COMMENT

(1)   This was a contract for services rather than a contract for employment; however, it is taken as the original authority for the proposition that the doctrine of frustration can apply to contracts of employment. If a contract is discharged in this way, then it is not terminated by either party and there is no dismissal for the purposes of an unfair dismissal claim.

(2)   There are two main situations in which it is commonly claimed that the contract of employment is frustrated: first, where the employee is ill (as in *Poussard* v *Spiers*), and second, where the employee has been sentenced to a term of imprisonment. In relation to illness, guidance was given in the following case.

Egg Stores Ltd v *Leibovici*

[1977] ICR 260 Employment Appeal Tribunal

An employee of 15 years' standing was injured in a road accident and was unfit to work for five months. He received sick pay for the first two months. When he asked to return to work, the employers refused because they had got a replacement. He claimed unfair dismissal, but the employers argued that they had not dismissed him: the contract had been frustrated.

Phillips J: ' ... it is obvious from this and other cases that the doctrine of frustration causes considerable difficulties. Accordingly, it may not be out of place if we add a word or two by way of assistance to the industrial tribunal which will have to decide the matter, and possibly to other industrial tribunals in other cases.

In general, we would adopt and endorse the statement of the law by Sir John Donaldson in the National Industrial Relations Court in *Marshall* v *Harland & Wolff Ltd*. It should be stressed (as is explained in that case, and as we have already stated in this judgment) that for frustration to be established it is not necessary to be able to show that the employers have taken some action in respect of it. The contract is terminated automatically by the event giving rise to frustration.

That being said, there is no doubt that difficulties in applying the doctrine do occur in the case of those contracts of employment which can be determined at short notice. In the case of a fixed-term contract of substantial length, no question can arise of the employer's terminating the contract and the doctrine of frustration is necessary if it has become impossible for the employee to continue to perform the contract. In the case of short-term periodic contracts of employment different considerations apply. Subject to the provisions of the [ERA 1996], the employer can terminate the contract of employment at short notice, and, if he does so, the only question will be whether in the circumstances such dismissal was unfair. This will usually turn on the question whether the time has been reached when the employer cannot be expected to wait any longer before permanently filling the absent employee's post. *Marshall* v *Harland & Wolff Ltd*, though of great value as a general statement of the law, perhaps does not deal in practical terms with the questions which will arise when frustration is considered in respect of such short-term periodic contracts. The question to be decided is summarised in that case in these words,

> "The question is and remains: 'Was the employee's incapacity, looked at before the purported dismissal, of such a nature, or did it appear likely to continue for such a period, that further performance of his obligations in the future would either be impossible or would be a thing radically different from that undertaken by him and accepted by the employer under the agreed terms of his employment?' "

That is helpful, but one needs to know in what kind of circumstances can it be said that further performance of his obligations in the future will be impossible? It seems to us that an important question to be asked in cases such as the present – we are not suggesting that it is the only question – is: "has the time arrived when the employer can no longer reasonably be expected to keep the absent employee's post open for him?" It will thus be seen that the sort of question which has to be considered when it is being decided whether a dismissal in such circumstances was unfair, and that which has to be considered when deciding whether the contract has been frustrated, are not dissimilar. For this reason, though we think that the industrial tribunal was wrong in what it stated in paragraph 10 about the consequences of the failure of the employers to take steps to terminate the employee's employment, we are not saying that in deciding whether a contract of employment has been frustrated it is irrelevant to consider what action the employer has taken or considered. Often it will be extremely relevant to note that the employer has not thought it right to dismiss the absent employee. The reason may be that he does not think that a sufficient length of time has elapsed to make it a proper course to take. If so, that view, represented by his failure to take action, will be one (but not the only) fact to be taken into consideration in deciding whether the contract has been frustrated.

It is possible to divide into two kinds the events relied upon as bringing about the frustration of a short-term periodic contract of employment. There may be an event (e.g. a crippling accident) so dramatic and shattering that everyone concerned will realise immediately that to all intents and purposes the contract must be regarded as at an end. Or there may be an event, such as illness or accident, the course and outcome of which is uncertain. It may be a long process before one is able to say whether the event is such as to bring about the frustration of the contract. But there *will* have been frustration of the contract, even though at the time of the event the outcome was uncertain, if the time arrives when, looking back, one can say that at some point (even if it is not possible to say precisely when) matters had gone on so long, and the prospects for the future were so poor, that it was no longer practical to regard the contract as still subsisting. Among the matters to be taken into account in such a case in reaching a decision are these: (1) the length of the previous employment; (2) how long it had been expected that the employment would continue; (3) the nature of the job; (4)

the nature, length and effect of the illness or disabling event; (5) the need of the employer for the work to be done, and the need for a replacement to do it; (6) the risk to the employer of acquiring obligations in respect of redundancy payments or compensation for unfair dismissal to the replacement employee; (7) whether wages have continued to be paid; (8) the acts and the statements of the employer in relation to the employment, including the dismissal of, or failure to dismiss, the employee; and (9) whether in all the circumstances a reasonable employer could be expected to wait any longer.'

(The case was remitted to a different tribunal for rehearing.)

COMMENT

(1) It will be seen that the guidance for judging whether an employer has unfairly dismissed an employee on grounds of illness is very similar to this, which raises the question of whether it is appropriate to use the doctrine of frustration in relation to this kind of situation. The arguments against treating this as a non-dismissal are the same as the arguments against allowing a concept of constructive resignation: namely, that it deprives the tribunal of an opportunity of reviewing the employer's decision (which is effectively what it is). Hence some commentators have argued that common law concepts such as frustration should not be used in interpreting a statutory labour code (see, for example, Hepple 'Restructuring Employment Rights' (1986) 15 ILJ 69; Collins *Justice in Dismissal* pp 44–45). However, such arguments were rejected by the Court of Appeal in *Notcutt* v *Universal Equipment*.

(2) A frustrating event is defined as one which occurs without the fault of either party. But a sentence of imprisonment which prevents the employee fulfilling her contract must involve fault on her part: does this mean that the contract is not frustrated?

Note that if this seemingly logical argument were accepted, it would mean that the employee would be better off through having been at fault in relation to the ending of the contract than she would be if she had not been at fault. For if the contract were genuinely frustrated, she would not be able to bring an unfair dismissal claim, but if she can successfully argue that she was at fault, she must have been dismissed through the employer refusing to hold the contract open.

(3) It was largely because of this 'affront to common sense' that when the Court of Appeal was faced with the issue in *Shepherd* v *Jerrom*, the judges held that the contract was capable of being frustrated by a term of imprisonment.

The fair reasons for dismissal

Employment Rights Act 1996

98. (1) In determining for the purposes of this Part whether the dismissal of an employee is fair or unfair, it shall be for the employer to show—
  (a) the reason (or, if more than one, the principal reason) for the dismissal, and
  (b) that it is either a reason falling within subsection (2) or some other substantial reason of a kind such as to justify the dismissal of an employee holding the position which the employee held.

(2)   A reason falls within this subsection if it—
   (a)   relates to the capability or qualifications of the employee for performing work of the kind which he was employed by the employer to do, or
   (b)   relates to the conduct of the employee, or
   (c)   is that the employee was redundant, or
   (d)   is that the employee could not continue to work in the position which he held without contravention (either on his part or on that of his employer) of a duty or restriction imposed by or under an enactment.

(3)   In subsection (2)(a)—
   (a)   'capability' means capability assessed by reference to skill, aptitude, health or any other physical or mental quality;
   (b)   'qualifications' means any degree, diploma or other academic, technical or professional qualification relevant to the position which the employee held.

(4)   Where the employer has fulfilled the requirements of subsection (1), the determination of the question whether the dismissal is fair or unfair (having regard to the reason shown by the employer)—
   (a)   depends on whether in the circumstances (including the size and administrative resources of the employer's undertaking) the employer acted reasonably or unreasonably in treating it as a sufficient reason for dismissing the employee; and
   (b)   shall be determined in accordance with equity and the substantial merits of the case.

COMMENT

(1)   Note that there are two elements in deciding whether a dismissal is unfair or not: whether the reason for it comes within one of the five specified categories, and if so, whether the employer acted reasonably in making the decision to dismiss. The burden of proof used to be on the employer for both elements. Since 1980, however, while the employer is still charged with proving the reason for the dismissal (and that it comes within one of the categories), the burden of proof with regard to reasonableness is neutral.

(2)   Apart from putting in a claim for unfair dismissal, an employee has an independent right to ask for the employer to provide information in writing as to what was the reason for the dismissal within two weeks of receiving the request (ERA s 92).

(3)   The employer may sometimes specify that the reason falls into more than one category, or may be unsure as to which category the reason is in. It is fairly common for underperformance to be categorised as either incapability or misconduct, and in the case of some kinds of restructuring resulting in job losses, the reason may be either redundancy or other economic reasons which will count as SOSR ('some other substantial reason ... '). This is permissible, although it may have repercussions as to the reasonableness of the dismissal (see *Trico-Folberth* v *Devonshire*, for example).

(4)   In practice, cases rarely turn on whether or not the reason has been established. The battleground is reasonableness. In deciding whether or not the employer behaved reasonably, different considerations may apply to the different categories of fair reason. Before these are considered in detail, however, a prior issue must be addressed: how

far can a tribunal go in overturning an employer's decision? And relatedly, how far can an appeal court (the Employment Appeal Tribunal or the Court of Appeal) go in overturning the decision of an industrial tribunal?

Iceland Frozen Foods v *Jones*

[1983] ICR 17 Employment Appeal Tribunal

Browne-Wilkinson J: ' ... Since the present state of the law can only be found by going through a number of different authorities, it may be convenient if we should seek to summarise the present law. We consider that the authorities establish that in law the correct approach for the industrial tribunal to adopt in answering the question posed by [ERA s 98(4)] is as follows: (1) the starting point should always be the words of [section 98(4)] themselves; (2) in applying the section an industrial tribunal must consider the reasonableness of the employer's conduct, not simply whether they (the members of the industrial tribunal) consider the dismissal to be fair; (3) in judging the reasonableness of the employer's conduct an industrial tribunal must not substitute its decision as to what was the right course to adopt for that of the employer; (4) in many, though not all, cases there is a band of reasonable responses to the employee's conduct within which one employer might reasonably take one view, another quite reasonably take another; (5) the function of the industrial tribunal, as an industrial jury, is to determine whether in the particular circumstances of each case the decision to dismiss the employee fell within the band of reasonable responses which a reasonable employer might have adopted. If the dismissal falls within the band the dismissal is fair: if the dismissal falls outside the band it is unfair ... '

COMMENT

(1)   This useful summary of the cases highlights the two crucial points by which an industrial tribunal must be guided. First, the greatest sin that a tribunal can commit is to hold that an employer was unreasonable because they would not have dismissed the employee in the same circumstances. This is defensible, for if that were the standard it would simply be substituting one subjective decision (that of the tribunal) for another (that of the employer) – whereas the use of the term 'reasonableness' implies an objective test.

(2)   More controversial, however, is the second point. The 'band of reasonable responses' doctrine, classically stated in *British Leyland* v *Swift*, holds that a dismissal is not unfair if the tribunal is convinced that other employers would not have dismissed in these circumstances. The idea is that reasonable people may yet reach different decisions on the same issue. Therefore the fact that one reasonable employer would have let the employee off with a warning, say, does not indicate that the employer who dismisses the employee on the same facts is unreasonable.

(3)   This means that the employer will only be acting unreasonably in dismissing if her decision lies wholly outside the range of reasonable responses to the case in hand. This gets uncomfortably close to encouraging a test which would categorise the employer's decision as unreasonable only if no reasonable employer would have acted in that way, although the Scottish EAT denied that it amounted to this in *Rentokil* v *Mackin*. However, it is fairly clear that the band of reasonable responses doctrine gives more scope to the managerial prerogative.

(4)   Tribunals are continually urged to start from the words of the statute rather than the decisions interpreting those words. Collins argues persuasively that the reason that the balance has tilted in favour of employers is because tribunals are now encouraged to consider whether the employer has acted *un*reasonably, where the statute asks whether the employer's decision was reasonable (see Collins, *Justice in Dismissal* pp 37–40).

(5)   Debate has also raged over how far the EAT should be able to interfere with the decision of an industrial tribunal. Appeals to the EAT lie on questions of law only (ITA s 21); this is in itself a limiting factor, as a narrow view is taken of what constitutes a question of law (see *O'Kelly* v *Trusthouse Forte*, p 97). The decision that a dismissal is fair or unfair involves drawing inferences from facts, but on the basis of a knowledge and understanding of law. Thus it could be argued that it is essentially factual, or that it is essentially legal (cannot be done if you do not know the law) or a mixture of the two. What is certain, however, is that from the point of view of appeals, it counts as a question of fact. This means that it will not be good grounds of appeal if you simply argue that the tribunal reached the wrong decision. The position is summarised and illustrated in the next case.

Piggott Bros v *Jackson*

[1991] IRLR 309 Court of Appeal

The employees began to suffer soreness and irritation from fumes given off by a consignment of PVC in the factory and were off sick for some weeks. The employer took advice from the Health and Safety Executive and improved ventilation, and although the cause of the problem was not identified, they were satisfied that there was no continuing danger to the employees. The employees, however, were not reassured, and refused to work with the material; after attempts to persuade them to reconsider had failed, they were dismissed.

An industrial tribunal found that the dismissals were unfair. The EAT allowed the employer's appeal and substituted a finding that the dismissals were fair. The employees appealed to the Court of Appeal, arguing that the EAT should not have interfered with the industrial tribunal's decision.

Lord Donaldson MR: ' ... There are, however, three categories of case where it is the duty of the EAT to interfere. They are stated by Lord Donaldson MR in *British Telecommunications* v *Sheridan* as follows:

"The Employment Appeal Tribunal can indeed interfere if it is satisfied that the tribunal (scil. the industrial tribunal) has misdirected itself as to the applicable law, or if there is no evidence to support a finding of fact, since the absence of evidence to support a finding of fact has always been regarded as a pure question of law. It can also interfere if the decision is perverse, as has been explained by May LJ in *Neale* v *Hereford & Worcester CC.*"

This last is an allusion to the now very familiar sentence:

"Deciding these cases is the job of industrial tribunals and when they have not erred in law neither the appeal tribunal nor this Court should disturb their decision unless one can say in effect, 'My goodness, that was certainly wrong' ."

I accept, as I must, the exposition of May LJ. Indeed, it has the added authority of, I think,

being derived, albeit expressed in more homely terms, from the speech of Lord Diplock in
R v *Secretary of State for Foreign and Commonwealth Affairs ex parte Council of Civil
Service Unions* where he said that a decision which was plainly wrong could found an
application for judicial review and that it was no longer necessary to resort to Viscount
Radcliffe's explanation in *Edwards* v *Bairstow* of irrationality as raising an inference of an
unidentifiable mistake of law.

Nevertheless, it is an approach which is not without its perils. A finding of fact which is
unsupported by *any* evidence clearly involves an error of law. The tribunal cannot have
directed itself, as it should, that findings of fact need *some* evidence to support them. The
danger in the approach of May LJ is that an appellate court can very easily persuade itself
that, as it would certainly not have reached the same conclusion, the Tribunal which did so
was "certainly wrong". Furthermore, the more dogmatic the temperament of the judges
concerned, the more likely they are to take this view. However, this is a classic non sequitur.
It does not matter whether, with whatever degree of certainty, the appellate court considers
that it would have reached a different conclusion. What matters is whether the decision
under appeal was a permissible option. To answer that question in the negative in the context
of employment law, the EAT will almost always have to be able to identify a finding of fact
which was unsupported by *any* evidence or a clear self-misdirection in law by the industrial
tribunal. If it cannot do this, it should re-examine with the greatest care its preliminary
conclusion that the decision under appeal was not a permissible option and has to be
characterised as "perverse"....

In my judgment the industrial tribunal were holding that the employers could reasonably
have been expected to do more with a view to obtaining a definitive answer than they did
and that, in the light of the employees' reasonable fears for their own health, until more had
been done and either an answer had emerged or it had become clear that nothing further
could be done, it was not reasonable to dismiss the employees. What the EAT was doing
was to decide that no reasonable employer could be expected to do more than rely upon the
Health and Safety Executive. That was not a decision for it.

I have no idea whether I would have reached the same conclusion as the industrial
tribunal, particularly as I do not know what evidence was given by the employees as to the
extent and basis of their fears, but that is in any event irrelevant. I can see no possible
grounds for holding that no reasonable industrial tribunal, properly directing itself, could have
reached such a conclusion and accordingly cannot and would not hold its decision to be
perverse.'

(Nicholls and Stuart-Smith LJJ agreed.)

COMMENT

(1)   Additionally the Court of Appeal held that if the decision had been perverse, the
proper course would have been for the EAT to remit the case for rehearing rather than
making its own finding.

(2)   The advice to tribunals that they should always start from the words of the statute
should be borne in mind while considering the next sections, where guidance on the
issue of reasonableness in relation to the different categories of fair reason will be
examined.

Capability or qualifications

Two separate situations fall under this category: cases where the employee is sick or injured and for that reason incapable of work, and cases of incompetence.

Links & Co Ltd v Rose

[1991] IRLR 353 Court of Session

The employee had worked at the company's snooker centre for six years. He suffered two heart attacks in August 1987 and remained unfit for work until April 1988 when he was dismissed. It was held that the dismissal was unfair because of the lack of warning or consultation with the employee before the decision was taken.

Lord McCluskey: ' ... The tribunal had been referred to a speech by Lord Bridge of Harwich in *Polkey* v *A E Dayton Services* containing an obiter passage which the tribunal considered afforded a clear indication as to the approach to be taken. As that dictum was also referred to by the Employment Appeal Tribunal and was the subject of some analysis in the submissions before us it should be quoted in full. It is as follows:

> "Employers contesting a claim of unfair dismissal will commonly advance as their reason for dismissal one of the reasons specifically recognised as valid by [ERA s 98(2)(a), (b) and (c)]. These, put shortly, are: (a) that the employee could not do his job properly; (b) that he had been guilty of misconduct; (c) that he was redundant. But an employer having prima facie grounds to dismiss for one of these reasons will in the great majority of cases not act reasonably in treating the reason as a sufficient reason for dismissal unless and until he has taken the steps, conveniently classified in most of the authorities as 'procedural', which are necessary in the circumstances of the case to justify that course of action. Thus in the case of incapacity, the employer will normally not act reasonably unless he gives the employee fair warning and an opportunity to mend his ways and show that he can do the job ..."

The first two sentences of that passage, which were not quoted by the tribunal, indicate that his Lordship was intending to indicate what the duty of employers was in relation to dismissal for a reason recognised as valid by paragraph (a) or (b) or (c) of [ERA s 98(2)]. The tribunal, having quoted the latter part of that passage, stated:

> "In accordance with our findings in fact which show (nos. 11 and 12) that there was no warning or opportunity as envisaged by Lord Bridge, the respondents (scil. the employers) must therefore be held to have dismissed the applicant unfairly in that they did not act reasonably in treating the reason as a sufficient reason for the dismissal in that they disregarded the steps described by Lord Bridge above...."

The law in relation to the duty of an employer who is considering dismissing an employee on the grounds of ill health, being ill health which appears to be such as to incapacitate the employee from performing the duties attached to his position, is not in dispute between the parties. We were referred to two cases where the employer's duty is described. It is sufficient to quote them. In the first, *East Lindsey District Council* v *Daubney*, Mr Justice Phillips said,

> "There have been several decisions of the Appeal Tribunal in which consideration has been given to what are the appropriate steps to be taken by an employer who is considering the dismissal of an employee on the ground of ill health. *Spencer* v *Paragon Wallpapers Ltd* and *David Sherratt Ltd* v *Williams* are examples. It comes to this. Unless there are wholly exceptional circumstances, before an employee is dismissed on the

ground of ill health it is necessary that he should be consulted and the matter discussed with him, and that in one way or another steps should be taken by the employer to discover the true medical position. We do not propose to lay down detailed principles to be applied in such cases, for what will be necessary in one case may not be appropriate in another. But if in every case employers take such steps as are sensible according to the circumstances to consult the employee and to discuss the matter with him, and to inform themselves upon the true medical position, it will be found in practice that all that is necessary has been done. Discussions and consultation will often bring to light facts and circumstances of which the employers were unaware, and which will throw new light on the problem."

In the second case, *Taylorplan Catering (Scotland) Ltd*, Lord McDonald said,

"There is no doubt that in the normal case a measure of consultation is expected of an employer before he decides to dismiss an employee for ill health. Apart from consider-ations of general courtesy the reason for this is to secure that the situation can be weighed up, balancing the employer's need for the work to be done on the one hand, against the employee's need for time to recover his health on the other."

It does not appear to us that the passage in the speech of Lord Bridge in *Polkey* is in any way inconsistent with these earlier cases. Lord Bridge was plainly addressing himself generally to cases of incapacity; that is clear from his reference to [s 98(2)(a)]. It is true that the concept of "fair warning and an opportunity to mend his ways" is not one which can be applied readily to a situation where the ill health which has rendered the employee unfit for the work he has been doing is of such a character that it is likely to be permanent. But it is easy enough to envisage cases in which an employee's incapacity might result from ill health which in turn flowed directly from some circumstance within the control of the employee himself. It might be, for example, that his ill health took the form of obesity and that with reasonable dieting he could cure his condition and restore his capacity to do the job. Another example would be one where the physical incapacity to perform the work could be remedied by a simple operation which the employee was, for no apparent reason, neglecting to take. It would be easy to multiply examples but it is not necessary to do so. Lord Bridge, in any event, qualified his remarks in this passage by the adverb, "normally". Accordingly the rel-evant law appears to us to be that stated by Mr Justice Phillips and Lord McDonald in the passages quoted. It follows, in our opinion, that an industrial tribunal, in approaching the question as to whether the employer acted fairly or unfairly must determine, as a matter of fact and judgment, what consultation if any was necessary or desirable in the known circumstances of the particular case, what consultation, if any, in fact took place, and whether or not that consultation process was adequate in all the circumstances. If it was not adequate the dismissal will be unfair, as explained by Lord Bridge … '

(The court decided to remit the case to the industrial tribunal for rehearing.)

COMMENT

(1) The decision of the House of Lords in *Polkey* v *Dayton Services* relating to the need for a fair procedure to be used is extremely important, and will be considered in more detail later. This decision relates its advice to sickness cases.

(2) An employer cannot generally require an employee to undergo a medical examination (*Bliss* v *SE Thames RHA*); furthermore, the employee has a right to see any report drawn up by her doctor for this purpose and can refuse to allow it to be sent

to the employer, under the Access to Medical Reports Act 1988. However, if the employers' genuine attempts to inform themselves about the state of the employee's health are frustrated by the employee's actions, the employers may act reasonably in deciding to go ahead with a dismissal.

(3)   Note the possible applicability of the Disability Discrimination Act 1995 to employees who have long-term illnesses. If the employee counts as a 'disabled person' within the meaning of that Act (see above, p 79) then the employer is at risk of liability for discrimination as well as unfair dismissal if insufficient efforts are made to redeploy her.

(4)   A problem frequently faced by employers is the situation where an employee has a poor attendance record caused by a variety of minor illnesses of short-term duration. The proper approach in such a case may be more like a disciplinary procedure, as the EAT pointed out in the next case.

International Sports Co Ltd v *Thompson*

[1980] IRLR 340 Employment Appeal Tribunal

The applicant was absent for about 25 per cent of the time over the last 18 months of her employment. Medical certificates covering the different periods revealed numerous ailments – dizzy spells, anxiety and nerves, bronchitis, virus infections, cystitis, althruigra of the knee, dyspepsia and flatulence – the last two accounting for a month's absence just before she was dismissed.

   The employers had an agreement with the trade union that absence levels above eight per cent were unsatisfactory, and accordingly she was given a series of warnings over the last year of her employment. Before dismissing her, the employers reviewed the medical evidence, but the company doctor concluded that there was no point in examining her as all the illnesses were of a transitory nature and had nothing in common.

Waterhouse J: '... It must be stressed that *Williamson* v *Alcan (UK) Ltd* and the earlier decisions followed in that judgment were all cases of incapability relating to ill-health. The industrial tribunal, in the present case, appears to have regarded those principles as applicable to all cases in which an employee is persistently absent on grounds of ill-health. We are unable to accept that as a correct proposition of law. In the *Williamson* case, the employee was still disabled by a slipped disc when he was dismissed. In *Spencer* v *Paragon Wallpapers Ltd* there was again continuing disability with back trouble, and in *East Lindsey District Council* v *Daubney* the employee had been continuously disabled following a stroke. Here, however, the employers did not purport to dismiss the employee on the ground of incapability. They were concerned with the impact of an unacceptable level of intermittent absences due to unconnected minor ailments.

   In such a case, it would be placing too heavy a burden on an employer to require him to carry out a formal medical investigation and, even if he did, such an investigation would rarely be fruitful because of the transient nature of the employee's symptoms and complaints. What is required, in our judgment, is, first, that there should be a fair review by the employer of the attendance record and the reasons for it; and, second, appropriate warnings, after the employee has been given an opportunity to make representations. If then there is no adequate improvement in the attendance record, it is likely that in most cases the employer will be justified in treating the persistent absences as a sufficient reason for dismissing the employee. It is to be noted, in the instant case, that the appellants did seek medical advice before they made the decision, and we can see no ground for criticism of the quality of that advice or of the appellants' acceptance of it. Accordingly, there was no chronic illness for them to investigate. Moreover, if the appellants had investigated the dyspepsia and flatulence further, they would no doubt have reached the conclusion that the symptoms should have been cured very quickly by a simple diet, which was the tribunal's own finding … '

(The EAT allowed the employer's appeal against the industrial tribunal's finding that the dismissal was unfair.)

COMMENT

(1)   In this case, the EAT considered that the facts indicated a dismissal on grounds of conduct rather than on capability. While it may be appropriate to use a quasi-disciplinary procedure in this sort of case, it is submitted that it is still properly to be regarded as a dismissal for incapability unless the employer is prepared to stigmatise the reasons for the absenteeism as malingering rather than genuine illness. Most employers are not prepared to do this, provided that they can get rid of the employee, because it introduces a different and unpleasant dimension to the case and is difficult to prove – even though they may secretly believe that the illnesses are not genuine.

(2)   The interface between dismissals for incapability and misconduct is blurred also in relation to incompetence.

Winterhalter Gastronom Ltd v Webb

[1973] ICR 245 National Industrial Relations Court

The employee was sales director of a company selling dishwashers. Sales were poor and the company lost money in its first full year of operation. While this was a concern to the three directors and the owner of the holding company, nothing was said to the effect that the employee would lose his job unless sales improved until July 1972, when he was asked to resign because of this. He refused, and was dismissed a month later. The industrial tribunal held the dismissal to be unfair because there had been no warning as recommended in the Code of Practice on Disciplinary Practices and Procedures in Employment.

Sir Hugh Griffiths: ' … It is right, as Mr Sedley points out, that those passages in the Code of Practice that refer to warning prior to dismissal relate to disciplinary procedures consequent upon misconduct. There is no provision in the Code of Practice that stresses the desirability of warning where performance is complained of rather than misconduct. Mr Sedley also points to a later passage in which the tribunal said: "Warning, which is so essential in a case of this sort under the [ERA], was never given." So Mr Sedley submits that the tribunal approached the matter on the basis that, if no warning was given, they were compelled to hold that the dismissal was unfair. We do not think that it would be right so to interpret the language of the tribunal. It is to be observed that they qualified their reference to the Code of Practice by saying that: " … the first step should generally be a warning". Nor do we think that in their reference to the [ERA] they were directing themselves that no dismissal could be fair unless prior warning had been given.

Mr Sedley, secondly, submits that, as the employee was a director, he was part of the mind of the company and would, therefore, be party to warning himself. This, Mr Sedley submits, is a ridiculous conception; and as the employee in his capacity as sales director was responsible for sales and knew the deplorable state of the sales, he must have appreciated that, if they did not improve, his job was in peril. Thus, argues Mr Sedley, with all these facts at his disposal and bearing in mind his capacity as a director, warning was neither necessary nor could it serve any useful purpose. Mr Sedley went so far as to submit that a warning can never be appropriate when the reason for dismissing a man is lack of capability. Warning, he says, is appropriate in the case of misconduct, because it lies within the man's own powers to rectify his conduct, but not his capability. We do not agree. There are many situations in which a man's apparent capabilities may be stretched when he knows what is demanded of him; many do not know they are capable of jumping the five-barred gate until the bull is close behind them. No doubt there may be cases in which giving warning to a director would be neither necessary nor achieve any useful purpose. But, each case must depend upon its own particular facts and it is, in the view of this court, quite impossible to say as a matter of law that there can never be circumstances in which it is necessary to give a warning to a director before dismissing him.'

(The employer's appeal was dismissed.)

COMMENT

(1) It must be remembered that cases turn on their facts and cannot be seen as providing hard and fast precedents. It is not always the case that warnings have to be given in incompetence cases: it may be pointless, because there is no way that the employee can change (as in *Dunning Ltd* v *Jacomb*), and in many cases, especially if the employee is senior, she should realise herself that her performance is not satisfactory.

(2) Once a warning has been given, then of course the employee must be permitted a reasonable period in which to show improvement – what is reasonable will depend on the work involved.

(3) Another important factor in incompetence cases is the adequacy of the training and support given to the employee. If the employee has a qualification which means she should be able to carry out a particular kind of work, the employer is not required to retrain her, but often companies will expect to have to train their workers for the jobs that they want them to do.

(4) Where the job involves a lot of responsibility, one mistake may be sufficient grounds for dismissal, as in *Alidair* v *Taylor*, where a pilot was dismissed after landing his plane badly and damaging it when there were no adverse conditions. The Court of Appeal in that case stated that the test was whether the employer could show that they had honestly lost faith in the employee's ability and that they had reasonable grounds for that belief.

Conduct

ACAS Code of Practice No 1 on Disciplinary Practices and Procedures in Employment

8. Employees should be made aware of the likely consequences of breaking rules and in particular they should be given a clear indication of the type of conduct which may warrant summary dismissal.

Essential features of disciplinary procedures

9. Disciplinary procedures should not be viewed primarily as a means of imposing sanctions. They should also be designed to emphasise and encourage improvements in individual conduct.

10. Disciplinary procedures should:
    (a) Be in writing.
    (b) Specify to whom they apply.
    (c) Provide for matters to be dealt with quickly.
    (d) Indicate the disciplinary actions which may be taken.
    (e) Specify the levels of management which have the authority to take the various forms of disciplinary action, ensuring that immediate superiors do not normally have the power to dismiss without reference to senior management.
    (f) Provide for individuals to be informed of the complaints against them and to be given an opportunity to state their case before decisions are reached.
    (g) Give individuals the right to be accompanied by a trade union representative or by a fellow employee of their choice.
    (h) Ensure that, except for gross misconduct, no employees are dismissed for a first breach of discipline.
    (i) Ensure that disciplinary action is not taken until the case has been carefully investigated.
    (j) Ensure that individuals are given an explanation for any penalty imposed.
    (k) Provide a right of appeal and specify the procedure to be followed.

The procedure in operation

11. When a disciplinary matter arises, the supervisor or manager should first establish the facts promptly before recollections fade, taking into account the statements of any available witnesses. In serious cases consideration should be given to a brief period of suspension while the case is investigated and this suspension should be with pay. Before a decision is made or penalty imposed the individual should be interviewed and given the opportunity to state his or her case and should be advised of any rights under the procedure, including the right to be accompanied.

12. Often supervisors will give informal oral warnings for the purpose of improving conduct when employees commit minor infringements of the established standards of conduct. However, where the facts of a case appear to call for disciplinary action, other than summary dismissal, the following procedure should normally be observed:
    (a) In the case of minor offences the individual should be given a formal oral warning or if the issue is more serious, there should be a written warning setting out the nature of the offence and the likely consequences of further offences. In either case the individual should be advised that the warning constitutes the first formal stage of the procedure.
    (b) Further misconduct might warrant a final written warning which should contain a statement that any recurrence would lead to suspension or dismissal or some other penalty, as the case may be.

     (c)   The final step might be disciplinary transfer, or disciplinary suspension without pay (but only if these are allowed for by an express or implied condition of the contract of employment), or dismissal, according to the nature of the misconduct. Special consideration should be given before imposing disciplinary suspension without pay and it should not normally be for a prolonged period.

13. Except in the event of an oral warning, details of any disciplinary action should be given in writing to the employee and if desired, to his or her representative. At the same time the employee should be told of any right of appeal, how to make it and to whom.

COMMENT

(1)   This advice is clear and comprehensive. It is further expanded in the ACAS Advisory Handbook, *Discipline at Work*.

(2)   Lay people frequently think that it is a rule of law that warnings should be given before a dismissal for misconduct. This is far from the case. The Code must be taken into account in all proceedings, but there may be circumstances where a failure to follow the provisions of the Code can be justified. It is not necessary to give a warning where the employee has committed gross misconduct; nor, apparently, if it is clear that a warning will make no difference to the employee (*Retarded Children's Aid Society* v *Day*).

(3)   The handling of misconduct situations can be difficult for an employer, particularly where the misconduct is a criminal offence, such as theft. The proper approach is set out in the well-known case, *BHS* v *Burchell*.

British Home Stores v Burchell

[1980] ICR 303 Employment Appeal Tribunal

The employee had been dismissed because the employers believed that she was fiddling on the staff discount purchase scheme.

Arnold J: ' … The case is one of an increasingly familiar sort in this tribunal, in which there has been a suspicion or belief of the employee's misconduct entertained by the employers; it is on that ground that dismissal has taken place; and the tribunal then goes over that to review the situation as it was at the date of dismissal. The central point of appeal is what is the nature and proper extent of that review. We have had cited to us, we believe, really all the cases which deal with this particular aspect in the recent history of this tribunal over the past three or four years; and the conclusions to be drawn from the cases we think are quite plain. What the tribunal have to decide every time is, broadly expressed, whether the employer who discharged the employee on the ground of the misconduct in question (usually, though not necessarily, dishonest conduct) entertained a reasonable suspicion amounting to a belief in the guilt of the employee of that misconduct at that time. That is really stating shortly and compendiously what is in fact more than one element. First of all, there must be established by the employer the fact of that belief; that the employer did believe it. Secondly, that the employer had in his mind reasonable grounds upon which to sustain that belief. And thirdly, we think, that the employer, at the stage at which he formed that belief on those grounds, at any rate at the final stage at which he formed that belief on those grounds, had carried out as much investigation into the matter as was reasonable in all the circumstances of the case. It is the employer who manages to discharge the onus of demonstrating those three matters, we think, who must not be examined further. It is not relevant, as we think, that the tribunal would themselves have shared that view in those circumstances. It is not relevant, as we think, for the tribunal to examine the quality of the material which the employers had before them, for instance to see whether it was the sort of material, objectively considered, which would lead to a certain conclusion on the balance of probabilities, or whether it was the sort of material which would lead to the same conclusion only upon the basis of being "sure", as it is now said more normally in a criminal context, or, to use the more old-fashioned term, such as to put the matter "beyond reasonable doubt". The test, and the test all the way through, is reasonableness; and certainly, as it seems to us, a conclusion on the balance of probabilities will in any surmisable circumstance be a reasonable conclusion ... '

COMMENT

(1)   Note that the issue is whether the employers were reasonable in reaching their conclusion on the facts as they appeared at the time of the decision to dismiss. Whether or not the employee is in fact guilty is beside the point as far as unfair dismissal is concerned – although dismissed employees find this difficult to accept and frequently want to take tribunal proceedings 'to clear my name'.

(2)   This approach, with the three requirements of honest belief, reasonable grounds for the belief, and a reasonable investigation, was expressly endorsed by the Court of Appeal in *Weddel* v *Tepper*. While being developed specifically in the context where an employee was suspected of a criminal offence, it is appropriate also in any situation where there is doubt as to what actually occurred. The following caveats should, however, be noted.

Boys and Girls Welfare Society v McDonald

[1996] IRLR 129 Employment Appeal Tribunal

Judge Clark: '...
The test of reasonableness
One starting point is the oft-cited *"Burchell test"*. British Home Stores Ltd v Burchell was decided by this Appeal Tribunal (Sir John Arnold presiding) on 20 July 1978. Although earlier reported in the Industrial Relations Law Reports it came to prominence after being cited with approval by the Court of Appeal in *Weddel & Co* v *Tepper*: see per Stephenson LJ and Cumming-Bruce LJ. The decision in *Burchell* was consequently published as a Note following the report of *Weddel* in the Industrial Cases Reports and has since come to be regarded as the leading authority on [s 98(4)] of the Act.

...

Whilst accepting unreservedly the importance of that test, we consider that a simplistic application of the test in each and every conduct case raised a danger of industrial tribunals falling into error in the following respects.

(1) The burden of proof
Burchell itself was decided on the provisions of para 6(8) of the First Schedule to the Trade Union and Labour Relations Act 1974, which provided that the question of reasonableness:

"... shall depend on whether the employer can satisfy the tribunal that in the circumstances (having regard to equity and the substantial merits of the case) he acted reasonably in treating it as a sufficient reason for dismissing the employee."

That wording was reproduced in the 1978 Act as originally drafted.

The amendment to s 57(3) affected by s 6 of the Employment Act 1980 produced the following wording:

"... The determination of the question whether the dismissal was fair or unfair, having regard to the reason shown by the employer, shall depend on whether in the circumstances ... the employer acted reasonably or unreasonably in treating it as a sufficient reason for dismissing the employee; and that question shall be determined in accordance with equity and the substantial merits of the case."

[The test in ERA s 98(4) is to the same effect, although expressed slightly differently.]

Thus, as a result of the 1980 amendment it was no longer necessary for the employer to satisfy the tribunal that it had acted reasonably. The burden of proof on the employer was removed. The question was now a "neutral" one for the industrial tribunal to decide.

The risk that by following the wording of Sir John Arnold's test in *Burchell* a tribunal may fall into error by placing the onus of proof on an employer to satisfy it as to reasonableness is not confined to industrial tribunals. In *Post Office (Counters) Ltd* v *Heavey*, this Appeal Tribunal, presided over by Wood J, reviewed the legislative history and observed:

"As the Court of Appeal has indicated on many occasions, the correct direction for an industrial tribunal to give themselves is to use the actual wording of the statute, and to remind themselves that there is no burden of proof on either party. A 'neutral' issue is indeed strange to those brought up with our adversarial system. It is not for the employer 'to show', nor for the tribunal 'to be satisfied' — each of which expressions indicate the existence of a burden of proof."

In the next paragraph of the judgment, Wood J acknowledges that it is all too easy to fall into the trap of applying the wrong burden of proof, as the Appeal Tribunal did in *Inner London Education Authority* v *Gravett*. ...

(2) Universal application of the Burchell *test*

Setting aside the question of onus of proof, it is apparent that the threefold *Burchell* test is appropriate where the employer has to decide a factual contest. The position may be otherwise where there is no real conflict on the facts. In *Royal Society for the Protection of Birds* v *Croucher*, a decision of the Employment Appeal Tribunal presided over by Waite J, the employee was suspected of dishonesty in relation to reimbursement of private petrol use by way of false expenses claims. He admitted the offences but said by way of mitigation that on earlier occasions he had omitted to claim genuine expenses. The industrial tribunal, applying the *Burchell* test, concluded that the employer had failed to carry out sufficient investigation and that the dismissal was unfair. On appeal the Employment Appeal Tribunal held that the employee having admitted the misconduct, there was little scope for further investigation and reversed the industrial tribunal's finding of unfairness. Waite J said:

"It is difficult to escape the impression that the source of error in the present case may have been their evident view that the test in *British Home Stores Ltd* v *Burchell*, was one which fell to be applied automatically whenever reasonableness was in issue at all events in cases of dishonesty, for the purposes of assessing whether a dismissal had been fair under [s 98(4)]. The *Burchell* case, it will be remembered, was a case which concerned instances in which there has been a suspicion or belief of the employee's misconduct entertained by the employers.

Here there was no question of suspicion or of questioned belief: there the dishonest conduct was admitted. There was very little scope, therefore, for the kind of investigation to which this appeal tribunal was referring in *Burchell*'s case; investigation, that is to say, designed to confirm suspicion or clear up doubt as to whether or not a particular act of misconduct has occurred. So we think that this may perhaps be another case where an industrial tribunal has fallen into error by a misplaced and artificial emphasis upon the guidelines in the *Burchell* case, something to which this appeal tribunal had recent occasion to refer in *Lintafoam (Manchester) Ltd* v *Fletcher.*

We repeat what we said then. The *Burchell* case remains, in circumstances akin to those that there were there under consideration, a most useful and helpful guideline; but it can never replace the soundness of an appraisal of all the circumstances of each particular case viewed in the round in the way that [s 98(4)] requires them to be viewed." ...

(3) The range of reasonable responses test
It should always be remembered that at the conclusion of the threefold test in *Burchell*, Sir John Arnold observed that it is the employer who manages to discharge the onus of demonstrating those three matters who must not be examined further. Leaving aside the onus of proof, we do not understand Sir John Arnold to be saying that the converse is necessarily true; that is to say, an employer who fails one or more of the three tests is, without more, guilty of unfair dismissal. In *British Leyland UK Ltd* v *Swift*, the Court of Appeal formulated the range of reasonable responses test. At paragraph 11 of the court's judgment Lord Denning MR said this:

"... It must be remembered that in all these cases there is a band of reasonableness, within which one employer might reasonably take one view: another quite reasonably take a different view. One would quite reasonably dismiss the man. The other would quite reasonably keep him on. Both views may be quite reasonable. If it was quite reasonable to dismiss him, then the dismissal must be upheld as fair: even though some other employers may not have dismissed him." ...'

COMMENT

(1)   This is a timely reminder that the *Burchell* test, like most guidelines, is not to be followed slavishly. It is always necessary to consider whether it is appropriate in the circumstances.

(2)   With reference to investigation of the facts, note the quotation from Lord Bridge's speech in *Polkey* v *Dayton Services*, p 305. A failure to give the employee a chance to offer an explanation or even a plea for mercy will almost certainly render a dismissal unfair, no matter how damning the apparent circumstances. If it turns out that the employee did indeed commit the misconduct, the dismissal will still be unfair, although that knowledge will be taken into account in assessing compensation.

(3)   This brings us to the important point about the stage at which the employer's decision to dismiss is to be judged. The position is dealt with in two vital decisions of the House of Lords.

Devis v Atkins

[1977] AC 931 House of Lords

The respondent had been employed as manager of the company's abattoir. Despite repeated instructions to buy animals directly from farmers, he persisted in buying animals through dealers. He was dismissed with pay in lieu of notice and an *ex gratia* payment of £6,000. He claimed that his dismissal was unfair. At the tribunal hearing, the employers attempted to introduce allegations that he had been taking a secret commission from the dealers, as they had discovered after his dismissal. The tribunal refused to admit this evidence and held the dismissal unfair for lack of warning. The employers' appeal had been dismissed by the High Court and the Court of Appeal.

Viscount Dilhorne: ' ... [The employers] not unnaturally resent the stigma which results from the tribunal's decision. In this appeal they do not challenge that decision on the evidence the tribunal heard, but they say the tribunal erred in refusing to hear evidence of the respondent's conduct which came to their knowledge after his dismissal and so in preventing them from establishing that the respondent was guilty of gross misconduct of such a character that, if they had had that information at the time and had acted on it, his dismissal would not have been unfair. In an action for damages for wrongful dismissal an employer can rely as justifying the dismissal on information only acquired after the dismissal: see *Boston Deep Sea Fishing and Ice Co* v *Ansell* and *Cyril Leonard & Co* v *Simo Securities Trust Ltd*. Why then should they not do so when the question at issue is, was the respondent unfairly dismissed? If they cannot do so, it must follow that a dishonest employee who up to the time of his dismissal has successfully concealed his dishonesty, may succeed in obtaining a decision that his dismissal was unfair which, apart from reflecting on his employers, may assist him in obtaining other employment when if the full facts had been known at the time of his dismissal, that would have been fully justified ...

Reverting now to paragraph 6(8) [the predecessor of ERA s 98(4)] it is to be observed that the paragraph does not require the tribunal to consider whether the complainant in fact suffered any injustice by being dismissed. If it had, then I see no reason to suppose that evidence subsequently discovered of the complainant's misconduct would not have been relevant to that question and admissible. The onus is on the employer to show what the reason was (paragraph 6(1)) and that it was a reason falling within paragraph 6(2) or some other substantial reason of a kind such as to justify the dismissal of an employee holding the position which that employee held. In this case the employer's reason fell within paragraph 6(2) as it related to the conduct of the respondent.

Then paragraph 6(8) requires the determination of the question whether the dismissal was unfair "having regard to the reason shown by the employer" to depend on whether in the circumstances the employer had acted "reasonably in treating it as a sufficient reason for dismissing the employee".

"It" must refer to the reason shown by the employer and to the reason for which the employee was dismissed. Without doing very great violence to the language I cannot construe this paragraph as enabling the tribunal to have regard to matters of which the employer was unaware at the time of dismissal and which therefore cannot have formed part of his reason or reasons for dismissing an employee.

Paragraph 6(8) appears to me to direct the tribunal to focus its attention on the conduct of the employer and not on whether the employee in fact suffered any injustice. If in the tribunal's view the employer has failed to satisfy it that he acted reasonably in treating the reason shown to be the reason for the dismissal as a sufficient reason for that dismissal, the conclusion will be that the dismissal was unfair.

Paragraph 6(8) replaced section 24 of the Act of 1971. Section 24(6) so far as material read as follows:

"... the determination of the question whether the dismissal was fair or unfair, having regard to the reason shown by the employer, shall depend on whether in the circumstances he acted reasonably or unreasonably in treating it as a sufficient reason for dismissing the employee; and that question shall be determined in accordance with equity and the substantial merits of the case."

In that section too attention was focused on the conduct of the employer and not on whether the employee in fact suffered an injustice.'

(On these grounds, the House of Lords also considered that the after-discovered information could not be taken into account and dismissed the employers' appeal.)

COMMENT

(1)   At this time, the law on unfair dismissal was contained in TULRA Schedule 1. Paragraph 6(8) is not in exactly the same terms as ERA s 98(4), but the differences are not material for the issue in hand.

(2)   At least three members of the House of Lords expressed some concern at their conclusion in this case, because at that time there was an irreducible minimum basic award equivalent to two weeks' pay in any case where a dismissal was found to be unfair. It was felt that this could amount to a 'rogues' charter' in situations where employees had successfully concealed their misdeeds while still employed. These rules have now been changed so that in such a case, the employee can be awarded nothing.

(3)   Despite the rule in *Devis* v *Atkins*, in considering the reasonableness of employers' decisions to dismiss, a 'no-difference' rule grew up – known as 'the rule in *British Labour Pump* v *Byrne*' after one of its standard formulations. The effect of the rule was that even if the employer's decision to dismiss was not reasonable in the light of the circumstances known *at the time* of the dismissal, because of some failure of procedure, yet the dismissal could still be held to be fair if, on the facts as (subsequently) proved, the industrial tribunal concluded that the employer would still have decided to dismiss even if she had followed a fair procedure. Critics complained that this amounted to using after-acquired knowledge to justify the dismissal – which was precisely what *Devis* v *Atkins* said should not happen. However, the *British Labour Pump* v *Byrne* rule had gained support in the Court of Appeal, and thus could only be overturned in the House of Lords.

Polkey v *Dayton Services Ltd*

[1988] AC 344 House of Lords

The company employed four van drivers, including the applicant. It was decided to replace the four drivers with two van salespeople. Only one of the existing drivers was thought capable of carrying out the selling as well as the driving function, so the other three were made redundant. The first Polkey knew of any of this was when he was called into the office, told that he was redundant, and sent home. There was no warning, consultation or discussion with the three beforehand – however, the industrial tribunal held, in accordance with the *British Labour Pump* v *Byrne* principle, that any such consultation would have made no difference: he would still have been sacked. Thus they found his dismissal was fair. He appealed to the House of Lords.

Lord Mackay LC: ' ... This appeal raises an important question in the law of unfair dismissal. Where an industrial tribunal has found that the reason for an applicant's dismissal was a reason of a kind such as could justify the dismissal and has found that there has been a failure to consult or warn the applicant in accordance with the Code of Practice, should the tribunal consider whether, if the employee had been consulted or warned before dismissal was decided upon, he would nevertheless have been dismissed? ...

[T]he tribunal in the present case were bound by a stream of authority applying the so-called *British Labour Pump* principle: *British Labour Pump Co Ltd* v *Byrne*. Browne-Wilkinson J in *Sillifant* v *Powell Duffryn Timber Ltd* thus described the principle,

> "even if, judged in the light of the circumstances known at the time of dismissal, the employer's decision was not reasonable because of some failure to follow a fair procedure yet the dismissal can be held fair if, on the facts proved before the industrial tribunal, the industrial tribunal comes to the conclusion that the employer could reasonably have decided to dismiss if he had followed a fair procedure."

It is because one of its statements is contained in *British Labour Pump Co Ltd* v *Byrne* that it has been called the *British Labour Pump* principle although it did not originate in that decision. In *Sillifant's* case the Employment Appeal Tribunal were urged to hold that the principle was unsound and not to give effect to it. After referring to the cases which introduced this principle, namely *Charles Letts & Co Ltd* v *Howard*, a decision relating only to compensation, *Lowndes* v *Specialist Heavy Engineering Ltd*, *British United Shoe Machinery Co Ltd* v *Clarke* and the *British Labour Pump* case itself. Browne-Wilkinson J continued,

> "Apart therefore from recent Court of Appeal authority and the *Lowndes* case, the *British Labour Pump* principle appears to have become established in practice without it being appreciated that it represented a fundamental departure from both basic principle and the earlier decisions. If we felt able to do so we would hold that it is wrong in principle and undesirable in its practical effect. It introduces just that confusion which *Devis* v *Atkins* was concerned to avoid between the fairness of the dismissal (which depends solely upon the reasonableness of the employer's conduct) and the compensation payable to the employee (which takes into account the conduct of the employee whether known to the employer or not). In our judgment, apart from the authority to which we are about to refer, the correct approach to such a case would be as follows. The only test of the fairness of a dismissal is the reasonableness of the employer's decision to dismiss judged at the time at which the dismissal takes effect. An industrial tribunal is not bound to hold that *any* procedural failure by the employer renders the dismissal unfair: it is one of the factors to be weighed by the industrial tribunal in deciding whether or not the dismissal was reasonable within [ERA section 98(4)]. The weight to be attached to such procedural failure should depend upon the circumstances known to the employer at the time of dismissal, not on the actual consequence of such failure. Thus in the case of a failure to give an opportunity to explain, except in the rare case where a reasonable employer could properly take the view on the facts known to him at the time of dismissal that no explanation or mitigation could alter his decision to dismiss, an industrial tribunal would be likely to hold that the lack of 'equity' inherent in the failure would render the dismissal unfair. But there may be cases where the offence is so heinous and the facts so manifestly clear that a reasonable employer could, on the facts known to him at the time of dismissal, take the view that whatever explanation the employee advanced it would make no difference: see the example referred to by Lawton LJ in *Bailey* v *BP Oil (Kent Refinery) Ltd*. Where, in the circumstances known at the time of dismissal, it was not reasonable for the employer to dismiss without giving an opportunity to explain but facts subsequently discovered or

proved before the industrial tribunal show that dismissal was in fact merited, compensation would be reduced to nil. Such an approach ensures that an employee who could have been fairly dismissed does not get compensation but would prevent the suggestion of "double standards" inherent in the *British Labour Pump* principle. An employee dismissed for suspected dishonesty who is in fact innocent has no redress: if the employer acted fairly in dismissing him on the facts and in the circumstances known to him at the time of dismissal the employee's innocence is irrelevant. Why should an employer be entitled to a finding that he acted fairly when, on the facts known and in the circumstances existing at the time of dismissal, his actions were unfair but which facts subsequently coming to light show did not cause any injustice? The choice in dealing with [section 98(4)] is between looking at the reasonableness of the employer or justice to the employee. *Devis* v *Atkins* shows that the correct test is the reasonableness of the employer: the *British Labour Pump* principle confuses the two approaches."

I gratefully adopt that analysis. The Employment Appeal Tribunal, however, went on to hold that they were bound by the decision of the Court of Appeal in *W & J Wass Ltd* v *Binns* which held that the *British Labour Pump* principle is good law ... '

The industrial tribunal asked themselves the wrong question when they applied the *British Labour Pump* principle. It is not apparent what their answer would have been if they had asked themselves the correct question. In my opinion the proper course is to remit this case to a new industrial tribunal for consideration in the light of your Lordships' judgment. The respondents must bear the appellant's costs in the Court of Appeal and in this House.

Lord Bridge: 'My Lords, I have had the advantage of reading in draft the speech of my noble and learned friend the Lord Chancellor and I agree with it. I add some short observations of my own because of the importance of the case.

Employers contesting a claim of unfair dismissal will commonly advance as their reason for dismissal one of the reasons specifically recognised as valid by [section 98(2)(a), (b) and (c) of the Employment Rights Act 1996]. These, put shortly are: (a) that the employee could not do his job properly; (b) that he had been guilty of misconduct; (c) that he was redundant. But an employer having prima facie grounds to dismiss for one of these reasons will in the great majority of cases not act reasonably in treating the reason as a sufficient reason for dismissal unless and until he has taken the steps, conveniently classified in most of the authorities as "procedural", which are necessary in the circumstances of the case to justify that course of action. Thus, in the case of incapacity, the employer will normally not act reasonably unless he gives the employee fair warning and an opportunity to mend his ways and show that he can do the job; in the case of misconduct, the employer will normally not act reasonably unless he investigates the complaint of misconduct fully and fairly and hears whatever the employee wishes to say in his defence or in explanation or mitigation; in the case of redundancy, the employer will normally not act reasonably unless he warns and consults any employees affected or their representative, adopts a fair basis on which to select for redundancy and takes such steps as may be reasonable to avoid or minimise redundancy by redeployment within his own organisation. If an employer has failed to take the appropriate procedural steps in any particular case, the one question the industrial tribunal is *not* permitted to ask in applying the test of reasonableness posed by [section 98(4)] is the hypothetical question whether it would have made any difference to the outcome if the appropriate procedural steps had been taken. On the true construction of [section 98(4)] this question is simply irrelevant. It is quite a different matter if the tribunal is able to conclude that the employer himself, at the time of dismissal, acted reasonably in taking the view that, in the exceptional circumstances of the particular case, the procedural steps normally appropriate would have been futile, could not have altered the decision to dismiss and therefore could be dispensed with. In such a case the test of reasonableness under [section 98(4)] may be satisfied.

My Lords, I think these conclusions are fully justified by the cogent reasoning of Browne-Wilkinson J in *Sillifant* v *Powell Duffryn Timber Ltd*, to which my noble and learned friend the Lord Chancellor has already drawn attention.

If it is held that taking the appropriate steps which the employer failed to take before dismissing the employee would not have affected the outcome, this will often lead to the result that the employee, though unfairly dismissed, will recover no compensation or, in the case of redundancy, no compensation in excess of his redundancy payment. Thus in *Earl* v *Slater & Wheeler (Airlyne) Ltd* the employee was held to have been unfairly dismissed, but nevertheless lost his appeal to the National Industrial Relations Court because his misconduct disentitled him to any award of compensation, which was at that time the only effective remedy. But in spite of this the application of the so-called *British Labour Pump* principle tends to distort the operation of the employment protection legislation in two important ways. First, as was pointed out by Browne-Wilkinson J in *Sillifant's* case, if the industrial tribunal, in considering whether the employer who has omitted to take the appropriate procedural steps acted reasonably or unreasonably in treating his reason as a sufficient reason for dismissal, poses for itself the hypothetical question whether the result would have been any different if the appropriate procedural steps had been taken, it can only answer that question on a balance of probabilities. Accordingly, applying the *British Labour Pump* principle, if the answer is that it probably would have made no difference, the employee's unfair dismissal claim fails. But if the likely effect of taking the appropriate procedural steps is only considered, as it should be, at the stage of assessing compensation, the position is quite different. In that situation, as Browne-Wilkinson J put in *Sillifant*'s case,

"There is no need for an "all or nothing" decision. If the industrial tribunal thinks there is a doubt whether or not the employee would have been dismissed, this element can be reflected by reducing the normal amount of compensation by a percentage representing the chance that the employee would still have lost his employment."

The second consideration is perhaps of particular importance in redundancy cases. An industrial tribunal may conclude, as in the instant case, that the appropriate procedural steps would not have avoided the employee's dismissal as redundant. But if, as your Lordships now hold, that conclusion does not defeat his claim of unfair dismissal, the industrial tribunal, apart from any question of compensation, will also have to consider whether to make any order under [ERA s 115]. It is noteworthy that an industrial tribunal may, if it thinks fit, make an order for re-engagement under that section and in so doing exercise a very wide discretion as to the terms of the order. In a case where an industrial tribunal held that dismissal on the ground of redundancy would have been inevitable at the time when it took place even if the appropriate procedural steps had been taken, I do not, as at present advised, think this would necessarily preclude a discretionary order for re-engagement on suitable terms, if the altered circumstances considered by the tribunal at the date of the hearing were thought to justify it.

For these reasons and for those given by my noble and learned friend the Lord Chancellor I would allow the appeal and remit the case to be heard by another industrial tribunal.'

(Lords Keith, Ackner and Brandon agreed.)

COMMENT

(1)   In this decision, the House of Lords expressly overruled *British Labour Pump* v *Byrne* and *Wass* v *Binns*.

(2)   The effect of *Polkey* has been a renewed emphasis on the importance of using correct procedures in relation to all kinds of dismissals, and the guidance of Lord Bridge has been particularly relied on. However, note the point that the 'no difference' principle can – and should – come into play in considering the appropriate remedy. It has been argued that *Polkey* is of limited effect: certainly the employee may get a decision that the dismissal was unfair, but she may still end up without a remedy.

(3)   Where the failure to follow procedure means that the employer may not be fully apprised of the facts before deciding to dismiss, the dismissal is virtually certain to be unfair. However, not every failure of procedure is of this type: see *Bailey* v *BP Oil*, where the employee was spotted on holiday in Mallorca when he was claiming to be away sick. The disciplinary procedure required that the full-time trade union official should be notified before any dismissal. As he was not available, the employers dismissed the employee anyway: this was the only respect in which they did not follow the agreed procedure. It was held by the Court of Appeal that the failure to follow the procedure in this situation did not render the dismissal unfair.

(4)   Note Lord Bridge's implication that a dismissal where procedural steps are not followed could still be fair if 'the employer himself, at the time of the dimissal, acted reasonably in taking the view that, in the exceptional circumstances of the particular case, the procedural steps normally appropriate would have been futile, could not have altered the decision to dismiss and therefore could be dispensed with.' This is considered further in the next case.

Duffy v *Yeomans & Partners Ltd*

[1995] ICR 1 Court of Appeal

This case, like *Polkey*, concerned an employee made redundant without warning or consultation.

Balcombe LJ: '… It has been suggested that the speeches in *Polkey*, and in particular that of Lord Bridge, establish that, unless an employer leads evidence to show that he considered the question of consultation and decided that it would be useless, he can never be said to have acted reasonably. A submission to this effect was made to this court in *Hooper* v *British Railways Board*, but was not accepted as being a sufficient basis for refusing to remit the case to the industrial tribunal on the grounds that the industrial tribunal must inevitably find that the dismissal was unfair. Ralph Gibson LJ, who gave the leading judgment said:

"… I do not consider that there is any distinction in substance between the principles formulated by Lord Mackay LC and that discernible in the speech of Lord Bridge. If there was any such distinction, we would have to give effect to that stated by Lord Mackay LC with which their Lordships all agreed. It is, I think, clear that Lord Bridge did not take the view that he was stating any different test. He was, in my judgment, emphasising one aspect of the principle stated by Lord Mackay LC, namely that the reasonableness of the action taken by the employer is to be judged by reference to the facts and factors known to the employer at the time of making the decision."

However, the suggestion has found favour with the Employment Appeal Tribunal in Scotland. In *Robertson* v *Magnet Ltd* Lord Coulsfield said:

> "As we understand what Lord Bridge said, the exception will normally only be available to the employer where the employer has himself considered whether consultation would be useful, and reached the conclusion that it would not. The speech of Lord Mackay LC ... seems to be to the same effect. In the present case, there is no hint in the findings of the industrial tribunal, nor was there, so far as we can tell from the statement of reasons for the decision, any hint in the evidence that the employers had considered whether or not to consult the appellant and come to the conclusion that it would have been futile to do so. The employers were of course placed in circumstances of difficulty, and were under stress and pressure. Nevertheless, as we understand the position, consultation is a very important requirement in redundancy dismissals, and is one which should not be over-looked or allowed to go by default. Accordingly, whatever the pressures, consultation is one of the points which an employer should consider, and if he does not do so, then normally it is likely that he will be held to have acted unfairly. In the present case it seems to us that that is the position. The employers did not consider consultation and there was certainly no consultation in fact. The circumstances were urgent, but were not so urgent that the employee could not have been given some opportunity to have his say or make his contribution. The majority of the industrial tribunal have, in our view, paid attention to the difficult circumstances affecting the employers but have not taken sufficient account of the fact that the employers did not, on the findings, apply their minds to the question of consultation at all. In these circumstances, we have come to the conclusion that there was a failure to consult, that that failure made the dismissal unfair, and that the conclusion of the majority of the industrial tribunal was in error."

The editor of *Harvey on Industrial Relations and Employment Law*, vol 3, p Q/438, after referring to the decision of the appeal tribunal in the present case, says:

> "On the other hand, the more normal approach (requiring a deliberate decision by that employer that consultation would be useless) was subsequently applied by the Scottish EAT in *Robertson* v *Magnet Ltd*; it is submitted that this is the better view, but the matter now needs an authoritative ruling."

In my judgment there is no warrant for the proposition that there *must* be a deliberate decision by the employers that consultation would be useless, with the corollary that, in the absence of evidence that such a decision was made, a finding by an industrial tribunal that a dismissal for redundancy was reasonable is necessarily wrong *in law*. There is nothing in the wording of [ERA s 98(4)], or in its exposition by Lord Mackay LC in *Polkey* v *AE Dayton Services Ltd*, to lead to such a result; if and in so far as that is the effect of Lord Bridge's speech, then I agree with the judgment of Ralph Gibson LJ in *Hooper* v *British Railways Board*, cited above, that we must give effect to the principles formulated by Lord Mackay LC, with which all the other law lords agreed.

As counsel for the employer put it succinctly in their skeleton argument: the industrial tribunal is asked to judge what the employer did and not what it might have done. It is what the employer (as a reasonable employer) could have done which is required to be tested; so the tribunal must ask whether an employer, acting reasonably, could have failed to consult in the given circumstances. I agree, and I reach this conclusion without reluctance, since I fear there is a grave danger that this area of the law is becoming oversophisticated, and that there is an attempt to lay down as rules of law matters which are no more than factors which an industrial tribunal should take into account in reaching its decision whether the employer acted reasonably in the circumstances of the particular case. ...'

(Saville LJ agreed. Sir Roger Parker delivered a concurring judgment.)

COMMENT

(1)   Since no evidence is necessary that the employer should have actually considered the matter and consciously decided that procedural steps would be futile, a number of commentators have expressed concern that tribunals could again slip into applying the 'no-difference' rule, even though ostensibly they are focusing only on what the employer knew at the time.

(2)   An issue requiring some thought in the light of *Devis* v *Atkins* and *Polkey* is the proper approach to appeals against dismissal. The Code of Practice recommends that employers should have an appeal procedure and, among large organisations, it can be elaborate and entail a relatively formal hearing. It is quite likely that other information will come to light. Is this 'after-acquired' information which should not be taken into account?

West Midlands Co-operative Society Ltd v *Tipton*

[1986] ICR 192 House of Lords

The employee had an appalling attendance record. He received clear warnings that he would be dismissed if it did not improve. There was no improvement, and ultimately he was summarily dismissed. The employers then refused to hear his appeal against dismissal, in breach of the agreed contractual procedure. The industrial tribunal found the dismissal unfair because of the refusal to entertain his appeal; this upheld by the EAT, but reversed by the Court of Appeal.

Lord Bridge: ' ... I can see nothing in the language of the statute to exclude from consideration in answering [the] question "in accordance with equity and the substantial merits of the case" evidence relevant to show the strength or weakness of the real reason for dismissal which the employer had the opportunity to consider in the course of an appeal heard pursuant to a disciplinary procedure which complies with the statutory Code of Practice. The apparent injustice of excluding, in relation to this question, misconduct of the employee which is irrelevant to the real reason for dismissal is mitigated, as I have earlier pointed out, by the provisions relating to compensation in such a case. But there is nothing to mitigate the injustice to an employee which would result if he were unable to complain that his employer, though acting reasonably on the facts known to him when he summarily dismissed the employee, acted quite unreasonably in maintaining his decision to dismiss in the face of mitigating circumstances established in the course of the domestic appeal procedure which a reasonable employer would have treated as sufficient to excuse the employee's offence on which the employer's real reason for the dismissal depended. Adopting the analysis which found favour in *J. Sainsbury Ltd* v *Savage*, if the domestic appeal succeeds the employee is reinstated with retrospective effect; if it fails the summary dismissal takes effect from the original date. Thus, in so far as the original dismissal and the decision on the domestic appeal are governed by the same consideration, sc. the real reason for dismissal, there is no reason to treat the effective date of termination as a watershed which separates the one process from the other. Both the original and the appellate decision by the employer, in any case where the contract of employment provides for an appeal and the right of appeal is invoked by the employee, are necessary elements in the overall process of terminating the contract of employment. To separate them and to consider only one half of the process in determining whether the employer acted reasonably or unreasonably in treating his real reason for dismissal as sufficient is to introduce an unnecessary artificiality into proceedings on a claim of unfair dismissal calculated to defeat, rather than accord with, the "equity and the substantial merits of the case" and for which the language of the statute affords no warrant.

This is the conclusion I should reach as a matter of construction, taking due account of the decision in the *Devis* case, if there were no other authority to guide me. But the conclusion is powerfully reinforced by the series of decisions of the Employment Appeal Tribunal, to which I have earlier referred, with which it is in full accord. The relevant cases are *Rank Xerox (UK) Ltd* v *Goodchild*; *Quantrill* v *Eastern Counties Omnibus Co Ltd*; *National Heart and Chest Hospitals Board of Governors* v *Nambiar*; *Sillifant* v *Powell Duffryn Timber Ltd*; and *Greenall Whitley Plc* v *Carr*. I need only quote certain key passages from the judgments.

In *National Heart and Chest Hospitals Board of Governors* v *Nambiar* Waterhouse J said,

"In this context it is necessary to distinguish the case where an employee is dismissed for reason A and evidence at an internal appeal invalidates reason A but demonstrates that a different reason B would justify dismissal. It is clear that in such circumstances the original dismissal ought not to stand and the employer must look at the matter afresh in order to decide whether a later dismissal on the new information is appropriate. In the more usual case, however, where the employer confirms the decision to dismiss for reason A, following the appeal, we consider that it is right for an industrial tribunal to look at the information that came to light in the course of the appeal.

The date of the decision to dismiss and the principal reason for it are established before an internal appeal, but an industrial tribunal has to consider whether the employer can satisfy them that, in the words of [ERA s 98(4)]: 'in the circumstances (having regard to equity and the substantial merits of the case) he acted reasonably in treating it as a sufficient reason for dismissing the employee'. In our judgment these are words of broad application and we suggest that our interpretation does not do violence to the language. When an internal appeal body decides or recommends that a dismissal shall stand, it has to consider whether the reason is sufficient to justify confirmation of the dismissal in the light of any new information about it as well as the information available to the employer when the original decision was made; and it would be artificial to exclude the new material from consideration by an industrial tribunal adjudicating upon a decision to dismiss that the employer has confirmed."...

A dismissal is unfair if the employer unreasonably treats his real reason as a sufficient reason to dismiss the employee, either when he makes his original decision to dismiss or when he maintains that decision at the conclusion of an internal appeal. By the same token, a dismissal may be held to be unfair when the employer has refused to entertain an appeal to which the employee was contractually entitled and thereby denied to the employee the opportunity of showing that, in all the circumstances, the employer's real reason for dismissing him could not reasonably be treated as sufficient. There may, of course, be cases where, on the undisputed facts, the dismissal was inevitable, as for example where a trusted employee, before dismissal, was charged with, and pleaded guilty to, a serious offence of dishonesty committed in the course of his employment. In such a case the employer could reasonably refuse to entertain a domestic appeal on the ground that it could not affect the outcome. It has never been suggested, however, that this was such a case.

I would accordingly allow the appeal.'

(Lords Roskill, Brandon, Brightman and Mackay agreed.)

COMMENT

(1)   The conclusion reached seems correct, although a little convoluted. Note the relevance of this issue also in determining the date at which the dismissal is held to have taken place. This is important because the limitation period for lodging an unfair dismissal application is only three months from the effective date of termination.

(2)   In *Westminster CC* v *Cabaj* the EAT held that a dismissal was unfair because the employee's appeal was heard by only two people instead of three, as stipulated in his contract. The Court of Appeal, however, reversed: even though the procedural failure was also a breach of contract, this did not make it automatically unfair. The case was remitted on the issue of whether the procedural failure prevented the employee getting a fair hearing.

(3)   The misconduct for which the employee is dismissed will usually be something done at work. However, it is possible for conduct outside the workplace to constitute a fair reason for dismissal.

ACAS Code of Practice No 1 on Disciplinary Practice and Procedures in Employment

15.   Special consideration should be given to the way in which disciplinary procedures are to operate in exceptional cases. For example:
  (a) *Employees to whom the full procedure is not immediately available.* Special provisions may have to be made for the handling of disciplinary matters among nightshift workers, workers in isolated locations or depots or others who may pose particular problems for example because no one is present with the necessary authority to take disciplinary action or no trade union representative is immediately available.
  (b) *Trade union officials.* Disciplinary action against a trade union official can lead to a serious dispute if it is seen as an attack on the union's functions. Although normal disciplinary standards should apply to their conduct as employees, no disciplinary action beyond an oral warning should be taken until the circumstances of the case have been discussed with a senior trade union representative or full-time official.
  (c) *Criminal offences outside employment.* These should not be treated as automatic reasons for dismissal regardless of whether the offence has any relevance to the duties of the individual as an employee. The main considerations should be whether the offence is one that makes the individual unsuitable for his or her type of work or unacceptable to other employees. Employees should not be dismissed solely because a charge against them is pending or because they are absent through having been remanded in custody.

COMMENT

(1)   Because of the 'range of reasonable responses' doctrine, an employer has some degree of latitude in deciding whether or not an offence is relevant to the employee's duties: see *Mathewson* v *R B Wilson Dental Laboratory Ltd*, for example.

(2)   How far unacceptability to other employees should be relevant is moot: under ERA s 107, pressure taking the form of a threat to engage in industrial action is to be

disregarded in assessing whether a dismissal is fair. See the discussion by R A Watt in 'HIV, Discrimination, Unfair Dismissal and Pressure to Dismiss' (1992) 21 **ILJ** 280.

Redundancy

An employee of two years' standing who is made redundant will be entitled to a redundancy payment. Thus redundancy is a fair reason for dismissal, provided it is handled reasonably. Advice on how to handle redundancy situations was contained in the Industrial Relations Code of Practice 1972 (drawn up under the authority of the Industrial Relations Act 1971); but this was repealed in 1991. The interpretation of reasonableness in relation to redundancy has, however, brought back the concept of best practice in this area to some extent.

Williams v Compair Maxam Ltd

[1982] ICR 156 Employment Appeal Tribunal

The company, which had about two hundred employees, was in dire financial straits: the trade union was informed that redundancies would be necessary and that as there were insufficient volunteers, there would need to be compulsory redundancies. However, the union was not consulted over the criteria to be used, nor given the names in advance. In fact, the three managers of the different departments in the company were told to 'pick a team' of those to be retained in their department in order to keep the company viable. The employees thus selected for redundancy were given no prior warning. They sued for unfair dismissal.

Browne-Wilkinson J: '...The question we have to decide is whether a reasonable tribunal could have reached the conclusion that the dismissal of the applicants in this case lay within the range of conduct which a reasonable employer could have adopted. It is accordingly necessary to try to set down in very general terms what a properly instructed industrial tribunal would know to be the principles which, in current industrial practice, a reasonable employer would be expected to adopt. This is not a matter on which the chairman of this appeal tribunal feels that he can contribute much, since it depends on what industrial practices are currently accepted as being normal and proper. The two lay members of this appeal tribunal hold the view that it would be impossible to lay down detailed procedures which *all* reasonable employers would follow in *all* circumstances: the fair conduct of dismissals for redundancy must depend on the circumstances of each case. But in their experience, there is a generally accepted view in industrial relations that, in cases where the employees are represented by an independent union recognised by the employer, reasonable employers will seek to act in accordance with the following principles:

1. The employer will seek to give as much warning as possible of impending redundancies so as to enable the union and employees who may be affected to take early steps to inform themselves of the relevant facts, consider possible alternative solutions and, if necessary, find alternative employment in the undertaking or elsewhere.
2. The employer will consult the union as to the best means by which the desired management result can be achieved fairly and with as little hardship to the employees as possible. In particular, the employer will seek to agree with the union the criteria to be applied in selecting the employees to be made redundant. When a selection has been made, the employer will consider with the union whether the selection has been made in accordance with those criteria.

3. Whether or not an agreement as to the criteria to be adopted has been agreed with the union, the employer will seek to establish criteria for selection which so far as possible do not depend solely upon the opinion of the person making the selection but can be objectively checked against such things as attendance record, efficiency at the job, experience, or length of service.
4. The employer will seek to ensure that the selection is made fairly in accordance with these criteria and will consider any representations the union may make as to such selection.
5. The employer will seek to see whether instead of dismissing an employee he could offer him alternative employment.

The lay members stress that not all these factors are present in every case since circumstances may prevent one or more of them being given effect to. But the lay members would expect these principles to be departed from only where some good reason is shown to justify such departure. The basic approach is that, in the unfortunate circumstances that necessarily attend redundancies, as much as is reasonably possible should be done to mitigate the impact on the work force and to satisfy them that the selection has been made fairly and not on the basis of personal whim....

We must add a word of warning. For the purpose of giving our reasons for reaching our exceptional conclusion that the decision of the industrial tribunal in this case was perverse, we have had to state what in our view are the steps which a reasonable and fair employer at the present time would seek to take in dismissing unionised employees on the ground of redundancy. We stress two points. First, these are not immutable principles which will stay unaltered for ever. Practices and attitudes in industry change with time and new norms of acceptable industrial relations behaviour will emerge. Secondly the factors we have stated are *not* principles of law, but standards of behaviour. Therefore in future cases before this appeal tribunal there should be no attempt to say that an industrial tribunal which did not have regard to or give effect to one of these factors has misdirected itself in law. Only in cases such as the present where a genuine case for perversity on the grounds that the decision flies in the face of commonly accepted standards of fairness can be made out, are these factors directly relevant. They are relevant only as showing the knowledge of industrial relations which the industrial jury is to be assumed as having brought to bear on the case they had to decide.

For the reasons that we have stated, we allow the appeal and substitute a finding that the four applicants were unfairly dismissed. We will remit the case to a differently constituted tribunal to assess the compensation.'

COMMENT

(1)   This decision is one of the classic 'guidance' cases from the EAT, and it should be remembered that the Court of Appeal has frequently warned against this tendency and stressed that there should be no gloss on the words of the statute. Also, some reliance was placed in the decision on the terms of the 1972 Code of Practice, now repealed. However, despite these caveats, the principles of good practice stated here are widely accepted and may be adapted also for use in situations where there is no recognised trade union.

(2)   Employers have a statutory duty to consult over multiple redundancies and over transfers of undertakings: this is dealt with in Chapter 9.

(3) Note the emphasis on the need for objective criteria, objectively and fairly applied. It is partly because length of service is a completely objective criterion that it is favoured by trade unions for compulsory redundancies. Management, however, usually prefers a method which involves assessing performance so as to retain the best workers. This case illustrates the importance of being clear what is meant by 'best' in this context, and how it is to be judged.

(4) Failure to give adequate warning or to consult with affected employees is another situation where redundancy dismissals can be held to be unfair. This, indeed, is what occurred in *Polkey* v *Dayton Services* (p 305).

(5) The final situation in which a dismissal for redundancy is likely to be found to be unfair is where there has been a failure to try and find alternative employment for the employee.

Vokes Ltd v Bear

[1974] ICR 1 National Industrial Relations Court

Sir Hugh Griffiths: 'On December 1 1969 the employee commenced employment with the employers as works manager at a salary of £3,000 a year, plus a company car and a company house for which he paid a very low rent. By December 1972 he was 47 years of age with a daughter at university, three sons of school age and his salary had been increased to £4,000 per annum. In that month the employers were taken over by the Tilling Group. After the takeover the Tilling Group sent the managing director of one of their other companies to investigate their new acquisition the employer company. He was elected to the board and took over as chief executive. He came to the conclusion that the management was top heavy and would have to be pruned. He indicated this in general terms at a meeting of management at which the employee was present at the beginning of February. The employee did not, however, think that his job was at risk; he thought he had an important role to play in the future development of the company under its new ownership, and it was not unreasonable that he should have thought this as he had been actively engaged in future planning.

It came therefore as a profound shock to him when on March 2 he was called into the chief executive's office, told that he was redundant, asked to leave forthwith and not to return to the company premises during working hours. He was paid his redundancy payment of £180, three months' salary in lieu of notice and allowed to use the car for eight weeks and the house for three months. We have not seen any written contract he may have had with the employers but in the absence of such a contract this would appear to be the bare minimum to which he would be entitled at common law. By no stretch of imagination could they be described as generous severance terms.

No attempt whatever had been made by the chief executive or anyone else within the company or the Tilling Group to see if this middle aged family man could be employed somewhere else within the group. He was given no real warning that he might be dismissed and before the blow fell no assistance whatever to find alternative employment ...

Having decided that the employee was dismissed by reason of redundancy the tribunal then turned to consider whether nevertheless his dismissal was unfair by virtue of the provisions of [ERA s 98(4)]. The tribunal held that it was unfair because no attempt whatever had been made to see if the employee could have been fitted into some other position in the group before he was dismissed. The evidence showed that the Tilling Group consisted of some 300 companies and there was evidence that at least one of those companies was advertising for persons to fill senior management positions shortly after the employee's dismissal. The Tilling Group apparently had no centralised machinery for providing services to all the companies in the group and it was argued before the tribunal and before this court that in all the circumstances it would have been impracticable to have made any inquiries within the group to see if there was another position that the employee might fill. The tribunal would have none of this argument. They said:

"We do not think that such inquiries were impracticable. We think that some inquiries should have been made to see whether it was possible to help someone like [the employee] whose services had proved satisfactory to his employers in every respect. We think the [employers'] failure to consider the question of finding some other position for the [employee] in the group made the dismissal unfair."

We find ourselves in full agreement with the way in which the tribunal expressed themselves. It would have been the simplest of matters to have circulated an inquiry through the group to see if any assistance could be given to the employee in the very difficult circumstances in which he would shortly find himself ... '

COMMENT

(1)   This case is a good illustration of the sort of situation where the employer could be expected to make an effort to find alternative employment. Clearly it will depend on the size and resources of the organisation in each case.

(2)   In addition to these general grounds of unfairness, there are certain situations where selection for redundancy will automatically constitute unfair dismissal.

Employment Rights Act 1996

105.   (1)   An employee who is dismissed shall be regarded for the purposes of this Part as unfairly dismissed if—
  (a)   the reason (or, if more than one, the principal reason) for the dismissal is that the employee was redundant,
  (b)   it is shown that the circumstances constituting the redundancy applied equally to one or more other employees in the same undertaking who held positions similar to that held by the employee and who have not been dismissed by the employer, and
  (c)   it is shown that any of subsections (2) to (7) applies. ...

COMMENT

(1) Selection for redundancy will be automatically unfair if the reason or principal reason is one for which dismissal is automatically unfair: this section thus completes that protection.

(2) These reasons are: (a) pregnancy (s 99); (b) certain health and safety reasons (s 100); (c) protected shop workers (s 101); (d) acting as trustee of a pension scheme (s 102); (e) acting as an employee respresentative for consultation (s 103); (f) asserting a statutory right (s 104).

Breach of statute

Where continued employment would be in breach of statute, it will be fair to dismiss the employee provided that the employer acted reasonably. Thus where a particular qualification is necessary for a job (such as passing examinations for solicitors or accountants) an employee who fails may be fairly dismissed; although it may be reasonable to let them have another chance (see, for example, *Sutcliffe and Eaton Ltd* v *Pinney*).

'Some other substantial reason'

The final category of fair reason is not really a category at all. It can embrace a variety of reasons which are not taken up elsewhere, and its boundaries are not limited.

Hollister v *National Farmers' Union*

[1979] ICR 542 Court of Appeal

The applicant was employed as a group secretary by the union in Cornwall. Group secretaries received a small salary from the union and gained most of their income through commission on insurance sold to members through an associated insurance company. For historical reasons, the arrangements in Cornwall were different from the rest of the country, and the group secretaries complained that they were not so well off. It was finally decided to bring them into line with the rest of the country, which involved various changes to their contractual arrangements. The tribunal found that most conditions were as good or better than before, but pension arrangements were not as good. The applicant refused to accept the new arrangements and so his contract was terminated. He sued for unfair dismissal.

Lord Denning MR: ' ... The question which is being discussed in this case is whether the reorganisation of the business which the National Farmers' Union felt they had to undertake in 1976, coupled with Mr Hollister's refusal to accept the new agreement, was a substantial reason of such a kind as to justify the dismissal of the employee. Upon that there have only been one or two cases. One we were particularly referred to was *Ellis* v *Brighton Co-operative Society Ltd*, where it was recognised by the court that reorganisation of business may on occasion be a sufficient reason justifying the dismissal of an employee. They went on to say,

> "Where there has been a properly consulted-upon reorganisation which, if it is not done, is going to bring the whole business to a standstill, a failure to go along with the new arrangements may well – it is not bound to, but it may well – constitute 'some other substantial reason'."

Certainly, I think, everyone would agree with that. But in the present case Arnold J expanded it a little so as not to limit it to where it came absolutely to a standstill but to where there was some sound, good business reason for the reorganisation. I must say I see no reason to differ from Arnold J's view on that. It must depend on all the circumstances whether the reorganisation was such that the only sensible thing to do was to terminate the employee's contract unless he would agree to a new arrangement. It seems to me that that paragraph may well be satisfied, and indeed was satisfied in this case, having regard to the commercial necessity of rearrangements being made and the termination of the relationship with the Cornish Mutual, and the setting up of a new relationship via the National Farmers' Union Mutual Insurance Society Ltd. On that rearrangement being made, it was absolutely essential for new contracts to be made with the existing group secretaries: and the only way to deal with it was to terminate the agreements and offer them reasonable new ones. It seems to me that that would be, and was, a substantial reason of a kind sufficient to justify this kind of dismissal. I stress the word "kind" ... '

(Eveleigh LJ and Sir Stanley Rees agreed with Lord Denning that the dismissal in these circumstances was fair.)

COMMENT

(1) This authority has frequently been relied upon in relation to reorganisations. It is quite difficult to explain to employees how come they must abide by the terms of the contract while they cannot hold their employer to the agreed terms.

(2) Obviously employers will have genuine needs to reorganise, particularly in recessionary conditions. But how far is it fair to pass this on to the workforce? In *St John of God (Care Services) Ltd* v *Brooks* a hospital run by a charity was faced with the need to make massive cuts in order to stay open. They proposed that paid holidays should be reduced, overtime rates abolished, the generous sick pay arrangements replaced by the minimum statutory sick pay and no guarantee of linkage to national pay scales for the future. Employees who refused the new contracts were dismissed. An industrial tribunal found the dismissals unfair, in that this was not an offer which a reasonable employer could expect the workforce to accept. The EAT held that this was the wrong test: the question was whether the decision to dismiss was fair or unfair, judged in all the circumstances pertaining at that time. The case was therefore remitted to the tribunal; however, it provides a fairly extreme example of what may occur. Should dismissals be fair in these circumstances, bearing in mind that this will not count as a redundancy situation?

(3) Customer pressure has also been accepted as constituting some other substantial reason. However, the emphasis on justice to the employee is important, since the reason for the customer's reaction cannot be scrutinised in the same way as the employer's reason to dismiss by the tribunal (cf *Dobie* v *Burns International Security Services*). By the same token, a personality clash or unacceptability to other employees may constitute some other substantial reason (see *Treganowan* v *Knee*, for example). However, note the point made on p 313.

(4) Expiry of a fixed-term contract for a genuine short-term need has also been held to be some other substantial reason (*Terry* v *East Sussex CC*) and ERA s 106 provides that where a temporary replacement is taken on for someone on maternity leave or absent because of a medical suspension, their termination will be regarded as for some other substantial reason as long as the short-term nature of their engagement was notified to them in writing when they were taken on. However, as no unfair dismissal obligations are assumed until the employee has been employed for two years, this will rarely arise in practice. All such dismissals must still be tested against the standard of reasonableness.

Remedies for unfair dismissal

Reinstatement and re-engagement

Employment Rights Act 1996

114. (1) An order for reinstatement is an order that the employer shall treat the complainant in all respects as if he had not been dismissed.

(2) On making an order for reinstatement the tribunal shall specify—

(a) any amount payable by the employer in respect of any benefit which the complainant might reasonably be expected to have had but for the dismissal (including arrears of pay) for the period between the date of termination of employment and the date of reinstatement;

(b) any rights and privileges (including seniority and pension rights) which must be restored to the employee; and

(c) the date by which the order must be complied with.

(3) If the complainant would have benefited from an improvement in his terms and conditions of employment had he not been dismissed, an order for reinstatement shall require him to be treated as if he had benefited from that improvement from the date on which he would have done so but for being dismissed.
...

115. (1) An order for re-engagement is an order, on such terms as the tribunal may decide, that the complainant be engaged by the employer, or by a successor of the employer or by an associated employer, in employment comparable to that from which he was dismissed or other suitable employment ...

COMMENT

(1) Reinstatement and re-engagement are categorically stated to be the first remedies which should be considered; however, they are rarely awarded: the figure has remained constant at about one per cent of cases proceeding to a hearing. Explanations for this vary, but it seems that the remedy is sought by very few applicants, because they fear victimisation if they return to their old job.

(2) Re-employment should not be ordered against the wishes of the employee. Apart from that, the main limiting factor on making a re-employment order is the question of practicability. Under ERA s 116(5), the fact that the employer has taken on a permanent replacement for the dismissed employee does not render re-employment impracticable unless either it was not practicable to cover the work in any other way or a reasonable time had passed without the employee indicating that she would be seeking this remedy.

(3) The tribunal should also consider whether it is just to order re-employment in cases where the employee was to some extent responsible for the dismissal.

(4) Where an employer fails to comply with a re-employment order, the tribunal makes an additional award of compensation of between 13 and 26 weeks' pay – unless the employer can show that it was not practicable to comply with the order. Practicability thus falls to be considered at two different stages (see *Port of London Authority* v *Payne*).

Compensation

In general compensation is made up of two elements: a basic award and a compensatory award. If an employer fails to comply with a re-employment order, an additional award is made as well. Where a dismissal is related to automatically unfair reasons, a special award is payable.

The basic award (ERA s 119)

The basic award is calculated by a fixed mathematical formula:

$$\text{Years of service} \times \text{Week's pay} \times \text{Multiplier} (\tfrac{1}{2}, 1 \text{ or } 1\tfrac{1}{2})$$

COMMENT

(1)   Years of service refers to *complete* years of service, up to a maximum of twenty.

(2)   Week's pay refers to gross pay, but is limited to a maximum, which figure is subject to annual review. It stood at £210 in 1997.

(3)   The multiplier depends on age: employees get half a week's pay for every year in which they were aged under 22; one week's pay for every year in which they were aged between 22 and 41, and one and a half weeks' pay for every year in which they were aged 41 or more. The maximum is thus £6,300. A redundancy payment is calculated in almost exactly the same way as the basic award.

(4)   Once the employee reaches the age of 64, the basic award is reduced by one twelfth for every complete month over that age. It thus tapers down to nothing by the time the employee reaches 65: this relates to the fact that an employee over 65 will not be able to claim for unfair dismissal. The relation of the two provisions is demonstrable, though their fairness is not.

(5)   The basic award can be reduced by a percentage fixed by the tribunal on three grounds. First, where the employee has unreasonably refused an offer of reinstatement (not re-engagement) from the employer. Second, where the conduct of the employee makes it just and equitable to reduce the award. This refers to any conduct before the dismissal, even if the employer does not discover it until afterwards. This takes care of the problem noted in *Devis* v *Atkins*: if the employer dismisses unfairly, but later discovers grounds which would have justified the dismissal, the employee is entitled to a decision that the dismissal was unfair, but may well find that the compensation is reduced by 100 per cent because of this or her blameworthy conduct.

Third, if the dismissal is for redundancy and the employee is awarded, or has already been paid, a redundancy payment, this will be deducted from the basic award, to avoid double compensation.

(6)   Where the dismissal was for union membership reasons (that is, membership or non-membership of a trade union, including selection for dismissal on those grounds), acting as an employee representative or health and safety reasons, the basic award cannot be less than £2,770 (before any reductions on the grounds noted above). The

employee's stance on union membership is not conduct to be taken into account in this connection.

The compensatory award

Employment Rights Act 1996

123.   (1)   Subject to the provisions of this section and sections 124 and 126, the amount of the compensatory award shall be such amount as the tribunal considers just and equitable in all the circumstances having regard to the loss sustained by the complainant in consequence of the dismissal in so far as that loss is attributable to action taken by the employer.

COMMENT

(1)   The maximum possible compensatory award was £11,300 in 1997. It is also subject to annual review, but has not been raised annually. In a case where an employer has refused to implement a re-employment order, the compensatory award may be higher, to ensure that it is not cheaper for the employer to flout such an order than to comply with it.

(2)   While the statutory formulation seems to leave a wide discretion for the calculation of the compensatory award, in fact fairly detailed rules as to the proper approach have been developed through case law. The starting point is the decision of the National Industrial Relations Court in an early appeal on the subject. They refer to the equivalent provision to s 123 under the Industrial Relations Act 1971.

Norton Tool Co Ltd v *Tewson*

[1972] ICR 501 National Industrial Relations Court

Sir John Donaldson: ' ... In our judgment, the common law rules and authorities on wrongful dismissal are irrelevant. That cause of action is quite unaffected by the Industrial Relations Act 1971 which has created an entirely new cause of action, namely, the "unfair industrial practice" of unfair dismissal. The measure of compensation for that statutory wrong is itself the creature of statute and is to be found in the Act of 1971 and nowhere else. But we do not consider that Parliament intended the court or tribunal to dispense compensation arbitrarily. On the other hand, the amount has a discretionary element and is not to be assessed by adopting the approach of a conscientious and skilled cost accountant or actuary. Nevertheless, that discretion is to be exercised judicially and upon the basis of principle.

The court or tribunal is enjoined to assess compensation in an amount which is just and equitable in all the circumstances, and there is neither justice nor equity in a failure to act in accordance with principle. The principles to be adopted emerge from section 116 of the Act of 1971 [now ERA s 123]. First, the object is to compensate, and compensate fully, but not to award a bonus, save possibly in the special case of a refusal by an employer to make an offer of employment in accordance with the recommendation of the court or a tribunal. Secondly, the amount to be awarded is that which is just and equitable in all the circumstances, having regard to the loss sustained by the complainant. "Loss" in the context of [ERA s 123] does not include injury to pride or feelings.

In these circumstances, and in the light of the request of the parties to which we have already referred, we shall substitute our own award. In our judgment the employee is entitled to compensation in the sum of £375. This sum we regard as just and equitable in all the circumstances, having regard to the loss sustained by him. That loss falls to be considered under the following heads.

(*a*) *Immediate loss of wages*
The Contracts of Employment Act 1963, as amended by the Act of 1971, entitles a worker with more than ten years' continuous employment to not less than six weeks' notice to terminate his employment [see now ERA s 86]. Good industrial practice requires the employer either to give this notice or pay six weeks' wages in lieu. The employee was given neither. In an action for damages for wrongful, as opposed to unfair, dismissal he could have claimed that six weeks' wages, but would have had to give credit for anything which he earned or could have earned during the notice period. In the event he would have had to give credit for what he earned in the last two weeks, thus reducing his claim to about four weeks' wages. But if he had been paid the wages in lieu of notice at the time of his dismissal, he would not have had to make any repayment upon obtaining further employment during the notice period. In the context of compensation for unfair dismissal we think that it is appropriate and in accordance with the intentions of Parliament that we should treat an employee as having suffered a loss in so far as he receives less than he would have received in accordance with good industrial practice. Accordingly, no deduction has been made for his earnings during the notice period. We have no information as to whether the £25.60 per week is a gross or a take-home figure. The relevant figure is the take-home pay since this and not the gross pay is what he should have received from his employer. However, neither party took this point and we have based our assessment of this head of loss on six weeks at £25.60 per week or £153.60. The employee drew £3 unemployment benefit for a short period, but we were not asked to make any deduction for this and have not done so. Finally, we have taken no account of the extent to which the employee's income tax liability may be reduced by his period of unemployment, since we consider that the sums involved will be small and that such a calculation is inappropriate to the broad, common sense assessment of compensation which Parliament contemplated in the case of unfair dismissal of a man earning the employee's level of wages.

(*b*) *Manner of dismissal*
As the employee secured employment within four weeks of his dismissal and we have taken full account of his loss during this period, we need only consider whether the manner and circumstances of his dismissal could give rise to any risk of financial loss at a later stage by, for example, making him less acceptable to potential employers or exceptionally liable to selection for dismissal. There is no evidence of any such disability and accordingly our assessment of the compensation takes no account of the manner of his dismissal. This took place during a heated exchange of words between him and one of the directors.

(*c*) *Future loss of wages*
There is no evidence to suggest that the employee's present employment is any less secure than his former employment, and we have therefore taken no account of possible future losses due to short-time working, lay-off or unemployment, apart from loss of rights in respect of redundancy and unfair dismissal which are considered separately below.

(*d*) *Loss of protection in respect of unfair dismissal or dismissal by reason of redundancy*
These losses may be more serious. So long as the employee remained in the employ of the employers he was entitled to protection in respect of unfair dismissal. He will acquire no

such rights against his new employers until he has worked for them for two years (see [ERA s 108(1)]. Accordingly, if he is unfairly dismissed during that period, his remedy will be limited to claiming damages for wrongful dismissal, which are unlikely to exceed six weeks' wages and may be less. Furthermore, upon obtaining further employment he will be faced with starting a fresh two-year period. This process could be repeated indefinitely, so that he was never again protected in respect of unfair dismissal. Whilst it is impossible for us to quantify this loss, which must be much affected by local conditions, we think that we shall do the employee no injustice if we include £20 in our assessment on account of it.

The loss of rights under [ERA Part XI] is much more serious ...'

COMMENT

(1)   Immediate loss of wages refers to the net benefits the employee would have received: it can therefore include overtime payments where overtime is regularly worked. The statement that no deduction should be made to take account of anything earned by the employee during his or her notice period must be read subject to the general principle that the award is intended to compensate and that the employee must mitigate his or her loss. It has therefore been modified occasionally where the employee would seem to be over-compensated by application of this rule.

(2)   State benefits received by the employee are ignored by the tribunal in assessing loss up to the time of the tribunal hearing; the employer will be required to pay that part of the award back to the state under the recoupment regulations. The recoupment regulations do not apply where the parties themselves settle compensation, and so the employer can make a saving by agreeing a private settlement if found liable. This is facilitated by most tribunals, who often adjourn proceedings after deciding liability so that the parties can reach an agreement.

(3)   Amounts awarded under the rubric of future loss cannot be quantified precisely if the employee has not found another job; in a time of rising unemployment and recession, tribunals are often criticised for taking too optimistic a view of the employee's chances of re-employment at a similar level.

(4)   As well as wages, the loss of any other benefits received by virtue of the occupation must be compensated. This includes such things as use of a company vehicle, private health insurance, subsidised meals or accommodation, tips, share schemes and so on. An extremely important matter under this heading is the employee's occupational pension entitlement.

(5)   While manner of dismissal can be taken into account where it makes it more difficult for the employee to find another job, injury to feelings is not compensatable.

(6)   At the time of this decision, there was no basic award for unfair dismissal, only a compensatory award. Hence the reference at the end of the extract to the serious loss of redundancy rights. It was to reflect the fact that that accrued service entitlement was lost through an unfair dismissal that the basic award (calculated like a redundancy payment) was introduced. However, it remains the case that the employee will have to get in two years' service before he or she will receive any protection from unfair dismissal or redundancy in a new job. A small conventional sum continues to be awarded to reflect this – probably in the region of £100–£150.

(7) The compensatory award is also subject to reduction on account of the employee's conduct.

(8) In 1994–95, the median compensatory award was £2,389.

The additional award

An additional award of between 13 and 26 weeks' pay (subject to the £210 maximum on a week's pay) is made in a situation where the employer has failed to comply with a reinstatement or re-engagement order. If the dismissal was contrary to the Sex Discrimination Act or Race Relations Act, the additional award is between 26 and 52 weeks' pay (ERA s 117).

The special award

Special rules to deal with union membership reasons were introduced by the Employment Act 1982. As part of the campaign against the closed shop, the idea was to make the dismissal of an employee for refusing to belong to a trade union prohibitively expensive in order to deter such dismissals. The special award is the main vehicle for this. Provisions whereby third parties could be joined in such proceedings meant that any order for compensation could be passed on to the trade union which had instigated the dismissal, if appropriate.

Given the link seen by the Government between the right to belong to a trade union and the right not to belong, it was felt that these two situations should be treated equally. Thus a dismissal of an employee for being a member of a trade union or taking part in its activities at an appropriate time also qualifies for enhanced compensation.

Under TULRCA s 158, the special award is payable where the employee is unfairly dismissed for one of the union membership reasons and seeks re-employment. If the tribunal decides not to make such an order, the special award will be 104 weeks' pay, subject to a minimum of £13,775 and a maximum of £27,500. If the tribunal does make such an order, and the employer does not comply, the special award will be 156 weeks' pay, subject to a minimum of £20,600. There is no maximum limit on this. All these figures are subject to annual review, although not usually changed that frequently.

In 1993 this provision was extended to employee representatives dismissed on certain health and safety grounds (s 100), and subsequently it has been applied to employees who act as pension fund trustees (s 102) or as representatives for statutory consultation purposes (s 103).

ENFORCEMENT OF THE CONTRACT OF EMPLOYMENT

The relatively low levels of compensation for unfair dismissal coupled with the virtual dead letter of the re-employment order has prompted a rekindled interest in actions at common law in situations of dismissal or threatened dismissal in the search for a more effective remedy.

Irani v *Southampton and SW Hants HA*

[1985] ICR 590 Chancery Division

The employee was an ophthalmologist who worked part-time at a hospital run by the authority. His contract therefore incorporated National Health Service terms and conditions ('the blue book') which contained a procedure dealing with disputes between employees (section 33) and a disciplinary procedure (section 40).

The employee quarrelled with the consultant ophthalmologist and the dispute escalated. Instead of following the procedures in the blue book, the authority used an *ad hoc* procedure and decided that the employee's contract should be terminated. This was because they considered that he and the consultant could no longer work together; they had no complaints about the employee's work. The employee brought an action for declarations that the dismissal was unlawful and that the procedure should have been followed, and an injunction to prevent the dismissal taking effect until the proper procedures had been implemented.

Warner J: 'Mr Clifford put forward as his primary submission that there was a clear rule that the court would not grant specific performance of a contract of employment or, in general, grant an injunction to restrain a breach of it and that there were no special circumstances here which would justify my granting an injunction the effect of which would be to compel the defendant authority to continue to employ Mr Irani until the trial or at all events until it had in the meantime completed the procedure under section 33.

The authorities that have been cited to me in the course of the argument evince three schools of thought among the judiciary as to the effect of the wrongful dismissal of a servant. Those three schools of thought are represented by the three members of the Court of Appeal in *Gunton* v *Richmond-upon-Thames London Borough Council*. Shaw LJ belonged to what I think is the old school, which holds that a wrongful dismissal constitutes a repudiation of the contract of employment and one which, exceptionally, brings the contract to an end even though it is not accepted by the other party to the contract, that is to say the employee. That was described during the argument before me as the "unilateralist" view. Buckley LJ took the opposite view that a contract of employment is no exception to the general rule that a repudiation of a contract by one party does not bring the contract to an end unless that repudiation is accepted by the other party. That has been described in the argument before me as the "acceptance" view. Brightman LJ took what seems to be a middle view, namely that the effect of the wrongful dismissal was to terminate the status or relationship of master and servant but not every provision of the contract.

In *Reg.* v *East Berkshire Health Authority, ex parte Walsh* May LJ expressed his agreement with the view of Browne-Wilkinson J as President of the Employment Appeal Tribunal in *Robert Cort & Son Ltd* v *Charman* that "this difficult question of the effect of an unaccepted wrongful dismissal is still unresolved". It was common ground between Mr Harwood-Stevenson and Mr Clifford that it would be right for me to leave it unresolved despite a powerfully reasoned judgment of Sir Robert Megarry V-C in *Thomas Marshall (Exports) Ltd* v *Guinle* in which he came down firmly in favour of the acceptance view. I was urged by both counsel to leave the resolution of that question for the purposes of the present case to the trial judge.

Mr Clifford's submission was that, even if the acceptance view was correct, I should apply the clear rule of this court that it would not grant specific performance of a contract of employment or in general grant an injunction to restrain a breach of such a contract. He submitted that *Hill* v *CA Parsons & Co Ltd* was the only case where that rule had been departed from to the extent of the court granting an injunction to compel an employer to continue employing an employee whom he had dismissed, that that case, as was emphasised in the case itself and in subsequent authorities, was quite exceptional and that the considerations underlying it did not apply here. I shall come to *Hill* v *CA Parsons & Co Ltd* in a moment but I think that I must approach the relevant authorities with the reasons for the general rule on which Mr Clifford relied in mind. They were expressed by Geoffrey Lane LJ in *Chappell* v *Times Newspapers Ltd* where he said:

"Very rarely indeed will a court enforce, either by specific performance or by injunction, a contract for services, either at the behest of the employers or of the employee. The reason is obvious: if one party has no faith in the honesty or integrity or the loyalty of the other, to force him to serve or to employ that other is a plain recipe for disaster."

It is not the case here that the defendant authority has no faith in the honesty or integrity or loyalty of Mr Irani....

I think the true position here is that the defendant authority would be willing to continue employing Mr Irani were it not for the fact that they are convinced that his and Mr Walker's continued employment are incompatible.

Mr Clifford more happily, I think, expressed the distinction between this case and the *Parsons* case in this way. He said that in the *Parsons* case the defendant fought the case because it was in fear of what the trade union might do if it did not, whereas here the defendant is fighting the case because it genuinely wants to be rid of Mr Irani. But, to revert to what I said earlier when I quoted from the judgment of Geoffrey Lane LJ in *Chappell* v *Times Newspapers Ltd*, it remains the fact that the defendant authority has perfect faith in the honesty, integrity and loyalty of Mr Irani.

Turning to Megarry J's second reason for the decision in the *Parsons* case, it seems to me that there is a comparable reason here. In the *Parsons* case, Mr Hill was seeking the protection of the Industrial Relations Act 1971. Here Mr Irani is seeking the protection of section 33 of the blue book to which he is entitled if the circumstances are appropriate.

Thirdly, as Mr Harwood-Stevenson has pointed out, this is a case – and I anticipate now on what I shall have to say in a moment about some subsidiary submissions of Mr Clifford – where damages would not be an adequate remedy.'

COMMENT

(1) This judgment highlights the two main issues in relation to the grant of equitable remedies to employees to prevent a breach of their contracts of employment. First, the idea that specific performance, or an injunction amounting to specific performance, should not be granted in relation to contracts involving personal service. Second, that in any case a dismissal in breach of contract cannot be prevented anyway, because the employer's action brings the contract to an end regardless of whether or not the employee accepts the situation.

(2) So far as the first issue is concerned, this case is typical of a number where temporary orders have been granted. The fact that the employer retains confidence in the employee has been treated as crucial in any situation where the employee is seeking reinstatement, although not necessarily where the aim is to force the employer to carry out a disciplinary procedure properly. Another condition appears to be that the plaintiff should seek not a permanent order, but just something that will enable the status quo to be maintained while the proper procedures are carried out. See also *Powell* v *Brent LBC* and *Robb* v *Hammersmith & Fulham LBC*.

(3)   Employees of public authorities, if they are able to show a sufficient 'statutory underpinning' of their contracts of employment, may be able to challenge dismissal by means of an action for judicial review: see, for example, *McLaren* v *Home Office*.

9   Redundancy and transfers of undertakings

In the 1960s, the overmanning of British industry was seen as a major problem. Today, the need to reduce staff costs in order for the business to survive and to have the flexibility necessary to respond quickly to technological developments or changing economic conditions are major reasons for shedding workers. Problems of this kind need not always result in dismissals: retraining and redeployment, reduced recruitment, early retirement, abolition of overtime, reduction in hours and even short-time working are examples of other measures which can be utilised. However, it is likely that at some point some staff will lose their jobs involuntarily.

By the mid-1960s a number of trade unions had concluded severance agreements with employers, providing for procedures to be followed and payments to be received when workers were made redundant. The Redundancy Payments Act 1965 institutionalised and spread the practice of compensating employees thrown out of work, building on what had happened in some sectors as a result of collective bargaining.

Lloyd v Brassey

[1969] 2 QB 98 Court of Appeal

Lord Denning MR: ' ... As this is one of our first cases on the Redundancy Payments Act, 1965, it is as well to remind ourselves of the policy of this legislation. As I read the Act, a worker of long standing is now recognised as having an accrued right in his job; and his right gains in value with the years. So much so that if the job is shut down he is entitled to compensation for loss of the job – just as a director gets compensation for loss of office. The director gets a golden handshake. The worker gets a redundancy payment. It is not unemployment pay. I repeat "not". Even if he gets another job straightaway, he nevertheless is entitled to full redundancy payment. It is, in a real sense, compensation for long service. No man gets it unless he has been employed for at least two years by the employer; and then the amount of it depends solely upon his age and length of service ... '

COMMENT

(1)   The main purpose of providing for compensation in case of redundancy was to sweeten the pill of job loss, in the hope of making redundancy situations more acceptable to employees and trade unions. The result is that the focus of trade union reaction to the announcement of redundancies has shifted from outright opposition and an attempt to get the decision reversed to negotiation about the terms on which the redundancies will be carried out.

(2) The law relating to redundancy is now consolidated as Part XI of the Employment Rights Act 1996. Between 1965 and 1972, when the action for unfair dismissal became available, a redundancy payment was the only statutory remedy obtainable on dismissal, and so the cases from that period involve employees claiming to be redundant while the employers argue that the dismissal was for some other reason. However, as compensation levels for unfair dismissal are distinctly higher than redundancy payments, since 1972 it is almost more common to find cases where the employer is the one arguing that the dismissal was for redundancy while the employee claims it was for a different reason – and unfair.

(3) This is another area where European Community law has had a considerable effect, although opinions are divided as to whether all the effects can be regarded as beneficial. The Acquired Rights Directive (EC/77/187) was enacted in English law through the Transfer of Undertakings (Protection of Employment) Regulations 1981. Its relationship with existing law on redundancy and unfair dismissal is not entirely clear, even now.

ENTITLEMENT TO CLAIM

The categories of worker entitled to claim redundancy payments is the same as for unfair dismissal, except that it also includes the police (see p 273). Most importantly, they must be employees and they must have been employed for two years. As with unfair dismissal, the burden of proof is on the applicant if there is any dispute as to whether the qualifying conditions have been met or whether the employee was dismissed. The definition of 'dismissal' for the purpose of a redundancy claim is found in ERA s 136; it is cast in the same terms as for unfair dismissal under s 95: on this, see pp 273ff. A particular problem in redundancy cases is presented where the employer, following good industrial relations practice, gives the workforce as much notice as possible of impending redundancies, and employees want to leave for other jobs ahead of the final shutdown.

Doble v Firestone Tyre and Rubber Co Ltd

[1981] IRLR 300 Employment Appeal Tribunal

The company announced in November that it would be closing its Brentford plant on 15 February, and that staff would receive redundancy notices to expire on that date as they became due. The staff were apparently entitled only to statutory notice periods, so the dates depended on length of service. The employee left early, and then claimed a redundancy payment. The employers argued that he had not been dismissed.

Waterhouse J: ' ... The broad submission made by counsel for the appellants is that that announcement constituted a notice of dismissal because a document of this kind amounts to notice of dismissal if either the date on which an individual employee's contract will be terminated is specified in the document or the announcement contains material from which that state can be identified with precision. In support of that proposition the appellant has relied principally upon the oft-cited judgment of Widgery J (as he then was) in *Morton Sundour Fabrics Ltd v Shaw*.

That case establishes that there can be no notice of dismissal unless the document relied upon specifies the actual date of termination of an individual employee's contract or the date can be ascertained precisely from the document. It is necessary to stress, however, that the finding by the Divisional Court in that case was that there was no such identifiable date in the document and that, therefore, the argument that there had been a dismissal could not be upheld. What the Divisional Court did not decide was that, if a document of this kind does indicate a date on which a factory is to close, or even when an individual employee's employment is likely to be terminated, the necessary conclusion is that there has been a dismissal or notice of dismissal. On the contrary, Widgery J, in dealing with one branch of the argument put forward on behalf of the appellant in that case, said

"It seems to me that however one looks at this case, the employee has the perfectly secure right if he thinks fit to wait until his contract is determined, to take his redundancy payment, and then see what he can do in regard to obtaining other employment. If he does, and one can appreciate that there may be compelling reasons, choose to leave his existing employment before the last minute in order to look for a new job before the rush of others competing with him comes, then that is up to him. The effect of the employer's warning is not in any way to derogate from his statutory rights but to give him an alternative which, if he is so minded, he can accept."

That was a helpful warning to employees who are faced with the kind of dilemma that faced the appellant in the present case, and it is perhaps unfortunate that the learned judge's words have not been more widely publicised.

Looking at the facts of the instant case, we are fully satisfied that the industrial tribunal were right to conclude that there was no dismissal; indeed, the conclusion was an inescapable one from the history that we have related.

The first reason for that conclusion is that we do not accept the argument that the date when this appellant's contract of employment was to be terminated was specified in the document or that it was ascertainable with precision therefrom. The passages that we have cited indicated that discussions were to take place and that the implementation of any necessary redundancies was to be a matter of consultation and review as the discussions progressed. It is unnecessary to cite all the relevant material but there was express reference to the fact that consultations were to take place with union representation in order to determine the selection for redundancy. Later in the statement it was said that it was planned to maintain production until 15.2.80, but that was not stated to be a final decision and the question whether any employees might be made redundant before 15.2.80 was still open to discussion, because the statement referred only to the "present" intention of the respondents at the time of the announcement; their plans would be kept under constant review. Again, the announcement stated that individual notices of termination of employment would be issued at appropriate times to those employees who were selected for redundancy. It seems to us quite impossible therefore to say that this statement resolved, so to speak, the position of the individual appellant and we cannot infer that it fulfilled even the first requirement considered by the Divisional Court in the *Morton Sundour Fabrics* case.

The second major reason for rejecting the argument on behalf of the appellant is that we do not consider that this statement to employees could be construed as a notice to individual employees in any event. It was not a statement directed to individual employees: it was handed to branch secretaries of the unions at the beginning of the consultation process in pursuance of s 99 of the Employment Protection Act 1975 [see now TULRCA s 188], and it was circulated by the branch secretaries for information to their own members. When the notices mentioned in the statement were issued later, they were individual notices addressed to the employees concerned and handed to them by departmental managers or other senior employees of the respondents.

The decision of the industrial tribunal on the interpretation of the statement of 14.11.79 was, therefore, correct and we are unable to uphold the appellant's arguments … '

COMMENT

(1)   In so far as the purpose of the redundancy legislation is to ease the process by making employees more willing to accept redundancy, it seems counter-productive to take such a strict approach to the giving of notice. The message for the employee is to hang on at all costs until the notice is actually given.

(2)   Where notice has actually been given to the employee, then he or she may give notice to leave early and yet retain his or her right to a redundancy payment. Provision is made for this under ERA s 142 – but it contains traps for the unwary. First, the employee's notice must be given within the 'obligatory period', which is that period of notice to which she is entitled by statute. Thus if under her contract she is entitled to, and is given, three months' notice, but her statutory entitlement would be only five weeks, she must give notice within the last five weeks if she wants to leave early but keep her redundancy payment. Second, the employer is not bound to accept the situation and can serve a further notice requiring the employee to stay to the end. If she does not do so, it will be up to the tribunal to decide what part, if any, of her redundancy payment she should receive.

(3)   Assuming that a dismissal is admitted or proved, the next stage is to consider whether it was for redundancy. As there is a statutory presumption of dismissal for redundancy under ERA s 163(2), it follows that it is for the employer to disprove this; a point made dramatically in the next case.

Willcox v Hastings

[1987] IRLR 298 Court of Appeal

Willcox and Lane both worked for a small business owned by Willcox's father. Willcox senior sold it to Mr and Mrs Hastings, who both intended to work in the business and therefore required one fewer employee. In fact, as they wanted their son to work in the business too, both Willcox and Lane were surplus to requirements. They both claimed redundancy payments.

Sir John Donaldson MR: ' … Returning to paragraph 7 of the industrial tribunal's reasons, they said:

"The question which now arises under that section is that, having found as a fact that the requirements for employees have diminished within the terms of that section, we still have to decide whether or not the dismissal of either or both of these applicants is attributable 'wholly or mainly' to that reduction. Here we find ourselves in serious difficulty again. It is certainly true that by virtue of Mrs Hastings' arrival as a working partner, there was a reduction of one in the requirements for employees. But the other reason for dismissal was clearly the introduction of Mr and Mrs Hastings' son into the business, which is thus another reason explaining the dismissal of these two applicants. It seems that the two reasons, redundancy on the one hand arising from the introduction of Mrs Hastings, and the introduction of her son on the other, operate equally in respect of both of these applicants. It is impossible to distinguish between them. We cannot look at either of these applicants and say 'He was dismissed by reason of redundancy' or that 'He was dismissed by reason of the introduction of the junior Mr Hastings'. The reasons are equal in their application. It seems an extremely narrow point, but we are unanimous that in the circumstances it is impossible for us to find that either of these applicants was dismissed 'wholly or mainly' by reason of the redundancy which arose because of the introduction of Mrs Hastings. In the circumstances we feel compelled to find that there is no entitlement to redundancy payment, but that we are precluded from considering whether or not either or both of these applicants could establish that he was unfairly dismissed."

What is said about that is that there is no trace whatsoever of the tribunal having taken account of [ERA s 163(1)], which provides as follows:

"Any question arising under this Part as to the right of an employee to a redundancy payment, or as to the amount of a redundancy payment, shall be referred to and determined by an industrial tribunal."

Then subsection (2), which is the important subsection:

"For the purposes of any such reference, an employee who has been dismissed by his employer shall, unless the contrary is proved, be presumed to have been so dismissed by reason of redundancy."

The Employment Appeal Tribunal on appeal from the Industrial Tribunal thought that, on a proper reading of paragraph 7, the contrary had been proved. For my part I do not think that that is right.

The reasons given by an industrial tribunal, like the reasons given by a judge in his judgment, are not to be construed with the exactitude of a statute. The question is what is the message which is being conveyed by the judgment or, in this case, by the reasons of the tribunal. The message that I get from paragraph 7 is quite simply this. Two people were dismissed. Two people had to be dismissed because there was a reduction in the requirements of the business to the extent of one employee, and another employee had to make way for the proprietor's son. That is uncontroverted. They then go on to say, "There is no way in which we can decide which reason operated in respect of which employee. We are simply left with two employees leaving the service of the employer and two reasons, each of which could have been the cause of the departure of one such employee. In those circumstances, we just do not know. Maybe both operated on each. We just do not know." Had they then added in the presumption, they must, as I think, have reached the conclusion that the employer had failed to rebut it. As is accepted by Mr Marr-Johnson, appearing for the employers, each case has to be looked at individually. This is not a bulk application. Mr Lane is entitled to say on the findings of the industrial tribunal, "They do not know whether I was dismissed wholly or mainly on account of redundancy. Therefore I am entitled to rely on the presumption." Mr Willcox junior is similarly able to say, "They do not know. I can rely on the presumption."

It is an unsatisfactory feature of this particular case that the Solomonic answer is without doubt that there should be one redundancy payment to be divided between the two applicants. It is an injustice if neither applicant can claim a redundancy payment. It is an injustice to the employers if they have to pay two redundancy payments. But we have to administer the law as it is, and, in my judgment, if the presumption in [ERA s 163(2)] is brought into account, as it does not appear to have been brought into account by the industrial tribunal, then these two applicants succeed.

I would allow the appeal accordingly.'

(Nourse and Glidewell LJJ agreed.)

THE DEFINITION OF REDUNDANCY

Two situations count as redundancy under the legislation. They may loosely be described as first, dealing with the shutdown of the business (or part of it) and second, dealing with overmanning.

Cessation of business

Employment Rights Act 1996

139. (1) For the purposes of this Act an employee who is dismissed shall be taken to be dismissed by reason of redundancy if the dismissal is wholly or mainly attributable to—
    (a) the fact that his employer has ceased or intends to cease—
        (i) to carry on the business for the purposes of which the employee was employed by him, or
        (ii) to carry on that business in the place where the employee was so employed, ...

Moon v *Homeworthy Furniture (Northern) Ltd*

[1977] ICR 117 Employment Appeal Tribunal

Kilner Brown J: ' ... The appeal raises a novel and important issue under the new legislation.

It was a case where a complete factory was closed down and the whole of the work force made redundant. Mr Stephenson, counsel for the employees, made it plain at the outset that there was a challenge to the validity of the redundancy process and that there was not a genuine redundancy situation. There was no suggestion that it was a contrived redundancy in any sinister sense but that the employees did not accept that it was justifiable to say that the factory was not economically viable. Broadly put, they considered that it was unfair to the work force to close down the factory, unfair to declare redundancy and therefore dismissals resulting therefrom must also be unfair.

With admirable perspicacity the chairman of the industrial tribunal recognised the inherent difficulties in this line of argument. He inquired how far the industrial tribunal could go into policy decisions of a board of directors on trading and economic matters. He had in mind, and kept in mind, that the definition of redundancy was to be found in [ERA s 139(1)]. Redundancy arises where in fact the employer has ceased or intends to cease to carry on business or where there is a reduced requirement of labour. However, in order to determine the scope of the inquiry and to delineate the area of the evidence it was agreed to call a director of the employers, Mr Bullard, to give evidence as to what had happened and why it had happened and he was cross-examined along the lines of the general views and beliefs of the work force. One thing emerged with clarity and that was that there was a history of unhappy industrial relations, an involvement of trade union representatives on a local and national level, and an enlistment of the services of the local Member of Parliament. It is obvious, therefore, that when matters have reached this sort of pitch nothing that the employers did would be likely to be acceptable and a trading decision would be regarded as a cloak for an industrial relations decision. As a result of Mr Bullard's evidence it must have seemed plain to most people that there were genuine economic problems. It was still not accepted by the employees that they were sufficiently genuine to oust all political or industrial reasons. Nevertheless one common factor emerged and that was that, whatever the rights and wrongs of the original and persistent labour troubles, the economic difficulties both preceded and succeeded the labour difficulties. It was a classic instance of the age old problem as to whether or not the chicken or the egg came first. The irrelevance and futility of the question is matched only by the irrelevance and futility of the answer ...

There are no reported decisions on the critical issue in the present case. The cases referred to under the previous jurisdiction concern the application of a redundancy situation on the grounds of unfair operation of redundancy notices either by method or by selection. In *Ram v Midland Motor Cylinder Co Ltd* Sir Hugh Griffiths, in the National Industrial Relations Court, said:

"Although it is an unlikely situation the court does not exclude the possibility of a redundancy dismissal being unfair albeit it was because a particular works was closed."

Those remarks may well have had significance under the Industrial Relations Act 1971, and in any event were made in passing and merely touching upon a hypothetical situation unlikely to arise. We are now faced with such a situation in reality, unhampered and unsupported by any authority.

After the evidence of Mr Bullard was given, the chairman of the industrial tribunal with acute cogency asked Mr Stephenson whether or not he accepted that there was a cessation of work and therefore a closure. With integrity and common sense Mr Stephenson conceded the point. Technically, therefore, a redundancy situation was proved up to the hilt. But Mr Stephenson hung on to his proposition that if the reason of redundancy was relied on it ought to be open to challenge the declaration of redundancy on its merits ...

Notwithstanding the care and the ability with which Mr Stephenson put his case, we are unable to criticise the way in which the chairman handled the matter or to find fault with his reasoning. However we would prefer to put the matter on a much broader and, in our view, more important basis.

The employees were and are seeking to use the industrial tribunal and the Employment Appeal Tribunal as a platform for the ventilation of an industrial dispute. This appeal tribunal is unanimously of the opinion that if that is what this matter is all about then it must be stifled at birth, for it was this imaginary ogre which brought about the demise of the National Industrial Relations Court. The Act of 1974 has taken away all powers of the courts to investigate the rights and wrongs of industrial disputes and we cannot tolerate any attempt by anybody to go behind the limits imposed on industrial tribunals.

The result is therefore that whether this appeal is considered upon the basis on which it was argued or on the more fundamental basis of jurisdiction, the decision of the industrial tribunal was right and there could not and cannot be any investigation into the rights and wrongs of the declared redundancy. There are no grounds for finding any error of law and the appeals are dismissed.'

COMMENT

(1) The unwillingness of the tribunal to get drawn into anything which might look political is clearly demonstrated here, as is their equal unwillingness to usurp the managerial prerogative. It is open to employees claiming unfair dismissal, as these were, to argue that the real reason for their dismissal was something other than what the employer claims. However, it seems that if the employer has gone as far as closing down, an objectively verifiable fact, then there can be no going behind the reason.

(2) The position is less clear where the closure is partial and the issue is whether the business has ceased 'in the place where the employee was so employed'. Many employees will have express mobility clauses in their contracts: even if not express,

there may be an implied mobility term. In such a situation, is it open to either the employer or the employee to argue that it is not a true redundancy because the contract permits the employee to be moved to another place of work which has not shut down?

High Table Ltd v Horst

[1997] IRLR 513 Court of Appeal

The company provided catering services to firms in the City of London. The three applicants had worked for a number of years as waitresses at Hill Samuel until being dismissed by the company in 1993. The reason given by the company was redundancy: following a reduction in the catering service required by Hill Samuel, they were no longer needed at that venue. They argued that they were not redundant because there was an express mobility clause in their contracts, so they could have been deployed elsewhere. Thus, they claimed that their dismissals were unfair.

Peter Gibson LJ: '... Before us two main issues have emerged. The first is whether (ERA s 139(1)] imposes a contractual test, as contended for by Mr O'Dempsey, or a primarily factual test, as contended for by Mr Underwood, to determine "the place where the employee was so employed". The second is whether the reasons given by the industrial tribunal were adequate.

...

Mr O'Dempsey pointed out that in [s 139(1)] the word "employed", not "worked", was used and he submitted that it connotes "employed under the contract of employment". He said that, in the context of the subsection and having regard to the definitions of "employee" and "employer", the question, what is the place where the employee was so employed, ie by the employer, must be determined by reference to the contract of employment; if the contract contains a mobility clause, allowing the employer to require the employee to work elsewhere, "the place where the employee was so employed" extends to every place where the employee may be required to work. He sought to rely on the decision of this court in *Mumford v Boulton and Paul (Steel Construction) Ltd* as supporting the contractual test. In that case, a steel constructor worked for many years for his employer in and around London. When his employer required him to to to a site 77 miles from London, the employee refused. His employer dismissed him, claiming that he was in breach of contract in refusing. It was held that, because he had been employed on terms that only required him to work in and around London, he had not repudiated his contract but was dismissed for redundancy. But the reasoning of this court which relied on the terms of the contract went only to the question whether the employee was bound to obey the requirement to work out of the London area. None of it was directed to the question, what was the place where the employee was employed by the employee, and it is important to have in mind that, under [ERA s 163(2)], "an employee who has been dismissed by his employer shall, unless the contrary is proved, be presumed to have been so dismissed by reason of redundancy". The contrary was not proved. That decision does not assist Mr O'Dempsey.

I would add that *O'Brien v Associated Fire Alarms Ltd* was decided by this court in a similar way. Again, the question was whether employees (of a contract electricity firm) who had been employed for some years in jobs within commuting distance of their homes, and who refused the employer's requirement to work further afield, were in breach of contract justifying dismissal. Again, it was in that context that the terms of contract were considered. This court implied a term that the employees' area of work was within commuting distance of their homes and concluded that the employees were not in breach of contract and so the presumption under [s 163(2)] applied. Salmon LJ specifically referred to, but found it unnecessary to decide, "the rather difficult point as to whether the words ... 'the place where the employee was so employed' refer to the place where the employee actually worked or to the place where, under his contract of employment, the employee could be required to work".

...

Mr Underwood submitted that what he called a "plain words" construction of the statute was appropriate, the words "the place where he was so employed" clearly referring to the place where the employee actually worked and not where in theory the employer could require the employee to work. He relied in particular on the decision of the Employment Appeal Tribunal in *Bass Leisure Ltd* v *Thomas*. In that case the employee was based at Coventry, but in the contract of employment the employer reserved the right to relocate the employee. When the employer closed its Coventry depot, the employee was expected to operate from a different location 20 miles away. After an unsuccessful trial, she left her employment and claimed a redundancy payment. The Employment Appeal Tribunal upheld the industrial tribunal's finding that she was entitled to that payment. Judge John Hicks QC, in a judgment which I have found most helpful, considered the language of [s 139(1)] and said:

> "We begin with the obvious but nevertheless important point that the question 'Where is X employed?' is on the fact of it a factual question. Indeed, where there is no contractual term – express or implied – requiring mobility, we do not see how it can be answered other than factually; that is to say as being equivalent to 'Where does X work?'
>
> It is arguable that that is all that needs to be said, but for ourselves we should not be disposed to maintain that contractual provisions are irrelevant, or that 'Where does X work?' is always an adequate paraphrase. The use of the words 'so employed', relating back to the phrase 'employed by [the employer]', directs attention to the relationship between the parties, and the definite article in 'the place' suggests a certain fixity which tends against equating the place of employment with, for instance, each location of a peripatetic 'place of work' successively. Without needing to consider or decide whether the parties could arbitrarily define the 'place where the employee is employed' in terms outside the limits of the objective realities, we see no reason why there cannot be valid and effective contractual terms, express or implied, evidencing or defining the place of employment and its extent within those limits, so that (for example) the place where a steel erector is employed could be the area within which he can be required to attend at construction sites to perform his duties. That is supported by the fact that the preposition before the expression to be construed is 'in' not 'at'.
>
> A construction which looks beyond those bounds and treats the 'place where the employee is employed' as including any place where he or she can contractually be required to work, whatever the nature of the term under which that requirement is imposed, whatever the limits to be observed, and whatever the conditions to be complied with before the power to impose it can be exercised, seems to us to raise substantial difficulties."

And a little later:

> "We appreciate that if a distinction such as we have recognised is drawn between different types of contractual provision there will be debatable borderline cases, but that simply reflects the infinite variety of factual situations and contractual terms, and the difficulty of applying to them a statutory test which requires the identification of a unique 'place where the employee was ... employed'.

It seems clear to us that the references to 'the place where [the employee] was ... employed' in [s 139(1)(a) and (b)] require that the location and extent of that 'place' be ascertainable, whether or not the employee is in fact to be required to move, and therefore before any such requirement is made (if it is) and without knowledge of the terms of any such requirement, or of the employee's response, or of whether any conditions upon the making of such a requirement have been complied with."

The judge carefully reviewed the authorities, finding particular assistance in the decision of the Divisional Court (Lord Parker CJ, Diplock LJ and Ashworth J) in *McCulloch* v *Moore*. There the existence of a mobility clause had been held not to prevent an employee, who had worked for his employer in Sussex and whose work there had come to an end, but who declined the employer's offer of employment elsewhere, from being entitled to a redundancy payment. The judge chose not to follow *Sutcliffe* v *Revlon Overseas Corporation* and *UK Atomic Energy Authority* v *Claydon* and concluded that the place where the employee was employed for the purposes of [s 139(1)] "is to be established by a factual inquiry, taking into account the employee's fixed or changing place or places of work and any contractual terms which go to evidence or define the place of employment and its extent, but not those (if any) which make provision for the employee to be transferred to another."

I am in broad agreement with this interpretation of the statutory language. The question it poses – where was the employee employed by the employer for the purposes of the business? – is one to be answered primarily by a consideration of the factual circumstances which obtained until the dismissal. If an employee has worked in only one location under his contract of employment for the purposes of the employer's business, it defies common sense to widen the extent of the place where he was so employed, merely because of the existence of a mobility clause. Of course, the refusal by the employee to obey a lawful requirement under the contract of employment for the employee to move may constitute a valid reason for dismissal, but the issues of dismissal, redundancy and reasonableness in the actions of an employer should be kept distinct. It would be unfortunate if the law were to encourage the inclusion of mobility clauses in contracts of employment to defeat genuine redundancy claims. Parliament has recognised the importance of the employee's right to a redundancy payment. If the work of the employee for his employer has involved a change of location, as would be the case where the nature of the work required the employee to go from place to place, then the contract of employment may be helpful to determine the extent of the place where the employee was employed. But it cannot be right to let the contract be the sole determinant, regardless of where the employee actually worked for the employer. The question what was the place of employment is one that can safely be left to the good sense of the industrial tribunal.

In my judgment, a remission on the first issue is not justified. It is plain that for all of the employees the place where they were employed by the employers was Hill Samuel and that there was a redundancy situation there which caused the employees to be dismissed ...'

(Hobhouse and Evans LJJ agreed.)

COMMENT

(1) In an important extension of the concept of redundancy the Court of Appeal here comes down in favour of the factual approach to deciding what is the place of work. In this case, of course, the effect of holding that it was redundancy was to the disadvantage of the employees because it defeated their unfair dismissal claim. But what if the company had asked them to move because of the reduction of work at Hill

Samuel and they had refused, in breach of the mobility clause? Would this be a dismissal for refusal to obey a lawful and reasonable order, or would it be a dismissal for redundancy?

(2) The question is not clearly answered here, because the point did not arise in that fashion. However, it is submitted that the tenor of the judgment suggests that such a situation should be treated as redundancy. Thus, if an employer tells an employee to move, pursuant to a mobility clause in the contract, and the employee is dismissed for refusing, it may now be necessary to ask why the employer was making the employee move. If the reason was because of a reduction of work at that workplace, the employee would appear to be entitled to a redundancy payment. This may come as a surprise to the employer, who may well think it is simply a dismissal for misconduct.

(3) This must be read in the light of ERA s 141, which provides that an employee will not be entitled to a redundancy payment if she unreasonably refuses an offer of suitable alternative employment (discussed below, p 352). An offer of the same or similar work in a different place is very likely to be a suitable alternative.

Surplus labour

Employment Rights Act 1996

139.   (1)   For the purposes of this Act an employee who is dismissed shall be taken to be dismissed by reason of redundancy if the dismissal is attributable wholly or mainly to—

...

(b)   the fact that the requirements of that business—
   (i)   for employees to carry out work of a particular kind, or
   (ii)   for employees to carry out work of a particular kind in the place where he was employed by the employer,
have ceased or diminished or are expected to cease or diminish.

Delanair Ltd v *Mead*

[1976] ICR 522 Employment Appeal Tribunal

The company manufactured car heaters for Fords. A lengthy strike at Fords in 1974 led to a knock-on problem for the company, resulting in decreased demand and severe financial difficulties. It was therefore decided that it was necessary to reduce the number of employees by 10 per cent and to alter working methods so that the work could be carried out by fewer people. The applicant was an electronics engineer who was the lamb chosen for sacrifice from his department, where one employee had to go. He successfully claimed at an industrial tribunal that this was not a redundancy and that his dismissal was unfair. The employers appealed.

Cumming-Bruce J: ' ... It is submitted by Mr Irvine, on behalf of the employers, that the industrial tribunal have applied the wrong test and have confused the diminution of work of a particular kind with the diminution of the requirement of the business for employees to carry out such work. It is clear that those two concepts differ in important respects, because the volume of work may remain the same though the requirement of the business for employees to carry it out has diminished. There are two obvious examples: (1) when a new machine is introduced which enables the same volume of work to be carried out by fewer men; (2) where there is over-manning such that on reorganisation of duties or terms and conditions of work the same volume of work is carried out by a slimmed down work force. Mr Irvine submits that this case illustrates a third example, namely, where for reasons of economy the employers introduce a new structure of management and supervision, and so reallocate duties that the same volume of work is carried out without the requirement of a foreman/supervisor to organise and oversee its performance. That such reallocation of duties may give rise to dismissal by reason of redundancy is illustrated by *Sutton* v *Revlon Overseas Corporation Ltd* and *Scarth* v *Economic Forestry Ltd*. As Sir Hugh Griffiths said in the latter case,

> "... the fallacy ... is to equate the requirement to achieve an end with the requirement ...of the business to have employees in order to achieve the end...."

Mr Newman submits that the crucial finding is the conclusion:

> "We find that the principal reason for the [employee's] dismissal was a managerial decision to reduce the number of monthly paid staff in order to save money, and we hold that his dismissal was unfair."

He submits that it is not open to a company which needs to save money to dismiss a man and claim that the reason is redundancy without attempting to decide whether the requirement of the company for that man's work has in fact diminished or is expected in the future to diminish ...

The relevant question of fact for determination is whether the employers have shown that the decision to dispense with the services of a foreman/electrician in the maintenance department was the result of an appraisal of the requirement of the business for employees to carry out that work. If such an appraisal was made and a decision taken that the work formerly done by the employee could be redistributed over the remaining staff, that reallocation of his work brought about his dismissal on the ground of redundancy. On the other hand, if a decision was taken that a monthly paid worker had to be dismissed somewhere in the business irrespective of the question whether it was practicable to redistribute his work over the remaining staff, such dismissal was on the ground of economy without such regard to the requirements of the business for employees to carry out the particular type of work as to constitute redundancy within the meaning given in [ERA s 139 (1)(b)]. We accept the criticism made by Mr Irvine of the test apparently applied by the industrial tribunal. On its face it was the wrong test, as the industrial tribunal concentrated upon the question whether there had been a diminution in the type of work and not upon the question whether the requirement of the business for employees to carry out the type of work had diminished ... '

(The EAT remitted the case for rehearing in the light of this advice.)

COMMENT

(1) Employees often feel that they are not really redundant when they see their work distributed among other people, and to some extent this decision seems to go along with that. However, it has been criticised on the ground that it involves going into the *motive* for the decision to make do with fewer staff, rather than the *fact* that this is what has been decided. If management has taken this decision, then the business's requirements for employees has diminished.

(2)   In considering this argument, however, it must also be borne in mind that in an unfair dismissal claim – as this was, and where the issue is most likely to arise – the employer has to establish the true reason for the dismissal. This does invite an examination of motives. At the very least, the employers will have to convince the tribunal that they were in a state of financial exigency and were not simply using an excuse to get rid of the applicant.

(3)   In a later decision, another EAT has explained *Delanair Ltd* v *Mead* as follows:

> 'The distinction taken in the *Delanair* case was between a decision merely to reduce the workforce without considering any redistribution of work and hence require-ment for staff; and the case where the employer did assess the situation, did decide that there was a requirement for less staff, and in particular for the employee concerned; in which case there was a redundancy ...'

(*Association of University Teachers* v *University of Newcastle*).

(4)   The employee may not be better off by persuading the tribunal that this was a situation of economising rather than redundancy. If the former, it is likely that it will be held to be a dismissal for 'some other substantial reason' and could be fair (see p 318). If so, the employee will not even get a redundancy payment.

Johnson v Notts Combined Police Authority

[1974] ICR 170 Court of Appeal

Lord Denning MR: 'Miss Johnson and Mrs Dutton were employed as clerks at a police station in Nottinghamshire. They had been so employed for over 20 years, each of them. Their hours of work were 9.30 am to 5 pm or 5.30 pm on five days of the week – Monday to Friday, inclusive. They typed reports. They filed papers. They did accounts. They answered the telephone. Before they arrived, a police officer was on duty answering the telephone, and so forth. Likewise after they left.

In 1972 the police authorities determined to reorganise the system. They wished to release police officers from the office work and put them on to the police work for which they had been trained. They proposed that the two ladies should work on separate shifts. One should work from 8 am to 3 pm for six days in the week. The other should work from 1 pm to 8 pm on those six days. Then the next week they would change over. Making allowance for meal times, this would mean a 38-hour week, which was the same number of hours as they had been working before. Their actual work would be just the same as before, but at different hours.

The ladies were offered the new hours. Each refused to accept them. Each had good reason for her refusal. She could not fit in the new hours with her duties in her home: whereas previously she had been able to do so. As each refused the new hours, the police authority gave them due notice to terminate their employment on August 11, 1972. They left. The police authority appointed two other ladies who were ready to do the new hours and accepted the employment.

The two ladies whose employment had been terminated claimed redundancy payments. The industrial tribunal rejected their claim. On appeal, the Industrial Court did likewise. The ladies now appeal to this court.

The case raises directly the meaning of the words "work of a particular kind ... "

Typical of redundancy situations are these. There may be a recession in trade so that not so many men are needed. There may be a change in the kind of work done, as from wood to fibre glass, so that woodworkers are no longer needed: see *Hindle* v *Percival Boats Ltd.*

The business may be no longer profitable so that the employer has to cut down somewhere. Or he may be overstaffed. The employer may meet such a situation by dispensing with the services of some of the men: or alternatively he may lower the wages: or put men on part time. If he does it by making a change in the terms and conditions of employment, it is due to a redundancy situation. Those who lose or leave their work in consequence are entitled to redundancy payments.

It is often difficult to know whether the employer's proposals are due to a redundancy situation or not. But at this point the statute comes in to help the employee by providing that he is presumed to be dismissed by reason of redundancy: see [ERA s 163(2)]. So in all the cases where there is a change in the terms and conditions of employment, it is for the employer to prove that it was done for efficiency, and not so as to meet a redundancy situation.

It remains to apply these principles to a change in hours of work. It is a change in the terms and conditions of employment. It does not automatically give rise to a right to redundancy payments. If the employer proves that it was due to a reorganisation so as to achieve more efficient working, the man is not entitled to redundancy payments. The decision of the Industrial Court in Scotland of *Blakeley* v *Chemetron Ltd* was, I think, correct.

A change in the hours of work is very different from a change in the place of employment. The statute expressly provides that if the requirements for employees at "the place" cease or diminish, there is a redundancy situation: see [ERA s 139(1)(b)]. But it says nothing of the like effect as to "hours" of work. If the employers require the same number of employees as before – for the same tasks as before – but require them at different hours, there is no redundancy situation. If the change in hours is unfair to a particular employee in the situation in which she finds herself, it might give rise to a claim for unfair dismissal under the Industrial Relations Act 1971: but it does not give rise to a redundancy payment.

In the present case the police authorities proved that the change in the hours of work was not due to a redundancy situation, but to a reorganisation in the interests of efficiency. The same work was done by two ladies afterwards as it was before. But they did it at different hours. I think that the industrial tribunal and the Industrial Court were quite right. I would dismiss the appeal.'

(Cairns and Stephenson LJJ agreed.)

Robinson v *British Island Airways Ltd*

[1978] ICR 304 Employment Appeal Tribunal

Before the reorganisation of the company, the applicant had been the flight operations manager, responsible to the general manager operations and traffic (Mr Owen), who was himself responsible to the general manager. Under the reorganisation, the post of general manager operations and traffic was replaced by a post of operations manager and the post of flight operations manager was abolished. The holder of the new post had to have a pilot's licence, which ruled out Mr Owen. The applicant was judged unsuitable for the new post, so both he and Mr Owen were made redundant. He claimed that it was unfair dismissal.

Phillips J: '... Cases concerning redundancy arising out of a re-organisation always cause difficulties. Certain passages in some of the judgments in *Johnson* v *Nottinghamshire Combined Police Authority* and *Lesney Products & Co Ltd* v *Nolan* have been taken as suggesting that if a dismissal has been caused by a re-organisation the reason for the dismissal cannot be redundancy. We do not think that this is the meaning of the passages, or what was intended. In truth a re-organisation may or may not end in redundancy; it all depends on the nature and effect of the re-organisation. In *Johnson* v *Nottinghamshire Combined Police Authority* there was no redundancy because in the opinion of the Court of Appeal the change in the hours of work involved in that case did not change the particular kind of work being carried on. In *Lesney Products & Co Ltd* v *Nolan* there was no redundancy because on the correct analysis of the facts (it was in the analysis of the facts that the appeal tribunal and the industrial tribunal were in error) there was no cessation or diminution of the requirement for employees to carry out work of a particular kind. The number of employees, and the nature of the work, remained the same, and all that changed was the ability to earn overtime. What has to be done in every case is to analyse the facts and to match the analysis against the words of [ERA s 139]. In doing this it is of no assistance to consider whether as a matter of impression there was or was not a "redundancy situation". The question is whether the definition is satisfied....

... There is no doubt that the employee was dismissed. To what was his dismissal attributable? It seems to us that the work done by the flight operations manager was of a "particular kind", and that the work done by the general manager operations and traffic was of a "particular kind", and that each kind was different from the other. It seems to us that the work done by the operations manager was of a "particular kind" and of a kind different from that done by the general manager operations and traffic and different from that done by the flight operations manager. Thus in our judgment it can truly be said that the dismissal of the employee was attributable to the fact that the requirements of the business for employees to carry out work of a particular kind had ceased or diminished and that each was redundant.

If this were wrong, we should be inclined to say that the circumstances constituted "some other substantial reason of a kind such as to justify the dismissal of an employee holding the position which that employee held". It seems to us that where there is a genuine re-organisation which has dislodged an employee who cannot be fitted into the re-organisation it must be open to the employer to dismiss him. But we prefer to think that in those circumstances he will usually be redundant, and thus entitled to a redundancy payment.

COMMENT

(1)   These cases illustrate some of the difficulties in applying the statutory definition. The fact that it emphasises the work to be done rather than the job package of the employee results in situations like *Johnson* or *Lesney Products* not constituting redundancy. What is particularly surprising is the apparent conclusion that dismissing more senior workers for people who can be paid less is not redundancy, nor, seemingly, unfair dismissal.

(2)   How different does the new job have to be before one can say that the employee who did the old job is redundant? In some ways, it is difficult to reconcile *Robinson* v *BIA* with *North Riding Garages* v *Butterwick*.

North Riding Garages v Butterwick

[1967] 2 QB 56   Queen's Bench Divisional Court

The employee had been employed at the garage for 30 years, becoming workshop manager. As the staff was small, he spent quite a lot of time actually working as a mechanic repairing cars. In 1965 new owners took over, who put more emphasis on the sales side of the business, which involved him in more paperwork, which he was not good at. They introduced new methods, which he had trouble adapting to. After eight months, they dismissed him, and he claimed that he was redundant. The employers argued that he had been dismissed for inefficiency and incompetence. An industrial tribunal found that it was a dismissal for redundancy.

Widgery J: 'It is, we think, important to observe that a claim under [ERA s 139(1)(b)] is conditional upon a change in the requirements of the business. If the requirement of the business for employees to carry out work of a particular kind increases or remains constant no redundancy payment can be claimed by an employee, in work of that kind, whose dismissal is attributable to personal deficiencies which prevent him from satisfying his employer. The very fact of dismissal shows that the employee's services are no longer required by his employer and that he may, in a popular sense, be said to have become redundant, but if the dismissal was attributable to age, physical disability or inability to meet his employer's standards he was not dismissed on account of redundancy within the meaning of the Act. For the purpose of this Act an employee who remains in the same kind of work is expected to adapt himself to new methods and techniques and cannot complain if his employer insists on higher standards of efficiency than those previously required; but if new methods alter the nature of the work required to be done it may follow that no requirement remains for employees to do work of the particular kind which has been superseded and that they are truly redundant. Thus, if a motor manufacturer decides to use plastics instead of wood in the bodywork of his cars and dismisses his woodworkers, they may well be entitled to redundancy payments on the footing that their dismissal is attributable to a cessation of the requirement of the business for employees to carry out work of a particular kind, namely, woodworking.

If one looks at the primary facts disclosed by the evidence in this case it is difficult to see what is the particular kind of work in which a requirement for employees has ceased or diminished. The vehicle workshop remained, as did the requirement for a workshop manager, and we do not understand the tribunal to have found that the volume of repair work had diminished to such an extent as to make the respondent's dismissal wholly or mainly attributable to that fact. The only possible conclusion which appears to us to have been open to the tribunal on the evidence was that the respondent was dismissed because he could not do his job in accordance with the new methods and new standards required by the appellants.

The tribunal seems to base its decision on the fact that a requirement for a workshop manager "of the old type" had ceased. This is probably a reference to the fact that the respondent had been required by the appellants to estimate costs, which the former owner had done for himself, but the mere fact that a reorganisation has transferred this work to the respondent does not show that the requirement of the business for employees to do this, or any other, kind of work has diminished. The only possible relevance of this evidence would be to show that the volume of repair work had been run down to such an extent that the respondent could no longer occupy his whole time in it, but the tribunal, on the totality of the evidence, does not seem to take that view.

We think that the tribunal has fallen into error by applying the wrong test in that they have not looked at the overall requirements of the business but at the allocation of duties between individuals. It is irrelevant that the duties of the new manager are not identical with the duties formerly undertaken by the respondent if the overall requirements of the business are unchanged.

The court will accordingly allow the appeal and remit the matter to the tribunal to enable the hearing to be continued in the light of this opinion.'

COMMENT

(1)   It is really quite difficult to see a distinction between this case and *Robinson*. One contrast is that here the employer wanted the employee to do the new job, unlike *Robinson*, but that should not make a difference: in theory what is being tested is the objective issue of whether there is a redundancy within the statutory definition.

(2)   It does look to some extent as if there is some flexibility which allows greater scope for the managerial prerogative. That is, if management forms the view that following reorganisation the employee is unsuitable for the new job, that will be accepted by the tribunal who will find that the employee is redundant. If management decides to give the employee the new job, the employee will be unable to argue that it involves such differences from her previous job that she is in fact redundant (in the context of technological change, see also *Cresswell* v *Board of Inland Revenue*, p 129).

(3)   Finally, it is worth noting that at the time of *Robinson*, employers were relatively willing to declare employees as redundant even in borderline cases, because they could get back half of the redundancy payment through the state Redundancy Fund. That rebate system has now been abolished, which may lead to employers taking a more rigorous approach.

(4)   One rule of thumb which is implicit in these cases is that where there is an overall reduction in staff, this tends to indicate that there is indeed a redundancy. However, this should not be applied without more consideration: it is not always the case.

(5)   What if the job which the employee has been doing disappears, but there is other work available which the employee could contractually be required to do? Can it be said in these circumstances that the employee is not redundant?

Safeway Stores plc v *Burrell*

[1997] IRLR 200 Employment Appeal Tribunal

The applicant had been employed as petrol station manager at a Safeway store site until his dismissal. The company decided to restructure its managerial organisation to reduce the layers of management. The post of petrol station manager disappeared in this reorganisation, although there was a lower-paid post of petrol station controller which was similar in some respects to the former post.

At the industrial tribunal, the applicant argued successfully that he was not really redundant: the work he had been doing was still there to be done and the restructuring was in his view 'just a cost-cutting exercise'. Safeway appealed.

Judge Peter Clark: 'What is redundancy? The basic question arises in this case, thirty years after the passing of the Redundancy Payments Act 1965, mainly due to the various tests purportedly propounded by the courts over the years. Our unavoidable task is to seek to resolve what may at first blush appear to be conflicting lines of authority in order to identify the true test or tests for deciding what is a dismissal by reason of redundancy ....

Free of authority, we understand the statutory frame-work of [s 139(1)(b)] to involve a three-stage process:

    (1)   was the employee dismissed? If so,

    (2)   had the requirements of the employer's business for employees to carry out work of a particular kind ceased or diminished, or were they expected to cease or diminish? If so,

    (3)   was the dismissal of the employee (the applicant before the industrial tribunal) caused wholly or mainly by the state of affairs identified at stage 2 above?

The position is, however, not free of authority. Far from it. It is therefore to those authorities, with the assistance of counsel, which we must now turn.

The authorities

Over the years the authorities in the Court of Appeal and this appeal tribunal and its predecessors (there is no relevant House of Lords authority) have spawned what commentators have variously dubbed "the overall requirement test", "the kind of employee test", "the contract test", "the function test", and "bumped redundancies". Can they all flow from one comparatively simple sub-subsection of an Act of Parliament; are they inconsistent with each other; if so, which is right and which is wrong?

   ...

Reduction in the work

From time to time the mistake is made of focusing on a diminution in the work to be done, not the employees who do it. One example will suffice. In *Carry All Motors Ltd* v *Pennington* the applicant before the industrial tribunal, employed as a transport clerk, was dismissed by his employers following their decision that his depot was overstaffed; they concluded that the work of the transport manager and transport clerk could be carried out by one employee only. The transport manager was retained and the applicant dismissed.

On his complaint of unfair dismissal the employer relied on redundancy as the reason for dismissal. An industrial tribunal held that the requirements of the business for employees to carry out particular work had not ceased or diminished. The same work remained. Accordingly, there was no redundancy but simply a reorganisation. The dismissal was unfair.

On appeal the Employment Appeal Tribunal reversed the industrial tribunal's findings. It held that the question was not whether the requirement for particular work had diminished, but whether the requirement for employees to do that work had diminished. Since one employee was now doing the work formerly done by two, the statutory test of redundancy had been satisfied. In reaching that conclusion, the Employment Appeal Tribunal followed and applied the approach of the National Industrial Relations Court in the case of *Sutton* v *Revlon Overseas Corporation*.

In our view *Pennington* and *Sutton* correctly applied the law to the facts in those cases. It is necessary to look at the overall requirement for employees to do work of a particular kind; not at the amount of work to be done.

Business reorganisation

A complication has arisen where there is a business reorganisation followed by dismissals. The fact that there has been a reorganisation does not of itself answer the stage 2 question one way or the other. It is simply part of the factual background. It may be relevant to an alternative ground of some other substantial reason if that is advanced by the employers.

In *Robinson* v *British Island Airways Ltd* the applicant employee worked as flight operations manager, reporting to the general manager operations and traffic. A reorganisation took place in the interests of efficiency and economy. The two former posts mentioned above were abolished and replaced by a single post of operations manager. That was a more important post than the two previous posts combined; both original postholders were dismissed and a new employee appointed operations manager. Before the industrial tribunal the applicant complained that he was not redundant and had been unfairly dismissed. The tribunal dismissed his complaint, holding that he had been dismissed fairly by reason of redundancy. The applicant's appeal to the Employment Appeal Tribunal was dismissed. In giving the judgment of this tribunal, Phillips J said this:

> "…Cases concerning redundancy arising out of a reorganisation always cause difficulties. Certain passages in some of the judgement in *Johnson* v *Nottinghamshire Combined Police Authority* and *Lesney Products & Co Ltd* v *Nolan* have been taken as suggesting if a dismissal has been caused by a reorganisation, the reason for dismissal cannot be redundancy. We do not think that this is the meaning of the passages, or what was intended. In truth, a reorganisation may or may not end in redundancy; it all depends upon the nature and effect of the reorganisation. In *Johnson* v *Nottinghamshire Combined Policy Authority* there was no redundancy because in the opinion of the Court of Appeal, the change in the hours of work involved in that case did not change the particular kind of work being carried on. In *Lesney Products & Co Ltd* v *Nolan* there was no redundancy because on the correct analysis of th facts (it was in the analysis of the facts that the appeal tribunal and the industrial tribunal were in error), there was no cessation or diminution of the requirement for employees to carry out work of a particular kind. The number of employees, and the nature of the work, remained the same, and all that changed was the ability to earn overtime. What has to be done in every case is to analyse the facts and to match the analysis against the words of [ERA s 139]. In doing this, it is of no assistance to consider whether as a matter of impression there was or was not a 'redundancy situation'. The question is whether the definition is satisfied."

Again, we adopt that analysis as a correct statement of the law, dealing as it does with the effect of the earlier Court of Appeal decisions in *Johnson* v *Lesney*, themselves consistent with the previous decision of the Court of Appeal in *Chapman* v *Goonvean*, where withdrawal of a free bus service for seven employees, who were constructively dismissed and claimed redundancy payments, was held not to give rise to dismissals by reason of redundancy, since the work continued to be performed by an identical number of new employees, recruited to replace the seven who had left.

The contract and function tests

The picture built up so far appears to us to present a clear and consistent approach to the question of whether a dismissal is by reason of redundancy, based as it is on the words of the statute. We now enter more troubled waters: the so-called "contract test".

The starting point for the development of the contract test is the Court of Appeal decision in *Nelson* v *BBC (No 1)*. In that case Mr Nelson, who conducted his own case, was employed by the BBC as a producer under the terms of their standard form contract of employment. Clause 8 was in wide terms: it gave the employer the right to direct the employee to serve wherever he may be required. In 1974 he was working under his contract of employment in the Caribbean service in a managerial, production and editorial capacity. In the interests of economy the BBC decided to terminate the Caribbean service. Mr Nelson was directed to transfer to a post of equivalent grade in overseas regional service, subject to a report being made on his suitability after three months in the new post. Mr Nelson did not like that proposal. He protested. An ultimatum was given; move or be dismissed by reason of redundancy. He still refused. Accordingly, he was dismissed.

He brought a complaint of unfair dismissal; the BBC responded by saying that he was dismissed by reason of redundancy and that the dismissal was fair. Mr Nelson contended that redundancy was not the reason for his dismissal.

The industrial tribunal apparently found that it was a term of the contract of employment that he should be employed only for programmes for the Caribbean. The tribunal went on to find that the dismissal was by reason of redundancy and that the dismissal was fair.

The Employment Appeal Tribunal dismissed Mr Nelson's appeal, reluctantly upholding the tribunal's finding that the reason for dismissal was redundancy.

The Court of Appeal reversed the decisions below. Roskill LJ concluded that the tribunal was wrong to find that redundancy was the reason for dismissal. He expressed his reasoning thus:

> "The corporation's case before the industrial tribunal was simplicity itself: 'This man was employed for the purpose of the Caribbean Service. The Caribbean Service was being shut down as a result of Treasury demands for economy. Therefore we could no longer keep him there; his services were not required; and therefore he became redundant; and because he became redundant he cannot claim to have been unfairly dismissed.'
>
> The industrial tribunal, as I said at the beginning of this judgment, accepted that argument and rejected the claim. They went into the matter with very great care. They held that Mr Nelson had become redundant. They reached that conclusion because of an argument that was apparently put forward that it was a term of Mr Nelson's employment that he should be employed for, and for all practical purposes only for, programmes for the Caribbean. That emerges very clearly from the industrial tribunal's reasons. It was said that, notwithstanding the very wide words of clause 8 of the agreement, none the less (and I read):
>
> > 'We think it was a term of Mr Nelson's contract of employment, arising by necessary implication or inference from the primary facts, that he was employed for the purposes of broadcasts to the Caribbean.'
>
> With very great respect to the tribunal, that seems to me to be an impossible conclusion as a matter of law, for this reason: it is a basic principle of contract law that if a contract makes express provision (as clause 8 did) in almost unrestricted language, it is impossible in the same breath to imply into that contract a restriction of the kind that the industrial tribunal sought to do."

Browne and Megaw LJJ agreed with the conclusion of Roskill LJ as to redundancy, but without adding any reasoning of their own.

The matter came back before the Court of Appeal following remission to an industrial tribunal for a remedies hearing: *Nelson* v *BBC (No 2)*. During the course of his judgment in the second appeal, Brandon LJ explained the basis of the first court's reasoning in this way:

> "That judgment [in *Nelson (No 1)*] shows that the attitude adopted by the corporation through its officers was substantially wrong in law, and the attitude adopted by Mr Nelson substantially right in law. By that I mean that the corporation were wrong in law in treating Mr Nelson as a person who, because the work which he was employed to do had come to an end, was redundant; and further wrong in law in asserting that the proposal which they were making to him was an offer of alternative employment rather than a proposal for reassignment under his existing contract. What the corporation was really doing, because they took an erroneous view of the legal position, was to use an unjustifiable threat of making Mr Nelson redundant as a means of persuading him to give his consent to a misdescribed proposal for which his consent was not in law required.
>
> By contrast, Mr Nelson was right in law in maintaining that, because the work which he was employed to do continued to exist, he was not redundant; and further right in law in asserting that the proposal which the corporation were making to him was not in reality an offer of alternative employment, but a proposal to reassign him to other work within

the scope of his existing contract of employment, which they were entitled to do irrespective of any consent on his part. What Mr Nelson was doing, therefore, was to assert correctly, and stand firmly on, his legal rights under his contract of employment."

What we understand the effect of *Nelson (No 1)* to be is this. Although a potential redundancy situation existed when it was decided to close the Caribbean service, because, contrary to the industrial tribunal's finding, Mr Nelson's contract of employment provided that he could be directed to serve wherever he was required, his eventual dismissal was not by reason of the closure of the Caribbean service but because of his refusal to transfer as directed. That was not a dismissal by reason of redundancy. The effective cause of his dismissal was his refusal to transfer. The reason why the BBC lost their case was on a pleading point. The only reason which they advanced for the dismissal was redundancy; no alternative reason was advanced, and in the absence of establishing a prescribed reason it followed that the dismissal was unfair.

It seems to us that *Nelson* is authority for no more than this proposition: where a redundancy situation arises and a potentially redundant employee is directed to transfer to other work within the scope of his contract of employment, if he refuses that transfer and is then dismissed, the reason for dismissal will not be redundancy.

We turn next to *Cowen* v *Haden Carrier Ltd*. There the employee was a quantity surveyor by profession. He commenced employment with the employer in June 1977 as regional surveyor – southern region. His work in that post took him as far afield as Nigeria. In August 1978 he suffered a mild heart attack, causing him to be off work for two months. Upon his return to work, his employers wished to lighten his load by reducing the amount of travelling which he had previously carried out. He therefore agreed to accept a new post of divisional contracts surveyor, assisting the divisional surveyor, Mr O'Donnell. Subsequently, a Mr Richmond was appointed regional surveyor.

Later, the employers were looking for reductions in expenditure. Mr O'Donnell decided that there was no need for a divisional contracts surveyor; there was no alternative employment available for the employee. He was dismissed. He complained to an industrial tribunal that his dismissal was unfair.

The industrial tribunal expressed their conclusion as to the reason for dismissal with admirable conciseness in two sentences:

"We are satisfied on the evidence that the employers no longer had a requirement for a divisional contracts surveyor. There was a redundancy within the meaning of [ERA s 139]."

They found the dismissal to be fair.

The employee appealed to the Employment Appeal Tribunal; like Mr Nelson, he conducted his own case. The judgment of Browne-Wilkinson J appears at p. 225 of the report. The basis of the employee's appeal is set out at 226, 10–12:

"The employee argues that that decision involves a misdirection in law by the industrial tribunal. He submits that it cannot be said that he was redundant under [s 139(1)(b)] unless the employers have shown a diminution in the requirements of their business for employees to carry out work, not only of the kind done by a divisional contracts surveyor, but of the kind which under his contract of employment he could have been required to do. He submits, plainly correctly, that the industrial tribunal have not applied that test but have directed themselves simply to the question 'was there any longer a requirement for a divisional contracts surveyor?' The industrial tribunal had no regard to any other work which the employee under his contract of employment could have been required to carry out. Therefore, he says that there has been a fundamental misdirection in law in that the reason for dismissal under [ERA s 98(2)] has not been shown to be redundancy.

If the matter were free from authority, we would have had little hesitation in dismissing the employee's submission on that point. If one simply reads the words of [s 139] themselves, there is nothing in them which requires one to look at the terms of the particular claimant's contract of employment. What the Act on its face requires is that one should look at the business of the employer to see whether there is a diminution in the requirements of that business for employees to carry out work of a particular kind, unrelated to any definition of the work which the particular employee who is making the claim can be required to do. In practice, in the experience of all of us on this tribunal a redundancy is accepted as having been shown where it is demonstrated that the actual job which the claimant was carrying out had ceased to exist. In our experience, nobody has previously sought to say: 'Even though my job has gone, look at what I might otherwise have been required to do' and to go on to submit, as the employee does in this case, that an employer cannot show that there is a redundancy under [s 139 (1)(b)] unless he is able to show that there is a diminution in the employer's requirements, not only for the work that the claimant was actually doing, but for all types of work that he could be required to do. That is our experience of recent practice.

There being nothing in the words of the Act to support the employee's submission, and, the submission running contrary to the way in which (so far as we are aware) for a considerable time the section has been applied in practice, we would not have upheld his submission."

Pausing there, we should have thought that the Employment Appeal Tribunal's initial view, expressed by Browne-Wilkinson J, was plainly and obviously correct.

However, the appeal tribunal did not maintain that preliminary view. It went on to hold that it was bound by the Court of Appeal decision in *Nelson* to arrive at a conclusion which did not accord with its view of the correct construction of the statute. That conclusion is expressed in this way:

"We are unable to treat the composite effect of those two decisions of the Court of Appeal [in *Nelson*] as being other than a decision binding on us that in considering [ERA s 139(1)(b)] it is not sufficient in order to establish redundancy to show merely that the requirements of the employers for employees to carry out work of the kind on which the employee was actually engaged has ceased or diminished: it is necessary to show such diminution or cessation in relation to any work that he could have been asked to do."

The employee's appeal was allowed and leave was given to the employer to go to the Court of Appeal.

The Court of Appeal allowed the appeal and restored the decision of the industrial tribunal. In reaching that decision, the Court of Appeal did not decide any of the arguments advanced in the original notice of appeal, but allowed the appeal solely on a further ground introduced by way of amendment during the hearing of the appeal. ...

In our judgment, the approach of both the majority and minority members of the tribunal and the submissions of counsel must be rejected.

The correct approach

Like the appeal tribunal in *Cowen* v *Haden Carrier*, we started by looking at the statute and construing the words free of authority. Similarly, we have looked at the authorities. Unlike that tribunal, we return to our original approach and conclude first that it was correct, and secondly that no binding authority causes us to abandon that position. We would summarise it as follows:

(1)   There may be a number of underlying causes leading to a true redundancy situation;

our stage 2. There may be a need for economies; a reorganisation in the interests of efficiency; a reduction in production requirements; unilateral changes in the employees' terms and conditions of employment. None of these factors are themselves determinative of the stage 2 question. The only question to be asked is: was there a diminution/cessation in the employer's requirement for *employees* to carry out work of a particular kind, or an expectation of such cessation/diminution in the future [redundancy]? At this stage it is irrelevant to consider the terms of the applicant employee's contract of employment. That will only be relevant, if at all, at stage 3 (assuming that there is a dismissal).

(2) At stage 3 the tribunal is concerned with causation. Was the dismissal attributable wholly or mainly to the redundancy? Thus –

   (a) Even if a redundancy situation arises, as in *Nelson*, if that does not cause the dismissal, the employee has not been dismissed by reason of redundancy. In *Nelson* the employee was directed to transfer to another job as provided for in his contract. He refused to do so. That was why he was dismissed.

   (b) If the requirement for employees to perform the work of a transport clerk and transport manager diminishes, so that one employee can do both jobs, the dismissed employee is dismissed by reason of redundancy. See *Pennington*. The same explanation applies, on the facts, to the eventual decision in *Robinson*. In *Cowen* v *Haden Carrier* the requirement for employees to do the work of a divisional contracts surveyor ceased. The postholder was dismissed. That was a dismissal by reason of redundancy.

   (c) Conversely, if the requirement for employees to do work of a particular kind remains th same, there can be no dismissal by reason of redundancy, notwithstanding any unilateral variation to their contracts of employment. See *Chapman, Lesney* and *Johnson*.

   (d) The contract versus function test debate is predicated on a misreading of both the statute and the cases of *Nelson* and *Cowen* v *Haden Carrier*. Save for the limited circumstances arising from *Nelson* where an employee is redeployed under the terms of his contract of employment and refuses to move, and this causes his dismissal, the applicant/employee's terms and conditions of employment are irrelevant to the questions raised by the statute.

   (e) This explains the concept of "bumped redundancies". Take this example: an employee is employed to work as a fork-lift truck driver, delivering materials to six production machines on the shop floor. Each machine has its own operator. The employer decides that it needs to run only five machines and that one machine operator must go. That is a stage 2 redundancy situation. Selection for dismissal is done on the LIFO principle within the department. The fork-lift truck driver has the least service. Accordingly, one machine operator is transferred to driving the truck; the short-service truck driver is dismissed. Is he dismissed by reason of redundancy? The answer is yes. Although under both the contract and function tests he is employed as a fork-lift driver, and there is no diminution in the requirement for fork-lift drivers, nevertheless there is a diminution in the requirement for employees to carry out the operators' work and that has caused the employee's dismissal. See, for example, *W Gimbert & Sons Ltd* v *Spurett; Elliot Turbomachinery* v *Bates*. In our judgment, the principle of "bumped" redundancies in statutorily correct, and further demonstrates the flaw in the "contract test" adumbrated in *Pink*.

   (f) Our approach is also consistent with the decision of the Court of Appeal in *Murphy* v *Epsom College*. There, the applicant was one of two plumbers employed by a school. His work consisted mainly of general plumbing work. The employers decided to employ a heating technician to maintain their improved heating system. They then decided to dismiss one of the two plumbers and selected the employee for dismissal. The Court of Appeal upheld the majority view of the industrial tribunal that the reason for dismissal was redundancy. The employer originally had two plumbers; now it only required one. The employee was dismissed by reason of redundancy.

The instant case
In our judgment the tribunal fell into error in the following respects:
(1) The majority failed to apply the correct statutory test in finding that the applicant's dismissal was not by reason of redundancy. It failed to ask itself whether there was a stage 2 redundancy situation, looking at the overall requirement of the employer for employees to carry out work of a particular kind, and then to consider whether that redundancy situation caused the applicant's admitted dismissal.
(2) The majority failed to consider whether Safeway had, in the alternative, established some other substantial reason for dismissal.
(3) It follows that the tribunal made no finding as to whether or not the employer acted reasonably in treating the true reason for dismissal as a sufficient reason.

The appeal is allowed.'

COMMENT

(1) This judgment is a brave attempt to rid the law of heresy, and the argument is convincing. If the employee is redundant, his or her dismissal may yet be unfair if the employer makes no effort at redeployment. However, the fact that the employee could be redeployed under his or her contract does not mean that the employee is not redundant just because he or she is not so redeployed.

(2) This approach raises another issue, however. If the employee's regular job disappears and he or she is directed to do other work which is within the terms of his or her contract, can the employee decline and claim a redundancy payment? *Nelson* v *BBC*, as explained here, suggests not. But consider the analogy with *High Table Ltd* v *Horst*, above, p 336.

OFFER OF SUITABLE ALTERNATIVE EMPLOYMENT
Employment Rights Act 1996

141. (1) This section applies where an offer (whether in writing or not) is made to an employee before the end of his employment—
     (a) to renew his contract of employment, or
     (b) to re-engage him under a new contract of employment,
     with renewal or re-engagement to take effect either immediately on, or after an interval of not more than four weeks after, the end of his employment.
     (2) Where subsection (3) is satisfied, the employee is not entitled to a redundancy payment if he unreasonably refuses the offer.
     (3) This subsection is satisfied where—
     (a) the provisions of the contract as renewed, or of the new contract, as to—

(i) the capacity and place in which the employee would be employed, and

(ii) the other terms and conditions of his employment,

would not differ from the corresponding provisions of the previous contract, or

(b) those provisions of the contract as renewed, or of the new contract, would differ from the corresponding provisions of the previous contract but the offer constitutes an offer of suitable employment in relation to the employee.

COMMENT

(1) Note that there are two separate questions here: first, whether the employment offered is suitable, and second, whether the employee acted unreasonably in refusing it. The first suggests an objective examination of the offer while the second permits consideration of the personal equation; however, in *Spencer* v *Gloucestershire CC* it was pointed out that many of the factors relevant to both questions are the same, and that in practice it may be difficult, and perhaps not desirable, to attempt to draw a line between them.

Taylor v *Kent CC*

[1969] 2 QB 560 Queen's Bench Divisional Court

The applicant had been headmaster of a boys' school which was merged with a girls' school; his appointment was therefore terminated. He was offered a post as one of a pool of mobile teachers to be sent out to schools as and when required: his salary entitlement would remain the same. The council opposed his claim for a redundancy payment on the ground of his refusal to accept this offer.

Lord Parker CJ: '... Let me say at once, suitability is almost entirely a matter of degree and fact for the tribunal, and not a matter with which this court would wish to or could interfere, unless it was plain that they had misdirected themselves in some way in law, or had taken into consideration matters which were not relevant for the purpose. It is to be observed that so far as age was concerned, so far as qualifications were concerned, so far as experience was concerned, they negative the suitability of this offer, because he is going to be put into a position where he has to go where he is told at any time for short periods, to any place, and be put under a headmaster and assigned duties by him.

The only matter which can be put against that as making this offer suitable is the guarantee of salary under Scale Q. One would think, speaking for myself, that for a headmaster of this experience, he would think an offer which, while guaranteeing him the same salary, reduced his status, was quite unsuitable. To go to quite a different sphere of activity, a director under a service agreement of a company is offered on dismissal a job as a navvy, and it is said: but we will guarantee you the same salary as you have been getting. I should have thought such an offer was plainly unsuitable ...

But for my part I feel that the tribunal have here misdirected themselves in law as to the meaning of "suitable employment". I accept, of course, that suitable employment is as is said: suitable employment in relation to the employee in question. But it does seem to me here that by the words "suitable employment", suitability means employment which is substantially equivalent to the employment which has ceased. RPA s 2(3) [broadly equivalent to ERA s 141(3)(a)] which I read at the beginning is dealing with the case where the fundamental terms are the same, and then no offer in writing is needed, but when they differ, then it has to be put in writing and must be suitable. I for my part think that what is meant by "suitable" in relation to the employee means conditions of employment which are reasonably equivalent to those under the previous employment, not the same, because then subsection (2) would apply, but it does not seem to me that by "suitable employment" is meant employment of an entirely different nature, but in respect of which the salary is going to be the same. Looked at in that way, it seems to me that there could be only one answer in this case, and that is that this man was being asked to do something utterly different; as I have said, just as if a director under a service agreement with a company was being asked to do a workman's job, albeit at the same salary ...'

(Melford Stevenson and Willis JJ agreed.)

COMMENT

(1)   The importance of equivalent status as well as equivalent salary is here stressed. Other relevant factors are whether or not retraining will be necessary – and how likely it is that the employee will be able to retrain successfully; travelling time and distance (compare *O'Brien* v *Associated Fire Alarms*); domestic circumstances, and whether it is necessary for the employee to relocate. If it is, how far the employer is prepared to assist will also be relevant.

(2)   Much the same sort of things will be relevant to the question of whether the employee acted reasonably in refusing.

Thomas Wragg & Sons Ltd v Wood

[1976] ICR 313 Employment Appeal Tribunal

The employee, who was aged 56, had been given notice of redundancy on 24 October which would expire on 6 December. He found another job to start the following Monday. On 5 December he received an offer of alternative employment from his employer, which he refused.

Lord McDonald: 'The short point for decision, therefore, is whether or not the employee acted unreasonably in refusing the employers' offer of alternative employment, which indeed was the course which he adopted.

The tribunal have taken the view that the employee did not act unreasonably in refusing that offer. Their reasons for so concluding are summarised in their decision, in the following terms:

"The tribunal feels that [the employee] having committed himself to the new job, and having all the fears of a man of 56 who faces unemployment, and having received the offer not too late but ... as late in the day as within 24 hours of the expiration of his notice, was not unreasonable in refusing the offer and, consequently, he succeeds in his claim."

Counsel for the employers argued before us that this reason involved three factors and that two of those factors, as matter of law, should not be considered. The three factors were: first, that the employee had committed himself to accept a new job; secondly, that one of his reasons for refusing the employers' offer was fear of unemployment in the future in a contracting industry; and thirdly, the lateness of the offer of alternative employment.

So far as the second and third of those factors are concerned, counsel for the employers argued that those fell to be discounted completely as they were not factors which, in law, should be considered. In connection with the fears of the employee that he would or might become redundant in the near future if he accepted the employers' offer of re-engagement, our attention was directed to *James & Jones* v *National Coal Board*. That was a case in which it was certainly held that it was unreasonable on the part of employees to refuse an offer of re-engagement simply because they considered that the industry was a contracting one and that their futures were not assured. There does not appear to have been any other factor, such as the acceptance on their part of another job elsewhere, or any other consideration which fell to be taken into account; and in that situation an industrial tribunal took the view that the refusal was not reasonable. We do not, however, extract from that case the proposition that the situation in a particular industry may not be a factor which, together with others, could properly be taken into account in deciding whether or not the refusal was reasonable.

So far as the lateness of the offer is concerned, it was argued that if the statute had intended that this should be a factor falling to be taken into account in assessing reasonableness, it would have said so. On the contrary, the statute lays down a time limit and the offer was made within that time limit, albeit very late in the day. We would accept that if this was the only single factor which an employee relied upon to justify his refusal to accept an offer, and if no other factor existed, that would not be sufficient; but we do not consider that it is a matter which automatically falls to be ignored, if other considerations exist and, in particular, if the employee, as here, has sought and gained alternative employment and has accepted an offer of such alternative employment from another employer.

Accordingly the two factors which have been criticised by counsel for the employers as being wholly irrelevant as matters of law are not, in our view, irrelevant to that extent. They are factors which we consider can be taken into account, provided other factors also exist.

It is clear in the present case that a third factor does exist and it is one which counsel for the employers accepted may competently be taken into account, although he argued that standing by itself it would not suffice. That factor, of course, is the acceptance by the employee of different employment before the expiry of his notice of dismissal. Our attention in this connection was directed to *McNulty* v *T Bridges and Co Ltd*. It was stated in that case that the fact that an employee accepts the offer of employment outside his employer's company, before an offer of alternative employment by that company was made, does not necessarily mean that his refusal of the company's offer is to be treated as reasonable. We would not quarrel with that proposition, but it is very clearly a factor which is to be taken into account when considering the element of reasonableness, and that is stated in terms in the decision of the tribunal in that particular case.

In the case with which we are concerned today, this third factor is in our opinion one of great importance. The employee obviously acted with some diligence and was successful in obtaining other employment which was due to commence at the termination of his employment with the employer. In our opinion, in doing so he acted very sensibly and very reasonably. Faced at the end of his period of notice with the sudden offer of re-engagement by his employers, we consider that he did not act unreasonably in refusing that offer, having regard to the fact that he had already engaged himself in this other job.

Accordingly we consider that the tribunal did not err in law in approaching the matter as they did, namely, considering all three factors as a whole rather than considering each in isolation. For these reasons, therefore, we dismiss the appeal.'

Trial periods

Under ERA s 138, where the employer offers the employee alternative employment which is different from her previous job, the employee has a four-week trial period in the new post without prejudice to her redundancy claim. If, during this four-week period, either the employee decides for any reason to leave, or the employer dismisses her, the termination will be treated as a dismissal on the date the original contract ended, for the reason for which that contract ended (i.e. redundancy).

This means that by opting to try a new job the employee has not waived her claim for a redundancy payment (or even, perhaps, to claim unfair dismissal). It may be felt that four weeks is a rather short period in which to judge a new job. However, the statutory period has been interpreted strictly (see, e.g. *Benton* v *Sanderson Keyser*). In the next case, the possibility of a common law trial period was canvassed.

Turvey v *C W Cheney & Son Ltd*

[1979] ICR 341 Employment Appeal Tribunal

Ms P Smith: '... The four employees in this case worked as polishers for C W Cheney & Son Ltd, the employers. In May 1977, following a decline in the trade, work in the polishing department where they worked had diminished and was about to cease. The employees were so informed on June 1 and each was offered a job in a different department.

From the notes of evidence at the industrial tribunal it appears that three of the four employees said that they would take the different jobs they were offered on trial; that is to say, they did not at once make a new contract or renew the contract of employment by agreeing to the variation in its terms, namely, that they should work in a different job which under their existing contract the employers could not require them to do. The evidence of the fourth suggests (though the note shows that this aspect of the problem was not fully explored) that she worked at the new job with an implied reservation that she was doing so, like the other three, on trial.

All worked in the new jobs for more than four weeks and then, finding that the new jobs did not suit them, left of their own accord. All applied to the industrial tribunal for redundancy payments. The basis of their applications was that the employers' action in informing them that there would be no more work for them in the polishing department (the only work which the employers were entitled as a matter of contract to require them to do) amounted to a repudiation of their contracts of employment; that in the circumstances they were entitled to treat their contracts as at an end themselves and did so; and that accordingly by the operation of [ERA s 136(1)(c)] they were to be treated as having been dismissed by the employers ...

It is clear law that where one party to a contract acts in such a way as to show he no longer intends to be bound, the other party can decide at his option whether or not to treat the contract as at an end. Moreover he does not necessarily have to make up his mind at once but is entitled to a reasonable time in which to do so.

The application of this common law principle to contracts of employment is illustrated in *Shields Furniture Ltd* v *Goff*, where Brightman J said that the mere fact that an employee started to work under the terms of a new contract offered him by the employer did not constitute an acceptance of the new contract so that he must be regarded as having made up his mind not to rely on the repudiation of the old contract. You have to see whether the employee is accepting the new contract by his conduct, or whether he is giving it a try to see whether he will accept it or not.

If, as in this case with the three employees, the employee says that he is giving it a trial, clearly he has not accepted the new contract simply by doing that. If having started by expressly giving it a trial he goes on working under the new terms without any more being said about it, the time will come when a reasonable time for making up his mind has expired, and he will be taken to have made a new contract or renewed the old one with variations, and he will no longer be able to rely on [s 136(1)(c)] and say: "You dismissed me." Each case will depend on its own facts, and it will be for the industrial tribunal to say whether or not, on the facts which it finds, a new contract has been made or the old contract has been renewed with variations. Since the answer must vary with the circumstances we will call the period which at common law the employee has to make up his mind period X ...'

COMMENT

(1)   It is clear that the common law trial period may be longer than the statutory trial period, although whether it was in this particular case was not decided. The EAT remitted the case for rehearing in the light of their decision.

LAY-OFF AND SHORT-TIME WORKING

Employment Rights Act 1996

147.   (1)   For the purposes of this Part an employee shall be taken to be laid off for a week if—
- (a)   he is employed under a contract on terms and conditions such that his remuneration under the contract depends on his being provided by the employer with work of the kind which he is employed to do, but
- (b)   he is not entitled to any remuneration under the contract in respect of the week because the employer does not provide such work for him.

(2)   For the purposes of this Part an employee shall be taken to be kept on short-time for a week if by reason of a diminution in the work provided for the employee by his employer (being work of a kind which under his contract the employee is employed to do) the employee's remuneration for the week is less than half a week's pay.

COMMENT

(1)   An employee who is laid off or kept on short-time for four consecutive weeks, or any six weeks within a 13-week period, may leave and claim a redundancy payment (ERA s 148). However, ERA ss 148 and 149 contain conditions for the exercise of this right, in terms of notice and counter-notice, which render this course of action potentially dangerous for an unrepresented employee, as failure to comply strictly with the rules will result in forfeiture of the right to claim.

(2)   Remember that it will be a fundamental breach of contract if the employer lays off workers or puts them on short-time without paying them unless there is an express or implied term permitting this.

CALCULATION OF THE REDUNDANCY PAYMENT

Employment Rights Act 1996

162. (1) The amount of a redundancy payment shall be calculated by—
    (a) determining the period, ending with the relevant date, during which the employee has been continuously employed,
    (b) reckoning backwards from the end of that period the number of years of employment falling within that period, and
    (c) allowing the appropriate amount for each of those years of employment.

    (2) In subsection (1)(c) "the appropriate amount" means—
    (a) one and a half weeks' pay for a year of employment in which the employee was not below the age of forty-one,
    (b) one week's pay for a year of employment (not within paragraph (a)) in which he was not below the age of twenty-two, and
    (c) half a week's pay for each year of employment not within paragraph (a) or (b).

    (3) Where twenty years of employment have been reckoned under subsection (1), no account shall be taken under that subsection of any year of employment earlier than those twenty years.

COMMENT

(1) This is virtually the same as the method for calculating the basic award for unfair dismissal, and the present maximum payment is the same: £6,300 (£210 x 30).

(2) For employees aged 64, the payment is reduced by one-twelfth for every month above that age. This means that it will taper to almost nothing if they have nearly reached retirement age by the time they are made redundant.

(3) The payment may also be reduced, or even extinguished, if the employee takes part in a strike or is dismissed for misconduct while on notice of dismissal for redundancy (ERA s 140).

(4) In the event of the employer being insolvent (which is a common cause of redundancy) the payment will be met by the Department of Employment. At one time there was a Redundancy Fund into which all employers contributed through national insurance payments. The Redundancy Fund met the obligations of insolvent employers but also paid a rebate to other employers, which at one time covered half the cost of a redundancy payment. The proportion was whittled down, then abolished in 1989.

TIME OFF TO LOOK FOR WORK

Employment Rights Act 1996

52. (1) An employee who is given notice of dismissal by reason of redundancy is entitled to be permitted by his employer to take reasonable time off during the employee's working hours before the end of his notice in order to—
    (a) look for new employment, or
    (b) make arrangements for training for future employment.

(2)   An employee is not entitled to take time off under this section unless, on whichever is the later of—
    (a) the date on which the notice is due to expire, and
    (b) the date on which it would expire were it the notice required to be given by section 86(1),
    he will have been (or would have been) continuously employed for a period of two years or more.

(3)   For the purposes of this section the working hours of an employee shall be taken to be any time when, in accordance with his contract of employment, the employee is required to be at work.

COMMENT

(1)   This seemingly generous provision is qualified by the fact that the maximum payment is two days' pay! Employees must have been employed for two years to be entitled to time off to look for work.

TRANSFERS OF UNDERTAKINGS

The sale of a business from one owner to another has redundancy implications in two main ways. First, the new owner may require fewer employees than the old owner and so the surplus workers will be redundant. Second, even if the new owner wants all the employees, a contract of employment is personal. This means that if the business is sold, the employee's contract of employment with the first owner ceases and there is a separate contract with the new owner. The ending of the first contract comes within the first limb of the definition of redundancy (cessation of business).

Consequently, the redundancy payments legislation has always made some special provision for this situation. However, the position has been complicated through the intervention of European Community law. EC/77/187, usually called the Acquired Rights Directive, was passed in order to protect the position of employees where the business is sold over their heads. It was unpopular with both political parties in the UK, and was only implemented after threats of action before the ECJ. The implementation, three years late, was carried out through the Transfer of Undertakings (Protection of Employment) Regulations 1981 (TUPE). Unfortunately, no one bothered to ensure that the regulations made sense in the context of existing redundancy law. The result is two overlapping sets of provisions whose operation may be inconsistent.

When do the Regulations apply?
Transfer of Undertakings (Protection of Employment) Regulations 1981

3.   (1)   Subject to the provisions of these Regulations, these Regulations apply to a transfer from one person to another of an undertaking situated immediately before the transfer in the United Kingdom or a part of one which is so situated.
        ...
      (4)   It is hereby declared that a transfer of an undertaking or part of one—
          (a) may be effected by a series of two or more transactions; and
          (b) may take place whether or not any property is transferred to the transferee by the transferor.

COMMENT

(1)   Regulation 2 states that, ' "Undertaking" includes any trade or business'. The original qualification, which excluded any undertaking which was not in the nature of a commercial venture, was repealed in 1993, when it became clear beyond peradventure that it was contrary to European Community law.

(2)   One of the criticisms levelled at the regulations is that they do not cover the take over of a business which is effected through a sale of shares in the business. As a company is distinct in law from its members, the identity of the employer in such a situation remains the same: the company. Yet clearly, if control of the company passes to new owners, it is very likely that there will be considerable changes in the conditions for employees. As most sales of businesses in this country are made in this way, it is argued that the regulations may have little practical effect. While this is no doubt the case, in this respect the TUPE Regulations are in accordance with the Acquired Rights Directive.

(3)   The concept of 'transfer of an undertaking' has been the subject of numerous references to the ECJ, whose decisions are vitally important to the interpretation of TUPE. The test was classically stated by the ECJ in the next case.

Spijkers v *Gebroeders Benedik Abattoir CV*

[1986] 2 CMLR 296

The plaintiff had been employed as assistant manager at an abattoir owned by Colaris. At the end of December 1982, Colaris sold the land, slaughterhouse premises and other offices to Benedik. By that stage, Colaris had ceased to carry on its commercial activity and there was no longer any goodwill in the business; Colaris was declared insolvent the following March.

Benedik began to operate an abattoir at the premises from February 1983, so that there was a gap in trading. While Benedik took on all the Colaris employees except for Spijkers and one other, it did not take over the customers of Colaris. Did the Acquired Rights Directive apply to this situation? The Dutch court referred the following specific questions to the ECJ:

(1)   Is there a transfer within the meaning of Article 1(1) of the Acquired Rights Directive where buildings and stock are taken over and the transferee is thereby enabled to continue the business activities of the transferor and does in fact subsequently carry on business activities of the same kind in the buildings in question?

(2)   Does the fact that at the time when the buildings and stock were being sold the business activities of the vendor had entirely ceased and that in particular there was no longer any goodwill in the business to prevent there being a 'transfer' as defined in question 1?

(3)   Does the fact that the circle of customers is not taken over prevent there being such a transfer?

Judgment of the Court: '... [8] Mr Spijkers submits that there is a transfer of an undertaking within the meaning of Article 1(1) of Directive 77/187 if the means of production and activities of the enterprise are transferred as a unit by one owner to another, and that it is unnecessary to decide whether, at the date of the transfer, the transferor's activities were interrupted or whether the goodwill (circle of customers and brand image) had already disappeared.

[9]   The Dutch and British Governments, as well as the Commission, consider on the other hand that the existence or otherwise of a transfer of an undertaking within the meaning described above must be assessed in the light of all the circumstances of the transaction in question such as the transfer or otherwise of tangible (buildings, movables, stocks) and intangible assets (know-how, goodwill), the nature of the activities and the cessation or not, as the case may be, of those activities at the date of transfer. However, none of these factors is decisive on its own.

[10]   In this connection the British Government and the Commission suggest that the essential criterion of the concept should be determined by reference to whether the transferee is given possession of an undertaking which is still in existence and the activities of which he can continue, or at least activities of the same type. The Dutch Government emphasises that, having regard to the social objective of the directive, the concept of transfer assumes that the transferor's activities are actually continued by the transferee in the framework of the same undertaking.

[11]   The last-mentioned view should be accepted. It appears from the general structure of Directive 77/187 and the wording of Article 1(1) that the directive aims to ensure the continuity of existing employment relationships in the framework of an economic entity, irrespective of a change of owner. It follows that the decisive criterion for establishing the existence of a transfer within the meaning of the directive is whether the entity in question retains its identity.

[12]   Consequently it cannot be said that there is a transfer of an enterprise, business or part of a business on the sole ground that its assets have been sold. On the contrary, in a case like the present, it is necessary to determine whether what has been sold is an economic entity which is still in existence, and this will be apparent from the fact that its operation is actually being continued or has been taken over by the new employer, with the same economic or similar activities.

[13]   To decide whether these conditions are fulfilled it is necessary to take account of all the factual circumstances of the transaction in question, including the type of undertaking or business in question, ithe transfer or otherwise of tangible assets such as buildings and stocks, the value of intangible assets at the date of transfer, whether the majority of the staff are taken over by the new employer, the transfer or otherwise of the circle of customers and the degree of similarity between activities before and after the transfer and the duration of any interruption in those activities. It should be made clear, however, that each of these factors is only a part of the overall assessment which is required and therefore they cannot be examined independently of each other.

[14]   The factual appraisal which is necessary to establish whether there is or is not a transfer as defined above is a matter for the national court, taking account of the detailed interpretation which has been given.

[15]   For these reasons the answers to the questions referred to the Court should be that Article 1(1) of Directive 77/187 must be interpreted to the effect that the expression "transfer of an undertaking, business or part of a business to another employer" envisages the case in which the business in question retains its identity. In order to establish whether or not such a transfer has taken place in a case such as that before the national court, it is necessary to consider whether, having regard to all the facts characterising the transaction, the business was disposed of as a going concern, as would be indicated *inter alia* by the fact that its operation was actually continued or resumed by the new employer, with the same or similar activities. …'

Dr Sophie Redmond Stichting v Bartol

[1992] IRLR 366 European Court of Justice

The Dr Sophie Redmond Stichting was a (non-commercial) Dutch foundation providing services to drug addicts. The foundation's grant was withdrawn and given to another organisation, Sigma, which took over the premises, clients and work of the foundation, and offered employment to some of the foundation's staff. The ECJ was asked whether the Acquired Rights Directive applied to this transfer.

Judgment of the Court: '... It should be recalled that in *Abels* the Court held that the scope of the provision of the Directive at issue cannot be appraised solely on the basis of a textual interpretation because of the differences between the various language versions of that provision and because of the divergences between the national legislation defining the concept of a contractual transfer.

In consequence the Court gave a sufficiently broad interpretation to that concept to give effect to the purpose of the Directive, which is to ensure that the rights of employees are protected in the event of a transfer of their undertaking, and held that that Directive was applicable wherever, in the context of contractual relations, there is a change in the legal or natural person who is responsible for carrying on the business and who incurs the obligations of an employer towards employees of the undertaking (see most recently *Bork International*).

In particular, the Court has held that the scope of the Directive covers the leasing of an establishment followed by the rescinding of that lease and the taking over of the operation by the owner herself (*Ny Mølle Kro*), the leasing of a restaurant followed by the rescinding of that lease and the conclusion of a new lease with a new lessee (*Daddy's Dance Hall*), and finally the transfer of a bar-discotheque by means of a lease-purchase agreement and the restoration of the undertaking to its owner as the result of a judicial decision (*Berg*).

As is stressed in *Bork*, where a lessee who is also the employer ceases to be the employer and a third party becomes the employer thereafter under a contract of sale concluded with the owner, the resulting transaction may fall within the scope of the Directive as defined in Article 1(1) thereof. The fact that in such a case the transfer is effected in two stages, in as much as the undertaking is first returned from the lessee to the owner and the latter then transfers it to the new owner, does not prevent the Directive from applying.

As described in the Order for reference, the transaction to which the preliminary questions put by the Kantonrechter of Groningen relate is governed by comparable reasoning. This is in fact a situation in which a local authority which finances, by a subsidy, the activities of a foundation engaged in providing assistance to drug dependants, decides to terminate this subsidy, as a result of which the activities of that foundation are terminated, in order to switch the subsidy to another foundation pursuing the same activities.

It is true that the judge making the reference asks, in his sixth question, whether the fact that the decision to make the switch is taken unilaterally by the public body, and does not result from an agreement concluded by it with the body subsidised, prevents the Directive from applying in this case.

This question must be answered in the negative.

Therefore, the reply to the questions or parts of questions relating to the interpretation of the concept of 'legal transfer' within the meaning of Article 1(1) of Directive 77/187, must be that the text must be interpreted as meaning that this concept covers the situation in which a public body decides to terminate a subsidy paid to one legal person, as a result of which the activities of that legal person are fully and definitively terminated, and to transfer it to another legal person with similar aims.'

COMMENT

(1)   Thus the fact that there is no connection between the transferor and transferee will not prevent the regulations from applying, nor the fact that there is no actual transfer of property between the parties. This paved the way for the next development.

Contracting out

Rask v ISS Kantineservice

[1993] IRLR 133 European Court of Justice

The plaintiffs had originally been employed by Philips A/S in Denmark to work in one of the four canteens at its works. In 1988 Philips made an agreement with ISS whereby Philips paid ISS a fixed monthly fee in return for which ISS took over the management of the canteens, including employment of the relevant staff. Philips provided the premises, along with heating, electricity, water, etc free of charge to ISS. Staff who were taken over were guaranteed the same salary and seniority rights.

Following a dispute over a unilateral variation in her contract of employment, Rask was dismissed. Did the Acquired Rights Directive apply to this situation?

Judgment of the Court: ' ...
On the first and second questions
By its first and second preliminary questions the national court seeks in substance to ascertain whether Article 1(1) of the Directive must be interpreted as meaning that the Directive can apply to a situation where the owner of an undertaking entrusts to the owner of another undertaking, by means of a contract, the responsibility of providing a service intended for employees, which it had previously operated directly, in return for a fee and various other benefits the terms of which are determined by the agreement made between them.

Mrs Rask and Mrs Christensen, as well as the Commission, suggest an affirmative answer to the questions as they are put. They maintain that such an agreement transfers the responsibility for the provision of the services concerned to the other contracting party which acquires, by reason of the transfer, the quality of employer of the employees assigned to provide these services. The plaintiffs in the main proceedings also maintain that the transfer affects a 'part of a business', within the meaning of the Directive, since the services which are transferred constitute an autonomous economic entity within the transferor undertaking.

The defendant in the main proceedings is of the opinion that, on the contrary, an agreement such as that described by the judge making the reference does not constitute a 'transfer of an undertaking' within the meaning of the Directive, unless one is to give to the Directive an excessively broad scope. It maintains, on the one hand, that an agreement of this type does not effect any transfer within the meaning intended by the Directive since it does not confer on the other contracting party either full and entire responsibility for the provision of the services, particularly insofar as the customers and the fixing of prices is concerned, nor ownership of the assets necessary for the provision of these services. It maintains, on the other hand, that an agreement such as this relates to services which cannot be called 'an undertaking' within the meaning of the Directive, taking into account the fact that they are ancillary to the activity of the transferor.

According to the case law of the Court (see the judgment [in] *Berg*), the Directive is applicable in any case where, following a legal transfer or merger, there is a change in the legal or natural person who is responsible for carrying on the business and who by virtue of that fact incurs the obligation of an employer vis à vis the employees of the undertaking, regardless of whether or not ownership of the undertaking is transferred.

Under Article 1(1), the protection provided by the Directive applies, in particular, where the transfer only concerns a business or part of a business, that is to say a part of an undertaking. It therefore concerns the employees assigned to that part of the undertaking since, as the Court held in *Bötzen*, the employment relationship is essentially characterised by the link existing between the employee and the part of the undertaking to which he is assigned to carry out his duties.

Thus, where the owner of an undertaking entrusts, by means of an agreement, the responsibility for providing a service to his undertaking, such as a canteen, to the owner of another undertaking who assumes, by reason of it, the obligations of an employer vis à vis the employees who are engaged in the provisions of that service, the resulting transaction is capable of falling within the scope of the Directive as defined in Article 1(1). The fact that, in such a case, the activity transferred is only an ancillary activity of the transferor undertaking not necessarily related to its objects cannot have the effect of excluding that transaction from the scope of the Directive. Similarly, the fact that the agreement between the transferor and the transferee relates to the provision of services provided exclusively for the benefit of the transferor in return for a fee, the form of which is fixed by the agreement, does not prevent the Directive from applying either.

It is for the national judge to assess whether all the factual circumstances as described in his Order for Reference are characteristic of a "transfer of an undertaking" within the meaning of the Directive. That is why, as a point of information, he should be reminded that he must take into account the following considerations (see, most recently, [*Dr Sophie*] *Redmond* [v *Bartol*]).

On the one hand, the decisive criterion for establishing whether there is a transfer within the meaning of the Directive is whether the business retains its identity, as would be indicated, in particular, by the fact that its operation was either continued or resumed.

On the other hand, in order to determine whether those conditions are fulfilled, it is necessary to consider all the factual circumstances characterising the transaction in question, including the type of undertaking or business concerned, whether the business's tangible assets, such as buildings and movable property, are transferred, the value of its intangible assets at the time of the transfer, whether or not the majority of its employees are taken over by the new employer, whether or not its customers are transferred and the degree of similarity between the activities carried on before and after the transfer and the period, if any, for which those activities are suspended. It should be noted, however, that all those circumstances are merely single factors in the overall assessment which must be made and cannot therefore be considered in isolation.

For these reasons, the reply to the first two preliminary questions must be that Article 1(1) of the Directive must be interpreted as meaning that the Directive may apply to a situation in which the owner of an undertaking entrusts to the owner of another undertaking by means of a contract the responsibility of providing a service for employees, previously operated directly, in return for a fee and other benefits the terms of which are determined by the agreement made between them. ...'

COMMENT

(1)   The combination of *Dr Sophie Redmond Stichting* v *Bartol*, making it clear that the Directive applied to non-commercial activities, which could include governmental activities, and *Rask*, which showed that the Directive applied to the contracting-out of services, had a dramatic effect in the United Kingdom. Under the Local Govern-

ment Act 1988 local authorities were required to identify activities which could be put out to tender on a regular basis to see whether they could be performed more economically by the private sector. Many other public bodies, such as hospitals, engaged in a similar process.

(2)   The process of compulsory competitive tendering (CCT) implied that at two- or three-year intervals the supplier of services might change. Of course, where the contracted services involve the use of labour but virtually nothing else, the only way one supplier can provide services more cheaply than another is either by paying their workers less or else by requiring the same amount of work from fewer people.

(3)   But if the Acquired Rights Directive applied, this meant that the new supplier would have to take on the workers of the old supplier *on the same terms and conditions* as they enjoyed before. This seemed to frustrate the purpose of the exercise, and led the then Conservative Government to make strenuous efforts to try to get the Directive altered. Before any change was made, however, the ECJ took a hand in another landmark decision.

Süzen v Zehnacker Gebäudereinigung GmbH Krankenhausservice

[1997] IRLR 255 European Court of Justice

Süzen worked as a cleaner for Zehnacker at a school where Zehnacker had the cleaning contract. The school terminated the arrangement with Zehnacker and contracted the cleaning to a different company, Lefarth. Zehnacker therefore dismissed Süzen and seven other cleaners.

Süzen claimed that this was a transfer of an undertaking within the meaning of the Directive and that therefore she should not have been dismissed. The German court referred two questions to the ECJ:

'(1)   On the basis of the judgments of the Court of Justice in *Schmidt* v *Spar-und Leikhasse* and *Dr Sophie Redmond Stichting* v *Bartol*, is Directive 77/187/EEC applicable if an undertaking terminates a contract with an outside undertaking in order then to transfer it to another outside undertaking?

(2)   Is there a legal transfer within the meaning of the Directive in the case of the operation described in Question 1 even if no tangible or intangible business assets are transferred?'

Judgment of the Court: ' … Article 1(1) of the Directive provides: "This Directive shall apply to the transfer of an undertaking, business or part of a business to another employer as a result of a legal transfer or merger."

In *Schmidt* [v *Spar- und Leikhasse*] the Court held that that provision must be interpreted as covering a situation, such as that outlined in the order for reference, in which an undertaking entrusts by contract to another undertaking the responsibility for carrying out cleaning operations which it previously performed itself, even though, prior to the transfer, such work was carried out by a single employee. Earlier, in *Redmond Stichting*, the Court took the view in particular that the term "legal transfer" covers a situation in which a public authority decides to terminate the subsidy paid to one legal person, as a result of which the activities of that legal person are fully and definitively terminated, and to transfer it to another legal person with a similar aim.

By its two questions, which it is appropriate to consider together, the national court asks whether the Directive also applies to a situation in which a person who had entrusted the cleaning of his premises to a first undertaking terminates his contract with the latter and, for the performance of similar work, enters into a new contract with a second undertaking without any concomitant transfer of tangible or intangible business assets from one undertaking to the other.

The aim of the Directive is to ensure continuity of employment relationships within a business, irrespective of any change of ownership. The decisive criterion for establishing the existence of a transfer within the meaning of the Directive is whether the entity in question retains its identity, as indicated inter alia by the fact that its operation is actually continued or resumed (*Spijkers* and, most recently, *Merckx and Neuhuys*; see also the advisory opinion of the Court of the European Free Trade Association in *Ulstein and Røiseng*).

Whilst the lack of any contractual link between the transferor and the transferee or, as in this case, between the two undertakings successively entrusted with the cleaning of a school, may point to the absence of a transfer within the meaning of the Directive, it is certainly not conclusive.

As has been held – most recently in *Merckx and Neuhuys* – the Directive is applicable wherever, in the context of contractual relations, there is a change in the natural or legal person who is responsible for carrying on the business and who incurs the obligations of an employer towards employees of the undertaking. Thus, there is no need, in order for the Directive to be applicable, for there to be any direct contractual relationship between the transferor and the transferee: the transfer may also take place in two stages, through the intermediary of a third party such as the owner or the person putting up the capital.

For the Directive to be applicable however, the transfer must relate to a stable economic entity whose activity is not limited to performing one specific works contract (*Rygaard*). The term entity thus refers to an organised grouping of persons and assets facilitating the exercise of an economic activity which pursues a specific objective.

In order to determine whether the conditions for the transfer of an entity are met, it is necessary to consider all the facts characterising the transaction in question, including in particular the type of undertaking or business, whether or not its tangible assets, such as buildings and movable property, are transferred, the value of its intangible assets at the time of the transfer, whether or not the majority of its employees are taken over by the new employer, whether or not its customers are transferred, the degree of similarity between the activities carried on before and after the transfer, and the period, if any, for which those activities were suspended. However, all those circumstances are merely single factors in the overall assessment which must be made and cannot therefore be considered in isolation (see, in particular, *Spijkers* and *Redmond Stichting*).

As observed by most of the parties who commented on this point, the mere fact that the service provided by the old and the new awardees of a contract is similar does not therefore support the conclusion that an economic entity has been transferred. An entity cannot be reduced to the activity entrusted to it. Its identity also emerges from other factors, such as its workforce, its management staff, the way in which its work is organised, its operating methods or indeed, where appropriate, the operational resources available to it.

The mere loss of a service contract to a competitor cannot therefore by itself indicate the existence of a transfer within the meaning of the Directive. In those circumstance, the service undertaking previously entrusted with the contract does not, on losing a customer, thereby cease fully to exist, and a business or part of a business belonging to it cannot be considered to have been transferred to the new awardee of the contract.

It must also be noted that, although the transfer of assets is one of the criteria to be taken into account by the national court in deciding whether an undertaking has in fact been transferred, the absence of such assets does not necessarily preclude the existence of such a transfer (*Schmidt* and *Merckx*).

As pointed out [above], the national court, in assessing the facts characterising the transaction in question, must take into account among others things the type of undertaking or business concerned. It follows that the degree of importance to be attached to each criterion for determining whether or not there has been a transfer within the meaning of the Directive will necessarily vary according to the activity carried on, or indeed the production or operating methods employed in the relevant undertaking, business or part of a business. Where in particular an economic entity is able, in certain sectors, to function without any significant tangible or intangible assets, the maintenance of its identity following the transaction affecting it cannot, logically, depend on the transfer of such assets.

The United Kingdom Government and the Commission have argued that, for the entity previously entrusted with a service contract to have been the subject of a transfer within the meaning of the Directive, it may be sufficient in certain circumstances for the new awardee of the contract to have voluntarily taken over the majority of the employees specially assigned by his predecessor to the performance of the contract.

In that regard, it should be borne in mind that the factual circumstances to be taken into account in determining whether the conditions for a transfer are met include in particular, in addition to the degree of similarity of the activity carried on before and after the transfer and the type of undertaking or business concerned, the question whether or not the majority of the employees were taken over by the new employer (*Spijkers*).

Since in certain labour-intensive sectors a group of workers engaged in a joint activity on a permanent basis may constitute an economic entity, it must be recognised that such an entity is capable of maintaining its identity after it has been transferred where the new employer does not merely pursue the activity in question but also takes over a major part, in terms of their numbers and skills, of the employees specially assigned by this predecessor to that task. In those circumstances, as stated in *Rygaard*, the new employer takes over a body of assets enabling him to carry on the activities or certain activities of the transferor undertaking on a regular basis.

It is for the national court to establish, in the light of the foregoing interpretative guidance, whether a transfer has occurred in this case.

The answer to the questions from the national court must therefore be that Article 1(1) of the Directive is to be interpreted as meaning that the Directive does not apply to a situation in which a person who had entrusted the cleaning of his premises to a first undertaking terminates his contract with the latter and, for the performance of similar work, enters into a new contract with a second undertaking, if there is no concomitant transfer from one undertaking to the other of significant tangible or intangible assets or taking over by the new employer of a major part of the workforce, in terms of their numbers and skills, assigned to his predecessor to the performance of the contract. ...

COMMENT

(1)   It is frankly difficult to reconcile this decision with *Schmidt*. What the Court appears to be getting at is the distinction between the genuine transfer of an economic entity and 'the mere loss of a service contract to a competitor'. However, not only is the distinction unclear, it should be noted that from the point of view of the employee the distinction has little meaning. Given the purpose of the Directive, it is submitted that the wider, pre-*Süzen*, interpretation was desirable.

(2)   The renewed emphasis on a transfer of assets raises the danger that in labour-

intensive industries (frequently low-paid manual work, such as cleaning) a new contractor will be able to avoid liability under TUPE by the simple expedient of refusing to take on the workforce of the old contractor.

(3) The effects of *Süzen* were swiftly seen when it was considered by the Court of Appeal.

Betts v Brintel Helicopters Ltd

[1997] IRLR 362 Court of Appeal

Kennedy LJ: 'This is an appeal by KLM, the second defendants in the action, from a decision of Scott Baker J, who on 28 July 1995 granted declarations to the plaintiffs but dismissed their application for an injunction.

Facts

The relevant facts are not contentious and are clearly set out in the judgment of the trial judge. For present purposes I can abridge his account.

At all material times the first defendants (Brintel) provided helicopter services to Shell (UK) Ltd, transporting men and goods to and from oil rigs in the North Sea. There were three contracts between Brintel and Shell covering separate sectors of the North Sea, one for each of three Brintel mainland helicopter bases, namely Aberdeen, Sumburgh and Beccles (Norfolk). All three contracts expired on 30 June 1995. This case is concerned only with Beccles, where, prior to 30 June 1995, Brintel employed 66 people including all seven plaintiffs, four of them on administration and three as engineers. When the contracts were due to expire, tenders were invited for the new contracts, and Brintel obtained the new contracts for Aberdeen and Sumburgh, but the southern sector contract went to the second defendants (KLM). KLM did not take over any staff or equipment from Brintel, and moved the Norfolk base from Beccles to Norwich Airport. Some 13 Brintel staff were redeployed, but 38 (including all seven plaintiffs) were surplus to requirements. It seems clear that, but for the threat of these or similar proceedings, KLM might have taken on some Brintel staff, but with the proceedings hanging over them they considered it imprudent to do so.

Prior to 30 June 1995, Brintel had 25 helicopters servicing all three contracts. Five were normally at Beccles, but it was not always the same five. Routine maintenance could be done there, but larger jobs were done at Aberdeen. Fifty-three of the 66 staff at Beccles were permanent and the rest, including some helicopter crews, were temporary, from other bases and elsewhere to meet the increased demands of the summer season. Beccles is a former RAF airfield, and except for occasional other jobs it was used solely to service the Shell contract.

When KLM began their operations, they used different types of helicopter, and they operated from a sophisticated airport with fire service, security and other services, which at Beccles Brintel had had to provide for themselves.

...

General effect of legislation

As Mr Carr QC, for the appellants, said at the start of his submissions, the general effect of the 1981 regulations is that where company A sells its business to company B two things happen – first, A's employees by operation of law become B's employees on the same terms, and secondly, any dismissal of an employee will be deemed unfair if the transfer or a reason connected with it is the reason or principal reason for his dismissal. The employee can seek relief before an industrial tribunal. But of course, Mr Carr's principal submission is that the situation with which we are concerned is not one to which the regulations applied. Here there was no sale of a business by Brintel and KLM, KLM acquired no assets which had previously belonged to Brintel unless – as Mr Goudie QC, for the respondents, contends – the right to land on Shell Oil rigs and to use their facilities can be regarded as an asset, and certainly KLM, as a matter of policy, did not employ anyone who had previously been employed by Brintel.

Non-re-engagement by KLM

Mr Goudie invites us to look with a critical eye at KLM's decision not to employ anyone who had worked for Brintel. It was, he submits, a transparent device to reduce the risk of an adverse finding under the 1981 Regulations. In *Litster* v *Forth Dry Dock & Engineering Co Ltd*, the receiver of the transferor dismissed the employees of the transferor one hour before the transfer. Regulation 5(3) as it was worded at that time only gave protection to those employed "immediately before the transfer", but the House of Lords, recognising that the regulations were "designed to give effect to Council Directive 77/187 EEC" (per Lord Keith), adopted a construction of the relevant regulations "which accords with the decisions of the European Court upon the corresponding provisions of the Directive to which the regulation was intended by Parliament to give effect". By implication words were added to reg 5(3) to indicate that an employee unfairly dismissed would be deemed still to be employed in the undertaking immediately before the transfer.

In my judgment, the decision in *Litster* is of limited assistance to us in this case. It demonstrates the lengths to which English courts at the highest level will go to ensure that regulations designed to give effect to a Directive (as interpreted by the European Court) attain their objective, but no one has submitted to us that the problems that arise in the present case can be resolved by reading words into a regulation.

The issues

There are, as the trial judge recognised, two critical issues in this case, namely:

    (1)   Prior to 30 June 1995, was Brintel's Beccles operation an undertaking or part of an undertaking for the purposes of reg 3(1) of the 1981 Regulations (as properly understood in the light of European jurisprudence)?

    (2)   If so, was that undertaking transferred so that it retained its identity in the hands of KLM?

...

In *Kenny and another* v *South Manchester College*, an education officer and a lecturer were employed by a local education authority which from 1 April 1993 was to cease to provide educational services at a young offenders' institution, that obligation having been acquired by the defendant corporation following competitive tendering. The matter came before the court on agreed facts to determine, as a preliminary issue, whether on 1 April 1993 the plaintiffs would automatically become employed by the defendants pursuant to the 1981 Regulations and/or the Directive. Sir Michael Ogden QC, sitting as a deputy judge, reviewed the authorities and concluded that he had to consider all the factual circumstances and assess whether they were characteristic of a transfer of an undertaking within the meaning of the Directive. He determined the issue in favour of the plaintiffs.

Mrs Schmidt was a cleaner at a branch of a German bank who decided to contract out the cleaning of that branch to a firm which already cleaned most of its other premises. The national court posed two questions for the European Court, namely:

"(1)   May an undertaking's cleaning operations, if they are transferred by contract to a different firm, be treated as part of the business within the meaning of the Directive 77/187 EEC?

(2)   If the answer to question (1) is in principle in the affirmative, does that also apply if prior to the transfer the cleaning operations were undertaken by a single employee?"

In giving judgment, the Court said:

"The decisive criterion for establishing whether there is a transfer for the purposes of the Directive is whether the business in question retains its identity. According to case law, the retention of that identity is indicated inter alia by actual continuation or resumption by the new employer of the same or similar activities."

In paragraph 20, the Court said that the Directive:

"... is to be interpreted as covering a situation ... in which an undertaking entrusts by contract to another undertaking the responsibility for carrying out cleaning operations which it previously performed itself, even though prior to the transfer such work was carried out by a single employee."

So, as Mr Goudie submitted, *Kenny* and *Schmidt* demonstrate that the 1981 Regulations can apply to what is sometimes called first-generation contracting-out.

In *Dines* v *Initial Services*, the applicants were eleven members of the staff of a company (Initial) which undertook cleaning work at a hospital pursuant to a fixed-term contract. As a result of competitive tendering, when the contract expired the new contract went to a new provider (Pall Mall). Initial declared all 98 cleaners and day supervisors redundant, and terminated their employment. Nearly all of them were engaged by Pall Mall on less favourable conditions. The industrial tribunal and the Employment Appeal Tribunal held that there had been no relevant transfer of an undertaking within the meaning of the 1981 Regulations. But this court allowed the appeal. Neill LJ said:

"the European cases demonstrate that the fact that another company takes over the provision of certain services as a result of competitive tendering does not mean that the first business or undertaking necessarily comes to an end."

At 341 he continued:

"I consider that, on the agreed facts, there was a transfer of an undertaking for the purposes of the 1981 Regulations. It took place in two phases – (a) the handing back by Initial to the authority on 30 April 1991 of the cleaning services at the hospitals; and (b) the grant or handing over by the authority to Pall Mall on 1 May 1991 of the cleaning services as from that date which were operated by essentially the same labour force."

That is a decision on which, for obvious reasons, Mr Goudie places considerable reliance. It is, as he points out, like the present case, an example of second-generation contracting-out, where one fixed-term contract for services comes to an end, and another fixed-term contract to provide essentially similar services is put in its place, but it is to be noted that although Pall Mall did not take over any plant or materials from Initial, they did operate with essentially the same labour force on the same premises for the same authority, and as Neill LJ observed hospital cleaning is not an operation which lends itself to the employment of many different techniques. ...

The plaintiffs in *Merckx* v *Ford Motor Company* were employed as salesmen by the Ford-owned dealership in Brussels when that dealership was transferred by Ford to an independent company. There was no transfer of tangible assets, but the transferor sent a letter of recommendation to its customers. The European Court said:

"It is settled case law that the decisive criterion for establishing whether there is a transfer for the purposes of the Directive is whether the entity in question retains its economic identity, as indicated inter alia by the fact that its operation is actually continued or resumed."

The Court reviewed the factors in favour of and against a finding that the transfer of the dealership fell within the scope of the Directive. In favour of that conclusion was the continuity of the activity, evidenced by the sale of Ford motor cars in the same territory without interruption, with the transferee company (recommended to customers by letter) taking on part of the transferor's staff. As against that conclusion there were a number of factors – the lack of transfer of any assets, or of any organisation, the movement of the dealership to a different site, the fact that the Ford-owned dealership ceased to trade, the fact that the majority of the staff were dismissed, and the fact that there was no contractual link between transferor and transferee. Even cumulatively, those adverse factors were held not to be decisive, and so, Mr Goudie submits, the emphasis must be on the activities of the transferor and the transferee. The force of that submission in the light of the line of authorities to which I have referred seems to me to be self-evident, but it may be that as time went on the width of the *Spijkers* test was being to some extent overlooked. If so, that was put right by the final decision in the European Court to which I must now refer, namely the recent case of *Ayse Süzen* in which judgment was delivered on 11 March 1997. ...

Mr Goudie's basic submission was that prior to the decision of the European Court in *Süzen* it could be seen from the authorities to which I have already referred that in order to discover what constituted an economic entity or an undertaking it was necessary to look at what was done. If after the alleged transfer activities were substantially the same, then it could be concluded that the undertaking had been transferred so that it retained its identity in the hands of the transferee. That, Mr Goudie submits, was well established by decisions which were cited in *Süzen* and not disapproved. It was an approach which was understood by employers and employees, it was predictable and enforceable, it enabled the consultation provisions of the 1981 Regulations to operate, and so far as possible *Süzen* should be read as not interfering with that approach. Mr Goudie submitted that where national legislation mirrors but does not go beyond the Directive there might, as a result of the decision in *Süzen*, be a difference between cases of first-generation contracting-out (to which the approach for which he contends could still apply) and cases of second-generation contracting-out, of which *Süzen* and the present case are examples; but, save that first-generation contracting-out involves a contractual relationship between transferor and transferee, Mr Goudie could not advance any logical reason for such a distinction, and I do not accept that it can exist.

The real distinction, as it seems to me, is between (1) labour-intensive undertakings, of which *Dines* is an example, in which if the staff combine to engage in a particular activity which continues or is resumed with substantially the same staff after the alleged transfer the court may well conclude that the undertaking has been transferred so that it has retained its identity in the hands of the transferee; and (2) other types of undertaking in relation to which the application of the *Spijkers* test involves a more wide-ranging inquiry. Consequently I have no difficulty in accepting as appropriate to its facts the approach adopted by this court in *Dines*. In the circumstances of this case a different approach is called for, leading, as it seems to me, to a different conclusion.

Mr Goudie did not expressly concede that if *Süzen* applies it cannot be distinguished, although in reality that must be the case. But, as Mr Goudie points out, *Süzen* is a decision of the European Court in relation to the Directive. It is not a decision of an English court in relation to the 1981 Regulations which, Mr Goudie submits, may go beyond the Directive. I can find no basis upon which to conclude that they do. If I were not of that opinion then it would be necessary to consider Mr Carr's submission that in so far as the Regulations exceed the requirements of the Directive they are ultra vires the enabling legislation, namely s 2 of the European Communities Act 1972. Mr Goudie submitted that the words "related to" in s 2(2)(b) of the 1972 Act give the Secretary of State a wide measure of discretion, as found by the Divisional Court in *R* v *Secretary of Trade and Industry ex parte Unison*, but he acknowledges that the decision in the *Unison* case was not followed by the Employment Appeal Tribunal in Scotland which, in *Addison* v *Denholm Ship Management*, expressed the view that if the 1981 Regulations went beyond the requirements of the Directive they would be ultra vires. In my judgment, it is unnecessary in this case to resolve that conflict and I say no more about it.

Mr Goudie's alternative submission is that if the *Süzen* approach must now be followed in English law then, on the facts, we should reach the same conclusion as the trial judge, because some assets which formed part of Brintel's undertaking were acquired by KLM – namely, the right to land on oil rigs and use oil rig facilities – and some Brintel employees might, and Mr Goudie submits that we should find would, have been engaged by KLM if KLM had not chosen to exclude them from consideration. Once the Brintel Beccles undertaking is defined in the way that I have defined it when dealing with the submissions made by Mr Carr, it seems to me that, even if Mr Goudie's identification of transferred assets is accepted, a transfer of such a limited part of the undertaking could not lead to the conclusion that the Brintel Beccles undertaking itself was transferred so that it retained its identity in the hands of KLM.

Conclusion

I accept that the decision in *Süzen* does represent a shift of emphasis, or at least a clarification of the law, and that some of the reasoning of the earlier decisions, if not the decisions themselves, may have to be reconsidered. With the benefit of the judgment in *Süzen*, which was not available to the trial judge, I am satisfied that the proper approach to this case is to consider first the nature of Brintel's Beccles operation. For the reasons I have given I accept that there was an undertaking or an economic entity. I turn then to the second question, namely whether that undertaking was transferred so that it retained its identity in the hands of KLM. In my judgment, the answer to that question is now clear, namely that there was no such transfer. I would therefore allow this appeal.

In his skeleton argument, Mr Carr set out examples of absurd results which, he contended, could result from an unfettered application of the law as contended for by Mr Goudie. That argument was not developed orally, so I do not dwell on it, but it looks persuasive on paper and could constitute a further reason for reaching the conclusion at which I have arrived. I add that by way of postscript to make it clear that the policy arguments have in fact played no part in my decision.

(Auld LJ and Sir Roger Parker agreed with Kennedy LJ.)

Effect of the transfer on contracts of employment

Transfer of Undertakings (Protection of Employment) Regulations 1981

5.   (1)   Except where objection is made under paragraph (4A) below, a relevant transfer shall not operate so as to terminate the contract of employment of any person employed by the transferor in the undertaking or part transferred but any such contract which would otherwise have been terminated by the transfer shall have effect after the transfer as if originally made between the person so employed and the transferee.

(2)   Without prejudice to paragraph (1) above, but subject to paragraph (4A) below, on the completion of a relevant transfer—

(a)   all the transferor's rights, powers, duties and liabilities under or in connection with any such contract, shall be transferred by virtue of this Regulation to the transferee; and

(b)   anything done before the transfer is completed by or in relation to the transferor in respect of that contract or a person employed in that undertaking or part shall be deemed to have been done by or in relation to the transferee.

(3)   Any reference in paragraph (1) or (2) above to a person employed in an undertaking or part of one transferred by a relevant transfer is a reference to a person so employed immediately before the transfer, including, where the transfer is effected by a series of two or more transactions, a person so employed immediately before any of those transactions.

(4)   Paragraph (2) above shall not transfer or otherwise affect the liability of any person to be prosecuted for, convicted of and sentenced for any offence.

(4A)   Paragraphs (1) and (2) above shall not operate to transfer his contract of employment and the rights, powers, duties and liabilities under or in connection with it if the employee informs the transferor or the transferee that he objects to becoming employed by the transferee.

(4B)   Where an employee so objects the transfer of the undertaking or part in which he is employed shall operate so as to terminate his contract of employment with the transferor but he shall not be treated, for any purpose, as having been dismissed by the transferor.

(5)   Paragraphs (1) and (4A) above are without prejudice to any right of an employee arising apart from these Regulations to terminate his contract without notice if a substantial change is made in his working conditions to his detriment; but no such right shall arise by reason only that, under that paragraph, the identity of his employer changes unless the employee shows that, in all the circumstances, the change is a significant change and is to his detriment.

COMMENT

(1)   As a contract of employment is personal, at common law the transfer of a business from one employer to another would involve the termination of the employee's contract of employment and a new contract with the new employer (*Nokes v Doncaster Amalgamated Collieries*). Under ERA s 218, continuity of employment is preserved in such a situation provided it is a transfer of business and not a transfer of assets.

(2)   Regulation 5 originally went further than this and in effect reversed *Nokes v Doncaster Amalgamated Collieries* by providing that where there was a transfer of a business or part of a business, employees' contracts of employment were *automatically* transferred to the new employer, regardless of the employees' agreement. This was seen as a strange derogation from existing rights in regulations which were intended to provide *protection* for employees. There was, of course, nothing to stop the employee leaving if she hated the transfer, but she would not qualify for any statutory compensation in such circumstances. The only mitigation of this was in reg 5(5).

(3)   Following the ECJ decision in *Katsikas* v *Konstantinidis*, it became clear that there had been a misunderstanding of what the Directive actually required. Hence the introduction, through TURERA, of subparagraphs (4A) and (4B). Unfortunately, however, the inclusion of (4B) makes an employee *worse* off, by negating the possibility of claiming against the transferor. There will no doubt be arguments in future about whether an employee who leaves objecting to the transfer comes under subparagraph (4A) or (5) – for in the latter case the employee can still claim at least a redundancy payment.

(4)   If the new employer (the transferee) does not want all the workers, the usual effect of reg 5 will be that anyone made redundant will be entitled to a redundancy payment from the new employer, not the old one. However, the protection afforded by the regulations goes further than this.

Transfer of Undertakings (Protection of Employment) Regulations 1981

8.   (1)   Where either before or after a relevant transfer, any employee of the transferor or transferee is dismissed, that employee shall be treated for the purposes of Part V of the 1978 Act and Articles 20 to 41 of the 1976 Order (unfair dismissal) as unfairly dismissed if the transfer or a reason connected with it is the reason or principal reason for his dismissal.

         (2)   Where an economic, technical or organisational reason entailing changes in the workforce of either the transferor or the transferee before or after a relevant transfer is the reason or principal reason for dismissing an employee—
               (a)   paragraph (1) above shall not apply to his dismissal; but
               (b)   without prejudice to the application of section 57(3) of the 1978 Act or Article 22(10) of the 1976 Order (test of fair dismissal), the dismissal shall for the purposes of section 57(1)(b) of that Act and Article 22(1)(b) of that Order (substantial reason for dismissal) be regarded as having been for a substantial reason of a kind such as to justify the dismissal of an employee holding the position which that employee held.

         (3)   The provisions of this Regulation apply whether or not the employee in question is employed in the undertaking or part of the undertaking transferred or to be transferred. ...

Berriman v *Delabole Slate Ltd*

[1985] ICR 546 Court of Appeal

The business in which the applicant was employed as a quarryman was transferred to the respondent company. They wanted to harmonise the employees' conditions of employment with their own workforce, and this meant reducing the amount of guaranteed basic pay that the applicant received. He refused the offer and left, claiming unfair dismissal.

Browne-Wilkinson LJ: 'The combined effect of these regulations and the [Employment Rights Act 1996] is as follows. On the transfer of a business, the employees of the transferor become the employees of the transferee. An employee has the right to treat himself as constructively dismissed by any detrimental change in his working conditions (regulation 5(5)) but the question whether his dismissal is fair is dealt with by regulation 8. Under regulation 8(1), if any employee is dismissed in connection with the transfer, the dismissal is unfair unless the reason or principal reason for dismissing the employee is an "economic, technical or organisational reason entailing changes in the workforce". In this event the case is taken out of the automatic unfairness provision of regulation 8(1) and the employer is treated as having demonstrated some other potentially fair reason for his dismissal thereby satisfying the requirements of [ERA s 98(1)]. The question will still remain whether, in the circumstances of the particular case, the dismissal of that employee was in fact fair for the purposes of [section 98(4)].

Applying those provisions to the present case, the first question was whether the employee was constructively dismissed by the employers' attempt to impose on him a lower guaranteed wage. The industrial tribunal held that he was constructively dismissed and the employers did not challenge this finding in the appeal tribunal. The next question was whether the employers' reason for dismissing the employee was the transfer of the undertaking to the employers or a reason connected with it so as to bring the case within regulation 8(1). The industrial tribunal held that it was and that accordingly the dismissal was rendered unfair by regulation 8(1). The next question was whether the case was taken out of the automatic unfairness provision by regulation 8(2) in that the employers' reason or principal reason for dismissing the employee was an "economic, technical or organisational reason entailing changes in the workforce". The industrial tribunal held that the employers' reason for dismissal was such a reason, but the appeal tribunal reversed them on this point holding that, although the reason for dismissal was an economic, technical or organisational reason, such reason did not "entail changes in the workforce". Finally, the industrial tribunal decided that the dismissal of the employee was fair within the meaning of [section 98(4)]. That finding was challenged before the appeal tribunal who did not decide the point: there is no respondent's notice raising the point before us.

The only point we have to decide therefore is whether, as a matter of law, the industrial tribunal were entitled to hold that the case fell within regulation 8(2) in that the employers' reason for dismissal was a reason "entailing changes in the workforce" of the employers.

Mr Tabachnik, for the employers, does not persist in the argument which he unsuccessfully advanced at the appeal tribunal that the words "changes in the workforce" were wide enough to cover changes in the terms and conditions of the workforce. He accepts that what must be shown are changes in the number of the workforce or possibly changes in the job descriptions of the constituent elements of the workforce which, although involving no overall reduction in numbers, involves a change in the individual employees which together make up the workforce. But, says Mr Tabachnik, it is necessary to ask the question "what was the reason for dismissal" as at the date of the constructive dismissal, i.e. 28 January 1983. At that date the reason for dismissal was not solely the employers' desire to standardise rates of pay, but also included the employee's refusal to accept the proposed change and his notice terminating his employment. Therefore, says Mr Tabachnik, the reason for dismissal entailed a change in the workforce since it entailed the constructive dismissal of the employee.

We do not accept these submissions. First, in our judgment, even in a case of constructive dismissal, [ERA s 98(1)] imposes on the employers the burden of showing the reason for dismissal, notwithstanding that it was the employee, not the employers, who actually decided to terminate the contract of employment. In our judgment, the only way in which the statutory requirements of the Act ... can be made to fit a case of constructive dismissal is to read [section 98(1)] as requiring the employers to show the reasons for their conduct which entitled the employee to terminate the contract thereby giving rise to a deemed dismissal by the employers. We can see nothing in the decision in *Savoia* v *Chiltern Herb Farms Ltd* which conflicts with this view.

If that is right, when one turns to regulation 8(2) and asks the question, "What was the reason or principal reason for dismissing the employee?", in a case of constructive dismissal attention has to be focused on the employers' reasons for presenting the employee with the ultimatum changing his guaranteed rates of pay. It is the employers' reasons for their conduct not the employee's reaction to that conduct which is important. In the present case the reason for the employers' ultimatum was to produce standard rates of pay – not in any way to reduce the number in their workforce.

Then, in order to come within regulation 8(2), it has to be shown that *that* reason is an economic, technical or organisational reason entailing changes in the workforce. The reason itself (i.e. to produce standardisation in pay) does not involve any change either in the number or the functions of the workforce. The most that can be said is that such organisational reason *may* (not must) lead to the dismissal of those employees who do not fall into line coupled with the filling of the vacancies thereby caused by new employees prepared to accept the conditions of service. In our judgment that is not enough. First, the phrase "economic, technical or organisational reason entailing changes in the workforce" in our judgment requires that the change in the workforce is part of the economic, technical or organisational reason. The employers' plan must be to achieve changes in the workforce. It must be an objective of the plan, not just a possible consequence of it.

Second, we do not think that the dismissal of one employee followed by the engagement of another in his place constitutes a change in the "workforce". To our minds, the word "workforce" connotes the whole body of employees as an entity: it corresponds to the "strength" or the "establishment". Changes in the identity of the individuals who make up the workforce do not constitute changes in the workforce itself so long as the overall numbers and functions of the employees looked at as a whole remain unchanged.

We are supported in this view by the fact that, if Mr Tabachnik is right, any case in which an employee is dismissed for an economic, technical or organisational reason will fall within regulation 8(2) and the words "entailing changes in the workforce" are otiose. Regulation 8(2) is dealing exclusively with cases where an employee has been dismissed for economic, technical or organisational reasons. Therefore, by definition there has, for a short while at least, been a reduction of one in the number of people employed. If that temporary reduction falls within the words "entailing changes in the workforce" then regulation 8(2) will cover every dismissal for an economic, technical or organisational reason and the words "entailing changes in the workforce" are given no effect whatsoever. That in our judgment could not be a proper construction of the regulation.

Mr Tabachnik points out that, if the construction we favour is correct, following a transfer of an undertaking employers will be precluded from imposing on the employees taken over necessary changes in their conditions of employment which, if there had been no transfer, could properly have been imposed on their existing workforce; see *Hollister* v *National Farmers' Union*. This, says Mr Tabachnik, would be an undesirable result. We do not find this argument persuasive. Regulation 8(1) will only render unfair a dismissal for failure to accept new conditions of service if the reason for dismissal is a reason connected with the transfer of the undertaking. If the reason for seeking to impose, say, standard conditions of service is connected with the transfer, it is far from clear that it was the intention of the legislature (or of Council Directive (77/187/EEC) which required the Regulations to be made) that immediately following a transfer the employees of the transferred undertaking could be made to accept new terms of service. The purpose of the directive was "the safeguarding of employees' rights in the event of transfers" and the Regulations themselves include in their name the words "protection of employment". Amongst the most crucial rights of employees are their existing terms of service. We are not satisfied that there is a clear statutory intention to ensure that, following a transfer, the transferee company can insist on equating the terms and conditions of the "transferred" employees to those of his existing employees notwithstanding the fact that such alteration may constitute a detriment to the transferred employees.

For these reasons, which are much the same as those given by the appeal tribunal, we dismiss the appeal. It follows that under regulation 8(1) the dismissal of the employee was unfair and as the appeal tribunal directed, in default of agreement the amount of compensation must be remitted to the industrial tribunal for assessment.'

COMMENT

(1)   The judgment of the Court of Appeal in this case shows a welcome purposive approach to the interpretation of the regulations, indicating that they may well have increased protection for employees in at least some types of restructuring.

(2)   One problem, however, is that reg 8(2) says that if there is a dismissal for an economic, technological or organisational reason, it will be treated as 'some other substantial reason' for dismissal. This could be taken to mean that in such a situation the employee would not even get a redundancy payment. However, in *Gorictree* v *Jenkinson* the EAT held that TUPE did not affect entitlement to a redundancy payment.

(3)   Since the thrust of TUPE is to pass all responsibility – and liability – in respect of employees to the new owner, it is not surprising that parties looked for ways round it. The new owner does not necessarily want the whole workforce of the old employer, and the old employer will want their business to be as attractive as possible to the new employer. Under reg 5(3), the regulations only apply to someone 'employed immediately before the transfer': the answer, therefore, seemed to be to make sure that the old employer dismissed the employees before that time.

Litster v *Forth Dry Dock and Engineering Co Ltd*

[1989] ICR 341 House of Lords

The respondent company, FDD, was in receivership. A new company, Forth Estuary Engineering, had been set up with a view to taking over FDD's business, but the promoters had no wish to take over FDD's workforce as they were planning to employ the redundant workforce of another shipyard who would come for lower rates. The two companies therefore agreed that FDD should dismiss the workforce before the transfer, and this in fact occurred an hour before the transfer went through.

Lord Oliver: '... It will be seen that, as is to be expected, the scope and purpose of both the Directive and the Regulations are the same, that is, to ensure that on any transfer of an undertaking or part of an undertaking, the employment of the existing workers in the undertaking is preserved or, if their employment terminates solely by reason of the transfer, that their rights arising out of that determination are effectively safeguarded. It may, I think, be assumed that those who drafted both the Directive and the Regulations were sufficiently acquainted with the realities of life to appreciate that a frequent – indeed, possibly, the most frequent – occasion upon which a business or part of a business is transferred is when the original employer is insolvent, so that an employee whose employment is terminated on the transfer will have no effective remedy for unfair dismissal unless it is capable of being exerted against the transferee. It can hardly have been contemplated that, where the only reason for determination of the employment is the transfer of the undertaking or the relevant part of it, the parties to the transfer would be at liberty to avoid the manifest purpose of the Directive by the simple expedient of wrongfully dismissing the workforce a few minutes before the completion of the transfer. The European Court of Justice has expressed, in the clearest terms, the opinion that so transparent a device would not avoid the operation of the Directive, and if the effect of the Regulations is that under the law of the United Kingdom it has that effect, then your Lordships are compelled to conclude that the Regulations are gravely defective and the Government of the United Kingdom has failed to comply with its mandatory obligations under the Directive. If your Lordships are in fact compelled to that conclusion, so be it; but it is not, I venture to think, a conclusion which any of your Lordships would willingly embrace in the absence of the most compulsive context rendering any other conclusion impossible ...'

The prohibitory nature of Article 4 was emphasised again in *Foreningen af Arbejdsledere i Danmark* v *Daddy's Dance Hall A/S* where the court in the course of its judgment observed:

"... Directive (77/187/EEC) aims at ensuring for workers affected by a transfer of undertaking the safeguarding of their rights arising from the employment contract or relationship. As this protection is a matter of public policy and, as such, outside the control of the parties to the employment contract, the provisions of the Directive, in particular those relating to the protection of workers against dismissal because of transfer, must be considered as mandatory, meaning that it is not permissible to derogate from them in a manner detrimental to the workers."

(See also *Landsorganisationen i Danmark* v *Ny Mølle Kro*.)

In a subsequent case, *P Bork International A/S* v *Foreningen af Arbejdsledere i Danmark* the question arose whether the Directive applied to a situation where the workforce had been dismissed upon the termination by the employer of the lease of the premises on which the undertaking was carried on, the assets of the business having been purchased shortly afterwards by the new lessee of the premises, which re-engaged over half the original workforce. The court held that the Directive applied and in relation to the question of whether workers dismissed before the transfer could claim the benefit of the Directive as against the transferee, said,

"the only workers who may invoke Directive [(77/187/EEC)] are those who have current employment relations or a contract of employment at the date of transfer. The question whether or not a contract of employment or employment relationship exists at that date must be assessed under national law, subject, however, to the observance of the mandatory rules of the Directive concerning the protection of workers against dismissal by reason of the transfer. It follows that the workers employed by the undertaking whose contract of employment or employment relationship has been terminated with effect on a date before that of the transfer, in breach of Article 4(1) of the Directive, must be considered as still employed by the undertaking on the date of the transfer with the consequence, in particular, that the obligations of an employer towards them are fully transferred from the transferor to the transferee, in accordance with Article 3(1) of the Directive. In order to determine whether the only reason for dismissal was the transfer itself, account must be taken of the objective circumstances in which the dismissal occurred and, in particular, in a case like the present one, the fact that it took place on a date close to that of the transfer and that the workers concerned were re-engaged by the transferee. The factual assessment needed in order to determine the applicability of the Directive is a matter for the national courts, *having regard to the interpretative criteria laid down by the court.*" (Emphasis added.)

It does not appear that the impact of Article 4 (and thus of regulation 8) on the construction and effect of Article 3 (or regulation 5) in relation to the employee's rights has previously fallen to be considered in any of the reported cases in the United Kingdom ...

[In *Secretary of State for Employment* v *Spence*] the transferor company was in receivership and the receivers had been negotiating a transfer of the business under a threat by the company's major customer to withdraw its work unless a transfer of the business had been agreed by 24 November 1983. No sale had been agreed by that date and although on 28 November 1983 the negotiations were continuing, the receivers had to decide whether it was proper in the interests of the debenture holders to continue to employ the workforce and to continue trading. Since there was no guarantee that the negotiations would be successful, the decision was taken to cease trading immediately and, at 11 am on that morning the employees were notified that they were dismissed with immediate effect. In fact, the negotiations were successful and an agreement for the sale of the undertaking was signed at 2 pm on that day. The employees were in fact re-employed by the transferee but claimed redundancy payments from the redundancy fund under [ERA s 166]. The claim was resisted on the ground that, since the claimants were employed "immediately before the transfer" their employment was continued with the transferee of the business by regulation 5(1), following the decision in the *Anchor Hotel* case. It is worth noting that it was found as a fact by the industrial tribunal, first, that the sequence of events was the result of independent action by the receivers and the transferees and that there was no collusion between them and, secondly, that the reason why the receivers decided to dismiss the workforce was that, until a contract could be renegotiated with the company's principal customer, there was no prospect of any work for the business. It follows from these findings that the reason for the dismissal was not one connected with the transfer but was due to economic considerations, with the result that regulation 8(1) did not render the dismissals unfair. The only question for decision, therefore, was whether having regard to the very short time which in fact elapsed between the dismissals taking effect and the conclusion of the transfer agreement, the workforce was employed "immediately before the transfer". After a careful analysis of the cases, the Court of Appeal rejected the approach of the Employment Appeal Tribunal in *Apex* and *Anchor Hotel* and held that regulation 5(1) can apply only where, at the very moment of transfer, the contract of employment (in the sense of the existing relationship of employer and employee) is still subsisting. If it is not, then there is nothing upon which the regulation can bite, even though the employment has been determined only a matter of minutes (or, it may be, seconds) before the transfer. My Lords, for my part, I can detect no flaw in the reasoning by which Balcombe LJ, who delivered the leading judgment in the Court of Appeal, reached the conclusion on the facts of that case that regulation 5(1) did not operate to transfer the obligations of the original employer to the transferee. Where, before the actual transfer takes place, the employment of an employee is terminated for a reason unconnected with the transfer, I agree that the question of whether he was employed "immediately" before the transfer cannot sensibly be made to depend upon the degree of temporal proximity between the two events, except possibly in a case where they are so closely connected in point of time that it is, for practical purposes, impossible realistically to say that they are not precisely contemporaneous. Either the contract of employment is subsisting at the moment of the transfer or it is not, and if it is not, then, on the pure textual construction of regulation 5, neither paragraph (1) nor paragraph (2) (which is clearly subsidiary to and complementary with paragraph (1)) can have any operation. But *Spence's* case was decided – and quite properly decided – entirely without reference to the effect of regulation 8(1) and in the context of the two important findings of fact by the industrial tribunal to which I have drawn attention. The Court of Appeal did not consider, and was not called upon to consider, a position where, whether under a collusive bargain or otherwise, an employee is dismissed from his employment solely or principally because of the prospective transfer of the undertaking in which he is employed, so that his dismissal is statutorily deemed to be unfair; and, of course, the case was decided without reference to the important *Bork* case already referred to which had not been decided at the date of the Court of Appeal's judgment and which had not been reported at the time when the instant case was argued before the Court of Session.

It is, I think, now clear that under Article 4 of the Directive, as construed by the European Court of Justice, a dismissal effected before the transfer and solely because of the transfer of the business is, in effect, prohibited and is, for the purpose of considering the application of Article 3(1), required to be treated as ineffective. The question is whether the Regulations are so framed as to be capable of being construed in conformity with that interpretation of the Directive....

Having regard to the manifest purpose of the Regulations, I do not, for my part, feel inhibited from making an implication in the instant case. The provision in regulation 8(1) that a dismissal by reason of a transfer is to be treated as an unfair dismissal, is merely a different way of saying that the transfer is not to "constitute a ground for dismissal" as contemplated by Article 4 of the Directive and there is no good reason for denying to it the same effect as that attributed to that article. In effect this involves reading regulation 5(3) as if there were inserted after the words "immediately before the transfer" the words "or would have been so employed if he had not been unfairly dismissed in the circumstances described in regulation 8(1)". For my part, I would make such an implication which is entirely consistent with the general scheme of the Regulations and which is necessary if they are effectively to fulfil the purpose for which they were made of giving effect to the provisions of the Directive. This does not involve any disapproval of the reasoning of the Court of Appeal in *Spence*'s case which, on the facts there found by the industrial tribunal, did not involve a dismissal attracting the consequences provided in regulation 8(1).'

(Lords Keith and Templeman delivered concurring judgments. Lords Brandon and Jauncey concurred. It was held that the transferee, Forth Estuary Engineering, were liable to the applicants for unfair dismissal.)

COMMENT

(1) This is a prime example of the purposive approach being invoked in order to give effect to an EC Directive. However, note that it does not mean that in every case where employees are employed until very shortly before the transfer reg 8 will be taken to apply. It will depend on whether the dismissals of the workers are linked to the transfer or not: here, there was collusion between transferor and transferee. That was not the case in *Spence*.

(2) Lord Oliver's analysis of the effects of a purported termination by the transferor was applied by the Court of Appeal in the following joined appeals.

Wilson v St Helens BC

Meade v British Fuels Ltd

[1997] IRLR 505 Court of Appeal

Problems arose in both cases because initially it was not appreciated that TUPE applied. In the first case, Lancashire County Council transferred the running of a children's home to St

Helens because it could no longer afford to run it. St Helens required certain financial guarantees before taking it on, and to meet the economic criteria the size of the operation was much reduced. The staff who stayed working at the school were made redundant by the county council and then given new contracts, on less favourable terms and conditions, by St Helens.

Eighteen months later the employees argued that, as it was a transfer to which TUPE applied, they should have continued on their former contracts, with the more favourable terms and conditions.

In the second case, the employees worked for a subsidiary of British Coal Corporation (BCC) called NFD. BCC bought another company and merged it with BCC; the new company was British Fuels Ltd. The NFD employees were given notice of redundancy, paid their redundancy payments, and offered new contracts, on less favourable terms and conditions, with British Fuels. Some 21 months later, Meade sought a declaration that his terms and conditions were still those which applied under NFD, as TUPE applied to the merger.

Both cases raised the question of whether the Acquired Rights Directive, and therefore TUPE, prohibited a change in terms and conditions caused by the transfer when this was agreed to by the employees. Arguably, they also raised the wider question as to how long after a transfer employees can continue to insist on their original terms and conditions. However, the Court of Appeal saw the case as being essentially about the validity of the termination of the employees' contracts in both cases. Giving the judgment of the Court, Beldam LJ quoted extensively from *Litster* before reaching the following conclusions:

Beldam LJ: '... From Lord Oliver's opinion, and the judgments in the European Court of Justice he cites, I would draw the following propositions.

(1) The purpose of the Directive is intended to ensure as far as possible that the employment relationship continues unchanged with the transferee and to protect workers against dismissals motivated solely by the fact of the transfer.

(2) That the existence or otherwise of the contract of employment on the date of the transfer within the meaning of Article 3(1) of the Directive must be established on the basis of the rules of national law, subject however to observance of the mandatory provisions of the Directive and more particularly Article 4(1) concerning the protection of employees against dismissal by the transferor or transferee by reason only of the transfer.

(3) It is for the national courts to decide whether or not on the date of transfer the employees in question were linked to the undertaking by virtue of a contract of employment or employment relationship.

(4) That under Article 4 the transfer does not by itself justify dismissal by the transferor or transferee unless such dismissal is for economic, technical or organisational reasons entailing changes in the workforce ... the employer who dismisses an employee for one of the reasons specified in Article 4(1) can thus justify the dismissal.

(5) In order to determine whether the only reason for dismissal was the transfer itself, account must be taken of the objective circumstances in which the dismissal occurred, in particular whether it took place on a date close to the transfer and whether the workers concerned were re-engaged by the transferee.

(6) A dismissal effected before the transfer and solely because of the transfer of the business is in effect prohibited and when considering the application of Article 3(1) is required to be treated as ineffective.

(7) That the crucial question is what is meant by a contract of employment being terminated "by" a transfer. To answer this question it is necessary to decide what is the effective reason for the termination of the contracts of employment.

In short, neither the former employer nor the succeeding employer may dismiss the employees simply because of the transfer, but they are not prohibited from terminating their contracts of employment on the occasion of the transfer if they do so on economic, technical or organisational grounds.

In implementing the provisions of Article 4 of the Directive, the draftsman of the Regulations has separated the effect of a relevant transfer on contracts of employment in reg. 5 from the provisions relating to the dismissal of the employee because of the relevant transfer in reg. 8. Nevertheless, the two regulations must, unless their language makes it impossible, be interpreted to give effect to the Directive as explained in the decisions of the European Court of Justice.

I would reject the submission of BFL, adopted also by St Helens, that the provisions of reg. 8(1) can be so applied to a dismissal before a relevant transfer that the transferor may validly, albeit unfairly, terminate his employees' contracts of employment so that they are not employed "immediately before" the transfer. Regulation 8(1) presupposes that the transfer is the reason or principal reason for the termination of the employee's contract and in that event reg. 5 provides that the transfer is not to determine the contract which is to have effect as if made with the transferee. The Regulations have to be read as a whole and the court or tribunal must seek the reason for the termination of the contract and not the manner in which it is effected by the employer. To uphold the employer's argument would deprive the employee of the benefit of his contract of employment and leave him only with remedies to enforce secondary obligations. Moreover, the submission is inconsistent with the interpretation of reg. 5(3) in *Litster*'s case that a person unfairly dismissed is to be regarded as employed in the undertaking immediately before the relevant transfer.

Regulation 8 clearly envisages dismissal both before and after a relevant transfer; before transfer such a dismissal could only be effected by the transferor. The regulation draws a distinction between those dismissals which are unfair, because the reason or principal reason for them is the transfer or a reason connected with it, and those which are to be regarded as not unfair because the reason or principal reason for them is an economic, technical or organisational reason entailing changes in the workforce. Thus if the contract of employment is terminated for such a reason, it is not to be regarded as terminated by the transfer itself though the termination may occur on the occasion of the transfer.

The decision in the *St Helens* appeals

I return to the facts of this case as found by the industrial tribunal and interpret its reasoning differently to the appeal tribunal. I do not think that it is correct to say that the industrial tribunal held that the transfer was the reason for the variation in the terms and conditions of employment of the employees. ...

How then should the findings of the industrial tribunal be interpreted? In my view, the tribunal effectively held that, whether by the transferor or transferee, the reason or principal reason why the contracts of employment were terminated was an economic or organisational reason. Accordingly, the Regulations had to be interpreted in a way which was consistent with Article 4(1) of the directive so that the provisions of reg. 5 did not apply to continue the contracts of employment with St Helens. On that basis, when the employees took up their new positions on 2 October 1992, they did so on the terms and conditions of the new contracts. Accordingly, I would hold that St Helens did not make unlawful deductions from the employees' wages and I would allow the appeals.

The decision in the *British Fuel Ltd* appeal

Although the appeal tribunal posed to itself the correct question in saying, "What falls to be decided is the effect in law of the purported notice of dismissal on 20 August 1992," I consider the tribunal was wrong to hold that the dismissal was effective in law to terminate the contract of employment, albeit unfairly. ...

The European Court of Justice has confirmed the mandatory effect of the rules of the Directive concerning the protection of workers against dismissal by reason of the transfer in subsequent cases, for example in *Rask* and in *Rotsart de Hertaing*, and in *Daddy's Dance Hall* itself. Nor do I think it correct to say that the words added in reg. 5(3) to give full effect to the Directive in *Litster's* case: "... necessarily reflect as a premise the validity of the dismissal subject to deemed unfairness, and subject to deemed liability therefor on the part of the transferee." In *Litster's* case, the appellant employees were no longer employed by the transferee, who had taken on different employees. Accordingly, no question of the terms and conditions of continued employment could arise. As Lord Oliver said, there only remained the secondary obligations to comply with the available remedies. But the effect of implying the additional words was that employees unfairly dismissed are to be regarded as employed immediately before the transfer and accordingly reg. 5(1) applies to their contracts of employment.

In my view, the appeal tribunal should have approached its decision by asking whether the transfer of the undertaking itself was the reason for the dismissal of the employees. On the evidence before the industrial tribunals, it was. If it had then considered the consequences, it could only have concluded that the purported dismissal was ineffective and that the contracts of employment continued as if originally made with BFL.

Accordingly, construing regs. 5 and 8 of the Regulations consistently with the Directive as interpreted by the European Court of Justice, the employees continued to be employed by BFL on the terms and conditions of their contracts of employment with NFD. ...'

(Waite and Swinton Thomas LJJ agreed.)

Consultation over transfers and redundancies

Both the Collective Dismissals Directive (75/129/EEC) and the Acquired Rights Directive (77/187/EEC) require employers to consult with workers' representatives. In British law this obligation was implemented by requiring consultation with recognised trade unions, which meant, of course, that where there was no recognised trade union, employees did not have a right to consultation. In 1994, in *EC Commission* v *United Kingdom*, the ECJ confirmed that this was a breach of the Directives. As a result, the Collective Redundancies and Transfers of Undertakings (Protection of Employment) (Amendment) Regulations 1995 were passed, to amend the existing consultation requirements.

Transfer of Undertakings (Protection of Employment) Regulations 1981

10. ... (2) Long enough before a relevant transfer to enable the employer of any affected employees to consult all the persons who are appropriate representatives of any of those affected employees, the employer shall inform those representatives of—

(a) the fact that the relevant transfer is to take place, when, approximately, it is to take place and the reasons for it; and

(b) the legal, economic and social implications of the transfer for the affected employees; and

(c) the measures which he envisages he will, in connection with the transfer, take in relation to those employees or, if he envisages that no measures will be so taken, that fact; and

(d) if the employer is the transferor, the measures which the transferee envisages he will, in connection with the transfer, take in relation to such of those employees as, by virtue of Regulation 5 above, become employees of the transferee after the transfer or, if he envisages that no measures will be so taken, that fact.

(2A) For the purposes of this Regulation the appropriate representatives of any employees are—

(a) employee representatives elected by them; or

(b) if the employees are of a description in respect of which an independent trade union is recognised by the employer, representatives of the trade union,

or (in the case of employees who both elect employee representatives and are of such a description) either employee representatives elected by them or representatives of the trade union, as the employer chooses.

(3) The transferee shall give the transferor such information at such a time as will enable the transferor to perform the duty imposed on him by virtue of paragraph (2)(d) above.

(4) The information which is to be given to the appropriate representatives shall be given to each of them by being delivered to them, or sent by post to an address notified by them to the employer, or (in the case of representatives of a trade union) sent by post to the union at the address of its head or main office.

(5) Where an employer of any affected employees envisages that he will, in connection with the transfer, be taking measures in relation to any such employees he shall consult all the persons who are appropriate representatives of any of the affected employees in relation to whom he envisages taking measures with a view to seeking their agreement to measures to be taken.

(6) In the course of those consultations the employer shall—

(a) consider any representations made by the appropriate representatives; and

(b) reply to those representations and, if he rejects any of those representations, state his reasons.

(6A) The employer shall allow the appropriate representatives access to the affected employees and shall afford to those representatives such accommodation and other facilities as may be appropriate.

(7) If in any case there are special circumstances which render it not reasonably practicable for an employer to perform a duty imposed on him by any of paragraphs (2) to (6), he shall take all such steps towards performing that duty as are reasonably practicable in the circumstances.

(8) Where—

(a) the employer has invited any of the affected employees to elect employee representatives, and

(b) the invitation was issued long enough before the time when the employer is required to give information under paragraph (2) above to allow them to elect representatives by that time,

the employer shall be treated as complying with the requirements of this Regulation in relation to those employees if he complies with those requirements as soon as is reasonably practicable after the election of the representatives.

Trade Union and Labour Relations (Consolidation) Act 1992

188. (1) Where an employer is proposing to dismiss as redundant 20 or more employes at one establishment within a period of 90 days or less, the employer shall consult about the dismissals all the persons who are appropriate representatives of any of the employees who may be so dismissed.

(1A) The consultation shall begin in good time and in any event—
   (a) where the employer is proposing to dismiss 100 or more employees as mentioned in subsection (1), at last 90 days, and
   (b) otherwise, at least 30 days,
   before the first of the dismissals takes effect.

(1B) For the purposes of this section the appropriate representatives of any employees are—
   (a) employee representatives elected by them, or
   (b) if the employees are of a description in respect of which an independent trade union is recognised by the employer, representatives of the trade union,
   or (in the case of employees who both elect employee representatives and are of such a description) either employee representatives elected by them or representatives of the trade union, as the employer chooses.

(2) The consultation shall include consultation about ways of—
   (a) avoiding the dismissals,
   (b) reducing the numbers of employees to be dismissed, and
   (c) mitigating the consequences of the dismissals,
   and shall be undertaken by the employer with a view to reaching agreement with the appropriate representatives.

COMMENT

(1) The duties to consult under TUPE reg 10 and TULRCA s 188 are in parallel terms, but there are some important differences. Under TUPE, the duty to consult applies to both transferor and transferee and the scope of the consultation is wider, covering the legal, social and economic implications of the transfer.

(2) The mechanism for consulting employee representatives other than trade union representatives was introduced by the 1995 Regulations to comply with the decision of the ECJ. Note that the employer could choose to consult non-union representatives even where there is a recognised trade union, although this may be unlikely to happen in practice. Provided that the employer invites employees to elect representatives in good time, there is no affirmative obligation to ensure that an election takes place – in which case, employees could still find that they are not represented.

(3) This was one of the main grounds on which the 1995 Regulations were challenged by three trade unions in *R* v *Secretary of State, ex p Unison*. However, the Divisional Court held that no breach of the Directives had taken place.

(4) For redundancy consultation, the obligation to consult now arises only where 20 or more are due to be made redundant over a 90-day period. Until amendment in 1995, the obligation applied to every single redundancy. However, when it was obliged by the ECJ to amend TULRCA s 188, the then Conservative Government took the

opportunity to limit the obligation in this way, which is permitted by the Collective Dismissals Directive.

(5)   Note the differences in the timing of the consultation: no specific period is laid down in TUPE, provided that it is 'long enough before ...'. TULRCA s 188 used to require consultation 'at the earliest opportunity', but was also watered down by the 1995 Regulations. Under TUPE the duty to consult arises only when a transfer has been decided upon. Under s 188, it is when the employer proposes to dismiss workers for redundancy. What is meant by 'proposing to dismiss', and is this in accordance with the Collective Dismissals Directive?

Hough v Leyland DAF Ltd

[1991] IRLR 194 Employment Appeal Tribunal

The applicants had been employed as security staff by the company. In May 1987 the company accepted a report from its security manager recommending that security arrangements should be contracted out. The employees' union, APEX was not informed until September 1987; the redundancies took effect at the end of December 1987. The employees claimed unfair dismissal (and were successful: this aspect of the case is not extracted), and the trade union complained of a failure to consult in breach of what is now TULRCA s 188.

Knox J: '... It was submitted to us on behalf of Leyland that the requirements in subsection [(4)] for disclosure of various matters indicated that the proposals will have reached a fairly advanced stage before the employer can be said to be "proposing" for the purposes of subsection (1) so as to be under an immediate duty to consult. We agree that [s 188] read as a whole contemplates that matters should have reached a stage where a specific proposal has been formulated and that this is a later stage than the diagnosis of a problem and the appreciation that at least one way of dealing with it would be by declaring redundancies. Beyond that we doubt whether it is helpful to try and analyse conceptually the precise stage that an employer must have reached to be "proposing" for the purposes of subsection (1) because the section has to cover a large multiplicity of possible situations which would be susceptible of very widely differing types of treatment. In that state of affairs it seems to us better to stick to the words of the section ...'

COMMENT

(1)   In *R* v *British Coal, ex p Vardy*, Glidewell LJ expressed the view that s 188 did not properly implement the Collective Dismissals Directive:

'I say this because in the Directive consultation is to begin as soon as an employer contemplates redundancies, whereas under the Act it only needs to begin when he proposes to dismiss as redundant an employee. The verb "proposes" in its ordinary usage relates to a state of mind which is much more certain and further along the decision-making process than the verb "contemplate" ...'

His comments were *obiter* but seem correct. However, this point was not taken in *EC Commission* v *UK* or *R* v *Secretary of State, ex p Unison*.

The special circumstances defence

In TULRCA s 188(7) and in TUPE reg 10(7) an employer has a defence where special circumstances render prior consultation not reasonably practicable. When will this apply?

Clarks of Hove Ltd v Bakers' Union

[1978] ICR 1076 Court of Appeal

The company, which had a bakery and retail business, found itself in serious financial trouble in late summer 1976. It sought a buyer for some of its shops in order to raise essential capital, but in October, its main prospect pulled out on seeing an auditors' report and on 24 October the last hope in the shape of another buyer also collapsed. The same day the directors put up a notice informing the employees that they were dismissed. The company argued that the financial situation amounted to special circumstances excusing their failure to consult.

Geoffrey Lane LJ: '...What, then is meant by "special circumstances"? Here we come to the crux of the case. In this aspect, also, the decisions under the Road Traffic Acts appear to me to be unhelpful. The decisions are too well known to need reference. The basis of them all is probably *Whittal* v *Kirby, per* Lord Goddard CJ,

"A special reason ... is one ... special to the facts of the particular case ... special to the facts which constitute the offence.... A circumstance peculiar to the offender as distinguished from the offence is not a special reason ..."

In so far as that means that the special circumstance must be relevant to the issue then that would apply equally here, but in these circumstances, the Employment Protection Act 1975 [now TULRCA s 188], it seems to me that the way in which the phrase was interpreted by the industrial tribunal is correct. What they said, in effect, was this, that insolvency is, on its own, neither here nor there. It may be a special circumstance, it may not be a special circumstance. It will depend entirely on the cause of the insolvency whether the circumstances can be described as special or not. If, for example, sudden disaster strikes a company, making it necessary to close the concern, then plainly that would be a matter which was capable of being a special circumstance; and that is so whether the disaster is physical or financial. If the insolvency, however, were merely due to a gradual run-down of the company, as it was in this case, then those are facts on which the industrial tribunal can come to the conclusion that the circumstances were not special. In other words, to be special the event must be something out of the ordinary, something uncommon; and that is the meaning of the word "special" in the context of this Act.

Accordingly it seems to me that the industrial tribunal approached the matter in precisely the correct way. They distilled the problem which they had to decide down to its essence, and they asked themselves this question: do these circumstances, which undoubtedly caused the summary dismissal and the failure to consult the union as required by [section 188], amount to special circumstances; and they went on, again correctly, as it seems to me, to point out that insolvency simpliciter is neutral, it is not on its own a special circumstance. Whether it is or is not will depend upon the causes of the insolvency. They define "special" as being something out of the ordinary run of events, such as, for example, a general trading boycott – that is the passage which I have already read. Here, again, I think they were right.'

(Roskill LJ delivered a concurring judgment and Stephenson LJ agreed.)

COMMENT

(1)   The decision that the reason for a sudden insolvency, and not merely its existence, is of the first importance and has been widely applied since (e.g. *Re Hartlebury Printers Ltd*). Note that even if the full consultation period is impossible, employers should still strive so far as feasible to comply by engaging in consultation as soon as they can.

(2)   It is common for counsel to argue by analogy to the use of similar words in other statutes when a statutory phrase comes up for interpretation, but the attempt to use the Road Traffic Acts by way of analogy seems singularly inappropriate.

(3)   Under TULRCA s 189, the remedy for failure to consult is for the trade union to apply for protective award on behalf of the employees. The maximum award possible corresponds to the minimum consultation periods for multiple redundancies in s 188. This may be contrasted with the maximum protective award of four weeks' pay available for breach of the duty to consult under TUPE. Since the amendments by TURERA, the two protective awards should not be set off against each other when both are payable; nor are they to be set off against any contractual severance payment.

10 Freedom of association

FREEDOM OF ASSOCIATION AND THE STATE

Freedom of association is regarded as an aspect of human rights, since it covers not merely freedom to belong to bodies like trade unions, but also political parties, religious groups and other kinds of organisation. Hence a right to associate is to be found in many treaties on human rights as well as in the Conventions of the International Labour Organization which are directly concerned with employment standards.

Treaties are addressed to states: under international law a state which ratifies a treaty has an obligation to change its municipal law to accord with it. Treaties do not generally apply directly.

Universal Declaration of Human Rights 1948

Article 20

(1)   Everyone has the right to freedom of peaceful assembly and association.
(2)   No one may be compelled to belong to an association.

COMMENT

(1)   The Universal Declaration of Human Rights has achieved general acceptance and can be taken to represent international law. As it is both brief and general it was intended that the standards should be filled out by later treaties. The International Covenants on Economic, Social and Cultural Rights and on Civil and Political Rights represent this next stage (cf Article 8 ICESCR and Article 22 ICCPR).

European Convention on Human Rights 1950

Article 11

1.   Everyone has the right to freedom of peaceful assembly and to freedom of association with others, including the right to form and to join trade unions for the protection of his interests.
2.   No restrictions shall be placed on the exercise of these rights other than such as are prescribed by law and are necessary in a democratic society in the interests of national security or public safety, for the prevention of disorder or crime, for the protection of health or morals or for the protection of the rights and freedoms of others. This Article

shall not prevent the imposition of lawful restrictions on the exercise of these rights by members of the armed forces, of the police or of the administration of the State.

COMMENT

(1)   Unlike most international treaties, the ECHR may be enforced through legal proceedings. A UK citizen who believes that the state is in breach of the Convention may complain to the European Commission on Human Rights. If the Commission believes that the case is likely to succeed and that it has fulfilled other conditions (like exhausting internal remedies first) it can refer the case to the European Court of Human Rights, which sits at Strasbourg. An example of this is *Young, James and Webster* v *UK*, p 419.

ILO Convention No 87 (1948)

Freedom of Association and Protection of the Right to Organize

PART I. FREEDOM OF ASSOCIATION
Article 1

Each Member of the International Labour Organization for which this Convention is in force undertakes to give effect to the following provisions.

Article 2

Workers and employers, without distinction whatsoever, shall have the right to establish and, subject only to the rules of the organization concerned, to join organizations of their own choosing without previous authorisation.

Article 3

1.   Workers' and employers' organizations shall have the right to draw up their constitutions and rules, to elect their representatives in full freedom, to organize their administration and activities and to formulate their programmes.
2.   The public authorities shall refrain from any interference which would restrict this right or impede the lawful exercise thereof.

Article 4

Workers' and employers' organizations shall not be liable to be dissolved or suspended by administrative authority. …

Article 9

1.   The extent to which the guarantees provided for in this Convention shall apply to the armed forces and the police shall be determined by national laws or regulations.
2.   In accordance with the principle set forth in paragraph 8 of article 19 of the Constitution of the International Labour Organization the ratification of this Convention by any Member shall not be deemed to affect any existing law, award, custom or agreement in virtue of which members of the armed forces or the police enjoy any right guaranteed by this Convention. …

Article 11

Each Member of the International Labour Organization for which this Convention is in force undertakes to take all necessary and appropriate measures to ensure that workers and employers may exercise freely the right to organize. …

Article 16

1. A Member which has ratified this Convention may denounce it after the expiration of ten years from the date on which the Convention first comes into force, by an act communicated to the Director-General of the International Labour Office for registration. Such denunciation shall not take effect until one year after the date on which it is registered.

2. Each Member which has ratified this Convention and which does not, within the year following the expiration of the period of ten years mentioned in the preceding paragraph, exercise the right of denunciation provided for in this Article, will be bound for another period of ten years and, thereafter, may denounce this Convention at the expiration of each period of ten years under the terms provided for in this Article.

ILO Convention No 98 (1949)

Application of the Principles of the Right to Organize and to Bargain Collectively

Article 1

1. Workers shall enjoy adequate protection against acts of anti-union discrimination in respect of their employment.

2. Such protection shall apply more particularly in respect of acts calculated to—
   (a) make the employment of a worker subject to the condition that he shall not join a union or shall relinquish trade union membership;
   (b) cause the dismissal of or otherwise prejudice a worker by reason of union membership or because of participation in union activities outside working hours or, with the consent of the employer, within working hours.

Article 2

1. Workers' and employers' organizations shall enjoy adequate protection against any acts of interference by each other or each other's agents or members in their establishment, functioning or administration.

2. In particular, acts which are designed to promote the establishment of workers' organizations under the domination of employers' organizations, or to support workers' organizations by financial or other means, with the object of placing such organizations under the control of employers or employers' organizations, shall be deemed to constitute acts of interference within the meaning of this Article.

COMMENT

(1) The provisions for coming into force and the denunciation of this Convention are the same as for Convention No 87.

(2) It will be noted that states may make exceptions for the police and armed forces, a permission taken up by the UK. The police and armed forces may not belong to

trade unions. No other group of staff is specifically forbidden by law, but one group of civil servants had their rights restricted in recent years.

Council of Civil Service Unions v Minister for the Civil Service

[1985] ICR 14 House of Lords

Government Communications Headquarters (GCHQ) was responsible for ensuring the security of official and military communications and for monitoring foreign signals for intelligence services. Employees belonged to various civil service unions which were members of the Council of Civil Service Unions (CCSU). In 1984, the Secretary of State announced without warning or consultation that all employees would have to cease membership of national trade unions. This was because they had taken part in a number of one-day strikes at their unions' behest between 1979 and 1981, which, in the view of the Government, endangered national security. The CCSU challenged the decision because of the lack of consultation.

Lord Fraser:
'National security
The issue here is not whether the minister's instruction was proper or fair or justifiable on its merits. These matters are not for the courts to determine. The sole issue is whether the decision on which the instruction was based was reached by a process that was fair to the staff at GCHQ. As my noble and learned friend Lord Brightman said in *Chief Constable of the North Wales Police* v *Evans,* "Judicial review is concerned, not with the decision, but with the decision-making process."

I have already explained my reasons for holding that, if no question of national security arose, the decision-making process in this case would have been unfair. The respondent's case is that she deliberately made the decision without prior consultation because prior consultation "would involve a real risk that it would occasion the very kind of disruption [at GCHQ] which was a threat to national security and which it was intended to avoid". I have quoted from paragraph 27(i) of the respondent's printed case. Mr Blom-Cooper conceded that a reasonable minister could reasonably have taken that view, but he argued strongly that the respondent had failed to show that that was in fact the reason for her decision. He supported his argument by saying, as I think was conceded by Mr Alexander, that the reason given in paragraph 27(i) had not been mentioned to Glidewell J and that it had only emerged before the Court of Appeal. He described it as an "afterthought" and invited the House to hold that it had not been shown to have been the true reason.

The question is one of evidence. The decision on whether the requirements of national security outweigh the duty of fairness in any particular case is for the Government and not for the courts; the Government alone has access to the necessary information, and in any event the judicial process is unsuitable for reaching decisions on national security. But if the decision is successfully challenged, on the ground that it has been reached by a process which is unfair, then the Government is under an obligation to produce evidence that the decision was in fact based on grounds of national security. Authority for both these points is found in *The Zamora*. The former point is dealt with in the well known passage from the advice of the Judicial Committee delivered by Lord Parker of Waddington,

"Those who are responsible for the national security must be the sole judges of what the national security requires. It would be obviously undesirable that such matters should be made the subject of evidence in a court of law or otherwise discussed in public."

The second point, less often referred to, appears at p 108 where this passage occurs:

"In their Lordships' opinion the order appealed from was wrong, not because, as contended by the appellants, there is by international law no right at all to requisition ships or goods in the custody of the court, but because the judge had before him *no satisfactory evidence* that such a right was exercisable." (Emphasis added.)

The evidence in support of this part of the respondent's case came from Sir Robert Armstrong in his first affidavit, especially at paragraph 16. Mr Blom-Cooper rightly pointed out that the affidavit does not in terms directly support paragraph 27(i). But it does set out the respondent's view that to have entered into prior consultation would have served to bring out the vulnerability of areas of operation to those who had shown themselves ready to organise disruption. That must be read along with the earlier parts of the affidavit in which Sir Robert had dealt in some detail with the attitude of the trade unions which I have referred to earlier in this speech. The affidavit, read as a whole, does in my opinion undoubtedly constitute evidence that the Minister did indeed consider that prior consultation would have involved a risk of precipitating disruption at GCHQ. I am accordingly of opinion that the respondent has shown that her decision was one which not only could reasonably have been based, but was in fact based, on considerations of national security, which outweighed what would otherwise have been the reasonable expectation on the part of the appellants for prior consultation. In deciding that matter I must with respect differ from the decision of Glidewell J but, as I have mentioned, I do so on a point that was not argued to him.

Minor Matters
The judge held that had the prior consultations taken place they would not have been so limited that he could confidently say that they would have been futile. It is not necessary for me to reach a concluded view on this matter, but as at present advised I am inclined to differ from the learned judge, especially because of the attitude of two of the trade union members of CCSU which declared that they were firmly against any no-strike agreement.

The Court of Appeal considered the proper construction of certain international labour conventions which they cite. I respectfully agree with Lord Lane CJ who said that "the correct meaning of the material articles of the Conventions is by no means clear", but I do not propose to consider the matter as the Conventions are not part of the law in this country ...'

(The union's appeal over the failure to consult was dismissed. Lords Scarman, Diplock, Roskill and Brightman delivered concurring opinions.)

COMMENT

(1)   Those civil servants who refused to give up their union membership were ultimately dismissed in 1988. The case was referred to the ILO, whose Committee of Experts considered that there was a breach of Convention No 87. However, the Conservative Government ignored its recommendations. See further Ewing, *Britain and the ILO* (IER 1989) and Brown and McColgan, 'UK Employment Law and the ILO' (1992) 21 ILJ 265. One of the first acts of the Labour Government elected in May 1997 was to restore the right of GCHQ staff to belong to trade unions.

(2)   The case was referred also to the European Commission on Human Rights, but failed because, as can be seen from ECHR Article 11(2), those concerned with the administration of the state can be exempted.

(3)   Clearly, where states accept their obligations to guarantee freedom of association

they must limit the power of employers to victimise employees because of union membership – otherwise the freedom is meaningless.

FREEDOM OF ASSOCIATION AND THE EMPLOYER

Dismissal and action short of dismissal on grounds of union membership

Trade Union and Labour Relations (Consolidation) Act 1992

146. (1)   An employee has the right not to have action short of dismissal taken against him as an individual by his employer for the purpose of—
  (a)   preventing or deterring him from being or seeking to become a member of an independent trade union, or penalising him for doing so,
  (b)   preventing or deterring him from taking part in the activities of an independent trade union at an appropriate time, or penalising him for doing so, or
  (c)   compelling him to be or become a member of any trade union or of a particular trade union or of one of a number of particular trade unions.

  (2)   In subsection (1)(b) 'an appropriate time' means—
  (a)   a time outside the employee's working hours, or
  (b)   a time within his working hours at which, in accordance with arrangements agreed with or consent given by his employer, it is permissible for him to take part in the activities of a trade union;
  and for this purpose 'working hours', in relation to an employee, means any time when, in accordance with his contract of employment, he is required to be at work.
  ...
  (5)   An employee may present a complaint to an industrial tribunal on the ground that action has been taken against him by his employer in contravention of this section.

COMMENT

(1)   TULRCA s 152, in parallel terms to s 146, states that it is automatically unfair to dismiss an employee on the same grounds as specified in s 146. Selection for redundancy on these grounds is also automatically unfair, although note the limitation in *O'Dea* v *ISC Chemicals Ltd*.

(2)   While TULRCA ss 137, 146 and 152 seem to provide a coherent and comprehensive protection of freedom of association as against an employer, the history of these provisions shows that the thinking behind them is not so logical. The protection against dismissal has been around in some form or another since the original unfair dismissal provisions of the Industrial Relations Act 1971. In 1975, when the Employment Protection Act introduced a range of positive employment protection rights concurrent with the contract of employment, protection against action short of dismissal was instituted. However, it was only in the 1990 Employment Act that the protection was extended to recruitment.

(3)   Note that these provisions protect against *refusal* to belong to a trade union as

well: this aspect will be considered further in the section on the closed shop, below.

(4)   The leading case on the meaning of 'action short of dismissal' is the following decision of the House of Lords.

Associated Newspapers Ltd v *Wilson* ; *Associated British Ports* v *Palmer*

[1995] ICR 406 House of Lords

Both cases resulted from the desire of the employers to move employees on to 'personal contracts' away from collectively agreed terms and conditions. In *Wilson*'s case, the company terminated the collective agreement with the union in April 1989. Employees who were willing to sign individual contracts were given a pay rise of 4.5 per cent from October 1989. Those (including Wilson) who declined and remained on the collectively agreed terms were told that they could expect no increase until the next salary review in October 1990. In *Palmer*'s case the company did not terminate collective bargaining, but offered a significant increase in pay to any employees who would opt for an individual contract; Palmer was one of those who refused to do so. Both applicants argued that the omission to give the pay rise to them constituted action short of dismissal for the purpose of deterring their trade union membership.

Lord Bridge: '...
The new point of law
[Section 298 of TULRCA] provides that:

" In this Act ... except so far as the context otherwise requires –
'act' and 'action' each includes omission and references to doing an act or taking action shall be construed accordingly ..."

The courts below were bound by authority to accept that the application of this definition to [s 146(1)] has the effect that, if an employer confers a benefit on employee A which he withholds from employee B, the omission to confer the benefit on B may, if the circumstances warrant such a finding, amount to "action (short of dismissal) taken against" B for one of the purposes prohibited by [s 146(1)], irrespective of the question whether B had any reasonable expectation of receiving that benefit. This proposition is established by the decision of the Court of Appeal in *National Coal Board* v *Ridgway and Fairbrother*. In that case the board employed miners belonging to rival unions, the National Union of Mineworkers ("the NUM") and the Union of Democratic Mineworkers ("the UDM"), at the same colliery. The board agreed to pay increased wages to members of the UDM but not to members of the NUM. On application by members of the NUM, the Industrial Tribunal held that withholding the increase from the applicants was an "omission" amounting to "action (short of dismissal) taken against" them for the purpose of penalising them for being members of the NUM and thus was a contravention of [s 146(1)(a)]. This decision was upheld by the Court of Appeal by a majority (Nicholls and Bingham LJJ, May LJ dissenting). May LJ said:

"There must, at the least, have been some obligation to pay or some expectation of receipt to enable one to categorise the non-payment of UDM rates to these applicants as an 'omission' on the part of the board to make such payments."

The majority view was expressed by Nicholls LJ, where he said:

"For an act to constitute 'action' within [s 146] there does not need to be any reasonable expectation by the employee that the employer would not so behave. This being so, I see no justification for adding this requirement as a gloss on the language of the statute in the case of an 'omission'. To be within [s 146], the conduct complained of has to have been done 'for the purpose of'. If it is for one of the requisite purposes that an employer omits to do something vis-à-vis the complainant employee as an individual then, whatever is the nature of the omission, it is impermissible."

The novel question, raised for the first time before your Lordships, is whether the extended meanings of the word "action" and of the phrase "taking action" provided by [s 298] are properly to be applied to [s 146(1)] or whether this is a case where "the context otherwise requires". The crucial phrase to be construed in [s 146(1)] is "the right not to have action ... taken against him". If this phrase is to be construed as embodying the extended meaning, one must first expand the language so as to include the verb "omit" or the noun "omission" to see how it reads. The attempt to do this grammatically, without substantially recasting the phrase and introducing additional words, at once exposes the difficulty. If the concept of taking action *against* some person is to embrace the concept of omitting to act, the omission must be an omission to act in that person's favour. I cannot believe that any competent Parliamentary draftsman, intending that an omission by an employer to take action in favour of an employee should have the same consequences as positive action taken against him, would fail to spell out the circumstances in which the obligation to take action in favour of the employee was to arise. Otherwise he creates an obvious ambiguity, as the difference of judicial opinion in *National Coal Board* v *Ridgway* well illustrates. To put it no higher, the question whether [s 146(1)] should be rewritten in some way so as to spell out expressly the meaning of "action" as including omission, or whether the context requires that the definition be not applied, gives rise to a "real and substantial difficulty" in the interpretation of the statute "which classical methods of construction cannot resolve" and thus entitles us to go behind the [EPCA] 1978 to derive whatever assistance we can in resolving the difficulty from the legislative history: see *Farrell* v *Alexander* per Lord Wilberforce.

The previous Acts consolidated by the Act of 1978 included the Trade Union and Labour Relations Act 1974 and the Employment Protection Act 1975. The definition of "act" and "action" now found in s 153(1) of the [EPCA 1978, now TULRCA s 298] was previously in s 30(1) of the Act of 1974 but did not appear anywhere in the Act of 1975. Section 23 of [the EPCA 1978, now TULRCA s 146], however, re-enacts s 53 of the Act of 1975. Thus, prior to the 1978 consolidation, there was no question of applying any definition giving an extended meaning to the word "action" in the context in which we now have to construe it.
...

... if the definition of "action" in [s 298] is applied to [s 146(1)], not only do we encounter the grammatical difficulty to which I have already referred, but we must also conclude that a consolidation Act has substantially altered the pre-existing law in a way that neither the draftsman nor Parliament can have intended. It seems to me plain that both the draftsman of the consolidation bill and the committee who approved it must have been satisfied that the definition of "act" and "action" taken from the Act of 1974 were excluded by the context of the phrase "the right not to have action taken against him" in s 53 of the Act of 1975.

Counsel for the respondents in the ABP appeal sought to surmount this hurdle by submitting that the policy of the relevant employment legislation has consistently outlawed discrimination in any form against employees on account of their union membership and that the language of [s 146(1)], even if not extended by definition to apply to omissions, should nevertheless be construed liberally as having the same effect as that attributed to it by the majority in *National Coal Board* v *Ridgway*. So far from supporting this submission it seems to me that a closer examination of the legislative history conclusively refutes it. The original enactment, which did indeed embody just such an anti-discrimination policy as that for which counsel now contends, was s 5 of the Industrial Relations Act 1971 which provided, so far as material:

"...

(2) It shall accordingly be an unfair industrial practice for any employer, or for any person acting on behalf of an employer –

...

    (b)   to dismiss, penalise or otherwise *discriminate against* a worker by reason of his exercising any such rights, or

    (c)   ...

(3) ...

(4) Where an employer offers a benefit of any kind to workers as an inducement to refrain from exercising a right conferred on them by subsection (1) of this section, and the employer—

    (a)   confers that benefit on one or more of those workers who agree to refrain from exercising that right,

        and

    (b)   withholds it from one or more of them who do not agree to do so,

the employer shall for the purposes of this section be regarded, in relation to any such worker as is mentioned in paragraph (b) of this subsection, as having thereby *discriminated against* him by reason of his exercising that right." [Emphasis added.] ...

... The language of this previous provision must clearly have been present to the draftsman's mind and, if his intention had been to achieve the same legislative consequence, it is, to my mind, inconceivable that he should not have used either the same language or language substantially to the like effect. In fact, as we have seen, he did not even use the word "discriminate" or adopt the extended definition of "action" used in the Act of 1974. ...

The line of reasoning which I have followed in three foregoing paragraphs was discussed in the course of argument and was criticised as unduly literalistic. It was even submitted that the Labour Government which introduced the Act of 1975 could not have intended to provide less effective protection for trade union members than the Act of 1971. A purposive construction to resolve ambiguities of statutory language is often appropriate and necessary. But this is the first time I have heard it suggested that the policy of an enactment to be presumed from the political complexion of the government which introduced it may prevail over the language of the statute. The courts' traditional approach to construction, giving primacy to the ordinary, grammatical meaning of statutory language, is reflected in the Parliamentary draftsman's technique of using language with the utmost precision to express the legislative intent of his political masters and it remains the golden rule of construction that a statute means exactly what it says and does not mean what it does not say.

For all these reasons I find it quite impossible to hold that withholding from the respondents to these two appeals the benefits conferred on some of their fellow employees, whatever its purpose may have been, was capable of amounting to a contravention of [s 146(1)]. It follows that I would also overrule the decision of the Court of Appeal in *National Coal Board* v *Ridgway*. ...'

(Lord Keith and Lord Browne-Wilkinson agreed with Lord Bridge. Lord Lloyd, with whom Lord Slynn agreed, dissented on this point.)

Lord Lloyd (dissenting on this point): '... I return now to the preliminary question, raised by your Lordships in the course of the hearing, whether the withholding of the 4.5% in *Wilson's* case and of the pay increase in *Palmer's* case was "action … taken" against the applicants within the meaning of [s 146(1)(a)]. On this I regret that I have reached a different conclusion from Lord Bridge of Harwich.

It is said that to read "action" in [s 146(1)(a)] as if it included "omission" presents a grammatical difficulty, and that therefore the context of [s 146(1)(a)] excludes the application of the definition in [s 298]. I accept at once that the inclusion of omissions within the scope of [s 146(1)(a)] means that the phrase has to be substantially recast. It is not possible to substitute one word for the other. For you cannot "take" an omission. But this is no bar to the application of [s 298]. It was foreseen by the draftsman. That is why it is provided by [s 298] that "taking action" is to be "construed accordingly". I cannot easily visualise a context in which "taking action" has to be construed so as to include an omission which would *not* involve substantial recasting.

…

Is there anything else in the wider context which requires us to exclude the definition? I think not. Indeed, it would create a surprising gap in the protection afforded by [s 146(1)(a)] if "action" did not include "omission". In *National Coal Board* v *Ridgway* the industrial Tribunal construed "action" as including "omission" in accordance with the definition. It never occurred to the employers to argue in that case, whether in the Appeal Tribunal or in the Court of Appeal, that the definition did not apply. It was common ground that it did. The dispute in *National Coal Board* v *Ridgway* on which the Court of Appeal was split was not whether the definition applied but whether, applying the definition, a failure to act could constitute an omission in the absence of some obligation to act, or expectation of action. The difference of judicial opinion in that respect does not indicate any difficulty in applying the definition as such. It would arise in whatever context the definition came to be applied. So I see no reason not to apply the definition on that ground. …'

COMMENT

(1)   As the majority held that 'action short of dismissal' did not include omission to act, the employers' appeals succeeded. The point involves a difficult exercise in statutory interpretation. Do you think that the right result was reached? If an omission on the employer's part results in a state of affairs which is a deterrent to union membership, would that be within the mischief at which this provision is aimed?

(2)   Alan applies for promotion. His employer rejects the application because of Alan's union activities. Action or omission? Belinda considers which of her employees is deserving of promotion and decides against Chris because of his union activities. Action or omission? Should it matter?

(3)   A separate question raised by this case is whether the employer's actions were 'for the purpose of' preventing or deterring union membership. Of course, there was no direct attack on this in either case. It was argued, however, that union membership includes the necessary incidents of union membership, such as making use of the union's services; an argument based on the EAT's decision in *Discount Tobacco* v *Armitage*. This is considered next.

Associated Newspapers Ltd v Wilson ; Associated British Ports v Palmer

[1995] ICR 406 House of Lords

Lord Bridge: '...

The membership issue

Much of the argument in the courts below and in both appeals before your Lordships was directed to questions relating to the relevant purpose of the employers. It was less than clear in either case what precisely the Industrial Tribunal had found the employers' purpose to be, leaving it open to argument whether the Tribunal had intended to find as a fact in favour of the applicants that the employers' purpose was to deter them from being "members of an independent trade union" or to penalise them for being such members and, if so, whether there was evidence to support such a finding. Having reached a conclusion on the new point which is decisive of both appeals, I do not find it necessary to go into these questions in any detail, but I think it appropriate to add some observations relating to one aspect of the approach of the courts below to the question of purpose in respect of a complaint under [s 146(1)(a)].

Sections 11 to 16 of the Employment Protection Act 1975 embodied a complex statutory code, the details of which do not now matter, which enabled a trade union to obtain "recognition" by an employer for the purpose of collective bargaining with him on behalf of its members. But these provisions were repealed by the Employment Act 1980 and since then an employer has been at liberty to decide for himself whether or not to enter into or to continue in force an agreement with a trade union providing for collective bargaining.

Whatever the purpose of ANL may have been, having given notice to terminate their house agreement with the NUJ, in offering an inducement to employees to sign individual contracts before the notice expired, the only witness called by the employers before the Industrial Tribunal gave evidence that the management had no intention of deterring their employees from continuing as members of the NUJ; the Industrial Tribunal's decision does not indicate that they rejected this evidence and in fact the majority of the employees have continued to be members of the NUJ ever since.

In the ABP case it was plain that the employers were seeking by means of an attractive offer to induce their employees voluntarily to quit the union's collective bargaining umbrella and to deal in future directly with the employers over their terms and conditions of employment, but I can see nothing in the evidence recited in the Industrial Tribunal's decision to suggest that the employers were seeking to induce the employees to give up their union membership.

The Industrial Tribunal, in the ABP case, in reaching the conclusion that the employers' relevant purpose contravened [s 146(1)(a)], relied expressly on *Discount Tobacco & Confectionery Ltd* v *Armitage* which, they said, "is authority for the proposition that there is no genuine distinction between membership of a union, on the one hand, and making use of the essential services which that union has to offer, such as representation, on the other." This approach was analysed and criticised in the judgment of the Employment Appeal Tribunal. But in the Court of Appeal the *Armitage* case provided an important link in the chain of reasoning relied on to affirm the decisions of the Industrial Tribunals in both cases.

Mrs Armitage had been engaged on 1 February 1988 and was dismissed on 15 July 1988. She applied to an Industrial Tribunal complaining that she had been dismissed by reason of her union membership in contravention of [s 152]. The evidence showed that she had written to her employers on 23 May asking for a statement of her terms of employment but had received no reply. She had then invoked the assistance of her union representative who wrote on her behalf on 23 June complaining of the failure to answer her letter and of various other matters in regard to her terms of employment. The employers gave evidence before the Industrial Tribunal that Mrs Armitage was dismissed on the ground of her unsuitability or incapacity, but the Industrial Tribunal disbelieved this evidence and found in terms that she had been dismissed "by reason of membership of an independent trade union". On the employer's appeal the Employment Appeal Tribunal concluded that there was material to support this finding. In reaching this conclusion the following passage appears in the judgment delivered by Knox J:

> "The evidence, therefore, in relation to union membership that was before the Industrial Tribunal, was that Mrs Armitage made use of her union membership by getting Mr McFadden to help in elucidating and attempting to negotiate the terms of her employment. He did not get very far in the latter because the dismissal supervened so soon but that, Mr West accepted, was what in fact she did and the question for this Tribunal is whether on that evidence of union involvement, to use a neutral expression, it was possible for the Industrial Tribunal to reach the conclusion that her dismissal was for membership of the union. Mr West drew a distinction between membership of the union, on the one hand, and resorting to the services of a union officer to elucidate and negotiate the terms of employment, on the other, and he accepted that there was evidence of the latter but said that it did not or could not amount to evidence of the former, membership of the union.
>
> We find ourselves unconvinced of that distinction. In our judgment, the activities of a trade union officer in negotiating and elucidating terms of employment is, to use a prayer book expression, the outward and visible manifestation of trade union membership. It is an incident of union membership which is, if not the primary one, at any rate a very important one and we see no genuine distinction between membership of a union, on the one hand, and making use of the essential services of a union, on the other.
>
> Were it not so, the scope of [s 152(1)(a)] would be reduced almost to vanishing point, since it would only be just the fact that a person was a member of a union, without regard to the consequences of that membership, that would be the subject matter of that statutory provision and, it seems to us, that to construe that paragraph so narrowly would really be to emasculate the provision altogether."

In the Court of Appeal Dillon LJ, with whose judgment Butler-Sloss and Farquharson LJJ agreed, relied on this passage in relation to both appeals. He said in addressing the ANL appeal,

> "But the decision on 'purpose' is or the Industrial Tribunal and *Discount Tobacco & Confectionery Ltd* v *Armitage* is authority that an industrial tribunal is entitled to conclude robustly that an employee who has been dismissed or penalised for invoking the assistance of his or her union in relation to his or her employment has been dismissed or penalised for being a member of the union."

I do not question the correctness of the Employment Appeal Tribunal's decision in the *Armitage* case. Once the Industrial Tribunal had rejected the employers' evidence as to their reason for Mrs Armitage's dismissal, it was an obvious inference that she had been dismissed because the employers resented the fact that she had invited the union to intervene on her behalf. In this narrow context the reasoning of Knox J may have been a legitimate means of refuting a particular argument advanced by counsel for the employers. But if the passage cited is held to establish as a general proposition of law that, in the context of [TULRCA ss146 and 152], membership of a union is to be equated with using the "essential" services of that union, at best it puts an unnecessary and imprecise gloss on the statutory language, at worst it is liable to distort the meaning of these provisions which protect union membership as such.

A union which has a collective bargaining agreement with employers is in a position to offer its members the service of negotiating their terms and conditions of employment. A union which has no such agreement with employers is unable to offer its members that service, but is able to offer them other important and valuable services. Thus, it cannot be said that the service of collective bargaining is an essential union service or that membership of a union unable to offer that service is valueless or insignificant. Accordingly, it seems to me that the reasoning of Knox J in the *Armitage* case could not properly be applied to the circumstances of the two cases with which we are concerned. Even if the construction put on [s 146(1)(a)] by the majority in *National Coal Board* v *Ridgway* were correct, I do not think that in either of these cases the withholding by the employers from employees who did not sign individual contracts of the benefits conferred on those who did, was by itself capable of supporting a finding that the employers' purpose was to deter those in the latter group from being members of a union or to penalise them for being such members.'

(Lord Lloyd and Lord Keith agreed with Lord Bridge on this point. Lord Browne-Wilkinson expressly reserved his position. Lord Slynn took a wider view, referring here to *ABP* v *Palmer*.)

Lord Slynn: '… Like Dillon LJ I do not consider that action "preventing or deterring" someone from being a member of a trade union or penalising him for doing so is limited to action taken in respect of his status as a member; the fact that he has or wants to have a union membership card. It may include action to prevent or deter him from, or action penalising him for, exercising his rights as a member of a trade union. The exercise of such rights is not necessarily included in a the phrase "taking part in the activities" of a trade union, words more apt to cover such activities as attending union meetings or acting as an official of the union.

In the present case, however, the right to be represented in collective bargaining by the union was a right granted contractually by the employers which could be terminated on notice. Ceasing to recognise the union was not an action taken to prevent or deter the employees from exercising their rights as members of the trade union. The fact that in Mr Palmer's case, unlike Mr Wilson's case, the workers had the option whether to go on being represented by the union or to accept a personal contract did not mean that those who accepted a personal contract were being prevented or deterred from exercising their union rights or penalised for doing so.

In any event it does not seem to me that, having accepted that the reason that the employers needed flexibility and more efficient conduct of their business was an honest reason, the Tribunal was entitled on the evidence to say that flexibility was their "objective" rather than their "purpose". Their purpose and their objective were to achieve flexibility; and the means to achieve it were by offering a higher salary for those who were prepared to give up union representation.'

COMMENT

(1)   Thus four out of five Law Lords considerd that the employers here did not have the purpose of deterring trade union membership. However, the Court of Appeal had taken a different view when the cases were before that court in 1993. An amendment was therefore hastily added to TURERA in order to neutralise that decision. Thus TULRCA s 148(3) now provides that the effect on union membership is to be disregarded if the employer also had the purpose of changing its relationship with all or any class of employees, and the means adopted to that end were not such that no reasonable employer would have used for that purpose.

(2)   Note also *Gallacher* v *Department of Transport*, where the argument that the employers' purpose must be taken to include the inevitable consequence of its action was rejected by the Court of Appeal.

(3)   In *Specialty Care* v *Pachela*, on facts similar to *Discount Tobacco* v *Armitage*, the EAT suggested that since the Law Lords were not in total agreement on this issue and, strictly, any opinions they expressed on it were *obiter*, it was still open to a tribunal to hold that an employee dismissed for invoking the assistance of her union had been dismissed for union membership.

(4)   Alternatively, could this be regarded as participation in a union activity? The boundary between union membership and union activities is not clear-cut. Nor, perhaps, is the distinction between union activities and misconduct.

Bass Taverns Ltd v Burgess

[1995] IRLR 595 Court of Appeal

Burgess was employed as the manager of a public house owned by the company and was also shop steward of his union, the National Association of Licensed House Managers. He had the status of trainer manager, which meant that he received extra pay for giving presentations on the company's training courses for new managers. On the first day of these courses, the company always allowed the union to make a presentation on its role, which could be a forum for recruitment. On one particular course, Burgess made the union presentation, in the course of which he made disparaging remarks about the company, suggesting that only the union would fight on behalf of managers injured by inebriated customers and that the company was more interested in profits than the safety of its employees. The management took a dim view of this and decided that he should no longer be a trainer manager. The demotion meant a loss of pay as well. Burgess resigned, and claimed that he had been constructively dismissed for his participation in union activities.

Pill LJ: '... Miss Slade QC for the company bases her submission upon the wording of [s 152(2)(b)] and a limitation upon the consent given. It was permissible for the industrial tribunal to conclude that the permission to recruit granted to the respondent had been exceeded. As the tribunal of fact they were entitled to conclude that the contents of the respondent's speech were, in the circumstances, outside the permitted scope of the meeting and that the consent had been exceeded. The circumstances relied upon were the context of the meeting, the first day of an induction course for trainee managers. Reliance is also placed upon the respondent's admission that he had "gone over the top". It is not suggested that the contents of the speech were dishonest or actuated by malice or that if delivered on a different trade union occasion, would have been other than taking part in the activities of an independent trade union. No malice or ill-feeling was involved, the industrial tribunal found.

The consent was subject, it is submitted, to an implied limitation that the occasion would not be used to criticise the company or to undermine the company in the eyes of the trainees. The industrial tribunal were entitled to conclude that the contents of the speech, as the tribunal found them to be, were outside the scope of the consent and therefore outside the scope of [s 152(1)]. Miss Slade concedes that a finding in the company's favour depends upon the presence of an implied limitation upon the ambit of the consent given to the respondent. There was no evidence of any express limitation. While they were not referred to [s 152(2)], the industrial tribunal were entitled to and did find such a limitation. ...

"We do not say that every such act is protected. For example, wholly unreasonable, extraneous or malicious acts done in support of trade union activities might be a ground for a dismissal which would not be unfair."

The argument in relation to a limitation upon the consent is now augmented by reference to [s 152(2)(b)]. No reference to that paragraph appears in the employer's written response to the original claim or in the evidence or submissions before the industrial tribunal. The company's case has hitherto been put simply on the basis that the conduct of the respondent in addressing the trainee managers as he did should not be regarded as taking part in the activities of a trade union. The company were not legally represented before the industrial tribunal. Having regard to their findings of fact, it was not, in my judgment, a permissible option for the industrial tribunal to find that the dismissal was other than for taking part in trade union activities. The respondent was permitted to use the meeting as a "forum for recruitment". I will consider the alleged limitation on the consent later.

On the face of it, a consent to recruit must include a consent to underline the services which the union can provide. That may reasonably involve a submission to prospective members that in some respects the union will provide a service which the company does not. On the assumption that I am prepared to make that the life of a manager of licensed premises has its dangers and licensees are from time to time injured by members of the public, a union existing to protect the interests of licensees is entitled to claim that if such a situation arises it is the union and not the company whcih will fight the licensee's cause. Indeed, to bring a claim on behalf of members arising out of personal injuries is an important function of many trade unions and the service can properly be emphasised at a recruiting meeting.

In the findings of the industrial tribunal as to what the respondent said, I find nothing beyond the rhetoric and hyperbole which might be expected at a recruiting meeting for a trade union or, for that matter, some other organisation or cause. Neither dishonesty nor bad faith are suggested. While harmonious relations between a company and a union are highly desirable, a union recruiting meeting cannot realistically be limited to that object. A consent which at the same time prevents the recruiter from saying anything adverse about the employer is no real consent. Given that there was consent to use the meeting as a forum for recruitment, it cannot be regarded as an "abuse of privilege" to make remarks to employees which are critical of the company. An industrial tribunal may be surprised at the situation which developed, but it was the employers who, at the start of their induction course, put the respondent in the position of being both trainer manager and recruiter. Having put him in that position, they cannot reasonably expect his activities in the latter role to be limited by the fact that he also was performing the role of trainer manager.

It appears to me that the industrial tribunal did base their decision on an implied term of the kind now contended for, albeit not in the same way. The company's case is not, in my judgment, improved by the present reliance upon an implied term that the recruiter should say nothing to criticise or disparage the company or upon the presence of the word "consent" and the word "permissible" in [s 152(2)(b)]. One has only to consider the likely reaction if the company had attempted to make the term expressed. It is difficult to envisage any trade union official accepting a limitation upon his activites at a recruiting meeting that he should say nothing critical about his employer. Indeed, it is difficult to envisage a sensible employer attempting to require such a term. It is wholly unrealistic, in my judgment, to believe that such a term can be implied in the present context. The respondent's admission that he had "gone over the top" does not, in my judgment, provide a basis for a finding that during his speech he was not taking part in trade union activities. That is an expression sometimes used colloquially in situations when that moderation and balance normally shown in social intercourse is perceived to have been exceeded. In the circumstances of the present case, however, it was not an admission that could form the basis for a conclusion that in law the contents of the speech were outside the scope of trade union activities. The Employment Appeal Tribunal correctly concluded that the industrial tribunal had fallen into error.

I would base the decision on this appeal upon the grounds already expressed rather than upon the Employment Appeal Tribunal's reliance on a verbal inconsistency between the industrial tribunal's finding that the respondent was "taking part in the activities of an independent trade union at an appropriate time" and their subsequent finding that he was not dismissed for trade union reasons. I would add that in dealing with the facts of this case, I am very far from saying that the contents of a speech made at a trade union recruiting meeting, however malicious, untruthful or irrelevant to the task in hand they may be, come within the term "trade union activities" in [s 152].'

COMMENT

(1)   It was held, therefore, that Burgess had been unfairly dismissed for trade union activities.

(2)   Note the suggestion in argument that the status of the activity depended to some extent on the time at which it was done. This is important in the following cases.

Zucker v Astrid Jewels Ltd

[1978] ICR 1088 Employment Appeal Tribunal

The employee appealed against an industrial tribunal's finding that her trade union activities had not been undertaken at an appropriate time.

Phillips J: '... According to paragraph 3 of the industrial tribunal's decision the matters primarily relied on by the employee as being the times when, as she said, she was engaged in trade union activities at an appropriate time, and in respect of which she was dismissed, are summarised as follows: talking with her colleagues about the question of trade union membership during the tea break in the morning from 10 to 10.20, during the tea break in the afternoon, and also at times like the lunch break. In addition to that she said that on the occasion of two lunch breaks she had left the premises, which she was allowed to do, and attended the office of her trade union in connection with her trade union activities. Over and above that, she said that while working on her machine, in the course of conversation with others working near her, she spoke of trade union matters and encouraged recruitment, and so on. No doubt the employers' case was that she engaged in these activities at unreasonable hours and in an unsuitable and disruptive manner. We do not know anything about that because there are no findings of fact about it.

But what the industrial tribunal did, having referred themselves to the new definition [in TULRCA s 152(2)], was to say that it divided "appropriate time" into two, either time outside working hours, or time inside working hours when there had been an agreement; that as to the times mentioned it was within working hours because " ' working hours' ... means any time when, in accordance with his contracted employment, the employee is required to be at work". In effect they took the view that any time in respect of which the employee was paid, and when she was on the premises, was a time when she was required to be at work. The only exception they make is for what they call the "lunch half hour break", in respect of which not only was she not working, but also was not paid.

Well, now, the decision is only a satisfactory decision if those conclusions are right in point of law, and the industrial tribunal correctly directed themselves. In our judgment they misdirected themselves. The relevant authority on the first point is *Post Office* v *Crouch* a decision of the House of Lords on the somewhat similar provision in section 5 of the Industrial Relations Act 1971. In his speech there, Lord Reid makes it quite clear that an employee is not necessarily required to be at work, and therefore, within the terms of the definition, is not within working hours, merely because he is on the premises, or, indeed, merely because he is on the premises during a time in respect of which he is being paid. It is not necessary to read it all, but his opinion makes it quite clear that it is not sufficient merely to be on the premises. He says, of the employee,

"He arrives at his employer's premises some time before he starts work. He leaves some time after his day's work is done. And I should think that in almost all cases he is not expected to work non-stop. There are recognised breaks for meals and perhaps other purposes during which he does and is expected to remain on his employer's premises."

He then goes on to explain the expression "in accordance with his contract", and concludes that paragraph by saying:

"… in my judgment, the Act entitles a worker who is a member of a trade union to take part in the activities of his union while he is on his employer's premises but is not actually working."

To anticipate our conclusion, we find it necessary to remit the matter to be re-heard by a differently constituted industrial tribunal. We do not wish to circumscribe their freedom, because they will decide the matter on the evidence which they have heard. But they will obviously guide themselves by the authority of the House of Lords in *Post Office* v *Crouch*. By way of further guidance we can say that on the facts so far as they appear in this decision, there seems every reason to suppose that the circumstances of the morning tea break at all events (the circumstances of the afternoon tea break are not so clearly stated) seem to be such that that tea break, like the lunch half hour break, was a recognised break for a meal: and ordinarily one would have thought, therefore (though the final decision must rest with the industrial tribunal upon the facts as they emerge), that those breaks would be times during which the employees, albeit they were being paid, were not required to be at work and therefore were not doing whatever they did "during working hours". But we repeat, the final decision must be for the industrial tribunal.

There is another point where we think the industrial tribunal misdirected themselves. It may be the case that some of the employee's activities took place, as we have already indicated, while she was working, in the course of conversation with others also working. The industrial tribunal will want to consider all the circumstances in relation to that. But we do not think that it is a right conclusion, from *Post Office* v *Crouch*, to say that activities of that kind *cannot* be activities undertaken in accordance with arrangements agreed with or consent given by the employer.'

Marley Tile Co Ltd v *Shaw*

[1980] ICR 72 Court of Appeal

The employee was appointed as shop steward for the maintenance section at the factory despite having worked for the company for only two months. When he raised a problem over wage differentials with management, he was told that the company did not accept him as shop steward because he had not been there long enough. Annoyed by this, the employee responded that he was going at once to telephone his district official and call a meeting of the other five maintenance men. The factory manager made no response to this. The employee made his 'phone call and held his meeting, which ended with an hour's stoppage of work. He was subsequently dismissed, and claimed it was because of his trade union activities. The employers argued that the activities were not protected because they had taken place in working hours without consent.

Goff LJ: '... The matter then rests on the question of consent. It is not necessary to decide whether arrangements can only be express because this was not something done pursuant to any general arrangement. The question turns on the word "consent". In my judgment, in a proper case, consent may be implied but this is not such a case. I accept the view of the majority of the appeal tribunal, "... that the consent of the employers can [not] be deduced from their silence", I add of Mr Wright, "when Mr Shaw announced that he was going to call a meeting of his members and telephone Mr Garwell". I accept the minority view of Mr Clement-Jones,

"... unless there is a general agreement or arrangement which covers it, the shop steward unaccredited by the management at the relevant time cannot be taken to have implied permission to call such a meeting in working hours; particularly one which ends in an hour's stoppage of the shop floor workers, even if that was not intended by the shop steward. Furthermore, Mr Clement-Jones does not agree that an arrangement for the conduct of shop steward's duties can be reasonably assumed to exist either by extension from other factories in the Marley Group, or by having regard to custom and practice at their Dewsbury plant, inasmuch as it was found by the industrial tribunal that neither had the AUEW hitherto nominated a shop steward nor had the TGWU done so for their membership on production in the factory."

Mr Rose submitted that the calling out of the maintenance men to discuss the unexpected situation which had arisen was incidental to the original approach to the management to discuss the fitters' differential, which the employers had agreed should be in working time by giving the employee an appointment for that purpose and should, therefore, be treated as covered by that consent. I do not think that is right because it was not necessary to do this in working time and because it involved a much more significant interference with the work of the factory in which all five men were involved and not the employee only.

Alternatively, he relied on the speech of Lord Reid in *Post Office* v *Crouch* where, dealing with the precisely similar wording of section 5 of the Industrial Relations Act 1971, his Lordship said:

"But again this must be applied reasonably. It is one thing to ask an employer to incur expense or submit to substantial inconvenience. That the worker may not do. But it is a different matter to use facilities which are normally available to the employer's workers or to ask him to submit to some trifling inconvenience. Men carrying on activities of their union on their employer's premises must do so in a manner which does not cause substantial inconvenience either to their employer or to fellow workers who are not members of their trade union – and employers must tolerate minor infringements of their strict legal rights which do them no real harm. In my view the industrial tribunals are well fitted to deal with disputes about matters of that kind."

He argued that this applied to the present case and the employee's conduct was no more than that little inconvenience which employers must accept. In my judgment, however, it was much more than that, and I think the industrial tribunal thought so too, when they said, in paragraph 17:

"Such a meeting must mean that the men are not as readily available for work as they would otherwise be, even if in this particular case these men were maintenance workers and would still be on call when in the canteen."

In my view there is no ground for inferring an implied consent to all the maintenance men being suddenly called from their place of work to a meeting, particularly one such as in the present case where the problem which had arisen did not call for a desperately urgent solution. In my judgment, therefore, even if the conduct for which the employee was dismissed was taking part in trade union activities, which I have assumed, it was not at an appropriate time because it was carried out in working hours and was not in accordance with the arrangements agreed with or consent given by the company. For these reasons, I would allow this appeal, discharge the orders of the industrial tribunal and the appeal tribunal and dismiss the employee's application.

COMMENT

(1)   These cases give guidance on what constitute protected union activities as well as what is an appropriate time. However, it is now necessary to note some important limitations on the protection for trade union activities.

Carrington v Therm-A-Stor Ltd

[1983] ICR 208 Court of Appeal

The TGWU recruited some 60 of the 70 employees of the company and then applied to the managing director, Morris, for recognition. His reaction was to instruct his chargehands to select 20 employees – any 20 – for dismissal. As they had not been employed long enough to claim unfair dismissal on the usual grounds, the employees claimed that they had been dismissed for their union activities.

Sir John Donaldson MR: '... As I see it, the first question for consideration is whether the fact that the chargehands undertook the selection for dismissal means that the chargehands' reason – probably last in first out – was the reason for the men's dismissal. Mr Tabachnik submits that so to conclude is to confuse the reason for dismissal with the basis for selection. As he rightly points out they are two quite different things and are so treated in [TULRCA s 153] in relation to redundancy. Where redundancy is the reason for the dismissal, the dismissal is not necessarily unfair. However, the method of selection for dismissal can make the dismissal unfair. For my part I think this is right and that the intervention of the chargehands can be disregarded as being concerned solely with selection and not with the reason for dismissal.

So far so good, but the four employees still have obstacles in their way. The industrial tribunal did not find that the employers or Mr Morris decided to dismiss the group of 20 men because any or all of them had joined the union or proposed to do so or had taken part in union activities or proposed to do so. He decided to dismiss them by way of reaction to the union's letter seeking recognition. The reason for the dismissals was the union's plea for recognition....

Tempted as I am to provide the four employees with a remedy for what was an indefensible reaction to a simple request for union recognition, which could have been granted or politely refused, I cannot construe [s 152] as being intended to deal with such a situation. The section is not concerned with an employer's reactions to a trade union's activities, but with his reactions to an individual employee's activities in a trade union context.

With regret, I would allow the appeal and restore the decision of the industrial tribunal.

(May and Watkins LJJ agreed.)

COMMENT

(1)   The gap in protection revealed in *Carrington* v *Therm-A-Stor Ltd* arises from the fact that the remedy is provided for individuals yet the activity is collective in nature.

(2)   See also *Chant* v *Aquaboats*, where the dismissed employee had instigated a round robin among union members about safety matters. As he was not a union official and the letter was not from the union to the employer, it was held that this was not a union activity and he was outside the protection of s 152. In this situation today the employee might try to claim that his dismissal was automatically unfair by virtue of ERA s 100 (dismissal in health and safety cases), although it is not clear that it would be covered on the facts.

(3)   If a claim for action short of dismissal is upheld, the tribunal must make a declaration and may award such compensation as is just and equitable, having regard to the loss suffered by the employee and the nature of the infringement of his or her right. In *Cleveland Ambulance NHS Trust* v *Blane* the EAT held that this could include a sum for injury to feelings. If the tribunal finds that the employee has been unfairly dismissed for trade union activities, a special regime of compensation applies (see TULRCA ss 155–159). In particular, the basic award cannot be less than £2,770, and there are heavy penalties if the employer wrongfully refuses to reinstate or re-engage the employee.

(4)   What if action is taken against the employee, not because of union activities in this employment, but because of union activities in the past? This was the issue in the next case.

Fitzpatrick v *British Railways Boad*

[1992] ICR 221   Court of Appeal

The applicant had been dismissed by BRB after working for them for only nine months, after a manager saw a report in the *Evening Standard* about union troubles at Ford Motors and British Telecom, which identified the applicant as a union activist having links with ultra-left Trotskyite groups, including Socialist Action. While she had disclosed her previous employment at British Telecom, she had deliberately not mentioned her brief employment at Ford on her application form for BRB, and she was ostensibly dismissed for this deceit. The tribunal found that the real reason was her previous union activities, which caused her employer to view her as a fomenter of trouble; however, they held that this was not covered by s 152.

Woolf LJ: '... In the course of their decision the Industrial Tribunal subjected the decision in *City of Birmingham District Council* v *Beyer* to careful scrutiny. It was the majority of the Industrial Tribunal's understanding of the effect of that decision which caused them to come to the conclusion that the appellant did not fall within [s 152(1)(6)]. The minority, the third member of the Industrial Tribunal, came to the conclusion that the appellant fell within the language of the relevant part of that subsection.

Superficially the facts in the *Beyer* case are very similar to those on this appeal. Mr Beyer, who was the respondent before the Employment Appeal Tribunal, was a noted trade union activist. He had applied on two different occasions to the district council in order to obtain employment. On the first occasion he had used a false name and a bogus reference. When this was discovered he was summarily dismissed for gross misconduct. On the second occasion he did not disguise his identity but he was able to obtain employment on a site where he was unknown. When within a couple of hours the officials of the corporation discovered the true facts he was again dismissed on the grounds that he had grossly deceived the corporation when he made his previous application.

The Industrial Tribunal held that "Mr Beyer had been dismissed for the inadmissible reason of his having taken part in trade union activities on the basis that he had to resort to deceit because he knew that his trade union activities in the past would bar him from employment and that therefore his act of deceit was a trade union activity." I draw particular attention to the basis of the Industrial Tribunal's decision that the act of deceit by Mr Beyer was a trade union activity. On any showing, in my judgment, an act of deceit, of the sort that was being considered by the Industrial Tribunal in the *Beyer* case, could not be considered to be a trade union activity.

In the Employment Appeal Tribunal, Mr Justice Kilner Brown started his judgment by reciting the facts. He then went on to say that:

"… with some justification Mr Beyer feels deeply aggrieved, although he does not even now seem to appreciate that he is largely the author of his own misfortune. Anyway he has convinced himself that the deception which he practised was justifiable. He feels that he is blacklisted on account of his trade union activities, he is being victimised and unfair discrimination is exercised against him. This may well be true, but with the state of the law as it is at present there is nothing that he can lawfully and properly do about it."

Mr Justice Kilner Brown having referred to the relevant statutory provisions added:

"We find it surprising that the Tribunal could have erred and misdirected themselves to the extent which they did. It ought to be obvious that the situation envisaged by the paragraph in question is some trade union activity [and I would add "or proposed trade union activity"] after employment has commenced. It could not conceivably refer to activities outside and before the employment began. The matter if not previously clear is put beyond doubt by the definition of 'appropriate time' now introduced … We assume that the Industrial Tribunal appreciated this and that is why they indulged in what appears to us to be defective reasoning."

Subject to a very minor caveat which I would make to what was said by Mr Justice Kilner Brown in relation to proposed activities, I find that paragraph of his judgment perfectly acceptable and as making clear that the activities referred to in [s 152(1)(b)] are activities in the employment of the employee from which he or she alleges that he or she has been unfairly dismissed. It is not referring to a past employment from which he or she may have previously been dismissed. If there was any doubt as that interpretation so far as [s 152(1)] is concerned, in my judgment subsection (2) would remove that doubt.

I do not, however, regard the decision of the Employment Appeal Tribunal as meaning that what has happened in previous employment can have no relevance to whether or not a person has been unfairly dismissed, in accordance with [s 152(1)], from a subsequent employment. What happened in a previous employment may form the reason for the dismissal in subsequent employment and therefore can be highly relevant to the question which a Tribunal has to answer under [s 152(1)]. The effect of the *Beyer* case on [s 152] is to make clear that if an employee obtained an employment by deceit and the employer dismisses that employee for the deceit, that is not an employment which is terminated within the language of [s 152(1)(b)], albeit that the deceit was about previous trade union activities.

In this case British Rail purported to dismiss the appellant on the basis of her deceit in concealing her previous trade union activities. If the Industrial Tribunal had accepted that it was her deceit which caused them to dismiss her, or if that was the primary reason for her dismissal, then the situation is that she would not have been able to bring herself within the language of [s 152(1)(b)]. However, as already indicated, all three members of the Industrial Tribunal accepted that it was not the deceit which was the operative cause for her dismissal.

What the majority concluded was, and I read here from paragraph 27 of the decision:

"It was the [appellant's] previous trade union (and possibly her political) activities, which gave her a reputation for being a disruptive force; and that was the prime reason for her dismissal."

That paragraph, in my judgment, discloses a failure on the part of the Industrial Tribunal to answer the critical question. The fact that the appellant had a reputation with regard to trade union activities was, as Miss Booth in her argument made clear, only relevant to British Rail in so far as it would have an effect on what she did while whe was employed by them. Miss Booth submits, clearly with justification, that British Rail did not suggest and would not in fact seek to dismiss the appellant merely in order to punish her for her previous trade union activities. Miss Booth submits that what the Industrial Tribunal failed to do was to identify why it was that because of her previous trade union, and possibly political, activities British Rail decided to dismiss the appellant. If the Tribunal had asked the question the answer would have been obvious. It would be that they would fear a repetition of the same conduct while employed by them.

The reason that the majority of the Industrial Tribunal did not address the critical question is probably because of their understanding of the *Beyer* decision. They say, having examined that decision, that so far as proposed activities are concerned it must, and I quote: "involve some cogent and identifiable act and not some possible trouble in the future". In other words the Industrial Tribunal are saying that in order to comply with the provisions of [s 152(1)(b)] there must have been some activity on the part of the employee to which they took exception, which was not a mere possibility but something which was sufficiently precise to be identifiable in her present employment.

In my judgment, to adopt this approach is to read into the language of [s 152(1)(b)] a restriction which Parliament has not identified. To limit the language, in the way which the Industrial Tribunal did, would prevent the actual reason for the dismissal in a case such as this from being considered by the Industrial Tribunal. As long as the reason which motivated the employer falls within the words "activities that the employee ... proposed to take part in", there is no reason to limit the language. The purpose of the subsection, in so far as (b) is concerned, is to protect those who engage in trade union activities and I can see no reason why that should not apply irrespective of whether the precise activities can be identified.

If an employer, having learnt of an employee's previous trade union activities, decides that he wishes to dismiss that employee, that is likely to be a situation where almost inevitably the employer is dismissing the employee because he feels that the employee will indulge in industrial activities of a trade union nature in his current employment. There is no reason for a rational and reasonable employer to object to the previous activities of an employee except in so far as they will impinge upon the employee's current employment. ...'

COMMENT

(1)   It was held, therefore, that she had been unfairly dismissed for proposing to take part in trade union activities.

(2)   The difference between *Fitzpatrick* and *Beyer* is that in the former case, the

tribunal found as a fact that the employee's deceit was not the true reason for the dismissal, whereas in the latter it was.

(3)   At the time of *City of Birmingham* v *Beyer* there was nothing to prevent discrimination on grounds of union membership or activities at the point of entry to employment. Some protection was introduced by the Employment Act 1990, and we turn to that.

Refusal of employment on grounds of trade union membership
Trade Union and Labour Relations (Consolidation) Act 1992

137.   (1)   It is unlawful to refuse a person employment—
    (a)   because he is, or is not, a member of a trade union, or
    (b)   because he is unwilling to accept a requirement—
        (i)   to take steps to become or cease to be, or to remain or not to become, a member of a trade union, or
        (ii)   to make payments or suffer deductions in the event of his not being a member of a trade union.
    (2)   A person who is thus unlawfully refused employment has a right of complaint to an industrial tribunal.

COMMENT

(1)   The major difference between s 137 and ss 146 and 152 is that it does not cover trade union activities. It will therefore be critical to know how far the concept of union membership can be stretched (see above, p 399ff).

(2)   In the first reported case on this section, *Harrison* v *Kent CC*, the applicant had been rejected because he was a union activist. The situation was much like *Fitzpatrick* or *Beyer*, save that he had not actually got the job. The EAT, relying on *Discount Tobacco* v *Armitage*, held that the concept of union membership could embrace this also: however, this decision was shortly before the House of Lords gave its judgment in *Associated Newspapers* v *Wilson*. Their comments in that case on membership may strictly have been *obiter*, but they must put the correctness of *Harrison* v *Kent CC* in considerable doubt.

Contracts between employers
Trade Union and Labour Relations (Consolidation) Act 1992

144.   A term or condition of a contract for the supply of goods and services is void in so far as it purports to require that the whole, or some part, of the work done for the purposes of the contract is done only by persons who are, or are not, members of trade unions or of a particular trade union.

COMMENT

(1)   The main reason for introducing this provision (in the Employment Act 1982) was to deter contractual requirements that suppliers should only use unionised labour forces: it will be referred to again in the context of the closed shop.

FREEDOM OF ASSOCIATION AND TRADE UNIONS

In this context, the question is whether an individual should be able to rely on freedom of association to give a right to belong to an association where the association does not wish to admit her. Refer back to ILO Convention No 87 Articles 2 and 3.

Admission to trade unions

Faramus v Film Artistes' Association

[1964] AC 925 House of Lords

Rule 4(2) of the union's rules provided that no one who had been convicted of an offence (other than a motoring offence not punishable by imprisonment) was eligible for membership. Faramus concealed his two convictions when he applied and was treated as a member for eight years, even serving on the executive committee. When his convictions came to light, he was excluded.

Lord Evershed: 'My Lords, like the learned judge who tried this case at first instance and like all the judges in the Court of Appeal I find it indeed difficult not to be most sympathetic to the appellant in this case. True it is that in the year 1938, when aged 17 years, he was convicted by a court of law in St. Helier, where he was born, of the criminal offence of taking and driving away the motor-cars of others without their consent; and for that offence he was sentenced to three months' imprisonment with hard labour. It is true also that two years later, during the period of the German occupation of Jersey, he was convicted by the local court of obtaining certain moneys by falsely stating that his wife was unemployed: and for this offence he was imprisoned for six months with hard labour. It appears that about the same time he was imprisoned for a further month for being in possession of propaganda literature. Indeed, for these last two offences he paid a penalty far more severe than the terms of imprisonment imposed upon him, for he was deported to Germany and there suffered the appalling horrors of being placed in the concentration camp with the ill-omened name of Buchenwald, and other similar places, and was so adversely affected by this treatment that his weight was reduced to less than half its proper amount. Since that date, however, and more particularly since he came to this country and sought in the year 1950 to join the respondents' union, his conduct, so far as is known, has been quite exemplary. Certainly there is no suggestion that during this latter period he has ever committed any criminal offence or ever been guilty of dishonest conduct. Yet if the respondents' argument is right the appellant has not now, and never had, the necessary qualification for election to their union, so that his election was wholly void ...'

Lord Pearce: ' ... Since this union has a monopoly, exclusion from its membership prevents a man from earning his living in this particular profession. An absolute rule that so prevents any person who may have suffered a trivial conviction many years before is in restraint of trade and unreasonable. It is therefore void unless it is saved by section 3 of the Trade Union

Act, 1871, which provides that: "The purpose of any trade union shall not, by reason merely that they are in restraint of trade, be unlawful so as to render void … any agreement or trust." It is argued that this rule is not a "purpose of the union" and that therefore section 3 does not touch it. But the rule clearly helps to achieve one at least of the objects of the association. It would be detrimental to the position and status of film artistes if they had among their numbers persons convicted of serious or frequent crimes of fraud. Also it might create trouble between member and managers or between member and member if such dishonest persons could roam the changing rooms as of right. Rule 4(2) in a more precise form is at least desirable for the objects of the association. Moreover, the evidence shows that one of the purposes of the union in support of its expressed objects is to cut down the number of persons engaged in this particular walk of life. For, if all who wished were admitted, there would not be an adequate living for any. This rule is partly directed to that purpose and it is no more unfair to keep out one man because he has been convicted albeit trivially and so to put another in his place, than to keep persons out simply because there is no room for them. Merely because a desirable rule is too far-reaching, it does not cease, in my opinion, to be one of the purposes of the union. The question here is, would the agreement (that is to say, the rules) or any part of it (or them) be void merely because the purpose of the union is in restraint of trade? If so, it is protected by section 3. In my opinion rule 4(2) would be void merely for that reason and for no other, and it is therefore protected … '

(Lords Reid, Hodson and Devlin concurred.)

COMMENT

(1) The modern version of the Trade Union Act 1871 s 3, which prevents the rules of trade unions being held to be in restraint of trade, is TULRCA s 11.

(2) There are few cases about the legality of refusal of admission precisely because there are no obvious legal grounds on which a disappointed applicant could claim. Faramus thought he was claiming for expulsion, but it was held that he had never been validly admitted.

(3) Lord Denning led a crusade to allow a claim where there was a closed shop, based on an alleged right to work (see p 134 and *Nagle* v *Feilden*, *Edwards* v *SOGAT*). It was where refusal of membership restricted job opportunities that the issue was seen as really important, and in 1980 legislation was introduced to deal with the situation.

(4) The Employment Act 1980 provided that in closed shop situations, an employee should not be unreasonably excluded or expelled from a trade union. Compliance with the union's own rules was not to be considered conclusive proof of reasonableness.

(5) However, when the closed shop ceased to be enforceable the Conservative Government turned its attention instead to the Bridlington Principles. The Bridlington Principles were adopted by the TUC at its 1939 Conference in Bridlington to deal with possible inter-union conflicts which could arise if more than one union was seeking to recruit the same group of workers.

(6) The Bridlington Principles provided that unions should not accept into membership someone who had previously belonged to another union without checking first that the former union did not object. Where one union already had a substantial

presence in a business, another union should not try to muscle in and 'poach' the workers. Arguments between unions were referred to the TUC's internal Disputes Committee.

(7)   The Bridlington Principles could be regarded as limiting workers' choice as to which union they belonged to. This was how the Conservative Government chose to present it, and in 1993 TURERA amended TULRCA in such a way as radically to transform the right of a union to choose whom to admit.

Trade Union and Labour Relations (Consolidation) Act 1992

174.   (1)   An individual shall not be excluded or expelled from a trade union unless the exclusion or expulsion is permitted by this section.

(2)   The exclusion or expulsion of an individual from a trade union is permitted by this section if (and only if)—

(a)   he does not satisfy, or no longer satisfies, an enforceable membership requirement contained in the rules of the union,

(b)   he does not qualify, or no longer qualifies, for membership of the union by reason of the union operating only in a particular part or particular parts of Great Britain,

(c)   in the case of a union whose purpose is the regulation of relations between its members and one particular employer or a number of particular employers who are associated, he is not, or is no longer, employed by that employer or one of those employers, or

(d)   the exclusion or expulsion is entirely attributable to his conduct.

(3)   A requirement in relation to membership of a union is "enforceable" for the purposes of subsection (2)(a) if it restricts membership solely by reference to one or more of the following criteria—

(a)   employment in a speficied trade, industry or profession,

(b)   occupational description (including grade, level or category of appointment) and,

(c)   possession of speficied trade, industrial or professional qualifications or work experience.

(4)   For the purposes of subsection (2)(d) "conduct", in relation to an individual, does not include—

(a)   his being or ceasing to be, or having been or ceased to be—

(i)   a member of another trade union,

(ii)   employed by a particular employer or at a particular place, or

(iii) a member of a political party, or

(b)   conduct to which section 65 (conduct for which an individual may not be disciplined by a trade union) applies or would apply if the references in that section to the trade union which is relevant for the purposes of that section were references to any trade union.

(5)   An individual who claims that he has been excluded or expelled from a trade union in contravention of this section may present a complaint to an industrial tribunal.

COMMENT

(1)   Instead of stating certain reasons for which someone may not be excluded or

expelled from a union, this section now starts from the other end and states that it is *only* if one of these reasons applies that a union may exclude someone who wishes to join or expel an existing member. Should trade unions be regulated so extensively as to whom they admit? Note that even before this was passed, the ILO had expressed the view that the level of legislative interference with the internal affairs of trade unions was a breach of ILO Convention No 87 Article 3.

(2)   This section applied to expulsion from unions as well as refusal to admit. There is therefore a considerable overlap with TULRCA s 65, dealing with unjustifiable discipline, which is explicitly referred to in s 174(4)(b). This aspect will be considered in Chapter 11, below.

(3)   The limitation on enforceable membership requirements in s 174(3) and the explicit statement in s 174(4) that membership of another union is not an acceptable ground for exclusion rendered the Bridlington Principles in their old form unenforceable. A revised version now states that affiliated unions must accept a binding committment that 'they will not knowingly and actively seek to take into membership the present "recent" members of another union' (see B Simpson, 'Bridlington "2" ' (1994) 23 ILJ 170).

(4)   There is just one respect in which the present version of s 174 is narrower than the previous formulation: there is no reference to reasonableness. Thus if a union refuses admission to someone because of an enforceable membership requirement, she or he would have no right to complain even if the union's decision was wholly unreasonable.

THE CLOSED SHOP

Otto Kahn-Freund *Labour and the Law* (2nd ed, 1977)

'... In many countries the freedom not to organise is put on a par with the freedom to organise. If everyone, so it is argued, has the fundamental right to join a union, he has the equally fundamental right not to do so. The law should not prevent anyone from being a union member, nor should it compel him to enter a union. But this is not enough. Just as the law must see that people can effectively exercise their freedom of association, and take positive steps to ensure this, so it is not enough to reject the principle of legally compulsory unionism (which in this country no one has ever advocated). The law must also protect people from being in fact constrained or pressed to join. No one must be exposed to the dilemma between joining a union he does not want to join, and not obtaining or holding a job he wants to obtain or to hold. This is as obnoxious as exposing him to the dilemma between getting or holding a job and joining or remaining in the union of his choice. For many people this reasoning appears to be intellectually attractive. Its symmetry is superficially satisfying ...

There are strong arguments in favour of banning or at least restricting the closed shop – arguments far stronger than the shallow legalism of the reasoning from analogy with the freedom to organise. Access to jobs should be free. This is in the interest of the development of the economy and of the optimal use of manpower. To exclude the non-unionist may mean to exclude the best man for the job. And if there are to be restrictions of access they should be imposed by organs of government responsible through democratic processes, and not by private organisations who are not publicly responsible. The closed shop is, if not a relic, then an image of the medieval guild organisation, or, if you like, of the Elizabethan Statute of Apprentices and it may produce job reservations for privileged minorities. This may not only restrict the supply of (especially skilled) labour, it may also, exactly like educational privileges, cause waste and frustration by robbing people of their opportunities, and it may subject the individual too much to the power of trade union officials. Where several unions compete, it may mean that minorities are suppressed by majorities, or the other way. In France the closed shop was banned in 1956, partly to protect minority unions against the powerful *Confédération Générale du Travail*. Lastly – the evidence received by the Donovan Commission was to this effect – there are small groups of people who have conscientious objections to joining unions, mainly on religious grounds ...

The argument which is most frequently advanced in favour of the closed shop is "he who does not sow, neither shall he reap". The non-unionist enjoys the fruit of the union's negotiations with the employer – it is neither desirable nor practicable for the employer to differentiate between union members and others – but he does not pay his share of the cost. The main significance of this argument is that it is so widely held, and that it has an emotional appeal. It is not a very strong argument in itself because foreign experience (the 'solidarity contribution' system in Switzerland, and the 'agency shop' in America), shows that one can substitute for the obligation to join the union a contribution to its funds, not involving membership. Moreover, though the analogy may not be strong, it is, as McCarthy points out, a fact that people constantly reap the benefit of voluntary efforts to which they make no contribution: not only those who pay their annual subscription to the National Trust enjoy the scenery and the architecture it preserves.

The case for the closed shop can only be made in terms of the need for an equilibrium of power. It cannot be attacked or defended in terms of general ethical sentiments, but only in terms of social expediency. Moreover – and this is not the same point – the case for legislation against it can also only be made in these terms: strictly in terms of utility and nothing else. It was for reasons of expediency that, after weighing the arguments *pro* and *contra*, the Donovan Commission decided not to recommend legislation against it. In the view of at least some employers it was in the mutual interest: it reduces friction on the shop floor and thus a whole range of causes of disputes and it ensures that the union represents the whole of the work force. The scene of the struggle between groups among the workers, between militant and less militant wings is shifted away from the workplace. Further, there are branches of the economy where there can be no equilibrium without a closed shop, either because (as with seamen, road haulage workers and others) recruitment for membership is technically impossible, or because (as in large parts of the building industry) no collective regulation can be made effective without the entire work force being subject to union discipline. Even the Industrial Relations Act 1971, which on principle prohibited the closed shop, permitted it under very restricted conditions in order to take account of the needs of some of the unions facing the first of these situations.

What is (to me) perhaps the most powerful argument not in favour of the closed shop, but against legislation seeking to suppress it, is that formal closed shop agreements are less frequent than informal arrangements. The experience made under the Industrial Relations Act has shown that the law cannot suppress practices based on informal and generally shared understandings of the workers, and for good reasons, tolerated, and sometimes even welcomed by employers.

There is a case for the closed shop, not necessarily the pre-entry closed shop, in the interest of creating or maintaining that equilibrium of power on which the system of labour relations rests. But there may be a case for it in the interest of management as well as of labour, and indeed of the public in general. This is especially the case where the closed shop prevents secession, the formation of breakaway unions ...

Yet, it is said, the protection of human freedom comes first. If, during the Second World War, conscientious objectors were exempt from joining the Forces, then surely, whatever the general interest, no one should, as a condition for getting or holding a job be made to join a voluntary association, if he does not wish to do so. No one has, I think, ever suggested that a closed shop agreement should be legally enforceable so as to order a worker into a union by means of a mandatory injunction. This would be absurd, and it is not the point. Compulsory unionism is as undesirable as compulsory voting at elections which exists in some countries, but will not, one hopes, ever be introduced here. The analogy is valid. In the occupational existence of most people trade unions are, as I have said, the equivalent of the franchise in their political existence. The law should encourage, but not compel, men and women to take an active part in determining the conditions in which they and their fellows live and work – to say the least it should neither discourage them nor allow others to do so. Conscientious objectors should be given the chance of staying outside without disadvantage but also without benefit to themselves, and, as we shall see, the law takes account of this consideration. Beyond this, I cannot see that it is the office of the law, by suppressing the closed shop, to discourage union membership …'

Report of the Royal Commission on Trade Unions and Employers' Associations 1965–68 ('the Donovan Commission') Cmnd 3623

588.   We consider first the operation of the closed shop. This is a term with varying meanings. We use it in the sense in which it is used in Dr McCarthy's book on the subject, namely 'a situation in which employees come to realise that a particular job is only to be obtained and retained if they become and remain members of one of a specified number of trade unions'. Dr McCarthy shows that in 1964 about 3¾ million members of trade unions, that is about 2 out of every 5, worked in a closed shop. In some cases a person may have to be a member of a trade union before he can obtain the job he seeks. This is a 'pre-entry' closed shop. In other cases he may be obliged to join a trade union within a short time of beginning the job he has secured. This is the 'post-entry' closed shop. The pre-entry is less common than the post-entry closed shop, but at the time of Dr McCarthy's study it included about ¾ million workers. The diagram on the following page [not reproduced here] shows the extent of both types of closed shop on the basis of these estimates.

589.   Since 1964 the numbers employed in some industries where the closed shop is common have gone down, but there is evidence that it has spread in other industries. The total extent of the closed shop therefore probably remains about the same today as when Dr McCarthy studied it.

590.   A justification for the closed shop commonly put forward by trade unionists is that the benefits of agreements negotiated with employers apply to employees irrespective of whether they are union members or not. Consequently non-members, who pay no trade union subscriptions, are receiving benefits at the union's expense; they should therefore be obliged to contribute. However, as Dr McCarthy has shown, this is not the main reason for its existence. Admittedly some unions insist upon the closed shop wherever they have the strength to enforce it, but there are others which tolerate a minority of non-members even where they could take action to force them to join the union or lose their jobs.

591.   Whether a closed shop will be imposed or not depends on the particular circumstances of the industry, and of the undertaking. If it seems probable that a closed shop will add considerably to the bargaining strength of the union or of a group of

workers, then the closed shop is likely to be imposed. On the other hand, if non-unionists are not a serious source of weakness, then their presence will be tolerated.

The Case for the Closed Shop

592.   The two most convincing arguments for the closed shop refer only to the first group of employments, and depend upon the close link between effective collective bargaining and strong trade unions. The first is that in some industries it is impossible or difficult for a union to establish effective and stable organisation without the help of the closed shop; the second is that even where membership can be recruited and retained without its assistance there are instances where it is needed to deploy the workers' bargaining strength to the full.

593.   There are, however, other arguments which can apply even where these two lack force. London Transport told us that they saw advantage in the closed shop, since, as they put it, it ensured that in dealings with the union they were meeting an organisation 'which does represent all your people'.

A similar argument is that the closed shop helps to secure the observance of agreements, since it adds to the power of the union to discipline those who ignore them.

594.   It must not be supposed, however, that good industrial relations are the invariable accompaniment of the closed shop. On the contrary the closed shop is widespread in motor manufacturing, shipbuilding, coal-mining and the docks, the four industries in which strikes in breach of agreement have been most common in recent years.

The Case against the Closed Shop

595.   Against the closed shop, it is argued that it reduces the individual's freedom in a number of ways. If he is to obtain or retain employment where there is a closed shop, he has no choice but to join the trade union and to pay a subscription. The trade union may refuse to accept him as a member, and is answerable to nobody for its decision. Once a member of the union, the individual has to comply with any relevant decisions it may make; if he does not he may be disciplined, and if things go too far he may eventually be expelled and lose his job in consequence. So far as he is concerned, therefore, the trade union is no longer a 'voluntary' organisation, at least in the normal sense, and he cannot register his disagreement with the union in the normal way open to members of voluntary organisations – by resignation – unless he is prepared also to face losing his job.

596.   The importance of the loss of individual freedom is reinforced by the extent to which, as we show elsewhere, power in trade unions rests with work groups. Where matters are left to work groups to settle, they may need to support their decisions with some authority. Unions' disciplinary procedures designed with the needs of the branch in mind sometimes appear irrelevant to the work group when shop floor questions are at issue. As a result informal disciplinary measures, such as ostracism, may be used. Occasionally, trade union authority is wholly usurped; for example, there have been cases where the closed shop has been used to hound a man out of his job even when he had not formally been expelled, as in the case which reached the courts as *Huntley* v *Thornton.*

597.   The second principal objection advanced against the closed shop concerns its economic effects. Essentially, what is at issue here is entry to the skilled trades. It is argued that the craft unions use the closed shop to restrict to their own members,

or certain classes of their own members, the right to do skilled work; and because they limit the number of entrants they will allow to be trained in the requisite skills, or refuse to recognise as eligible to do skilled work members who have not served apprenticeships, they cause shortages of skilled labour which are economically damaging.

COMMENT

(1)   The references in both extracts are to McCarthy's classic study, *The Closed Shop in Britain* (Blackwell, 1964). Dunn and Gennard (*The Closed Shop in British Industry* (Macmillan 1984)) found that in 1978 the number of employees covered by closed shop arrangements had risen to 5.2 million, or 23 per cent of the workforce. As total employment had declined in industries where the closed shop had traditionally been strong, the increase was the more significant. They found the most notable rises in the nationalised industries and in white collar employment.

(2)   Both Kahn-Freund and the Donovan Commission (of which Kahn-Freund was a member) favoured restricting rather than abolishing the closed shop, by providing safeguards for individuals with genuine reasons for not joining. It is noticeable that one reason for not prohibiting it, put forward by both, is that it would be impossible to do so. This was to reckon without the determination to deal with the issue displayed by the Conservative Government of the 1980s, who regarded it as a focal point of many of the things they deplored about trade unions. The Conservative Government had already begun to legislate against manifestations of the closed shop in the Employment Act 1980 when it found itself in the odd position of defending the legislative position that had pertained under the Labour Government before the European Court of Human Rights.

Young, James and Webster v *United Kingdom*

[1981] IRLR 408 European Court of Human Rights

The three plaintiffs had all been dismissed from their jobs with British Rail because of their refusal to join the appropriate trade union. At all times British Rail had operated a closed shop agreement with the rail unions which followed exactly the pattern permitted by the law of unfair dismissal on who was exempt from the requirement to join. None of the plaintiffs came in an excepted category.

Judgment of the majority:

'1.   *The existence of an interference with an Article 11 right*

A substantial part of the pleadings before the Court was devoted to the question whether Article 11 guarantees not only freedom of association, including the right to form and to join trade unions, in the positive sense, but also, by implication, a "negative right" not to be compelled to join an association or a union.

Whilst the majority of the Commission stated that it was not necessary to determine this issue, the applicants maintained that a "negative right" was clearly implied in the text. The Government, which saw the Commission's conclusion also as in fact recognising at least a limited negative right, submitted that Article 11 did not confer or guarantee any rights not to be compelled to join an association. They contended that this right had been deliberately excluded from the Convention and that this was demonstrated by the following passage in the *travaux préparatoires*:

"On account of the difficulties raised by the 'closed shop system' in certain countries, the Conference in this connection considered that it was undesirable to introduce into the Convention a rule under which 'no one may be compelled to belong to an association' which features in [Article 20 s 2 of] the United Nations Universal Declaration (Report of 19.6.50 of the Conference of Senior Officials, Collected Edition of the *Travaux Prépara-toires*, vol IV, p 262)."

The Court does not consider it necessary to answer this question on this occasion.

The Court recalls, however, that the right to form and to join trade unions is a special aspect of freedom of association (see the *National Union of Belgian Police* judgment); it adds that the notion of a freedom implies some measure of freedom of choice as to its exercise.

Assuming for the sake of argument that, for the reasons given in the above-cited passage from the *travaux préparatoires*, a general rule such as that in Article 20 s 2 of the Universal Declaration of Human Rights was deliberately omitted from, and so cannot be regarded as itself enshrined in, the Convention, it does not follow that the negative aspect of a person's freedom of association falls completely outside the ambit of Article 11 and that each and every compulsion to join a particular trade union is compatible with the intention of that provision. To construe Article 11 as permitting every kind of compulsion in the field of trade union membership would strike at the very substance of the freedom it is designed to guarantee (see, *mutatis mutandis*, the *Belgian Linguistic* case, the *Golder* judgment and the *Winterwerp* judgment).

The Court emphasises once again that, in proceedings originating in an individual application, it has, without losing sight of the general context, to confine its attention as far as possible to the issues raised by the concrete case before it (see, *inter alia*, the *Guzzardi* judgment). Accordingly, in the present case, it is not called upon to review the closed shop system as such in relation to the Convention or to express an opinion on every consequence or form of compulsion which it may engender; it will limit its examination to the effects of that system on the applicants.

As a consequence of the agreement concluded in 1975 the applicants were faced with the dilemma either of joining NUR (in the case of Mr James) or TSSA or NUR (in the cases of Mr Young and Mr Webster) or of losing jobs for which union membership had not been a requirement when they were first engaged and which two of them had held for several years. Each applicant regarded the membership condition introduced by that agreement as an interference with the freedom of association to which he considered that he was entitled; in addition, Mr Young and Mr Webster had objections to trade union policies and activities coupled, in the case of Mr Young, with objections to the political affiliations of the specified unions. As a result of their refusal to yield to what they considered to be unjustified pressure, they received notices terminating their employment. Under the legislation in force at the time, their dismissal was "fair" and, hence, could not found a claim for compensation, let alone reinstatement or re-engagement.

The situation facing the applicants clearly runs counter to the concept of freedom of association in its negative sense.

Assuming that Article 11 does not guarantee the negative aspect of that freedom on the same footing as the positive aspect, compulsion to join a particular trade union may not always be contrary to the Convention.

However, a threat of dismissal involving loss of livelihood is a most serious form of compulsion and, in the present instance, it was directed against persons engaged by British Rail before the introduction of any obligation to join a particular trade union.

In the Court's opinion, such a form of compulsion, in the circumstances of the case, strikes at the very substance of the freedom guaranteed by Article 11. For this reason alone, there has been an interference with that freedom as regards each of three applicants.

Another facet of this case concerns the restriction of the applicants' choice as regards the trade unions which they could join of their own volition. An individual does not enjoy the right to freedom of association if in reality the freedom of action or choice which remains available to him is either non-existent or so reduced as to be of no practical value (see, *mutatis mutandis*, the *Airey* judgment).

The Government submitted that the relevant legislation not only did not restrict but also expressly protected freedom of action or choice in this area; in particular, it would have been open to the applicants to form or to join a trade union in addition to one of the specified unions. The applicants, on the other hand, claimed that this was not the case in practice, since such a step would have been precluded by British Rail's agreement with the railway unions and by the Bridlington Principles; in their view, joining and taking part in the activities of a competing union would, if attempted, have led to expulsion from one of the specified unions. These submissions were, however, contested by the Government.

Be that as it may, such freedom of action or choice as might have been left to the applicants in this respect would not in any way have altered the compulsion to which they were subjected since they would in any event have been dismissed if they had not become members of one of the specified unions.

Moreover, notwithstanding its autonomous role and particular sphere of application, Article 11 must, in the present case, also be considered in the light of Articles 9 and 10 (see, *mutatis mutandis*, the *Kjeldsen, Busk Madsen and Pedersen* judgment).

Mr Young and Mr Webster had objections to trade union policies and activities, coupled, in the case of Mr Young, with objections to the political affiliations of TSSA and NUR. Mr James' objections were of a different nature, but he too attached importance to freedom of choice and he had reached the conclusion that membership of NUR would be of no advantage to him.

The protection of personal opinion afforded by Articles 9 and 10 in the shape of freedom of thought, conscience and religion and of freedom of expression is also one of the purposes of freedom of association as guaranteed by Article 11. Accordingly, it strikes at the very substance of this Article to exert pressure, of the kind applied to the applicants, in order to compel someone to join an association contrary to his convictions.

In this further respect, the treatment complained of – in any event as regards Mr Young and Mr Webster – constituted an interference with their Article 11 rights.'

COMMENT

(1)   Six judges who concurred with the majority would have gone further and held that the right not to belong should in all respects be treated as on an equal footing with the right to belong. Three judges dissented, largely because it was clear from the *travaux préparatoires* that the drafters of the Convention had specifically intended to leave out the closed shop because of the lack of consensus between states on the issue.

(2)   Until the law of unfair dismissal was introduced the courts had not been involved with the closed shop. Since an employer could dismiss for any reason (provided notice was given), a dismissal because someone refused to join a union was perfectly legitimate, as was refusing to recruit a worker on that ground.

(3)   During the 1980s the Government pursued salami tactics against the closed shop, introducing more and more exceptions to the basic rule that a dismissal in a closed

shop situation was automatically fair, until the exceptions had virtually swallowed up the rule. In 1988 the basic rule was finally abolished by the Employment Act 1988 so that any dismissal for refusing to belong to a union became automatically unfair. This is now found in TULRCA s 152. Additionally, refusal to recruit on grounds of non-membership and discrimination against non-unionists are prohibited by TULRCA ss 137 and 146, which treat them on a par with union protection rights. Note also that in these cases special rules apply in relation to compensation (see p 325 on the special award). If the dismissal has come about at the behest of the trade union, it can be joined as a party in the unfair dismissal proceedings and compelled to pay part or all of the compensation (TULRCA ss 142, 160).

(4)   Thus while the closed shop is not illegal, it is no longer legally enforceable. A steep decline in trade union membership in general, coupled with high unemployment in traditional industries and the antipathy to union recognition which the Conservative Government had encouraged must mean that the number of employees now covered by closed shop arrangements has dropped considerably.

THE STATUS OF TRADE UNIONS IN LAW

The present legal status of trade unions is explicable to some extent in terms of their past; however, the history of trade unions is beyond the scope of this work. Pelling, *A History of British Trade Unionism* (Macmillan, 5th edn, 1992), is a readable account.

In English law, two kinds of person are recognised: natural persons and legal persons. Legal persons are corporations: registered companies are the most obvious example of these. A company has a separate existence from its members and owns property, enters contracts etc., in its own right. A trade union is not a company: it is an unincorporated association of individual natural persons; however, the House of Lords decided in an historic decision in 1901 that it had certain quasi-corporate characteristics.

Taff Vale Railway v Amalgamated Society of Railway Servants

[1901] AC 426 House of Lords

The railway company sued for an injunction to prevent strike action being taken by the union. In an unprecedented move, the company sued the union in its own name. The union argued that, as an unincorporated association, it could not be sued as if it were a legal person. Farwell J found for the company, but his decision was reversed by the Court of Appeal. The company appealed to the House of Lords. In view of the references to Farwell J's judgment by members of the House of Lords, it is also extracted.

Farwell J: 'The defendant society have taken out a summons to strike out their name as defendants, on the ground that they are neither a corporation nor an individual, and cannot be sued in a quasi-corporate or any other capacity. Failing this, they contend that no injunction ought to be granted against them. I reserved judgment last week on these two points, because the first is of very great importance, and counsel were unable to assist me by citing any reported case in which the question had been argued and decided.

Now it is undoubtedly true that a trade union is neither a corporation, nor an individual, nor a partnership between a number of individuals; but this does not by any means conclude the case. A trade union, as defined by s 16 of the Trade Union Act, 1876, "means any combination, whether temporary or permanent, for regulating the relations between workmen and masters, or between workmen and workmen, or between masters and masters, or for imposing restrictive conditions on the conduct of any trade or business, whether such combination would or would not, if the principal Act had not been passed, have been deemed to have been an unlawful combination by reason of some one or more of its purposes being in restraint of trade". It is an association of men which almost invariably owes its legal validity to the Trade Union Acts, 1871 and 1876 ...

Now, the Legislature in giving a trade union the capacity to own property and the capacity to act by agents has, without incorporating it, given it two of the essential qualities of a corporation – essential, I mean, in respect of liability for tort, for a corporation can only act by its agents, and can only be made to pay by means of its property. The principle on which corporations have been held liable in respect of wrongs committed by its servants or agents in the course of their service and for the benefit of the employer – qui senti commodum sentire debet et onus – (see *Mersey Docks Trustees* v *Gibbs*) is as applicable to the case of a trade union as to that of a corporation. If the contention of the defendant society were well founded, the Legislature has authorised the creation of numerous bodies of men capable of owning great wealth and of acting by agents with absolutely no responsibility for the wrongs that they may do to other persons by the use of that wealth and the employment of those agents. They would be at liberty (I do not at all suggest that the defendant society would so act) to disseminate libels broadcast, or to hire men to reproduce the rattening methods that disgraced Sheffield thirty or forty years ago, and their victims would have nothing to look to for damages but the pockets of the individuals, usually men of small means, who acted as their agents. That this is a consideration that may fairly be taken into account appears from the opinion of the judges given to the House of Lords in the *Mersey Docks Case*: "We cannot think that it was the intention of the Legislature to deprive a shipowner who pays dues to a wealthy trading company, such as the St. Catherine's Dock Company for instance, of all recourse against it, and to substitute the personal liability of a harbourmaster, no doubt a respectable person in his way, but whose whole means, generally speaking, would not be equal to more than a very small percentage of the damages, when there are any." The proper rule of construction of statutes such as these is that in the absence of express contrary intention the Legislature intends that the creature of the statute shall have the same duties, and that its funds shall be subject to the same liabilities as the general law would impose on a private individual doing the same thing. It would require very clear and express words of enactment to induce me to hold that the Legislature had in fact legalised the existence of such irresponsible bodies with such wide capacity for evil. Not only is there nothing in the Acts to lead me to such a conclusion, but ss 15 and 16 of the Act of 1871 imposing penalties on the trade union, and ss 8 and 15 of the Act of 1876 point to a contrary intention; nor do I see any reason for saying that the society cannot be sued in tort in their registered name ...'

Earl of Halsbury LC: 'My Lords, in this case I am content to adopt the judgment of Farwell J, with which I entirely concur; and I cannot find any satisfactory answer to that judgment in the judgment of the Court of Appeal which overruled it. If the Legislature has created a thing which can own property, which can employ servants, and which can inflict injury, it must be taken, I think, to have impliedly given the power to make it suable in a Court of Law for injuries purposely done by its authority and procurement.

I move your Lordships that the judgment of the Court of Appeal be reversed and that of Farwell J restored.'

Lord Macnaghten: '... The substantial question, therefore, as Farwell J put it, is this: Has the Legislature authorised the creation of numerous bodies of men capable of owning great wealth and of acting by agents with absolutely no responsibility for the wrongs they may do to other persons by the use of that wealth and the employment of those agents? In my opinion, Parliament has done nothing of the kind. I cannot find anything in the Acts of 1871 and 1876, or either of them, from beginning to end, to warrant or suggest such a notion. It is perhaps satisfactory to find that nothing of the sort was contemplated by the minority of the members of the Royal Commission on Trade Unions, whose views found acceptance with the Legislature. In paragraph 4 of their report they say: "It should be specially provided that except so far as combinations are thereby exempted from criminal prosecution nothing should affect ... the liability of every person to be sued at law or in equity in respect of any damage which may have been occasioned to any other person through the act or default of the person so sued." Now, if the liability of every person in this respect was to be preserved, it would seem to follow that it was intended by the strongest advocates of trade unionism that persons should be liable for concerted as well as for individual action; and for this purpose it seems to me that it cannot matter in the least whether the persons acting in concert be combined together in a trade union, or collected and united under any other form of association.

Then, if trade unions are not above the law, the only remaining question, as it seems to me, is one of form. How are these bodies to be sued? I have no doubt whatever that a trade union, whether registered or unregistered, may be sued in a representative action if the persons selected as defendants be persons who, from their position, may be taken fairly to represent the body....

The further question remains: May a registered trade union be sued in and by its registered name? For my part, I cannot see any difficulty in the way of such a suit. It is quite true that a registered trade union is not a corporation, but it has a registered name and a registered office. The registered name is nothing more than a collective name for all the members. The registered office is the place where it carries on business. A partnership firm which is not a corporation, nor, I suppose, a legal entity, may now be sued in the firm's name. And when I find that the Act of Parliament actually provides for a registered trade union being sued in certain cases for penalties by its registered name, as a trade union, and does not say that the cases specified are the only cases in which it may be so sued, I can see nothing contrary to principle, or contrary to the provisions of the Trade Union Acts, in holding that a trade union may be sued by its registered name.

I am, therefore, of opinion that the appeal should be allowed and the judgment of Farwell J restored with costs, here and below.'

(Lords Shand, Brampton and Lindley delivered concurring opinions.)

COMMENT

(1) The policy reasons for deciding the case in this manner are obvious. Its impact in the field of industrial action is discussed later (p 494).

(2) Trade unions had been legalised by the Trade Union Act 1871 (amended 1876) which had provided the embryonic form of registration by which some store was set in this case. The position is essentially the same today, with present definitions dating from the repeal of the Industrial Relations Act 1971 by TULRA 1974.

(3) The fact that trade unions are still not corporations having a separate legal

personality has two important consequences: first, they have to have certain quasi-corporate characteristics (like the right to own property) conferred on them by statute; second, they are defined in terms of their *purposes*, unlike companies, which are defined in terms of their *constitutions*.

Trade Union and Labour Relations (Consolidation) Act 1992

1.   In this Act a 'trade union' means an organisation (whether temporary or permanent)—

    (a)   which consists wholly or mainly of workers of one or more descriptions and whose principal purposes include the regulation of relations between workers of that description or those descriptions and employers or employers' associations; or

    (b)   which consists wholly or mainly of—

       (i)   constituent or affiliated organisations which fulfil the conditions in paragraph (a) (or themselves consist wholly or mainly of constituent or affiliated organisations which fulfil those conditions), or

      (ii)   representatives of such constituent or affiliated organisations, and whose principal purposes include the regulation of relations
between workers and employers or between workers and employers' associations, or the regulation of relations between its constituent or affiliated organisations.

   ...

10.   (1)   A trade union is not a body corporate but—

    (a)   it is capable of making contracts;

    (b)   it is capable of suing and being sued in its own name, whether in proceedings relating to property or founded on contract or tort or any other cause of action; and

    (c)   proceedings for an offence alleged to have been committed by it or on its behalf may be brought against it in its own name.

   (2)   A trade union shall not be treated as if it were a body corporate except to the extent authorised by the provisions of this Part.

   (3)   A trade union shall not be registered—

    (a)   as a company under the Companies Act 1985, or

    (b)   under the Friendly Societies Act 1974 or the Industrial and Provident Societies Act 1965;

and any such registration of a trade union (whenever effected) is void.

Electrical, Electronic, Telecommunication and Plumbing Union v *Times Newspapers Ltd*

[1980] 1 All ER 1097   Queen's Bench Division

The union sued the owners of *The Times* for libel in respect of statements defamatory of the union which had appeared in the newspaper: the issue before the court was whether a trade union could maintain an action for defamation.

O'Connor J: ' Now it is important to have clearly in mind that these issues are concerned with the law touching the action of defamation. The issues are in no way concerned with any of the law which may or may not touch on industrial disputes. It is the law of defamation with which I am concerned. As was said by Denning LJ in the Court of Appeal in his dissenting judgment in *Bonsor* v *Musicians' Union*:

> "A libel is, of course, in its very nature a wrong to the person, not a wrong to property; and it is apparent that it is only by attributing legal personality to a trade union that it can be permitted to sue for a libel on itself."

That is only applying to a trade union a much broader principle that the action for defamation is a personal matter because it is the reputation of the person which is defamed, and unless one can attach a personality to a body, it cannot sue for defamation....

Now where stands a trade union? It is not necessary for the purposes of this judgment to go into a detailed analysis of the history of trade unions in our law. It is well known that, before they were legalised, they ran foul of the law because they were unlawful combinations in the restraint of trade and suffered disabilities. But that is in the long and distant past. The Trade Union Acts since 1871 have recognised trade unions, but they were without question unincorporated associations, and as such one would have thought that they could neither sue in their own names, nor be sued, and as such could not be defamed in their proper name.

In 1901 in *Taff Vale Railway Co* v *Amalgamated Society of Railway Servants*, the House of Lords got over this difficulty, but in circumstances which were disliked by the trade union movement, by introducing what has come to be called a quasi-corporation, or a near corporation. Quite shortly, what happened was this. Looking at the registration of a trade union under the 1871 Act, and seeing the various matters dealt with in that statute, the House of Lords came to the conclusion that the trade union had a sufficient personality for that reason so that it could be sued in its own name and its funds charged in the action.

The reverse of that coin necessarily followed; if it could be sued so also it could maintain an action in its own name and, as we shall see in a moment, unions soon did so and perfectly properly. The immediate effect of the *Taff Vale* decision was to call for a change in the law to give protection to trade unions (nothing whatever to do with actions of libel, but in their industrial capacity), and in 1906 Parliament passed the Trade Disputes Act in order to reverse the decision of the House of Lords in the *Taff Vale* case: that is, to reverse the decision which had enabled the plaintiffs in that case to sue the union in tort. And in 1906, in the Trade Disputes Act, Parliament passed a blanket section relieving trade unions of liability in tort.

It left quite unaffected the decision of the House of Lords that this unincorporated body, because of the effect of the statute to which it was subject, had a quasi- corporate personality and thus we find that trade unions brought actions in their own name and, I have been told, that they sued for libel as early on as 1913; but it is unnecessary to examine that because the matter was decided, in a decision which is binding on me, in 1945, in *National Union of General and Municipal Workers* v *Gillian* ...

In 1965 a Royal Commission was appointed to inquire into the position of the trade unions, under the chairmanship of Lord Donovan. In its report it considered the position of trade unions and it found that there were certain anomalies and recommended that the position be clarified by passing legislation requiring or saying that trade unions should be bodies corporate. It also made recommendations about the immunity in tort because there were all sorts of matters which were quite outside industrial relations, e.g. personal injuries that a visitor to union premises might suffer. It has got nothing whatever to do with the industrial capacity of a trade union. There were difficulties, which were set out in the report; and in the Industrial Relations Act 1971 effect was given certainly to the recommendation that unions should be bodies corporate. Now it is well known that that statute met with determined opposition from the trade unions and in due course it was repealed and replaced by the statute which governs their positions today. It is unnecessary, other than the statement which I have made, to look further at the 1971 Act because it has been repealed, and the present position, and the difficulty with which I am confronted, has been created by the Trade Union and Labour Relations Act 1974 [now repealed and replaced by TULRCA 1992] ...

Section 2 [cf TULRCA s 10], the side note to which reads, "Status of trade unions", provides:

(1) A trade union which is not a special register body shall not be, or be treated as if it were, a body corporate ...

In my judgment, those are absolutely clear words. One must remember the position in law at that time. At that time, trade unions if they were registered were not necessarily corporate bodies; they were made corporate bodies. If they were on the provisional register they had the attributes of corporate bodies and could properly be called quasi-corporate associations, and the whole background of the position of trade unions until 1971 was that they were quasi-corporate bodies. It was a matter which was as much in their interest as any possible disability. Nevertheless here we find Parliament telling us what a trade union may not be: it "shall not be, or be treated as if it were, a body corporate"...

If the words "or be treated as if it were" were not in [s.10(2)] there would be absolutely no difficulty because all those powers which are attributed and given to trade unions make it quite clear that if they are, as the section would say, not a body corporate, they had the attributes of one and they were to be treated as one, so that they could possess the necessary personalities which they could protect by the action of defamation; but the words are there, and the words are saying that that is exactly what is not to be done. I do not find any ambiguity in them.

The tort of libel, as I have already demonstrated, must be founded on possession of a personality which can be libelled and [s.10] has removed that personality from trade unions. I find nothing in the statute to show that those words are ambiguous. There are many attributes which, but for the presence of the words "or be treated as if it were" in [s.10(2)] would simply confirm that a trade union enjoyed a quasi-corporate personality and could bring an action in libel in its own name for the protection of its own reputation, and, as I have said, I am quite clear that apart from the law anybody would say that a trade union has a separate reputation and should be entitled to protect it; but there it is. Parliament has deprived trade unions of the necessary personality on which an action for defamation depends; and to the first question which I have to decide which is:

Can a trade union (not being a special register body) maintain an action in its own name for damages for defamation in relation to its reputation as a legal entity whether or not such entity is separate and distinct from its individual members?

the answer is: "No. It cannot."

As I have said, I regret that I have to arrive at that decision but, I repeat, it seems to me that I am driven to it by the clear words of the statute ...'

COMMENT

(1) This illustrates that the 1974 definition of trade unions did not (as had perhaps been intended) simply return trade unions to the status that they had enjoyed before the Industrial Relations Act 1971.

(2) As will be seen, the total immunity in torts conferred on trade unions by the Trade Disputes Act 1906 has now been abolished (see Chapter 13).

(3)   While the definition of a trade union is narrowed by reference to an organisation consisting of workers (thus excluding solicitors: *Carter* v *Law Society*), on the whole it is a very wide definition. Trade unions may now incur extensive liabilities if they organise industrial action, which gives considerable importance to the fact that the definition may include temporary organisations.

Midland Cold Storage v Turner

[1972] ICR 230 National Industrial Relations Court

Midland found that it had been made the subject of a blacking order (meaning that its goods would not be handled) by a shop stewards' committee operating on the London docks. While the members of the committee were shop stewards of recognised unions, their committee had no official status within the unions and it was not recognised by the employers. Its activities were confined to the organisation or discontinuation of industrial action on the docks.

Sir John Donaldson: '... This brings us to the respondent committee. The habitual use of threatening notes over the name of the committee, the photograph of the chairman and the secretary visiting the picket line, and the complete absence of any repudiation by the committee of the pickets' authority, clearly point to the action of the pickets as being action taken on behalf of the committee. It must, therefore, seem strange that we are unable to make any order against the committee. The reason is this. The general law is that only individual men or women or corporations can be sued. Midland have taken proceedings against Mr Steer and Mr Turner as individuals but have not named any other individual members of the committee as being responsible for the threats of "blacking". Instead, they have taken proceedings against the committee as if it was a corporation, which it is not. Counsel for Midland admits that the committee is not a corporation, but he submits that s 154(2) of the 1971 Act justifies Midland in treating it as if it was, because it is an "organisation of workers". Section 154 certainly has that effect if the committee is an organisation of workers. But is it? An "organisation of workers" is defined in s 61(1) of the 1971 Act as,

> an organisation (whether permanent or temporary) which either – (a) consists wholly or mainly of workers of one or more descriptions and is an organisation whose principal objects include the regulation of relations between workers of that description or those descriptions and employers or organisations of employers, or (b) is a federation of workers' organisations [cf TULRCA s 1].

It follows that if Midland are to obtain an order against the committee they must satisfy us that (a) it is an organisation; (b) it consists wholly or mainly of workers; (c) its principal objects include the regulation of relations between workers of that description and employers.

We have no doubt at all that the committee exists and has great influence in the London docks. We have no evidence as to its composition, other than the fact that it has a chairman and secretary, and that, as we infer from its name and our general knowledge of organisation in the docks, it is composed wholly or mainly of trade union shop stewards. It is not recognised by employers, although they are well aware of its existence and may take account of its activities. Furthermore, there is no evidence that it seeks recognition by employers as a bargaining agent for any bargaining unit or as a representative body for or of any union or unions. It is proved to be an influential pressure group. Our general knowledge of the industry tells us that its activities are to some extent co-ordinated with those of other shop stewards' committees in other docks by a national dock shop stewards' committee, but that those other committees may have different compositions and functions. If we have to be able to point to evidence to confirm what as members of an industrial court we ought to know and do know, it was provided at a late stage in the hearing by the production of a printed leaflet, purporting to be issued by the committee, referring to support from the national committee. Its most apparent activity seems to consist of recommending the taking or abandonment of industrial action in the London docks and organising any such action which may be decided on. Thereafter it does not seem to enter into negotiations with the employers but leaves this task to the established union machinery.

Against this background, we are satisfied that prima facie the committee is an organisation and that it consists wholly or mainly of workers as defined in the 1971 Act. However, we are not satisfied that there is a prima facie case for holding that its principal objects include the regulation of relations between workers of that description (namely registered dock workers) and employers. No body whose principal objects included such regulation could fail at least to seek recognition from employers and of such an attempt we have no evidence. Accordingly, we are unable to make any order against the committee as such ...'

COMMENT

(1)   Had the purposes of this ad hoc committee been different, it would have incurred liability. However, it is conceivable that there could be some scope for trade unions to delegate organisation of industrial action to non-union organisers in such a way as to avoid liability. It would be difficult, because of the wide canons of vicarious liability applied; but not wholly impossible.

(2)   While the union is able to own property in perpetuity by virtue of TULRCA s 12, it seems that according to the general law there is nothing to prevent branches owning their own funds separately. Now that union funds are frequently at risk when industrial action is taken, this also could be important, as the next case shows:

News Group Newspapers Ltd v Society of Graphical and Allied Trades 1982

[1986] ICR 716 Court of Appeal

In the wake of industrial action, a sequestration order was made against the funds of the union because of its contempt of court. While the union had over £5 million in its central funds, branch funds amounted to more than £6 million. This was an action by the sequestrators to get at the £279,297 held by the London branch.

Lawton LJ: 'The union, which is registered under the Trade Union and Labour Relations Act 1974 was formed in 1982, being an amalgamation of two unions in the printing industry. It has about 200,000 members. Its objects are the usual ones of large trade unions, that is to say, collective bargaining, safeguarding working conditions and the provision of benevolent funds and services for its members. It is organised in branches. Every member has to belong to a branch and in every place of employment where two or more members work they have to form and join a chapel.

Each branch has a considerable degree of independence as rule 1(3) of SOGAT 1982's General Rules 1984 shows:

For the convenience of members, branches shall be formed in such towns as may be found necessary. Each branch shall be at liberty to elect its own officers, conduct its own business, and be empowered to frame its own local, superannuation and distress fund rules and regulations, provided they are approved by the executive council and in conformity with the general rules.

Branches are empowered to "raise funds for local purposes": see rule 39(2). Rule 39(5) distinguishes between a branch's funds and property and the union's because there is a prohibition against any branch "disposing of the society's funds or property otherwise than by these rules allowed". There is the same indication in rule 1(4) which envisages that on the secession or dissolution of a branch the union's funds, books and property shall be delivered to the general secretary but the branch shall be entitled to keep "purely provident, local, superannuation and distress funds, books and properties".

All members of the union have to contribute to its funds and to branch funds, if there are any, and to chapel funds. By rule 41 local funds "shall be the property of the branch". The branches are responsible to the union for the collection of the contributions to the union's funds. In practice members pay a composite sum at prescribed intervals which is made up of what is to go to the union and what to the local funds. Of that which is to go to the union, as a matter of convenience before forwarding it, the branches deduct 40 per cent which they use to help pay for the cost of administering the branches. In the case of the London branch this percentage is not enough to cover all their administrative expenses and is supplemented by payments out of its local funds. In the past the London branch has not differentiated in its bank accounts between what is due to the union and what it can keep as its local funds. Mr Mowbray on behalf of the London branch and the chapel, accepted that any identifiable sums in those accounts which belong to the union must be held to the order of the commissioners as must, as long as the order of sequestration is in operation, all contributions to union funds which its members may pay it. The rules of the London branch set out how its branch funds are to be spent, that is to say "to finance the activities and benefits of the branch", in specified ways which are all concerned with the activities and interests of its members, not of the union as such. As already recounted trustees of the funds and property have been appointed. Any decision relating to "the use, disbursement or investments of the assets of the branch is to be exclusively that of the branch committee to whose decision the trustees are bound to conform".

In my judgment, when the rules of both the union and the London branch are construed, not as if they were in a statute or deed but as the terms of a contract, the intention manifested by the words used was that the local funds of the London branch were to be used solely for the benefit of such of its members as it had at any one time, provided that any expenditure was for purposes in conformity with the objects of the union ...

In my judgment the issue in this case is to be decided on the construction of the rules of the union and of the London branch. Since, as I adjudge, both sets of rules provide that the property and funds of the London branch are to be held for benefit of that branch, it follows that its property and funds are not the property of the union and are not subject to the order of sequestration.

I would allow the appeal.'

(Lloyd and Glidewell LJJ delivered concurring judgments.)

LISTING AND INDEPENDENCE OF TRADE UNIONS

Listing

Trade Union and Labour Relations (Consolidation) Act 1992

2.   (1)   The Certification Officer shall keep a list of trade unions containing the names of—

        (a) the organisations whose names were, immediately before the commencement of this Act, duly entered in the list of trade unions kept by him under section 8 of the Trade Union and Labour Relations Act 1974, and

        (b) the names of the organisations entitled to have their names entered in the list in accordance with this Part.

    (2)   The Certification Officer shall keep copies of the list of trade unions, as for the time being in force, available for public inspection at all reasonable hours free of charge.

    (3)   A copy of the list shall be included in his annual report.

    (4)   The fact that the name of an organisation is included in the list of trade unions is evidence (in Scotland, sufficient evidence) that the organisation is a trade union.

    (5)   On the application of an organisation whose name is included in the list, the Certification Officer shall issue it with a certificate to that effect.

    (6)   A document purporting to be such a certificate is evidence (in Scotland, sufficient evidence) that the name of the organisation is entered in the list.

COMMENT

(1) Registration under the Trade Union Act 1871, mentioned in the *Taff Vale* case, was replaced one hundred years later by registration under the Industrial Relations Act 1971. The consequences, however, were very different: under the Industrial Relations Act, registered trade unions became corporate bodies, suable in tort and subject to a great deal of regulation of their internal affairs. Non-registration therefore became the rallying call of trade union opposition to that Act. In 1974, when the Industrial Relations Act was repealed, the word 'register' had too many unpleasant connotations to be used and so it was replaced by the more innocuous 'list'.

(2) There are certain minor tax advantages for trade unions in being listed; however, the main reason for seeking listing is that it is an essential first step before establishing the union's status as an independent and recognised trade union.

Independent trade unions

Trade Union and Labour Relations (Consolidation) Act 1992

5.   In this Act an 'independent trade union' means a trade union which—

        (a) is not under the domination or control of an employer or group of employers or of one or more employers' associations, and

        (b) is not liable to interference by an employer or any such group or association (arising out of the provision of financial or material support or by any other means whatsoever) tending towards such control;

    and references to 'independence', in relation to a trade union, shall be construed accordingly.

COMMENT

(1) A listed trade union may apply to the Certification Officer for a certificate of independence, which will be issued if the above definition is satisfied. An appeal from the Certification Officer's decision lies to the EAT.

(2) The reason for the emphasis on independence is to guard against employers encouraging what the Americans graphically term 'sweetheart unions'. A company may encourage workers to join an organisation in which it pulls the strings: it will then be entirely happy to grant exclusive negotiating rights to this body and will use it as an excuse to refuse to recognise any other union.

(3) The criteria used by the Certification Officer were described with approval by the EAT in the first appeal against a refusal to grant a certificate of independence.

Blue Circle Staff Association v *Certification Officer*

[1977] ICR 224 Employment Appeal Tribunal

Cumming-Bruce J: 'In response to a question from the tribunal the Certification Officer described his approach. He stated that he had found no nice clear yardstick which could be laid against each case, but that it was a case of looking at the factors and doing a balancing act. He then indicated certain criteria which he found useful. In view of the novelty and importance of the subject matter we set out these criteria as the witness described them, though we do not think it would give a fair impression of his evidence if we suggested that he presented them either as comprehensive, or of similar weight in any two cases.

1. *Finance*: If there is any evidence that a union is getting a direct subsidy from an employer, it is immediately ruled out.
2. *Other assistance*: The Certification Officer's inspectors see what material support, such as free premises, time off work for officials, or office facilities a union is getting from an employer, and attempt to cost them out.
3. *Employer interference*: If a union is very small and weak and gets a good deal of help, then on the face of it its independence must be in danger and liable to employer interference.
4. *History*: The recent history of a union, important in the case of Blue Circle Staff Association which before February 1976 was dominated by the employers, is considered. It was not unusual for a staff association to start as a "creature of management and grow into something independent". The staff association had started on this road but still had a way to travel.
5. *Rules*: The applicant union's rule book is scrutinised to see if the employer can interfere with or control it, and if there are any restrictions on membership. If a union is run by people near the top of a company it could be detrimental to rank and file members.
6. *Single company unions*: While they were not debarred from getting certificates, because such a rule could exclude unions like those of miners and railwaymen, they were more liable to employer interference. Broadly based multi-company unions were more difficult to influence.
7. *Organisation*: The Certification Officer's inspectors then examine the applicant union in detail, its size and recruiting ability, whether it is run by competent and experienced officers, the state of its finance, and its branch and committee structure. Again, if the union was run by senior men in a company, employer interference was a greater risk.
8. *Attitude*: Once the other factors had been assessed, inspectors looked for a "robust

attitude in negotiation" as a sign of genuine independence, backed up by a good negotiating record. They may find a single company union with little resources which may have behaved in a robust or even militant way. It did not seem common sense to say that a union which has constantly caused trouble for an employer is dependent on that employer. However, that did not mean he favoured militancy, because, if a union dealt with a good, tactful and sensitive employer who paid well and its members had little to be militant about, it could be extremely difficult for it to demonstrate its robustness and militancy or, consequently, its independence ...

Squibb UK Staff Association v Certification Officer

[1979] ICR 235 Court of Appeal

In 1973 white collar staff at E R Squibb & Sons Ltd formed a staff association, which 231 out of a potential 290 employees joined. In 1976 it applied for a certificate of independence. The Certification Officer rejected the application because of the association's dependence on facilities provided free by the employer – free office and meetings accommodation, free stationery, telephone, photocopying and internal mailing, and so on. Given the narrow membership base of the association and its limited resources, the Certification Officer thought that it would find it extremely difficult to function if these facilities were withdrawn. In consequence, he concluded that it was 'liable to interference' within the meaning of TULRCA s 5.

Lord Denning MR: 'The Certification Officer interpreted the words "liable to interference" as meaning "vulnerable to interference" or "exposed to the risk of interference" by the employer. Whereas Mr Irvine for the association suggested that it meant "likely" or "not unlikely" to be subjected to interference by the employer. The Employment Appeal Tribunal preferred Mr Irvine's interpretation. They said:

"We feel that Mr Irvine's approach ... is the better one and that the words must be construed as meaning that, in the circumstances and on the facts of each case, it is not unlikely that interference will take place and, that when it does, it is not unlikely to have the effect of some degree of control by the employer."

Applying that test, which I may call "the likelihood of interference" test, the appeal tribunal held that there should be a certificate of independence. They said,

"... on the evidence we have heard and the documents we have read, there is no real likelihood either of the facilities being withdrawn, or, if they were, of this in any way affecting the independence of the union from employer interference, and that therefore the union has successfully rebutted the presumption."

So there it is. They decided because there was no real "likelihood of interference by the employer".

I agree that there are two possible meanings of the word "liable". It is a very vague and indefinite word. Having heard very good arguments on both sides, it seems to me that the Certification Officer's interpretation of "liable" is correct and the staff association's interpretation is not correct. One has to envisage the possibility that there may be a difference of opinion in the future between the employers and the staff association. It does not matter whether it is likely or not – it may be completely unlikely – but one has to envisage the possibility of a difference of opinion. It may be on the amount of pay; it may be on the question of a pension; it may be on the safeguards; and the like. Whatever it may be, there may be a difference of opinion. It may be a mere possibility. But when it arises, the questions have to be asked. What is the strength of the employers? What pressures could they bring to bear against the staff association? What facilities could they withdraw? [TULRCA s 5] contemplates that the association may be liable to interference arising out of "the provision of financial or material support or by any other means whatsoever".

The employers could take away the four facilities which the Certification Officer mentioned in his reasons. They could take away the facility of time off for meetings. They could take away the facility of free use of office accommodation, and so forth. Those are pressures which the employers could bring to bear on their side. On the other side, this association is rather weak. It has a narrow membership base. It has small financial resources. Weighing the two sides, one against the other, the Certification Officer came to the conclusion that the association was liable to interference in this way: the association was so weak that it was vulnerable, in that it was exposed to the risk of interference tending towards control by the employers.

The Employment Appeal Tribunal reversed the Certification Officer. It seems to me that it misdirected itself. It concentrated too much on the "likelihood of interference" whereas it should have had regard to the "vulnerability to interference". I would therefore allow the appeal and restore the decision of the Certification Officer ...'

(Shaw and Brandon LJJ agreed.)

COMMENT

(1)   Some of the consequences of the status of independent trade unions have now disappeared. From the point of view of the union, the main importance is in relation to the rights of recognised trade unions (dealt with in Chapter 5, above), which are only granted to recognised *independent* trade unions.

(2)   There are also advantages for employees in that the protection against dismissal or action short of dismissal on grounds of union membership or activities applies only to members of independent trade unions (TULRCA ss 146, 152; contrast s 137).

11 Trade unions and their members

Generally when you join an organisation such as a club or a political party or the National Trust, you agree to abide by the rules of that organisation. If you don't like the rules, you have two choices: either don't join, or else join and work from the inside to persuade the necessary majority to your point of view. The law basically keeps out of the affairs of private organisations, except in so far as the law of trusts may regulate their financial affairs.

This may be contrasted with the position relating to companies: the basic principle behind our company law is that entrepreneurs should be free to get on with business in whatever way they think fit, provided that they meet certain minimum standards, in particular of disclosure. Thus the formation of companies is closely regulated and they have to submit regular statements of their financial affairs for public inspection as well as inspection by their members; however, beyond that the board of directors has great discretion in what the organisation does.

Should trade unions be treated like private organisations or like companies? In a sense, neither model is wholly appropriate. While a trade union is a voluntary (in the sense that you do not have to join one) unincorporated association like a club or a political party, it could be argued that it is too important in working life to be left outside legal regulation; also, it does have quasi-corporate characteristics, as we saw in the last chapter. But the model of the registered company is inapposite also: companies are top-down organisations whose members have almost no interest either in its day-to-day affairs or in broad policy-making. Trade unions receive their direction from the grass roots, and members are not only closely involved in making policy, but are also affected by and participate in their day-to-day affairs.

In this chapter we will consider the law's regulation of the internal affairs of trade unions in three areas: first, the political activities of trade unions; second, common law supervision of trade union rules, and finally the increasing statutory intervention in the relationship of union and member.

EXPENDITURE FOR POLITICAL PURPOSES

When trade unions were first legalised by the Trade Union Acts 1871–76, nothing was stated about the use of trade union funds for political purposes.

Amalgamated Society of Railway Servants v Osborne

[1910]   AC 87   House of Lords

In 1903 the union added to its list of purposes, 'to secure parliamentary representation' and in 1906, that sponsored candidates should be subject to the Labour party whip. A member challenged the legality of the rules.

Lord Atkinson: '... The contentions relied upon to establish the validity of the impeached rule are, as I understand it, first, that the definition contained in clause 16 of the Trade Union Amendment Act of 1876 is not, as it is said, exhaustive, and that therefore a trade union, though registered, may have amongst its objects, in addition to one or more of the objects named in the section, any object whatever not in itself illegal, and accordingly that, provided it be created to effect one or more of the objects named, it is in other respects in the same position as any individual or voluntary association of individuals, and is therefore at liberty to expend its funds to procure the return of members of Parliament, and to maintain them there, as freely as an individual or such an association of individuals is to devote his or its moneys to a like purpose; and, second, that, even if such a union be not free to aim at all legal objects not named in the section, parliamentary representation, on the conditions prescribed in the rule, is the most effective means of attaining the objects which are named, and may therefore be lawfully provided for in the mode prescribed....

Now it is not contended that it is a matter of necessity for registered trade unions to secure parliamentary representation on the lines indicated in this rule, or on any other lines. Their whole history refutes such a suggestion. But it is contended that it is only fair to imply that they have this power, because such a representation would afford the most effective means of accomplishing the objects mentioned in s 16, inasmuch as legislation might be introduced to help or hinder them in the prosecution of those objects, and that it is vital to their interests to have in Parliament members in sympathy with their views to support the one form of legislation and to oppose the other; and, further, that they cannot procure the return of such members unless they pay out of their funds the election expenses of chosen candidates, and by the same means maintain them if returned to Parliament.

The answer to that argument is, I think, this. Trade unions are in this respect in precisely the same position as all corporations, municipal or commercial, including in the latter all limited liability companies created under the Act of 1862. These bodies, like the trade unions, may by legislation be helped or hindered in carrying out the objects which they were formed to carry out. Their most vital interest may be seriously prejudiced by taxation which the Legislature may impose, or enabling statutes, general in character, may be introduced calculated to enlarge their powers, increase their privileges, or remove restraints upon their action, or again some of them may be under the necessity of promoting private Bills to meet their own special needs. If, despite all this, the intention never has been and cannot be imputed to the Legislature to confer upon such corporations as these power or authority to devote their funds to the procurement of parliamentary representation in the manner in this case contended for, how can such an intention be imputed to it in the case of quasi-corporations such as registered trade unions? And if this intention cannot be imputed to the Legislature in the case of registered trade unions, as in my view it cannot be, there can be no such thing as an implied grant of the desired powers, because an addition to a grant is only introduced by implication in order to carry out the presumed intention of the grantor. During the argument I asked to be informed on what principle the case of registered trade unions was to be differentiated from that of other corporations such as I have named, and why the former were to be permitted, by an alteration of their rules, to convert themselves into political organisations, while a similar privilege was to be denied to the latter. No satisfactory reply was given to me, because none could, I believe, be given. I know of no such principle myself.

It is not disputed that up to 1903, at all events, members of trade unions were not on joining required to subscribe to any political creed, or submit to any political test, no more than are persons who become shareholders in a railway company, and, for all that appears, there may be as great a diversity of political views amongst the members of the one class as of the other. Freedom of opinion was probably permitted amongst the members of both classes because it was not the business of either of the bodies to which they respectively belonged to support particular political parties or to promote a particular political policy. It would be as unjust and oppressive as, in my view, it is illegal to compel, by passing rules such as that impeached, a member of a trade union, who like the respondent joined in the days when freedom of action was permitted, either to contribute to the promotion of a political policy of which he might possibly disapprove, or be expelled from the union to which he belonged for so many years and forfeit all benefit from the money he had subscribed.

I am therefore of opinion that power and authority such as are in this case claimed for the appellants have not been conferred upon them expressly or by implication; that the impeached rule is ultra vires; that the decision appealed from was on this point right and should be upheld, and the appeal dismissed with costs ...'

(The Earl of Halsbury and Lord Macnaghten delivered concurring speeches. Lord James concurred on a different ground and Lord Shaw expressly refrained from deciding this issue.)

COMMENT

(1)   This decision and *Taff Vale* are probably the most famous cases in the annals of trade union history. Both were regarded as attacks on the trade union movement. Note the emphasis in the opinion on the analogy with the position of registered companies.

(2)   The Liberal Government of the day took prompt action to reverse the effects of the decision. However, trade unions were not given a free hand to spend their funds on political activities. The Trade Union Act 1913 required that a separate political fund should be set up, and political purposes financed from this alone. These requirements were substantially modified by the Trade Union Act 1984, and the present position is to be found in the Trade Union and Labour Relations (Consolidation) Act 1992 Chapter VI.

Trade Union and Labour Relations (Consolidation) Act 1992

71.   (1)   The funds of a trade union shall not be applied in the furtherance of the political objects to which this Chapter applies unless—
(a)   there is in force in accordance with this Chapter a resolution (a 'political resolution') approving the furtherance of those objects as an object of the union (see sections 73 to 81), and
(b)   there are in force rules of the union as to—
(i)   the making of payments in furtherance of those objects out of a separate fund, and
(ii)   the exemption of any member of the union objecting to contribute to that fund,
which comply with this Chapter (see sections 82, 84 and 85) and have been approved by the Certification Officer....

72. (1) The political objects to which this Chapter applies are the expenditure of money—
      (a) on any contribution to the funds of, or on the payment of expenses incurred directly or indirectly by, a political party;
      (b) on the provision of any service or property for use by or on behalf of any political party;
      (c) in connection with the registration of electors, the candidature of any person, the selection of any candidate or the holding of any ballot by the union in connection with any election to a political office;
      (d) on the maintenance of any holder of a political office;
      (e) on the holding of any conference or meeting by or on behalf of a political party or of any other meeting the main purpose of which is the transaction of business in connection with a political party;
      (f) on the production, publication or distribution of any literature, document, film, sound recording or advertisement the main purpose of which is to persuade people to vote for a political party or candidate or to persuade them not to vote for a political party or candidate.
    (2) Where a person attends a conference or meeting as a delegate or otherwise as a participator in the proceedings, any expenditure incurred in connection with his attendance as such shall, for the purposes of subsection (1)(e), be taken to be expenditure incurred on the holding of the conference or meeting....
73. (1) A political resolution must be passed by a majority of those voting on a ballot of the members of the trade union held in accordance with this Chapter.
    (2) A political resolution so passed shall take effect as if it were a rule of the union and may be rescinded in the same manner and subject to the same provisions as such a rule.
    (3) If not previously rescinded, a political resolution shall cease to have effect at the end of the period of ten years beginning with the date of the ballot on which it was passed. ...

COMMENT

(1)   The requirement that there should be a re- ballot every ten years (s 73(3)) was introduced in 1984 in such a way that unions which already had funds (usually set up shortly after 1913) had to re-ballot within a year. All were endorsed by the members. Since then, no union has lost a political fund ballot.

(2)   Members who are against the political fund in effect get counted twice: they may vote against in the ballot, but even if the ballot goes against them, they can be exempt from payment (s 71(1)(b)(ii)).

(3)   The secret ballot must be conducted according to rules approved by the Certification Officer (s 74) and must be fully postal (that is, ballot papers sent out and returned by post) (s 77). There must be an independent, qualified scrutineer, whose name must appear on the ballot paper (ss 75, 77(2)). All members of the union must be given the right to vote (s 76). The scrutineer's report on the ballot, including information on the numbers of ballot papers sent out, votes, spoiled papers and so on, must be sent to all members (s 78). A member believing that the ballot has been conducted in breach of these requirements may make an application to the Certification Officer or to the court (ss 80, 81).

(4)   Since TURERA, the scrutineer is required to inspect the membership register of the union where it is suspected of being inaccurate or not up-to-date.

(5)   These are the requirements which must be followed when the union wishes to spend money on 'political objects' as defined by s 72. The original 1913 list was extended in 1984. It follows that if the activity is outside the political objects, the union may use any general funds to finance it; conversely, if the activity is within the political objects, a union which does not have a political fund is prohibited from spending any money on it.

Paul and Fraser v *National and Local Government Officers' Association*

[1987] IRLR 413 Chancery Division

NALGO ran a campaign called 'Make People Matter' in 1987 (which was designated by the TUC as Public Services Year). The campaign highlighted cuts in public services. Two members claimed that the expenditure on the campaign was unlawful because NALGO did not have a political fund.

Browne-Wilkinson V-C: '... The next leaflets were not issued to the public until April of this year, that is to say a month before the local government elections. They each deal with a separate topic or sector of public service. The first says, "Decent public services make all the difference." On the back it says, "I used to catch a bus to the shops. Now I have to walk to the shops to get a bus." Then it refers to "cut-backs in day centres and the number of home helps make it harder for elderly people to cope ... sheltered housing for those who need it has been cut too. More than 36,000 National Health Service beds – one in 10 of the total – have been cut since 1979. People are waiting longer and longer for treatment – some die before they reach the top of the queue." In another passage it refers to "private contractors, encouraged by the Government to compete to run services, cut corners in order to cut costs". Then they refer to it being a time to invest, and at one point say, "Spending on health and education creates five times as many jobs as tax cuts." At the bottom it says, "You have a voice. You have a vote. Make people matter." In a box against a pink background the nature of NALGO is described, and this passage (which also appears in all subsequent leaflets) appears: "NALGO is not affiliated to any political party and is not seeking or opposing the election of any particular candidate or group of candidates. NALGO is campaigning so people can judge for themselves how important our public services are – to themselves and to the country as a whole." I will refer to that as "the disclaimer". The next leaflet is headed on its front, "Getting to the truth behind the promises. Questions to ask before you vote." At the back it starts: "It's election time! On 7 May council elections take place." It goes on to say that "every party will claim they are determined to improve your local services, and that the others have got it wrong. So who's telling the truth?" Then there are a number of specimen questions which the elector is invited to ask his candidate. "If I vote for you, will you publicly support the case for more investment in the NHS, public education, low-cost housing and public transport?" ...

  The question is not whether the purposes being pursued by NALGO in this campaign are political; by any conceivable standard they are obviously political. The question is whether they are involved in the publication and distribution of literature, the main purpose of which is to persuade people not to vote for a political party.

  The plaintiffs' case is that this literature, read in its context, can only be read as an attempt to persuade people to vote against the Conservative Party. I would for myself emphasise in

(f) the use of the words "to vote for or not to vote for". A crucial feature of any political purpose within [TULRCA s 72(1)(f)] is an element of persuasion to vote. Mere persuasion of people's minds to a particular viewpoint unconnected with the exercise of a vote at an election is not covered by this. What is precluded is the attempt to persuade somebody to exercise a vote one way or the other. I am not dealing with a case where there is a publicity campaign disconnected from an election and without an invitation to vote. The facts of this case are much nearer the line than that. What the plaintiffs have to show is that the *main* purpose was to persuade people not to vote for a particular party, namely the Conservative Party ...

I will now turn to consider the literature which is complained of in this case, the effect of which I have sought to summarise. I have no doubt whatsoever that one purpose of the literature, particularly the leaflets, is to persuade people not to vote for the Conservative Party. The burden of the literature is to criticise the record of the Conservative Government which is said to be the run-down of the public services. That censure on the Conservative Government is confined to the Conservative Government. Though Mr Monks said, as I am sure is the case, that NALGO have been complaining of government cut-backs since before 1979, it is notable that in no place in the literature is any reference made to any cut-backs earlier than 1979. Each leaflet refers to the Conservative Government only and each leaflet refers to its policies and the implementation of its policies unfavourably. It does not refer to any other government critically or unfavourably, and it contains nothing critical of any other party. What is more, it takes matters of policy which are known to be Conservative Party policy, such as privatisation, and decries them.

The leaflets then go on, having given that one-sided view of the effect of the Conservative policy and its non-coincidence with NALGO policy, to invite the electorate to think and then to vote. Every one of the leaflets complained of expressly invites the member receiving the leaflet to vote. The inference to my mind from the leaflet itself is really overwhelming. It says that the Government's policies since 1979 are bad, you have to think about it, and having thought about it you have to vote. The only rational message to be drawn from that is, "If you accept the message of the leaflet vote against the Conservatives."

Each leaflet contains the disclaimer, saying we are not inviting you to vote this way or that. I think where a message is as clear as this one a disclaimer of that kind is no more effective to avoid liability than is a disclaimer where in a libel case it is said that nobody in this book bears any resemblance to anybody in real life. It is not effective to escape liability once one looks at the purpose of the document as a whole. Therefore I have no doubt that one purpose of the literature was to persuade people to vote against the Conservative Party....

To sum up, in my judgment what we have here is literature which gives one side of the political argument. It attributes a bad record to the Conservative Party (admittedly indirectly by calling it the Government). That literature is then timed to be published at the time of an election. The same literature invites people to vote, taking into account that one-sided version of the issues involved. In those circumstances it seems to me impossible to say that the main purpose was not to influence the voting. While I have no explanation as to how the reference to voting crept in the fact is that it did. In those circumstances in my judgment the expenditure was unlawful as being in breach of [TULRCA s 71] ...

Finally I would like to say that nothing in this judgment should be taken as suggesting that a publicity campaign organised by a union at times other than an election and therefore at a time when neither directly nor indirectly can the union be inviting anyone to exercise a vote at the time, is unlawful, merely because it expresses disapproval of the Government's policy. Unions, like anybody else, are entitled to disapprove of government policy and to say so. The vice in this case to my mind is that they have linked this disapproval in a biased way with an invitation to vote at the time of an election ...'

COMMENT

(1) Despite the statement in the last paragraph extracted, this judgment alarmed many public sector unions and persuaded many that they needed to set up a political fund in order to be able to campaign around issues affecting their members.

(2) The requirements for unions to use funds for political purposes may be contrasted with those applicable to companies. Under the Companies Act 1985, the annual Directors' Report must disclose political donations above £200 in amount. There is no requirement for any approval to be given by shareholders. Short of voting down the accounts (a wholly unrealistic scenario) there is no way that shareholders can prevent such expenditure. They have no individual opt-out clause such as exists for union members.

(3) Union members who opt out of paying the political subscription are protected from discrimination on that account by TULRCA s 82, which states that they shall not on that account be disadvantaged or excluded from any office, except in relation to the management or control of the political fund.

Birch v National Union of Railwaymen

[1950] Ch 602 Chancery Division

Rule 21(8) of the defendant union provided that members who did not contribute to the political fund would not be under any disability compared with other members, except that they could take no part in the control or management of that fund and would be ineligible for any office involving such control or management. The union's rules had been approved by the Registrar in this form.

 Birch, who contracted out of the political fund, had been elected as branch chairman. The general secretary of the union ruled that he was ineligible for this office because it inevitably involved management of the political fund. He sought a declaration that this was in breach of the Act.

Danckwerts J: '... It is to be observed that, when first read, the rule appears to follow the requirements of that paragraph and confine discrimination and ineligibility to positions involving control or management of the political fund, which is the exception mentioned in the paragraph. It is not until it is discovered that an exempted member is disqualified from holding the office of chairman because that office involves control or management of the political fund as well as the general fund, that doubts begin to rise.

 Sir Walter Monckton contended (as I understood his argument) that (1) as a matter of practical administration of the affairs of the branch it is necessary to combine the control and management of the general fund and the political fund in the hands of the same officials of the branch, and (2) accordingly, the exempted member must suffer the disability or disadvantage of exclusion from office by reason of the exception permitting disability or disadvantage where the control or management of the political fund is involved. There is, he said, no provision confining the exception to functions concerned with control or management of the political fund. This is an ingenious argument, but be it observed that the effect is to exclude an exempted member from any part in the affairs of his branch as an officer or a representative by reason of the fact that the same persons administer (as the rules are constituted) both the general and the political funds. This appears to me to be equivalent to the exception swallowing the provisions [of s 82(1)(c)] which were primarily designed to prevent disability from being imposed on the exempted member. In other words, as long as the constitution of the union fails to separate the control and management of the political fund from other functions of the union, there is no limit to the area of the exception and an exempted member might find himself excluded from practically all the activities of his branch. I cannot believe that this is the result of an exception introduced into a provision designed to protect the exempted member. It is entirely reasonable that a non-contributor should be excluded from control or management of the political fund; it is quite another matter that he should be excluded from any office in his union or branch.

I reach the conclusion, therefore, that r 21(8) in conjunction with the other rules of the union, offends against the provisions of [TULRCA s 82(1)(c)] ...'

COMMENT

(1)   It would appear that unions must separate entirely control of the political fund from any other office within the union.

(2)   Members of the union must be informed what amount is payable to the political fund (s 85). It remains the case that members must opt out of payment (rather than opting in if they want to make political contributions), but they are to be reminded of their right to opt out every time the political resolution comes up for renewal (s 84(2)).

(3)   Where the employer automatically deducts the employee's union subscription from pay and forwards it to the union (the check-off system), the employee may at any time give notice of exemption from liability to pay and the employer must implement this at once (s 86). However, a member who wants to be exempt remains liable to the union to pay the political subscription for the rest of the calendar year, unless she has opted out within a month of the original political resolution ballot (s 84(4)). It will be virtually impossible for the union to collect in these circumstances.

(4)   TURERA amended TULRCA s 68 so that employees have to re-authorise their employer to deduct union subscriptions every three years. The *employer* is obliged to give the employee notice of any increase in subscription rates, and at the same time to remind the employee of her right to withdraw from payment. The extra adminis-trative burden was a clear disincentive for employers to agree to maintain check-off procedures, certainly where they did not charge the union for this facility. It was also likely that the forces of inertia would deter employees from renewing their authority to deduct, and so would reduce the number of members contributing to the political fund. A large number of unions responded by persuading members to change to a direct debit system instead.

UNION RULES AT COMMON LAW

The rules of a trade union form a contract between the union and the member. There are two major ways in which the courts have exercised control over union rules: first, in relation to their interpretation; second, in insisting that the rules of natural justice apply.

Interpretation of the rule book

At the outset, it is worth recalling the oft-quoted words of Lord Wilberforce in *Heatons Transport* v *TGWU*:

'... But trade union rule books are not drafted by parliamentary draftsmen. Courts of law must resist the temptation to construe them as if they were; for that is not how they would be understood by the members who are the parties to the agreement of which the terms, or some of them, are set out in the rule book, nor how they would be, and in fact were, understood by the experienced members of the court. Furthermore, it is not to be assumed, as in the case of a commercial contract which has been reduced into writing, that all the terms of the agreement are to be found in the rule book alone: particularly as respects the discretion conferred by the members upon committees or officials of the union as to the way in which they may act on the union's behalf. What the members understand as to the characteristics of the agreement into which they enter by joining a union is well stated in the section of the TUC Handbook on the Industrial Relations Act which gives advice about the content and operation of unions' rules. Paragraph 99 reads as follows:

"Trade union government does not however rely solely on what is written down in the rule book. It also depends upon custom and practice, by procedures which have developed over the years and which, although well understood by those who operate them, are not formally set out in the rules. Custom and practice may operate either by modifying a union's rules as they operate in practice, or by compensating for the absence of formal rules. Furthermore, the procedures which custom and practice lays down very often vary from workplace to workplace within the same industry, and even within different branches of the same union." '

In the past 20 years, trade union rule books have been much revised, and the effects of statute are such that it may be that custom and practice have less of a place than once was the case. However, in an important recent decision, *Heatons Transport* v *TGWU* was relied on to support a finding that the union had an *implied* power to discipline and expel members.

McVitae v *Unison*

[1996] IRLR 33 Chancery Division

Unison came into existence on 1 July 1993 on the amalgamation of three unions: COHSE, NALGO and NUPE. The four plaintiffs, members of Unison, had previously been members of the Liverpool branch of NALGO. At the time of the amalgamation they were subject to internal disciplinary proceedings because of alleged intimidation and sexual harassment of other members which had not been completed. After the amalgamation, they were charged with offences under the Unison rule book instead. They argued that it was beyond the powers of the union to take this disciplinary action against them for events which occurred while they were NALGO members, because there was no rule which permitted this. The union argued, *inter alia*, for an implied rule to that effect.

Harrison J: '... The main thrust of the argument between the parties centred on whether a disciplinary power relating to pre-inception conduct could be implied into the contract between the Unison members. If such a term were not to be implied there would, in effect, be an amnesty for all offences committed before the vesting day but which had not by that date resulted in a penalty being imposed.

...

Mr King drew my attention to the following passage in *Harvey on Industrial Relations and Employment Law*, volume II, paragraph M 2652, where it is stated:

"The power of a union to discipline a member depends upon the express terms of the rulebook. A power to discipline or expel will not be implied."

Three authorities are quoted for those propositions: *Dawkins* v *Antrobus, Abbott* v *Sullivan*, and *Spring* v *National Amalgamated Stevedores' and Dockers' Society*. Mr Langstaff QC, who appeared on behalf of the defendant, submitted that the three cases are not authority for the propositions quoted in *Harvey*.

Mr King, on the other hand, told me that he had not been able to find any case where the court had implied a power to discipline. He reminded me that the evidence on behalf of the plaintiffs was that if the charges were proved against them they may be deprived of their jobs and it would have a serious effect on their personal reputations and their future employability. He therefore relied on the following passage in the judgment of Sedley J at p 9A of the transcript:

"... where disciplinary proceedings are concerned there is a limit to the amount of relaxation which the courts are prepared to allow of the close reading of their provisions. The reason for this is equally obvious: such provisions within the domestic context of a trade union are truly penal and need to be therefore read down rather than up and read with caution rather than with excessive liberality. This is a balance, therefore, that needs to be argued out at trial more fully than has been possible or appropriate today."

... Mr Langstaff submitted that common sense dictated that Unison should have the power to discipline, for instance, a dishonest official whose financial irregularity had come to light after the vesting day. He suggested that Sedley J, when dealing with that situation, had not dealt with the real purpose of the disciplinary rules, which is not to punish or to recover money but to regulate the people who are entitled to be members and officers of the union.

So far as the law is concerned, Mr Langstaff relied in particular on the well-known passage in the judgment of MacKinnon LJ, in *Shirlaw* v *Southern Foundries (1926) Ltd* when he stated:

"Prima facie that which in any contract is left to be implied and need not be expressed is something so obvious that it goes without saying; so that, if, while the parties were making their bargain, an officious bystander were to suggest some express provision for it in their agreement, they would testily suppress him with a common 'Oh, of course!' "

Reliance was also placed on the words of Lord Wilberforce in *Liverpool City Council* v *Irwin* when, in dealing with implied terms, he said:

"The present case, in my opinion, represents a fourth category, or I would rather say a fourth shade on a continuous spectrum. The court here is simply concerned to establish what the contract is, the parties not having themselves fully stated the terms. In this sense, the court is searching for what must be implied."

Mr Langstaff submitted that, whether it was the *Moorcock* test, the officious bystander test or Lord Wilberforce's test, the power of Unison to discipline members for pre-inception conduct complied with it. It was, he said, necessary to have an implied term for enabling Unison to have such a power, otherwise how else, he asked, could it discipline or expel a dishonest or racist member for conduct before the vesting day? ...

... I should say straight away that I recognise the force of the arguments that have been raised by both sides on the jurisdiction point. It is a difficult issue with much to be said on both sides. The starting point, it seems to me, must be to consider whether the statement in *Harvey on Industrial Relations and Employment Law* that a power of a union to discipline or expel a member will not be implied is correct because, if it is, it would effectively dispose of the point. I have considered those three cases cited in support of that proposition but I am not satisfied that they are authority for such a widely stated proposition. In the case of *Dawkins* v *Antrobus* the Court of Appeal refused to interfere with a decision of a members' club expelling a member from the club. I do not find anything in the judgments in the Court of Appeal in that case to justify the general assertion that a power to discipline or expel will not be implied. In the case of *Abbott* v *Sullivan* a committee of corn porters, which had no written constitution, resolved to remove the plaintiff's name from the register of corn porters for striking a trade union official. The Court of Appeal held that the resolution was invalid because there was no evidence of a contract, express or implied, to show that they had jurisdiction to take that action. In deciding whether or not the plaintiff could claim damages from members of the committee, the court, Denning LJ dissenting, held that there could not be implied a contract between the plaintiff and the committee that the members of the committee would not do anything which was beyond their jurisdiction. The plaintiff was not therefore entitled to claim damages for breach of contract. I do not find that case to be authority for the general proposition that there can be no implied power to discipline a trade union member. It was a case decided on its own facts involving a committee which had no written constitution but which existed as a matter of custom and practice.

Finally, in the case of *Spring* v *National Amalgamated Stevedores' and Dockers' Society* the plaintiff's union excluded him from membership of the union as a result of an award by the Trades Union Congress that the union should exclude those members, including the plaintiff, who had been admitted to the union in breach of the Bridlington Agreement dealing with the relationship between trade unions. The court refused to imply a term of the plaintiff's contract of membership of the union that the union should have the right to do anything necessary and proper to comply with the Bridlington Agreement because the plaintiff did not know of the Bridlington Agreement when he became a member of the union. Furthermore the Agreement contained no rules about what a trade union member should do or abstain from doing and it contained no power of expulsion. That again was a case decided on its own particular facts which I do not read as laying down any general proposition that there can be no implied power to discipline or expel.

I therefore conclude that the statement in *Harvey on Industrial Relations and Employment Law* that a power of a union to discipline or expel a member will not be implied is too broadly stated and is not supported by the three cases which are cited as authority for it. In my view, the court can imply such a disciplinary power, although the court's power to do so is one which should be exercised with care and only where there are compelling circumstances to justify it. The reason why the court should be slow to imply a disciplinary power is that it is penal and could include serious consequences affecting the reputation and livelihood of the union member.

...

Having decided that, as a matter of principle, the court can imply a power by a union to discipline a member, the next question is whether, in the particular circumstances of this case, there can be implied a power by the defendant to discipline the plaintiffs for their alleged conduct occurring before the amalgamation.

It is quite clear from the evidence that although there were extensive negotiations between the amalgamating unions prior to the amalgamation, the Unison rulebook did not cover all matters covering the relationship between the union and its members. In a complex amalgamation involving three large unions I do not find that surprising. The evidence showed that there were various matters, Including the continuation in office of the shop stewards and branch secretaries after the vesting day, the continuation of representation and legal assistance and the inclusion of membership of a member's former union as qualifying for a member's benefits, which were not included in the Unison rulebook but which were to be implied because they were generally assumed to be authorised. It is therefore clear that the Unison rulebook does not contain the whole of the contract between the union and its members. The principle of some terms being implied must therefore be accepted. There is nothing unusual in that, as can be seen from the case of *Heatons Transport* v *TGWU.*

It is clear that the existence of an implied power to discipline for pre-inception conduct must depend on the presumed intention of the parties. ...

I cannot conceive that it was intended that there should be a complete amnesty for pre-inception conduct. There is certainly no evidence of such an intention and common sense suggests that it would not have been intended. It offends against common sense that a member who has, for instance, done something dishonest before amalgamation which contravenes both the rules of his former union and the rules of Unison should escape penalty simply as a result of the amalgamation. As a responsible union, Unison would be just as intent on ensuring that such conduct was disciplined as would have been the former union. It is not in the interests of Unison that they should be unable to regulate their membership or the holding of office in such circumstances. In my judgment, it would have been the expectation of members in such circumstances that the union should be able to take disciplinary action. If they had been asked about it, they would have said that it was so obvious that it must have been intended to form part of the agreement between Unison and its members.

Such a conclusion does not cause any prejudice to the plaintiffs because they would have been subject to the disciplinary proceedings anyway under the Nalgo rules if the amalgamation had not taken place. A contrary conclusion would have meant that they would have been the lucky beneficiaries of a technicality. Those considerations in themselves are relevant to what must be presumed to have been the intention of members of the union.

Although, as I have said, the court should be slow to imply disciplinary powers, it should equally be slow to reach a decision which, on the fact of it, is contrary to what both the members and common sense would have expected. I have come to the conclusion, for the reasons that I have given, that the particular circumstances of this case are sufficiently compelling to warrant a disciplinary power being implied in relation to pre-inception conduct. ...'

COMMENT

(1) This case bucks the trend of judicial decisions on the interpretation of union rules, especially those relating to discipline and expulsion, where the tendency has been to construe rules very strictly. It also illustrates the continuing relevance of the common law in this area, despite increased statutory regulation.

(2) As the rules constitute a contract, the courts have the opportunity to say what the contract means.

Lee v *The Showmen's Guild of Great Britain*

[1952] 2 QB 329 Court of Appeal

A dispute arose between Lee and another member of the union as to which of them was entitled to a particular site at Bradford Fair for his Noah's Ark roundabout. An internal union committee decided in favour of the other member but Lee refused to accept this and took the site instead. The union committee found Lee guilty of unfair competition contrary to the union's rules and fined him £100. Lee sought to challenge this by way of an action for a declaration.

Denning LJ: 'The jurisdiction of a domestic tribunal, such as the committee of the Showmen's Guild, must be founded on a contract, express or implied. Outside the regular courts of this country, no set of men can sit in judgment on their fellows except so far as Parliament authorises it or the parties agree to it. The jurisdiction of the committee of the Showmen's Guild is contained in a written set of rules to which all the members subscribe. This set of rules contains the contract between the members and is just as much subject to the jurisdiction of these courts as any other contract ...

Although the jurisdiction of a domestic tribunal is founded on contract, express or implied, nevertheless the parties are not free to make any contract they like. There are important limitations imposed by public policy. The tribunal must, for instance, observe the principles of natural justice. They must give the man notice of the charge and a reasonable opportunity of meeting it. Any stipulation to the contrary would be invalid. They cannot stipulate for a power to condemn a man unheard.

Another limitation arises out of the well-known principle that parties cannot by contract oust the ordinary courts from their jurisdiction: see *Scott* v *Avery, per* Alderson B and Lord Cranworth LC. They can, of course, agree to leave questions of law, as well as questions of fact, to the decision of the domestic tribunal. They can, indeed, make the tribunal the final arbiter on questions of fact, but they cannot make it the final arbiter on questions of law. They cannot prevent its decisions being examined by the courts. If parties should seek, by agreement, to take the law out of the hands of the courts and put it into the hands of a private tribunal, without any recourse at all to the courts in case of error of law, then the agreement is to that extent contrary to public policy and void ...

The question in this case is: to what extent will the courts examine the decisions of domestic tribunals on points of law? This is a new question which is not to be solved by turning to the club cases. In the case of social clubs, the rules usually empower the committee to expel a member who, in their opinion, has been guilty of conduct detrimental to the club; and this is a matter of opinion and nothing else. The courts have no wish to sit on appeal from their decisions on such a matter any more than from the decisions of a family conference. They have nothing to do with social rights or social duties. On any expulsion they will see that there is fair play. They will see that the man has notice of the charge and a reasonable opportunity of being heard. They will see that the committee observe the procedure laid down by the rules; but they will not otherwise interfere: see *Labouchere* v *Earl of Wharncliffe* and *Dawkins* v *Antrobus*.

It is very different with domestic tribunals which sit in judgment on the members of a trade or profession. They wield power as great as, if not greater than, any exercised by the courts of law. They can deprive a man of his livelihood. They can ban him from the trade in which he has spent his life and which is the only trade he knows. They are usually empowered to do this for any breach of their rules, which, be it noted, are rules which they impose and which he has no real opportunity of accepting or rejecting. In theory their powers are based on contract. The man is supposed to have contracted to give them these great powers; but in practice he has no choice in the matter. If he is to engage in the trade, he has to submit to the rules promulgated by the committee. Is such a tribunal to be treated by these courts on the same footing as a social club? I say no. A man's right to work is just as important to him as, if not more important than, his rights of property. These courts intervene every day to protect rights of property. They must also intervene to protect the right to work.

But the question still remains: to what extent will the courts intervene? They will, I think, always be prepared to examine the decision to see that the tribunal has observed the law. This includes the correct interpretation of the rules. Let me give an illustration. If a domestic tribunal is given power by the rules to expel a member for misconduct, such as here for "unfair competition," does that mean that the tribunal is the sole judge of what constitutes unfair competition? Suppose it puts an entirely wrong construction on the words "unfair competition" and finds a member guilty of it when no reasonable person could so find, has not the man a remedy? I think that he has, for the simple reason that he has only agreed to the committee exercising jurisdiction according to the true interpretation of the rules, and not according to a wrong interpretation....

My conclusion, therefore, is that the court has power in this case to intervene in the decision of the committee of the Showmen's Guild if no facts were adduced before them which could reasonably be considered to be "unfair competition" within rule 15(c), which says that "no member of the guild shall indulge in unfair competition with regard to the renting, taking, or letting of ground or position. ...The judge held that there was nothing of "unfair competition" in the plaintiff's conduct, and I agree with him. It may have been very reprehensible of him not to abide by the previous ruling of the guild. He should have given way to Shaw: but he can hardly be said to have been guilty of unfair competition. There was no undercutting or anything of that sort. He only accepted the position allotted to him and stood on it. Inasmuch as the facts are not reasonably capable of being "unfair competition" it follows that the committee had no jurisdiction to find him guilty of it ...'

(Somervell and Romer LJJ delivered concurring judgments.)

COMMENT

(1)   Note that there are several grounds on which intervention by the court is here said to be justified: the other grounds will be examined later.

(2)   The standard justification for intervention – the risk of loss of livelihood if expelled from the union – is also laid out. Today, that risk is in theory no longer applicable, as the closed shop may not be enforced. However, informal closed shop arrangements may exist, and in any case, there are other reasons for belonging to a trade union – such as participation in collective bargaining – which would justify at least some control over a union's decision to expel a member.

(3)   However, it is interesting to contrast the approach to review of a union's decision with the infinitely more limited powers of an industrial tribunal to review an employer's decision to dismiss and of the EAT to review the decision of an industrial tribunal.

Leigh v National Union of Railwaymen

[1970] Ch 326 Chancery Division

The plaintiff's nomination for election as president was rejected by the general secretary on the grounds that he was not a member of the Labour Party as required by the union rules.

When the plaintiff challenged this decision, the union argued, among other things, that he had no right to start legal proceedings without exhausting internal remedies first.

Goff J: '… Next, it was submitted on behalf of the defendants that the plaintiff is not entitled to relief because he has not exhausted or, indeed, embarked upon the domestic remedies afforded by the rules. On this point I extract from *White* v *Kuzych* in the Privy Council, and *Lawlor* v *Union of Post Office Workers* in this court, two propositions. The first is that even where there is an express provision in the rules that the plaintiff must first exhaust his domestic remedies, the court is not absolutely bound by that because its jurisdiction cannot be ousted, but the plaintiff will have to show cause why it should interfere with the contractual position. This is consonant with the rule in the case of a submission to arbitration where the court always has a discretion whether to stay an action but cause must be shown why it should not. The second proposition is largely the converse of the first, namely, that in the absence of such a provision the court can readily, or at all events more readily, grant relief without prior recourse to the domestic remedies, but may require the plaintiff to resort first to those remedies. Thus, in *Lawlor*'s case Ungoed-Thomas J said,

> "Trade union rules clearly cannot oust the jurisdiction of the courts. Contracts, including a contract constituted by trade union rules, may provide that recourse to domestic tribunals shall be exhausted before there is recourse to the courts, and the courts may recognise and give effect to that contract; but that does not oust its jurisdiction. So in this case, the court has jurisdiction, and here there is no contractual provision requiring domestic remedies to be exhausted before resort to the courts. Should that jurisdiction be exercised now, or should it be withheld, in the circumstances, pending appeal to annual conference?
>
> This case involves the construction of the rules of the trade union, and it is for the courts, and not a domestic body, to decide questions of construction, as matters of law. It involves questions of natural justice, which again are matters for the courts to decide."

The plaintiff's counsel concedes that he cannot, on the evidence on this motion, show cause why an express provision, if there be one, requiring that domestic remedies should be first utilised should be disregarded, and the defendants submit that the rules, and in particular rules 3(6) and 9(4), have that effect. I must therefore first determine whether this is so, and I am not prepared to accept that submission. The rules purport to exclude the jurisdiction of the court altogether and to that extent are void on the authority of *Lee* v *Showmen's Guild of Great Britain*, but that is no reason for construing them as requiring recourse to the domestic tribunal first. The two things are inconsistent.

Then ought I, notwithstanding the absence of such a provision, to refuse relief because the domestic remedies have not been adopted? In my judgment, on the facts of this case, I ought not. it is true that *Lawlor*'s case was one of expulsion and infringement of the rules of natural justice, and is therefore much stronger than the present. On the other hand, this is at least one of refusing the opportunity of election to an office of honour and profit, and it is one turning on construction, which, as Ungoed-Thomas J observed in the passage I have quoted, is peculiarly appropriate for the court. Moreover, having regard to the union's decision in Bowman's case, the plaintiff could not reasonably expect to succeed, if at all, by the domestic remedies, short of an appeal to the annual general meeting, which would have meant driving the matter up to the very meeting at which the election should take place, and so have left him virtually no chance of obtaining relief through the court until after the election. This would not, as a matter of law, prevent him from obtaining relief at all, because he could apply to set it aside and for an injunction restraining the union and the successful candidate from acting on the vote, but it might well prejudice his position in fact on a subsequent election.'

COMMENT

(1)   There is now a limitation on rules requiring internal procedures to be exhausted first: if the member makes an application to the union and the matter is not wrapped up within six months, the member is entitled to go to the court without further delay (TULRCA s 63, introduced originally by the Employment Act 1988).

(2)   It is no longer possible for the rules to require that the president, general secretary or any member of the principal executive committee of the union should be a member of a particular party; however, it is possible to prescribe that they must *not* be members of a particular party or parties (TULRCA s 47, introduced in 1984).

Natural justice

The rules of natural justice have been developed in public law to lay down minimum standards of procedural justice for bodies carrying out quasi-judicial functions. There are essentially two elements: first, that you should know the charge against you and have an opportunity to counter it; second, that the body making the decision should be unbiased.

Stevenson v United Road Transport Union

[1977] ICR 893 Court of Appeal

The plaintiff, a member of the union, was appointed as regional officer for an indefinite period in 1970. In 1974, friction arose between him and other officers and members of the union. It resulted in the general secretary writing to him on 10 June suspending him on full pay until a disciplinary hearing to be held on 9 July. The letter stated that the disciplinary hearing would be about allegations contained in a report by the officer to whom he was responsible of non-cooperation and failure to carry out instructions.

   The union declined to send him a copy of the relevant report, saying that he knew what it was about. At the disciplinary hearing, at which the plaintiff was not permitted legal representation, the charges were presented. He asked for a copy in writing in order to prepare his defence, and made no attempt at that hearing to give his side of the story. The committee nevertheless decided to serve him with three months' notice.

   Although the plaintiff was an employee of the union, he was also a member of it, and the court considered that the rules of natural justice applied.

Buckley LJ: '... So, in our judgment, the judge was right in his conclusion that the executive committee was bound to comply with the rules of natural justice. He went on to consider whether they had sufficiently done so. He rejected a suggestion by the plaintiff that the committee were biased against him. This is not an issue on this appeal.

   Mr Rose has submitted that cases to which the rules of natural justice apply can be divided into three categories: (1) cases in which the rules may be said to apply in their full rigour, so that the accused party is entitled to notice and full particulars of the charges against him, perhaps with discovery, and to a hearing with or without witnesses, and perhaps with professional representation; (2) cases in which the accused party is merely entitled to an opportunity to state his own case; and (3) cases in which the only requirement is that the tribunal must act fairly, honestly and without bias. It is true that what natural justice requires may vary according to the circumstances of each case, but we think that it is undesirable to attempt to classify them. In *Russell* v *Duke of Norfolk* Tucker LJ said:

"The requirements of natural justice must depend on the circumstances of the case, the nature of the inquiry, the rules under which the tribunal is acting, the subject matter that is being dealt with, and so forth. Accordingly, I do not derive much assistance from the definitions of natural justice which have been from time to time used, but, whatever standard is adopted, one essential is that the person concerned should have a reasonable opportunity of presenting his case. I think from first to last the plaintiff did have such an opportunity."

We gratefully adopt that statement. A case may be of so uncomplex a character and the issues may be so well known to all parties concerned that no more particular notice of any charges may be required, an opportunity for the party of whom complaint is made to state his case being sufficient. *Russell* v *Duke of Norfolk* was such a case but the present one is not, for the judge found as a fact that on July 9, 1974, the plaintiff did not know, when the hearing began, what charges were to be made against him. Mr Rose accepted in this court that what occurred at the meeting between Mr Moore and the plaintiff on May 23, 1974, was not enough to tell the plaintiff in sufficient detail the nature of all the charges he had to meet.

As was pointed out in *Kanda* v *Government of Malaya* if the right to be heard is to be a real right which is worth anything, it must carry with it a right for the party of whom complaint is made to know the case which is made against him (and see *Ridge* v *Baldwin*): and, since the purpose of that requirement is to enable that party to defend himself or answer the complaint, it must follow that the notice must be sufficient to enable him adequately to prepare his defence or answer. We agree with the judge in thinking that the plaintiff should have been supplied with a fair statement, by which we mean a sufficiently specific statement, of the charges which it was proposed to lay before the executive committee a reasonable time before the meeting of July 9. This was not done. The plaintiff then asked, as he was entitled to do, for the charges to be formulated and for a sufficient adjournment to enable him to prepare his defence. He was not allowed either. The judge found that the members of the executive committee assumed on July 9 that the plaintiff then knew with what he was charged, but this, although it may explain the denial of what the plaintiff was fairly entitled to, cannot excuse it. Consequently, in our judgment, the proceedings on July 9 did not conform to the requirements of natural justice and were defective ...'

(Orr and Goff LJJ concurred in this judgment.)

COMMENT

(1)   It seems that the rules of natural justice do not require that the 'accused' should be entitled to legal representation: *Enderby FC* v *Football Association*.

Roebuck v National Union of Mineworkers (No 2)

[1978] ICR 676 Chancery Division

Templeman J: 'The following principal material facts are pleaded by the plaintiffs and admitted by the union. In 1974 the president of the union, Mr Scargill, brought an action for libel against a newspaper. The libel action was commenced and conducted by Mr Scargill, on behalf of the union, pursuant to a resolution of the area council. At the trial of the libel action, Mr Roebuck and Mr O'Brien gave evidence for the newspaper. After a trial which lasted from March 8 to 24, 1976, Mr Scargill was awarded £3,000 damages for libel and he has since accounted for those damages to the union. Shortly after the conclusion of the trial of the libel action, Mr Scargill prepared and signed a report, which was dated March 29, 1976 ...

The report expressed the belief of Mr Scargill that Mr Roebuck's actions were clearly detrimental to the interests of the union; that the actions of Mr O'Brien could only be described as a very serious offence; and were clearly detrimental to the interests of the union; and that both as regards Mr Roebuck and Mr O'Brien, the matters set out in the report were of such magnitude and seriousness that Mr Scargill would be failing in his duty if he did not reflect it to the area council and include it in the report.

In this court, counsel for the union submitted that the statement in the report that Mr Scargill believed the action of Mr O'Brien could only be described as a very serious offence and was clearly detrimental to the interests of the union (thus foreshadowing and echoing the words of rule 42) only amounted to an indication that Mr Scargill believed that a prima facie case had been established. I am bound to say that to me those words read more like judgment before trial.

On April 12, 1976, the area council met, under the chairmanship of Mr Scargill. Although Mr Scargill's report had not been considered by the executive committee, and if the executive committee took a certain course would inevitably, or probably, be referred to the area council for review, Mr Scargill read his report aloud to the area council. The area council then referred the actions of Mr Roebuck and Mr O'Brien to the area executive committee. The area executive committee held a meeting, under the chairmanship of Mr Scargill, and attended by Mr Roebuck; and they resolved to charge Mr Roebuck with conduct detrimental to the union, in that he gave a signed statement to the union solicitors, and yet when he appeared under subpoena at the Sheffield High Court he completely contradicted that statement. In doing this, the charge alleged, Mr Roebuck misled the union and his action was of assistance to the newspaper in its defence against the union in the libel action.

The area executive committee held another meeting under the chairmanship of Mr Scargill and resolved to charge Mr O'Brien with conduct detrimental to the union, in that he gave a voluntary statement to the solicitors acting on behalf of the newspaper, which was of assistance to the newspaper in their defence against the union in the libel action; and in that he allowed the solicitors acting on behalf of the newspaper to see private correspondence between the area president and a branch of the union, which was directly concerned with the libel action; and in the view of the executive committee these letters were of assistance to the newspaper, in their defence against the union, in the libel action.

At a subsequent meeting of the area executive committee, under the chairmanship of Mr Scargill, and attended by Mr O'Brien, first of all the charges against Mr O'Brien were found to be proved; and Mr O'Brien was suspended from his office as branch secretary for a period of two years. At that or at a subsequent meeting on the same day, the charges against Mr Roebuck were found to be proved and he was declared to be ineligible for any office or committee of the union, for a like period of two years.

The area council held a meeting on May 24, 1976, under the chairmanship of Mr Scargill. Mr Roebuck and Mr O'Brien attended. Mr Scargill read and explained to the delegates a statement of facts which was based on his report; and, in the case of Mr Roebuck, the statement of facts said, inter alia, that the statement that Mr Roebuck had made to the solicitors of the newspaper was clearly in contradiction of the statement he had made to the union's solicitors; and on the basis of the evidence presented by Mr Roebuck himself, it was clear that the charge had been proved. In the case of Mr O'Brien, the statement of facts said, inter alia, that it was clear that the charges which had been put to Mr O'Brien at the meeting of the executive committee had been proved, on the basis of Mr O'Brien's admissions to the executive committee. The area council affirmed the convictions and punishments of Mr Roebuck and Mr O'Brien.

At the relevant meetings of the executive committee and the area council, Mr Scargill participated in the questioning of Mr Roebuck and Mr O'Brien, and participated in the deliberations of the executive committee and the area council, in each case outside the presence of Mr Roebuck and Mr O'Brien; but it is common ground that when the relevant resolutions were voted upon by the executive committee and the area council, Mr Scargill did not cast a vote. I do not know whether he had a vote to cast in his position as president; but whether because he had no power to vote, or because he did not choose to vote, the admitted fact is that he did not vote.

Those are the admitted facts; and Mr Turner-Samuels who appeared on behalf of the union, submitted – as indeed is true – that it is a strong thing to find against a defendant on admissions in the pleadings and he submitted that the union were entitled to a full trial. The object of that trial, as I understood him, was to produce evidence that Mr Scargill was not biased against Mr Roebuck or Mr O'Brien; that the presence and conduct of Mr Scargill did not inhibit or hinder Mr Roebuck or Mr O'Brien in the conduct of their defence; that the members of the executive committee and the area council reached their conclusions freely, conscientiously, and independently; and, in short, that Mr Scargill's presence and conduct had no influence on the result.

But, in my judgment, all those matters, which may be capable of proof, and on which I cannot and do not express any concluded view, are irrelevant. Mr Roebuck and Mr O'Brien were entitled to be tried by a tribunal whose chairman did not appear to have a special reason for bias, conscious or unconscious, against them. True it is that all the members of the executive committee and the area council, in common with all members of a domestic tribunal where the interests of their own organisation are at stake, have a general inclination to defend the union and its officers against attack from any source; this fact, every trade unionist and every member of a domestic organisation knows and accepts.

But Mr Scargill had a special position, which clearly disqualified him from taking the part in the critical meetings of the executive committee and the area committee which he did take. I say that as a question of fact and not as a question of criticism. It is a fact that Mr Scargill, as plaintiff, had clearly borne the heat and burden of the libel action. It is clear from the admissions that his cross-examination had been complicated and made difficult by the actions of Mr Roebuck and Mr O'Brien. It is clear that Mr Scargill was a witness to what had happened and to what Mr Roebuck and Mr O'Brien had said and done in the course of the libel action in the High Court. Whether or not those actions of Mr Roebuck and Mr O'Brien, before and during the High Court proceedings, were detrimental to the interests of the union, it is quite plain that they must have been gall and wormwood to Mr Scargill before, during and after the trial. Mr Scargill was a plaintiff and a witness – an important witness – in the High Court proceedings. Then he reappeared as the complainant, the pleader, the prosecutor, the advocate and the chairman in the union proceedings, which followed swiftly. It is impossible to know what would have happened if Mr Scargill had recognised his impossible position and had not acted as he did. But his presence as chairman, and his conduct (admitted conduct) undoubtedly gave the impression that the dice were loaded against Mr Roebuck and Mr O'Brien. No amount of evidence can remove that impression, or establish affirmatively that the end result was unaffected by natural resentment and prejudice in the mind of Mr Scargill for prolonging his cross-examination and jeopardising the success of the action which, true enough, affected the union, but in addition vitally affected Mr Scargill, as president of the union, and as a private individual, who had been libelled. Whether he recognised the fact or not, Mr Scargill must inevitably have appeared biased against Mr Roebuck and Mr O'Brien. The appearance of bias was inevitable; the exercise of bias, conscious or unconscious, was probable. I am content to rest my judgment on the ground that it was manifestly unfair to Mr Roebuck and Mr O'Brien that Mr Scargill should have acted as chairman, and should have played the part which he admits to have played at the relevant meetings of the executive committee and the area council ...'

COMMENT

(1)   These cases illustrate the requirements of natural justice. However, there may be exceptional circumstances where an expulsion may be permitted without the necessity of complying with these rules. In *Cheall* v *APEX* it was argued that the plaintiff should not be expelled from the union without a hearing. However, the rules expressly stipulated for expulsion to comply with a ruling of the TUC Disputes Committee. In these circumstances, it was held that he had no action on this ground.

(2)   While decisions of unions may still be subject to supervision by the courts on the grounds discussed in this section, there has now been a great deal of statutory intervention in this area, which means that resort to the common law is more rare.

Enforcing the rules

The cases examined so far have involved the personal rights of members in relation to discipline and expulsion. If the member seeks to enforce observance of other rules, which do not affect her as directly or particularly as a disciplinary decision, some difficulties will be encountered. The miners' strike 1984–5 gave rise to a number of cases where this area was explored, and also provides some explanation for subsequent legislation.

Taylor and Foulstone v National Union of Mineworkers (Yorkshire Area)

[1984] IRLR 445 Chancery Division

The National Union of Mineworkers is composed of a number of area unions, with members of the area unions also being members of the national union. In interlocutory proceedings the plaintiffs, members of the Yorkshire Area union, sued both the area union and the National Union of Mineworkers, alleging that the strike had been called in breach of the national and area rules (Rules 43 and 51 respectively) which required a ballot before strike action and a 55 per cent majority in favour. (Under national rule 41 there was also provision for the national executive of the union to sanction strike action in an area.)

In January 1981 there had been a ballot in the Yorkshire Area where over 85 per cent had voted in favour of strike action; subsequently there had been three national ballots where the required majority in favour had not been achieved. In March 1984, the national executive committee of the union stated that proposed strike action in Yorkshire would be official.

Nicholls J: '... Finally I come to the relief concerned with the claim that the strike in the Yorkshire Area is invalid. On this the plaintiffs first seek, in short, injunctions restraining the defendant Unions from instructing or seeking to persuade the plaintiffs or other members of the Yorkshire Union to strike or not to cross picket lines by describing the strike or picket lines as official or by threatening disciplinary action. That the strike is not lawful national action is self-evident; rule 43 has not been complied with. But can the strike be justified as lawful area action under Yorkshire Union rule 53 and NUM rule 41? The plaintiffs submit in effect that although sought to be dressed up as area by area action, what the Yorkshire Union and the NUM have entered upon is, and is alone, national action. Hence it cannot be justified in Yorkshire under rule 41. Moreover, even considered on an area by area basis as the NUM would seek to do, the strike in the Yorkshire Area did not comply with rule 53: an Area ballot was needed, and none was held, the 1981 ballot being too remote in time and there having been too much change in the branch membership of the Area since then for that ballot to be capable of justifying a call to strike action two and a half years later.

This is not the trial of the action. Suffice it for me to say that in my view on the evidence that I have referred to above the plaintiffs have a highly arguable case on these points in support of a claim that the strike is in breach of the rules and constitution of the two Unions and as such is unlawful.

Since what is at issue is the right of the plaintiffs to go to work and earn their living, I have no hesitation in concluding that this is a proper case in which to grant injunctive relief as sought pending the trial. The plaintiffs have been kept from working now for many months. They have constant police protection and their houses are surrounded by police officers. Conversely if, despite the injunction, the Unions wish to continue to describe the strike as official in the Yorkshire Area then, as was pointed out by Mr Burton for the plaintiffs, they have a remedy in their own hands: ballot their members. The Unions can then let the majority votes determine their policy, as the NUM president said when successfully proposing a reduction in the majority required on a ballot in April of this year.

But on this part of the case the plaintiffs go further and ask for a mandatory order that the NUM do now conduct a national ballot. For me to grant such an order I would have to find in the rules of the NUM, expressly or impliedly, a positive legal obligation on the NUM to hold such a ballot, of which obligation it was currently in breach. The only relevant rule is rule 43. The relevant part of the rule is expressed in negative terms. It limits the circumstances in which if national action is proposed by the NUM a national strike may be entered upon. The limit, the pre-requisite of a valid national strike, is a ballot vote taken in pursuance of a resolution of Conference and (as recently amended) a simple majority of those voting on the ballot being in favour of such a strike. In short, a national strike shall not be declared unless the national ballot condition is satisfied. Thus if, in contravention of that rule, the NUM declares (or 'enters upon') a national strike without the national ballot condition being satisfied, the NUM is acting beyond its powers and unlawfully, and it can be restrained from so doing. What for my part I at present do not see (and I choose my words bearing in mind that this is not the trial of the action and it is not for me on this motion to seek to decide the point) is how, if the NUM does act *ultra vires* and unlawfully, by calling for a national strike without a national ballot being held pursuant to an appropriate resolution of a NUM Conference, there then arises a positive obligation on the NUM to conduct such a ballot regardless of whether Conference has resolved that there be a ballot or not. The NUM's acts will not be lawful unless and until it does duly hold a national ballot which shows a majority in favour of the strike. But, as at present advised, I am unable to spell out of rule 43 by implication any such positive obligation entitling a member to compel the NUM to hold a ballot. The member's right under the Rules is confined to being able to insist that a national strike cannot lawfully be held without a national ballot; but he has no greater right than that in respect of a national ballot. The point is, I accept, arguable, but following the approach to the grant of a mandatory injunction which I have stated above, I do not think I should on this interlocutory application make a mandatory order for the NUM to hold a national ballot …'

COMMENT

(1)   This shows that at best a member can exercise a negative restraint – by preventing action in breach of the rules – but cannot positively require the union to do something if there is no positive obligation in the rules.

(2)   Union members now have a statutory right to restrain any kind of industrial action without a prior ballot, regardless of what is in the union's rules (TULRCA s 62), but it remains the case that there is no mechanism to force the union to hold a ballot, unless there is a positive obligation in the rules.

(3)   A further restraint is to be found in the Rule in *Foss* v *Harbottle*. This is a company law rule, derived from a nineteenth century case. The rule states that where a wrong is done to the company, such as action being taken in breach of the company's own rules, then if the wrong is capable of being ratified, no individual member of the company may bring legal action to complain of it.

The rationale of the rule is that it would be pointless to allow an individual member to bring an action if a majority of the other members could simply ratify the wrongful act and thus scupper the legal proceedings. Note that it is not necessary that the majority actually carry out such a ratification: the mere possibility is enough. The other rationale for the rule is practical: the company should be protected from unnecessary litigation. If the majority do not wish to take action, the company should not be at the mercy of an individual shareholder who does.

There are two issues: does this company law rule apply to trade unions, and when are breaches of the rules non-ratifiable?

Taylor v National Union of Mineworkers (Derbyshire Area)

[1985] IRLR 99 Chancery Division

Taylor (a different Taylor), who was a member of the Derbyshire union, had already obtained a declaration that the strike in Derbyshire had been called in breach of the rules. In this action the plaintiff claimed that £1.7 million spent by the Derbyshire union on the strike was *ultra vires* (beyond the powers) of the union and was thus a misapplication of union funds.

Vinelott J: '... In *Edwards* v *Halliwell* the plaintiff, a member of the same union, claimed that a resolution increasing the contributions of employed members was invalid. Under the rules such a resolution required a two-thirds majority obtained at a ballot vote. The purported resolution was passed without a ballot. The Court of Appeal held that the rule in *Foss* v *Harbottle* did not apply to bar the plaintiff's right to sue. The failure to hold a ballot was not a mere irregularity. Any member was entitled to refuse to pay an increased subscription unless made payable by a valid resolution. In a classic exposition of the rule in *Foss* v *Harbottle,* which is often cited but which I shall cite again, Jenkins LJ said:

"The rule in *Foss* v *Harbottle*, as I understand it, comes to no more than this. First the proper plaintiff in an action in respect of a wrong alleged to be done to a company or an association of persons is *prima facie* the company or the association of persons itself. Secondly, where the alleged wrong is a transaction which might be made binding on the company or association and on all its members by a simple majority of the members, no individual member of the company is allowed to maintain an action in respect of that matter for the simple reason that, if a mere majority of the members of the company or association is in favour of what has been done, then *cadit quaestio*. No wrong has been done to the company or association and there is nothing in respect of which anyone can sue. If, on the other hand, a simple majority of members of the company or association is against what has been done, then there is no valid reason why the company or association itself should not sue. In my judgement, it is implicit in the rule that the matter relied on as constituting the cause of action should be a cause of action properly belonging to the general body of corporators or members of the company or association as opposed to a cause of action which some individual member can assert in his own right.

The cases falling within the general ambit of the rule are subject to certain exceptions. It has been noted in the course of argument that in those cases where the act complained of is wholly *ultra vires* the company or association the rule has no application because there is no question of the transaction being confirmed by any majority. It has been further pointed out that where what has been done amounts to what is generally called in these cases a fraud on the minority and the wrongdoers are themselves in control of the company, the rule is relaxed in favour of the aggrieved minority who are allowed to bring what is known as a minority shareholders' action on behalf of themselves and all others. The reason for this is that, if they were denied that right, their grievance would never reach the court because the wrongdoers themselves, being in control, would not allow the company to sue. Those exceptions are not directly in point in this case, but they show, especially the last one, that the rule is not an inflexible one and it will be relaxed where necessary in the interests of justice."

I have read that passage in full, because Jenkins LJ makes it clear that the protection afforded by the rule in *Foss* v *Harbottle* to a company and a trade union does not extend to cases where the plaintiff seeks to prevent or remedy an application of the funds of the body which is outside the powers conferred by its constitution. The reason is that such an application cannot be ratified by a mere majority of the members or indeed by any majority, however large. Any member is entitled to insist that the funds of the body be used exclusively in furtherance of its objects, those objects to be inferred from its constitution ...

It seems to me that if the rules of a union provide expressly for allowances to be made to members on what I will for convenience call an "official strike" – that is, one called in accordance with the procedures prescribed by the rules – it is impossible to imply consistently with that a power for officers to make a precisely similar allowance to members on "unofficial strike" – that is, one called or followed in breach of the rules of the union. Every member of the union, as he has an interest in preserving the funds of the union, is, it seems to me, entitled to prevent the funds of the union being used in that way. That was quite clearly the approach of the Court of Appeal and the House of Lords in *Howden's* case, and although there is no doubt that today a more liberal approach to the construction of the rules of a union is appropriate, that principle seems to me equally applicable.

If that is the right conclusion, then it seems to me that it must follow that any payment to a member on unofficial strike whether by way of weekly allowance or by way of intermittent payment or by meeting expenses directly or in any other way with a view to making good the wages lost by the member on unofficial strike must be equally impermissible. So also must payments to pickets be impermissible ...'

COMMENT

(1) This decision has attracted two quite separate criticisms. First, it is argued by Lord Wedderburn that since a trade union is not, *and is not to be treated as if it were*, a corporation, the doctrine of *ultra vires*, which is a company law doctrine, should not be applied to it – by parity of reasoning with *EETPU* v *Times Newspapers* (see (1985) 14 ILJ 127).

Second, if the plaintiffs had the right to take individual action in this case, the judge really had no warrant for refusing to make the order sought.

(2) Note the exceptions when the rule in *Foss* v *Harbottle* will not apply, outlined in the judgment. Cases involving discipline or expulsion of union members will always fall under the exception for personal rights: that is, it is the member's personal right which is infringed by the alleged failure to follow the rules, not just a wrong to the union. However, the most recent case where the issue was argued, *Wise* v *USDAW*, Chadwick J seemed to imply that this exception applied to all breaches of the rules. In that case, the president of the union brought an action challenging two decisions which had been taken by the union's national executive council against her advice. The decisions related to elections in which she had no particular interest, in that she was not standing as a candidate, and the union therefore argued that the rule in *Foss* v *Harbottle* precluded her claim. The judge said:

'… the basis upon which a member of the union … agrees to be bound by the decisions of the executive council … is that those decisions will be made and elections for those offices will be held in accordance with the rules … Accordingly, as it seems to me, the right of a member to complain of a breach of the rules is a contractual right which is individual to that member; although of course, that member holds the right in common with all other members having the like right.'

It seems, therefore, that it will be an exceptional case where the rule will prevent an action.

(3) Before leaving common law regulation of union rule books to examine statutory regulation, it is worth noting that the Commissioner for the Rights of Trade Union Members has, since 1990, had power to assist individual union members in taking action against their union in virtually all areas governed by the common law, including discipline and expulsion (TULRCA s 109(2)).

STATUTORY REGULATION OF TRADE UNION RULES

The miners' strike provided an impetus, and many of the ideas, for the reform of trade unions' internal rules.

Accounts

Trade Union and Labour Relations (Consolidation) Act 1992

30. (1) A member of a trade union has a right to request access to any accounting records of the union which are available for inspection and relate to periods including a time when he was a member of the union.

   In the case of records relating to a branch or section of the union, it is immaterial whether he was a member of that branch or section.

 (2) Where such access is requested the union shall—

   (a) make arrangements with the member for him to be allowed to inspect the records requested before the end of the period of twenty-eight days beginning with the day the request was made,

   (b) allow him and any accountant accompanying him for the purpose to inspect the records at the time and place arranged, and

(c) secure that at the time of the inspection he is allowed to take, or is supplied with, any copies of, or of extracts from, records inspected by him which he requires.

COMMENT

(1)   A member refused her rights under s 30 may apply to the court for an order. As with all the statutory rights of union members, the Commissioner for the Rights of Trade Union Members has power to give assistance.

(2)   This provision can be traced to *Taylor* v *NUM (Derbyshire Area) (No 2)*, where the plaintiff had attempted to inspect the union's accounts accompanied by an accountant. It was held that if the rules gave a right to inspect (as they did), this impliedly included the right to do so with a professional agent. As a result the NUM altered its rules expressly to exclude the right to professional accompaniment.

(3)   In 1990 allegations were made about the use of NUM funds during the 1984–5 miners' strike. Gavin Lightman QC was appointed by the union to investigate and he identified a number of improper dealings. Criminal proceedings were started, but the charges were dismissed when the court held that evidence uncovered by the Lightman inquiry was inadmissible.

This gave the Government the ammunition it needed to introduce further controls on union finances and to extend penalties for their breach.

(4)   TURERA gave the Certification Officer (CO) power to investigate the financial affairs of a trade union or any of its branches. It introduced a new s 37A into TULRCA giving power to require the production of documents and a new s 37B allowing the CO to appoint an inspector to investigate and report in any case where the CO suspects fraud, misfeasance or other misconduct or non-compliance with accounting and auditing requirements.

A new s 45A provides a series of criminal offences which will be committed by trade union officials who obstruct any such inquiry and under the new s 45B, anyone convicted of such an offence will be disqualified from holding office as president, general secretary or national executive member for up to ten years.

(5)   Analogies may be drawn with the rules applying to companies here, except that shareholders would have a much more difficult time in challenging perceived misfeasance and there is no public official comparable to the Commissioner for the Rights of Trade Union Members to give them assistance.

(6)   Again, TURERA's introduction of a new s 32A into TULRCA requiring unions to provide an annual return to all members summarising the union's financial affairs can be compared with the similar right for shareholders. However, union members have the right to know the exact amounts of remuneration being paid to the president, general secretary and national executive members of the union: no such right exists presently for shareholders in respect of directors and senior managers.

Discipline and expulsion

In Chapter 10 we examined TULRCA s 174, which greatly restricts the grounds on which a trade union can refuse to admit a member. As we noted then, s 174 applies to *expulsion* from a union as well as exclusion. One of the grounds on which expulsion or exclusion is permitted is misconduct. This links with TULRCA s 64 which gives union members a right not to be unjustifiably disciplined for certain kinds of conduct: s 174 also provides that expulsion or exclusion on these grounds is unlawful. The kinds of conduct protected are defined in s 65.

Trade Union and Labour Relations (Consolidation) Act 1992

65. ... (2)   This section applies to conduct which consists in—

(a)   failing to participate in or support a strike or other industrial action (whether by members of the union or by others), or indicating opposition to or a lack of support for such action;

(b)   failing to contravene, for a purpose connected with such a strike or other industrial action, a requirement imposed on him by or under a contract of employment;

(c)   asserting (whether by bringing proceedings or otherwise) that the union, any official or representative of it or a trustee of its property has contravened, or is proposing to contravene, a requirement which is, or is thought to be, imposed by or under the rules of the union or any other agreement or by or under any enactment (whenever passed) or any rule of law;

(d)   encouraging or assisting a person—

   (i)   to perform an obligation imposed on him by a contract of employment, or

   (ii)   to make or attempt to vindicate any such assertion as is mentioned in paragraph (c); or

(e)   contravening a requirement imposed by or in consequence of a determination which infringes the individual's or another individual's right not to be unjustifiably disciplined;

(f)   failing to agree, or withdrawing agreement, to the making from his wages (in accordance with arrangements between his employer and the union) of deductions representing payments to the union in respect of his membership;

(g)   resigning or proposing to resign from the union or from another union, becoming or proposing to become a member of another union, refusing to become a member of another union, or being a member of another union;

(h)   working with, or proposing to work with, individuals who are not members of the union, or who are or are not members of another union;

(i)   working for, or proposing to work for, an employer who employs or who has employed individuals who are not members of the union or who are or are not members of another union; or

(j)   requiring the union to do an act which the union is, by any provision of this Act, required to do on the requisition of a member.

...

(5)   This section does not apply to an act, omission or statement comprised in conduct falling within subsection (2), (3) or (4) above if it is shown that the act,

omission or statement is one in respect of which individuals would be disciplined by the union irrespective of whether their acts, omissions or statements were in connection with conduct within subsection (2) or (3) above.

(6) An individual is not unjustifiably disciplined if it is shown—
  (a) that the reason for disciplining him, or one of them, is that he made such an assertion as is mentioned in subsection (2)(c), or encouraged or assisted another person to make or attempt to vindicate such an assertion,
  (b) that the assertion was false, and
  (c) that he made the assertion, or encouraged or assisted another person to make or attempt to vindicate it, in the belief that it was false or otherwise in bad faith,

and that there was no other reason for disciplining him or that the only other reasons were reasons in respect of which he does not fall to be treated as unjustifiably disciplined.

COMMENT

(1) The most important thing to be included under this section is strike-breaking. This is traditionally seen as a most serious offence by trade unions, given the crucial importance of solidarity if industrial action is to have a chance of success. However, as *Esterman* v *NALGO* indicates, courts have been reluctant to uphold expulsions on such a ground.

(2) Note that by s 64(5), rights under this section are specifically stated to be additional to any other rights. Thus the member is free to pursue also any common law claims.

(3) There is a clear overlap here also with s 174 (preventing unreasonable expulsion). Where the disciplinary measure falls short of expulsion, only s 64 may be used. If the expulsion is for anything other than misconduct, as here defined, an action under s 174 is the only possibility. However, in those cases where a member is expelled for conduct which comes within the definition of unjustifiable discipline in s 65, then a claim under either section is possible. This overlap is dealt with by providing that an action may only be brought under one of the sections and, if successful, may not form the basis for a claim under the other.

Remedies under the two sections are very similar: a declaration plus compensation, which may not be less than £5,000 in any case where the union has refused to re-admit the member. The main difference is in relation to the limitation period, which is six months for s 174 as against the more usual three months for s 64.

(4) In *Bradley* v *NALGO* the EAT awarded eight applicants who had been expelled for strike-breaking the minimum award, because in the absence of a closed shop, they considered that their job prospects were not affected detrimentally. The point that they were thereby excluded from participation in the collective bargaining process does not seem to have been considered.

(5) Note, however, that strike-breaking must be distinguished from acting contrary to the policy of the union, which is conduct for which a member may properly be dismissed.

Knowles v *Fire Brigades Union*

[1996] IRLR 617 Court of Appeal

The union was in dispute with employers over the use of retained firefighters. Where a station is not permanently staffed, there are firefighters on stand-by duty (retained firefighters). At one time, full-time firefighters did this in their spare time, which was a way of earning extra money. The union considered it drove down full-time wages (because it was assumed that everyone was doing retained duties too), and that it was a safety risk. It was successful in getting the employing councils to agree to end the practice in 1977. However, towards the end of the 1980s, councils started looking at this again, and in 1990 Shropshire CC decided to reintroduce the use of retained firefighters. K and J, who were full-time firefighters at a station which was not staffed at night, were offered jobs as retained firefighters at the same place for nights. They accepted. They were then expelled from the union for breach of union policy. They claimed that they had been expelled for refusing to take part in industrial action, and that this was unjustifiable discipline within the meaning of s 65. An industrial tribunal upheld their claim, but its decision was reversed by the EAT.

Neill LJ: '... It was argued on behalf of the appellants that in the absence of any statutory definition the question of whether there was or was not "other industrial action" was a question of fact which an industrial tribunal was particularly suited to determine.

Counsel for the appellants drew our attention to the decision of the Court of Appeal in [*Power Packing Casemakers Ltd* v *Faust*]. In that case the Court of Appeal upheld the decision of the Employment Appeal Tribunal, who had decided that employees who had refused a request by their employers to work overtime had taken part in "other industrial action" within the meaning of [TULRCA s 238].

The question in issue in that case was whether the industrial tribunal had any jurisdiction to determine whether the dismissal was fair or unfair. In the course of his judgment Stephenson LJ approved the refusal of the Employment Appeal Tribunal to define the phrase "other industrial action" in [s 238] and their decision that the matter should be left to the good sense of industrial tribunals. Earlier in his judgment Stephenson LJ said:

"An industrial tribunal and the lay members of an appeal tribunal may be trusted to recognise industrial action when they see it, and that was how both tribunals, as well as one appellant and one other witness, described the employees' refusal to work overtime."

...

It was argued in the alternative on behalf of the appellants that, if the question of what was meant by "other industrial action" were to be more properly regarded as a mixed question of fact and law rather than a question of pure fact, the industrial tribunal did not misdirect themselves and there was no proper basis for the intervention by the Employment Appeal Tribunal. It was to be noted that the industrial tribunal made specific reference in paragraph 8 of the reasons to the decision in *Rasool and others* v *Hepworth Pipe Co Ltd (No 2)*, and that in paragraph 10 they had distinguished it on the basis that the steps taken by the union were not, as in *Rasool*'s case, merely acts preparatory to ascertaining the feelings of the employees towards industrial action.

In *Rasool* v *Hepworth Pipe Co Ltd*, supra, the Employment Appeal Tribunal was concerned with an argument that the attendance of employees at an unauthorised mass meeting for the purpose of ascertaining the views of the workforce with regard to impending wage negotiations constituted 'other industrial action' within the meaning of the predecessor to [EPCA s 62, now TULRCA s 238]. Waterhouse J said:

"It is sufficient for us to say that it is probably incorrect to attempt to interpret the expression [other industrial action] narrowly in terms of specific intention and that the nature and effect of the concerted action are probably of greater importance. Nevertheless, in our judgment, attendance at an unauthorised meeting for the purpose indicated by the majority of the tribunal in the instant case falls short of 'other industrial action'. As the majority of the tribunal found, it is more properly regarded as trade union activity, even though a degree of disruption of the manufacturing process resulted."

In addition counsel drew our attention to a phrase in the judgment of Ralph Gibson LJ in *Ticehurst* v *British Telecommunications plc* where he referred to the fact that Mrs Ticehurst had participated in "the concerted action" devised by the union. It was said that in the present case the appellants had failed to participate in the concerted action which the union had devised, namely that full-time fire fighters should refuse to enter into retained contracts. A refusal to enter into retained contracts was analogous to a refusal to operate machines. Pressure was applied to the employers who suffered inconvenience and incurred the expense of employing new retained fire fighters.

On behalf of the union on the other hand it was argued that what constituted "other industrial action" was plainly a mixed question of law and fact. In reaching their conclusions the industrial tribunal had failed to distinguish between:

(a)   acts preparatory to industrial action;

(b)   threats of industrial action; and

(c)   actual industrial action.

By failing to make this distinction they had reached a conclusion which was perverse on the facts found. It was important to note that the industrial tribunal stated in their reasons that they had heard no evidence as to whether the policy of the union "might financially inconvenience the local authorities". On the findings the effect of the policy went no further than to prevent the local authorities from carrying out the reorganisation of the fire service in the manner in which they might wish to do. The union had done no more than seek to persuade the Shropshire County Council not to offer retained contracts to whole-time fire fighters. No "action" had been taken against the employers by the union nor had there been any threats of action.

It was accepted that a breach of contract was not a necessary prerequisite for a finding that there had been industrial action, though normally industrial action does amount to or involve a breach of contract. Counsel referred us to the decision of the Employment Appeal Tribunal in *Midland Plastics* v *Till*. In that case the employers had been informed by a member of the works committee that if the demands for a specified minimum wage were not met in full it was the workers' intention to take industrial action as from 11.00 am that day. In the interval between the receipt of the letter and 11.00 am four employees were asked by the management what action they were going to take if the demands were not met.

They replied that they were going to abide by the wishes of the workforce. They were immediately dismissed. By a majority the industrial tribunal concluded that the letter and the surrounding circumstances did not amount to "other industrial action" within [TULRCA s 238]. The Employment Appeal Tribunal dismissed the employers' appeal. Browne-Wilkinson J said:

"The majority of the industrial tribunal have referred to the actions which, in normal contemplation, might be thought of as industrial action: walk out, go slow, working to rule, banning of overtime, picketing. They are far from saying that that is a comprehensive list. But if the employers are to succeed, as it seems to us they must be able to show that the threat of taking industrial action can itself amount to taking industrial action. We reject that view."

Later he continued:

> "Unfortunately a substantial factor in industrial relations negotiations in this country is a display of power by one side in response to which the other side either does or does not yield to the wishes of the person displaying such power. The actual taking of industrial action is the last stage and is quite distinct from the stage at which the threat of it is being used as a negotiating weapon. Throughout the period of a strike notice what is bearing upon the employer is the risk to his business. We can see no distinction between what occurred in this case and the ordinary strike notice. In neither case had the matter matured into taking part in industrial action."

Conclusion

I accept that the words "other industrial action" are not to be narrowly construed. But they have to be looked at in a context where the transition from negotiations to action may have far-reaching consequences. We are not dealing in the present case with part V of the Act of 1992 which is concerned with industrial action, or with s 226 in part V which provides that an act done by a trade union to induce a person to take part in industrial action is not protected unless the industrial action has the support of a ballot. But it is to be noted that one of the rights conferred on trade union members by chapter V in part I is the right to a ballot before industrial action takes place: see s 62.

Industrial action can take many forms, but, in the absence of any statutory definition, I do not think that any attempt at a paraphrase is likely to be useful. In my judgment the question of what is industrial action for the purposes of s 65 of the Act of 1992 is a mixed question of fact and law. In large measure it is a question of fact, but the facts have to be judged in the context of the Act which plainly contemplates that industrial action is a serious step.

It is necessary to look at all the circumstances. These circumstances will include the contracts of employment of the employees and whether any breach of or departure from the terms of the contract are involved, the effect on the employer of what is done or omitted and the object which the union or the employees seek to achieve.

In the present case it seems to me that the following factors are relevant:

(a)   At the date when the appellants were expelled from the union the policy had been in force for over 18 months. The object to be achieved by the union's policy was to prevent a unilateral departure from the terms which had been agreed in 1977.

(b)   The policy did not require full-time workers to break or to depart from the terms of their existing contracts. The policy merely required fire fighters not to undertake additional work under new contracts.

(c)   There is no evidence to suggest that either the county council or the union contemplated that the "pressure" exerted by the union required the support of a ballot.

(d)   There was some discussion at the hearing as to whether any of the other full-time fire fighters in Shropshire had actually refused offers of retained contracts. Even in the absence of express evidence to this effect, however, it is reasonable to assume that some of the 45 other fire fighters did so refuse. But their compliance with the union's policy does not seem to me on the facts of this case to amount to a clear indication that the union and its members had crossed the threshold into taking industrial action within the meaning of s 65.

(e)   The evidence of Mr Bryant, as recorded in paragraph 6 of the reasons, shows that negotiations were being continued and that though the union were making clear that they intended to adhere to their policy, the breakdown which is almost implicit in the taking of industrial action had not occurred. As Browne-Wilkinson J said in *Midland Plastics v Till*, supra, in the passage which I have already cited, "the actual taking of industrial action is the last stage and is quite distinct from the stage at which the threat of it is being used as a negotiating weapon." One must also take account of the reaction of the lay members of the Employment Appeal Tribunal in the present case to the suggestion that the mere fact that an employer may feel himself inhibited as a result of pressure applied to him means that industrial action has been taken.

In my judgment the Employment Appeal Tribunal were justified in concluding that the industrial tribunal had misdirected themselves in treating pressure plus inhibition as a sufficient test of industrial action. Furthermore I think that counsel for the union was correct in her submission that the industrial tribunal failed sufficiently to distinguish between conduct which fell short even of a threat and actual "industrial action" within the meaning of s 65. Accordingly I would dismiss this appeal.'

(Millett and Phillips LJJ agreed with Neill LJ.)

Election of trade union officials

Which officials must be elected?

Trade unions typically have two kinds of officials. First, those active members who have volunteered or stood for election and take on trade union duties while remaining employees: this includes all shop stewards and usually members of the union's executive committees and the president and vice-presidents. Second, however, there are those officials who carry out the day-to-day administration of the union's affairs as area, regional or even branch officials and who work full time for the union. They are career trade unionists, they are employees of the union, and they usually include the general secretary.

In theory, policy-making is carried out in committees and conferences with a high involvement of members of the union. However, since policy-making often starts with a discussion paper and the best-informed are the best able to influence policy, there is no doubt that full-time officials are likely to have a significant input to the direction of union policy; nor is this in any way sinister.

Again, the traditional pattern has been that lay officials (those who are not full-time employees of the union) have been elected to their position, but that full time officials, whose whole job is working for the union, have been appointed in the same way that any other employee is appointed (that is, usually after success in a competitive interview).

Until 1984, these were treated strictly as internal matters for the union. However, the Government was concerned that some important officials either were never elected, or once elected, held office indefinitely (the president of the NUM being the example that sprang most readily to mind).

Trade Union and Labour Relations (Consolidation) Act 1992

46. (1) A trade union shall secure—
    (a) that every person who holds a position in the union to which this Chapter applies does so by virtue of having been elected to it at an election satisfying the requirements of this Chapter, and
    (b) that no person continues to hold such a position for more than five years without being re-elected at such an election.

    (2)   The positions to which this Chapter applies (subject as mentioned below) are—
       (a)   member of the executive,
       (b)   any position by virtue of which a person is a member of the executive,
       (c)   president, and
       (d)   general secretary;
       and the requirements referred to above are those set out in sections 47 to 52 below.

COMMENT

(1)   The original provision introduced by the Trade Union Act 1984 only required *voting* members of the national executive committee to offer themselves for re-election every five years. On the whole, this sufficed to bring in democracy while not requiring employees of the union to have to put their jobs at risk every five years. However, it also meant that it could be circumvented by an official giving up his right to vote: which is what the president of the NUM did. Thus the Employment Act 1988 introduced the so-called 'Scargill clause' extending the requirement to its present form.

(2)   Note that it applies only to members of the principal executive committee of the union (called the national executive in most unions). Thus members of other influential committees in the union need not be subject to election within the terms of the Act (see *Paul* v *NALGO*).

Candidates for office

Trade Union and Labour Relations (Consolidation) Act 1992

47.   (1)   No member of the trade union shall be unreasonably excluded from standing as a candidate.
      (2)   No candidate shall be required, directly or indirectly, to be a member of a political party.
      (3)   A member of a trade union shall not be taken to be unreasonably excluded from standing as a candidate if he is excluded on the ground that he belongs to a class of which all the members are excluded by the rules of the union.
          But a rule which provides for such a class to be determined by reference to whom the union chooses to exclude shall be disregarded.

COMMENT

(1)   TULRCA s 48 continues the policy of preventing discrimination between candidates: the union must circulate election addresses from each candidate and any facilities offered for producing an address must be afforded equally to all candidates. The costs must be borne by the union.

(2)   Before the Trade Union Act 1984 it was common for members of the national executive to be elected by the annual national conference of the union rather than by the whole membership directly. This process can be seen either as assisting the perpetuation of a self-selecting oligarchy somewhat to the left of the general mem-

bership, or as a sensible method of indirect representative democracy which ensured that the electorate was knowledgeable about the candidates.

(3) While direct democracy is now required for these posts, it appears that it is still lawful for the union to hold a ballot at its annual conference and to inform the membership that these candidates are official or endorsed by conference (and see also *Paul* v *NALGO*).

The conduct of the ballot

The first requirement for a valid ballot is that there must be an independent scrutineer to supervise the conduct of the ballot and report on it at the end. The role of the independent scrutineer was critical in the Conservative Government's strategy of ensuring that ballots were conducted properly. Under TURERA her role was strengthened by requiring her to inspect the membership register of the union according to which the ballot papers have been distributed; where a member requests this because of a suspicion that the register is not up to date, the scrutineer must inspect the register unless she considers that the suspicions are unfounded.

However, as *Veness* v *National Union of Public Employees* indicates, there may be advantages for the union in having to delegate the conduct of the election to an independent scrutineer. In that case, members complained under what is now TULRCA s 49 alleging, among other things, that only 100 out of 1,150 members at one branch and only 11 members out of 2,200 members at another branch had received ballot papers. The union had, as required by the law and its own rules, delegated the conduct of the ballot to the Electoral Reform Society. The members' claim against the union was therefore struck out as disclosing no cause of action.

Trade Union and Labour Relations (Consolidation) Act 1992

50. (1) Subject to the provisions of this section, entitlement to vote shall be accorded equally to all members of the trade union.
    (2) The rules of the union may exclude entitlement to vote in the case of all members belonging to one of the following classes, or to a class falling within one of the following—
      (a) members who are not in employment;
      (b) members who are in arrears in respect of any subscription or contribution due to the union;
      (c) members who are apprentices, trainees or students or new members of the union....
51. (1) The method of voting must be by the marking of a voting paper by the person voting.
    (2) Each voting paper must—
      (a) state the name of the independent scrutineer and clearly specify the address to which, and the date by which, it is to be returned,
      (b) be given one of a series of consecutive whole numbers every one of which is used in giving a different number in that series to each voting paper printed or otherwise produced for the purposes of the election, and
      (c) be marked with its number.

(3) Every person who is entitled to vote at the election must—
   (a) be allowed to vote without interference from, or constraint imposed by, the union or any of its members, officials or employees, and
   (b) so far as is reasonably practicable, be enabled to do so without incurring any direct cost to himself.

(4) So far as is reasonably practicable, every person who is entitled to vote at the election must—
   (a) have sent to him by post, at his home address or another address which he has requested the trade union in writing to treat as his postal address, a voting paper which either lists the candidates at the election or is accompanied by a separate list of those candidates; and
   (b) be given a convenient opportunity to vote by post.

(5) The ballot shall be conducted so as to secure that—
   (a) so far as is reasonably practicable, those voting do so in secret, and
   (b) the votes given at the election are fairly and accurately counted.
   For the purposes of paragraph (b) an inaccuracy in counting shall be disregarded if it is accidental and on a scale which could not affect the result of the election.

(6) The ballot shall be so conducted as to secure that the result of the election is determined solely by counting the number of votes cast directly for each candidate.

(7) Nothing in subsection (6) shall be taken to prevent the system of voting used for the election being the single transferable vote, that is, a vote capable of being given so as to indicate the voter's order of preference for the candidates and of being transferred to the next choice—
   (a) when it is not required to give a prior choice the necessary quota of votes, or
   (b) when, owing to the deficiency in the number of votes given for a prior choice, that choice is eliminated from the list of candidates.

COMMENT

(1) It was previously possible to have part-postal voting – where ballot papers were distributed at the workplace but then returned by post. Full postal voting was introduced by the Employment Act 1988.

(2) Where it is alleged that there has been a breach of the election rules, the aggrieved member has a choice of complaining to the Certification Officer or to the High Court. Proceedings before the Certification Officer are likely to be quicker and less formal; however, his powers are limited to making a declaration. The right to complain to the High Court is independent and applies even if the Certification Officer has found against the member's complaint. The High Court does have power to order the defect to be remedied, for example, by requiring a re-run of the election.

(3) Needless to say, the assistance of the Commissioner for the Rights of Trade Union Members may be sought in such cases.

12 Industrial action I

When industrial action is taken the employer principally affected has two possible targets for any legal action: the employees on strike and the organisers of the strike (who may be employees, but will frequently include the employees' trade union and some trade union officials who are not employees). As the employer is unlikely to be linked to the strike organisers by contract (unless there is a legally enforceable collective agreement between the employer and the union), any legal action will probably have to be based on tort. Such tortious liability depends in large measure on whether the actions of the employees are unlawful or not: in consequence, this issue will be examined first.

INDUSTRIAL ACTION AND INDIVIDUAL RIGHTS

Strikes and the contract of employment

The issue here is whether going on strike is a breach of an employee's contract of employment: within that question is a subsidiary issue as to whether the answer is affected by the employees giving notice of their intention to strike.

Morgan v Fry

[1968] 2 QB 710 Court of Appeal

The plaintiff sued the defendant, an official of the TGWU, for the tort of intimidation. The defendant had threatened strike action unless members of a breakaway union (including the plaintiff) were dismissed. A central question before the court was whether the threatened strike action would have been a breach of contract for the employees involved.

Denning MR: '... This brings me, therefore, to the crux of the case: was the "strike notice" in this case the threat of a breach of contract? If it had been a full week's notice by the men to terminate the employment altogether, it would not have been a threat to commit a breach of contract. Every man was entitled to terminate his contract of employment by giving a week's notice. But the "strike notice" in this case was not a notice to terminate the employment. It was a notice that they would not work with non-unionists. That looks very like a threat of a breach of contract: and, therefore, intimidation. In *Stratford (JT) & Son Ltd v Lindley*, I stated the argument in this way:

> "Suppose that a trade-union officer gives a 'strike notice'. He says to an employer: 'We are going to call a strike on Monday week unless you ... dismiss yonder man who is not

a member of the union.' … Such a notice is not to be construed as if it were a week's notice on behalf of the men to terminate their employment, for that is the last thing any of the men would desire. They do not want to lose their pension rights and so forth by giving up their jobs. The 'strike notice' is nothing more nor less than a notice that the men will not come to work' – or, as in this case, that they will not do their work as they should – in short, that they will break their contracts.… In these circumstances … the trade-union officer, by giving the 'strike notice,' issues a threat to the employer. He threatens to induce the men to break their contracts of employment unless the employer complies with their demand. That is a threat to commit a tort. It is clear intimidation.…"

It is difficult to see the logical flaw in that argument. But there must be something wrong with it: for if that argument were correct, it would do away with the right to strike in this country. It has been held for over 60 years that workmen have a right to strike (including therein a right to say that they will not work with non-unionists) provided that they give sufficient notice beforehand: and a notice is sufficient if it is at least as long as the notice required to terminate the contract.

There have been many cases where trade-union officials have given "strike notices" of proper length, and no one has suggested there was anything illegal about them …

What then is the legal basis on which a "strike notice" of proper length is held to be lawful? I think it is this: The men can leave their employment altogether by giving a week's notice to terminate it. That would be a strike which would be perfectly lawful. If a notice to terminate is lawful, surely a lesser notice is lawful: such as a notice that "we will not work alongside a non-unionist". After all, if the employers should retort to the men: "We will not accept this notice as lawful", the men can at once say: "Then we will give notice to terminate." The truth is that neither employer nor workmen wish to take the drastic action of termination if it can be avoided. The men do not wish to leave their work for ever. The employers do not wish to scatter their labour force to the four winds. Each side is, therefore, content to accept a "strike notice" of proper length as lawful. It is an implication read into the contract by the modern law as to trade disputes. If a strike takes place, the contract of employment is not terminated. It is suspended during the strike: and revives again when the strike is over.'

(Davies and Russell LJJ concurred in the result, but on different grounds.)

COMMENT

(1)   The judgment of Lord Denning that the contract is suspended where the strike notice is of an equivalent length to that needed to terminate the contract was a novelty. Neither of the other judges in the case decided it on those grounds. The argument was considered by the Donovan Commission in its contemporaneous report.

Royal Commission on Trade Unions and Employers' Associations 1965–68 (the Donovan Commission)

936.   Strikes may be preceded by no notice or some notice given by or on behalf of the employees concerned.

937.   If no notice is given, then ignoring special cases such as an engagement from day to day where no notice is required, a breach of the contract of employment will normally result. The same is true even if notice of the intention to strike is given, whether the notice be shorter, or longer, or the same length as the notice required by the contract for its termination.

938.   If however the notice is in terms a notice to terminate the contract and is of the required length, and the employee works the notice out before ceasing work, no breach of contract occurs. On the contrary the contract has been fulfilled according to its terms.

939.   It is sometimes said that this situation does not reflect the true intentions of the parties. Where notice of a stoppage of work is given, not being a notice to terminate the contract, it is true that the employees concerned are in breach of the contract. Under that contract they are bound to go on rendering service until some event has occurred upon which it was agreed that the contract should end, as for example the giving of due notice to terminate it. Yet by ceasing to work without giving such a notice, the employees are not, it is argued, really intending to repudiate the contract altogether – they simply want it modified. Nor does the employer in such a case regard the cessation of work as a repudiation of the contract, entitling him to rescind it. He really wants the contract to continue and he hopes to be able to come to terms over the modification which his employees are seeking. Only if this hope is finally dashed will questions of repudiation and consequent rescission arise.

940.   Similarly when due notice to end the contract is given prior to the strike, the notice being to the effect that the employee will cease work on its expiry, neither side, it is said, really wishes to put an end to the contract. One party simply wants different terms; the other hopes to come to some agreement about them.

941.   It has accordingly been proposed by some that this situation should be reflected in the law and that, if the intention of the parties is simply to suspend the contract for the period of the strike, then the law of contract should produce that effect; for one of the purposes of the law, after all, is to give effect to the intentions of the contracting parties.

942.   To this end it has been suggested that strikes should merely suspend the contract of employment without breaking it, or terminating it. In practice this would mean creating a new right of unilateral suspension, since either side to the contract of employment could exercise the right without the consent of the other, the employee by striking, the employer by locking out.

943.   The concept is not as simple as it sounds: and before any such new law could be formulated problems of some difficulty would have to be faced and solved. They include the following:

(a)   To what strikes would it apply? To unofficial and unconstitutional as well as to official strikes? How would strikes be defined for this purpose?

(b)   Would it also apply to other industrial action such as a ban on overtime in breach of contract or to a 'go slow'?

(c)   Would it apply to 'lightning strikes' or only to strikes where at least *some* notice was given, though less than the notice required for termination of the contract? If so, what length of notice should be required?

(d)   Would the new law apply to the gas, water, and electricity industries, which at present are subject to the special provisions of section 4 of the Conspiracy and Protection of Property Act 1875? What also would be the position under section 5 of the same Act?

(e)   Would the employer still be allowed instantly to dismiss an employee for grave misconduct during the course of the strike? (Note: this is the case under French law where strikes are treated as suspending the contract of employment.) If so, what kind of acts would constitute 'grave misconduct'?

(f)   Would 'contracting out' of the new law be permissible, e.g. in collective bargains, or in individual contracts of employment?

(g) Would strikers be free to take up other employment while the contract was suspended? If so, would any obligations of secrecy in the suspended contract be suspended too?

(h) If all efforts to end the strike failed, upon what event would the suspension of the contract cease and be replaced by termination?

944. This list is not exhaustive, but is perhaps sufficient to show that considerable technical difficulties would be encountered if the doctrine of unilateral suspension of contracts of employment by strike action were to be made part of our law.'

COMMENT

(1) In the light of present circumstances, it may be felt that the difficulties outlined in para 943 are overstated. There is now a clear distinction in law between official and unofficial industrial action (see p 494); it would seem clearly inappropriate to apply the concept to industrial action short of a complete withdrawal of labour, and the questions of short notice and public utilities present no theoretical problems. If French law can cope with a concept of dismissal for gross misconduct during a strike, presumably English law could too: there is provision relating strikes and redundancy as seen already (see p 358). An enforceable collective agreement could be a suitable alternative mechanism; the question of strikers working for other employers while on strike does not cause insuperable problems in American law and nor should the issue of a final termination.

(2) That said, however, the classic view expressed here by the Donovan Commission that a strike, whether or not notice is given, is a fundamental breach of contract entitling the employer to dismiss at common law is generally preferred to the Denning approach.

(3) It is admitted on all sides, however, that if employees all give notice to *terminate* their contracts on the same day, then even if they are acting in concert in order to pressurise their employer, they are not acting in breach of contract. But it must be clear that this is the true construction of the facts.

Boxfoldia v National Graphical Association (1982)

[1988] ICR 752 Queen's Bench Division

Saville J: 'At a meeting held on 20 February 1985 the National Council of the National Graphical Association (1982) endorsed a recommendation made to them by Mr Harding, a national officer of this trade union, that 14 days' notice of withdrawal of labour should be served on Boxfoldia Ltd in respect of those employees of that company who were members of that trade union. By a letter dated 21 February 1985, Mr Harding wrote to the managing director of Boxfoldia Ltd in the following terms:

"Further to our meeting in your offices on Friday, 1 February, I gave a full report on the breakdown of our negotiations to our national council at its meeting on 20 February. Our council have taken the decision to fully support our members' aspirations as far as Boxfoldia are concerned. Therefore I have been instructed to write giving the company 14 days' notice of withdrawal of all NGA members' labour from the company as from Monday, 25 February. Therefore, this would become effective as of Monday, 11 March."

The NGA sent copies of this letter to their local branch and to the union chapel officials at Boxfoldia. It is common ground that by acting as they did, the NGA called for an official strike of its members working for this company to begin on 11 March 1985.

On that day 39 employees of Boxfoldia who were members of the NGA failed to report to work. Later on the same day the company wrote to each of those employees, stating in effect that those whose absence meant that they were taking part in the strike were dismissed with immediate effect. In truth, with two exceptions resulting from ill- health, the failure of those employees to report for work was indeed because they were taking part in the strike called by their union, and it is also common ground that the NGA, by calling an official strike, induced those employees to act as they did ...

On behalf of the NGA, Mr Goudie's principal submission was that his clients had not induced the majority of the employees concerned to break their contracts of employment. He pointed out, as was the fact, that in the case of all but nine of the employees, the contracts of employment provided for two weeks' notice of termination; and his submission was that this contractual notice had been given on behalf of those employees by the NGA in their letter dated 21 February 1985. Thus, argued Mr Goudie, the NGA had done no more than to induce those employees to bring their contracts to a lawful end, something which it is accepted the union were perfectly entitled to do. As to the remaining nine employees, whose contracts provided for four weeks' notice of termination, Mr Goudie submitted that no loss was proved to have flowed from the termination of those contracts alone, a submission which Mr Mitting for the company did not seek to dispute.

In these circumstances, the central issue in the case is whether the letter of 21 February 1985 is properly to be treated as one written on behalf of the employees concerned giving contractual notice of the termination of their contracts of employment ...

In my judgment, it would not be right to approach any given case on the basis that the one construction is automatically to be preferred to the other. Whether or not a strike notice is properly categorised as one giving notice of termination in accordance with the terms of the employment contracts depends in my view on the meaning and effect of the words used in the context in which they were used, that is to say by the application of the ordinary and well established rules of law developed to deal with contractual and other matters of this kind.

I turn, therefore, to consider the letter itself. This was written in the context of a long-standing and unresolved trade dispute between local officials of the NGA and the company over terms and conditions of employment of members of the NGA employed by the company. Indeed, for many months past the dispute had resulted from time to time in various forms of industrial action (short of a strike) against the company. The employer (the company) was anxious for the matter to be considered by the NGA at national level, but negotiations at this level which took place eventually at the beginning of February 1985 were not successful. This led to Mr Harding, who was the national officer of the NGA involved in the negotiations, to make a report and recommendations to the national council of the NGA. The result was the decision of the national council (who clearly constituted responsible persons within the meaning of section 15 of the Employment Act 1982) to call the official strike.

In my judgment, the letter cannot be categorised as a notice given pursuant to the termination provisions of the respective contracts of employment, that at the end of the stipulated notice period the contracts of employment would come to an end. To have this effect it seems to me that the letter would have to be capable of being reasonably read and understood in its context as one written by the NGA as agent for the employees concerned, communicating the decision of those employees to implement the termination provisions and giving on their behalf the appropriate notice of termination. On its face the letter fulfils none of these requirements. It does not purport to be written on behalf of or as agent for those employees; it does not purport to communicate the decision of those employees to bring their contracts to an end; and it does not purport on their behalf to give the appropriate termination notice stipulated in their contracts. On the contrary, the material part of the letter on its face is written by Mr Harding on the instructions of the national council (not the employees) communicating the decision of that council (not the employees) to call an official strike on 14 days' notice. While I agree with Mr Goudie that the phrase "withdrawal of labour" is in itself theoretically capable of being read as referring to notice of contractual termination, in the context in which it was used in this case I consider that it cannot sensibly bear that meaning ...

There is no evidence in the present case, nor is it suggested, that any of the members concerned gave any specific authority to the NGA to act as agent to give contractual notice of termination of the employment contracts on their behalf. There is nothing in the union rules which vests the union with any such authority. On the contrary, rule 40(2) of the rules of the NGA provides that if a dispute cannot be settled by conciliatory means and where the sanction of the national council has been obtained, all members working in offices affected by the dispute and paying full subscriptions must give notice to terminate their engagements. Thus, so far from the NGA being authorised to give contractual (or other) notices of termination on behalf of and as agent for the members, it is the latter who by the rules have agreed to give such notice themselves if instructed by their union to do so. To my mind this provision, which forms part of the terms and conditions of the contract of union membership, is quite inconsistent with and indeed the antithesis of the authority which it is suggested was impliedly conferred on the union by its members ...'

COMMENT

(1) As the union had not balloted its members it had no immunity from tortious liability for inducing breaches of the employees' contracts of employment. But if the employees had lawfully terminated their contracts by giving notice, no tort would have been committed and it would not have mattered that the union had not held a ballot. However, since then the utility of this has been reduced by the introduction of two rights to restrain even lawful industrial action if there has not been a ballot first. Under TULRCA s 62 (originally introduced by the Employment Act 1988) a member of a union who is called upon to take part in industrial action can seek an order from the court to stop the action if there has not been a valid ballot, and in 1993 TURERA extended a similar right to any individual affected by industrial action through the disruption of the supply of goods or services to him or her (TULRCA s 235A).

(2) The case is of interest also in relation to the question of agency of a trade union (see p 168).

Industrial action short of a strike

Go-slow

General Engineering Services v Kingston and St Andrew Corporation

[1989] ICR 88 Privy Council

The judgment of their Lordships was delivered by Lord Ackner:

'The plaintiff carries on the business of mechanical and electrical engineering and at all material times owned 27, Dunrobin Avenue, Kingston, St Andrew, where they stored specialised medical-electrical equipment and other material connected with their business. At about 5.45 am on 13 October 1977 Mrs Enid Holding, who lived at 29, Dunrobin Avenue, heard a slight crackling sound coming from no. 27. On looking through her bedroom window she saw smoke and flames coming from a section of the building. She dialled the fire brigade at Half Way Tree, which is only one and a half miles away, involving a journey which normally takes the fire engine no more than three and a half minutes. When some 15 minutes later the fire brigade had not arrived, she telephoned again and was told the unit was on its way. It arrived shortly after the telephone call, having taken some 17 minutes to drive this short distance. It was common ground that if the fire brigade had arrived with its usual expedition, the fire would have been speedily extinguished and the complete destruction not only of the office and store room, but also of its contents involving a total loss of approximately $6.2 million, would have been avoided.

The reason why it took some five times longer for the fire brigade to reach this fire than normally was that the firemen, in furtherance of an industrial dispute, were operating a "go slow" policy in order to bring pressure upon their employer to satisfy their grievances. Mrs Holding, who became very anxious at the non-arrival of the fire brigade after making her second telephone call, went up the road along which she was expecting them to arrive. She saw them turn the corner, enter Dunrobin Avenue and then noticed the fire engine slowly moving forward, then stopping, then moving slowly again and then once more stopping. Evidence was given by Mr Dixon, the plaintiff's managing director, who arrived at the scene of the fire about an hour later, that he asked the chief officer in charge of the fire brigade "Why did you let the place burn down?" This question elicited the reply "We are on a go-slow and even if my mother was in there, it would have to burn down. I want my raise of pay." Although this reply was denied, Mr Cotran, on behalf of the plaintiff, did not seek to challenge that the clear inference from the facts was that the firemen had, in pursuance of their go slow policy, decided to take so long to get to the fire that by the time of their arrival the property would have been substantially destroyed.

On 17 August 1978 the plaintiff issued a writ against the defendant alleging that, under the Kingston and St. Andrew Fire Brigade Act, the defendant had a statutory duty to extinguish this fire, that in breach of this duty, it failed to respond promptly to the emergency call and was vicariously responsible for the negligence of the members of the fire brigade. Had the defendant complied with its statutory duty and had the fire brigade travelled to the scene of the fire with due expedition, the fire, so it was alleged, would have been extinguished with minimal damage and loss to the plaintiff ...

It is of course common ground that a master is not responsible for a wrongful act done by his servant unless it is done in the course of his employment. Further it is well established that the act is deemed to be so done if it is either (1) a wrongful act authorised by the master or (2) a wrongful and unauthorised mode of doing some act authorised by the master. Mr Cotran contended that the conduct of the members of the fire brigade could properly be categorised as a wrongful and unauthorised mode of doing some act, i.e. driving to the scene of a fire, which was authorised by the defendant, their employer ...

Their Lordships have no hesitation in agreeing with the unanimous decision of the Court of Appeal, upholding that of Malcolm J that the members of the fire brigade were not acting in the course of their employment when they, by their conduct described above, permitted the destruction of the building and its contents. Their unauthorised and wrongful act was so to prolong the time taken by the journey to the scene of the fire, as to ensure that they did not arrive in time to extinguish it, before the building and its contents were destroyed. Their mode and manner of driving – the slow progression of stopping and starting – was not so connected with the authorised act, that is driving to the scene of the fire as expeditiously as reasonably possible, as to be a mode of performing that act.

For all the practical difference that it would have made, they might, after answering Mrs Holding's call, just as well have waited in the fire station, until they were confident that the building and its contents were beyond saving and then to have proceeded expeditiously to the scene of the fire: or having arrived expeditiously, then to have refused to take any action until it was too late. The negligence which would then have been asserted, namely the failure to answer the alarm or extinguish the fire with proper expedition, could not have been said to have been so connected with the authorised act, that is, immediately answering the alarm, or extinguishing the fire on arrival at the scene, as to be a mode of performing the acts.

Here the unauthorised and wrongful act by the firemen was a wrongful repudiation of an essential obligation of their contract of employment, namely the decision and its implementation not to arrive at the scene of the fire in time to save the building and its contents. This decision was not in furtherance of their employer's business. It was in furtherance of their industrial dispute, designed to bring pressure upon their employer to satisfy their demands, by not extinguishing fires until it was too late to save the property. Such conduct was the very negation of carrying out some act authorised by the employer, albeit in a wrongful and unauthorised mode. Indeed in preventing the provision of an essential service, members of the fire brigade were, by virtue of the provisions of the Jamaican Labour Relations and Industrial Disputes Act, guilty of a criminal offence.

Their Lordships will accordingly humbly advise Her Majesty that the appeal should be dismissed. The plaintiff must pay the defendant's costs.'

COMMENT

(1)   The issue here was whether the employer was vicariously liable for the action (or inaction) of the employees. However, the finding that the go-slow was a fundamental breach of contract carries the clear corollary that the employer would be justified in dismissing the employee summarily on this ground.

Work-to-rule
Secretary of State v ASLEF (No 2)

[1972] 2 QB 455 Court of Appeal

Under the Industrial Relations Act 1971 the Secretary of State for Employment had power to invoke emergency procedures in case of a strike, or industrial action short of a strike, thought to be injurious to the national economy. Three rail unions, ASLEF, NUR and TSSA had ordered their members to work strictly to rule and also to ban overtime and rest day working in pursuit of a pay claim. The Secretary of State in these proceedings sought to enforce the emergency procedures.

Lord Denning MR: '... Now for the next requisite, "irregular industrial action short of a strike". Before any ballot is ordered, it must appear to the Secretary of State under [the Industrial Relations Act] section 141(1)(a) that "any irregular industrial action short of a strike has begun or is likely to begin". It is said that the Secretary of State has misdirected himself in the law on the meaning of the words "irregular industrial action" and that it could not reasonably appear to him that there was any irregular industrial action.

I turn, therefore, to the definition in the Act of "irregular industrial action short of a strike". It is contained in section 33(4). The primary requisite is that there should be a concerted course of conduct by a group of workers "with the intention of ... interfering with the production of goods or the provision of services". That primary requisite is here fulfilled. The three unions have combined together to order the men to work to rule. They readily admit that their intention is to disrupt the railway service. But there is a further requisite, I will call it the secondary requisite, in section 33(4)(b). This requires that "in the case of some or all" of the group of workers the concerted course of conduct is carried on in "breach of their contracts of employment".

For this purpose, of course, we must consider what their contracts of employment are and see whether this conduct is in breach of those contracts. So we have been referred to the contracts of employment. They are contained in a series of collective agreements made by the Railways Board with the trade unions. The terms are set out in some books which have been put before us. They contain detailed provisions on all sorts of matters, such as hours of duty, meal times, rates of pay, rest days and so forth.

The rule book is entirely different. It has 280 pages and 239 rules with many sub-rules. Each man signs a form saying that he will abide by the rules. But these rules are in no way terms of the contract of employment. They are only instructions to a man as to how he is to do his work. Some of them are quite out of date, such as that the coal on the engine must not be stacked too high. Others contain trivial details, such as that the employees must on duty be neat in appearance. A few are important in this case, particularly rule 2(1), which says that employees must see that the safety of the public is their chief care under all circumstances, a rule to which all would subscribe. Rule 126(i), which was specially emphasised in the instructions to the men, says: "The driver and fireman MUST ... satisfy themselves that the engine is in proper order". Rule 176 is a compendious rule which is worth noting: "Inspectors, shunters, guards, drivers, signalmen and all others concerned, must make every effort to facilitate the working of trains and prevent any avoidable delay."

Those rules are to be construed reasonably. They must be fitted in sensibly the one with the other. They must be construed according to the usual course of dealing and to the way they have been applied in practice. When the rules are so construed the railway system, as we all know, works efficiently and safely. But if some of those rules are construed unreasonably, as, for instance, the driver takes too long examining his engine or seeing that all is in order, the system may be in danger of being disrupted. It is only when they are construed unreasonably that the railway system grinds to a halt. It is, I should think, clearly a breach of contract first to construe the rules unreasonably, and then to put that unreasonable construction into practice ... the principal discussion before us (and it is the most important discussion for the purposes of the case) was as to the general instruction to the men to "work to rule", or, as it is put more fully in the instructions, "Strictly observe all BRB rules." The meaning of that instruction is not in doubt. It is well known to everyone in the land. The instruction was intended to mean, and it was understood to mean, "Keep the rules of your employment to the very letter, but, whilst doing so, do your very utmost to disrupt the undertaking." Is that a breach of contract?

Now I quite agree that a man is not bound positively to do more for his employer than his contract requires. He can withdraw his goodwill if he pleases. But what he must not do is wilfully to obstruct the employer as he goes about his business. That is plainly the case where a man is employed singly by a single employer. Take a homely instance, which I put in the course of argument. Suppose I employ a man to drive me to the station. I know there is sufficient time, so that I do not tell him to hurry. He drives me at a slower speed than he need, with the deliberate object of making me lose the train, and I do lose it. He may say that he has performed the letter of the contract; he has driven me to the station; but he has wilfully made me lose the train, and that is a breach of contract beyond all doubt. And what is more, he is not entitled to be paid for the journey. He has broken the contract in a way that goes to the very root of the consideration; so he can recover nothing. Such a case is akin (it has been said we have had no authorities on the subject) to the many cases where there is an implied term not wilfully to prevent the carrying out of the contract …

So much for the case when a man is employed singly. It is equally the case when he is employed, as one of many, to work in an undertaking which needs the service of all. If he, with the others, takes steps wilfully to disrupt the undertaking, to produce chaos so that it will not run as it should, then each one who is a party to those steps is guilty of a breach of his contract. It is no answer for any one of them to say "I am only obeying the rule book", or "I am not bound to do more than a 40-hour week". That would be all very well if done in good faith without any wilful disruption of services; but what makes it wrong is the object with which it is done. There are many branches of our law when an act which would otherwise be lawful is rendered unlawful by the motive or object with which it is done. So here it is the wilful disruption which is the breach. It means that the work of each man goes for naught. It is made of no effect. I ask: Is a man to be entitled to wages for his work when he, with others, is doing his best to make it useless? Surely not. Wages are to be paid for services rendered, not for producing deliberate chaos. The breach goes to the whole of the consideration …'

Buckley LJ: '… With regard to the direction to the men to work strictly in accordance with the rules, the contracts of employment between the board and the railwaymen are entered into as part of the board's commercial activity. Such contracts have commercial objectives and are based on commercial considerations. Just as, where a contract is entered into the performance of which requires the continued existence of a particular state of affairs, the wilful act of one party in bringing that state of affairs to an end so as to render the performance of the contract impossible constitutes a breach of an implied term of the contract, so, in my judgment, in the case of a contract of a commercial character the wilful act of one party which, although not, maybe, departing from the literal letter of the agreement, nevertheless defeats the commercial intention of the parties in entering into the contract, constitutes a breach of an implied term of the contract to perform the contract in such a way as not to frustrate that commercial objective.

Assuming in the appellants' favour that the direction to work to rule avoided any specific direction to commit a breach of any express term of the contract, the instruction was, nevertheless, directed, and is acknowledged to have been directed, to rendering it impossible, or contributing to the impossibility, to carry on the board's commercial activity upon a sound commercial basis, if at all. The object of the instruction was to frustrate the very commercial object for which the contracts of employment were made. It struck at the foundation of the consensual intentions of the parties to those contracts, and amounted, in my judgment, to an instruction to commit what were clearly breaches or abrogations of those contracts. These are or would be, in my judgment, breaches of an implied term to serve the employer faithfully within the requirements of the contract. It does not mean that the employer could require a man to do anything which lay outside his obligations under the contract, such as to work excess hours of work or to work an unsafe system of work or anything of that kind, but it does mean that within the terms of the contract the employee must serve the employer faithfully with a view to promoting those commercial interests for which he is employed. The contrary view is, in my opinion, one which proceeds upon much too narrow and formalistic an approach to the legal relations of employer and employee and is an approach which, I may perhaps add, seems to me to be unlikely to promote goodwill or confidence between the parties …'

Roskill LJ: '… The fact that under normal conditions railways operate satisfactorily when the rule book is interpreted as it clearly is normally interpreted suggests to me that over the years a course of dealing and common understanding in the performance of the instructions has arisen, from which an employee is not free arbitrarily to depart. Mr Wedderburn said this morning that there was no evidence of any such course of conduct. With respect, that seems to me to be wrong. There is ample evidence, for it is a matter of common knowledge that the railways work satisfactorily and efficiently in normal times when the rule book is observed as it normally is observed. An implied term can only be implied if it is both reasonable and necessary to make the implication so as to ensure that the contract works. The courts are rightly slow to write into contracts terms for which the parties have not themselves made provision. The courts do not, cannot, and must not re-write contracts so as to make them, as some may think, more reasonable than they are if they are construed as the parties have provided.

Mr Wedderburn this morning, in a happy phrase, said that the implication which the Crown and the Railways Board sought was designed not to make the contract work, but to make the workers work. If I thought that that aphorism accurately stated the position I would not hesitate to refuse to imply any such term. The courts will only imply a term when it is so clear that the only reason why it has not been expressly included is because the parties thought the need for the provision was self-evident. Mr Pain has referred more than once, and again finally this morning, to the well-known illustration of the officious bystander. I have endeavoured, following Mr Pain's line of argument, to attempt to apply that test by imagining an officious bystander watching an interview between a responsible officer of the Railways Board about to engage a highly articulate and intelligent driver or guard and that driver or guard. I have imagined a copy of the rule book being handed over the table and the onlooker asking the former why he has not said to the latter: "You do understand, don't you, that you must not operate these instructions so as to disrupt the entire running of the railways system of the country?" Traditionally it is enough if the answer to that hypothetical question is a testy "of course". Were such a question put I doubt if the driver's or guard's response would have been limited, in MacKinnon LJ's famous phrase, to such a testy "Oh, of course". I think he might well have been forgiven if he had replied to such a question in more vigorous and less restrained language.

Notwithstanding the skill with which the contrary view has been urged upon us, I regard it as self-evident that each party to each service agreement must, as rational beings, be taken to have assumed as a matter of course, when each service contract was entered into, that the employee would never seek so to interpret and act upon the rules as to disrupt the entire railway system. Accordingly, I have no hesitation in implying a term into the contract of service that each employee will not, in obeying his lawful instructions, seek to obey them in a wholly unreasonable way which has the effect of disrupting the system, the efficient running of which he is employed to ensure. I prefer to rest my decision that work to rule is a breach of contract on this ground rather than on the alternative ground, clearly equally tenable, advanced by the Solicitor-General, that work to rule involves a breach of the positive obligation of faithful service owed by employee to his master.

COMMENT

(1)   Notice that each judge gives a different reason for saying that the work-to-rule is a breach of contract. These judgments are important also in relation to the development of implied terms in employment contracts (see Chapter 4).

Blacking and part-performance

One way in which trade unionists have traditionally given support to other unionists engaged in a trade dispute is to 'black' – that is, to refuse to handle – goods supplied by, or destined for, the employer in dispute. Blacking is thus usually a form of sympathy action.

Related to it, in the sense that it also involves employees not doing all their work, is part-performance, where the tactic used is to refuse to do certain duties while remaining ready and willing to do everything else. This is often resorted to where the dispute is over whether these duties can properly be regarded as part of the employees' work (cf *Cresswell* v *Board of Inland Revenue*, p 129). However, it may also be used in order to put pressure on the employer over some other matter, as in the following case.

Miles v *Wakefield MDC*

[1987] ICR 368 House of Lords

Lord Templeman: 'My Lords, the respondent plaintiff is the superintendent registrar of births, deaths and marriages for the district of Wakefield. The plaintiff was appointed by the appellant defendants, Wakefield Metropolitan District Council. The plaintiff is paid a salary by the council, and he works a 37-hour week. One of the most important functions of the plaintiff as superintendent registrar is to conduct civil wedding ceremonies, and the most popular time for such weddings is Saturday morning when the registry office provided by the council is open for three hours between nine o'clock and midday. On instructions from his trade union, NALGO, the plaintiff, by way of industrial action, refused to conduct weddings on Saturday morning. The object of the union was, by inconveniencing the public, to obtain publicity and support for the campaign conducted by the union in the interests of its members for a higher scale of salary to be paid to superintendent registrars. The plaintiff remained willing to work a 37-hour week and to work on Saturday but he refused to conduct weddings on Saturday. By a letter dated 8 October 1981, the council:

> "made it clear to the registration officers that whilst ever they are not prepared to undertake the full range of their duties on Saturdays they are not required to attend for work and accordingly will not be paid. If the registrars attend at their offices on Saturdays that is entirely a matter for them."

Thus the council treated the plaintiff as being under a duty to work three out of his 37 hours on Saturday morning for the purpose of conducting weddings if required. The plaintiff refused to conduct weddings on Saturday and the council treated him as working for only 34 hours. In refusing to conduct weddings on Saturday, the plaintiff, as he now frankly concedes, acted in breach of his duties as superintendent registrar. The council deducted $\frac{3}{37}$ths of the salary of the plaintiff while he remained unwilling to conduct weddings on Saturday, between August 1981 and October 1982, when the salary dispute was settled. The plaintiff now seeks payment of the sums deducted, amounting to £774. Nicholls J decided against the plaintiff. The Court of Appeal by a majority (Parker and Fox LJJ) held that the plaintiff was entitled to be paid his full salary unless and until he was dismissed ...

My Lords, industrial action involves a worker, in conjunction with all or some of his fellow workers, declining to work or declining to work efficiently in each case with the object of harming the employer so that the employer will feel obliged to increase wages or improve conditions of work or meet the other requirements put forward by the workers' representatives. The form of industrial action which consists of declining to work is a strike. The form of industrial action which consists of declining to work efficiently has many manifestations including the "go slow" and the refusal by the plaintiff to carry out some of his functions on Saturday. In essence, the plaintiff was employed by the public and his industrial action took the form of declining to work efficiently on Saturday with the object of inconveniencing the public and advancing the claim of his union for higher salaries. Industrial action is an effective method of enhancing the bargaining power of the workers' representatives. The courts are not competent to determine and are not concerned to determine whether a strike or other form of industrial action is justified or malicious, wise or foolish, provoked or exploited, beneficial or damaging; history has proved that any such determination is speculative and liable to be unsound. Any form of industrial action by a worker is a breach of contract which entitled the employer at common law to dismiss the worker because no employer is contractually bound to retain a worker who is intentionally causing harm to the employer's business....

My Lords, I would allow this appeal.'

(Lords Brightman, Brandon, Bridge and Oliver agreed that the Council's appeal should be allowed.)

COMMENT

(1)   Lord Templeman's statement that 'any form of industrial action by a worker is a breach of contract ...' would seem to be too wide, unless the courts are to take the view that the motive of a worker can turn otherwise lawful conduct into a breach of contract. However, refusing to carry out part of one's duties is clearly a breach, though capable of being waived by the employer.

(2)   In *Wiluszynski* v *Tower Hamlets* the principle in this case was extended so as to deny any payment at all to local government officers who had refused to answer queries from local councillors although carrying out all their other duties during a trade dispute. In this case, the employer had not physically barred them from the premises in order to prevent them carrying out their other duties, but it had been made clear to them that part-performance was not acceptable and that any work they did while refusing to carry out all their duties would be regarded as having been done on a purely voluntary basis. These decisions are likely to reduce the attractiveness of this form of industrial action, which had initially looked like a tactic which could be used without employees losing as much pay as they would in an all-out strike.

(3)   Blacking has not been the subject of decisions on individual contracts, but has been treated without discussion as a breach of workers' contracts of employment in a number of cases concerned with the liability of trade unions for organising industrial action (see, for example, *Thomson* v *Deakin*, p 496).

Overtime ban
National Coal Board v *Galley*

[1958] 1 WLR 16 Court of Appeal

The defendant was employed as a pit deputy – in effect a kind of supervisor – at a mine in Derbyshire. His contract of employment stated that his terms and conditions were 'regulated by such national agreement and the county wages agreement for the time being in force ...' Galley's union, NACODS, had concluded an agreement replacing the previous overtime arrangement and providing that, 'deputies shall work such days and part days in each week as may reasonably be required by the management in order to promote the safety and efficient working of the pit ...'

All the deputies refused to work the Saturday morning shift. In the absence of proper supervision, the pit could not be operated and all production was lost.

The judgment of the court was given by Pearce LJ: '...We come now to the central point in this appeal, namely, whether the defendant became in breach of his contract of employment when he refused to obey his employer's request to work the Saturday voluntary shift on June 16, 1956. He had already worked 11 shifts on the preceding 11 days. Could he reasonably be required to work a twelfth day before having two days off? In other words, was it reasonable to require him to work 12 days in the fortnight? It is, of course, clear that the court is in no way concerned with what are reasonable hours in the abstract. Its task is to consider the agreement made in 1952 and to determine on the evidence whether or not the defendant was being required to work in breach of that agreement. The only yardstick stated in the agreement is what is reasonably required by the management in order to promote the safety and efficient work of the pit and to comply with statutory requirements. But this clearly is not the only yardstick, since the hours of work a deputy could reasonably be required to work for these purposes would depend on the number of deputies employed. Ultimately the question must be whether the defendant himself was being required to work reasonable hours. If, of course, he was being required to work longer hours than other deputies, that, in the absence of some exceptional circumstances, would be evidence that the requirement made on him was unreasonable. There is, however, no suggestion of that in this case.

[His Lordship reviewed the evidence and said that the court had come to the conclusion that there was no evidence to justify the contentions that the defendant was being required to work in breach of the 1952 agreement.]

COMMENT

(1) In this case it was held that overtime was required by the contract of employment. However, if it were purely voluntary, it must be the case that the employee would commit no breach of contract in refusing to work overtime and would not be liable to dismissal at common law. However, the position as regards unfair dismissal is different (cf *Power Packing Casemakers* v *Faust*, below).

(2) This case was unusual in that the employer sued the employees directly for damages for breach of contract (rather than attempting to sue the union for organising it).

Strikes and unfair dismissal

Special provision has always been made in unfair dismissal legislation for employees dismissed while taking part in industrial action. The basic principle has always been that tribunals will have no jurisdiction to hear unfair dismissal complaints unless the employer has discriminated between those taking part in the action by dismissing some and not others (or dismissing all, but then taking back some and not others).

Trade Union and Labour Relations (Consolidation) Act 1992

238. (1) This section applies in relation to an employee who has a right to complain of unfair dismissal (the 'complainant') and who claims to have been unfairly dismissed, where at the date of the dismissal—
   (a) the employer was conducting or instituting a lock-out, or
   (b) the complainant was taking part in a strike or other industrial action.

   (2) In such a case an industrial tribunal shall not determine whether the dismissal was fair or unfair unless it is shown—
   (a) that one or more relevant employees of the same employer have not been dismissed, or
   (b) that a relevant employee has before the expiry of the period of three months beginning with the date of his dismissal been offered re-engagement and that the complainant has not been offered re-engagement. ...

   (3) For this purpose 'relevant employees' means—
   (a) in relation to a lock-out, employees who were directly interested in the dispute in contemplation or furtherance of which the lock-out occurred, and
   (b) in relation to a strike or other industrial action, those employees at the establishment of the employer at or from which the complainant works who at the date of his dismissal were taking part in the action.

   Nothing in section 237 (dismissal of those taking part in unofficial industrial action) affects the question who are relevant employees for the purposes of this section. ...

COMMENT

(1)   This does not mean that these dismissals are fair: the tribunal simply does not have the power to investigate the fairness or otherwise of the dismissal. This is intended to preserve the neutrality of tribunals, so that they should not get drawn into pronouncing on the rights and wrongs of industrial disputes. The theoretical distinction is clear, although it may be hard to explain to a dismissed striker.

(2)   Equally, in those cases where the tribunal does have jurisdiction, because the employer has discriminated, it does not follow that the dismissal will be unfair. The employer may be able to justify the selection of some but not all of the strikers.

(3)   Note that s 238 is not stated to apply where the *reason* for the dismissal is the employee's participation in industrial action, but only where *at the time of dismissal* the employee is participating in industrial action. The test is temporal, not causative. Accordingly, s 238(2A) (omitted here) provides that in the latter situation, the dismissal will nonetheless be unfair if the main reason for it is pregnancy or childbirth, health and safety reasons within the meaning of ERA s 100 or acting as an employee representative.

(4)   Two main issues arise in relation to this provision: what is meant by a lock-out, strike or other industrial action, and with which other workers can the dismissed employees compare their treatment?

Lock-outs, strikes and other industrial action

No definition of these terms appeared in the main body of legislation until a definition

of 'strike' was included in TULRCA Part V. However, there were statutory definitions in the legislative provisions dealing with individuals' continuity of employment,
which are now found in ERA s 235.

Employment Rights Act 1996

235. ...(4)   ... 'lock-out' means—

    (a)   the closing of a place of employment,

    (b)   the suspension of work or,

    (c)   the refusal of an employer to continue to employ any number of persons
employed by him in consequence of a dispute.

done with a view to compelling persons employed by the employer, or to aid
another employer in compelling persons employed by him, to accept terms and
conditions of or affecting employment.

    (5)   ... 'strike' means—

    (a)   the cessation of work by a body of employed persons acting in combina-
tion, or

    (b)   a concerted refusal, or a refusal under a common understanding, of any
number of employed persons to continue to work for an employer in
consequence of a dispute,

done as a means of compelling their employer or any employed person or body
of employed persons, or to aid other employees in compelling their employer
or any employed person or body of employed persons, to accept or not to
accept terms or conditions of or affecting employment.

COMMENT

(1)   Until the consolidation of trade union law in TULRCA and individual employment law in ERA, the law on strikes and unfair dismissal and the provisions relating
to continuity were in the same statute: the Employment Protection (Consolidation)
Act 1978. Thus it is not surprising that it was argued that the definitions for continuity
purposes were relevant also to the meaning of those terms elsewhere in the Act.

Express and Star Ltd v *Bunday*

[1988] ICR 379 Court of Appeal

The print union, NGA, was implacably opposed to the introduction of new technology which
would allow journalists to type in copy directly instead of its being set by a typesetter. After
a breakdown in negotiations, the union told members not to use the new technology. The
employer therefore limited access to the premises to one entrance, where each employee
was asked before coming in if they were prepared to work without disruption. All those who
refused were suspended. Was it a strike or a lock-out?

May LJ: '... For my part, if it were material, I am quite clear that the definitions in Schedule
13 [now in ERA s 235] should be limited, at least in so far as their explicit terms are
concerned, to the provisions of the Schedule. I do not think that they can be applied generally
throughout the Act itself. I would respectfully adopt the dictum of Waterhouse J in his
judgment in *Rasool* v *Hepworth Pipe Co Ltd* that "it is impermissible to import into the
interpretation of industrial action ... definitions contained in other statutory provisions for
different purposes". However I would not be prepared to put the contents of paragraph 24

[now ERA s 235(4), (5)] completely on one side when construing the same words in other parts of the Act: I think that they may give an indication of the sort of ingredients that one should look for in order to determine whether a state of affairs does indeed amount to a "strike" or a "lock-out".

In these circumstances both counsel took us to the dictionary definitions of a "lock-out". For present purposes I merely quote that in the *Shorter Oxford English Dictionary*, because it seems to be the most modern of the editions to which our attention was drawn. It defines a "lock-out" as:

> "An act of locking out a body of operatives; i.e. a refusal on the part of an employer, or employers acting in concert, to furnish work to their operatives except on conditions to be accepted by the latter collectively."

For my part I would again be prepared to accept this dictionary definition as at least a reliable indication of what does constitute a lock-out in modern industrial relations. Nevertheless, I think that it would be wrong to treat the dictionary definition as if it were expressly contained in the statute and to seek to apply it word for word to any problem which may arise in this context. As has already been pointed out, each of these cases must be decided on its own facts and merits and, as will appear, subject to what I have already said, I have no doubt that the best appreciation of what is or is not a strike or lock-out will come from either an industrial tribunal, or on appeal the Employment Appeal Tribunal, highly experienced in these matters as these bodies respectively are ...

I would therefore allow this appeal, set aside the decision of the appeal tribunal and remit this case to the industrial tribunal with whatever directions we may think appropriate after further hearing counsel.'

Glidewell LJ: '... Since there is no statutory definition of the word "lock-out" where it appears in section 62 [now TULRCA s 238], it must be given its ordinary meaning. I agree with May LJ that the court is entitled to consider the definition in paragraph 24 of Schedule 13 [now ERA s 235(4), (5)] as a guide to the ordinary meaning, as well as the dictionary definition. If the appeal tribunal was in error in this respect, therefore, the error may not be material.

What is material is that in my view the ordinary meaning of the word "lock-out" comprehends not merely the act of the employer in refusing to allow his employees to work, but the reason why he so refuses. Suppose that a manufacturer has an urgent order from a valued customer, and that some of the employees threaten that they will "go slow" and not complete the order on time unless they receive double pay; if the employer refuses, and tells the employees that they may only continue to work for him provided that they work at the normal speed and for the agreed rate of pay, can he be said to lock-out his employees? I do not accept that he can.

Thus in my judgment the industrial tribunal, when deciding whether there had been a lock-out by the employer, was entitled as a matter of law to consider whether the adoption of the practice of "single keying" involved a change in the terms or conditions of the employees' contracts of employment. It decided, as a matter of fact, that it did not. The appeal tribunal concluded, in effect, that this was not a consideration relevant to the decision whether or not there was a lock-out. In my judgment this conclusion was wrong, and it was wrong in law. For this reason I would allow the appeal and adopt the order proposed by May LJ.'

(Croom-Johnson LJ delivered a concurring judgment.)

COMMENT

(1) Presumably this holds good even though the law on unfair dismissal and industrial action and the continuity provisions are in different statutes.

(2) TULRCA s 246 (with the side note, 'Minor definitions') provides,

'In this Part—

...

"strike" means any concerted stoppage of work ...'

This has been imported from the Trade Union Act 1984 s 11(11), where, however, it applied only to that particular section of that particular Act, dealing with ballots before industrial action. Its applicability now is much wider, and arguably goes beyond the mere consolidation purposes of the 1992 Act.

(3) This case gives useful guidance on the meaning of lock-out, in particular the relevance of motive and whether or not it must be a breach of contract. On the latter point, the reasoning was informed partly by the next case.

Power Packing Casemakers v *Faust*

[1983] ICR 282 Court of Appeal

The three employees were dismissed for refusing to work overtime. The company, which only had fifteen employees, had an important rush order to fulfil. It was clear that those who refused to work overtime were doing so because of a dispute over wages; however, the industrial tribunal found that they had no contractual obligation to work overtime.

Stephenson LJ: '... The industrial tribunal were not addressing their minds to [s 238] and the meaning of the words "industrial action" there. But I find that that makes the material provided by the evidence quoted, and the findings based on it, all the more impressive. An industrial tribunal and the lay members of the appeal tribunal may be trusted to recognise industrial action when they see it, and that was how both tribunals, as well as one appellant and one other witness, described the employees' refusal to work overtime.

Now Mr Jones submitted on the employees' behalf that they ought not to have described it so, because it was not a breach of contract. His point on construction is this: to constitute "industrial action", in the natural meaning of those words, on the part of an employee, there must be action in breach of his contract of employment. If he merely refuses to do something which he is not contractually bound to do, he cannot be taking part in industrial action. I would agree that if he refuses because he has a private commitment to visit a sick friend, or a personal preference for a football match, he is not taking industrial action. But that is not this case. If he refuses because he and others who refuse with him hope to extract an increase of wages out of his employers because their business will be disrupted if they do not grant it, that continued application of pressure is industrial action in the common sense of the words. I do not feel able to say any more about that argument of Mr Jones that that is not the natural meaning of "industrial action". And when the words come at the end of the phrase "taking part in a strike or other industrial action," they seem to me to cover even more clearly a refusal used as a bargaining weapon, whether it is a breach of contract or not....

Since the repeal in 1974 of the [Industrial Relations] Act 1971 there are no references in these statutory provisions to the requirement that the "other industrial action" should be "irregular" or in breach of contract, or, for that matter, "short of a strike"; and I respectfully agree with the view of Waterhouse J, giving the judgment of the appeal tribunal in *Rasool* v *Hepworth Pipe Co Ltd* that it is impermissible to import the earlier definition into the later provisions.

Why were those words left out? Why should they be put back? When they were put in, I agree with Mr Carr that Parliament was thereby indicating that without them "other industrial action" extended to action involving no breach of contract or irregularity. I would assume that the qualifying words and the definition of them were not accidentally omitted, that there was some reason for deliberately omitting them. I cannot take the words now used as shorthand for the words no longer used or for the now absent definition, and I can find no compelling reason for putting those in after their four years' absence. Subsequent statutes of 1980 and 1982 have not reinserted them. I can infer that the words "short of a strike" were left out as unnecessary or otiose, but why leave out "irregular" or the restriction to breaches of contract? Why, furthermore, should the industrial tribunal have to embark on an inquiry into the terms of a claimant's contract of employment, express and implied, in order to decide whether he was taking part in industrial action when he was dismissed?

Mr Jones submits that to give these words the extended (and what, contrary to his first submission, I have held to be the natural) meaning which they bear if not confined to breaches of contract, would do injustice and defeat the purpose and object of [s 238] and its predecessor in the Act of 1975, namely, to deprive an employee of his right to complain to an industrial tribunal of unfair dismissal if, and only if, he has been guilty of misconduct or has broken the terms of his contract. If Mr Jones's gloss – for such, contrary to his submission, it clearly is – upon the language of the section is rejected, unscrupulous employers will be allowed, so he submits, to dismiss unfairly and unjustly those who take legitimate industrial action, without any fear of the circumstances being investigated by the statutory tribunals, or of having to pay compensation or reinstate those unfairly dismissed employees. He calls attention to an obvious misunderstanding by the appeal tribunal of the effect of their interpretation of [s 238] ...

Mr Carr concedes that the criticisms of this part of May J's judgment are well founded, but counters the potential injustice relied on by Mr Jones by submitting that the purpose and object of the section is to avoid courts of law and tribunals being required to investigate the rights and wrongs, or to adjudicate on the merits, of trade disputes in the context of unfair dismissal applications. He referred us to what Lord Scarman said, in *NWL Ltd* v *Woods*, about the policy of the Act of 1974 to exclude trade disputes from judicial review by the courts and to substitute an advisory, conciliation and arbitration process; and he pointed out that such disputes are often complex and to give the determination of them to industrial tribunals would defeat the legislative aim of providing cheap and speedy hearings of unfair dismissal complaints by such tribunals. These considerations must, he submitted, have outweighed, with the legislature, the potential injustice created by the statutory ban imposed not only on determining complaints by strikers or those engaged in industrial action by [s 238(1)(b)], but imposed by [s 238(1)(a)] on determining complaints by employees locked out by employers at the date of dismissal.

I feel the force of these submissions, but no certainty as to the intention of the legislature in enacting this provision.

In threading my way from section and subsections to schedule and paragraphs, and from schedule back to section, I may have lost the way, or the thread, or sight of Parliament's aim and object, even if Parliament itself did not. But of this I have no doubt, that as there is no compelling reason why the words of the provision should not be given their natural and ordinary meaning, and good reason why they should not now be defined as once they were, we ought to give them that meaning and apply them, as the appeal tribunal did, to the undisputed facts of the case in favour of the employers. I would accordingly affirm their decision and dismiss this appeal.'

(Purchas LJ delivered a concurring judgment and Sir George Baker agreed.)

COMMENT

(1)   The difference between this case and *NCB* v *Galley* is that here overtime working was not required under the contract of employment, so that a refusal to work overtime was not a breach.

(2)   Even if employees manage to find a kind of industrial action which does not break their contracts of employment, this decision means that they will not be protected under the law of unfair dismissal. Should this be the case?

(3)   While it may not avail employees that their action is not a breach of contract, it is of considerable significance to trade unions in relation to their potential liability to employers.

Who are 'relevant employees'?

Since an employee dismissed for taking part in industrial action can only claim unfair dismissal if other 'relevant employees' were not dismissed, or were re-engaged, it is of great importance to know with whom comparisons may be made. The definition of 'relevant employees' is found in TULRCA s 238(3), above.

H Campey & Sons Ltd v Bellwood

[1987] ICR 311 Employment Appeal Tribunal

When employees refused to accept variations to their terms and conditions of employment, the employer locked them all out. A week later, the employer gave them an ultimatum to return to work the next day. Those who did not were dismissed, and claimed unfair dismissal on the grounds that the employer had taken back those who complied with the ultimatum.

Popplewell J: 'In *Stock* v *Frank Jones (Tipton) Ltd*, not dissimilar legislation had been considered. The House of Lords held that the fact that two employees, who had been on strike had returned to work before the complaining employees' dismissal rendered their dismissal unfair. The House of Lords decided that there was no justification for reading into the paragraph the words "at the date of the dismissal were taking part." No doubt as a result of that decision [s 238(3)(a)] was amended in its present form.

The distinction as to time in sub-paragraphs (a) and (b) is very marked and has been emphasised by the amendment to sub-paragraph (b). It is further emphasised by the absence of amendment as to time in relation to sub-paragraph (a).

In *Fisher* v *York Trailer Co Ltd*, the facts were that the workforce were deliberately working slowly. By letter of 7 February 1978 the company sought from the workforce an undertaking that they would work at a normal pace. They were told if they did not give the undertaking by signing they would be suspended. There was a meeting. All but seven of the employees signed the undertaking and subsequently they were dismissed. It was held,

"That on the true construction of the amended paragraph 7 of Schedule 1 to the Act of 1974 'relevant employees' were not confined to those who were actually locked out, but included those employees who were directly interested in the trade dispute; that the lock-out in the present case occurred when the 34 employees were told that they would not be allowed to work and did not work on 8 February and, since none of them had signed the undertaking on that date, they were all directly interested in the dispute and, therefore, 'relevant employees' for the purposes of the paragraph and, as they had not all been dismissed, the tribunal had jurisdiction in accordance with [s 238] to determine whether the six employees had been unfairly dismissed ..."

We would, ourselves, on the language of [s 238(3)(a)] without any further assistance have come to the same conclusion as the industrial tribunal. We are however fortified in our view by the reasoning and judgment in the *Fisher* case. It is the practice of this appeal tribunal, in so far as it is possible, to follow our own decisions and if there is to be a conflict it is to be resolved by the Court of Appeal. The decision in the *Fisher* case seems to us to be right in law and logic. It has been followed without criticism so far as we are aware for a number of years. In the world of industrial relations it is even more important than elsewhere that decisions which have been consistently relied on by employers and employees and acted on should not lightly be overturned.

We are also fortified in our conclusion by the legislative changes that have occurred since. We have already observed that [s 238(3)(b)] has been amended in order to identify the time in relation to a strike; no doubt to give effect to the observations of the House of Lords, that it was for Parliament to introduce legislation; to add words which previously had been missing. The absence of amendment to [subsection 3(a)] ... lends substance to the view that Parliament, and those responsible for drafting the legislation, did not think that the *Fisher* case had misinterpreted what Parliament intended. Nothing would have been easier than to have added "at the complainant's date of dismissal" to subparagraph (a) as well as to sub-paragraph (b).

Mr Hand has observed that the effect of the decision, by widening those who are directly interested, may cause grave difficulties to employers in the same way that the decision in *Stock* v *Frank Jones (Tipton) Ltd* did. The answer to that may well lie in the argument that if an employer chooses to exercise his right of lock-out, then the consequences are on his own head. We should not seek to do what the House of Lords said we must not do in order to remedy an alleged defect, but should seek to interpret the Act in accordance with the intention of Parliament. For these reasons we are unable to say that the *Fisher* case was wrongly decided or that it can be distinguished; indeed the effect of subsequent amendments is to strengthen the decision of the *Fisher* case and not to weaken it.

Accordingly we take the view that the industrial tribunal have properly directed themselves and their decision cannot be faulted.'

COMMENT

(1)   This decision emphasises the different test for who is a relevant employee according to whether the dismissal took place in the context of a strike or a lock-out. In the latter case, all those originally locked out are 'relevant'. In the former, it is only those still on strike at the time that this complainant was dismissed: not all the original strikers.

(2)   The amendment to this effect was made to the law following the House of Lords decision in *Stock* v *Jones*, as noted here.

(3)   The result of the present version of TULRCA s 238(3)(a) is that, faced with a strike, the employer can wait until some employees drift back to work and then give the rest an ultimatum. Anyone who does not then return may be safely dismissed.

Coates v Modern Methods & Materials Ltd

[1982] ICR 763 Court of Appeal

A dispute blew up at the employer's factory on 12 February over the compulsory transfer of workers. Coates and others were dismissed in March for taking part in industrial action. They claimed unfair dismissal, and argued that the tribunal had jurisdiction because Leith, another employee, had taken part in the strike but had not been dismissed.

Leith had arrived for work as usual on 12 February, but did not cross the picket line because she did not want to be subjected to the verbal abuse the pickets meted out to those who did go in to work. The following day, her doctor certified her as unfit to work because of back trouble, a state of affairs which lasted until late April when she returned to work. During her absence, she did not draw strike pay, but she attended some strike meetings 'to know what was going on'.

An industrial tribunal held that Leith did take part in the strike so it had jurisdiction to hear the employees' unfair dismissal claim. The EAT reversed that decision and the employees appealed.

Stephenson LJ: '... It is to be observed that the industrial tribunal's decision rests partly on the view that there was no good reason why Mrs Leith should withhold her labour and that she decided not to break the strike or did not break it. They must have held that to refuse to pass the pickets because she did not want the abuse meted out to Mrs Jessop and to stay outside the works gates in consequence with the others – some 40 in number according to the evidence – instead of going in to work with Mrs Jessop and, according to the evidence, one other, constituted taking part in the strike. There is no reference in their decision to Mrs Leith's reason, expressed to Mr Brearley, for declining strike pay not because she was disqualified by certificated sickness but because she was not on strike. And the tribunal cannot have regarded that or her explanation for attending strike meetings as of importance, if indeed they accepted her evidence on those two matters.

Can Mrs Leith reasonably be said to have taken part in this strike by yielding to her fear of abuse, and so withholding her labour – a dignified paraphrase of "not working" – and not breaking the strike either by braving the pickets and going to work, or by some protest or expression of dissent?...

I have found this a difficult case. It ought to be easy to decide what "taking part in a strike" means and whether on proved or accepted facts a particular employee was or was not taking part in a strike. The industrial tribunal seem to have found it easy, because they unanimously decided that Mrs Leith was taking part, and on an application for review the chairman thought the weight of the evidence showed that she was taking part and a review had no reasonable prospect of success. I know that the construction of a statute is a question of law; but the meaning of ordinary words is not, and the meaning of "taking part in a strike" seems to me to be just the sort of question which an industrial jury is best fitted to decide. No member of either tribunal has spelt out its meaning, perhaps because it was thought unwise or impossible to attempt a paraphrase of plain words. But I should be very reluctant to assume that any of them attributed to the words an unnatural meaning which they were incapable of bearing in their context, or to differ from their conclusion that Mrs Leith took part in the strike. Only the plainest error in law would enable me to differ from them on such a finding, particularly when the majority of the appeal tribunal, whose decision convicts them of such error, appear themselves to be influenced by an erroneous conception of their power to interfere with the industrial tribunal's decision. On the other hand, I think that on the evidence without argument and reflection I should have taken the view which Mrs Leith's employer appears to have taken that she was not on strike or striking or taking part in the strike. That view takes into account her state of mind, her intention, her motive, her wishes. Some support for doing that is to be found in what Talbot J said in giving the judgment of the appeal tribunal in *McCormick* v *Horsepower Ltd* about Brazier not being motivated by fear in refusing to cross the picket line and withdrawing his labour to aid the strikers: and also in what Lawton LJ, in the passage I have quoted from his judgment in the same case said obiter about giving help generally and about Brazier not being shown to have had a common purpose with the striking boiler-makers. Furthermore, it seems hard on an employer who takes the trouble to investigate an employee's motives and reasons for stopping work to be told "you were wrong to accept what she told you; you ought to have dismissed her and so prevented two other strikers from complaining to the industrial tribunal of unfair dismissal". On the other side it was said that it would be intolerable to impose on employers the burden, which this employer undertook with one employee, of looking into the mind of every employee withholding his or her labour before deciding whether to dismiss, in order to see if each had some reason for stopping work unconnected with the object of the strike.

I have come to the conclusion that participation in a strike must be judged by what the employee does and not by what he thinks or why he does it. If he stops work when his workmates come out on strike and does not say or do anything to make plain his disagreement, or which could amount to a refusal to join them, he takes part in their strike. The line between unwilling participation and not taking part may be difficult to draw, but those who stay away from work with the strikers without protest for whatever reason are to be regarded as having crossed that line to take part in the strike. In the field of industrial action those who are not openly against it are presumably for it. This seems to be the thinking behind the industrial tribunal's decision. If the words in question are capable of bearing that meaning, they are capable of being applied to Mrs Leith's actions on the morning of February 12, 1980, though her time outside the factory gates with the strikers was short and her reason for not entering the factory was accepted. In my judgment a reasonable tribunal could give that meaning to the statutory words and could apply them to Mrs Leith. The industrial tribunal did not, therefore, go wrong in law and it was the majority of the appeal tribunal who did. I would accordingly allow the appeal, set aside the decision of the Employment Appeal Tribunal and restore the decision of the industrial tribunal.'

(Kerr LJ delivered a concurring judgment; Eveleigh LJ dissented.)

P & O European Ferries (Dover) Ltd v *Byrne*

[1989] ICR 779 Court of Appeal

May LJ: '… The brief circumstances of the case are these. Some time last year a substantial number of employees of the employer took industrial action in the form of a strike. As a consequence the employer's contention is that all those employees were dismissed. There were offers of re-engagement but we need not go into that in this appeal. All 1,025 employees concerned applied for compensation for unfair dismissal.

The particular employee who is the applicant in this case, Mr Byrne, was the first to make a claim to the appropriate industrial tribunal and, when he did so, his employer countered by contending that the industrial tribunal should not hear the complaint by virtue of the provisions of [section 238].…

From what I have said it will be apparent that this is a case within [TULRCA s 238(1)], in that the employee concerned was dismissed at a time when he was taking part in a strike. Consequently, if there had been no discrimination amongst all the employees of the employer taking part in that strike, then subsection (2)(a) would be applicable and in those circumstances the industrial tribunal would not have been entitled to determine Mr Byrne's application.

When the employer took this point in its pleading, the applicant in his turn countered by alleging that at least one "relevant employee" had not in fact been dismissed at the material time and accordingly there had in fact been discrimination, whether the employer intended it or not, and accordingly his claim for compensation was not barred by the provisions of [s 238(2)(a)]. Understandably the employer at once asked for particulars of that allegation and especially for the identity of the single employee not dismissed, upon whose retention in employment the applicant relied to avoid the disqualification involved in [s 238(2)(a)]. Particulars giving the name of the one employee not dismissed have however been refused on the ground that to identify this employee would enable the employer, prior to the determination of the applicant's application by the industrial tribunal, to ensure that what may have been discrimination in fact no longer inures, by the simple course of dismissing forthwith the one employee so identified. In those circumstances the employer sought an order for the particulars on the ground that it was essential for it to know the identity of the one employee to enable it adequately to deal with the applicant's contention based, as I say, on [s 238(2)(a)].

When the application for these particulars came before the industrial tribunal it refused to order them on the basis that it would indeed enable the employer to put matters right, from the employer's point of view, in the sense that I have indicated in so far as the present applicant is concerned, on one particular construction of [s 238(2)(a)] in any event even on the alternative construction of the subsection, to give the particulars sought would enable the employer to put matters right vis-à-vis the other 1,024 employees whose claims for compensation for unfair dismissal still have to be heard ...

In so far as the reasons for not ordering particulars, which the industrial tribunal gave and in which it was supported by the appeal tribunal, are concerned, I respectfully disagree with both tribunals. It was, I think, an improper exercise of the discretion of the tribunals below not to order such particulars on the ground that to do so would enable the employer to put matters right, if one relevant employee had got through the net and was not dismissed at the time when the remaining 1,025 employees were dismissed. It is true that a party to litigation is not entitled to particulars solely for the purpose of ascertaining the names of his opponent's witnesses. But a party is entitled to particulars to enable him to know what case he has to meet, even though giving those particulars will identify one or more of the potential witnesses on behalf of the other party ...

The particular parts of [s 238(2)(a)] which require careful consideration are, first, the word "determine" in the earlier part of the subsection, and in the next line the words "unless it is shown". The use of the word "determine" is in my judgment arguably ambiguous. One speaks of a determination in the litigious context both of the final decision of the issues in that litigation and also of the actual hearing itself. In one sense a court determines by a trial from the time that the case is called on until the time when the court gives its ultimate decision. But there is no such ambiguity in the words "unless it is shown". Those words necessarily direct one's attention to the conclusion of the relevant hearing before the industrial tribunal and in my opinion require one to conclude that on its proper construction the material point in time is when the industrial tribunal either determines the substantive hearing which involves determining the jurisdiction point as well, or alternatively determines the jurisdiction point on a preliminary hearing prior to going on, or not going on, as the case may be, with the substantive hearing for compensation.

That in my judgment is the clear and plain meaning of the statutory provision and although we were pressed on the one side not to and on the other side to insert words into the subsection and also to adopt what was said to be a purposive construction of [s 238(2)(a)] to lead us to adopt a construction which looked to the start of the hearing rather than its conclusion as the material time, Mr Supperstone, who has said everything that could be said on behalf of the applicant with skill and cogency was in the end, as I think, almost bound to accept that the meaning of the statutory phrase was clear. When pressed to detail the respects in which he suggested that one should give the phrase a narrow rather than a wider construction, as he suggested at one point was the correct approach, he very properly and realistically found himself unable to do so.

I should just mention that Mr Supperstone also pointed to this potential difficulty if the construction for which he contended was not to be accepted and that is that in the circumstances the unknown Mr X is put in an invidious position. If he is called to give evidence to the effect that he was on strike but not dismissed, he would clearly know that the consequence would be that he would in fact immediately be dismissed so as to preclude the continuing existence of any discrimination under the provisions of [TULRCA s 238(2)(a)]. But this cannot affect what in my view is the clear and literal meaning of the subsection.

For my part I do not think that much more need be said on this appeal, although that is in no way intended to be disrespectful to the interesting arguments which counsel on both sides have addressed to the court. In my judgment the industrial tribunal, and the appeal tribunal following it, erred in directing themselves that it was a legitimate reason for refusing to order particulars which the employer had to have in order to meet the case made against it, that to do so might prejudice not only the applicant's claim but also perhaps the claim of the other 1,024 people and indeed might have a deleterious effect on the continued employment prospects of the unknown Mr X. The allegation had been made against the employer that there had been discrimination in that Mr X had not been dismissed and it was entitled to know who he was so that it could meet that case. It was entitled to know that at that stage in the litigation, particularly having regard to the proper construction of [s 238(2)(a)] which requires one to look to the end of the decision of the relevant determination by the industrial tribunal and not the start.

In those circumstances I would allow this appeal and, subject to hearing further from the counsel if necessary, make an order directing that the relevant particulars be given by the applicant to the employer.'

COMMENT

(1) It may be doubted whether the legislation was intended to operate in the way that it did in the last case. It would seem sensible to amend the statute so that a relevant employee would be one who was still employed at the date of the complainant's dismissal even if dismissed by the time of the application to the industrial tribunal.

(2) A converse situation to *P & O Ferries* v *Byrne* occurred in *Bigham and Keogh* v *GKN Kwikform Ltd*: all strikers, including B and K were dismissed, but B later applied for and got a job with a different branch of the company. He made no attempt to conceal the fact of his earlier dismissal and made no untrue statements in his application. Four weeks later, the employers made the connection and dismissed him. He and others of the original strikers then claimed unfair dismissal based on selective re-engagement: that is, the fact that B had, albeit briefly, been re-employed. The EAT

held that the employer should have known about his earlier employment history with them and that in the absence of fraud, where an employer with actual or constructive knowledge of the earlier dismissal re-engages a dismissed striker, the others may claim. B withdrew his appeal; it is unclear whether he could have claimed. (Note that where the applicant is relying on selective re-engagement, only an offer of re-engagement within three months of the original dismissal need be proved: note the difference of wording between s 238(2)(a) and s 238(2)(b).)

(3)   If the employer selectively re-engages strikers more than three months after their original dismissal, the other dismissed employees have no claim (s 238(2)(b)).

(4)   The Employment Act 1990 provided that unofficial strikers who were dismissed would not be able to claim unfair dismissal in any circumstances. This is now contained in TULRCA s 237. It is important to appreciate that in this context 'unofficial' means action not authorised or endorsed by the union within the meaning of TULRCA s 20 (see below, p 564), rather than contrary to the rules of the union. Employees who do not belong to a trade union and who engage in industrial action are not to be regarded as unofficial strikers unless any of those involved are union members. If some are unofficial strikers, all of them, including the non-members, will be so treated. Note also TULRCA s 223, by which industrial action will lose any immunity if it is taken in order to bring about the reinstatement of workers dismissed for participation in unofficial action.

(5)   The ILO has already concluded that UK law in relation to dismissals in connection with industrial action contravenes the Convention on Freedom of Association. However, this did not weigh heavily with the previous administration. It remains to be seen what the Labour Government will do.

THE RIGHT TO ORGANISE INDUSTRIAL ACTION

Industrial action does not merely involve workers breaking their contracts of employment. The organisers, individuals and trade unions, will also commit civil wrongs through bringing about these breaches and the knock-on interference with trading contracts. Until the House of Lords' decision in *Taff Vale* v *Amalgamated Society of Railway Servants* in 1901, it was thought to be practically impossible for technical reasons to sue trade unions in contract or tort. This meant that trade unions could organise industrial action with impunity. The individual officials could be liable, but in practice no employer would bother suing for damages an individual who would probably have very limited means.

The pattern that grew up, therefore, was for employers who thought that they had a cause of action in tort to sue for an injunction to get the action called off. As they could not sue the union, they sued the officials – usually choosing a top official such as the president or general secretary. While an injunction against an individual only binds that individual, in practice where an employer was successful, the union would accept the situation and treat it as if awarded against the union.

All this changed following *Taff Vale*, for if unions could be sued, their property could be seized to pay damages claims. Given the large financial costs which can quickly result from strike action, a union would risk swift bankruptcy whenever it became involved in industrial action. It is the belief that there should in some sense be a right to strike which justifies the law intervening to prevent that state of affairs.

The response of the Liberal government in 1906 was to pass the Trade Disputes Act 1906, giving trade unions *total* immunity from any action in tort, and giving *partial* immunity to individuals: they would be immune from liability for some torts provided that they were acting in contemplation or furtherance of a trade dispute. In 1982, the Conservative government abolished unions' immunity from tort actions and put them in the same position as individuals. Thus today, unions and individuals have *partial* immunity from liability for some torts, provided that they are acting in contemplation or furtherance of a trade dispute. At the same time, since 1980 the Government has increasingly squeezed the ambit of the immunity.

The result is that today, the question of legal liability for organising industrial action must be looked at in three stages: first, would the activity be unlawful at common law? If it is not tortious, then no one is going to be liable for doing it. Second, if the action does involve the commission of torts, is there immunity by statute for this? This entails two sub-questions: is the alleged tort one for which immunity is given, and if so, was the action 'in contemplation or furtherance of a trade dispute'? Finally, even if such immunity is established there is a third stage: has the immunity been lost for one of the specific statutory reasons? Each of these stages will be examined in turn.

Liability in tort

The first torts to be examined are those for which immunity is given, provided that the tortfeasors are acting in contemplation or furtherance of a trade dispute.

Inducement of breach of contract

Lumley v Gye

[1853] 2 E & B 216 Court of Queen's Bench

The plaintiff, manager of the Queen's Theatre in London, had hired the opera singer, Johanna Wagner, to sing exclusively at his theatre for three months. The defendant, knowing of this, persuaded her to refuse to perform the contract. The law at this time recognised a tort of enticing a servant away from a master, but it was doubtful that the singer could be regarded as the servant of the plaintiff.

Crompton J: '... The law as to enticing servants was said to be contrary to the general rule and principle of law, to be anomalous, and probably to have had its origin from the state of society when serfdom existed and to be founded upon, or upon the equity of, the Statute of Labourers. It was said that it would be dangerous to hold that an action was maintainable for persuading a third party to break a contract unless some boundary or limits could be pointed out; that the remedy for enticing away servants was confined to cases where the relation of master and servant, in a strict sense, subsisted between the parties; and that, in all other cases of contract, the only remedy was against the party breaking the contract.

Whatever may have been the origin or foundation of the law as to enticing of servants, and whether it be, as contended by the plaintiff, an instance and branch of a wider rule, or, as contended by the defendant, an anomaly and an exception from the general rule of law on such subjects, it must now be considered clear law that a person who wrongfully and maliciously, or, which is the same thing, with notice, interrupts the relation subsisting between master and servant by procuring the servant to depart from the master's service, or by harbouring and keeping him as servant after he has quitted it and during the time stipulated for as the period of service, whereby the master is injured, commits a wrongful act for which he is responsible at law. I think that the rule applies wherever the wrongful interruption operates to prevent the service during the time for which the parties have contracted that the service shall continue, and I think that the relation of master and servant subsists, sufficiently for the purpose of such action, during the time for which there is in existence a binding contract of hiring and service between the parties ...'

(Erle and Wightman JJ delivered concurring judgments; Coleridge J dissented.)

COMMENT

(1)   This was seen at the time as a considerable extension of the existing (and archaic) tort of enticement of a servant. Its applicability to trade disputes is obvious: organisers of industrial action are likely to persuade employees to break their contracts of employment, or they may try to persuade other employers not to deal with the employer in dispute.

(2)   In the direct form of the tort, as seen in this case where the defendant directly persuades the third party to break her contract with the plaintiff, it is necessary only that the persuasion was deliberate, and carried out with knowledge of the contract that would be broken.

(3)   What if the defendant does not simply *persuade* the third party not to perform her contract with the plaintiff, but actually *prevents* her from doing so? This may occur, for example, where a trade union calls out the workforce of one employer in order to prevent that employer performing a contract with the employer in dispute. Is this tortious conduct? The issue was first examined in the next case.

D C Thomson & Co Ltd v *Deakin*

[1952] Ch 646 Court of Appeal

Since the General Strike in 1926, the plaintiff printing company had refused to employ trade unionists, causing a dispute with the print union NATSOPA. NATSOPA called on other unions to support them, with the result that drivers and loaders working for Bowaters, who supplied paper to the plaintiffs, told Bowaters that they would black (refuse to handle) any supplies intended for Thomson's. Bowaters therefore contacted the plaintiffs and informed them that they would be unable to perform their contract to deliver paper to them. Bowaters, to avoid trouble, did not actually ask any of their loaders or drivers to supply paper to the plaintiff company.

Jenkins LJ: '... Direct persuasion or procurement or inducement applied by the third party to the contract breaker, with knowledge of the contract and the intention of bringing about its breach, is clearly to be regarded as a wrongful act in itself, and where this is shown a case of actionable interference in its primary form is made out: *Lumley* v *Gye*.

But the contract breaker may himself be a willing party to the breach, without any persuasion by the third party, and there seems to be no doubt that if a third party, with knowledge of a contract between the contract breaker and another, has dealings with the contract breaker which the third party knows to be inconsistent with the contract, he has committed an actionable interference: see, for example, *British Industrial Plastics Ltd* v *Ferguson*, where the necessary knowledge was held not to have been brought home to the third party; and *British Motor Trade Association* v *Salvadori*. The inconsistent dealing between the third party and the contract breaker may, indeed, be commenced without knowledge by the third party of the contract thus broken; but, if it is continued after the third party has notice of the contract, an actionable interference has been committed by him: see, for example, *De Francesco* v *Barnum*.

Again, so far from persuading or inducing or procuring one of the parties to the contract to break it, the third party may commit an actionable interference with the contract, against the will of both and without the knowledge of either, if, with knowledge of the contract, he does an act which, if done by one of the parties to it, would have been a breach. Of this type of interference the case of *GWK Ltd* v *Dunlop Rubber Co Ltd* affords a striking example.

Further, I apprehend that an actionable interference would undoubtedly be committed if a third party, with knowledge of a contract and intent to bring about its breach, placed physical restraint upon one of the parties to the contract so as to prevent him from carrying it out.

It is to be observed that in all these cases there is something amounting to a direct invasion by the third party of the rights of one of the parties to the contract, by prevailing upon the other party to do, or doing in concert with him, or doing without reference to either party, that which is inconsistent with the contract; or by preventing, by means of actual physical restraint, one of the parties from being where he should be, or doing what he should do, under the contract.

But here the acts complained of as constituting the actionable interference do not amount to a direct invasion of the plaintiffs' contractual rights. The plaintiffs' case, as regards paper, is that the defendants persuaded, induced or procured employees of Bowaters (that is, drivers employed by Bowaters Sales Company Ltd, and loaders employed by Bowaters Mersey Mills Ltd) to break their contracts of employment by refusing to drive lorries loaded with, or to load lorries with, paper destined for the plaintiffs, with the object and intention of causing Bowaters to break, or making it impossible for them to fulfil, their contract for the supply of paper to the plaintiffs; and that the defendants did in fact, by the means I have stated, produce the intended result ...

Now, the plaintiffs' case, as I have stated it, does seem to me to involve an extension of the range of actionable interference with contractual rights beyond any actual instance of this type of wrong to be found in the decided cases. Here there is no direct invasion of the plaintiffs' rights under the contract. It was no part of their contract that these particular employees, or any particular employees, should be employed by Bowaters for the purpose of effecting deliveries of paper to them. Thus the breaches by these men of their contracts of services with Bowaters (if made out on the facts) did not in themselves involve any breach of Bowaters' contract with the plaintiffs. The breaches of the contracts of service (if made out) were, so to speak, at one remove from the breach of contract complained of. Nevertheless, I think that in principle an actionable interference with contractual relations may be committed by a third party who, with knowledge of a contract between two other persons and with the intention of causing its breach, or of preventing its performance, persuades, induces or procures the servants of one of those parties, on whose services he relies for the performance of his contract, to break their contracts of employment with him, either by leaving him without notice or by refusing to do what is necessary for the performance of his contract, provided that the breach of the contract between the two other persons intended to be brought about by the third party does in fact ensue as a necessary consequence of the third party's wrongful interference with the contracts of employment.

I take this view because I see no distinction in principle for the present purpose between persuading a man to break his contract with another, preventing him by physical restraint from performing it, making his performance of it impossible by taking away or damaging his tools or machinery, and making his performance of it impossible by depriving him, in breach of their contracts, of the services of his employees. All these are wrongful acts, and if done with knowledge of and intention to bring about a breach of a contract to which the person directly wronged is a party, and, if in fact producing that result, I fail to see why they should not all alike fall within the sphere of actionable interference with contractual relations delimited by Lords Macnaghten and Lindley in *Quinn* v *Leathem*.

But, while admitting this form of actionable interference in principle, I would hold it strictly confined to cases where it is clearly shown, first, that the person charged with actionable interference knew of the existence of the contract and intended to procure its breach; second, that the person so charged did definitely and unequivocally persuade, induce or procure the employees concerned to break their contracts of employment with the intent I have mentioned; third, that the employees so persuaded, induced or procured did in fact break their contracts of employment; and, fourth, that breach of the contract forming the alleged subject of interference ensued as a necessary consequence of the breaches by the employees concerned of their contracts of employment.

I should add that by the expression "necessary consequence" used here and elsewhere in this judgment I mean that it must be shown that, by reason of the withdrawal of the services of the employees concerned, the contract breaker was unable, as a matter of practical possibility, to perform his contract; in other words, I think the continuance of the services of the particular employees concerned must be so vital to the performance of the contract alleged to have been interfered with as to make the effect of their withdrawal comparable, for practical purposes, to a direct invasion of the contractual rights of the party aggrieved under the contract alleged to have been interfered with, as, for example (in the case of a contract for personal services), the physical restraint of the person by whom such services are to be performed.

I make the above reservations in regard to the scope of this newly propounded form of actionable interference with contractual rights for these reasons: It is now well settled that, apart from conspiracy to injure, no actionable wrong is committed by a person who, by acts not in themselves unlawful, prevents another person from obtaining goods or services necessary for the purposes of his business, or who induces others so to prevent that person by any lawful means. It follows, in my view, that (again apart from conspiracy to injure) there is nothing unlawful, under the law as enunciated in *Allen* v *Flood* and subsequent cases, in general appeals to others to prevent a given person from obtaining goods or services, for that is a purpose capable of being lawfully carried out, and there can, therefore, be nothing unlawful in advocating it, unless unlawful means are advocated. The result of such advocacy may well be that unlawful means are adopted by some to achieve the purpose advocated, but that is not to say that a person who advocates the object without advocating the means is to be taken to have advocated recourse to unlawful means. If by reference to the form of actionable interference with contractual rights now propounded, general exhortations issued in the course of a trade dispute, such as "Stop supplies to X", "Refuse to handle X's goods", "Treat X as 'black' ", and the like, were regarded as amounting to actionable interference, because persons reached by such exhortations might respond to them by breaking their contracts of employment and thereby causing breaches of contracts between their employers and other persons, and because the person issuing such exhortations must be taken constructively to have known that the employers concerned must have contracts of some kind or other with other persons, and that his exhortations (general as they were) might lead to breaches of those contracts through breaches of contracts of employment committed by persons moved by his exhortations, then, the proposition must be accepted, that it is an actionable wrong to advocate objects which can be achieved by lawful means, because they can also be achieved by unlawful means; and to that proposition I decline to subscribe.

Furthermore, as the judge in effect pointed out in his judgment, almost every strike, if to any extent successful, must cause breaches of contracts between the employer against whom it is directed and the persons with whom he is doing business, the very object of the strike being to bring his business to a standstill or himself to terms. Again, many a strike embarked on in support of a strike in progress in some other concern must have had for its immediate object the cutting off of supplies to, or prevention of distribution of the products of, or the application of similar pressure upon, that other concern.

Yet we have been referred to no case in which the persons inciting a strike have been held liable for actionable interference with contractual relations between the strikers' employers and the persons with whom they deal; and in principle I do not think that the inciters of the strike could be held so liable in the absence of proof that they knew of the existence of a particular contract, and, with a view to bringing about its breach, counselled action by employees in itself necessarily unlawful (as, for example, breach of their contracts of employment) designed to achieve that end.

To hold otherwise would, in my view, be to admit not only an addition to the means whereby actionable interference with contractual rights may be compassed (which addition, as I have said, I am in principle prepared to accept), but also an enlargement of the character and scope of the tort itself (which I cannot agree to).

Finally, not every breach of a contract of employment with a trading or manufacturing concern by an employee engaged in services required for the performance of a contract between his employer and some other person carries with it as a necessary consequence (in the sense above indicated) the breach of the last mentioned contract. For instance, A induces B, C's lorry driver, to refuse, in breach of his contract of employment, to carry goods which C is under contract to deliver to D, and does so with a view to causing the breach of C's contract with D. C could, if he chose, engage some other lorry driver, or arrange alternative means of transport, but does not do so. He fails to deliver the goods, telling D he is prevented from doing so by B's breach of contract. In such circumstances, there has been no direct invasion by A of C's rights under his contract with D, and, although A has committed an actionable wrong against C, designed to bring about the breach of C's contract with D, and a breach has in fact occurred, it cannot be said that the breach has in fact been caused by A's wrongful act, and therefore D cannot, in my view, establish as against A an actionable interference with his rights under his contract with C.

It remains briefly to relate the foregoing considerations to the facts of the present case. [His Lordship reviewed the evidence and held that the plaintiffs had not established a case against any of the defendants.]'

(Evershed MR and Morris LJ delivered concurring judgments.)

COMMENT

(1)   The reason that the tort was not made out here was because the loaders and drivers for Bowaters had never actually committed a breach of contract: Bowaters did not ask them to handle supplies for Thomson's and so they never had to refuse.

(2)   Note that blacking is here treated as a breach of contract without discussion. It will usually involve refusal to obey lawful and reasonable orders.

(3)   This decision established the existence of the tort of inducing breach of contract in an indirect form: where the defendant (third party in Jenkins's terminology) puts it out of the contractor's power to perform the contract with the plaintiff. The Court insists that such prevention will only be tortious if *unlawful means* are used: it was settled in the famous House of Lords decision in *Allen* v *Flood* that if you compel the third party to act to the detriment of the plaintiff by using lawful means, there is no liability even though you intended to damage the plaintiff.

(4)   The distinction between direct and indirect inducement of breach of contract is thus crucial. If the defendant has *directly* invaded the rights of one party to the contract, it is not necessary to prove unlawful means in addition. The distinction was critical in the next case.

Middlebrook Mushrooms Ltd v Transport and General Workers' Union

[1993] IRLR 232   Court of Appeal

The employers had dismissed 89 workers who had been involved in industrial action arising from a dispute over pay and conditions. Their union decided to mount a publicity campaign to elicit public sympathy and support for the dismissed workers. They produced a leaflet to be distributed by the dismissed workers at supermarkets which stocked the employers' products. It was in the following terms:

> "89 ladies were dismissed from Middlebrook Mushrooms for refusing to accept a pay cut.
>   Over the last two years these ladies have accepted 300 redundancies, changes to working practices and last year a pay freeze. The company now want them to accept a pay cut; and because they have refused they have been dismissed. Other sections have been told they will not have to accept the same pay cut.
>   This is unfair. Please support the ladies by refusing to buy Middlebrook Mushrooms when you shop at this store, and please sign our petition.
>   Thank you."

The employers argued that this amounted to the tort of direct inducement of breach of contract.

Neill LJ: '... Counsel for the employers made it clear that in his submission the distribution of the leaflets outside supermarkets brought the case within the four corners of the *Lumley* v *Gye* principle.
    Counsel developed his argument as follows:

(a)   The correct approach was to look first at the position of the supermarket manager, who is in a position to decide whether or not to break his contract with the employers. If, as is very likely in the present situation, he chooses not to perform the contract, one asks the reason why. The answer would be that he was apprehensive of the effect on the public of the leaflets and he wanted to avoid any embarrassment to his business.

(b)   In a case such as the present the breach of contract would be brought about by a conscious decision of one of the parties to the contract who would have been influenced to break it by the words or conduct of the third party.

(c)   The true demarcation line in cases of interference with contractual relations is between cases where one of the parties to a contract is influenced to break it by the actions of a third party, and cases where the actions of a third party have rendered further performance of the contract impossible. The test of causation in cases of the latter type is different from the test where a party to the contract breaks the contract himself. Cases of physical restraint therefore fall on the other side of this demarcation line from cases such as the present where the hypothetical supermarket manager will have made a decision himself to break his contract with the employers. In the instant case the actions of the "pickets" would communicate pressure or persuasion to the mind of the supermarket manager. It was his perception of the effect of the leaflets on the public which was important rather than the actual effect on the supermarkets' customers themselves. Accordingly this was a clear case of direct persuasion where influence was brought to bear on the mind of one of the parties to the contract.

(d) The appellants must have been aware that the employers' produce reaches the shelves of the supermarkets through the medium of contracts. Moreover, the evidence contained in the affidavits and exhibits, including the affidavit of Mr Brothers and the newspaper reports attributing statements to the appellants, demonstrated the plain intention of the appellants to bring about a boycott of the employers' products if necessary on a national scale.

In my view Mr Pardoe was right to underline the importance of causation, but I am quite unable to accept his submission that it is enough for the employers to prove that one or more supermarket managers may have been influenced in his decision to break his contract with the employers by the distribution of the leaflets outside the doors of the supermarkets. If the case is to fall within the *Lumley* v *Gye* category the persuasion has to be directed at one of the parties to the contract. It is therefore necessary in every case to examine the form or nature of the communication on which a plaintiff relies.

In the present case the leaflet was directed to the customers. There was no message in the leaflets for the management of the supermarket. They were not exhorted to take any action or to desist from taking any action. In my judgment it is most important not to extend the *Lumley* v *Gye* principle outside its proper limits. This category of interference is concerned with the *direct* persuasion of one of the parties to the contract to break his contract. In the present case it is an important fact that the suggested influence was exerted, if at all, through the actions or the anticipated actions of third parties who were free to make up their own minds. Though counsel for the appellants did not place any specific reliance on Article 10 of the European Convention on Human Rights and Fundamental Freedoms, it is relevant to bear in mind that in all cases which involve a proposed restriction on the right of free speech the court is concerned, when exercising its discretion, to consider whether the suggested restraint is necessary. In the present case, however, one does not reach the question of the exercise of discretion. In my judgment the distribution of these leaflets in the way proposed does not fall within the *Lumley* v *Gye* principle at all.

In the course of the argument I drew Mr Pardoe's attention to the example of interference given by Sir Raymond Evershed MR in *D C Thomson & Co* v *Deakin*. He said:

"My instance was of a contract between A and B, whereby A contracted to sell his house to B at a price beneficial to A. I will assume that it will have been disclosed by A to B that there was in fact a public right of way passing close to the property, but that B had been informed, correctly, that the use of such right of way had become so slender that it was of little, if any, practical significance. Then let it be supposed that some third party, desiring to cause B to resile from the contract with A and to deprive A of the benefit of the contract, persuaded a number of individuals in the neighbourhood to resume the use of the right of way, so that there then passed near the premises a considerable stream of persons, all legitimately using the right of way as such, as a result of which B decided that the amenities of the premises were so damaged that he was no longer willing to continue."

The Master of the Rolls expressed the opinion that it was difficult to see how the intervener in such circumstances would be liable. In my judgment, the example of the right of way is a good illustration of the limits which, as a matter of policy, the courts must place on the *Lumley* v *Gye* principle. Where the direct pressure is brought to bear on strangers to the contract, such as Bowaters' drivers in *D C Thomson & Co Ltd* v *Deakin* and the effect on the contracting party is indirect, it is necessary to show that some unlawful means have been employed if the conduct is to be actionable. ...'

(Mann LJ agreed with Neill LJ; Hoffman LJ delivered a concurring judgment.)

COMMENT

(1) The employers presumably did not attempt to argue for the indirect inducement to breach of contract here because no unlawful means were used: the workers' attendance at the protest at the supermarket was lawful. Note that the workers involved in the distribution of leaflets had been dismissed. Would it make a difference if they were still employed when taking part in this action?

(2) It is interesting to see the reference by Neill LJ to the ECHR and the value to be placed on freedom of speech in this judgment. As the activity was more in the nature of a demonstration than what is normally regarded as 'picketing', TULRCA s 220 (below, p 570) was not relevant. They were not acting unlawfully, and so had no need of the protection which that section confers on those who act within its limits.

(3) The Court of Appeal is here concerned not to allow the tort of direct interference to spread beyond its existing boundaries. However, despite the comments of Jenkins LJ in *Thomson* v *Deakin* that the four conditions for indirect inducement should be interpreted tightly, they have been considerably relaxed over the years. The first condition was that the defendant should have knowledge of the contract which would be broken by the use of the unlawful means.

Merkur Island Shipping Corporation v Laughton

[1983] ICR 490 House of Lords

Lord Diplock: '... Such facts as it is necessary to recount in order to dispose of this appeal can be stated briefly. The respondents ("the shipowners") own the *Hoegh Apapa* ("the ship"), a Liberian registered ship, of which the majority of the crew were Filipinos. On July 15, 1982, she arrived at a dock in Liverpool for loading. ITF (of which the individual appellants are officials), having previously learnt that the shipowners were paying less than the rate of wages approved by ITF persuaded the tugmen employed by a company known as Rea Towing ("the tugowners") to refuse, in breach of their contract of employment with the tugowners, to move the ship out of the dock so as to enable her to sail.

The ship was let by the shipowners to Leif Hoegh and Co ("the charterers") under a time charter ("the charter") in the New York Produce Exchange form with certain additional clauses, to two of which it will be necessary to refer. The charterers in turn had sub-chartered the ship to Ned Lloyd under a six-month time charter ("the sub-charter") containing similar clauses. Both charter and sub-charter provided that the charterers thereunder should,

> "provide and pay for all … port charges, normal pilotages, agencies, commissions, consular charges … and all other usual expenses… . but when the vessel puts into a port for causes for which vessel is responsible, then all such charges incurred shall be paid by the owners."

Pursuant to this clause in the sub-charter, the sub-charterers, who have a running contract with the tugowners for the provision of tugs to all their vessels using the port of Liverpool, made through their agent a specific contract with the tugowners for the provision of tugs to take the ship into and out of the dock at which the ship was to be loaded. As a result of the blacking of the vessel, however, on completion of the loading on July 16 the tugmen employed by the tugowners, in breach of their contracts of employment, refused to move the ship except to a lay berth …

I turn to the four elements of the tort of actionable interference with contractual rights as Jenkins LJ stated them, but substituting "interference with performance" for "breach", except in relation to the breaking by employees of their own contracts of employment where such breach has as its necessary consequence the interference with the performance of the contract concerned.

The first requirement is actually two-fold, (1) knowledge of the existence of the contract concerned and (2) intention to interfere with its performance.

As respects knowledge, ITF had been given an actual copy of the charter on July 19, 1980, three days after the " blacking" started but two days before the application to Parker J was made. Quite apart from this, however, there can hardly be any one better informed than ITF as to the terms of the sort of contracts under which ships are employed, particularly those flying flags of convenience. I agree with what was said by the Master of the Rolls on the question of ITF's knowledge:

> "Whatever the precise degree of knowledge of the defendants at any particular time, faced with a laden ship which, as they well knew, was about to leave port, the defendants must in my judgment be deemed to have known of the almost certain existence of contracts of carriage to which the shipowners were parties. The wholly exceptional case would be that of a ship carrying the owner's own goods. Whether that contract or those contracts consisted of a time charter, a voyage charter or one or more bill of lading contracts or some or all of such contracts would have been immaterial to the defendants. Prima facie their intention was to immobilise the ship and in so doing to interfere with the performance by the owners of their contract or contracts of carriage – immobilising a laden ship which had no contractual obligation to move would have been a pointless exercise, since it would have brought no pressure to bear on the owners."

The last sentence of this citation deals also with intention. It was the shipowners upon whom ITF wanted to bring pressure to bear, because it was they who were employing seamen at rates of pay lower than those it was the policy of ITF to enforce. The only way in which income could be derived by the shipowners from the ownership of their ship was by entering into contracts with third parties for the carriage of goods under which a primary obligation of the shipowners would be to prosecute the contract voyages with the utmost dispatch, and their earnings from their ship would be diminished by its immobilisation in port. Diminishing their earnings under the contract of carriage was the only way in which pressure could be brought to bear on the shipowners …'

COMMENT

(1)   This case was actually based on interference with contract rather than inducement of breach of contract (see below), but the requirements laid down by Jenkins LJ are considered to apply with the substitution of 'interference with performance' for breach.

(2)   The defendants here actually had a copy of the contract and thus could not argue ignorance of its contents; however, what is interesting is that the court is prepared to act on what, in their view, the defendants 'must have known' without proof of their actual knowledge.

(3)   In *Dimbleby & Sons Ltd* v *NUJ*, Lord Diplock went further: in that case it was argued by the union that there was no evidence to show that the contract to print newspapers between Dimbleby's and a printing company would be broken through the journalists' refusal to supply copy. Lord Diplock considered that it was enough that the union had an intention to prevent the printing contract being performed regardless; also that there was evidence of other contracts, such as advertising contracts, which would be broken if the newspapers failed to appear. The interesting point is that he makes no reference to whether the union had knowledge of these contracts, nor what level of knowledge was necessary for the union to be fixed with liability.

(4)   The second condition was stated by Jenkins L J to be that the defendant 'did definitely and unequivocally persuade, induce or procure the employees to break their contracts of employment with the intent I have mentioned' – a condition he then expands upon.

J T Stratford & Son Ltd v Lindley

[1965] AC 269 House of Lords

The facts of this case reveal a similar scenario to that in *Thomson* v *Deakin*. The commercial contract whose breach was brought about was one between the hirers of barges who should have returned them after hire to the plaintiff, but were prevented from doing so by the refusal of their employees to handle them.

Lord Pearce alone addressed the issue of persuasion: '... Did the defendants induce the breach? Albeit with expressions of regret, the defendants made it clear to the Association of Master Lightermen, which in effect represented the hirers (by letter of November 8, 1963), that the hirers could not return the barges to the plaintiffs. The fact that an inducement to break a contract is couched as an irresistible embargo rather than in terms of seduction does not make it any less an inducement. The defendants were in effect saying to the hirers: "You shall not carry out your contract with the plaintiffs, and we have taken steps which will make it impossible, though we regret the inconvenience to you." If thereby the hirers were induced to break the contract, the tort is established ...'

Torquay Hotel Co Ltd v *Cousins*

[1969] 2 Ch 106 Court of Appeal

The facts of this case are given with the longer extract from it below.

Only Winn LJ addressed the issue of persuasion: '... It was one of Mr Pain's main submissions that mere advice, warning or information cannot amount to tortious procurement of breach of contract. Whilst granting arguendi causa that a communication which went no further would, in general, not, in the absence of circumstances giving a particular significance, amount to a threat or intimidation, I am unable to understand why it may not be an inducement. In the ordinary meaning of language it would surely be said that a father who told his daughter that her fiancé had been convicted of indecent exposure, had thereby induced her, with or without justification, by truth or by slander, to break her engagement. A man who writes to his mother-in-law telling her that the central heating in his house has broken down may thereby induce her to cancel an intended visit ...'

COMMENT

(1)   This also seems to suggest a lower standard than the words of Jenkins L J.

(2)   The requirement of an actual breach of contract (see the third and fourth conditions) has been significantly watered down, with the recognition of a tort of *interference* with contract, dealt with next.

(3)   In a situation like *Thomson* v *Deakin*, Bowaters could have sued the defendant also (had their employees actually committed breaches of contract) because the direct form of the tort would have been committed against them, as well as the indirect form against Thomson's. Bowaters chose not to sue. But could anyone else having a contract with the employer in dispute claim for disruption of *their* contract, even though there was no specific intention to harm them?

Falconer v *ASLEF and NUR*

[1986] IRLR 331 Sheffield County Court

Because of a one-day rail strike, the plaintiff was compelled to travel from Doncaster to London one day early for an appointment and to return one day later, necessitating expenditure on overnight accommodation. He sued the unions for inducing a breach of his contract with British Rail.

Judge Henham: '... It is the defendants' case that it has not been proved that the action (admitted) by the defendants was aimed at the plaintiff or that they intended to cause him harm. Any such harm was a consequence (and not the object) of pressure intended to be brought upon the BR Board. That the defendants were not, and have not been shown to be, deliberately selecting the plaintiff or any other as specific instruments through which to damage or harm the BR Board.

It is the defendants' conclusion that liability in tort only arises where the plaintiff can show he was the party ultimately aimed at or the object of the action or that he was deliberately selected as the instrument through which to cause injury to the BR Board. The Court has been invited to compare the allied tort of intimidation where the plaintiff must be the person whom the defendants intended to injure. I do not find any assistance from this comparison.

The defendants also submit that to extend liability in tort would be unacceptable and contrary to authority.

I find myself in respectful agreement with the late Lord Diplock in the *Merkur Island* case, as indeed were the majority of members of the House of Lords hearing the appeal, that many of the cases referred to, although of some value, are of dubious benefit. I am content, as he was, to accept the statement of Jenkins LJ in *Thomson* v *Deakin* as authoritative law in this matter.

Of the matters which it was stated form the elements of the tort in this case (i.e. arising from the indirect action of a third party) and which must be proved, I find as follows:

1st element

1. *That the defendants knew of the existence of the contract and intended to interfere with its performance.*

They were without doubt aware of the published contractual terms between BR and its passengers.

In my view the plaintiff was *one of a definite* and *identifiable* group of people in contractual relationship with the BR Board. The fact that his actual name and description were unknown to the defendants at the time does not preclude him from beginning the action and succeeding in his claim *provided* he satisfies the Court in regard to other matters which must be proved....

I accept the argument advanced on behalf of the plaintiff that it is sufficient to show that the defendants knew there were existing contracts between the Board and the group or class of persons (passengers) of which the plaintiff was one. He has satisfied the Court that the defendants did know of this.

As to the need to prove the defendants intended to procure a breach of, or interference with the performance of, those contracts, I find no sympathy for the argument that the plaintiff was not the object or instrument of the action taken when the strike was called. Undoubtedly, it was the intention of the defendants to cause the BR Board to be rendered incapable of performing its contractual obligations with the plaintiff and other passengers but to suggest that the effect upon them (i.e. the passengers) was merely consequential is, in my view, both naïve and divorced from reality. It was clearly the intention of the defendants in calling the strike to direct its effect upon the plaintiff and others and that by so doing create pressure upon the Board by the plaintiff and others and thus to induce the Board to accede to the defendants' wishes.

In any event the defendants were in my view undoubtedly reckless (in the sense that they knew and appreciated the effects of the action upon the plaintiff but nevertheless pursued it).

2nd element

2. *That the defendants induced or procured the BR employees to breach their contract of employment with the Board with the intention mentioned above.*

There is an admission as to the intended inducement and, if there be any doubt as to the intention behind the induced breach of contract of employment, I have no difficulty in saying that I am more than satisfied this was the intended consequence and that it was achieved. No evidence has been called by the defendants to the contrary.

3rd element

3. *That the employees did in fact break their contracts of employment.*

I have already answered this argument.

4th element

4.   That the interference with the performance of the contract between the BR Board and the plaintiff ensued as a necessary consequence of the breaches by the employees of their contracts of employment.

Jenkins LJ in *Thomson* v *Deakin* described "necessary consequence" as meaning that by reason of the withdrawal of the employees' services, the contract breaker (the Board) was unable, as a matter of *practical possibility*, to perform his contract. The *continuance of the services* must be *vital* to the performance of the contract.

I accept that in purchasing the return ticket on 16.1.85 the plaintiff was in contractual relationship with BR Board subject to the conditions set out in the Conditions of Carriage.

It seems to me unarguable that the ability of BR to carry out its contractual obligations to provide carriage by train (subject to paragraph 17 referred to later) was directly precluded, prevented and interfered with as a result of the breach of service contract induced by the defendants. The submission that the contract merely creates an expectation to provide transport but no primary obligations to do so does not find favour with me. There is no evidence to show that, the effect of such withdrawal of services apart, BR were not at all times willing and able to perform its part of the contract with the plaintiff.

Furthermore, the services of its employees were *unquestionably vital* to the ability of the Board to discharge its contractual obligation to the plaintiff …'

(The plaintiff was awarded £173 by way of damages.)

Barretts & Baird (Wholesale) v *Institution of Professional Civil Servants*

[1987] IRLR 3 Queen's Bench Division

Fatstock officers (FOs) employed by the Meat and Livestock Commission (MLC) have the job of dealing with the certification process in respect of livestock and deadstock at abattoirs. In pursuit of a regrading claim, their union, the IPCS, organised a series of one-day strikes. The plaintiffs were meat trade companies whose business was disrupted because of the interruption to the certification process. They claimed that the industrial action was an interference with their trade by unlawful means.

Henry J: '… The next necessary ingredient in this still relatively undeveloped tort of interfering with the trade or business of a person by unlawful means is what we have called the "intent to injure". That is useful shorthand but insufficiently precise to be useful as a legal test here. To make an individual striker liable in tort to any third party damaged by that strike the test, in my judgment, must in Lord Diplock's words in *Lonrho Ltd* v *Shell Petroleum (No. 2)* be that the striker's predominant purpose must be injury to the plaintiffs rather than his predominant purpose being his own self-interest….

Even though there is no evidence from Mr Knowles or from any of the other 630 FOs for the good reason that he was finally joined too late and they are not parties, it seems to me on the evidence that it is plain that the industrial action being taken here is perfectly straightforward industrial action taken for improved pay. The FOs are based at abattoirs nationwide, it is a national strike. There is no evidence of any independent, let alone predominant, desire to injure the plaintiffs at whose premises they work. Naturally, the effect of their withdrawal of their labour will damage the plaintiffs. Naturally, the union, when sending out the ballot papers, will refer, with apparent satisfaction, to the 'major disruption caused by the first one-day stoppage'. But the primary purpose of the breach of their contracts of employment by the FOs was to seek an improvement in their pay and conditions. Clearly, damage to the various plaintiffs was an unavoidable by-product of that withdrawal of labour and was a readily foreseeable consequence and, perhaps, in the case of some FOs, a not undesired consequence on the basis that the greater the disruption caused the greater the pressure for a satisfactory settlement with the MLC and the sooner the return to normal working. But there is no evidence to suggest that the FOs would not have struck if their industrial action had not injured these plaintiffs. On the evidence the desire to strike was the cause of the injury to the plaintiffs rather than the desire to injure the plaintiffs being the cause of the strike. It seems to me abundantly clear that the predominant purpose of this strike was the FOs' desire to achieve a speedy and satisfactory settlement to their regrading claim. On the evidence before me I would regard the contrary as being unarguable ...'

COMMENT

(1)   Although *Barretts & Baird* v *IPCS* concerns the tort of interference with trade or business by unlawful means rather than inducing breach of contract, it is likely that the requirements in terms of intention and knowledge are the same (cf *Merkur Island Shipping*).

(2)   These two cases give opposing views. County court decisions are rarely reported and are not regarded as establishing binding precedents. However, the decision of a single High Court judge is not binding on other High Court judges either. Thus it would be correct to say that this important issue awaits further clarification.

(3)   It was to deal with situations similar to *Falconer* v *ASLEF* that TULRCA s 235A was introduced, giving individuals a right to restrain either unlawful industrial action or action organised by a union without a valid ballot, where the action disrupts the supply of goods or services to him or her. This statutory right does not depend on the individual being able to show that she or he would have a right to sue at common law. See G S Morris, 'Industrial action: public and private interests', (1993) 22 ILJ 194. Note also the role of the Commissioner for Protection Against Unlawful Industrial Action (see, p 11). This official would now have power to assist in cases like these.

(4)   There is some evidence to suggest that there is a defence of justification for this tort (*Brimelow* v *Casson*). However, objecting to a cut in wages apparently would not constitute such justification (*South Wales Miners' Federation* v *Glamorgan Coal Company*).

(5)   Where the tort of inducement of breach of contract is committed by people acting in contemplation or furtherance of a trade dispute, they will qualify for immunity at Stage 2 by virtue of TULRCA s 219(1)(a).

Interference with contract

The conditions laid down by Jenkins L J in *Thomson* v *Deakin* required that an actual breach of contract should have been induced as a result of the defendants' actions. The requirement was soon relaxed.

Torquay Hotel Co Ltd v Cousins

[1969] 2 Ch 106 Court of Appeal

The Transport and General Workers' Union was attempting to organise hotel workers in Torquay and to get recognition from hotels. In the course of the resulting dispute, the manager of the Imperial Hotel was reported in the press as having made some remarks which inflamed the situation. The union decided to spread the strike to the Imperial Hotel and telephoned Esso Petroleum, who supplied the hotel with oil, to inform them that the hotel was blacked.

Esso had a contract to supply the hotel with all the fuel oil it required: however, the contract contained a *force majeure* clause.

Lord Denning MR: '... The Imperial Hotel had a contract with Esso under which the Imperial Hotel agreed to buy their total requirements of fuel-oil from Esso for one year, the quantity being estimated at 120,000 gallons, to be delivered by road tank wagon at a minimum of 3,000 gallons a time. Under that contract there was a *course of dealing* by which the Imperial Hotel used to order 3,000 gallons every week or 10 days, and Esso used to deliver it the next day. But there was a *force majeure* or *exception* clause which said that

"neither party shall be liable for any failure to fulfil any term of this agreement if fulfilment is delayed, hindered or prevented by any circumstance whatever which is not within their immediate control, including ... labour disputes."

It is plain that, if delivery was hindered or prevented by labour disputes, as, for instance, because their drivers would not cross the picket line, Esso could rely on that exception clause as a defence to any claim by Imperial. They would not be liable in damages. And I am prepared to assume that Esso would not be guilty of a breach of contract. But I do not think that would exempt the trade union officials from liability if they unlawfully hindered or prevented Esso from making deliveries. The principle of *Lumley* v *Gye* extends not only to inducing breach of contract, but also to preventing the performance of it. That can be shown by a simple illustration taken from the books. In *Lumley* v *Gye*, Miss Wagner, an actress, was engaged by Mr Lumley to sing at Her Majesty's Theatre. Mr Gye, who ran Covent Garden, procured her to break her contract with Mr Lumley by promising to pay her more: see *Lumley* v *Wagner*. He was held liable to Mr Lumley for inducing a breach of contract. In *Poussard* v *Spiers & Pond* Madam Poussard was under contract with Spiers to sing in an opera at the Criterion Theatre. She fell sick and was unable to attend rehearsals. Her non-performance, being occasioned by sickness, was not a breach of contract on her part: but it was held to excuse the theatre company from continuing to employ her. Suppose now that an ill-disposed person, knowing of her contract, had given her a potion to make her sick. She would not be guilty of a breach herself. But undoubtedly the person who administered the potion would have done wrong and be liable for the damage suffered by them. So here I think the trade union officials cannot take advantage of the force majeure or exception clause in the Esso contract. If they unlawfully prevented or hindered Esso from making deliveries, as ordered by Imperial, they would be liable in damage to Imperial, notwithstanding the exception clause ...

The interference is not confined to the procurement of a *breach* of contract. It extends to a case where a third person *prevents* or *hinders* one party from performing his contract, even though it be not a breach ...'

COMMENT

(1)   Russell and Winn L J J delivered judgments reaching the same result, but they were of the view that the *force majeure* clause excused liability for breach, rather than stopped a breach occurring. In other words, from their point of view, the full tort of

inducement of breach of contract was made out. However, since 1969 it has become clear that interference with performance of the contract is enough.

(2)   This is an important staging post on the way to the development of the so-called 'super-tort' – interference with trade or business by unlawful means (see below).

(3)   Where the tort of interference with contract is committed by people acting in contemplation or furtherance of a trade dispute, they will qualify for immunity at Stage 2 by virtue of TULRCA s 219(1)(a).

Intimidation
Rookes v *Barnard*

[1964] AC 1129   House of Lords

Rookes was employed by BOAC as a draughtsman and belonged to the Association of Engineering and Shipbuilding Draughtsmen (AESD). The union maintained a closed shop at BOAC, but Rookes became dissatisfied with the union and left. The union then put pressure on BOAC to dismiss him. Threatened with strike action by the union, BOAC gave Rookes due notice to terminate his contract of employment.

Lord Reid: '... This case, therefore, raises the question whether it is a tort to conspire to threaten an employer that his men will break their contracts with him unless he dismisses the plaintiff, with the result that he is thereby induced to dismiss the plaintiff and cause him loss. The magnitude of the sum awarded by the jury shows that the appellant had every prospect of retaining his employment with BOAC if the respondents and the other conspirators had not interfered: leaving the Trade Disputes Act, 1906, out of account, if BOAC had been induced to dismiss the appellant in breach of their contract with him then there is no doubt that the respondents would have committed a tort and would have been liable in damages (*Lumley* v *Gye*). Equally, there is no doubt that men are entitled to threaten to strike if that involves no breach of their contracts with their employer, and they are not trying to induce their employer to break any contract with the plaintiff. The question in this case is whether it was unlawful for them to use a threat to break their contracts with their employer as a weapon to make him do something which he was legally entitled to do but which they knew would cause loss to the plaintiff.
    The first contention of the respondents is very far reaching. They say there is no such tort as intimidation. That would mean that, short of committing a crime, an individual could with impunity virtually compel a third person to do something damaging to the plaintiff which he does not want to do but can lawfully do: the wrongdoer could use every kind of threat to commit violence, libel or any other tort, and the plaintiff would have no remedy. And a combination of individuals could do the same, at least if they acted solely to promote their own interests. It is true that there is no decision of this House which negatives that argument. But there are many speeches in this House and judgments of eminent judges where it is assumed that that is not the law and I have found none where there is any real support for this argument. Most of the relevant authorities have been collected by Pearson LJ and I see no need to add to them. It has often been stated that if people combine to do acts which they know will cause loss to the plaintiff, he can sue if either the object of their conspiracy is unlawful or they use unlawful means to achieve it. In my judgment, to cause such loss by threat to commit a tort against a third person if he does not comply with their demands is to use unlawful means to achieve their object.

That brings me to the second argument for the respondents, which raises a more difficult question. They say that there is a distinction between threats to commit a tort and threats to break a contract. They point out that a person is quite entitled to threaten to do something which he has a legal right to do and they say that breach of contract is a private matter between the contracting parties. If the plaintiff cannot sue for loss to him which results from an actual breach of a contract to which he is not a party, why, they ask, should he be entitled to sue for loss which results from a threat to break a contract to which he is not a party?

A somewhat similar argument failed in *Lumley* v *Gye*. The defendant had induced a singer to break her contract with the plaintiff and he knew that this would cause loss to the plaintiff. The plaintiff had his action against the singer for breach of contract and he was held also to have a cause of action against the defendant for the tort of unjustifiably interfering so as to cause him loss. The fact that the direct cause of the loss was a breach of a contract to which the defendant was not a party did not matter. So, too, the plaintiff's action in the present case does not sound in contract: in fact there was no breach of contract because BOAC gave in.

The appellant in this case could not take a benefit from contracts to which he was not a party or from any breach of them. But his ground of action is quite different. The respondents here used a weapon in a way which they knew would cause him loss, and the question is whether they were entitled to use that weapon – a threat that they would cause loss to BOAC if BOAC did not do as they wished. That threat was to cause loss to BOAC by doing something which they had no right to do, breaking their contracts with BOAC. I can see no difference in principle between a threat to break a contract and a threat to commit a tort. If a third party could not sue for damage caused to him by the former I can see no reason why he should be entitled to sue for damage caused to him by the latter. A person is no more entitled to sue in respect of loss which he suffers by reason of a tort committed against someone else than he is entitled to sue in respect of loss which he suffers by reason of breach of a contract to which he is not a party. What he sues for in each case is loss caused to him by the use of an unlawful weapon against him – intimidation of another person by unlawful means. So long as the defendant only threatens to do what he has a legal right to do he is on safe ground. At least if there is no conspiracy he would not be liable to anyone for doing the act, whatever his motive might be, and it would be absurd to make him liable for threatening to do it but not for doing it. But I agree with Lord Herschell (*Allen* v *Flood*) that there is a chasm between doing what you have a legal right to do and doing what you have no legal right to do, and there seems to me to be the same chasm between threatening to do what you have a legal right to do and threatening to do what you have no legal right to do. It must follow from *Allen* v *Flood* that to intimidate by threatening to do what you have a legal right to do is to intimidate by lawful means. But I see no good reason for extending that doctrine. Threatening a breach of contract may be a much more coercive weapon than threatening a tort, particularly when the threat is directed against a company or corporation, and, if there is no technical reason requiring a distinction between different kinds of threats, I can see no other ground for making any such distinction.

I have not set out any of the passages cited in argument because the precise point which we have to decide did not arise in any of the cases in which they occur, and it does not appear that any of the authors of these passages had this point in mind. Sometimes the language seems to point one way and sometimes another and it would. I think, be wrong in such circumstances to use a judge's language as authority for a proposition which he did not have in mind. The Court of Appeal in this case were unwilling to go beyond existing authorities. Sellers LJ said: "Unless authority requires it, I would resist enlarging the tort of intimidation in the manner sought before and accepted by the judge," and Pearson LJ said: "Should this obscure, unfamiliar and peculiar cause of action, which has its roots in cases of physical violence and threats of violence, be extended to cover a case in which there is only a threat to break a contract?" I am afraid I take a different view. Intimidation of any kind appears to me to be highly objectionable. The law was not slow to prevent it when violence and threats of violence were the most effective means. Now that subtler means are at least equally effective I see no reason why the law should have to turn a blind eye to them. We have to tolerate intimidation by means which have been held to be lawful but these I would stop. Accordingly, I would hold that on the facts found by the jury the respondents' actions in this case were tortious ...'

(Lords Evershed, Devlin, Hodson and Pearce delivered concurring opinions.)

COMMENT

(1)   This is a bit like the situation in *Thomson* v *Deakin* except that there was no breach of the contract between the party in the position of Thomson's (Rookes) and the party in the position of Bowaters (BOAC). However, for the tort of intimidation, the fact that the third party's action causing detriment to the plaintiff is lawful does not prevent the tort being committed if the means used to *coerce* the third party to behave in this way are unlawful. It is possible to see why this was seen as a significant extension of liability.

(2)   Despite the union's argument, the tort of intimidation had been considered to exist before this case, but had been invoked only where there were threats of violence (see *Tarleton* v *M'Gawley*, for example). To say that a threat of a breach of contract was enough was the turning point which suddenly made the tort relevant to trade disputes.

(3)   The real sting from this case was that whereas there was an immunity for inducing breach of contract, there was no immunity for intimidation. To trade unions, this looked like the courts outflanking their immunity from action through 'discovering' new causes of action which could be applicable. The result was that in the following year, immunity was extended to this tort by the Trade Disputes Act 1965. Today, where the people involved are acting in contemplation or furtherance of a trade dispute, there is immunity at Stage 2 by virtue of TULRCA s 219(1)(b).

(4)   Again, this extension of liability helped pave the way for the 'super-tort', to be considered next.

Interference with trade or business by unlawful means
Merkur Island Shipping Corporation v Laughton

[1983] ICR 490 House of Lords

The facts of the case are given on p 502.

Lord Diplock: '... The shipowners' writ includes claims in tort for damages under two alternative heads:

(1)   Damages for deliberate interference with and/or threat to the performance of a time charter dated February 12, 1982, between the plaintiffs and Leif Hoegh and Co. Aktiesel-

skab, such interference and/or threat being brought about by unlawful means, namely wrongfully procuring and/or inducing and/or threatening to procure or induce lock-keepers and/or tugmen and/or pilots and/or boatmen and/or linesmen and/or others concerned with the free passage and operation of vessels at Liverpool to refuse to assist the free passage or working of the *Hoegh Apapa* at Liverpool.

(2)   Damages for deliberate interference with and/or threat to the trade and business of the plaintiffs, such interference and/or threat being brought about by unlawful means namely wrongfully procuring and/or inducing and/or threatening to procure or induce lock-keepers and/or tugmen and/or pilots and/or boatmen and/or linesmen and/or others concerned with the free passage and operation of vessels at Liverpool to refuse to assist the free passage or working of the *Hoegh Apapa* at Liverpool.

It was under the first head that Parker J held that on the evidence before him the ship-owners had shown a cause of action at common law in respect of which it was unlikely the ITF would succeed in establishing an immunity from liability under the Act of 1974 as modified by the Act of 1980.

Before the Act of 1980 came into force the question whether "blacking" was lawful in any particular case involved a two-stage approach. Stage 1 was to determine whether the plaintiff had established that what was done in the course of the "blacking" would, if the Act of 1974 had not been passed, have given him a cause of action in tort. If so, stage 2 was to determine whether that cause of action was removed as against individual defendants by section 13 of the Act of 1974. To that two-stage process the Act of 1980 added one further stage, stage 3. This was to determine whether that cause of action which had been removed by the Act of 1974 was restored by section 17 of the Act of 1980 ...

The common law tort relied upon by the shipowners under head (1) of the writ is the tort of interfering by unlawful means with the performance of a contract. The contract of which the performance was interfered with was the charter, the form the interference took was by immobilising the ship in Liverpool to prevent the captain from performing the contractual obligation of the shipowners under clause 8 of the charter to "prosecute his voyages with the utmost dispatch". The unlawful means by which the interference was effected was by procuring the tugmen and the lockmen to break their contracts of employment by refusing to carry out the operations on the part of the tugowners and the port authorities that were necessary to enable the ship to leave the dock....

DC Thomson & Co Ltd v *Deakin* was a case in which the only interference with contractual rights relied upon was procuring a *breach* by a third party of a contract between that third party and the plaintiff. That is why in the passage that I have picked out for citation Jenkins LJ restricts himself to that form of actionable interference with contractual rights which consists of procuring an actual breach of the contract that formed the subject matter of interference, but it is evident from the passages in his judgment which precede the passage I have cited and are themselves set out in the judgment of O'Connor LJ, that Jenkins LJ though using the expression "breach", was not intending to confine the tort of actionable interference with contractual rights to the procuring of such non-performance of primary obligations under a contract as would necessarily give rise to secondary obligations to make monetary compensation by way of damages. All prevention of due performance of a primary obligation under a contract was intended to be included even though no secondary obligation to make monetary compensation thereupon came into existence, because the second obligation was excluded by some force majeure clause.

If there were any doubt about this matter, it was resolved in 1969 by the judgments of the Court of Appeal in *Torquay Hotel Co Ltd* v *Cousins*. That was a case in which the contract the performance of which was interfered with was one for the delivery of fuel. It contained a force majeure clause excusing the seller from liability for non-delivery if delayed, hindered or prevented by (inter alia) labour disputes. Lord Denning MR stated the principle thus,

> "...there must be *interference* in the execution of a contract. The interference is not confined to the procurement of a *breach* of contract. It extends to a case where a third person *prevents* or *hinders* one party from performing his contract, even though it be not a breach...." (The emphasis is that of Lord Denning.)

Parliamentary recognition that the tort of actionable interference with contractual rights is as broad as Lord Denning MR stated in the passage I have just quoted is, in my view, to be found in section 13(1) of the Act of 1974 itself which refers to inducement not only "to break a contract", but also "to interfere with its performance", and treats them as being pari materia.

On the stage 1 point I accordingly agree with the Court of Appeal that the shipowners, upon the evidence that was before Parker J, have made out a strong prima facie case that ITF committed the common law tort of actionable interference with contractual rights....'

COMMENT

(1)   There is a strong suggestion that the elements of the tort in relation to knowledge, intention, etc, are as laid down by Jenkins L J in *Thomson* v *Deakin*. Lord Diplock suggests that the tort of interference with trade or business by unlawful means may be regarded as a genus, or general species, of tort, of which torts such as inducement of breach of contract or intimidation are sub-species. This obscures the fact that the development of the tort has been inductive (working from the particular to the general) rather than deductive.

(2)   The last passage from the judgment refers to the immunity contained in TULRA 1974 s 13. This was the source of the basic immunity until the consolidation in TULRCA. It is now in TULRCA s 219, but not in the same form as referred to here, which is why the original references have been left. Most importantly, s 13(2), which gave immunity from interference with trade or business (for the avoidance of doubt, since it was not clear in 1974 whether such a tort would be recognised by the courts), was repealed in 1982, albeit after the events giving rise to this case.

(3)   The tort may now be regarded as established; however, there is doubt as to its ambit, in particular in relation to the meaning of 'unlawful means': see *Lonrho Ltd* v *Shell Petroleum (No 2)* and *Lonrho* v *Fayed*.

Conspiracy

Since unions are combinations of people, and since the organisation of industrial action will inevitably involve a number of people working together, it is not surprising to find charges of conspiracy, which depend on concerted action, being used against them. Indeed, at the beginning of the nineteenth century, trade unions were treated as criminal conspiracies. Criminal liability for conspiracy was effectively removed by the Trade Union Act 1871, but there remained the *tort* of conspiracy, which was used instead. There are two forms of the tort of conspiracy: conspiracy to injure, and conspiracy to use unlawful means.

Conspiracy to injure

This tort consists of two or more people acting together with the intention of harming the plaintiff. It is actionable even if no unlawful means are used.

Lonrho Ltd v Shell Petroleum (No 2)

[1982] AC 173 House of Lords

Following the illegal unilateral declaration of independence (UDI) by the Smith regime in Rhodesia in 1965, oil shipments to Rhodesia were banned by statutory regulation, breach of which was a criminal offence. Lonrho alleged that Shell and BP had continued to supply oil to Rhodesia, thus prolonging the existence of the illegal government and damaging the business of Lonrho. Lonrho had had extensive business interests in Rhodesia, including oil supply, which had been suspended during the period while sanctions had been imposed.

Lonrho's claim was based either on what Lord Diplock described as 'an innominate tort … of causing foreseeable loss by an unlawful act' or alternatively, on conspiracy.

Lord Diplock: '… Question 5(b), to which I now turn, concerns conspiracy as a civil tort. Your Lordships are invited to answer it on the assumption that the purpose of Shell and BP in entering into the agreement to do the various things that it must be assumed they did in contravention of the sanctions Order, was to forward their own commercial interests; *not* to injure those of Lonrho. So the question of law to be determined is whether an intent by the defendants to injure the plaintiff is an essential element in the civil wrong of conspiracy, even where the acts agreed to be done by the conspirators amount to criminal offences under a penal statute. It is conceded that there is no direct authority either way upon this question to be found in the decided cases; so if this House were to answer it in the affirmative, your Lordships would be making new law.

My Lords, conspiracy as a criminal offence has a long history. It consists of " the agreement of two or more persons to effect any unlawful purpose, whether as their ultimate aim, or only as a means to it, and the crime is complete if there is such agreement, even though nothing is done in pursuance of it". I cite from Viscount Simon LC's now classic speech in *Crofter Hand Woven Harris Tweed Co Ltd v Veitch*.

Regarded as a civil tort, however, conspiracy is a highly anomalous cause of action. The gist of the cause of action is damage to the plaintiff; so long as it remains unexecuted the agreement, which alone constitutes the crime of conspiracy, causes no damage; it is only acts done in execution of the agreement that are capable of doing that. So the tort, unlike the crime, consists not of agreement but of concerted action taken pursuant to agreement.

As I recall from my early years in the law first as a student and then as a young barrister, during its chequered history between Lord Coleridge CJ's judgment at first instance in *Mogul Steamship Co Ltd v McGregor, Gow & Co* and the *Crofter* case, the civil tort of conspiracy attracted more controversy among academic writers than success in practical application. Why should an act which causes economic loss to A but is not actionable at his suit if done by B alone become actionable because B did it pursuant to an agreement between B and C? An explanation given at the close of the 19th century by Bowen LJ in the *Mogul* case when it was before the Court of Appeal was:

"The distinction is based on sound reason, for a combination may make oppressive or dangerous that which if it proceeded only from a single person would be otherwise."

But to suggest today that acts done by one street-corner grocer in concert with a second are more oppressive and dangerous to a competitor than the same acts done by a string of supermarkets under a single ownership or that a multinational conglomerate such as Lonrho or oil company such as Shell or BP does not exercise greater economic power than any combination of small businesses, is to shut one's eyes to what has been happening in the business and industrial world since the turn of the century and, in particular, since the end of World War II. The civil tort of conspiracy to injure the plaintiff's commercial interests where that is the predominant purpose of the agreement between the defendants and of the acts done in execution of it which caused damage to the plaintiff, must I think be accepted by this House as too well-established to be discarded however anomalous it may seem today. It was applied by this House 80 years ago in *Quinn* v *Leathem* and accepted as good law in the *Crofter* case where it was made clear that injury to the plaintiff and not the self-interest of the defendants must be the predominant purpose of the agreement in execution of which the damage-causing acts were done.

My Lords, in none of the judgments in decided cases in civil actions for damages for conspiracy does it appear that the mind of the author of the judgment was directed to a case where the damage-causing acts although neither done for the purpose of injuring the plaintiff nor actionable at his suit if they had been done by one person alone, were nevertheless a contravention of some penal law. I will not recite the statements in those judgments to which your Lordships have been referred by the appellants as amounting to dicta in favour of the view that a civil action for conspiracy does lie in such a case. Even if the authors' minds had been directed to the point, which they were not, I should still find them indecisive. This House, in my view, has an unfettered choice whether to confine the civil action of conspiracy to the narrow field to which alone it has an established claim or whether to extend this already anomalous tort beyond those narrow limits that are all that common sense and the application of the legal logic of the decided cases require.

My Lords, my choice is unhesitatingly the same as that of Parker J and all three members of the Court of Appeal. I am against extending the scope of civil tort of conspiracy beyond acts done in execution of an agreement entered into by two or more persons for the purpose not of protecting their own interests but of injuring the interests of the plaintiff. So I would answer Question 5(b): "No." ...'

(Lords Edmund-Davies, Keith, Scarman and Bridge agreed with Lord Diplock.)

Crofter Hand Woven Harris Tweed Co Ltd v *Veitch*

[1942] AC 435 House of Lords

Only tweed woven on the Island of Lewis could be described as Harris Tweed. Crofters on the island, most of whom belonged to the TGWU, spun the yarn and wove the tweed, but found that their prices and jobs were threatened by the activities of companies such as the appellants, who brought in yarn spun on the mainland, and sent the cloth there for finishing. The respondents, officials of the union, called on their members who were dockers to place an embargo on the import of yarn and the export of cloth. The appellants sought an order to stop the embargo.

Viscount Simon LC: '... However the origin of the rule may be explained, I take it to be clear that there are cases in which a combination of individuals to act in a certain way, resulting in deliberate damage to others, is actionable, even though the same thing, if done by a single individual without any element of combination, would not expose him to liability. In the present case, the evidence did not support an allegation that the defendants, or either of them, had procured a breach of contract, and if one of them, acting alone, had without employing unlawful means induced the dockers to refuse to handle the appellants' goods, I cannot see that any action would have lain against him. Everything turns, therefore, on whether the two respondents were engaged in a combination "to injure", in the sense in which that phrase is employed when liability results; it is to this question that I now address myself... .

The question to be answered, in determining whether a combination to do an act which damages others is actionable, even though it would not be actionable if done by a single person, is not "did the combiners appreciate, or should they be treated as appreciating, that others would suffer from their action", but "what is the real reason why the combiners did it?" Or, as Lord Cave puts it, "what is the real purpose of the combination?" The test is not what is the natural result to the plaintiffs of such combined action, or what is the resulting damage which the defendants realise or should realise will follow, but what is in truth the object in the minds of the combiners when they acted as they did. It is not consequence that matters, but purpose; the relevant conjunction is not ὥστε, "so that ... " but ἵνα "in order that".

Next, it is to be borne in mind that there may be cases where the combination has more than one "object" or "purpose". The combiners may feel that they are killing two birds with one stone, and, even though their main purpose may be to protect their own legitimate interests notwithstanding that this involves damage to the plaintiffs, they may also find a further inducement to do what they are doing by feeling that it serves the plaintiffs right. The analysis of human impulses soon leads us into the quagmire of mixed motives, and even if we avoid the word "motive", there may be more than a single "purpose" or "object". It is enough to say that if there is more than one purpose actuating a combination, liability must depend on ascertaining the predominant purpose. If that predominant purpose is to damage another person and damage results, that is tortious conspiracy. If the predominant purpose is the lawful protection or promotion of any lawful interest of the combiners (no illegal means being employed), it is not a tortious conspiracy, even though it causes damage to another person ...

I am content to say that, unless the real and predominant purpose is to advance the defendants' lawful interests in a matter where the defendants honestly believe that those interests would directly suffer if the action taken against the plaintiffs was not taken, a combination wilfully to damage a man in his trade is unlawful. Although most of the cases have dealt with trade rivalry in some form or other, I do not see why the proposition as to the conditions under which conspiracy becomes a tort should be limited to trade competition. Indeed, in its original sense, conspiracy as a tort was a combination to abuse legal procedure: see Winfield's *History of Conspiracy*, c. ii. I have used the word "directly" without seeking to define its boundaries as an indication that indirect gains, such as the subscription in the illustration above, would not provide a justification.

In the present case, the conclusion, in my opinion, is that the predominant object of the respondents in getting the embargo imposed was to benefit their trade-union members by preventing under-cutting and unregulated competition, and so helping to secure the economic stability of the island industry. The result they aimed at achieving was to create a better basis for collective bargaining, and thus directly to improve wage prospects. A combination with such an object is not unlawful, because the object is the legitimate promotion of the interests of the combiners, and because the damage necessarily inflicted on the appellants is not inflicted by criminal or tortious means and is not "the real purpose" of the combination. I agree with Lord Fleming when he says in his judgment that it is not for a court of law to consider in this connection the expediency or otherwise of a policy adopted by a trade union. Neither can liability be determined by asking whether the damage inflicted to secure the purpose is disproportionately severe: this may throw doubts on the bona fides of the avowed purpose, but once the legitimate purpose is established, and no unlawful means are involved, the quantum of damage is irrelevant. I move that this appeal be dismissed with costs.'

(Viscount Maugham and Lords Thankterton, Wright and Porter delivered concurring judgments.)

COMMENT

(1)   The predominant purpose doctrine as here interpreted has meant that in most trade disputes, there will be no liability for conspiracy to injure. The defendants' motive will usually be predominantly one of more or less ruthless pursuit of their own self-interest, which does not attract liability if only lawful means are used.

(2)   In any case, where the action is carried out by people acting in contemplation or furtherance of a trade dispute, it will attract the basic immunity under TULRCA s 219(2).

Conspiracy to use unlawful means

This tort is committed when two or more people combine to injure the plaintiff and use unlawful means to achieve their purpose.

Lonrho plc v Fayed

[1991] 3 All ER 303 House of Lords

Lonrho's attempt to take over the House of Fraser was referred by the Secretary of State to the Monopolies Commission. Lonrho gave an undertaking not to acquire more shares in the company before the Commission reported. While Lonrho was still bound by that undertaking, the Fayed brothers successfully bid for and bought the House of Fraser. Their bid was not referred to the Monopolies Commission. Lonrho sued the Fayeds, alleging that they had made fraudulent misrepresentations to the Secretary of State.

Lord Bridge: '... As against all the defendants, Lonrho's statement of claim pleads that their intention was both to benefit the Fayeds and Holdings by furthering their interest in the acquisition of HoF and to injure Lonrho by preventing them from acquiring HoF. Lonrho claims to have lost the opportunity to acquire HoF by bidding for the shares without competition from the Fayeds or Holdings and thereby to have suffered damage. Lonrho asserts that these facts are sufficient to establish a cause of action for the common law tort of interfering with business by unlawful means. But the statement of claim also relied additionally or alternatively on the same allegations of fact as establishing the tort of conspiracy to injure ...

Where conspirators act with the predominant purpose of injuring the plaintiff and in fact inflict damage on him, but do nothing which would have been actionable if done by an individual acting alone, it is in the fact of their concerted action for that illegitimate purpose that the law, however anomalous it may now seem, finds a sufficient ground to condemn their action as illegal and tortious. But when conspirators intentionally injure the plaintiff and use unlawful means to do so, it is no defence for them to show that their primary purpose was to further or protect their own interests; it is sufficient to make their action tortious that the means used were unlawful.

Did the House in *Lonrho Ltd* v *Shell Petroleum Co Ltd* depart from this reasoning and lay down for the first time a new principle that a plaintiff, seeking to establish the tort of conspiracy to injure, must in every case prove that the intention to injure him was the predominant purpose of the defendants, whether the means used were lawful or unlawful? ...

My Lords, I am quite unable to accept that Lord Diplock or the other members of the Appellate Committee concurring with him, of whom I was one, intended the decision in *Lonrho Ltd* v *Shell Petroleum Co Ltd* to effect, sub silentio, such a significant change in the law as it had been previously understood. The House, as is clear from the parties' printed cases, which we have been shown, had never been invited to take such a step. Moreover, to do so would have been directly contrary to the view of Lord Denning MR expressed in the judgment which the House was affirming and inconsistent with the dicta in what Lord Diplock described as "Viscount Simon LC's now classic speech in *Crofter Hand Woven Harris Tweed Co Ltd* v *Veitch*". I would overrule the *Metall* case in this respect.

It follows from this conclusion that Lonrho's acceptance that the pleaded intention on the part of the defendants to cause injury to Lonrho was not the predominant purpose of their alleged unlawful action is not necessarily fatal to the pleaded cause of action in conspiracy and therefore affords no separate ground for striking out that part of the pleading. If the defendants fail to establish that Lonrho's primary pleading asserting the tort of interference with business by unlawful means should be struck out, they are in no stronger position in relation to the pleaded cause of action in conspiracy. It is not, I think, necessary for present purposes to consider whether the pleaded conspiracy adds anything of substance or raises any significantly different issues from those on which the rest of the pleading depends. At this interlocutory stage it is sufficient to say that the two pleaded causes of action must stand or fall together. Either both should be struck out or both should go to trial.'

(Lords Brandon, Templeman, Goff and Jauncey agreed with Lord Bridge.)

COMMENT

(1)   The decision makes clear the distinction between the two forms of tortious conspiracy. In practice, conspiracy to use unlawful means is not of great significance, since it will either amount to interference with trade or business by unlawful means (in which case it is unnecessary to prove the element of combination) or it will not be actionable.

(2)   There is no specific immunity for this form of the tort, but as with interference with trade or business by unlawful means, if there is immunity for the unlawful means, it will not be possible to sue for conspiracy to use them.

Other torts

If it can be shown that industrial action involves the commission of torts for which there is no immunity, it will be actionable. Hence the search is on to discover different heads of liability.

Meade v Haringey Council

[1979] ICR 494 Court of Appeal

Lord Denning MR: 'On Monday, January 22, 1979, the caretakers at the schools in Haringey came out on strike. There were very few of them. Only one or two for a school of 500 or 600 children. Their duties were simple enough. To look after the buildings and the heating system. To unblock drains. To lock up at night and open up in the morning. And so forth. Yet by coming out on strike they succeeded in paralysing the educational system of the great London Borough of Haringey. The borough council closed over 100 schools for weeks on end. 37,000 children were deprived of the teaching they should have had. They were put back in their examinations and their careers. Some ran loose in the streets while their mothers were out working.

The parents of the children were much upset by all this. They went to their lawyers to see if there was any way to get the schools reopened. The lawyers looked up the statute and found that it was the duty of the borough council under section 8(1) of the Education Act 1944 "to secure that there shall be available for their area sufficient schools ... for providing ... full-time education" suitable to the requirements of the pupils. ...

Now comes the great question in this case: had the borough council any just cause or excuse for closing the schools as they did? On the evidence as it stands, the borough council were acting under the influence of the trade unions and indeed in combination with them. And the trade unions and their secretaries were, as I see it, acting quite unlawfully. They were calling upon the local authority to break their statutory duty – to close the schools instead of keeping them open as they should have done. Now [TULRCA s 219] gives them immunity if they induce a person to break a contract. But it gives them no immunity if they induce a local authority to break its statutory duty ...

On the evidence as it stands before us, it appears that the trade unions were the dominating influence in requiring the schools to be closed – and not re-opened: and the borough council closed them at the behest of the trade unions or in agreement with them. In so doing the borough council were breaking their statutory duty: and the trade unions' leaders were inducing them to break it. Such conduct was in my view unlawful: and the trade unions' leaders have no immunity in respect of it.

(Eveleigh LJ and Sir Stanley Rees delivered concurring judgments.)

COMMENT

(1)   Very many employments in the public sector are regulated to some extent by statute, which may give some scope for further exploitation of this tort. However, see *Associated British Ports* v *TGWU*, where the House of Lords was not prepared to accept easily that workers in breach of contract were also in breach of a statutory duty.

Prudential Assurance Co Ltd v Lorenz

[1971] 11 KIR 78 Chancery Division

In furtherance of a trade dispute, the union representing insurance agents working for the plaintiff company called on them not to submit accounts to the company.

Plowman J: '... Now, Mr Pain on behalf of the plaintiffs puts the plaintiffs' case in three ways. First of all he submits that the circular is an incitement to members to commit a breach of a duty to account which is implied by the general law independently of the agents' service agreement, with the consequence that notwithstanding the existence of a trade dispute in this case, the Trade Disputes Act, 1906, section 3 [now TULRCA s 219] affords no protection, and as authority for this proposition Mr Pain cited an unreported decision of Pennycuick's of May 13, 1969 in a case called the *Co-operative Insurance Society Limited* v *Quinlan and Others*. ...

With regard to Mr Pain's first submission Mr Oliver submitted that the circular went no further than to suggest an interference with the contractual obligation of the plaintiffs' agents to account, and he cited authority to show what an agent's liability to account, apart from express contract, is. However, as I understood it, he was constrained to admit that if he was right, the two *Co-operative Insurance Society* cases to which I have already referred must be wrong. But he pertinently pointed out that the authorities on which he relied, *Turner* v *Burkinshaw* and *The Earl of Hardwicke* v *Vernon* were not cited in the *Co-operative Insurance Society* cases. Well, it is certainly possible that Mr Oliver may be right in his submission and in due course the Court of Appeal may say so, but in this court I think that Mr Pain is entitled to rely on those two cases, at the very least to the extent of saying that they establish a sufficient *prima facie* case in his favour for the purposes of an interlocutory injunction …'

COMMENT

(1)   While inducing a breach of an equitable obligation to account is here regarded as tortious, it must be remembered that in interlocutory proceedings points are not fully argued. It seems that this probably does not apply in relation to all breaches of equitable obligation: in *Metall und Rohstoff AG* v *Donaldson, Lufkin & Jenrette Inc*, the Court of Appeal held that there was no such tort as inducing a breach of trust. (It was a different point in that case which was overruled by the House of Lords in *Lonrho* v *Fayed*).

Universe Tankships Inc of Monrovia v International Transport Workers' Federation

[1982] ICR 262 House of Lords

The case arose out of the long-running campaign by the ITF against ships which fly flags of convenience – that is, are registered in countries which do not require that they observe internationally agreed standards, in particular in relation to the terms and conditions of their crews.

The *Universe Sentinel* was blacked by the union on its arrival at Milford Haven and was thus unable to leave port. In order to get the blacking order lifted, the owners agreed to pay $6,480 to the union's welfare fund. Subsequently the owners tried to reclaim the money.

Lord Diplock: '… My Lords, I turn to the second ground on which repayment of the $6,480 is claimed, which I will call the duress point. It is not disputed that the circumstances in which ITF demanded that the shipowners should enter into the special agreement and the typescript agreement and should pay the moneys of which the latter documents acknowledge receipt, amounted to economic duress upon the shipowners; that is to say, it is conceded that the financial consequences to the shipowners of the *Universe Sentinel* continuing to be rendered off-hire under her time charter to Texaco, while the blacking continued, were so catastrophic as to amount to a coercion of the shipowners' will which vitiated their consent to those agreements and to the payments made by them to ITF. This concession makes it unnecessary for your Lordships to use the instant appeal as the occasion for a general consideration of the developing law of economic duress as a ground for treating contracts as voidable and obtaining restitution of money paid under economic duress as money had and received to the plaintiffs' use….

Commercial pressure, in some degree, exists wherever one party to a commercial transaction is in a stronger bargaining position than the other party. It is not, however, in my view, necessary, nor would it be appropriate in the instant appeal, to enter into the general question of the kinds of circumstances, if any, in which commercial pressure, even though it amounts to a coercion of the will of a party in the weaker bargaining position, may be treated as legitimate and, accordingly, as not giving rise to any legal right of redress. In the instant appeal the economic duress complained of was exercised in the field of industrial relations to which very special considerations apply.

My Lords, so far as is relevant to this appeal, the policy of Parliament, ever since the Trade Disputes Act 1906 was passed to overrule a decision of this House, has been to legitimise acts done by employees, or by trade unions acting or purporting to act on their behalf, which would otherwise be unlawful wherever such acts are done in contemplation or furtherance of a dispute which is connected with the terms and conditions of employment of any employees. I can confine myself to the kind of acts and the particular subject matter of the trade dispute that was involved in the instant case, and I use the expression "legitimise" as meaning that the doer of the act is rendered immune from any liability to damages or any other remedy against him in a court of justice, at the suit of a person who has suffered loss or damage in consequence of the act; save only a remedy for breach of contract where the act is done in breach of a direct contract between the doer of the act and the person by whom the damage is sustained... .

The use of economic duress to induce another person to part with property or money is not a tort per se; the form that the duress takes may, or may not, be tortious. The remedy to which economic duress gives rise is not an action for damages but an action for restitution of property or money exacted under such duress and the avoidance of any contract that had been induced by it; but where the particular form taken by the economic duress used is itself a tort, the restitutional remedy for money had and received by the defendant to the plaintiff's use is one which the plaintiff is entitled to pursue as an alternative remedy to an action for damages in tort.

In extending into the field of industrial relations the common law concept of economic duress and the right to a restitutionary remedy for it which is currently in process of development by judicial decisions, this House would not, in my view, be exercising the restraint that is appropriate to such a process if it were so to develop the concept that, by the simple expedient of "waiving the tort," a restitutionary remedy for money had and received is made enforceable in cases in which Parliament has, over so long a period of years, manifested its preference for a public policy that a particular kind of tortious act should be legitimised in the sense that I am using that expression.

It is only in this indirect way that the provisions of the Trade Union and Labour Relations Act 1974 are relevant to the duress point. The immunities from liability in tort provided by sections 13 and 14 are not directly applicable to the shipowners' cause of action for money had and received. Nevertheless, these sections, together with the definition of trade dispute in section 29, afford an indication, which your Lordships should respect, of where public policy requires that the line should be drawn between what kind of commercial pressure by a trade union upon an employer in the field of industrial relations ought to be treated as legitimised despite the fact that the will of the employer is thereby coerced, and what kind of commercial pressure in that field does amount to economic duress that entitles the employer victim to restitutionary remedies ...'

COMMENT

(1)   The House of Lords here recognises an action for economic duress, but only if illegitimate pressure is used. If the pressure takes the form of industrial action which would be immune under TULRCA s 219, no action may be brought.

(2)   Lord Diplock refers to TULRA ss 13, 14 and 29. TULRA s 14 gave trade unions an almost complete immunity from *any* kind of tort action: it was abolished by the Employment Act 1982. Since then trade unions have been on the same footing as individuals. TULRA ss 13 and 29 are now TULRCA ss 219 and 244 respectively.

(3)   In the event, the case turned on whether the pressure used (the blacking of the *Universe Sentinel*) attracted the immunity or not. By a majority, the House of Lords held it did not; thus the shipowners could recover their payment.

(4)   This position was extended by the House of Lords' decision in *Dimskal Shipping* v *ITF*, where the facts were similar but the money was paid in Sweden. The pressure used would have been lawful under Swedish law, although not under British law. Nonetheless, recovery of the money was allowed.

Criminal liability

Incitement to Disaffection Act 1934

1.   If any person maliciously and advisedly endeavours to seduce any member of His Majesty's forces from his duty or allegiance to His Majesty, he shall be guilty of an offence under this Act.

Police Act 1964

53.   (1)   Any person who causes, or attempts to cause, or does any act calculated to cause, disaffection amongst the members of any police force, or induces or attempts to induce, or does any act calculated to induce, any member of a police force to withhold his services or to commit breaches of discipline, shall be guilty of an offence and liable—
      (a)   on summary conviction, to imprisonment for a term not exceeding six months or to a fine not exceeding the prescribed sum, or to both;
      (b)   on conviction on indictment, to imprisonment for a term not exceeding two years or to a fine or to both.
  (2)   This section applies to special constables appointed for a police area as it applies to members of a police force.

Criminal Justice and Public Order Act 1994

127.   (1)   A person contravenes this subsection if he induces a prison officer—
      (a)   to withhold his services as such an officer; or
      (b)   to commit a breach of discipline.
  (2)   The obligation not to contravene subsection (1) above shall be a duty owed to the Secretary of State.
...

Post Office Act 1953

58.   (1)   If any person engaged in the business of the Post Office, contrary to his duty, opens, or procures or suffers to be opened, any postal packet in course of transmission by post, or wilfully detains or delays, or procures or suffers to be detained or delayed, any such postal packet, he shall be guilty of a misde-

meanour and be liable to imprisonment for a term not exceeding two years or to a fine, or to both: ...

COMMENT

(1)   National security is the reason for the restriction on organising industrial action by the police or armed forces and, most recently, prison officers. Prison officers were added to the groups of workers effectively precluded from striking following disputes and industrial action in prisons in the early 1990s. Although included in this section on 'Criminal Liability', it should be noted that the Criminal Justice and Public Order Act 1994 adopts the potentially more effective strategy of creating civil liability by establishing a duty owed to the Secretary of State. Thus, instead of the temporary martyrdom of a union official, a union organising industrial action by prison officers would run the risk of an action for substantial damages.

(2)   Other workers may commit criminal offences if they take the most obvious form of strike action; the Post Office Act provides an example of this, and there are similar offences in relation to telecommunications under the Telecommunications Act 1984 ss 44–46. However, it would be highly unusual to prosecute in such circumstances, and according to *Gouriet* v *UPOW*, private citizens cannot prosecute if the authorities are unwilling to take action.

(3)   The most startling example of criminal liability for industrial action used to be found in the Conspiracy and Protection of Property Act 1875, although it was never used. However, the provisions have been included in TULRCA, and it remains to be seen whether their new guise prompts a greater interest in their use.

Trade Union and Labour Relations (Consolidation) Act 1992

240.   (1)   A person commits an offence who wilfully and maliciously breaks a contract of service or hiring, knowing or having reasonable cause to believe that the probable consequences of his so doing, either alone or in combination with others, will be—
       (a)   to endanger human life or cause serious bodily injury, or
       (b)   to expose valuable property, whether real or personal, to destruction or serious injury.
   (2)   Subsection (1) applies equally whether the offence is committed from malice conceived against the person endangered or injured or, as the case may be, the owner of the property destroyed or injured, or otherwise.
   (3)   A person guilty of an offence under this section is liable on summary conviction to imprisonment for a term not exceeding three months or to a fine not exceeding level 2 on the standard scale or both.
   (4)   This section does not apply to seamen.

COMMENT

(1)   This is obviously potentially very wide. However, it has never been used in strikes by hospital workers, ambulance drivers, fire service workers and so on. Presumably, the reason is the fear of making martyrs of particular individuals.

(2) While s 240 does not apply to seafarers, it should be noted that under the Merchant Shipping Act 1970 s 30, merchant seafarers may not take industrial action while at sea.

(3) Is it right that some groups of workers should risk criminal liability for strike action while others do not? Should the police, prison officers and armed forces be permitted to strike, provided that safeguards, such as emergency cover, are in place?

(4) The last proposal of the Conservative Government on industrial action, contained in its Green Paper, *Industrial Action and Trade Unions*, Cm 3470, published in November 1996, was effectively to remove immunity from industrial action which contravened s 240.

13 Industrial action II

The three-stage approach to whether or not organising industrial action will attract tortious liability involves asking at Stage 1 whether or not the activity would be tortious at common law in the first place. If not, then of course there is no problem (although see the provisions about ballots on p 545). If it is, then the next stage is to ask whether it would come within the basic immunity in TULRCA s 219. As noted in the last chapter, Stage 2 breaks down into two sub-questions: first, does s 219 cover this tort, and second, is the other condition in s 219 met?

IMMUNITY UNDER TULRCA S 219

Trade Union and Labour Relations (Consolidation) Act 1992

219. (1) An act done by a person in contemplation or furtherance of a trade dispute is not actionable in tort on the ground only—
     (a) that it induces another person to break a contract or interferes or induces another person to interfere with its performance, or
     (b) that it consists in his threatening that a contract (whether one to which he is a party or not) will be broken or its performance interfered with, or that he will induce another person to break a contract or interfere with its performance.

    (2) An agreement or combination by two or more persons to do or procure the doing of an act in contemplation or furtherance of a trade dispute is not actionable in tort if the act is one which if done without any such agreement or combination would not be actionable in tort.

    (3) Nothing in subsections (1) and (2) prevents an act done in the course of picketing from being actionable in tort unless it is done in the course of attendance declared lawful by section 220 (peaceful picketing).

    (4) Subsections (1) and (2) have effect subject to sections 222 to 225 (action excluded from protection) and to sections 226 (requirement of ballot before action by trade union) and 234A (requirement of notice to employer of industrial action) and in those sections 'not protected' means excluded from the protection afforded by this section or, where the expression is used with reference to a particular person, excluded from that protection as respects that person.

COMMENT

(1)   As noted in Chapter 12, this means that the torts of inducement of breach of

contract, interference with contract, intimidation and conspiracy to injure receive direct protection.

(2) Interference with trade or business by unlawful means, conspiracy to use unlawful means and economic duress are not directly protected. However, there is an indirect immunity in that if the unlawful means attract immunity, they cannot be relied on as the necessary unlawful means. There is no immunity in respect of other torts.

(3) The other major requirement required by s 219 will here be examined: it is that the action must be 'in contemplation or furtherance of a trade dispute'. This phrase was first used in the Conspiracy and Protection of Property Act 1875. Its meaning, however, has changed over recent years, because of substantial amendment of the definition of trade dispute.

Trade Union and Labour Relations (Consolidation) Act 1992

244. (1) In this Part a 'trade dispute' means a dispute between workers and their employer which relates wholly or mainly to one or more of the following—
    (a) terms and conditions of employment, or the physical conditions in which any workers are required to work;
    (b) engagement or non-engagement, or termination or suspension of employment or the duties of employment, of one or more workers;
    (c) allocation of work or the duties of employment between workers or groups of workers;
    (d) matters of discipline;
    (e) a worker's membership or non-membership of a trade union;
    (f) facilities for officials of trade unions; and
    (g) machinery for negotiation or consultation, and other procedures, relating to any of the above matters, including the recognition by employers or employers' associations of the right of a trade union to represent workers in such negotiation or consultation or in the carrying out of such procedures....

    (3) There is a trade dispute even though it relates to matters occurring outside the United Kingdom, so long as the person or persons whose actions in the United Kingdom are said to be in contemplation or furtherance of a trade dispute relating to matters occurring outside the United Kingdom are likely to be affected in respect of one or more of the matters specified in subsection (1) by the outcome of the dispute....

    (5) In this section—
    'employment' includes any relationship whereby one person personally does work or performs services for another; and
    'worker', in relation to a dispute with an employer, means—
    (a) a person employed by that employer; or
    (b) a person who has ceased to be so employed if his employment was terminated in connection with the dispute or if the termination of his employment was one of the circumstances giving rise to the dispute.

'Workers and their employer'

Until amendment by the Employment Act 1982, a dispute could be between workers and employers generally (that is, the dispute did not have to be with your own employer) or between workers and workers. The limiting effect of the new wording may be seen in the next case.

Dimbleby & Sons Ltd v NUJ

[1984] ICR 386 House of Lords

The plaintiff company (referred to as 'Dimbleby' in the speech of Lord Diplock) published local newspapers ('the Dimbleby newspapers') and employed journalists who were members of the NUJ.

Lord Diplock: '... The Dimbleby newspapers were printed not by Dimbleby itself but by an associated company – an arrangement which your Lordships were informed is common in the case of publishers of provincial newspapers. That associated company, Dimbleby Printers Ltd, had been, and apparently still is, engaged in a trade dispute with a powerful trade union that enforces a "closed shop" in nearly all establishments engaged in the printing trade, the National Graphical Association ("NGA"). As a result of this trade dispute there was a strike by members of the NGA employed by Dimbleby Printers Ltd which stopped the Dimbleby newspapers from appearing after 19 August 1983. In order to resume publication of the Dimbleby newspapers, Dimbleby had to find an alternative printer for its newspapers who did not employ members of the NGA. It found one in TBF, which was an associated company of T Bailey Forman Ltd, the publishers of the *Nottingham Evening Post*, with whom the NUJ has been engaged in a trade dispute which started in 1979 and is still continuing. The two companies have parallel shareholding and are controlled by the same (third) company.

In the first week of October 1983, Dimbleby entered into an oral contract with TBF for the provision by Dimbleby to TBF of copy for the Dimbleby newspapers and the printing of the necessary quantities of those newspapers by TBF. On learning of this the NUJ, who apparently at that stage did not know that TBF was a different company from T Bailey Forman Ltd with which they were in long-standing dispute, instructed the NUJ journalists employed by Dimbleby to refuse to provide copy to Dimbleby for printing by TBF. With this instruction, given on 10 October 1983, the NUJ journalists complied. They refused to provide copy to their employer Dimbleby as their contracts of employment required them to do. As a result of that refusal which they persisted in, they were suspended from their employment and so remain.

My Lords, since this is only an interlocutory appeal and from the evidence given at the trial there may emerge a picture of the facts of the case different from that which is disclosed by the affidavits and documents that were before the judge. I shall confine myself (1) to mentioning the main grounds upon which it was contended by the NUJ that there was a likelihood that their defence, that their acts which were the subject of the suit, were done in contemplation or furtherance of a trade dispute, would succeed and that the balance of convenience lay in favour of refusing the injunction sought; and (2) to giving a brief indication of the reasons why, in my opinion, upon the evidence as it stands at present, none of these contentions is likely to succeed.

I start with the simplest argument advanced on behalf of the NUJ. This was: that the NUJ journalists' refusal, on the instructions of the NUJ, to provide copy to Dimbleby constituted in itself a trade dispute between workers and their employer as to the terms and conditions of their employment, within the meaning of section 29 of the Act of 1974 as amended by section 18 of the Act of 1982 [now TULRCA s 244] ...

There was, however, in the evidence before the judge no vestige of any claim by the NUJ itself or by the NUJ journalists that their current contracts of employment by Dimbleby – and it is only their *current* contracts that can be relevant to this argument – contained a term entitling them to refuse to comply with instructions given to them by Dimbleby to provide copy of the kind that they were employed to obtain, if they received instructions to the contrary from the NUJ. Indeed, it passes beyond the bounds of credibility that any responsible newspaper proprietor would agree to such a term in contracts of employment with his journalists. The evidence that was before the judge makes it perfectly clear that the NUJ journalists acknowledged that by refusing to provide copy for the Dimbleby newspapers so long as they were to be printed by TBF they were breaking their contracts, albeit they were doing so reluctantly upon the instructions, enforceable by disciplinary sanctions, that had been given to them by the NUJ. But for the fact that, contrary to the unanimous opinion of the Court of Appeal, the judge himself appears to have thought that there was a trade dispute between Dimbleby and the NUJ as to the terms and conditions of employment by Dimbleby of the NUJ journalists, I should not myself have thought that on this issue the evidence before the judge raised any arguable question to be tried; but having regard (as [TULRCA s 221(2)] commands me) to the likelihood of the NUJ's succeeding in this particular defence at the trial, I agree with the Court of Appeal that the likelihood is minimal.

Your Lordships were also invited to consider an alternative ground on which it was submitted that there existed a trade dispute between Dimbleby and the NUJ, viz "the allocation of work or the duties of employment between workers or groups of workers" within the meaning of [TULRCA s 244(1)(c)] the allocation sought to be relied upon being the allocation between workers employed by Dimbleby Printers Ltd (not Dimbleby itself) and workers employed by TBF.

This contention does not appear to have been advanced on behalf of the NUJ before either the judge or the Court of Appeal. Even if an argument to this effect could have been advanced with any degree of plausibility before the amendment of section 29 of the Act of 1974 by section 18 of the Act of 1982, all vestige of plausibility is removed by the amended definitions of "trade dispute" and "worker" found in subsections [(1)] and [(5)] respectively. The effect of subsection [(1)] is to redefine "trade dispute" as a dispute between workers and their employer wholly "or mainly related to" one or more of the matters listed in [s 244(1)]. Subsection [(5)], so far as relevant, provides that " 'worker' in relation to a trade dispute with an employer means a worker employed by that employer".

So allocation of work or duties of employment between workers or groups of workers as a possible subject of a trade dispute is now limited to demarcation issues between workers or groups of workers employed by the same employer. The likelihood of the NUJ succeeding in this particular defence is, in my view, nil.

It is not now disputed that in October 1983 when the NUJ journalists refused to provide copy to be printed by T Bailey Forman Ltd, there was still in existence a trade dispute between the NUJ and T Bailey Forman Ltd ...'

(Lords Fraser, Scarman, Bridge and Brandon agreed with Lord Diplock.)

COMMENT

(1)　There were three potential trade disputes in this case. The first was between the journalists and Dimbleby, their employer, over whether they should have to supply copy in contravention of their union's instructions. Lord Diplock effectively says that because they have no complaint about their own current terms and conditions, there is no trade dispute just because they are breaking their contracts of employment.

However, it could be argued that they were in dispute about whether there should be a *new* term in their contracts, that they should not have to disobey their union's instructions. Lord Diplock impliedly negatives this, but without much by way of argument. This point will be returned to.

(2) The journalists argued alternatively that they were in dispute with Dimbleby over allocation of work, which is a trade dispute issue under TULRCA s 244(1)(c). However, they were complaining about the allocation of work to TBF away from printers employed by a different employer, Dimbleby Printers Ltd. Because they did not work for the same employer as the journalists, the journalists could not be in dispute with *their* employer about them.

Dimbleby and Dimbleby Printers Ltd were, of course, associated companies with the same people controlling them: but legally they were different employers and the veil of incorporation has not been lifted in these circumstances – which provides a clear incentive for employers to structure their businesses as separate companies.

(3) The second dispute was between the printers and their employer, Dimbleby Printers Ltd: the dispute which led to Dimbleby Printers Ltd switching the work to TBF in the first place. This was clearly a trade dispute, and before 1982, this would have sufficed for the journalists' action to come within the immunity. Even under the new wording, the journalists could have said that they were acting in contemplation or furtherance of this dispute even though it was not their own dispute. The new wording only requires that *somewhere* there is a dispute between workers and their employer, and that this industrial action was organised in contemplation or furtherance of it. However, if the journalists were acting in furtherance of someone else's dispute, it would be sympathy action, and as we will see, immunity is lost in those circumstances.

(4) It is, however, worth noting that Lord Diplock accepts that demarcation disputes between groups of workers employed by the same employer will count as trade disputes. After the 1982 amendment, this had been doubted by some commentators, who thought that such a dispute would be one between workers and workers only. But, as others have pointed out, the employer is virtually bound to get involved.

(5) The third dispute is between the NUJ and T Bailey Forman Ltd. This is admitted on all sides to be a trade dispute. However, there are two problems about immunity here, following the 1982 amendment. First, action in furtherance of it is sympathy action by the journalists, which loses immunity on that account. Second, the company struck at was TBF – an associated company with T Bailey Forman Ltd, run by the same people, but having a separate identity in law. The House of Lords refused to treat them as the same, however, and consequently action taken against TBF was secondary action (which is a ground for losing immunity, as we will see below).

(6) It is clear that it is no longer sufficient just to be able to point at some industrial dispute somewhere. The parties need to be identified with some precision if there is to be immunity.

An existing dispute

Bents Brewery Co Ltd v *Hogan*

[1945] 2 All ER 570 Liverpool Assizes

The union, through its divisional officer, had sent out a questionnaire to the managers of public houses seeking information about takings, staff costs, etc., which it wanted for collective bargaining purposes. As some of it was confidential information, its disclosure by the managers would have been a breach of their contracts of employment. Sued for inducing breaches of contract, the union claimed that it was not liable because it was acting in contemplation or furtherance of a trade dispute.

Lynskey J: 'The next question I have to decide is whether the document was sent out by the defendant, or on his behalf, in contemplation or furtherance of a trade dispute. Long and detailed particulars were given by the defendant as to trade disputes alleged to be existing or in contemplation. I do not propose to go through these particulars or the evidence relating to them, as, in my opinion, they do not disclose any dispute either in being or imminent. The document was sent out to managers of brewery companies. No demand has been made for either better conditions or increased wages by any manager to any of the plaintiff brewery companies. No such demands had been made by the defendant, or his union, on behalf of such managers. The defendant in his evidence before me said he sent out the document containing the questionnaire to find out whether there was a trade dispute, and to find out whether the conditions and wages were satisfactory. In my opinion, a dispute cannot exist unless there is a difference of opinion between two parties as to some matter. There is no evidence before me that any dispute existed. The highest that it can be put on the evidence in favour of the defendant is that the document was sent out to obtain information which, after consideration of the information obtained, might lead to a request which, if not granted, might result in a dispute.

In *Conway* v *Wade*, Lord Loreburn LC dealt with the meaning of the words "an act done in contemplation or furtherance of a trade dispute". In his speech he said:

"I think they mean that either a dispute is imminent and the act is done in expectation of and with a view to it, or that the dispute is already existing, and the act is done in support of one side to it. In either case the act must be genuinely done as described and the dispute must be a real thing imminent or existing."

There was no dispute when the document was sent out which was a real thing, either imminent or existing. There was a possibility of a dispute at some future time, but no certainty that such a dispute would arise.

In my view there was no dispute existing at the time this questionnaire was sent and the result is that the protection given by [TULRCA s 219] does not help the defendant.'

COMMENT

(1)   One of the main reasons for restricting trade disputes to those between workers and their employer was the ITF campaign against flags of convenience, referred to already (see p 521). Frequently the crews themselves were happy with their wages, even though they were below ITF rates. Today the union would not be protected if it blacked a ship flying a flag of convenience if there was no existing dispute between the seafarers and their employer.

Subject-matter of the dispute

In order to be protected, the dispute must be about one or more of the issues in s 244(1). Disputes which put pressure on the government are often argued to be political rather than trade disputes.

National Sailors' and Firemen's Union v Reed

[1926] Ch 536 Chancery Division

This is the only reported case arising from the General Strike of 1926. Miners took strike action because their employers proposed to increase working hours and reduce wages. They called on other unions to assist, and the TUC called a general strike. The defendant officials of the Tower Hill branch of the union, without authority from the union executive, passed a motion supporting the strike and called on members to withdraw their labour.

Astbury J: '… According to the evidence before me certain members of the plaintiff Union have been misled and compelled in London by the defendants and their pickets to leave their ships and to suffer serious loss and damage, and have been placed in doubt as to their position as members of this Union. These acts on the part of the defendants have been done without the authority of the plaintiff Union and contrary to its rules and orders, and lastly, no strike has been called by the plaintiff Union, and no ballot of its members, as provided for by its rules, has been completed. In these circumstances the plaintiff Union seeks the injunction which I have referred to, and the learned counsel who has appeared for the Union bases his right to claim this injunction on two grounds: one, that the defendants have acted in breach of the rules and orders of the Union and are liable to be restrained as prayed, and secondly, that they have acted contrary to the common law of this country.

I will endeavour now to state what I apprehend is the law upon this matter. To take the more general ground first, it is evident from the facts above mentioned and from the rest of the evidence that has been filed that members of the plaintiff Union have been placed in a position of doubt and danger, and it is my duty, as I have been requested by the plaintiffs and defendants to do, to state shortly their rights and those of their Union. The so-called general strike called by the Trades Union Congress Council is illegal, and persons inciting or taking part in it are not protected by the Trade Disputes Act, 1906. No trade dispute has been alleged or shown to exist in any of the unions affected, except in the miners' case, and no trade dispute does or can exist between the Trades Union Congress on the one hand and the Government and the nation on the other. The orders of the Trades Union Congress above referred to are therefore unlawful, and the defendants are acting illegally in obeying them, and accordingly (for the reason I shall state under the other head) can be restrained by their own Union from doing so. The plaintiffs' counsel has contended that if the members of the plaintiff Union stay in their jobs and refuse to strike they cannot be deprived of their trade union benefits, and the defendants who have appeared before me have stated, and stated very properly, that it is important to them that their members should know their rights in this respect.

Now the law upon that matter is as follows. No member of the plaintiff Union or any other trade unionist in this country can lose his trade union benefits by refusing to obey unlawful orders, and the orders of the Trades Union Congress and the unions who are acting in obedience thereto in bringing about the so-called general strike are unlawful orders, and the plaintiff Union is entitled to have this fact made clear and brought to the attention of its members … '

COMMENT

(1)   This judgment prompted a famous article by Goodhart ('The Legality of the General Strike' (1926) 36 Yale L J 464, also in his *Essays in Jurisprudence and the Common Law*) which criticised the reasoning on two grounds. First, and most importantly, since every strike puts pressure on parties not directly involved, it should not be treated as political simply because the third party affected was the government. Second, since Astbury admitted that there was a genuine trade dispute between the miners and their employers, the others should have been within the immunity as they were acting in furtherance of it. As to this, as noted already, today sympathy action will lose immunity.

(2)   What if actions of the government have a direct effect on terms and conditions of employment?

Sherard v *AUEW*

[1973] ICR 421 Court of Appeal

The union called a one-day strike for 1 May 1973 in protest at the government's implementation of phase two of the Counter-Inflation (Temporary Provisions) Act 1972, which would have the effect of freezing pay. Some members, employed at government installations, sought an injunction to stop the strike, on the grounds (among other things) that it was political. (At this time the Industrial Relations Act 1971 was in force, but its definition of an 'industrial dispute' did not differ materially from the definition in TULRCA s 244.)

Lord Denning MR: '... I am of opinion that a dispute between the TUC, on the one hand, and the government, on the other hand, is not an industrial dispute. To that extent I would agree with the view expressed by Astbury J in *National Sailors' and Firemen's Union of Great Britain and Ireland* v *Reed*. At first sight this did appear to be a dispute between the TUC and the government. But Mr Irvine asks us to say that there is a dispute between workers in the employ of the government on the one hand and the government as employers on the other hand. The government as employers have decided to enforce phase two, which has frozen wages against the will of the workers. The men in the government employ object to this freezing of their wages. They – or some of them – are in dispute with their employers about it.

I think that this point made by Mr Irvine is arguable. If it is good, it means that the whole dispute is an "industrial dispute" and, therefore, not within the cognizance of these courts.

In *Conway* v *Wade* Lord Loreburn LC said:

"A dispute may have arisen, for example, in a single colliery, of which the subject is so important to the whole industry that either employers or workmen may think a general lock-out or a general strike is necessary to gain their point. Few are parties to, but all are interested in, the dispute."

Seeing that this is arguably an industrial dispute, I do not think we should grant an interlocutory injunction ...'

Roskill LJ: '... I ventured to ask Mr Campbell at an early stage of his argument what he meant by a "political strike". He replied "a strike which was not the subject of an accompanying industrial dispute". Although the phrase "political strike" has from time to time been used in reported cases, it is to my mind a phrase which should be used, at any rate in a court of law, with considerable caution, for it does not readily lend itself to precise or accurate definition. It is all too easy for someone to talk of a strike as being a "political strike" when what that person really means is that the object of the strike is something of which he as an individual subjectively disapproves …

There is only one other matter to which I would refer. At the outset of his submission Mr Campbell founded part of his argument upon the well-known (some might call it notorious) decision in *National Sailors' and Firemen's Union of Great Britain and Ireland* v *Reed*. He suggested when his attention was drawn to the fact that that case had been the subject of much extra-judicial criticism that that criticism had come from parties who might be regarded as not wholly disinterested. But, as Mr Irvine pointed out, that case was the subject of a very well-known article by Professor Goodhart over 45 years ago in (1927) 36 *Yale Law Journal*, p 464. I say no more than that. One day it may be necessary to reconsider in this court that decision of Astbury J. The present is not the occasion. I only mention the matter in deference to the arguments of counsel.

For the reasons I have given I too, would dismiss this appeal.'

COMMENT

(1)   There were only two judges sitting in the Court of Appeal for these interlocutory proceedings.

(2)   Lord Denning seems to have been swayed here by the argument that if employees of the government took part in the strike, they could definitely claim it was a trade dispute, and then the rest would be able to say that they were acting in furtherance of it. Today, the others would be taking part in sympathy action which would not be immune. Roskill LJ placed his decision on wider grounds.

(3)   As the immunity was originally formulated, action was regarded as in contemplation or furtherance of a trade dispute if it was 'connected with' one of the matters listed in s 244(1). However, the Employment Act 1982 introduced the present wording which requires that the dispute be 'wholly or mainly' about one of these matters. As the next case shows, this may increase the risks of a dispute being regarded as political.

Mercury Communications Ltd v *Scott-Garner*

[1984] ICR 74 Court of Appeal

At the beginning of the 1980s the government decided to break the Post Office monopoly on telecommunications. It passed the British Telecommunications Act 1981 establishing British Telecom and also empowering the Secretary of State to license rival telecommunications services. The Post Office Engineering Union was opposed to this policy of 'liberalisation' and also feared that privatisation, to which it was also opposed, was on the horizon. When a licence was granted to Mercury, the POEU instructed its members to disobey orders from their employer, British Telecom, to connect Mercury to the BT telecommunications system.

Mercury sought an injunction, claiming that the union's action did not enjoy the trade dispute immunity. The union argued that it was a dispute about termination of employment (cf s 244(1)(b)) – that they feared compulsory redundancies. Their evidence in this regard was undermined by the production, at a fairly late stage of the proceedings, of a Job Security Agreement concluded in 1980 where the employer had given a commitment that there would be no compulsory redundancies.

Sir John Donaldson MR: '... The most obvious way of finding out what a particular dispute is wholly or mainly about is to inquire what the men concerned – in this case primarily those who refuse to interconnect – said to management at the time. Unfortunately we have no evidence, but it is a fair inference from what we do know that they said that the interconnection was contrary to their union's instructions. This throws one back to what the dispute between the union and BT was wholly or mainly about. That was not, of course, a relevant dispute because the union is neither an employer nor a worker in this context, but the subject matter of the dispute between BT and its employees can legitimately be taken to be the same as that between the union and BT.

What the union's dispute with BT is about is the subject matter of paragraph 22 of Mr Stanley's first affidavit which I have already quoted:

"... BT have entered into an interconnection agreement with [Mercury]. It is over this that the union are in dispute with BT ... BT ... have ... allowed a rival organisation to inter-connect with its network. It is this fact which puts them at odds with my union ... The action which BT is taking is inconsistent with the desire of my members to retain the traditional monopoly over telecommunications facilities within BT. Once BT embarked upon a course of seeking to facilitate and implement liberalisation, they embarked upon a course which can only lead to a dispute between them and the union."

Mr Stanley goes on to say that the *cause* of the dispute is that BT wished his members to take a step which his members regarded as putting their jobs at risk (my emphasis) and a few sentences later this suffers a further change when he states that the subject matter of the dispute is the risk to jobs.

Well; which is the subject matter – facilitating and implementing liberalisation, agreeing to interconnect, ordering interconnection or the risk to jobs? Only the latter would enable the dispute to qualify as a trade dispute. The evidence has to be looked at as a whole, but I find it impossible to conclude on the evidence at present available that the risk to jobs was a major part of what the dispute was about. I say that because I find it inconceivable that if the dispute was wholly or mainly about jobs, the union would not have approached BT asking for a guarantee of job security or a strengthening of the Job Security Agreement. Yet nothing of the sort appears to have happened and the union did not even think that this agreement was relevant to the present proceedings. On the other hand there is massive evidence that the union was waging a campaign against the political decisions to liberalise the industry and to privatise BT.'

(May and Dillon LJJ delivered concurring judgments.)

British Broadcasting Corporation v *Hearn*

[1977] ICR 685 Court of Appeal

The Association of Broadcasting Staff was proposing to prevent transmission of the Cup Final by satellite to South Africa, because they argued that it would be seen as showing support for the South African policy of apartheid. The BBC sought an injunction to stop the union inducing breaches of contract by its staff on the grounds that this was not a trade dispute.

Lord Denning MR: '... So I come to the words "in contemplation or furtherance of a trade dispute." There comes the rub. Was a trade dispute in contemplation? This has been discussed in the courts. As long ago as 1908 one of my predecessors, Cozens-Hardy MR in *Conway* v *Wade* said:

"The words 'in contemplation' are difficult, but they must embrace an act done by a person with a view to bringing about a trade dispute. If, for example, a minister of religion says to an employer, 'If you do not tomorrow morning discharge all your workmen who are not of my sect, I will call out all my co-religionists', he may act with impunity."

That view was expressly rejected by the House of Lords. Lord Loreburn LC himself said he could not agree. And Lord Shaw of Dunfermline said that he "respectfully but totally" dissented from that view of the Master of the Rolls. Lord Shaw said:

"... I think the argument was well founded that the contemplation of such a dispute must be the contemplation of something impending or likely to occur, and that they do not cover the case of coercive interference in which the interviewer may have in his own mind that if he does not get his own way he will thereupon take ways and means to bring a trade dispute into existence."

Adapting those words to the illustration given by Cozens-Hardy MR it means that if shop stewards – who object to a man's religious belief – say to an employer, "Dismiss this man or we will go out on strike", that is not a trade dispute. It is coercive interference with the man's freedom of religion and with the employer's business. Take the case which I put in the course of argument: if printers in a newspaper office were to say: "We don't like the article which you are going to publish about the Arabs – or the Jews – or on this or that political issue – you must withdraw it. If you do not do so, we are not going to print your paper." That is not a trade dispute. It is coercive action unconnected with a trade dispute. It is an unlawful interference with the freedom of the press. It is a self-created power of censorship. It does not become a trade dispute simply because the men propose to break their contracts of employment in doing it. Even if the men have a strong moral case, saying, "We have a conscientious objection to this article. We do not want to have anything to do with it", that does not turn it into a trade dispute. The dispute is about the publication of the article, not about the terms and conditions of employment.

Applying those considerations to this case, all that was happening was that the trade union, or its officers, were saying: "Stop this televising by the Indian Ocean satellite, stop it yourself. If you don't, we will ask our own people to stop it for you." That is not a trade dispute. They were hoping, I suppose, that the BBC would give in; but, if they did not give in, they were going to order their members to stop the broadcast. That does not seem to me to be a trade dispute. To become a trade dispute, there would have to be something of the kind which was discussed in the course of argument before us: "We would like you to consider putting a clause in the contract by which our members are not bound to take part in any broadcast which may be viewed in South Africa because we feel that is obnoxious to their views and to the views of a great multitude of people. We would like that clause to be put in, or a condition of that kind to be understood." If the BBC refused to put in such a condition, or refused to negotiate about it, that might be a trade dispute. That, I think, is rather the way in which the judge approached this case. Towards the end of his judgment he said, putting it into the mouths of members through their union:

"We wish it established as a condition of employment that we shall not be required to take part in broadcasts to South Africa so long as the South African Government pursues its policy of apartheid."

If that request had been made, and not acceded to, there might be a trade dispute as to whether that should be a condition of the employment. But the matter never reached that stage at all. It never reached the stage of there being a trade dispute. There was not a trade dispute "in contemplation". It was coercive interference and nothing more. If that is the right view, it means that the trade union and its officers are not exempt from the ordinary rule of law – which is that men must honour their contracts, and must not unlawfully interfere with the performance of them ...'

(Roskill and Scarman LJJ delivered concurring judgments.)

COMMENT

(1) The last part of the judgment extracted seems to offer considerable scope for turning what otherwise might not be trade dispute matters into disputes over terms and conditions of employment. However, the House of Lords has shown some antipathy to this notion.

Universe Tankships Inc of Monrovia v International Transport Workers' Federation

[1982] ICR 262 House of Lords

The facts of this case are given on p 521. The company was reclaiming money paid to the union welfare fund, arguing that it had been paid under duress. One issue was whether the action came within the trade dispute immunity.

Lord Diplock: '... In my view, it is not enough in order to create the necessary connection between a dispute relating to terms and conditions of employment of employees of a particular employer, and a demand made upon that employer by a trade union acting on its own behalf and not on behalf of employees working for the employer, that the demand should be made at a time when the trade union is negotiating a collective agreement relating to the terms and conditions of employment of those employees, and the employer's yielding to that demand is made a condition precedent to the lifting of a blacking additional to the condition precedent that the employer should also agree to the terms of the collective agreement insisted on by the trade union. To take an extreme example, if a trade union were to demand as a condition precedent to lifting a blacking that the employer should make a contribution to a particular political party favoured by the union, or to a guerilla group in some foreign country, such a demand whenever it was made would not, in my opinion, have the necessary connection with any dispute about terms or conditions of employment in further-ance of which the blacking was imposed ...

In view of the difference of opinion between the members of this House upon the duress point it may be appropriate that before departing from the subject I should state that my opinion that the demand for a contribution to the welfare fund is not legitimised so as to deprive the shipowners of a restitutionary remedy would not necessarily be different if a requirement that the shipowners should make such a contribution were incorporated in the ITF Collective Agreement. [TULRCA ss 219 and 244] are not directly applicable to restitu-tional remedies; they are relevant only for such indications as they give of the public policy as to what kinds of demands ought to be regarded as legitimate in the field of industrial relations notwithstanding that compliance with them is induced by economic duress. The fact that ITF had also insisted that a term as to the requirement of payment to the welfare fund should be inserted in the ITF Collective Agreement would not, in my opinion, affect the public policy under which it is excluded from being legitimised.'

Lord Cross: '... I would add, although on the facts of this case the point does not arise for decision, that I fully concur with the view expressed by my noble and learned friend in the concluding paragraph of his speech, that in the case supposed it would have made no difference to the right of the appellants to recover the payments to the guerilla fund that ITF had insisted, as a condition of lifting the "blacking" of the vessel, that an undertaking by the appellants to make the payments should be inserted in the contracts of employment of each member of the crew and that the appellants had, under duress, entered into such undertakings with each member. A trade union cannot turn a dispute which in reality has no connection with terms and conditions of employment into a dispute connected with terms and conditions of employment by insisting that the employer inserts appropriate terms into the contracts of employment into which he enters ...'

(Lord Russell gave a speech agreeing with Lords Diplock and Cross; Lords Scarman and Brandon dissented on this point.)

COMMENT

(1)   Lord Cross's remarks are *obiter*. Why should it be impossible to conjure up a trade dispute in this way? Dealing obliquely with the argument in *Dimbleby v NUJ*, Lord Diplock said, '... it passes the bounds of credibility that any responsible newspaper proprietor would agree to such a term [that is, a term that they should not have to supply copy to a company blacked by their union] in contracts of employment with his journalists'. Yet the fact that an employer is most unlikely to agree a term does not mean that there cannot be a dispute over whether the employer *should* agree to it (think of some of the more optimistic wage claims that unions have submitted ...). Also, *Hadmor Productions Ltd v Hamilton* (another case where Lord Diplock delivered the principal speech in the House of Lords) affords an example of an employer (Thames Television) which had agreed a similar clause with its union.

(2)   Could the ABS have claimed that it was acting in contemplation or furtherance of a trade dispute between black South African workers and their employers? On these facts, no, because there was no evidence of any such dispute: it was rather a protest against the political system in South Africa. However, even if there were such a dispute, note the restriction on immunity in respect of overseas disputes in s 244(3). And there is the problem of sympathy action.

(3)   Not only political reasons take a dispute outside the 'trade dispute' formula: cf *Huntley v Thornton*, where it was held that union officials were pursuing a private vendetta against a member.

LOSS OF IMMUNITY

Until 1980, consideration of the legality of industrial action stopped at the end of the last section. However, the strategy of the Conservative Government which was in power from 1979–97 was to limit the ambit of lawful industrial action in two main ways. The first was to narrow the concept of trade dispute, and the effects of that were seen in the last section. The second was to introduce new conditions for lawful industrial action by providing that trade unions and individuals would forfeit immunity if they failed to comply with them.

Secondary action

The winter of 1978–79 was called by some sections of the press 'the winter of discontent' because of a number of highly-publicised national strikes which substantially affected the general public. The perceived failure of the then Labour Government to deal effectively with the situation was a major reason for its defeat in the 1979 general election and its replacement with a Conservative Government led by Margaret Thatcher.

Three important cases came to the Court of Appeal and House of Lords over that time (*NWL* v *Woods, Express Newspapers* v *McShane* and *Duport Steels* v *Sirs*). In each of them the Court of Appeal (or, to be more accurate, Lord Denning) attempted to develop a concept of remoteness and to withdraw immunity from action regarded as 'too remote' from the original dispute. In each case, the House of Lords reversed the Court of Appeal's decision on the ground that there was no justification for such a gloss on the statute – although most members of the House of Lords evinced overt or covert sympathy for the general aim of restricting union power.

The following extract is from the Court of Appeal decision in one of those cases. It is given because it is a good example of the kind of action which was seen to be the problem, and also because Lord Denning's concept of secondary action was taken up by the Conservative Government in its first piece of employment legislation, the Employment Act 1980.

Express Newspapers Ltd v McShane

[1979] ICR 210 Court of Appeal

Lord Denning MR: 'There are about 1,000 local newspapers published in this country. They are served by about 9,000 journalists of whom 8,500 belong to a trade union called the National Union of Journalists ("the NUJ"). Unfortunately there is a difference about their pay. The journalists feel that they are underpaid and that they ought to be paid more. The proprietors feel they cannot pay more because of the government's policy of the 5 per cent limit and their own financial situation. That difference has not been resolved. Feeling very upset about it, some journalists took disruptive action. The Bolton Evening News dismissed 105 NUJ members. In consequence the NUJ (through their national executive council) decided to take industrial action. The decision was taken by a majority vote of 14 to seven. It is the first time, we are told, in the 71 years of its existence that this union has called a strike. On 4th December 1978 (2½ weeks ago) the NUJ called a strike withdrawing all the services of their member journalists on the local newspapers, with the result that those journalists would not supply any news or copy for the local papers. That may be called the "primary" action taken by the NUJ. It brought pressure to bear directly on the employers.

But this strike did not put the local papers out of action altogether. Those papers do not depend solely on their journalists to feed them with news. They also get news copy through the important organisation called the Press Association. The Press Association have some 250 journalists on their staff. They collect news of all kinds (major and minor happenings, sporting items, Parliamentary items, items from these courts and the like). They send out these items in a continuous stream from their offices in Fleet Street by teleprinter to all the media in the country. It is sent to the national newspapers, the local newspapers, the broadcasters, and on tape to clubs, offices and institutions throughout the country.

In order to make the strike more effective, the NUJ wished to stop the news going out from the Press Association to the local newspapers. So they called on the journalists on the Press Association (many of whom are members of the union) to come out on strike as well. If they stopped work, it would mean that no news would be provided by the Press Association to anyone. It would affect not only the local newspapers with whom there was a dispute, but also the national newspapers, the media, clubs, and so forth, with whom there was no dispute. None of them would get their news from the Press Association. That may be called a "secondary" action taken by the union. It brought pressure to bear on the Press Association who were not involved in the dispute at all.

In order to induce the journalists on the Press Association to strike, the union promised to pay them £50 a week (much more than the hardship allowance paid to the provincial journalists). But even so many of the journalists on the Press Association were unwilling to strike. They did not wish to obey the orders of the national executive council. So they had a meeting to determine it. Out of the 250 journalists on the Press Association 162 attended. Eighty-six decided to ignore the call to strike. They stayed at work. Seventy-six came out on strike. The 86 were joined by others who were not members of the union. In rough figures, half the journalists on the Press Association remained at work and half came out on strike. The half who were still at work continued to send out news over the teleprinter to all the newspapers up and down the country and to all the media. So a good deal of news still got through to the local newspapers and enabled them to carry on, not fully, but partially.

At the same time the union took a further measure which may be described as a further "secondary" action. They had members working for the *Daily Express* and other national newspapers and also for the media. The union ordered these members to "black" the Press Association copy. That meant that they called on their members working for the *Daily Express* and other newspapers to refuse to use the copy which came through on the teleprinter from the Press Association. They told their members at the *Daily Express* not to handle it or make any use of it whatsoever. They allowed their members to get news from other sources. For instance, their members could telephone freelance journalists or other sources of information so as to get news for the *Daily Express*. But they were not to use any of the copy supplied by the Press Association. Their members were still to get their full pay from their employers, but were not to do their work properly ...

At the outset I would say that it is clear that there was a "trade dispute" between the local newspapers and the journalists employed by them. It was a dispute about their pay. But there was no other trade dispute at all. There was no dispute between the Press Association and the union. There was no dispute between the *Daily Express* and the union. The only dispute was with the local provincial newspapers.

The "primary" action was certainly taken by the union "in furtherance of" that dispute. They called out on strike their members who were employed by the local newspapers. That would bring direct pressure on the local newspapers. The first "secondary" action may also be said to be "in furtherance of" the dispute. The union called out on strike their members at the Press Association. That would also bring pressure to bear on the local newspapers because, by stopping copy going out from the Press Association, it would hamper the production of local newspapers, even though it might hamper the national newspapers also.

But what about the further "secondary" action? The act of calling on the member journalists employed by the *Daily Express* to "black" the copy supplied by the Press Association? That would not affect the local newspapers in the slightest degree. It would not bring any pressure to bear on them. It would not affect the Press Association either. The only persons whom it would affect would be the *Daily Express* and put them to great trouble, difficulty and expense. But not the local newspapers. Can such an act be said to be "in furtherance of" the dispute?

Before dealing with this point, I would draw attention to the very great power which the leaders of the trade unions have over their members, especially when there are "closed shops"...

It is said on behalf of the NUJ leaders that "furtherance" depended on their state of mind. If they genuinely and honestly believed that the "blacking" would advance the cause of the provincial journalists, then their acts were done "in furtherance of" the dispute. The judge did not accept that submission. Nor do I. "Furtherance" is not a merely subjective concept. There is an objective element in it. The Shorter Oxford Dictionary defines "furtherance" as "the fact or state of being helped forward". It seems to me that, for an act to be done "in furtherance of" a trade dispute, it must be reasonably capable of doing so, or have a reasonable prospect of it, in this way that it must help one side or the other to the dispute in a *practical* way by giving support to the one or bringing pressure to bear on the other. Such as in the common case where men, who are in dispute with their employer, withdraw their labour, or "black" materials coming to his factory, or are supported by pickets outside his gates. Those are practical measures which have an impact in *fact* on the employer. They directly damage the employer's business. Such acts have a different quality from those which do not directly damage the employer's business but serve only to improve the morale of the strikers or promote their confidence or encourage them in their efforts, or damage innocent people not parties to the dispute. If this is all they do, they are not "in furtherance of" the dispute. In ordinary speech we draw a distinction between giving moral support to a cause and practical support to it. To be "in furtherance of" a dispute, an act must give practical support to one side or the other and not merely moral support.

The trade union leaders put their case in this way. They say that, if they call on the journalists at the *Daily Express* to "black" the copy from the Press Association, that will improve the morale of the strikers. It will reinforce their determination to strike; and they hope it will persuade those who refuse to strike to join the strike. The effect is that it will support their cause in the strike …

In this case there is no evidence that the "blacking" at the *Daily Express* of the Press Association copy has had any effect on the only trade dispute there is, the dispute of the provincial journalists with the local newspapers. It has had no practical effect on it at all. It has not induced any more men at the Press Association to come out on strike, nor has it affected the supply of news from the Press Association to its subscribers. It has been going on for 2½ weeks now. There is no evidence from any strikers or non-strikers at the Press Association that it has had any effect on them. As far as one knows they are still about half and half at the Press Association, half on strike and half still remaining at work. I have no doubt that the acts were done "in connection with" the trade dispute with the local newspapers, but they were not done "in furtherance of" it.

It seems to me that the leaders of trade unions have been reading these words "in furtherance of" in a wide sense as if they extended to any acts done "in connection with" or "in consequence of" a trade dispute. But as the judge said they are narrower words and are to be given a narrower construction. A wide construction would confer far too wide an immunity …'

(Lawton and Brandon LJJ delivered concurring judgments.)

COMMENT

(1) The action taken by journalists at the Press Association and in turn by those employed by national newspapers was sympathy action: they had no particular dispute with their own employers at that time. However, previously this had been regarded as within the immunity because it was in contemplation or furtherance of the primary dispute – here, the dispute between the provincial papers and their employees.

(2)   Lord Denning described both the action at the Press Association and the action at the national papers as being 'secondary action'. However, it is notable that he thought that the action at the Press Association *was* capable of furthering the primary dispute – and would therefore be covered by the immunity. It is the secondary action (or tertiary action) at the national papers which, in his opinion, would have no effect one way or the other on the dispute.

(3)   This is important, because it was this pattern which was adopted by the Conservative Government in its first treatment of secondary action in the Employment Act 1980 s 17. Under that provision, the Press Association action would have been 'protected secondary action' – protected, because there was a contractual link between the Press Association and the employer in dispute. That meant it did not lose its immunity. The action at the national papers would not have been protected, because there was no contractual link between the employer in dispute (the provincial papers) and the employer whose employees were being induced to break their contracts of employment (the national newspapers). This was known as the 'first customer/first supplier' exception.

(4)   Under the Employment Act 1980 s 17, two other kinds of secondary action were protected: action taken against a company in the same group as the employer in dispute *provided* that the associated company was doing work that would normally have been done by the company in dispute. Thus to a limited extent, a union could 'follow' struck work and attempt to make the strike effective by stopping the employer in dispute from switching production elsewhere.

(5)   The other kind of protected secondary action was where it occurred in the context of lawful picketing: this will be considered in the section on picketing.

(6)   In a Green Paper in 1989, the Conservative Government gave its reasons for altering the law on secondary action.

Removing Barriers to Employment

Cm 655   March 1989

Paras 3.5–3.8 described the legal position as it then stood.

3.9.   The arrangements described above were framed in the light of circumstances in 1980, at a time when secondary industrial action had been much more widespread than it has been in more recent years. But it is now right to ask whether the immunities described in paragraphs 3.7 and 3.8 are still justified.

3.10.   The Government believe that the following considerations indicate that the present law needs amendment:

   –   In general there is no good reason why employers who are not party to a dispute should be at risk of having industrial action organised against them;

   –   Secondary action may deter employers from starting up for the first time in this country, with harmful effects on new investment and on jobs. For example, there might be a threat of secondary action being organised among workers of the new firm's customers or suppliers, with the aim of forcing the new enterprise to accept certain terms and conditions. This sort of threat was made when the American Ford Motor Company was planning to establish a new factory at Dundee. Regardless of whether they are lawful or unlawful under the present law, there is no good reason why any threats of this kind, or the organisation of action of this kind, should enjoy immunity;

— The law as it stands is complicated, and it could well be difficult for those involved to determine, in the absence of a court judgment, whether there would be immunity for organising certain secondary action. An example might be secondary action which involved a union inducing transport workers to refuse to move coal to power stations, or within power stations, in support of an industrial dispute between British Coal and its employees. If the coal was part of a shipment including other goods from other suppliers, it might be very difficult to know whether there would be immunity for refusal to move the shipment as a whole. The same would apply if the coal was unloaded and stored with coal from other suppliers, from which it could not be distinguished, and transport workers then refused to move any part of the store of coal.

COMMENT

(1) These were the arguments put forward to justify the complete removal of immunity from all forms of sympathy or solidarity action, the traditional strength of the trade union movement and indeed, their *raison d'être* in the eyes of many.

(2) The law was changed by the Employment Act 1990; the relevant provision is now found in TULRCA.

Trade Union and Labour Relations (Consolidation) Act 1992

224. (1) An act is not protected if one of the facts relied on for the purpose of establishing liability is that there has been secondary action which is not lawful picketing.

(2) There is secondary action in relation to a trade dispute when, and only when, a person—

(a) induces another to break a contract of employment or interferes or induces another to interfere with its performance, or

(b) threatens that a contract of employment under which he or another is employed will be broken or its performance interfered with, or that he will induce another to break a contract of employment or to interfere with its performance,

and the employer under the contract of employment is not the employer party to the dispute....

(5) An act in contemplation or furtherance of a trade dispute which is primary action in relation to that dispute may not be relied on as secondary action in relation to another trade dispute.

Primary action means such action as is mentioned in paragraph (a) or (b) of subsection (2) where the employer under the contract of employment is the employer party to the dispute.

COMMENT

(1) Thus the position now is that sympathy action loses its immunity at Stage 3. The only hope for trade unions will be to spread the primary dispute to more employers –

but clearly the motives of strikers and organisers will be closely scrutinised (*Mercury* v *Scott-Garner*, above, gives an example of this).

(2)   The only kind of secondary action which retains protection is that which occurs in the context of lawful picketing. This will be examined with picketing in general.

Failure to hold a ballot

Before the Trade Union Act 1984, unions were entitled to agree their own rules for calling industrial action. Obviously no union is likely to call action where the members do not support it, because it would ruin their credibility. But not all unions had rules like those of the National Union of Mineworkers, which not only required a ballot of all the members, but also a special majority of 55 per cent before action could be called.

The Trade Union Act did not mandate ballots in every case; however, it removed immunity from any industrial action where a proper ballot had not been held. The requirements for a proper ballot have become more complicated with subsequent legislation.

Trade Union and Labour Relations (Consolidation) Act 1992

226.   (1)   An act done by a trade union to induce a person to take part, or continue to take part, in industrial action

(a)   is not protected unless the industrial action has the support of a ballot, and

(b)   where section 226A falls to be complied with in relation to the person's employer, is not protected as respects the employer unless the trade union has complied with section 226A in relation to him.

In this section 'the relevant time', in relation to an act by a trade union to induce a person to take part, or continue to take part, in industrial action, means the time at which proceedings are commenced in respect of the act.

(2)   Industrial action shall be regarded as having the support of a ballot only if—

(a)   the union has held a ballot in respect of the action—

(i)   in relation to which the requirements of section 226B so far as applicable before and during the holding of the ballot were satisfied,

(ii)   in relation to which the requirements of sections 227–231A were satisfied, and

(iii)   in which the majority voting in the ballot answered 'Yes' to the question applicable in accordance with section 229(2) to industrial action of the kind to which the act of inducement relates;

(b)   such of the requirements of the following sections as have fallen to be satisfied at the relevant time have been satisfied, namely—

(i)   section 226B so far as applicable after the holding of the ballot, and

(ii)   section 231B, and

(c)   the requirements of section 233 (calling of industrial action with support of ballot) are satisfied. ...

(3)   Where separate workplace ballots are held by virtue of section 228(1)—

(a)   industrial action shall be regarded as having the support of a ballot if the conditions specified in subsection (2) are satisfied, and

(b)   the trade union shall be taken to have complied with the requirements relating to a ballot imposed by section 226A if those requirements are complied with, in relation to the ballot for the place of work of the person induced to take part, or continue to take part, in the industrial action.

(4) For the purposes of this section an inducement, in relation to a person, includes an inducement which is or would be ineffective, whether because of his unwillingness to be influenced by it or for any other reason.

COMMENT

(1) It is most important to note that the requirement to hold a ballot applies *only* to trade unions calling or approving industrial action. If non-union workers decide to engage in industrial action, they will be protected despite not holding a ballot first.

(2) Since not all industrial action involves the commission of torts (it is occasionally possible to organise action which does not break contracts of employment) it would seem that ballots are not necessary in all cases. An employer has no right to sue just because the union has not held a ballot: only if the union has committed a tort and not held a ballot first. For this reason, the following provision was introduced by the Employment Act 1988.

Trade Union and Labour Relations (Consolidation) Act 1992

62. (1) A member of a trade union who claims that members of the union, including himself, are likely to be or have been induced by the union to take part or to continue to take part in industrial action which does not have the support of a ballot may apply to the court for an order under this section.

...

(3) Where on an application under this section the court is satisfied that the claim is well-founded, it shall make such order as it considers appropriate for requiring the union to take steps for ensuring—
   (a) that there is no, or no further, inducement of members of the union to take part or to continue to take part in the industrial action to which the application relates, and
   (b) that no member engages in conduct after the making of the order by virtue of having been induced before the making of the order to take part or continue to take part in the action.

COMMENT

(1) No trade union can be absolutely sure that no single member will decide to challenge under this section. Thus, effectively, a trade union which wishes to call industrial action must hold a ballot first.

(2) As noted in Chapter 12 above, this concept was extended by TURERA to give third party individuals a right to restrain even lawful industrial action if it is organised by a trade union and there has not been a valid ballot first: this is contained in TULRCA s 235A.

(3) The numerous requirements for a valid ballot will be examined in turn. Reference should also be made to the *Code of Practice on Industrial Action Ballots and Notice to Employers* (1995).

Notice

Trade Union and Labour Relations (Consolidation) Act 1992

234A (1)   An act done by a trade union to induce a person to take part, or continue to take part, in industrial action is not protected as respects his employer unless the union has taken or takes such steps as are reasonably necessary to ensure that the employer receives within the appropriate period a relevant notice covering the act.

  (2)   Subsection (1) imposes a requirement in the case of an employer only if it is reasonable for the union to believe, at the latest time when steps could be taken to ensure that he receives such a notice, that he is the employer of persons who will be or have been induced to take part, or continue to take part, in the industrial action.

  (3)   For the purposes of this section a relevant notice is a notice in writing which—

  (a)   describes (so that he can readily ascertain them) the employees of the employer who the union intends to induce or has induced to take part, or continue to take part, in the industrial action ("the affected employees"),

  (b)   states whether industrial action is intended to be continuous or discontinuous and specifies—

  (i)   where it is to be continuous, the intended date for any of the affected employees to begin to take part in the action,

  (ii)   where it is to be discontinuous, the intended dates for any of the affected employees to take part in the action, and

  (c)   states that it is given for the purposes of this section.

  (4)   For the purposes of subsection (1) the appropriate period is the period —

  (a)   beginning with the day when the union satisfies the requirement of section 231A in relation to the ballot in respect of the industrial action, and

  (b)   ending with the seventh day before the day, or before the first of the days, specified in the relevant notice. ...

COMMENT

(1)   There is a prior notice requirement in TULRCA s 226A, which states that the union must give seven days' notice of a ballot to any employer whose employees would be entitled to vote, plus a sample of the voting paper three days in advance of the ballot. A major issue arising is, how much detail has to be given about the relevant employees?

Blackpool and The Fylde College v *NATFHE*

[1994] IRLR 227 Court of Appeal

A dispute had arisen between the college and the union and its members about the contracts on which new staff were employed. In January 1994 the union gave the college the first notice that it intended to ballot all its members at the college.

Bingham MR: '... On 10 February 1994 the union sent the college a notice in these terms:

"*Notice of industrial action*
Further to my letter dated 9 February 1994, I hereby give you notice as required by s 234A of the Trade Union and Labour Relations (Consolidation) Act 1992 that, having aggre-

gated the votes cast by all members in each of the Colleges Employers Forum-affiliated college institutions balloted, as the union is allowed to do by virtue of s 228(3) of the same Act, the union has instructed all its members employed by your institution to take part in discontinuous action. The first intended date of this industrial action, which will be on this occasion strike action, is 1 March 1994."

Those two notices were clearly and expressly intended to comply with ss 226A and 234A of the Act (as amended).

The short point taken by the college, which found favour with the judge, is that the notices do not comply with the sections. It is said that the notices which were given do not describe, so that the college can readily ascertain them, the college's employees whom the union intends to ballot or induce to take industrial action. The notices refer to "all our" – meaning the union's – "members employed in or by" the college, but that language, it is said, is not sufficiently precise to enable the college to ascertain who the employees are. If that submission is accepted, then it is common ground that the union does not enjoy immunity under s 219 for the action which it proposes to take. From that it follows that the proposed action is unlawful and that the grant of an injunction is appropriate.

The issue between the parties, therefore, is whether the notice that was given was sufficiently precise or specific in its terms to enable the college to ascertain the employees whom the union intended to ballot or call out. The factual foundation of the college's case is laid in an affidavit sworn by the principal of the college. He deposes – and these facts are not in issue – that of the 872 full-time and part-time lecturers employed by the college, the college does not know which belong to the union. What the college does know, because it was told in September 1993 by the branch secretary of the union at the college, is that 288 of the college's academic staff – that is, very roughly one-third of the total – were members of the union. What the college also knows is that there are 109 lecturers whose union dues are debited directly from their salaries before those salaries are paid. The college is, therefore, aware who those employees are, and no doubt assumes that they are among those balloted and induced to take strike action. That, however, only accounts for 109 out of the total of 872 members of the college's academic staff. It seems probable that 180 or so lecturers in addition to those 109 are likely to have been balloted or induced to take strike action as members of the union, and they may be any of the 760 remaining lecturers employed by the college whose identity is unknown to the college. Accordingly on that basis the college submits that the union's description in the two notices simply does not enable the college readily to ascertain who the employees are who were to be balloted and have been induced to take strike action. It is of course obvious that the college could simply ask all the members of its academic staff whether they are members of the union, whether they have been balloted and whether they have been instructed to take strike action. The college says that such an approach would cause great resentment and cause offence. But more significantly the college submits that that is not what the sections require. The union, on the other hand, submits that the college's argument in effect requires the union in this and similar situations to name its members within the college. That, it says, is deeply offensive to members of the union, who are entitled to keep their membership of the union private as between themselves and their union unless they choose to do otherwise. It is very strongly argued that to disclose these names against the wishes of the union's members would be in effect a breach of faith.

...

[Counsel for the union] addresses a powerful argument based on policy, and emphasises the offensiveness to union members of giving their names in this sort of situation, and fortifies that by reference to the Data Protection Act 1984 which would be, he says, breached if the names of members were to be disclosed without their consent. There are, I think, two conclusive answers to that argument. The first is that we are dealing with a later Act, and if its meaning is plain then it can only be construed as derogating from the general provisions of the earlier Act. The second answer is that if this can only be done with consent then the choice for the union, however difficult it may be in practice, is either to obtain consent or not to give the notice. It is also pointed out that the Data Protection Act does contain an exception covering information which has to be given by law.

Mr McMullen has drawn our attention to the European Convention of Human Rights and Fundamental Freedoms, and relies on Articles 8, 9, 10, 11, 13 and 14, arguing that the right to privacy of a trade union member should be protected and that in construing any ambiguous legislation we should bear in mind the desirability that the United Kingdom should conform with its obligations under the Convention. It is, of course, trite law that the Convention does not form part of our law, but if there were an ambiguity in this section I for my part would look very sympathetically towards the Convention if it provided help in construing the section. In my judgment there is in the present case no ambiguity in the section, and moreover I doubt if very much help is derived from the European Convention. The same, I think, is true of the ILO Conventions to which our attention was also drawn.

Mr McMullen has referred to the second volume of *Harvey on Industrial Relations and Employment Law*, in which volume, at division N on p 1898, the learned editors advance suggestions as to what should be an adequate description of employees to satisfy ss 226A and 234A. In my judgment, however, it all depends on the facts. There would be many situations that one could imagine in which a reference to all workers employed in this shop, or that shop, or this works, or that works, might give the employer sufficient information readily to ascertain who the employees in question were, but it must ultimately always be a question on the facts of a particular case as to whether the notice gives the employer that requisite knowledge or not. In this case it seems to me inescapable that the employer did not receive adequate information describing the employees so that he could readily ascertain who they were.

We have in this case the benefit of an extremely helpful and lucid judgment by the learned judge at first instance. He put his conclusion in the following way:

"Purely as a matter of construction, it seems to me that the words 'describing (so that he can readily ascertain them) the employees of the employer' can only mean that the union must, by specifying a category or by naming individuals or by a combination of the two, enable the employer readily to ascertain which of his employees are to be balloted, and subsequently to be called upon to take the relevant action. The wording set out above does not, I think, permit the interpretation contended for by Mr McMullen. It is not the description which the employer must readily ascertain, whatever that may mean; rather, it is the employees, because it is the employees who are to be described and ascertained. Whilst Parliament could have required a union always to name their members, by using the language it did I think that Parliament apparently allowed for the possibility that there would be occasions on which a union could properly identify the employees by category rather than by name."

I find myself in complete agreement with that and find it difficult to put the point more clearly or more succinctly.

The learned judge said that in coming to his conclusion he felt a degree of unease. If by that he meant that he was uneasy as to the practical implications of this construction, as to its effect on the shopfloor and on industrial relations, then it is possible to feel very considerable sympathy with his view. If, however, he meant (and I think that he did not) that he felt unease as to whether this was the correct construction, then I for my part do not share that unease, since, however unpalatable it may be, I regard the construction which he upheld as inescapable. For my part, therefore, I conclude that this appeal must be dismissed.'

(Neill and Steyn LJJ agreed.)

COMMENT

(1)   When the notice provisions were going through Parliament, it was denied that they would require the union always to provide an employer with a list of names. This decision suggests the opposite. The next case indicates what now appears to be standard practice. The main issue in this case, however, is about the effects of changes in the membership of the union after notices have been given.

London Underground Ltd v RMT

[1995] IRLR 636 Court of Appeal

Millet LJ: '...
The facts
The facts are not in dispute and may be shortly stated. There is a legitimate trade dispute between the parties, in furtherance of which the union has called on its members to take part in discontinuous industrial action consisting of a series of one- or two-day strikes. On 27 July, pursuant to s 226A of the Act, the union gave notice to the plaintiff of its intention to hold a ballot. The union served the plaintiff with a list of all its members (approximately 5,000) then in its employ who were entitled to vote in the ballot. The ballot was held between 4 and 17 August: 2,012 voted in favour of industrial action and 622 voted against.

On 17 August the union notified the plaintiff of the result of the ballot and pursuant to s 234A of the Act served notice of its intention to call for industrial action on dates between 25 August and 4 September. In the notice the union listed the names of its members upon whom it intended to call to take part in industrial action on those dates. The list included the names of 20 new members who had joined the union since the date of the ballot. They had not, of course, been balloted, nor had their names been included in the notice given to the plaintiff on 27 July.

In early September the union served a second notice under s 234A of the Act of further industrial action to take place on 20–22 September. The notice listed the names of its members whom it intended to call upon to take part in the industrial action on those dates. The list included the names of a further 672 new members who had joined the union since the date of the ballot. Of the 672 new members whose names appeared on the second s 234A notice, but not on the first, 244 had participated in one or more of the earlier stoppages, notice of which was given by the first notice. The inference is that their participation in those stoppages had been induced by the union.

The 692 new members who joined the union after the ballot included many key operatives whose participation was calculated to make industrial action more effective. They included, for example, 137 train staff concentrated on two lines. The plaintiff did not complain about the addition of the original extra 20 names; it regarded this as de minimis. The plaintiff does, however, complain of the addition of nearly 700 names. This is of wholly different order of magnitude and is clearly not de minimis.

The new members were not new employees of the plaintiff. They were existing employees who at the time of the ballot were either not members of any union or were members of another union, ASLEF. ASLEF was subject to an injunction restraining it from inducing its members to take industrial action. The judge considered it probable that they were persons who wished to take industrial action and joined the union in order to do so. According to the uncontradicted evidence to the plaintiff, the new members were persuaded to join the union as a result of an active recruitment campaign which it conducted among employees of the plaintiff.

Since the last s 234A notice, further new members have joined or have been recruited by the union. It is thought that there are now upwards of 800 members of the union who have never been balloted and whose names were not included on the original ballot list served on the plaintiff on 17 July but whom the union would wish to call upon to take part in any further stoppage.

...

The appeal: the 692

The question here is whether a trade union, without losing its immunity from suit, can call on a significant number of members to take part in industrial action who have joined the union since the date of the ballot and who have therefore not had an opportunity to vote in the ballot. A subsidiary question is whether it makes any difference that the new members have not joined the union by natural accretion during a long dispute, but have been actively recruited in order to make the industrial action more effective. The plaintiff insists that those who have been balloted represent the constituency of those who can be called on to take part in the action. If more than a de minimis number of members who have not been balloted are called upon to take part in industrial action, it is submitted that the action does not have the support of a ballot and the immunity is lost. It does not matter that the members in question joined the union after the ballot and so could not have been balloted. The union must take care to confine its call to take part in industrial action to those of its members who were balloted.

It is to be observed that the statutory immunity is conferred by s 219 in wide and general terms. It is not limited to trade unions and their members, but extends to *any person* who induces *another person* to commit a breach of contract. The withdrawal of immunity for want of a ballot, however, is in more limited terms. It is withdrawn only in respect of acts done *by a trade union*, and only in respect of acts to induce a person *to take part or continue to take part in industrial action*.

The question turns on the meaning of the critical words in s 226:

"(1) An act done by a trade union to induce a person to take part, or continue to take part, in industrial action—
(a) is not protected unless the industrial action has the support of a ballot ..."

The judge rightly concentrated on these words. He said:

"The key to all this lies in s 226(1), which provides that, for a trade union to be protected in respect of inducement to a person to take part in industrial action – which I read as meaning 'by the particular person induced' – must have the support of the ballot. The question is whether it can fairly be said that a particular industrial action *by a particular person* does have the support of a ballot [my emphasis]."

With respect, this is not only an unwarranted gloss on the words of the section but is syntactically incorrect and flies in the face of the plain meaning of the statutory language. What must have the support of a ballot is "the industrial action", that is to say, the industrial action referred to in the preceding line. That is not industrial action by a particular person (assuming for the moment that that is capable of being an accurate expression), but the industrial action *in which a particular person has been induced to take part*. If the opening words of s 226(1) are fully expanded, they read as follows:

"(1) An act done by a trade union to induce a person to take part, or continue to take part, in industrial action—

(a) is not protected unless the industrial action in which he has been induced to take part, or continue to take part, has the support of a ballot."

Industrial action is collective action. An individual does not take collective action; he takes part in it. Those who take part in it will normally be in breach of their contracts of employment. By inducing them to take part in it the union would be liable for the tort of inducing a breach of contract but for the immunity conferred by s 219. That immunity is withdrawn by the combined effect of s 219(4) and s 226(1) if the industrial action does not have the support of a ballot. But the participation of a particular individual in collective industrial action and the industrial action itself are two different things. It is the industrial action which must have the support of a ballot, not the participation of those who have been induced to take part in it.

This construction of the section is supported by the text of other provisions to be found in this part of the Act. Every person taking part in the ballot, for example, must be asked whether he is prepared to take part, or continue to take part, in industrial action (s 229(2)). If a majority of those who vote in the ballot answer "Yes", and the other requirements of the Act are satisfied, then "the industrial action shall be regarded as having the support of a ballot" (s 226(2)). The industrial action which is to be regarded as having the support of a ballot is not the industrial action of any particular individual, nor is it the action of those who voted "Yes". Even those who voted "No," but were outvoted, may be called upon to take part in the industrial action without the union losing its immunity. It is the industrial action in which a majority of those voting in the ballot have declared themselves prepared to take part. The collective action is treated as distinct from the participation of the individuals who are prepared to take part in it.

There is nothing in the very detailed requirements which Parliament has laid down for the conduct of the ballot which compels the union to restrict its call for industrial action to those of its members who were members at the date of the ballot and were given the opportunity to take part in it. Parliament must be taken to have appreciated that there would be constant changes in the membership of a large union, and that by normal accretion alone significant numbers of new members might join the union between the date of the ballot notice given to the employer under s 226A and the holding of the ballot, and between the holding of the ballot and the taking of industrial action. In the case of a lengthy dispute, the numbers in the latter case could be very large indeed.

But all this is expressly catered for. Section 226A requires the union to notify the employer of those of his employees who it is reasonable for the union to believe *at the time when it takes steps to give them notice* will be entitled to take part in the ballot. When the ballot is held, s 227(1) requires the union to ballot all those *of its members* who it is reasonable *at the time of the ballot* for the union to believe will be called upon to take part in the industrial action proposed and no others. If new members have joined since the service of the s 226A notice, they *must* be included in the ballot. There is nothing in s 227 which precludes the union from calling on them to take part in the industrial action. Non-members *must not* be included in the ballot.

If the union intends to call out signalmen but not train drivers, the signalmen *must* be balloted; the train drivers *must not*. The object is to prevent the union from distorting the result of the ballot by including militant members whom it does not intend to call upon to take part in industrial action. This is reinforced by subsection (2) which prevents the union from confining the ballot to militant members whom it does intend to call out and then changing its mind and calling out other less militant members. If it changes its mind and decides to extend the industrial action to members *who were members of the union at the time when the ballot was held* but who were not balloted, then it must hold a fresh ballot. But there is nothing in the section to preclude the union from including in the industrial action new members who were not balloted (and who could not lawfully be included in the ballot) because they were not members of the union at the time when the ballot was held.

...

Parliament's object in introducing the democratic requirement of a secret ballot is not to make life more difficult for trade unions by putting further obstacles in their way before they can call for industrial action with impunity, but to ensure that such action should have the genuine support of the members who are called upon to take part. The requirement has not been imposed for the protection of the employer or the public, but for the protection of the union's own members. Those who are members at the date of the ballot, and whom the union intends to call on to take industrial action, are entitled to be properly consulted without pressure or intimidation. There is no possible reason to extend the same protection to those who join after the ballot. They do so of their own volition and in the knowledge of the outcome of the ballot and of the imminence of industrial action in which they will be called upon to take part.

...

If inducing non-members to support industrial action by withdrawing their labour is to be distinguished from inducing members to take part in the industrial action called by the union, then it is an activity which attracts immunity under ss 219 and 220 but falls outside the withdrawal of the immunity in s 226(1). But even if the premise is not right, I think that the same conclusion is nevertheless correct. It would be astonishing if a right which was first conferred by Parliament in 1906, which has been enjoyed by trade unions ever since and which is today recognised as encompassing a fundamental human right, should have been removed by Parliament by enacting a series of provisions intended to strengthen industrial democracy and governing the relations between a union and its own members.

I conclude, therefore, that there is nothing in ss 226–235 which curtails a union's long-accepted right to induce non-members to support the industrial action called by the union by breaking their own contracts of employment. But if this is so, then there is no reason to deny the same right in respect of non-members who have subsequently joined the union. There is simply no objection to a small union, which has the support of a ballot of its own members, seeking to attract support from non-members.

The judge may also have been influenced by the fact that the union has obtained a large influx of new members by an active recruiting campaign. I am unable to see what objection there can be to such activity. A union is plainly free to campaign actively for new members before it holds the ballot in the hope that such members will support industrial action. If they become members before the ballot, they *must* be balloted, even though their views may affect the result of the ballot. I am unable to see why activity which is unobjectionable before the ballot is objectionable after it.

I would allow the appeal. ...'

(Ward and Butler-Sloss LJJ agreed.)

COMMENT

(1)   The trial judge also held, however, that the union was not entitled to call out the new members unless they had been identified in the s 234A notice. The union did not appeal against this, so the Court of Appeal did not consider the issue.

(2)   Note Millett L J's opinion that non-members may be called on to take part without being balloted first. Do you think that he is correct in his description of Parliament's intention in this matter?

(3)   In this case the Court of Appeal also rejected the different view about changes in the membership expressed by Donaldson MR in *Post Office* v *UCW* (below, p 562).

Who votes?
Trade Union and Labour Relations (Consolidation) Act 1992

227.   (1)   Entitlement to vote in the ballot must be accorded equally to all the members of the trade union who it is reasonable at the time of the ballot for the union to believe will be induced to take part or, as the case may be, to continue to take part in the industrial action in question, and to no others.

 (2)   The requirement in subsection (1) shall be taken not to have been satisfied if any person who was a member of the trade union at the time when the ballot was held and was denied entitlement to vote in the ballot is induced by the union to take part or, as the case may be, to continue to take part in the industrial action.

COMMENT

(1)   It was held in *British Railways Board* v *NUR* that inadvertent failure to give a member an opportunity to vote did not amount to a breach of s 227.

(2)   Under TULRCA s 230, as amended by TURERA, the ballot has to be fully postal: that is, the ballot papers must be sent out by post with pre-paid envelopes so that they can be returned by post as well.

(3)   The Code of Practice on Trade Union Ballots recommends that at least seven days should be allowed for a postal ballot where first class post is used, and at least fourteen days for second class post. Both seem somewhat optimistic: the net result is that it will be harder for unions to strike while the iron is hot.

(4)   Another change introduced by TURERA was a scrutiny requirement for all ballots where more than 50 members are entitled to vote (TULRCA ss 226B, 226C, 231B).

(5)   Generally speaking, however, the obligation to hold a ballot is strictly construed: in *Shipping Company Uniform Inc* v *International Transport Workers' Federation* the union had not held a ballot for the very good reason that the ITF was a federation of unions and had no individual members: therefore there was no one it could ballot. Rather than hold it was exempt from the requirement, Staughton J held that no ballot meant no immunity. The union had got to change its rules to allow the members of federated unions to become direct members of the ITF, so that ballots could be held in the future.

Separate workplaces
University of Central England v *NALGO*

[1993] IRLR 81 Queen's Bench Division

The two plaintiffs were formerly polytechnics, in which guise they had been members of the

Polytechnic and Colleges Employers' Forum, which negotiated on behalf of its members with the union. The union rejected a pay offer and balloted all its members on industrial action. There was a majority of 3,630 to 3,004 on a 59 per cent turn out.

The plaintiffs argued that there should have been separate ballots at each employer's workplace.

Latham J: '... The two plaintiffs are aggrieved by that decision for two reasons. One is that they consider that their own employees, who are members of the defendant union, were not themselves in favour of strike action; and that may or may not be factually correct. It certainly of itself has no legal significance. Their second grievance is that the ballot which was carried out was not a lawful ballot for the purposes of justifying, or to be more exact protecting, the defendants in relation to their strike call. The plaintiffs assert that, for the purposes of [TULRCA ss 226–232] the ballot had to be a ballot of each individual employer and it was not open to the defendants to protect their position by way of what one might loosely call the nationwide ballot ...

[Section 228] is dealing with the question of where members of the union have different places of work. Prima facie, where their members do have different places of work there must be a separate ballot in respect of each of those places of work.

Again, there is nothing in that subsection which helps expressly to determine whether the members have to be employed by the same employer or not. Equally, there is nothing which says that they must be. It, again, could be said that the phrase "different places of work" is more apt to describe the situation where the employers are the same employers, but on the other hand it could equally be that that is intended to ensure that not only where there are different employers, but where within the same employer there are different places of work, there has to be a separate ballot. The absence of the phrase or anything expressly dealing with employers really is, in one sense, neutral in that particular subsection.

As one goes through [ss 227–232], it is plain that up until the time we get to [s 228] there has never been any mention of the phrase 'by the same employer' until one gets to [s 228(3)(c)(ii)]. Up to that point it was at least arguable, even though the plain words of the section do not lead to that conclusion, that [s 228] is indeed only ever to be applied in respect of the members of the union who are employed by the one employer, who is the employer with whom they are in dispute for the purposes of the trade dispute.

But Parliament has used the phrase 'by the same employer' in that particular subsection, and nowhere else in [ss 226–232]. The more one reads through [ss 227–232], the more one appreciates in those circumstances that it would have been easy for Parliament, had it intended [those sections] to have the construction called for by Mr Hand on behalf of the plaintiffs, to have said so in a way which would have obviated the need for much of the verbiage which is found in those subsections.

Having considered carefully the argument put forward on behalf of the plaintiffs, I am quite satisfied that the clear indication given by the use of the phrase in one place and its absence elsewhere points against one being able to read into what are otherwise the clear words of [ss 226–232] the implication which the plaintiffs seek to bring into it, which is that the underpinning of the meaning of "trade dispute" somehow justifies that gloss on what would otherwise be the normal meaning of the words in the sections.

For that reason, I am quite satisfied that, provided the defendants can show that it was reasonable for them to believe, and they did believe, that there was some common factor relating to the terms or conditions of employment in respect of which the industrial action is called for, they are entitled to hold a ballot of all their members affected by that factor, whether they are employed by the same employer or not. I am comforted to note that the Code of Practice which was published together with the Act, although there is no doubt that it is to some extent deficient, generally speaking can only have meaning if the construction which

I have considered to be the appropriate construction of [ss 226–232] is that which was indeed intended by Parliament.

It follows that I refuse the applications for injunctions in these two actions. I am very grateful to both parties for their arguments.'

COMMENT

(1)   TULRCA s 228 could be one of the most obscure statutory provisions ever drafted. The gist of it is to stop unions defining the constituency of those voting in such a way that a militant group can outweigh moderate voters. However, at the same time it is recognised that the union is entitled to hold a single ballot for all those having the same interest in the dispute. Thus it will not often be applicable.

(2)   As long as there is national bargaining for employees, national ballots will continue to be possible, provided that the members have the same interest. The only limiting factor, noted by the judge, is that there must be a trade dispute, which means that there must be separate disputes with each employer.

(3)   The converse is also true: if employers move away from national collective bargaining to local bargaining, it becomes more likely that separate ballots will be necessary. The break-up of nationalised industries also has that potential, as the next case illustrates.

Intercity West Coast Ltd v RMT

[1996] IRLR 583 Court of Appeal

Union members who worked as train conductors at Manchester Piccadilly station were in dispute with ICWC over the non-reinstatement of four conductors. Following rail privatisation, two companies, ICWC and North West Regional Railways (NWRR), both wholly-owned subsidiaries of British Rail, ran services from the station. They operated from separate buildings next to the station, which was where conductors reported for work. However, the conductors actually carried out their work on the concourse and platforms at the station, which were owned by Railtrack. Railtrack allowed employees of the two rail companies on to the station under a licence agreement.

RMT balloted all the conductors working for both ICWC and NWRR on industrial action and got a large majority in favour. ICWC challenged the ballot, claiming that its employees had a separate workplace from NWRR employees, and so there should have been separate ballots. The crucial question was, what was their place of work? This is defined in TULRCA s 228(4) as 'the premises occupied by the employer at or from which that person works ...'. ICWC argued that their employees worked from their building, not the station; furthermore, since the station premises were owned by Railtrack, not ICWC, they did not *occupy* the station. These arguments succeeded at first instance, and the union appealed.

Morritt LJ: '... It seems to me that there are two questions to be decided. The first is to ascertain what premises were occupied by the plaintiff, and the second is to identify that place from which it can be said that the conductors work. Both depend upon the proper construction of s 228(4) of the Trade Union and Labour Relations (Consolidation) Act 1992, as applied to the facts of the case in so far as that can ascertained from the evidence before us.

In the nature of things that evidence is relatively incomplete. But the third affidavit of Mr Mitchell [ICWC's director of human resources], from which my Lord has already quoted, paragraph 2, states in terms that the concourse, track, platforms, etc, are not leased or exclusively licensed to any other person. As regards these, train operating companies such as ICWC have entered into formal access agreements, which give them a licence by themselves and their staff to use those parts of the station for the purpose of their business. Mr Mitchell then expresses the view that he does not consider that that results in ICWC occupying any part of the station. That of course is a question of the proper construction of the Act when applied to the facts.

A licence, as such, can come in many different forms. At one end of the scale is the case of permission to walk over the land of another; at the other end of the scale there is what is, in all but name and legal effect, a lease of the property because it is essential to have substantial control of it for the purposes of conducting your business at it. The evidence of Mr Mitchell leads me to think that we are entitled to infer that the relationship between Railtrack and ICWC comes at the latter end of the scale rather than the former.

It is also necessary to consider the purpose for which the legislation raises the question of occupation. The purpose is to identify by some formula the place of work of particular employees. Neither a place of work nor the concept of occupation requires exclusive possession or a lease or any other particular concept familiar to real property lawyers. What they do require is sufficient access to and sufficient control over the premises to enable the work to be carried on or the business of the employer to be carried out. It is true that in this case there are parts of the station which are let to others; for example, that part let to the newsagents or that part let to each of the individual operating companies. But so far as the concourse, track and platforms, etc, are concerned, these are not leased to others but they are the very essence of the business conducted by the operating companies. It seems to me that in those circumstances, those parts of Manchester Piccadilly, that is to say the parts referred to by Mr Mitchell, are indeed occupied by the operating companies and each of them, notwithstanding that they also occupy as lessees other parts of the station – that is to say the Tower Block or the Amenity Block respectively.

Given that construing the legislation in the light of the purpose for which it is enacted, one reaches as I do the conclusion that the operating companies do occupy those parts of the station, the problem then arises to identify that place from which, within the terms of the section, the conductors work. It seems to me that in every realistic sense of the word they work from the operating part of the station and not just from that bit where they clock on and clock off. In railway terms, any person asked where the conductor worked from would identify the station and not the particular place where he clocked on and clocked off. From the point of view of the operating company, the operating company is operating from the station, including the concourse, the platforms and the track, and not merely from the Amenity Block or the Tower Block. From the point of view of the work to be carried out by the conductors, which as the evidence recognises is primarily on the trains, that work takes place from the station as a whole and not from the individual parts of it.

In agreement with my Lord, I think with respect to Gage J, he reached the wrong conclusion in this respect, and I would allow the appeal.'

(Neill LJ delivered a concurring judgment; Pill LJ dissented.)

The ballot paper
London Underground Ltd v National Union of Railwaymen

[1989] IRLR 341 Queen's Bench Division

The union, in balloting its members, indicated that the dispute was about four issues, but asked only a single question about whether or not members were willing to strike. The company argued that this invalidated the ballot because three of the issues were no longer the subject of current negotiations.

Simon Brown J: '... Mr Lemon further argues that, even if all four issues are trade disputes, nevertheless it is impermissible and offensive to the scheme of [ss 226–232] to wrap them all up together in a single question. That part of his submissions I cannot accept. Mr Hendy's submission, advanced on behalf of the defendant union, is that it is not fatal to his client's right to invoke the statutory immunity even if the three subsidiary issues are found not to be trade disputes. He submits that, even if only one of the four issues is a trade dispute, that is sufficient to give immunity. That submission equally I reject. I recognise that it is arguable, but to my mind that is certainly not the unambiguous purport and meaning of the Act, and it would be surprising if the argument were right. If it were, then a majority of the voters at the qualifying ballot could well support strike action in regard to issues that were not trade disputes and for which, in the ordinary way, no [s 219] immunity would arise, and indeed be wholly against the notion of striking for the only issue capable of founding that immunity. Mr Hendy says that that is irrelevant: so long as members, for whatever reason, support a strike, then it is immaterial that that support is not in regard to the only legitimate reason, namely the trade dispute, for which the strike is called.

True, the only question that requires to be asked under [s 229(2)] is a simple question involving a yes or no answer. True too, all that the statute expressly requires to appear on the voting paper is the cautionary sentence: "If you take part in a strike ... you may be in breach of your contract of employment." But I am not inclined to construe [s 226(2)(a)] as being satisfied where the ballot poses a question which, either wholly or in part, asks whether the member is prepared to participate in a strike by reference to issues other than trade disputes.

The result of those conclusions is this. The defendants, although asserting that all four issues here constituted trade disputes, at this point cannot, to my mind, show that more probably than not they will succeed in that assertion. Were they to do so, then, in line with Lord Diplock's approach in *NWL Ltd* v *Woods*, and rejecting as I do Mr Lemon's wider submissions, I would refuse this application. As it is, however, it seems to me that the defendants are as likely to fail as to succeed in what I believe to be the necessary step in their argument for immunity of showing that all four issues constitute trade disputes. That being so, and all other factors to be weighed in the balance of convenience to my mind very firmly supporting the maintenance of the *status quo* and thus the calling off of Monday's strike, I believe that this injunction must be granted.

I add only this. Although inevitably that is a decision which I am driven to take at this late hour and after insufficient argument and certainly insufficient consideration, I am to some degree comforted by the thought that it may well not be the last word on this obviously important and by no means straightforward issue. For my part, however, I believe that the application is well-founded and that the relief sought should be granted.'

COMMENT

(1)   This case, again, involved emergency interlocutory proceedings held on a single day with judgment given late in the evening. It illustrates one of the endemic problems about the case law on industrial action: many are heard only as interlocutory proceedings, where the employer is seeking an injunction at short notice to prevent threatened action. They are heard in great haste, without proper evidence and without wholly

adequate argument. The decisions are thus sometimes not as fully considered as would be desirable. The notice provisions in ss 226A and 234A partially alleviate this.

(2)   That said, it seems that this judgment must accurately state the law: presumably it is for the union to convince the court that there was a genuine trade dispute issue, which perhaps relates more to s 219 than the balloting rules. However, it may be noted that the Code of Practice on Trade Union Ballots on Industrial Action (para 43) recommends that background information on the issues to which the dispute relates should be given to members.

(3)   TULRCA s 229 deals with the format of the ballot paper, and requires a 'health warning' to be included on every ballot paper reading, 'If you take part in a strike or other industrial action, you may be in breach of your contract of employment.' This is obviously intended to have a chilling effect on a worker's enthusiasm for action. While no comment is permitted on the ballot paper itself, it seems that it would be legitimate for a union to enclose separate literature with the ballot paper, pointing out, for example, that this is nothing new.

(4)   It is clear that s 229(2) requires two questions where the union is planning both strike action and action short of a strike (see *Post Office* v *UCW* below, p 562).

(5)   In *West Midlands Travel* v *TGWU* the union asked separate questions on all-out strike action and action short of a strike. On strike action, 1,265 were in favour, 1,225 were against and 147 left the question blank. On action short of a strike, 1,059 were in favour, 1,156 were against and 427 left if blank. Thus overall, 2,642 had taken part in the ballot by answering at least one of the questions. The employer therefore argued that a majority meant at least 1,322 in favour, and this had not been achieved. However, the Court of Appeal held that 'majority' meant a majority on each question, discounting those who chose not to vote (otherwise their abstentions would effectively count as 'no' votes).

Procedure after the ballot

After the ballot is held, TULRCA s 231 requires the union to provide all those entitled to vote with a breakdown of the result. Following amendment by TURERA, s 231A requires the union to provide the same information to all employers of members entitled to vote. The requirement for the scrutineer to produce a report on the ballot states that it must be made available to anyone entitled to vote, or the employer of such a person, during the six months following the ballot (s 231B).

TULRCA s 233 stipulates that subsequent industrial action will only be protected if the person specified on the ballot paper as having authority to call the action actually does so.

Tanks & Drums Ltd v Transport and General Workers' Union

[1992] ICR 1 Court of Appeal

The specified person on the ballot paper was Ron Todd, General Secretary of the TGWU. The company claimed that the strike was not immune because it had in fact been called by two shop stewards. Mr Todd gave evidence that the usual procedure was for the regional officer to inform him of the ballot result and he would then authorise the action and ask the regional official to inform the district organiser, who in turn should inform the members. In this case, the word had gone down to the district organiser that the action could start if the employer's stance did not change at a final negotiating meeting which was due the next day. The district organiser informed the shop stewards of this. At the meeting, the employers asked for more time to consider their position and were given four days. However, later the same day the shop stewards reached the conclusion that the employers were not serious about reconsidering their proposals and they called a meeting of the workforce at which it was decided to strike at once.

Neill LJ: '...On behalf of the plaintiff in this court it has been argued that in [TULRCA s 233] the call for a strike which is there envisaged is an unequivocal call by the specified person and one which is free from any conditions. It was said that that is not only the natural meaning of the subsection but is also consistent with the mischief against which this legislation is aimed. If in fact it was possible to impose conditions, it would mean that somebody other than the specified person would have a discretion and authority to decide whether the conditions had been met. The plain purpose of this legislation is that it is only at the end of the road, when negotiations have really reached a make or break point, that the specified person, with all the facts in front of him, should have an opportunity to make up his mind whether or not at that stage to call for a strike. That is Mr Supperstone's principal submission: he said that it meets the purpose of the Act.

For my part I am unable to accept that argument. Mr Supperstone was constrained to admit that in a case such as this if a specified person says "I call a strike" or "I call for industrial action" and then tells his subordinate union officers "If you have a successful meeting tomorrow you should not go ahead with the strike", that is something which is permissible and within the wording of the section, but what cannot be allowed is for the specified person to say "I call for or authorise a strike if the meeting tomorrow is not successful." It seems to me that such a distinction, which depends purely on the language which the specified person uses over the telephone, cannot be a proper distinction to be drawn in circumstances of this kind.

Clearly, as I see it, there must be a very close link in time between the call for a strike and the event, for example, an unsuccessful meeting, which precipitates the final action. Mr Hendy conceded that it certainly would not be within the purpose of this legislation if a general secretary or other specified person were to give a blanket authority for a local union official to go ahead with negotiations on the basis that a strike could then be treated as being authorised if things did not go well. It seems to me that, as was put in the course of argument, it is a question of fact and degree in each case. At the end of the day one has to answer the simple question: did the specified person call or call for the industrial action? This union decided to make the general secretary the specified person. This may be regarded as an indication that the union treats the legislation seriously and regards the calling of a strike as a serious matter which, before it is authorised, has to go to the highest level ...

It seems to me that one has to look at this evidence as a whole. For my part I pay particular attention to what Mr Todd himself said in his affidavit. He was saying: "I call for a strike if the meeting which the local officers are having tomorrow is not successful." It was on that basis and only on that basis that a condition was imposed on the strike. It seems to me that in the field of industrial relations it would be impracticable to leave matters in such a way that there was no possibility for the exercise of judgment on the ground. Some matters must be left for the judgment of those on the ground who have to decide how and when as a matter of common sense the call for action is to be put into operation. Therefore for those reasons I would reject Mr Supperstone's two primary arguments....'

(Russell LJ delivered a concurring judgment and Leggatt LJ agreed.)

COMMENT

(1)   The ostensible purpose of the 'specified person' provision was to stop minor officials (like shop stewards) jumping the gun and starting action as soon as the result of the ballot was announced. However, as this case shows, it has the potential for being one more trap which may result in the loss of immunity. The Court of Appeal shows a welcome realism in its decision.

(2)   Reference is made in the case to the time limit on the effectiveness of the ballot: s 234 provides that the ballot ceases to be effective four weeks after the date of the ballot. That limit is eroded by every new requirement to be fulfilled before action in the post-ballot period. For example, in *Associated British Ports* v *TGWU*, the union representing dockers wanted to organise a dock strike in protest at the proposed deregulation of the docks which was at that time going through Parliament (it eventually became the Dock Work Act 1989). A majority voted in favour of action in a ballot, but the employer subsequently sued for an interlocutory injunction, claiming that the action was outside the trade dispute immunity. By the time the House of Lords found in favour of the union and discharged the injunction against them, the original four-week mandate had expired. By the time another ballot could be held, the bill had been passed into law, and protest was too late. For this reason, what is now TULRCA s 234 was amended so that in such circumstances, the time limit can be extended – although this will not necessarily happen in every case.

(3)   The requirement to give employers seven days' notice of any action effectively reduces the four-week window to three weeks, since the notice cannot be given until after the ballot result is announced (s 234A(4)).

(4)   What if the action produces fresh negotiations with the employer and the action is suspended? Does there have to be a fresh ballot before action can be recommenced?

Monsanto plc v Transport and General Workers' Union

[1987] ICR 269 Court of Appeal

There was a dispute at the company over the use of temporary labour. The union held a ballot on 6 May, and action started the day after a result in favour of action was announced. On 12 June, the action was suspended because there were new meetings with the management in an attempt to settle the dispute. There was no settlement, and so on 23 June the union recommenced action.

Dillon LJ: '... Mr Goudie says first that once industrial action is discontinued, for whatever reason and even if it is only pending negotiations, it is spent and there must be a further ballot before it can legitimately be resumed. He says secondly that the initial ballot was in relation to the engagement of temporary employees, but that is no longer the issue causative of the industrial action from 23 June onwards, because the five employees have gone and so the ballot has been overtaken by subsequent events.

In considering that second submission I find it necessary first to look at the wording of [TULRCA s 226]. An act done by a trade union is actionable in tort on the ground that it induced a person to break his contract of employment or to interfere with its performance if the act was done without the support of a ballot. An act is to be taken as having been done with the support of a ballot if, and only if, the union has held a ballot in respect of the industrial action in the course of which the breach or interference occurred. So the instruction to break the contract or interfere with its performance and the obedience to that instruction are industrial action and one has to consider whether the course of industrial action in which they occurred was a course of industrial action in respect of which a ballot has been held. I look to see therefore what this ballot was about and I find that in the heading to the announced return, which says: "TGWU ballot in respect of industrial action in pursuit of a settlement of the dispute with Monsanto Ltd over the employment of temporary labour." Mr Goudie says that the industrial action was over the five temporary employees, but for the purposes of this interlocutory appeal I could not accept that because the employees were dismissed on 30 May and in the memorandum of 4 June the company was treating the dispute as still continuing, the central issue being temporaries which the company wished to resolve at an early stage. Therefore I do not read it for present purposes as limited to the employment of five individuals. It is also a ballot in respect of industrial action in pursuit of a settlement of the dispute. The matters which have led to the further outbreak of industrial action at 23 and 24 June are the arrangements in respect of pay during the time that the employees were acting in accordance with the union's instructions for industrial action, sick pay as a result of the countersanctions by the company and so forth and all that, as it seems to be, is part of the process covered by settlement of the dispute with the company over the employment of temporary labour, at any rate prima facie. We are not required on this appeal to express a concluded view, but we are required by [s 221] to have regard to the likelihood of the union succeeding at the trial.

In relation to Mr Goudie's first submission it seems to me that in the normal course of industrial relations where industrial action has been begun the employer is likely to say that he will not negotiate while the industrial action is continuing. The union may be prepared to suspend industrial action while negotiations take place, but the intention throughout would be that that is not a discontinuance of the industrial action but a temporary suspension for the purposes of negotiation so that the industrial action will be resumed if the negotiations fail. I do not for my part see that in such circumstances the statute or good industrial relations require a further ballot at each stage if there is a suspension for negotiations.

Proceeding from there it seems to me that as the matters which led to the outbreak of the further industrial action or the reimposition of it are matters within the scope of the settlement of the original dispute, the principle of which has not been answered either way – that is to say, the principle of the company's power as manager to employ temporary labour – this is a case in which on the facts, so far as we can discern them from the affidavit evidence in advance of the trial the union is considerably more likely than not to succeed at the trial of the action.

That being so, I disagree with the view which I take Gatehouse J to have formed in relation to [s 221(2)]. Having to balance the important factor of the union's prospects of success against the balance of convenience factors affecting the company which I mentioned earlier, I reach the conclusion feeling free to exercise a discretion having regard to the judge's approach to [s 221] that in the circumstances of this case the injunction ought not to be granted ...'

Neill LJ: '... In my view both as a matter of principle and on the facts of this case that submission cannot be sustained. To my mind it would be quite wrong not to allow to union officials the flexibility of being able to call off strike action or other action temporarily so that negotiations can continue and then reimpose it if, after a short period, the discussions fail to reach any fruitful result ...'

Post Office v Union of Communication Workers

[1990] ICR 258 Court of Appeal

Lord Donaldson MR:
'... *The effect of discontinuity of industrial action*

The intention of Parliament was quite clear that industrial action, whether taking the form of a strike or of industrial action short of a strike or both, should be begun, or its continuance endorsed, within a short period after the date of the ballot: see [TULRCA s 226(2)(c)]. The reason is clear. Industrial relations are essentially fluid and attitudes change quickly. Accordingly, authority obtained from a ballot may in fact, as distinct from law, become invalid within a relatively short time. Although the Act in terms only requires the action to be begun in the specified period of four weeks, it is implicit that, once begun, it shall continue without substantial interruption, if reliance is to continue to be placed upon the verdict of the ballot. This is a question of fact and degree, but the question which the court has to ask itself is whether the average reasonable trade union member, looking at the matter at or shortly after any interruption in the industrial action, would say to himself: "the industrial action has now come to an end", even if he might also say: "the union may want to call us out again if the dispute continues". This is to be contrasted with a situation revealed in *Monsanto Plc* v *Transport and General Workers' Union* where industrial action was "suspended" for a short period (14 days) in order to enable active negotiations to take place. The negotiations failed and any reasonable union member would have said, and this court did say, that the termination of the period of suspension restored the original and authorised industrial action.

On the facts of the present case, it is quite clear that the all out one day strike on 12 December 1988 ended the industrial action contemplated and authorised by the August 1988 ballot and that this is why no further such action took place for over nine months. Applying the analysis of the traditional firework display, various rockets and bangers were discharged between 12 October and 30 November 1988 with the set piece finale on 12 December 1988. This was followed by a complete change of tactics, namely, the mounting of a public relations campaign, with a reversion to a policy of industrial action only in September 1989, even if a decision or tentative decision to adopt this course was taken in May 1989. This represented entirely new and disconnected action which needed the support of a fresh ballot.

...

(Butler-Sloss LJ delivered a concurring judgment and Farquharson LJ agreed.)

COMMENT

(1) In *Post Office* v *UCW*, the union lost immunity on two grounds: the point discussed here, and also because it had asked just one question in relation to both strike action and action short of a strike. See also *Secretary of State for Scotland* v *Scottish Prison Officers' Association*.

(2) It should be clear that the requirements to be met for a valid ballot are both numerous and complicated. Should a union fail anywhere along the line, the industrial action will lose its immunity and be actionable in tort.

Action for prohibited reasons

The final strategy of the Conservative Government for reducing the ambit of lawful industrial action was to identify certain reasons as unlawful. Action in pursuit of these reasons will then lose its immunity. These provisions sit rather oddly with TULRCA s 244(1), as the grounds are recognised there as being valid subject-matter for a trade dispute.

Union membership and recognition requirements

Trade Union and Labour Relations (Consolidation) Act 1992

222. (1) An act is not protected if the reason, or one of the reasons, for which it is done is the fact or belief that a particular employer—
    (a) is employing, has employed or might employ a person who is not a member of a trade union, or
    (b) is failing, has failed or might fail to discriminate against such a person.

(2) For the purposes of subsection (1)(b) an employer discriminates against a person if, but only if, he ensures that his conduct in relation to—
    (a) persons, or persons of any description, employed by him, or who apply to be, or are, considered by him for employment, or
    (b) the provision of employment for such persons,
    is different, in some or all cases, according to whether or not they are members of a trade union, and is more favourable to those who are.

(3) An act is not protected if it constitutes, or is one of a number of acts which together constitute, an inducement or attempted inducement of a person—
    (a) to incorporate in a contract to which that person is a party, or a proposed contract to which he intends to be a party, a term or condition which is or would be void by virtue of section 144 (union membership requirement in contract for goods or services), or
    (b) to contravene section 145 (refusal to deal with person on grounds relating to union membership).

...

COMMENT

(1)   This means that industrial action taken to enforce the closed shop (subs (1)) or to spread it to other employers (subs (3)) will lose immunity.

(2)   In similar vein, TULRCA s 225 removes immunity from any action taken to enforce recognition requirements.

(3)   The genesis of both ss 222 and 225 was the practice of Labour-controlled councils to put union membership requirements in contracts offered for tender. That is, firms wanting to have local government contracts would sometimes have to undertake to maintain a closed shop, to use only union labour, etc. When it was proposed to outlaw such requirements in the Employment Act 1982, some councils began instead to insert recognition requirements: contractors would have to undertake to recognise the appropriate union in respect of their workers. All such requirements are now void (see TULRCA ss 186–187).

(4)   Compare TULRCA s 244(1)(e) and (g).

Reinstatement of unofficial strikers

Trade Union and Labour Relations (Consolidation) Act 1992

223.   An act is not protected if the reason, or one of the reasons, for doing it is the fact or belief that an employer has dismissed one or more employees in circumstances such that by virtue of section 237 (dismissal in connection with unofficial action) they have no right to complain of unfair dismissal.

COMMENT

(1)   The restrictions on lawful industrial action have made unions reluctant to call official action, which has led to an increase in unofficial action. We saw in Chapter 12 that workers dismissed for taking unofficial action have no claim for unfair dismissal in any circumstances: this goes further and removes immunity from any industrial action taken with a view to getting them reinstated.

(2)   Note that the immunity is lost in both this case and under ss 222 and 225 if only *one* of the reasons for action is a prohibited reason.

(3)   Compare TULRCA s 244(1)(b).

Who represents the union?

Where organising industrial action results in tortious liability, the individuals who have actually done the organising are personally liable. However, the employer normally wishes to claim against the union – whether the aim is to get damages or just to get the action called off. But who is the union? It cannot be every single member; is it the president or general secretary or national executive or what? Once the Employment Act 1982 removed the total immunity that unions had previously enjoyed and put them on the same footing as individuals, it became crucial to know the answer to this question. Unfortunately, there is not one answer, but two.

Trade Union and Labour Relations (Consolidation) Act 1992

20.   ...
  (2)   An act shall be taken to have been authorised or endorsed by a trade union if it was done, or was authorised or endorsed—
     (a)   by any person empowered by the rules to do, authorise or endorse acts of the kind in question, or
     (b)   by the principal executive committee or the president or general secretary, or
     (c)   by any other committee of the union or any other official of the union (whether employed by it or not).
  (3)   For the purposes of paragraph (c) of subsection (2)—
     (a)   any group of persons constituted in accordance with the rules of the union is a committee of the union, and
     (b)   an act shall be taken to have been done, authorised or endorsed by an

official if it was done, authorised or endorsed by, or by any member of, any group of persons of which he was at the material time a member, the purposes of which included organising or co-ordinating industrial action.

COMMENT

(1)   Note that this statutory regime applies only to liability for those torts for which immunity is given by virtue of s 244 (inducement of breach of contract, interference with contract, intimidation and conspiracy), and in assessing whether individuals are taking part in official or unofficial action in relation to s 237. For all other purposes, common law principles must apply.

(2)   Subsection (2) lists the officials whose authorisation (ahead of action) or endorsement of it (after it has started) will make the union liable. Those mentioned in (a) and (b) are obvious: the top officials are the ones who run the union and must therefore be taken to speak for it. If the rules add anyone else, then it makes sense that that should be given effect. Subsection (2)(c), however, goes much further: any other official would cover every shop steward in the country, which in the case of the large unions would run to thousands. Union liability was extended to this group by the Employment Act 1990.

(3)   There is a let-out for the union, where action is authorised or endorsed by these lesser officials: it can escape liability if it promptly repudiates the action. However, the conditions for a valid repudiation were made considerably more onerous by the Employment Act 1990.

Trade Union and Labour Relations (Consolidation) Act 1992

21.   (1)   An act shall not be taken to have been authorised or endorsed by a trade union by virtue only of paragraph (c) of section 20(2) if it was repudiated by the executive, president or general secretary as soon as reasonably practicable after coming to the knowledge of any of them.

(2)   Where an act is repudiated—
   (a)   written notice of the repudiation must be given to the committee or official in question, without delay, and
   (b)   the union must do its best to give individual written notice of the fact and date of repudiation, without delay—
      (i)   to every member of the union who the union has reason to believe is taking part, or might otherwise take part, in industrial action as a result of the act, and
      (ii)   to the employer of every such member.

(3)   The notice given to members in accordance with paragraph (b)(i) of subsection (2) must contain the following statement—

'Your union has repudiated the call (or calls) for industrial action to which this notice relates and will give no support to unofficial industrial action taken in response to it (or them). If you are dismissed while taking unofficial industrial action, you will have no right to complain of unfair dismissal.'

(4)   If subsection (2) or (3) is not complied with, the repudiation shall be treated as ineffective.

(5)   An act shall not be treated as repudiated if at any time after the union concerned purported to repudiate it the executive, president or general secretary has behaved in a manner which is inconsistent with the purported repudiation.

(6)   The executive, president or general secretary shall be treated as so behaving if, on a request made to any of them within three months of the purported repudiation by a person who—

    (a)   is a party to a commercial contract whose performance has been or may be interfered with as a result of the act in question, and

    (b)   has not been given written notice by the union of the repudiation,

    it is not forthwith confirmed in writing that the act has been repudiated.

(7)   In this section 'commercial contract' means any contract other than—

    (a)   a contract of employment, or

    (b)   any other contract under which a person agrees personally to do work or perform services for another.

COMMENT

(1)   The burdensome requirement in subsections (2)(b) and (3), to give individual written notices to affected members and employers, were 1990 amendments.

(2)   Subsection (6) was also introduced then. However, even before this, the courts had shown themselves astute to the possibility of a purported repudiation not being genuine: see *Express & Star Ltd* v *National Graphical Association (1982)*.

Trade Union and Labour Relations (Consolidation) Act 1992

22.   (1)   This section applies to any proceedings in tort brought against a trade union, except—

    (a)   proceedings for personal injury as a result of negligence, nuisance or breach of duty;

    (b)   proceedings for breach of duty in connection with the ownership, occupation, possession, control or use of property;

    (c)   proceedings brought by virtue of Part I of the Consumer Protection Act 1987 (product liability).

    (2)   In any proceedings in tort to which this section applies the amount which may be awarded against the union by way of damages shall not exceed the following limit—

Number of members of union	Maximum award of damages
Less than 5,000	£10,000
5,000 or more but less than 25,000	£50,000
25,000 or more but less than 100,000	£125,000
100,000 or more	£250,000

    (3)   The Secretary of State may by order amend subsection (2) so as to vary any of the sums specified; and the order may make such transitional provision as the Secretary of State considers appropriate.

...

COMMENT

(1)   These limits have not been raised since their introduction in 1982. TULRCA s 23 further provides that the union's political and benevolent funds (if any) will not be available for paying damages, provided that the rules of those funds prevent them being used to finance industrial action.

(2)   Note, however, that they apply only to actions in tort: s 20 has no relevance to contempt proceedings, for example. There is no limit on the amount of the fine which may be levied for contempt.

(3)   Equally, s 20 only indicates the people for whom the union is vicariously liable in proceedings for the economic torts there specified. Outside s 20, common law principles of agency must be invoked to discover whether the union will be liable for the actions of its officials.

Thomas v National Union of Mineworkers (South Wales Area)

[1985] ICR 886 Chancery Division

This case arose during the 1984–5 miners' strike. The plaintiffs sought an injunction against mass picketing at collieries where they worked, and picketing at the homes of working miners and at other industrial premises. The action was brought against the South Wales area union, the national union and against named members of the national coordinating committee.

Scott J: '... I now come to the question whether the defendants, or any of them, can be held responsible in law for the colliery gates picketing.
  I will deal first with the position of Mr Hendy's clients, the NUM and the members of the national co-ordinating committee. These defendants on the evidence I have seen played no part in organising the colliery gate picketing, or for that matter any other picketing within the South Wales area. They have no control over the picketing that goes on within the South Wales area. It follows that injunctions to control that picketing cannot be granted against any of them. Mr Blom-Cooper, I think, accepted that that was so.
  Next I want to deal with the position of the second to seventh defendants. The second, third and fourth defendants are, or were, the trustees of the South Wales union's funds. The fifth, sixth and seventh defendants are the union's principal officers. There was nothing in the evidence which links any of the trustees to the organisation of the colliery gate picketing. There is clearly no case for the grant of injunctions regarding colliery gate picketing against the second, third or fourth defendants. There is, however, some evidence that the three main officers of the union are responsible for the general picketing policy put into effect by the lodges ...
  The fifth, sixth and seventh defendants have the general control and management of the South Wales union. Each is an active officer. Each would in my view be responsible under the general law for taking appropriate steps to see that the union obeyed any order made against it. I propose therefore to leave their liability on that basis and not to make any order against them personally.
  The real question concerns the responsibilities of the lodges and through them of the South Wales union. There is, as I have said, a real question on the evidence as to the responsibility of the lodges and their respective officers for the nature and manner of the colliery gate picketing that is taking place. But none of the lodge officers is a defendant, so unless

responsibility can be imposed on the South Wales union for what is done by the lodge officers the plaintiffs' claim in this action for injunctive relief to control the colliery gate picketing must fail.

The lodges are constituent parts of the South Wales union. I have already referred to rule 27 of the rules. There are many other rules which refer to the lodges and their officers, but, otherwise than in respect of funds, contributions, accounts and other like matters, there is no rule which sets out the powers or duties of the lodges. These powers and duties are obviously and sensibly enough left to practice and custom. The rules do, however, provide for the objects of the South Wales union itself. The objects include under paragraph 3(b):

> "To advance and protect the interests of members in relation to questions of wages, hours, holidays, conditions of employment, safety, compensation and all other questions arising out of and/or in connection with the member's employment or occupation."

The object is plainly wide enough to cover the conduct of an official strike and, in my view, under the rules the overall responsibility for the conduct of any official strike rests with the union itself. The arrangements for local picketing at collieries and elsewhere may be left to the individual lodges, but in carrying out this function the lodges are, in my judgment, acting on behalf of the South Wales union for the purpose of enabling the union to pursue one of its own most important objects, namely the advancement of the interests of its members in connection with their employment.

Mr Scrivener referred me to *Heatons Transport (St Helens) Ltd* v *Transport and General Workers' Union* on this question of the union's vicarious responsibility for its lodges. The point in that case was whether a union against which an injunction had been granted was liable for contempt of court where one of its shop stewards had acted in breach of the order. The relationship between the union and its shop stewards was examined. The House of Lords, reversing the Court of Appeal, held the union liable, not on a vicarious footing for what the shop steward had done, but rather on the ground that the union had failed to take adequate steps to try and ensure that the order was obeyed. But as to the vicarious liability point Lord Wilberforce said,

> "In the Court of Appeal Lord Denning MR and Roskill LJ in considering the scope of the shop stewards' scope of authority placed considerable reliance on the fact that the shop stewards were agents rather than servants. But we think that is not an important factor in this case. No new development is involved in the law relating to the responsibility of a master or principal for the act of a servant or agent. In each case the test to be applied is the same: was the servant or agent acting on behalf of, and within the scope of the authority conferred by, the master or principal?: ... Usually a servant, as compared with an agent, has a wider authority because his employment is more permanent and he has a larger range of duties as he may have to exercise discretion in dealing with a series of situations as they arise. The agent in an ordinary case is engaged to perform a particular task on a particular occasion and has authority to do whatever is required for that purpose but has no general authority."

The application of the principle there expressed to the facts of the present case leads, in my judgment, to the conclusion that the South Wales union is responsible on ordinary principles of vicarious liability for what is done by the lodges and their officers in organising colliery gate and other local picketing on behalf of and in the name of the South Wales union. That leads me to the question of the responsibility of the lodges and their officers for the numbers who attend at the colliery gates and for the behaviour of those who attend.

Mr Scrivener impressed upon me that given the strength of the feeling in the South Wales mining towns and villages in support of the strike and of anger against those who are breaking the strike and returning to work, spontaneous attendance of large numbers at the collieries and expressions of abuse, anger and sometimes violence, were all to be expected. I follow that submission and it may very well be right. But it is reasonably clear that some degree of organisation by the lodges does regularly take place. The extent and nature of the organising are likely to vary from lodge to lodge, but, as I understand the evidence, the lodge officers regard it as the duty of the lodge to see that the colliery gates are picketed, there is usually a lodge officer in attendance on the picket line and the officer in attendance has an authority, as evidenced by his selection of the six who stand close to the colliery gates, which is respected by those present. Further, there is a telling lack in the evidence of any suggestion that on any occasion any lodge officer has discouraged the attendance at the colliery gates of large numbers. Further, there are minutes of meetings of the South Wales union's area executive council which appear to establish a policy of picketing in large numbers. At a meeting on 6 November it was agreed that "picketing at collieries will be stepped up significantly". It is not to be expected that this policy was not made known to the lodges and required to be implemented by the lodges.

At this interlocutory stage of the case, with affidavit evidence and no cross examination, I can and should come to no final conclusion as to the extent to which the picketing I regard as tortious has been arranged by the lodges. But that the lodges have played a significant part seems to me to be clear ...'

COMMENT

(1)   From 1971–74 unions could be sued under the Industrial Relations Act 1971. *Heatons Transport* v *TGWU* arose at that time, when the House of Lords held that the union's rules, supplemented by custom and practice, had devolved the power to call strikes to shop stewards. It was accordingly liable for their actions.

(2)   In the light of this, it is clearly essential for unions to review the powers of officials under their own rules, and to ensure that the rules are complied with.

(3)   As noted above, the risk for trade unions of unlawful action is not merely damages claims (and note that damages up to the limit can be awarded to each separate plaintiff) but also the risk of fines for contempt. In the miners' strike and in the printing strikes of the 1980s these were measured in hundreds of thousands of pounds.

PICKETING

The final aspect of industrial action to be considered is the law relating to picketing. Establishing a picket line is frequently seen as essential to the successful prosecution of industrial action, not only in making sure people do not work, but also in trying to ensure that supplies are not brought in nor products got out. Since it involves face-to-face confrontation, it can be a volatile, even a violent situation. Hence the criminal law as well as the civil law is frequently invoked against pickets.

Civil liability for picketing

If successful, pickets can induce breaches of contracts of employment (by persuading people not to work) and disrupt commercial contracts (if they stop deliveries) and would thus be liable in tort at Stage 1, if there were no immunity. However, they receive the basic immunity provided by TULRCA s 219 *provided* that the picketing is lawful under the terms of s 220.

Trade Union and Labour Relations (Consolidation) Act 1992

220. (1) It is lawful for a person in contemplation or furtherance of a trade dispute to attend—
      (a) at or near his own place of work, or
      (b) if he is an official of a trade union, at or near the place of work of a member of the union whom he is accompanying and whom he represents,
    for the purpose only of peacefully obtaining or communicating information, or peacefully persuading any person to work or abstain from working.

    (2) If a person works or normally works—
      (a) otherwise than at any one place, or
      (b) at a place the location of which is such that attendance there for a purpose mentioned in subsection (1) is impracticable,
    his place of work for the purposes of that subsection shall be any premises of his employer from which he works or from which his work is administered.

    (3) In the case of a worker not in employment where—
      (a) his last employment was terminated in connection with a trade dispute, or
      (b) the termination of his employment was one of the circumstances giving rise to a trade dispute,
    in relation to that dispute his former place of work shall be treated for the purposes of subsection (1) as being his place of work.

    (4) A person who is an official of a trade union by virtue only of having been elected or appointed to be a representative of some of the members of the union shall be regarded for the purposes of subsection (1) as representing only those members; but otherwise an official of a union shall be regarded for those purposes as representing all its members.

COMMENT

(1) The limitation of lawful picketing to picketing one's own place of work was introduced by the Employment Act 1980 to curb the use of 'flying pickets'. For strikers who have been sacked, it is their former place of work.

(2) Picketing other places will lose immunity: but of course, that will not matter if there is no tortious liability in the first place: see *Middlebrook Mushrooms Ltd* v *TGWU* above, p 500.

(3) The special provision for workers who do not work in one place, or whose place of work is inaccessible, might indicate a concern that everyone should have a place to picket. However, this is not how it has been interpreted.

News Group Newspapers Ltd v *SOGAT '82 (No. 2)*

[1987] ICR 181 Queen's Bench Division

The decision of Rupert Murdoch to remove his newspaper operations (including the *Sun*, the *News of the World*, *The Times* and *The Sunday Times*) from central London to Wapping, together with the streamlined practices he intended to introduce sparked a bitter war with the print unions, which intensified with the dismissal of 5,500 workers. As the operations had moved to Wapping, that is where the pickets went – but it was not where they had formerly been employed.

Stuart-Smith J: '... Mr Grabiner submits that three propositions are established on the evidence:

1. That those who attend at or near Wapping are not at or near their place of work.

I agree. Counsel on behalf of the defendants have submitted that because the dismissed workers previously did work in printing *The Sun*, *News of the World*, *The Times* and *Sunday Times* and that work has now been transferred to Wapping, Wapping has become their place of work. But it seems to me that place refers to a geographical location; and without special words in the section, a place where he has never worked cannot become one where he does. And this is made clear by [TULRCA s 220] which provides:

> "In the case of a worker who is not in employment where – (a) his last employment was terminated in connection with a trade dispute, or (b) the termination of his employment was one of the circumstances giving rise to a trade dispute subsection (1) above shall in relation to that dispute have effect as if any reference to his place of work were a reference to his former place of work."

This subsection makes it clear that the place of work of the dismissed men within the meaning of the section is Bouverie Street or Gray's Inn Road, as the case may be.

It follows from this that even if they are acting peacefully, that is to say, not abusing or threatening people or creating an obstruction or nuisance, official pickets and others not employed there who attend at Wapping will be committing the tort of interference with contract if they induce other persons to break their contracts of employment....

2. That the conduct complained of committed by those who attend at or near Wapping demonstrates that they are not there for the purpose only of peacefully obtaining or communicating information or peacefully persuading any person to work or abstain from working.

I agree. The contrary has not been argued.

3. That all those taking part in official pickets, daily demonstrations, marches, rallies and other demonstrations are picketing.

There is no definition of picketing in the relevant legislation. As I understand his submission, Mr Grabiner sought to spell out a definition from [s 220] the essential elements being a person who in contemplation or furtherance of a trade dispute attends at or near a place of work for the purpose of obtaining or communicating information or persuading any person to work or abstain from working. This definition accords with that in the *Oxford English Dictionary*, namely:

> "men acting in a body or singly who are stationed by a trades-union or the like, to watch men going to work during a strike or in non-union workshops, and to endeavour to dissuade or deter them."

Applying either of these tests it seems to me that there can be little doubt that the official pickets and daily demonstrators come within it. On the other hand I do not think that those who take part in marches and rallies, if they proceed peaceably along the Highway into Wellclose Square are picketing. The problem arises when they break ranks or disperse and commit the acts complained of to which I have referred. In my view the plaintiffs do have an arguable case that such people are picketing. They are attending at or near the plaintiffs' plant for the purpose, inter alia, of communicating information in the form of their views and abuse and persuading people to abstain from working.

These considerations are also relevant to the grant of interlocutory relief, since the court in exercising its discretion whether or not to grant the injunction must have regard to the likelihood of the defendants succeeding at the trial of the action in establishing the matter or matters which would, under the provisions of [s 219 and s 220] afford a defence to the action: see [s.221(2)]. For the two reasons which I have given I consider it unlikely that such defences will be established in relation to Wapping.'

COMMENT

(1)   The Court of Appeal dealt with a similar situation in the same way in *Union Traffic Ltd* v *TGWU*, where Bingham LJ said:

'... Underlying Mr Walker's submissions was, I thought, the premise that everyone must have somewhere where he can effectively picket. That is, in my judgment, not so, as a reading of [s 220] makes plain. One need only take the case of an employee who works, or normally works, at one place that is closed; it may then be futile to picket at that place, but it may nonetheless be the case that there are no other premises of his employer from which he works or from which his work is administered, and in that event there is nowhere he can effectively picket ...'

(2)   In *Rayware* v *TGWU* the Court of Appeal held that pickets were at or near their employer's premises on a private industrial estate when they were on the public road at the entrance to the estate, some 1,230 yards from the actual workplace. They could not go closer because they would have been trespassing.

(3)   Implicitly accepting this, the revised version of the Code of Practice on Picketing (1992) recommends that where the picket takes place at a place of work of more than one employer, the pickets should ensure that the workers who are not involved in the dispute are not interfered with. It also states that where there is a choice of locations which could be regarded as 'at or near' the place of work, that picketing should be confined to the closest.

(4)   The status of such pronouncements in the Code of Practice is problematic. While it is true that the Code must be taken into account in all relevant proceedings, yet it is also the case that its recommendations do not have the force of law. Therefore, it is submitted, if the picketing can properly be described as 'at or near', then it will not be rendered unlawful merely because it is not in fact at the nearest possible point.

(5)   A similar issue arises in relation to the well-known recommendation in the Code that no more than six pickets should be necessary at any one entrance. This is frequently treated by police on duty to keep the peace as if it were a legal requirement.

(6)   Pickets who are successful may persuade employees of employers other than the employer in dispute to break their contracts of employment. An obvious example would be if pickets persuaded lorry drivers not to deliver goods to the struck firm which the drivers' employers had contracted to deliver. Under TULRCA s 224(2) this is secondary action. But by virtue of s 224(1), it is protected secondary action. This is the only situation where workers will not lose immunity while engaging in secondary action.

(7)   Pickets who are lawful by the terms of s 220 receive the immunity from liability for the economic torts provided by s 219. However, there are other torts which may be committed on the picket line, and there is no immunity in respect of these. An extreme case, the Wapping dispute case referred to above, at least provides fairly comprehensive coverage.

News Group Newspapers Ltd v *SOGAT '82 (No 2)*

[1987] ICR 181 Queen's Bench Division

The reasons for the dispute are set out on p 570.

Stuart-Smith J:
'*The conduct complained of*
    The conduct complained of consists of allegedly unlawful and tortious acts committed in the course of activities organised by the various defendants. It is necessary to describe these activities at the various sites with which I am concerned and the tortious acts alleged.

Wapping
    Three forms of activity take place, which for convenience may be described as picketing, daily demonstrations, and marches, rallies and demonstrations. It should be emphasised that this is merely for ease of definition. It does not matter what people are called. What is relevant is what they do. The plaintiffs submit that there is really no difference between the activities of any of those who attend at or near the plant: they are all picketing....

Pickets
    These are sometimes described as official pickets. They are organised by the two defendant unions through the London District Council of SOGAT and the joint liaison committee of the unions. They consist of six pickets, two at least of whom are members of SOGAT and one at least NGA, together with a steward. They wear official armbands or other insignia. By agreement with the police they are stationed at the outer main gate. They are there 24 hours a day and have attended every day since the dispute began save perhaps for the first day or so. They change every four hours.

Daily demonstrators
    Estimates of their numbers vary to some extent between 50 and 200. They tend to be at their maximum in the morning and evening when the bulk of the plaintiffs' workforce are coming to and from work. In the main, they congregate on the north side of the Highway, behind crush barriers at a distance of some 80 yards from the main gate. There is a police presence at the north end of Virginia Street.
    There is a dispute in the evidence whether or not the daily demonstrators are organised by the defendants or any of them, particularly the unions. This is denied by the defendants' deponents ...
    This is clearly an important issue of fact which cannot be resolved without oral evidence, cross-examination and discovery. But to my mind the plaintiffs have at least a good arguable case that the daily demonstrators are, in fact, being organised by or on behalf of the defendant unions. Whatever may be the position in a remote mining village in South Wales, where it is not improbable that striking miners may assemble spontaneously and without organisation by their union at their pit at the beginning and end of a shift, I find it hard to believe that day after day for six months 50 to 200 dismissed print workers and some of their

families assemble spontaneously from all over London and maybe further afield, at their own expense to signify by their presence the depth of their feelings, unless they are organised. Obviously, it is not the same people who come each day, morning and evening, with lesser numbers during the rest of the day.

Rallies, marches and demonstrations

Every week on Wednesday and Saturday nights and sometimes at other times as well – for example, 1 and 5 May (the latter being apparently for the benefit of the local residents) – rallies, marches and demonstrations take place. They normally take the form of an assembly at some point, usually Tower Hill, then a procession to Wapping, where it moves into Wellclose Square and at this point is addressed by speakers who sympathise with the cause of the dismissed workers. Thereafter, those involved should disperse. That is what is supposed to happen. As will be seen, it seldom if ever works just like that. It is not disputed that these activities are organised by or on behalf of both unions. The numbers attending vary from about 700 or 800 to between 6,000 and 7,000. Generally there are more on Saturdays than on Wednesdays. Recently the numbers of those attending has tended to decrease ...

All these activities are supposed to take place in an orderly and peaceful way with the pickets peaceably attempting to persuade those who work there not to do so or imparting information to them and the demonstrators showing by their presence that they have a grievance and a just cause and appealing to the consciences of those in work and the plaintiffs' management for a more generous settlement of the dispute. That is the theory, and if that were the practice the plaintiffs would have no cause to complain. In fact, it is very far from the practice.

It is necessary to examine the evidence in some detail in relation to each place and kind of activity, though I do not intend to lengthen the judgment with detailed description of all the incidents.

Pickets and daily demonstrations at Wapping

There is overwhelming evidence that those of the plaintiffs' employees who pass both the pickets and daily demonstrators are almost invariably subjected to abuse and, frequently, to threats. They are called scabs, but that is the least of the insults. Vile and obscene language is used, particularly to women. Much of the abuse is of a personal nature, since many of the plaintiffs' employees, and particularly the journalists, are known by name and sight. There are also threats, such as "We'll get you" and "You can't hide forever." To add point to their meaning there have been other touches. Earlier in the dispute a coffin was suspended from a lamp post in Virginia Street. Several witnesses speak of being photo-graphed as they come and go at the gate and having the numbers of their cars taken. There was at one time a so-called roll of dishonour of those working, which gave their names and addresses. The significance of these matters will become clear later....

The marches and rallies

Very often, though not on every occasion, there have been incidents of violence and obstruction and not infrequently they have been of a serious nature. In the course of these forays journalists have been attacked in their cars and so have drivers of TNT lorries and vans. A particularly dangerous incident occurred when a sharpened stick was thrown through the back window of a car, showering the occupant of the back seat with glass. On another 40 yards of the perimeter fence was knocked over. Rockets, flares and stones have been directed against the plaintiffs' buildings. But in the main the violence has been directed against the police, who have had to be present in large numbers in order to try and protect the plaintiffs' premises and employees. They have borne the brunt of the casualties. It is quite clear that on occasions some of those who have attended have come armed with an assortment of offensive weapons in order to make a concerted attack. ...

The plaintiffs contend that the conduct complained of involves the commission of four separate torts – that is to say, nuisance, intimidation, harassment and interference with the performance of their commercial contracts. They then contend that the defendants are liable in respect of some or all of these torts ...

Nuisance

A nuisance may be a public nuisance actionable at the suit of a particular plaintiff or a private nuisance.

(a) Public nuisance

Public nuisance is a criminal offence which for the purpose of this case may be defined as an unlawful act which endangers lives, safety, health, property or comfort of the public or by which the public are obstructed in the exercise or enjoyment of any right common to all Her Majesty's subjects. It must materially affect the reasonable comfort and convenience of a class of Her Majesty's subjects who come within the sphere or neighbourhood of its operation: see *per* Romer LJ in *Attorney-General* v *PYA Quarries Ltd*. It is only actionable as a civil wrong if the plaintiff can show particular damage other than and beyond the general inconvenience suffered by the public. Such particular damage must be substantial, but it is not limited to special damage in the sense of provable pecuniary loss. ...

(b) Private nuisance

The owner of land adjoining the highway has a right of access to the highway from any part of his premises. Interference with this right is actionable; but where the interference is, as here, alleged obstruction, it is subject to the same qualification that the obstruction must be an unreasonable use of the highway. It is submitted that the third plaintiffs as owners of the land are entitled to sue at Wapping, the first and second at Bouverie Street and Gray's Inn Road, respectively, if the nuisance is thus made out.

How are these principles to be applied to the facts at the various places in question?

Wapping

I have no doubt that the conduct of the pickets and the daily demonstrators as described in the evidence amounts to an unreasonable obstruction of the highway. Moreover, it seems to me that unlike the working miners in *Thomas* v *National Union of Mineworkers (South Wales Area)* who were unable to establish special damage because they were driven into the pit in a bus provided by their employer and there was no other evidence of damage, both the seventh plaintiff and the other plaintiffs can establish damage peculiar to them. The seventh plaintiff describes how she no longer feels able to leave the plant during the day for a meal or similar break. She has to go by taxi or mini-cab instead of on foot and how she feels drained by the constant pressure of having to come to work through the picket line. These are all matters in my view capable of being regarded as substantial damage.

So far as the other plaintiffs are concerned, although it is not entirely clear who incurs the expense, the cost of busing their employees is £100,000 per month – by no means insubstantial damage. Moreover, Mr Wilson, the editor of *The Times*, has made it clear that the second plaintiffs have both lost some journalists and failed to attract others because of the conduct of the pickets and daily demonstrators. Journalists are the life blood of a newspaper and, in my view, this is very serious damage.

The third plaintiffs' cause of action in private nuisance is also established, it not being necessary to establish peculiar damage in that case.

So far as the twice-weekly marches, rallies and demonstrations are concerned, when they are peaceful and orderly no nuisance is created. But it is quite clear that on those occasions when the marches or demonstrations get out of control, attack the police, the employees of the plaintiffs and TNT and obstruct the highway by masses of people, that is not a reasonable use of the highway and amounts to a nuisance....

Intimidation

The tort of intimidation is committed when A delivers a threat to B that he will commit an act or use means unlawful against B, as a result of which B does or refrains from doing some act which he is entitled to do, thereby causing damage either to himself or C. The tort is one of intention and the plaintiff, whether it be B or C, must be a person whom A intended to injure: see *Clerk & Lindsell on Torts*, 15th ed. (1982), p 729....

The defendants submit, rightly in my view, that abuse, swearing and shouting does not amount to a threat of violence. They further submit that the threat has to be express or implied that if the person threatened does not do what is required he will be subjected to violence and that such threats as have been made do not amount to this. I disagree. The words, "Scab, we will get you", or words to the same effect, could mean, "We will assault you because you have been working for the plaintiffs." But, since the obvious intention is to dissuade people from continuing to work, the more likely meaning is, "We will get you if you do not stop working for the plaintiffs." There is ample evidence of such threats at Wapping from both the pickets and daily demonstrators. There is also some evidence to this effect in relation to those who attend at Bouverie Street and Gray's Inn Road.

If a threat is little more than idle abuse and is not to be taken seriously, then it would not be sufficient to found an action for intimidation. Indeed, the tort is not complete unless the person threatened succumbs to the threat and damage is suffered. But it is clear that injunctive relief can be granted to restrain the unlawful act and also threats to commit the unlawful act: *Clerk & Lindsell on Torts*, p 743, footnote 42. But in order for an injunction to be granted the threat or threats must be serious and taken seriously by those who receive them. It is in this context that, in my view, the evidence of what has happened away from the plaintiffs' premises is material. Where there is such an abundance of evidence of the employees being followed, molested, assaulted and subject to criminal damage to their cars and houses, to say nothing of the treatment meted out to TNT drivers, it is idle to suggest that the threats are not serious or to be taken seriously. The taking of photographs of employees, noting of numbers of their cars and the distribution of so-called rolls of dishonour is particularly significant in this context....

Harassment

In *Thomas v National Union of Mineworkers (South Wales Area)* Scott J, after holding that the conduct of the pickets at the colliery gates was intimidating in the ordinary sense of the word, said, ...

"Nuisance is strictly concerned with, and may be regarded as confined to, activity which unduly interferes with the use or enjoyment of land or of easements. But there is no reason why the law should not protect on a similar basis the enjoyment of other rights. All citizens have the right to use the public highway. Suppose an individual were persistently to follow another on a public highway, making rude gestures or remarks in order to annoy or vex. If continuance of such conduct were threatened no one can doubt but that a civil court would, at the suit of the victim, restrain by an injunction the continuance of the conduct. The tort might be described as a species of private nuisance, namely unreasonable interference with the victim's rights to use the highway. But the label for the tort does not, in my view, matter.

In the present case, the working miners have the right to use the highway for the purpose of going to work. They are, in my judgment, entitled under the general law to exercise that right without unreasonable harassment by others. Unreasonable harassment of them in their exercise of that right would, in my judgment, be tortious.

A decision whether in this, or in any other similar case, the presence or conduct of pickets represents a tortious interference with the right of those who wish to go to work to do so without harassment must depend on the particular circumstances of the particular case. The balance to which I have earlier referred must be struck between the rights of those going to work and the rights of the pickets."

The defendants criticise this statement of the law. They submit that Scott J should not have invented a new tort and that it is not sufficient to found liability that there has been an unreasonable interference with the rights of others, even though when a balance is struck between conflicting rights and interests the scale comes down in favour of the plaintiffs, unless those rights are recognised by the law and fall within some accepted head of tort.

I am bound to say that, with all respect to Scott J, I think there is force in these criticisms, especially where it does not appear that damage is a necessary ingredient of the tort. If, of course, damage peculiar to the plaintiff is established, then the tort is that of nuisance.

Since, in my view, the tort of nuisance is established and the tort of intimidation is threatened, it is unnecessary for me to express a final view on the question of harassment.

COMMENT

(1)   The judge also considered that the tort of interference with trade or business by unlawful means was made out, given that s 219 immunity did not apply to the picketing.

(2)   Note that since the torts concerned are not covered by TULRCA s 219, the question of the union's responsibility had to be settled by common law principles.

(3)   The case has been criticised on the ground that it makes the union liable for the activities of people it cannot possibly control: do you agree?

Criminal liability for picketing

Specific types of picketing have been criminal offences since the Conspiracy and Protection of Property Act 1875.

Trade Union and Labour Relations (Consolidation) Act 1992

241.   (1)   A person commits an offence who, with a view to compelling another person to abstain from doing or to do any act which that person has a legal right to do or abstain from doing, wrongfully and without legal authority—

(a)   uses violence to or intimidates that person or his wife or children, or injures his property,

(b)   persistently follows that person about from place to place,

(c)   hides any tools, clothes or other property owned or used by that person, or deprives him of or hinders him in the use thereof,

(d)   watches or besets the house or other place where that person resides, works, carries on business or happens to be, or the approach to any such house or place, or

(e)   follows that person with two or more other persons in a disorderly manner in or through any street or road.

(2)   A person guilty of an offence under this section is liable on summary conviction to imprisonment for a term not exceeding six months or a fine not exceeding level 5 on the standard scale, or both.

(3)   A constable may arrest without warrant anyone he reasonably suspects is committing an offence under this section.

COMMENT

(1)   Note that the activity in question must be independently wrongful before it becomes a criminal offence: *Ward Lock & Co Ltd* v *Operative Printers' Assistants' Society*.

(2)   These provisions were rarely used for a century, but a revival of interest came with the miners' strike 1984–85: see Wallington, 'Policing the Miners' Strike (1985) 14 ILJ 145.

(3)   Other statutory provisions which could well be applicable to pickets are contained in the Public Order Act 1986 and the Protection from Harassment Act 1997.

(4)   In practice, the most common offences committed by pickets are obstruction of the highway and obstruction of a police officer in the execution of his duty. The next case examines the ambit of the latter offence.

Piddington v *Bates*

[1960] 3 All ER 660 Queen's Bench Divisional Court

This was an appeal by way of case stated against the appellant's conviction for obstructing a police officer in the execution of his duty, contrary to what is now the Police Act 1964 s 51.

The police had been called to a printing works where a van containing about eighteen people arrived to picket the two entrances. They were refusing to permit more than two pickets at each entrance. What occurred next was reported as follows:

> "The respondent told the appellant three times that, in his view, two pickets at each entrance were sufficient. The appellant said, 'I'm going there and you can't stop me. I know my rights,' and, 'I can stand by the gate if I want to,' and finally, 'I'm going to join them. If you don't want me to you'd better arrest me.' The appellant then pushed gently past the respondent and was gently arrested. There was no obstruction of the highway in the vicinity of the premises, nor any disorder, nor any violence, threatened or offered, by any of the pickets or other persons present. In para (k) of the Case Stated it was found that the respondent arrived at his view that two pickets at each entrance were enough, on the grounds that that number was sufficient for peaceful picketing in view of the number of persons who might then, or later, leave the premises, and that picketing by persons in excess of that number might lead to intimidation and a breach of the peace.
>
> It was contended on behalf of the appellant that in the peaceful circumstances of the picketing the respondent had no right in law to restrict the number of pickets on the doors to two and that, accordingly, the appellant was not guilty of the offence charged."

Lord Parker CJ: '... The question here is whether the constables were acting in the course of the execution of their duty when, so it is said, they were obstructed. The court has been referred to a great number of cases, both Irish and English, dealing with the position when a police constable can be said to contemplate a breach of the peace and to take action to preserve it, but I find it unnecessary to refer to those cases. It seems to me that the law is reasonably plain. First, the mere statement by a constable that he did anticipate that there might be a breach of the peace is clearly not enough. There must exist proved facts from which a constable could reasonably have anticipated such a breach. Second, it is not enough that his contemplation is that there is a remote possibility but there must be a real possibility of a breach of the peace. Accordingly, in every case it becomes a question whether, on the particular facts, there were reasonable grounds on which a constable charged with this duty reasonably anticipated that a breach of the peace might occur…'.

(The judge held that in this case, the police officer had reasonable grounds for his belief and that the appellant was rightly convicted. Ashworth and Elwes JJ agreed.)

Hunt v Broome

[1974] ICR 84 House of Lords

Lord Reid: 'The facts are set out in the case stated by the justices:

"(a) On September 5, 1972, there was in progress a nationwide building workers' strike. On that day one Ronald Dickinson, a driver, called at a building site and was accosted by the respondent who was a trade union official. The respondent tried to dissuade Dickinson from entering the site, but it transpired that Dickinson was at the wrong site so he departed in his lorry for the correct site, which was in Short Street, and told the respondent of his intention. The respondent took a short cut to Short Street. (b) In Short Street the respondent held out a poster and asked Dickinson to draw into the side of the road which he did. In a brief conversation the respondent tried to dissuade Dickinson from entering the site for which his load was intended. He failed in his first attempt to persuade Dickinson to go away with his load. Dickinson manoeuvred his lorry to drive into the site. The respondent stood in front of the lorry with his poster, still shouting in an attempt to persuade Dickinson to refrain from delivering his load. Dickinson did not attempt to drive into the respondent but asked him to move. He did not move. (c) The appellant – a police inspector – arrived and spoke to Dickinson. He then told the respondent that Dickinson wanted to enter the site and the respondent said that he did not want Dickinson to enter the site. The appellant told the respondent that if he did not move he would be arrested. The respondent did not move and was immediately arrested. (d) Throughout the whole incident there were no angry words or violent actions. It was a peaceful picket. The whole incident in Short Street lasted only at the very most for nine minutes. At all material times the respondent was on the highway."

The justices' reason for dismissing the information is set out in the case stated:

"We were of opinion that a period of nine minutes at most interspersed with manoeuvring of the lorry and intervention by the police was not an unreasonably long time for the respondent to spend in exercising his statutory right peacefully to seek to persuade a person not to work and that his statutory right is meaningless unless the picket places himself in such a position that the person to be persuaded is obliged to stop and listen for a reasonable length of time and accordingly we dismissed the case …"

His attendance … is only made lawful by [s 220] if he attended only for the purpose of obtaining or communicating information or "peacefully persuading" the lorry driver. Attendance for that purpose must I think include the right to try to persuade anyone who chooses to stop and listen, at least in so far as this is done in a reasonable way with due consideration for the rights of others. A right to attend for the purpose of peaceful persuasion would be meaningless unless this were implied.

But I see no ground for implying any right to require the person whom it is sought to persuade to submit to any kind of constraint or restriction of his personal freedom. One is familiar with persons at the side of a road signalling to a driver requesting him to stop. It is then for the driver to decide whether he will stop or not. That, in my view, a picket is entitled to do. If the driver stops, the picket can talk to him but only for so long as the driver is willing to listen.

That must be so because if the picket had a statutory right to stop or to detain the driver that must necessarily imply that the Act has imposed on those passing along the road a statutory duty to stop or to remain for longer than they chose to stay. So far as my recollection goes it would be unique for Parliament to impose such a duty otherwise than by express words, and even if one envisages the possibility of such a duty being imposed by implication the need for it would have to be crystal clear. Here I can see no need at all for any such implication.

Without the protection of the section merely inviting a driver to stop and then, if he were willing to stop and listen, proceeding to try to persuade him not to go on, would in many cases be either an offence or a tort or both, particularly if more than a very few pickets were acting together. I see no reason to hold that the section confers any other right.

The justices speak of the appellant's "statutory right peacefully to seek to persuade". That is not an accurate or adequate statement of the provisions of the section. And their further statement that,

> "his statutory right is meaningless unless the picket places himself in such a position that the person to be persuaded is obliged to stop and listen for a reasonable length of time"

is for the reasons I have given wholly erroneous.

There was a suggestion that if a picket does not have a right to stop a driver or pedestrian the same result could be obtained lawfully by a large number of pickets gathering at the same place and doing nothing. The section does not limit the number of pickets and no limitation of numbers can be implied. So if a large number assemble it will not be physically possible in many cases for a driver or pedestrian to proceed.

But if a picket has a purpose beyond those set out in the section, then his presence becomes unlawful and in many cases such as I have supposed it would not be difficult to infer as a matter of fact that pickets who assemble in unreasonably large numbers do have the purpose of preventing free passage. If that were the proper inference then their presence on the highway would become unlawful. *Tynan's* case is a good example of this.

In this case it was not and could not reasonably be maintained that, if the law is as I have stated it, any other conclusion is possible than that the appellant committed the offence with which he has been charged.

I would therefore dismiss this appeal.'

(Lords Morris and Salmon and Viscount Dilhorne delivered concurring judgments; Lord Hodson agreed.)

COMMENT

(1)   This case illustrates the position that there is no positive right to picket: thus it does not excuse otherwise unlawful conduct.

(2)   The question of stopping vehicles generates much heat. If they cannot, pickets today are often rendered powerless to communicate; but to permit them to would be an infringement of the traveller's right not to stop. A practical compromise, where relations between police and pickets are good, is for the police to stop the vehicles, for a mutually agreed reasonable time. However, this common sense approach is arguably not justified in law.

(3)   In serious disputes, all manner of other crimes may also be committed, ranging from offences under the Public Order Act 1986 to grievous bodily harm or worse. However, as the cases selected illustrate, the most common offences for which pickets risk arrest are obstruction of the highway, obstruction of a police officer in the execution of his duty and conduct likely to cause a breach of the peace.